AS Level and A Level

# Chemistry

Brian Ratcliff, Helen Eccles, John Raffan
John Nicholson, David Johnson, David Acaster,
... ...man

## CAMBRIDGE
UNIVERSITY PRESS

CAMBRIDGE UNIVERSITY PRESS

Cambridge, New York, Melbourne, Madrid, Cape Town, Singapore, São Paulo, Delhi

Cambridge University Press
The Edinburgh Building, Cambridge CB2 8RU, UK

www.cambridge.org
Information on this title: www.cambridge.org/9780521544719

First published 2004
7th printing 2008

Printed in Dubai by Oriental Press

*A catalogue record for this publication is available from the British Library*

ISBN  978-0-521-54471-9 paperback

ACKNOWLEDGEMENTS
We are grateful to the following for permission to reproduce
photographs:

**Tick Ahearn** pp. 43*tr* and *cr*, 72*tr*, 318*r*, 321*bl*; **Bryan and Cherry
Alexander** p. 53*br*; **Allsport** (Gray Mortmore) p. 394; **Ancient Art
and Architecture Collection** pp. 40*cl* and *bl*; **Argonne National
Laboratory** p. 35; **Art Directors and TRIP Photo Library** p. 317*cr* ;
courtesy of **Aventis Pasteur MSD** pp. 19*tl*, 21, 277 and 282; **A–Z
Botanical Collection Ltd**) p. 321*cl* (Dan Sams), p.351*bl* (Alan
Gould); **Elenac/BASF** p. 184;  courtesy of **Baxter Haemoglobin
Therapeutics, USA** p. 126; **Billingham Ammonia Plant Terra
Nitrogen (UK) Ltd** p. 134; **Boeing/TRH Pictures** p. 208*tr*; **Michael
Brooke** pp. 78, 162*bl*, 165*tl* and *r*, 284, 288, 331, 348, 351*tl*, 355,
357, 358*tl* and *bl*; by kind permission of **Buxton Lime Industries** p.
72*l*; **Civil Aviation Authority International Fire Training Centre
UK** p. 332*l*; **John Cleare** p. 58; **Ecoscene**  pp. 262 (Nick Hawkes),
305*tr* (C.J. Bent), 314*bl* (Kieran Murray) and *br* (Schaffer); **James
Evans** p. 387*l*; **Garden Matters** pp. 151, 351*r* and 363; **Peter Gould**
pp. 44*l*, 46, 217*br* and 305*l*; **Geoscience Features Picture Library**
pp. 19*br*, 40*tl*, 43*l* and *cl* (Dr B. Booth), p. 30*t*, (A. Fisher), pp. 34, 45,
197*tl* and *cr*; courtesy of **Dr Jonathan Goodman, Department of
Chemistry, Cambridge University, using the program Eadfrith
(copyright J.M. Goodman, Department of Chemistry, Cambridge
University, 1994)/photo by Cambridge University Chemistry
Department Photographic Unit** p. 47*tl*; **Copper in Architecture** p.
67; **Leslie Garland Picture Library** pp. 217*tr* and 221*tl*; **Robert
Harding Picture Library** pp. 91, 246*br*, 312 (Paolo Koch) and 318*bl*
(FPG Int); **Holt Studios**  p. 261 (Nigel Cattlin); **Roger G. Howard**  p.
370; **ICI**  pp. 31*bl*, 382 and 385; **IFA** pp. 44*r* and 383*l*; **Image State**
p. 300*bl*; **La Belle Aurore**  pp. 157, 171 and 242; **Andrew Lambert**
pp. 1, 25, 59*tr*, 100, 101, 109, 110, 138*l*, 152, 165*bl*, 166, 168, 170,
208*cr* and *br*, 218, 219, 220 239, 240, 246*l*, *bl* and *bc*, 253, 274, 275,
276, 295, 296, 300*bl*, 302*r*, 321*c*, 325, 330, 337, 338, 339, 343, 347,
354, 360, 361, 371, 372, 373 and 379*tr*; **Frank Lane Picture Agency**
(B. Kuiter/Foto Natura Stock) p. 326; **Stefan Lesnianski** (**University
of Leeds**) p. 53*bl*; courtesy of **Lever Bros Ltd**  p. 362; **Life File**  pp.
59*br*(Barbara Berkowitz), 62(Jan Suttle), 72*br*, (Tim Fisher) and 273
(Barry Mayes); **Gordon Woods/Malvern School** p. 200*br*;  **Johnson**

**Matthey Environmental Catalysts and Technologies** p. 190;
**Manchester  University/Science and Society Picture Library** p. 4;
reproduced by kind permission of **Mercedes Benz**  p. 318*tl*; **Master
File** p. 323; **Natural History Museum** p. 33*tl*; **NSSDC/NASA** p. 17;
**www.osf.com**  (Mark Deeble & Victoria Stone) pp. 125 , (Martin
Chillmaid)  222 and (Rafi Ben-Shahar) 369*tl*; **Photo Library
International** p. 30*b*; **George Porter** p. 175; **Press Association**  p.
53*tr*; **Popperfoto** pp. 162*tl* and 379*tr*; **Brian Ratcliff**  pp. 33*br*, 97,
221*bl* and 306; **Ann Ronan Picture Library** pp. 81, 216, 268 and
313; courtesy of the **Library & Information Centre of the Royal
Society of Chemistry** p. 198; **RCSB Protein Data Bank** p.387*r*;
**Science Photo Library** pp. 20 (Heine Schneebeli), 31*tl*, 332*r* (NASA),
47*bl* (Dr Arthur Lesk, Laboratory of Molecular Biology), 71 (Astrid
& Hanns-Frieder-Michler), 132 (David Frazier), 175*l*(Jack Finch),
197*tc*, *cb*, *br*, *tr* and *cl* , 227, 260*l* (Keith Kent) 260*r* (Dr Jeremy
Burgess), 263*l* (Adam Hart-Davis), 263*br*, 305*br* (James Holmes), 315*l*
(Martin Bond), 316*l* (US Department of Energy) 317*tl* ((John
Mead),*tr* (Simon Fraser), 369*bl* (A. Barrington Brown), 383*r*(James
Holmes/Zedcor) and 391 (Cape Grin BAPS Simon Fraser); **Shell
Photo Service** pp. 310, 311; **www.shoutpictures. com** p. 379 *br*;
**Budd Titlow/Stop Pictures** p. 191; **University of Cambridge
Cavendish Laboratory** pp. 3 and 6; **USGS** p. 51; courtesy of **Van
den Berg Foods Ltd**  p. 302*bl*.

Front cover photograph: Science Photo Library (salt crystal)
Cover illustration by J.C.Revy, ISM/**Science Photo Library**

Past examination questions are reproduced by permission of the
University of Cambridge Local Examinations Syndicate.

# Contents

# Introduction

CIE Chemistry is derived from the highly successful Cambridge Advanced Sciences series developed for the UK market, Chemistry 1 and Chemistry 2. Chemistry 1 covers the AS part of the UK A level in Chemistry from OCR, whilst Chemistry 2 covers the A2 part. Both Chemistry 1 and Chemistry 2 were based on some of the earlier Cambridge Modular Sciences texts, but with the addition of much new material.

During the development of Chemistry 1 and Chemistry 2, the opportunity was taken to improve the design and make the language used more accessible than that used in more traditional A level Chemistry texts. They also contained many more illustrations and photographs in colour, demonstrating the way chemistry affects the lives of us all.

CIE Chemistry has continued this tradition of development and improvement, with new material being added to cover the learning outcomes of the CIE Chemistry syllabus.

The presentation of each chapter places AS material before A2 material. An additional chapter on spectroscopy from Chemistry 2 has been retained as it contains much useful material for the Spectroscopy option.

Each chapter contains self-assessment questions (SAQs). These are to help students think about what they have read and make sure they have understood it. Where new material has been introduced, new SAQs have been written. Answers to the SAQs can be found on pages 402–28.

Exam-type questions have been provided at the end of chapters.

Chemistry involves a number of technical terms. Each time a new term is introduced it is shown in **bold** and its meaning is explained. The Glossary (pages 429–34) contains definitions of the technical terms used.

## The presentation of units

You will find that the books in this series use a bracketed convention in the presentation of units within tables and on graph axes. For example, ionisation energies of $1000\,\text{kJ}\,\text{mol}^{-1}$ and $2000\,\text{kJ}\,\text{mol}^{-1}$ will be represented in this way:

| Measurement | Ionisation energy ($kJ\,mol^{-1}$) |
|---|---|
| 1 | 1000 |
| 2 | 2000 |

CIE examination papers use the solidus as a convention, thus:

| Measurement | Ionisation energy / $kJ\,mol^{-1}$ |
|---|---|
| 1 | 1000 |
| 2 | 2000 |

Any numbers appearing in brackets with the units, for example $(10^{-5}\,\text{mol}\,\text{dm}^{-3}\,\text{s}^{-1})$, should be treated in exactly the same way as when preceded by the solidus, $/10^{-5}\,\text{mol}\,\text{dm}^{-3}\,\text{s}^{-1}$.

# CHAPTER 1

# Atomic structure (AS)

## By the end of this chapter you should be able to:

1 recognise and describe *protons*, *neutrons* and *electrons* in terms of their relative charges and relative masses;

2 describe the distribution of *mass* and *charge* within an *atom*;

3 describe the contribution of protons and neutrons to atomic nuclei in terms of *atomic number* and *mass number*;

4 deduce the numbers of protons, neutrons and electrons present in both atoms and *ions* from given atomic and mass numbers;

5 describe the behaviour of protons, neutrons and electrons in electric fields;

6 distinguish between *isotopes* on the basis of different numbers of neutrons present;

7 explain the terms *first ionisation energy* and *successive ionisation energies* of an *element* in terms of 1 mole of gaseous atoms or ions;

8 explain that ionisation energies are influenced by *nuclear charge*, *atomic radius* and *electron shielding*;

9 predict the number of electrons in each principal *quantum shell* of an element from its successive ionisation energies;

10 describe the shapes of s and p *orbitals*;

11 describe the numbers and relative energies of the s, p and d orbitals for the principal quantum numbers 1, 2, 3 and also the 4s and 4p orbitals;

12 deduce the *electronic configurations* of atoms up to $Z = 36$ and ions, given the atomic number and charge, limited to s and p *blocks* up to $Z = 36$.

Chemistry is a science of change. Over the centuries people have heated rocks, distilled juices and probed solids, liquids and gases with electricity. From all this activity we have gained a great wealth of new materials – metals, medicines, plastics, dyes, ceramics, fertilisers, fuels and many more (*figure 1.1*). But this creation of new materials is only part of the science and technology of chemistry. Chemists also want to *understand* the changes, to find patterns of behaviour and to discover the innermost nature of the materials.

Our 'explanations' of the chemical behaviour of matter come from reasoning and model-building based on the limited evidence available from

● **Figure 1.1** All of these useful products, and many more, contain chemicals that have been created by applying chemistry to natural materials. Chemists must also find answers to problems caused when people misuse chemicals.

experiments. The work of chemists and physicists has shown us the following:

- All known materials, however complicated and varied they appear, can be broken down into the fundamental substances we call **elements**. These elements cannot be broken down further into simpler substances. So far, about 115 elements are recognised. Most exist in combinations with other elements in compounds but some, such as gold, nitrogen, oxygen and sulphur, are also found in an uncombined state. Some elements would not exist on Earth without the artificial use of nuclear reactions. Chemists have given each element a symbol. This symbol is usually the first one or two letters of the name of the element; some are derived from their names in Latin. Some examples are:

| Element | Symbol |
|---------|--------|
| carbon | C |
| lithium | Li |
| iron | Fe (from the Latin *ferrum*) |
| lead | Pb (from the Latin *plumbum*) |

- Groups of elements show patterns of behaviour related to their atomic masses. A Russian chemist, Dmitri Mendeleev, summarised these patterns by arranging the elements into a 'Periodic Table'. Modern versions of the Periodic Table are widely used in chemistry. (A Periodic Table is shown in the appendix on page 401 and explained, much more fully, in chapter 9.)
- All matter is composed of extremely small particles (**atoms**). About 100 years ago, the accepted model for atoms included the assumptions that (i) atoms were tiny particles, which could not be divided further nor destroyed, and (ii) all atoms of the same element were identical. The model had to give way to other models, as science and technology produced new evidence. This evidence could only be interpreted as atoms having other particles inside them – they have an internal structure.

Scientists now believe that there are two basic types of particles – 'quarks' and 'leptons'. These are the building-blocks from which everything is made, from microbes to galaxies. For many explanations or predictions, however, scientists find it helpful to use a model of atomic structure that includes three basic particles in any atom, the

electron, the **proton** and the **neutron**. Protons and neutrons are made from quarks, and the electron is a member of the family of leptons.

# Discovering the electron

## Effect of electric current in solutions (electrolysis)

When electricity flows in an aqueous solution of silver nitrate, for example, silver metal appears at the negative electrode (cathode). This is an example of **electrolysis** and the best explanation is that:

- the silver exists in the solution as positively charged particles known as **ions** ($Ag^+$);
- one silver ion plus one unit of electricity gives one silver atom.

The name 'electron' was given to this unit of electricity by the Irish scientist George Johnstone Stoney in 1891.

## Study of cathode rays

At normal pressures gases are usually very poor conductors of electricity, but at low pressures they conduct quite well. Scientists, such as William Crookes, who first studied the effects of passing electricity through gases at low pressures, saw that the glass of the containing vessel opposite the **cathode** (negative electrode) glowed when the applied potential difference was sufficiently high.

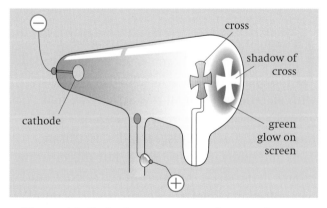

- **Figure 1.2** Cathode rays cause a glow on the screen opposite the cathode, and the 'Maltese Cross' casts a shadow. The shadow will move if a magnet is brought near to the screen. This shows that the cathode rays are deflected in a magnetic field. The term 'cathode ray' is still familiar today, as in 'cathode-ray oscilloscopes'.

A solid object, placed between the cathode and the glow, cast a shadow (*figure 1.2*). They proposed that the glow was caused by rays coming from the cathode and called these cathode rays.

For a while there was some argument about whether cathode rays are waves, similar to visible light rays, or particles. The most important evidence is that they are strongly deflected in a magnetic field. This is best explained by assuming that they are streams of electrically charged particles. The direction of the deflection (towards the positive pole) shows that the particles in cathode rays are negatively charged.

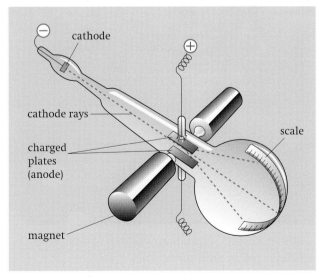

● **Figure 1.3** Joseph (J. J.) Thomson (1856–1940) using his cathode-ray tube.

## J. J. Thomson's *e/m* experiment

The great leap in understanding came in 1897, at the Cavendish Laboratory in Cambridge (*figures 1.3* and *1.4*). J. J. Thomson measured the deflection of a narrow beam of cathode rays in both magnetic and electric fields. His results allowed him to calculate the charge-to-mass ratio ($e/m$) of the particles. Their charge-to-mass ratio was found to be exactly the same, whatever gas or type of electrodes were used in the experiment. The cathode-ray particles had a tiny mass, only approximately 1/2000 th of the mass of a hydrogen atom. Thomson then decided to call them **electrons** – the name suggested earlier by Stoney for the 'units of electricity'.

## Millikan's 'oil-drop' experiment

The electron charge was first measured accurately in 1909 by the American physicist Robert Millikan using his famous 'oil-drop' experiment (*figure 1.5*). He found the charge to be $1.602 \times 10^{-19}$ C (coulombs). The mass of an electron was calculated to be $9.109 \times 10^{-31}$ kg, which is 1/1837 th of the mass of a hydrogen atom.

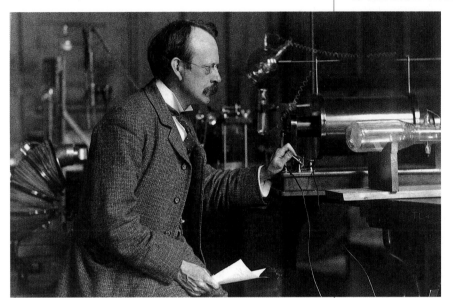

● **Figure 1.4** A drawing of Thomson's apparatus. The electrons move from the hot cathode (negative) through slits in the anode (positive).

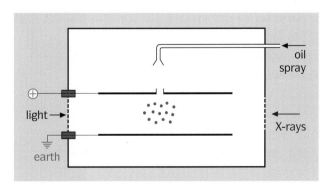

● **Figure 1.5** Robert Millikan's 'oil-drop' experiment. Millikan gave the oil drops negative charge by spraying them into air ionised by X-ray bombardment. He adjusted the charge on the plates so that the upward force of attraction equalled the downward force due to gravity, and a drop could remain stationary. Calculations on the forces allowed him to find the charges on the drops. These were multiples of the charge on an electron.

# Discovering protons and neutrons

## New atomic models: 'plum-pudding' or 'nuclear' atom

The discoveries about electrons demanded new models for atoms. If there are negatively charged electrons in all electrically neutral atoms, there must also be a positively charged part. For some time the most favoured atomic model was J. J. Thomson's 'plum-pudding', in which electrons (the plums) were embedded in a 'pudding' of positive charge (*figure 1.6*).

Then, in 1909, came one of the experiments that changed every-thing. Two members of Ernest Rutherford's research team in Manchester University, Hans Geiger and Ernest Marsden, were investigating how α-particles (α is the Greek letter alpha) from a radioactive source were scattered when fired at very thin sheets of gold and other metals (*figure 1.7*). They detected the α-particles by the small flashes of light (called 'scintillations') that they caused on impact with a fluorescent screen. Since (in atomic terms) α-particles are heavy and energetic, Geiger and Marsden were not surprised that most particles passed through the metal with only slight deflections in their paths. These deflections could be explained by the 'plum-pudding' model of the atom, as small scattering effects caused while the positive α-particles moved through the diffuse mixture of positive charge and electrons.

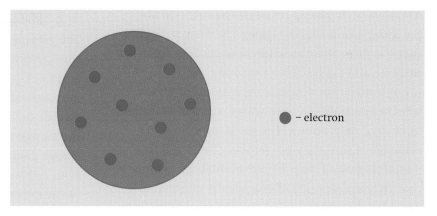

● **Figure 1.6** J. J. Thomson's 'plum-pudding' model of the atom. The electrons (plums) are embedded in a sphere of uniform positive charge.

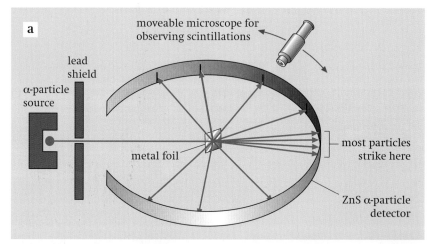

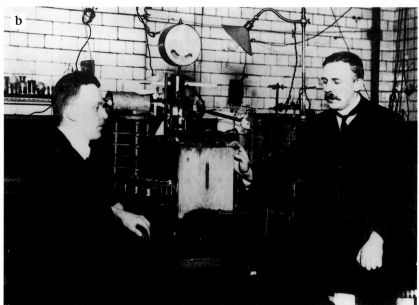

● **Figure 1.7** Geiger and Marsden's experiment, which investigated how α-particles are deflected by thin metal foils.
**a** A drawing showing the arrangement of the apparatus.
**b** Ernest Rutherford (right) and Hans Geiger using their apparatus for detecting α-particle deflections. Interpretation of the results led Rutherford to propose the nuclear model for atoms.

However, Geiger and Marsden also noticed some large deflections. A few (about one in 20 000) were so large that scintillations were seen on a screen placed on the same side of the gold sheet as the source of positively charged α-particles. This was unexpected. Rutherford said: 'it was almost as incredible as if you had fired a 15-inch shell at a piece of tissue paper and it came back and hit you!'

The plum-pudding model, with its diffuse positive charge, could not explain the surprising Geiger–Marsden observations. However, Rutherford soon proposed his convincing nuclear model of the atom. He suggested that atoms consist largely of empty space and that the mass is concentrated into a very small, positively charged, central core called the **nucleus**. The nucleus is about 10 000 times smaller than the atom itself – similar in scale to a marble placed at the centre of an athletics stadium.

Most α-particles will pass through the empty space in an atom with very little deflection. When an α-particle approaches on a path close to a nucleus, however, the positive charges strongly repel each other and the α-particle is deflected through a large angle (*figure 1.8*).

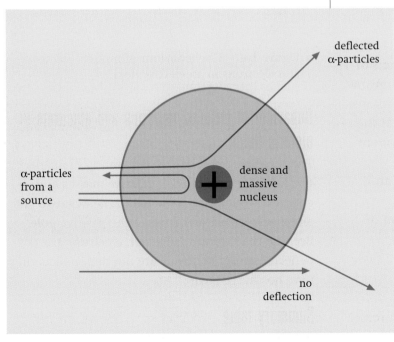

● **Figure 1.8** Ernest Rutherford's interpretation of the Geiger–Marsden observations. The positively charged α-particles are deflected by the tiny, dense, positively charged nucleus. Most of the atom is empty space.

## Nuclear charge and 'atomic' number

In 1913, Henry Moseley, a member of Rutherford's research team in Manchester, found a way of comparing the positive charges of the nuclei of elements. The charge increases by one unit from element to element in the Periodic Table. Moseley showed that the sequence of elements in the Table is related to the nuclear charges of their atoms, rather than to their relative atomic masses (see page 199). The size of the nuclear charge was then called the **atomic number** of the element. Atomic number defined the position of the element in the Periodic Table.

## Particles in the nucleus

### The proton

After he proposed the nuclear atom, Rutherford reasoned that there must be particles in the nucleus which are responsible for the positive nuclear charge. He and Marsden fired α-particles through hydrogen, nitrogen and other materials. They detected new particles with positive charge and the approximate mass of a hydrogen atom. Rutherford eventually called these particles **protons**. A proton carries a positive charge of $1.602 \times 10^{-19}$ C, equal in size but opposite in sign to the charge on an electron. It has a mass of $1.673 \times 10^{-27}$ kg, about 2000 times as heavy as an electron.

Each electrically neutral atom has the same number of electrons outside the nucleus as there are protons within the nucleus.

### The neutron

The mass of an atom, which is concentrated in its nucleus, cannot depend only on protons; usually the protons provide around half of the atomic mass. Rutherford proposed that there is a particle in the nucleus with a mass equal to that of a proton but with zero electrical charge. He thought of this particle as a proton and an electron bound together.

Without any charge to make it 'perform' in electrical fields, detection

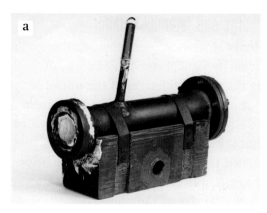

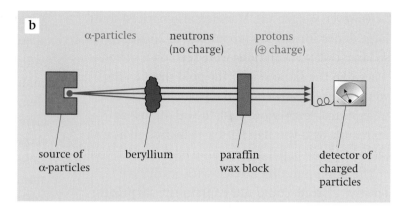

- **Figure 1.9**
- **a** Using this apparatus, James Chadwick discovered the neutron.
- **b** Drawing of the inside of the apparatus. Chadwick bombarded a block of beryllium with α-particles ($^4_2$He). No charged particles were detected on the other side of the block. However, when a block of paraffin wax (a compound containing only carbon and hydrogen) was placed near the beryllium, charged particles were detected and identified as protons (H⁺). Alpha-particles had knocked neutrons out of the beryllium, and in turn these had knocked protons out of the wax.

of this particle was very difficult. It was not until 12 years after Rutherford's suggestion that, in 1932, one of his co-workers, James Chadwick, produced sufficient evidence for the existence of a nuclear particle with a mass similar to that of the proton but with no electrical charge (*figure 1.9*). The particle was named the neutron.

# Atomic and mass numbers

## Atomic number (*Z*)

The most important difference between atoms of different elements is in the number of protons in the nucleus of each atom. The number of protons in an atom determines the element to which the atom belongs. The atomic number of an element shows:

- the number of protons in the nucleus of an atom of that element;
- the number of electrons in a neutral atom of that element;
- the position of the element in the Periodic Table.

## Mass number (*A*)

It is useful to have a measure for the total number of particles in the nucleus of an atom. This is called the **mass number**. For any atom:

- the mass number is the sum of the number of protons and the number of neutrons.

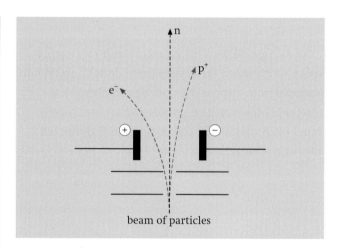

- **Figure 1.10** The behaviour of protons, neutrons and electrons in an electric field.

## Behaviour of protons, neutrons and electrons in electric fields

The three particles behave differently in an electric field, because of their relative masses and charges. Protons are attracted to the negative pole and electrons are attracted to the positive pole. Because they are much lighter, electrons are deflected more. Neutrons are not deflected as they have no charge (*figure 1.10*).

## Summary table

| Particle name | Relative mass | Relative charge |
|---|---|---|
| electron | negligible | −1 |
| proton | 1 | +1 |
| neutron | 1 | 0 |

# Isotopes

In Rutherford's model of the atom, the nucleus consists of protons and neutrons, each with a mass of one atomic unit. The relative atomic masses of elements should then be whole numbers. It was thus a puzzle why chlorine has a relative atomic mass of 35.5.

The answer is that atoms of the same element are not all identical. In 1913, Frederick Soddy proposed that atoms of the same element could have different atomic masses. He named such atoms **isotopes**. The word means 'equal place', i.e. occupying the same place in the Periodic Table and having the same atomic number.

The discovery of protons and neutrons explained the existence of isotopes of an element. In isotopes of one element, the number of protons must be the same, but the number of neutrons may be different.

Remember:

atomic number ($Z$) = number of protons

mass number ($A$) = number of protons + number of neutrons

Isotopes are atoms with the same atomic number, but different mass numbers. The symbol for isotopes is shown as

$$\frac{\text{mass number}}{\text{atomic number}}X \quad \text{or} \quad {}^{A}_{Z}X$$

For example, hydrogen has three isotopes:

|  | Protium, $^{1}_{1}H$ | Deuterium, $^{2}_{1}H$ | Tritium, $^{3}_{1}H$ |
|---|---|---|---|
| protons | 1 | 1 | 1 |
| neutrons | 0 | 1 | 2 |

It is also common practice to identify isotopes by name or symbol plus mass number only. For example, uranium, the heaviest naturally occurring element ($Z = 92$), has two particularly important isotopes of mass numbers 235 and 238. They are often shown as uranium-235 and uranium-238, as U-235 and U-238 or as $^{235}U$ and $^{238}U$.

## Numbers of protons, neutrons and electrons

It is easy to calculate the composition of a particular atom or ion:

number of protons = $Z$

number of neutrons = $A - Z$

number of electrons in neutral atom = $Z$

number of electrons in positive ion = $Z$ – charge on ion

number of electrons in negative ion = $Z$ + charge on ion

For example, magnesium is element 12; it is in Group II, so it tends to form doubly charged (2+) ions. The ionised isotope magnesium-25 thus has the full symbol $^{25}_{12}Mg^{2+}$, and

number of protons = 12

number of neutrons = 13

number of electrons = 10

## SAQ 1.1

**a** What is the composition (numbers of electrons, protons and neutrons) of neutral atoms of the two main uranium isotopes, U-235 and U-238?

**b** What is the composition of the ions of potassium-40 ($K^+$) and chlorine-37 ($Cl^-$)?

(Use the Periodic Table, page 401, for the atomic numbers.)

# Electrons in atoms

Electrons hold the key to almost the whole of chemistry. Protons and neutrons give atoms their mass, but electrons are the outer part of the atom and only electrons are involved in the changes that happen during chemical reactions. If we knew everything about the arrangements of electrons in atoms and molecules, we could predict most of the ways that chemicals behave, purely from mathematics. So far this has proved very difficult, even with the most advanced computers – but it may yet happen.

## SAQ 1.2

Suggest why the isotopes of an element have the same chemical properties, though they have different relative atomic masses.

What models are currently accepted about how electrons are arranged around the nucleus? The first simple idea – that they just orbit randomly around the nucleus – was soon rejected. Calculations showed that any moving, electrically charged particles, like electrons, would lose energy and fall into the nucleus.

A model you may have used considers the electrons to be arranged in shells. These 'shells' correspond to different energy levels occupied by the electrons.

## Arrangements of electrons: energy levels and 'shells'

There was a great advance in atomic theory when, in 1913, the Danish physicist Niels Bohr proposed his ideas about arrangements of electrons in atoms.

Earlier the German physicist Max Planck had proposed, in his 'Quantum Theory' of 1901, that energy, like matter, is 'atomic'. It can only be transferred in packets of energy he called quanta; a single packet of energy is a quantum. Bohr applied this idea to the energy of electrons. He suggested that, as electrons could only possess energy in quanta, they would not exist in a stable way, anywhere outside the nucleus, unless they were in fixed or 'quantised' energy levels. If an electron gained or lost energy, it could move to higher or lower energy levels, but not somewhere in between. It is a bit like climbing a ladder; you can only stay in a stable state on one of the rungs. You will find that, as you read more widely, there are several names given to these energy levels. The most common name is **shells**.

Shells are numbered 1, 2, 3, 4, etc. These numbers are known as **principal quantum numbers** (symbol $n$). Such numbers correspond to the numbers of rows (or Periods) in the Periodic Table.

We can now write the simple electronic configurations as shown in *table 1.1*. Remember that the atomic number tells us the number of electrons present in an atom of the element. For a given element, electrons are added to the shells as follows:

■ up to 2 electrons in shell 1;
■ up to 8 electrons in shell 2;
■ up to 18 electrons in shell 3.

Some of the best evidence for the existence of electron shells comes from ionisation energies.

## Ionisation energy

When an atom loses an electron it becomes a positive ion. We say that it has been ionised. Energy is needed to remove electrons and this is generally called **ionisation energy**. More precisely, the first ionisation energy of an element is the amount of energy needed to remove one electron from each atom in a mole of atoms of an element in the gaseous state.

The general symbol for ionisation energy is $\Delta H_i$ and for a first ionisation energy it is $\Delta H_{i1}$. The process may be shown by the example of calcium as:

$$Ca(g) \rightarrow Ca^+(g) + e^-; \qquad \Delta H_{i1} = +590 \, kJ \, mol^{-1}$$

(If the symbols seem unfamiliar at this stage, see page 73.)

The energy needed to remove a second electron from each ion in a mole of gaseous ions is the second ionisation energy. For calcium:

$$Ca^+(g) \rightarrow Ca^{2+}(g) + e^-; \qquad \Delta H_{i2} = +1150 \, kJ \, mol^{-1}$$

Note that the second ionisation energy is much larger than the first. The reasons for this are discussed on page 9.

We can continue removing electrons until only the nucleus of an atom is left. The sequence of first, second, third, fourth, etc. ionisation energies (or successive ionisation energies) for the first 11 elements in the Periodic Table are shown in *table 1.2*.

|  | Atomic number | Number of electrons in shell | | |
|---|---|---|---|---|
|  |  | $n = 1$ | $n = 2$ | $n = 3$ |
| H | 1 | 1 |  |  |
| He | 2 | 2 |  |  |
| Li | 3 | 2 | 1 |  |
| Be | 4 | 2 | 2 |  |
| B | 5 | 2 | 3 |  |
| C | 6 | 2 | 4 |  |
| N | 7 | 2 | 5 |  |
| O | 8 | 2 | 6 |  |
| F | 9 | 2 | 7 |  |
| Ne | 10 | 2 | 8 |  |
| Na | 11 | 2 | 8 | 1 |

● **Table 1.1** Electronic configurations of the first 11 elements in the Periodic Table.

| | | 1 | 2 | 3 | 4 | 5 | 6 | 7 | 8 | 9 | 10 | 11 |
|---|---|---|---|---|---|---|---|---|---|---|---|---|
| | | | | | | Electrons removed | | | | | | |
| 1 | H | 1310 | | | | | | | | | | |
| 2 | He | 2370 | 5250 | | | | | | | | | |
| 3 | Li | 520 | 7300 | 11800 | | | | | | | | |
| 4 | Be | 900 | 1760 | 14850 | 21000 | | | | | | | |
| 5 | B | 800 | 2420 | 3660 | 25000 | 32800 | | | | | | |
| 6 | C | 1090 | 2350 | 4620 | 6220 | 37800 | 47300 | | | | | |
| 7 | N | 1400 | 2860 | 4580 | 7480 | 9450 | 53300 | 64400 | | | | |
| 8 | O | 1310 | 3390 | 5320 | 7450 | 11000 | 13300 | 71300 | 84100 | | | |
| 9 | F | 1680 | 3470 | 6040 | 8410 | 11000 | 15200 | 17900 | 92000 | 106000 | | |
| 10 | Ne | 2080 | 3950 | 6120 | 9370 | 12200 | 15200 | – | – | – | 131400 | |
| 11 | Na | 510 | 4560 | 6940 | 9540 | 13400 | 16600 | 20100 | 25500 | 28900 | 141000 | 158700 |

● **Table 1.2** Successive ionisation energies for the first 11 elements in the Periodic Table (to nearest $10\,kJ\,mol^{-1}$).

We see that the following hold for any one element:

■ The ionisation energies increase. As each electron is removed from an atom, the remaining ion becomes more positively charged. Moving the next electron away from the increased positive charge is more difficult and the next ionisation energy is even larger.

■ There are one or more particularly large rises within the set of ionisation energies of each element (except hydrogen and helium).

Ionisation energies of elements are measured mainly by two techniques:

■ calculating the energy of the radiation causing particular lines in the emission spectrum of the element;

■ using electron bombardment of gaseous elements in discharge tubes.

We now know the ionisation energies of all of the elements.

These data may be interpreted in terms of the atomic numbers of elements and their simple electronic configurations.

Before doing so, we must consider the factors which influence ionisation energies.

## Factors influencing ionisation energies

The three strongest influences on ionisation energies of elements are the following:

■ *The size of the positive nuclear charge*
This charge affects all the electrons in an atom.

The increase in nuclear charge with atomic number will tend to cause an increase in ionisation energies.

■ *The distance of the electron from the nucleus*
It has been found that, if $F$ is the force of attraction between two objects and $d$ is the distance between them, then

$F$ is proportional to $1/d^2$
    (the 'inverse square law')

This distance effect means that all forces of attraction decrease rapidly as the distance between the attracted bodies increases. Thus the attractions between a nucleus and electrons decrease as the quantum numbers of the shells increase. The further the shell is from the nucleus, the lower are the ionisation energies for electrons in that shell.

■ *The 'shielding' effect by electrons in filled inner shells*
All electrons are negatively charged and repel each other. Electrons in the filled inner shells repel electrons in the outer shell and reduce the effect of the positive nuclear charge. This is called the **shielding effect**. The greater the shielding effect upon an electron, the lower is the energy required to remove it and thus the lower the ionisation energy.

Consider the example of the successive ionisation energies of lithium. We see a low first ionisation energy, followed by much larger second and third ionisation energies. This confirms that lithium has one electron in its outer shell $n = 2$, which is easier to remove than either of the two electrons in the inner shell $n = 1$. The large increase in ionisation energy indicates where there is a change from shell $n = 2$ to shell $n = 1$.

The pattern is seen even more clearly if we plot a graph of ionisation energies ($y$ axis) against number of electrons removed ($x$ axis). As the ionisation energies are so large, we must use logarithm to base 10 ($\log_{10}$) to make the numbers fit on a reasonable scale. The graph for sodium is shown in *figure 1.11*.

### SAQ 1.3

**a** In *figure 1.11* why are there large increases between the first and second ionisation energies and again between the ninth and tenth ionisation energies?

**b** How does this graph confirm the suggested simple electronic configuration for sodium of (2,8,1)?

Successive ionisation energies are thus helpful for predicting or confirming the simple electronic configurations of elements. In particular, they confirm the number of electrons in the outer shell. This leads also to confirmation of the position of the element in the Periodic Table.

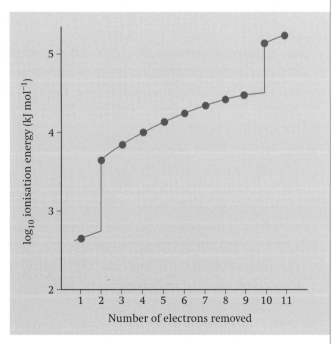

● **Figure 1.11** Graph of logarithm ($\log_{10}$) of ionisation energy of sodium against the number of electrons removed.

Elements with one electron in their outer shell are in Group I, elements with two electrons in their outer shell are in Group II, and so on.

### SAQ 1.4

The first four ionisation energies of an element are, in kJ mol$^{-1}$: 590, 1150, 4940 and 6480. Suggest the Group in the Periodic Table to which this element belongs.

## Need for a more complex model

Electronic configurations are not quite so simple as the pattern shown in *table 1.1*. You will see in chapter 9 (page 206) that the first ionisation energies of the elements 3 (lithium) to 10 (neon) do not increase evenly. This, and other, variations show the need for a more complex model of **electron configurations** than the Bohr model.

The newer models depend upon an understanding of the mathematics of quantum mechanics and, in particular, the Schrödinger equation and Heisenberg's uncertainty principle. Explanations of these will not be attempted in this book, but an outline of some implications for the chemist's view of atoms is given.

It is now thought that the following hold:

■ The energy levels (shells) of principal quantum numbers $n = 1, 2, 3, 4$, etc. do not have precise energy values. Instead, they each consist of a set of subshells, which contain **orbitals** with different energy values.

■ The subshells are of different types labelled s, p, d and f. An s subshell contains one orbital; a p subshell contains three orbitals; a d subshell contains five orbitals; and an f subshell contains seven orbitals.

■ An electron orbital represents a region of space around the nucleus of an atom, within which there is a high chance of finding that particular electron.

■ Each orbital has its own approximate, three-dimensional shape. It is not possible to draw the shape of orbitals precisely. They do not have exact boundaries but are fuzzy, like clouds; indeed, they are often called 'charge-clouds'. Approximate representations of orbitals are shown in *figure 1.12*. Some regions, where there is

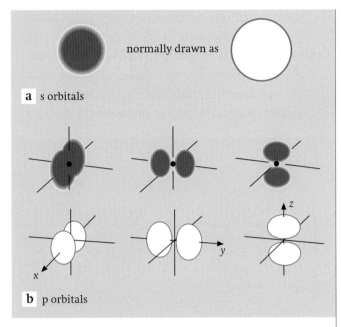

**a** s orbitals

**b** p orbitals

● **Figure 1.12** Representations of orbitals (the position of the nucleus is shown by the black dot):
**a** s orbitals with spherical symmetry;
**b** p orbitals, $p_x$, $p_y$ and $p_z$, with 'lobes' along $x$, $y$ and $z$ axes.

a greater chance of finding an electron, are shown as more dense than others. To make drawing easier, however, we usually show orbitals as if they have a boundary; this encloses over 90% of the space where you can find the electron. Note that there is only one type of s orbital but three different p orbitals ($p_x$, $p_y$, $p_z$). There are five different d orbitals and seven f orbitals.

## Orbitals: Pauli exclusion principle and spin-pairing

The shell $n = 1$ consists of a single s orbital called 1s; $n = 2$ consists of s and p orbitals in subshells called 2s and 2p; $n = 3$ consists of s, p and d orbitals in subshells called 3s, 3p and 3d.

There is an important principle concerning orbitals that affects all electronic configurations. This is the theory that any individual orbital can hold *one* or *two* electrons but *not more*. The principle was proposed by the Austro-Swiss physicist Wolfgang Pauli in 1921 and is called the Pauli exclusion principle.

You may wonder how an orbital can hold two electrons with negative charges that repel each other strongly. It is explained by the idea of spin-pairing. Along with charge, we say that electrons have a property called spin. We can visualise

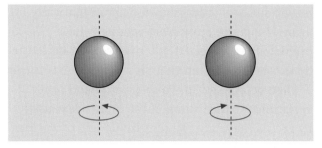

● **Figure 1.13** Representation of opposite spins of electrons.

spin as an electron rotating at a fixed rate. Two electrons can exist as a pair in an orbital through each having opposite spin (*figure 1.13*); this reduces the effect of repulsion (see also later in this chapter). Clockwise spin is shown as ↑, anticlockwise spin as ↓.

From all the known evidence, including the Pauli exclusion principle, scientists have decided that: shell $n = 1$ contains up to two electrons in an s orbital; shell $n = 2$ contains up to eight electrons, two in an s orbital and six in the p subshell, with two in each of the $p_x$, $p_y$, $p_z$ orbitals; shell $n = 3$ contains up to 18 electrons, two in an s orbital, six in the p subshell and ten in the d subshell, with two in each of the five orbitals.

## Order of filling shells and orbitals

In each successive element of the Periodic Table, the order of filling the shells and orbitals is the order of their relative energy. The electronic configuration of each atom is the one that gives as low an energy state as possible to the atom as a whole. This means that the lowest-energy orbitals are filled first. The order of filling is:

first 1s, then 2s, 2p, 3s, 3p, 4s, 3d, 4p, …

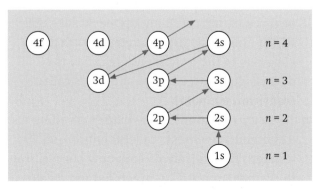

● **Figure 1.14** Diagram to show the order in which orbitals are filled up to shell $n = 4$.

As you see, the order (shown diagrammatically in *figure 1.14*) is not quite what we might have predicted! An expected order is followed up to the 3p subshell, but then there is a variation, as the 4s is filled before the 3d. This variation and other variations further along in the order are caused by the increasingly complex influences of nuclear attractions and electron repulsions upon individual electrons.

# Electronic configurations

## Representing electronic configurations

The most common way of representing the electronic configurations of atoms is shown below. For example, hydrogen has one electron in an s orbital in the shell with principal quantum number $n = 1$. We show this as

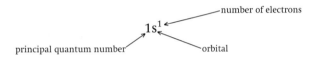

Helium has two electrons, both in the 1s orbital, and is shown as $1s^2$.

The electronic configurations for the first 18 elements (H to Ar) are shown in *table 1.3*.

For the set of elements 19 (potassium) to 36 (krypton), it is more convenient to represent part of the configuration as a 'noble-gas core'. In this case the core is the configuration of argon. For convenience we sometimes represent $1s^2\ 2s^2\ 2p^6\ 3s^2\ 3p^6$ as [Ar] rather than write it out each time. Some examples are shown in *table 1.4*.

The following points should be noted:

■ When the 4s orbital is filled, the next electron goes into a 3d orbital (see scandium). This begins a pattern of filling up the 3d subshell, which finishes at zinc. The elements that add electrons to the d subshells are called the d-block elements; a subset of these is called **transition elements**.

■ There are variations in the pattern of filling the d subshell at elements 24 (chromium) and 29 (copper). These elements have only one electron in their 4s orbital. Chromium has five d electrons, rather than the expected four; copper has ten d electrons rather than nine. This is the

outcome of the complex interactions of attractions and repulsions in their atoms.

■ From element 31 (gallium) to 36 (krypton) the electrons add to the 4p subshell. This is similar to the pattern of filling the 3p subshell from elements 13 (aluminium) to 18 (argon) in Period 3.

| 1 | H | $1s^1$ |
|---|---|---|
| 2 | He | $1s^2$ |
| 3 | Li | $1s^2\ 2s^1$ |
| 4 | Be | $1s^2\ 2s^2$ |
| 5 | B | $1s^2\ 2s^2\ 2p^1$ |
| 6 | C | $1s^2\ 2s^2\ 2p^2$ |
| 7 | N | $1s^2\ 2s^2\ 2p^3$ |
| 8 | O | $1s^2\ 2s^2\ 2p^4$ |
| 9 | F | $1s^2\ 2s^2\ 2p^5$ |
| 10 | Ne | $1s^2\ 2s^2\ 2p^6$ |
| 11 | Na | $1s^2\ 2s^2\ 2p^6\ 3s^1$ |
| 12 | Mg | $1s^2\ 2s^2\ 2p^6\ 3s^2$ |
| 13 | Al | $1s^2\ 2s^2\ 2p^6\ 3s^2\ 3p^1$ |
| 14 | Si | $1s^2\ 2s^2\ 2p^6\ 3s^2\ 3p^2$ |
| 15 | P | $1s^2\ 2s^2\ 2p^6\ 3s^2\ 3p^3$ |
| 16 | S | $1s^2\ 2s^2\ 2p^6\ 3s^2\ 3p^4$ |
| 17 | Cl | $1s^2\ 2s^2\ 2p^6\ 3s^2\ 3p^5$ |
| 18 | Ar | $1s^2\ 2s^2\ 2p^6\ 3s^2\ 3p^6$ |

● **Table 1.3** Electronic configurations for the first 18 elements in the Periodic Table.

| 19 | Potassium (K) | $[Ar]\ 4s^1$ |
|---|---|---|
| 20 | Calcium (Ca) | $[Ar]\ 4s^2$ |
| 21 | Scandium (Sc) | $[Ar]\ 3d^1\ 4s^2$ |
| ⋮ | | |
| 24 | Chromium (Cr) | $[Ar]\ 3d^5\ 4s^1$ |
| 25 | Manganese (Mn) | $[Ar]\ 3d^5\ 4s^2$ |
| ⋮ | | |
| 29 | Copper (Cu) | $[Ar]\ 3d^{10}\ 4s^1$ |
| 30 | Zinc (Zn) | $[Ar]\ 3d^{10}\ 4s^2$ |
| 31 | Gallium (Ga) | $[Ar]\ 3d^{10}\ 4s^2\ 4p^1$ |
| ⋮ | | |
| 35 | Bromine (Br) | $[Ar]\ 3d^{10}\ 4s^2\ 4p^5$ |
| 36 | Krypton (Kr) | $[Ar]\ 3d^{10}\ 4s^2\ 4p^6$ |

● **Table 1.4** Electronic configurations for some of the elements 19 to 36, where [Ar] is the electronic configuration of argon, $1s^2\ 2s^2\ 2p^6\ 3s^2\ 3p^6$.

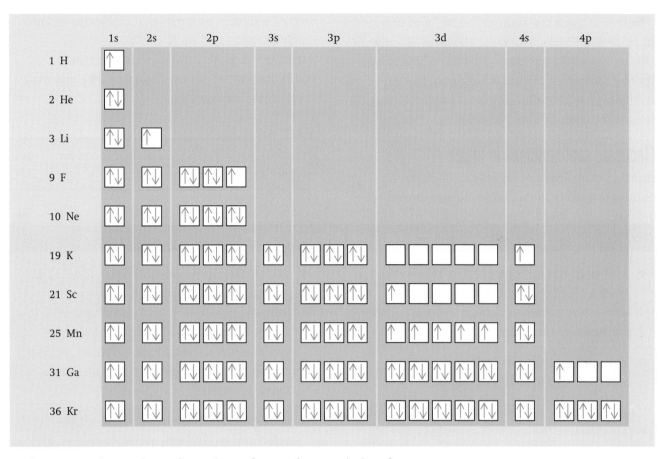

● **Figure 1.15** Electronic configurations of some elements in box form.

## Filling of orbitals

Whenever possible, electrons will occupy orbitals singly. This is due to the repulsion of electron charges. Electrons remain unpaired until the available orbitals *of equal energy* have one electron each. When there are more electrons than the orbitals can hold as singles, they pair up by spin-pairing. This means that, if there are three electrons available for a p subshell, one each will go to the $p_x$, $p_y$ and $p_z$ orbitals, rather than two in $p_x$, one in $p_y$ and none in $p_z$. When there are four electrons available, two will spin-pair in one orbital, leaving single electrons in the other orbitals. Similarly, five electrons in a d subshell

will remain unpaired in the five orbitals (see *figure 1.15*).

As an example, we can show how orbitals are occupied in atoms of carbon, nitrogen and oxygen as:

carbon (six electrons)     $1s^2\ 2s^2\ 2p_x^{\ 1}\ 2p_y^{\ 1}\ 2p_z^{\ 0}$
nitrogen (seven electrons)

$$1s^2\ 2s^2\ 2p_x^{\ 1}\ 2p_y^{\ 1}\ 2p_z^{\ 1}$$

oxygen (eight electrons)   $1s^2\ 2s^2\ 2p_x^{\ 2}\ 2p_y^{\ 1}\ 2p_z^{\ 1}$

(Normally electronic configurations are shown in less detail – as in *table 1.4*.)

## Electronic configurations of ions

The number of electrons in an ion is found from the atomic number of the element and the charge of the ion. Some examples are shown in *table 1.5*.

| | Sodium atom | Sodium ion | Fluorine atom | Fluoride ion |
|---|---|---|---|---|
| Symbol | Na | $Na^+$ | F | $F^-$ |
| Atomic number | 11 | 11 | 9 | 9 |
| Electrons | 11 | 10 | 9 | 10 |
| Configuration | $1s^2\ 2s^2\ 2p^6\ 3s^1$ | $1s^2\ 2s^2\ 2p^6$ | $1s^2\ 2s^2\ 2p^5$ | $1s^2\ 2s^2\ 2p^6$ |

● **Table 1.5**

Note that both the sodium ion Na$^+$ and the fluoride ion F$^-$ have the same electronic configuration as the noble gas neon. This has implications for the formation of, and bonding in, the compound sodium fluoride (see chapter 3, page 30 for a discussion of ionic bonding).

## Electronic configurations in boxes

Another useful way of representing electronic configurations is in box form. We can show the electrons as arrows with their clockwise or anti-clockwise spin as ↑ or ↓.

*Figure 1.15* (page 13) shows the electronic configurations of some of the first 36 elements represented in this way.

### SAQ 1.5

Draw box-form electronic configurations for: boron, oxygen, argon, nickel and bromine.

## SUMMARY (AS)

- Any atom has an internal structure with almost all of the mass in the nucleus, which has a diameter about $10^{-4}$ that of the diameter of the atom.

- The nucleus contains protons (+ charge) and neutrons (0 charge). Electrons (– charge) exist outside the nucleus.

- All atoms of the same element have the same atomic number ($Z$); that is, they have equal numbers of protons in their nuclei.

- The mass number ($A$) of an atom is the total number of protons and neutrons. Thus the number of neutrons = $A - Z$.

- The isotopes of an element are atoms with the same atomic number but different mass numbers. If neutral, they have the same number of protons and electrons but different numbers of neutrons.

- Electrons can exist only at certain energy levels and gain or lose 'quanta' of energy when they move between the levels.

- The main energy levels or 'shells' are given principal quantum numbers $n$ = 1, 2, 3, 4, etc. Shell $n$ = 1 is the closest to the nucleus.

- The shells consist of subshells known as s, p, d or f and each subshell consists of orbitals. Subshells s, p, d and f have one, three, five and seven orbitals respectively. Orbitals s, p, d, and f have different, distinctive shapes; we have looked at the shapes of s and p orbitals.

- Each orbital holds a maximum of two electrons, so that full subshells of s, p, d and f orbitals contain two, six, ten and fourteen electrons respectively. The two electrons in any single orbital are spin-paired.

- Electrons remain unpaired among orbitals of equal energy until numbers require them to spin-pair.

- The first ionisation energy of an element is the energy required to remove one electron from each atom in a mole of atoms of the element in the gaseous state.

- Successive ionisation energies are the energies required to remove first, second, third, fourth, etc. electrons from a mole of gaseous ions of an element.

- Large changes in the values of successive ionisation energies of an element indicate that the electrons are being removed from different shells. This gives evidence for the electronic configuration of atoms of the element and helps to confirm the position of the element in the Periodic Table.

# Questions (AS)

1 What are the electronic configurations of the following atoms or ions: $Li^+$, $K^+$, $Ca^{2+}$, $N^{3-}$, $O^{2-}$, $S^{2-}$, $Cl$ and $Cl^-$?

2 Chemists use a model of an atom that consists of subatomic particles (protons, neutrons and electrons).

   a State the relative mass and relative charge of each of these three particles.

   b The particles in each of the following pairs differ **only** in the number of protons **or** neutrons **or** electrons. Explain what the difference is within each pair.

   (i) $^6Li$ and $^7Li$

   (ii) $^{32}S$ and $^{32}S^{2-}$

   (iii) $^{39}K^+$ and $^{40}Ca^{2+}$

3 Hydrogen fluoride in water produces hydrofluoric acid. This acid is extremely corrosive and, because it reacts with glass, is often stored in nickel containers. This is possible because the hydrofluoric acid reacts with the nickel to form a protective coating of nickel(II) fluoride.

   a What is the electronic configuration of a nickel atom?

   b Predict the electronic configuration of a nickel(II) ion.

4 In 1911, a 40 kg meteorite fell in Egypt. Isotopic and chemical analysis of oxygen extracted from this meteorite showed a different relative atomic mass to that of oxygen normally found on Earth. This value matched measurements made of the Martian atmosphere by the Viking landing in 1976, proving that the meteorite had originated from Mars.

   a (i) Explain what you understand by the word **isotopes**.

   (ii) Oxygen has three main isotopes, $^{16}O$, $^{17}O$ and $^{18}O$. State the number of protons, neutrons and electrons in $^{16}O$ and $^{17}O$.

   (iii) Explain what you understand by the term **relative atomic mass**.

   (iv) Suggest why the relative atomic mass of Martian oxygen is different from that of oxygen obtained from Earth.

   b The first ionisation energy of oxygen is $1310 \, kJ \, mol^{-1}$.

   (i) Explain what is meant by the first ionisation energy of an element.

   (ii) Write an equation, including state symbols, to represent the first ionisation energy of oxygen.

   (iii) Suggest why there is very little difference between the first ionisation energies of $^{16}O$, $^{17}O$ and $^{18}O$.

5 Values of the successive ionisation energies of nitrogen are shown below:

| Ionisation energy | 1st | 2nd | 3rd | 4th | 5th | 6th | 7th |
|---|---|---|---|---|---|---|---|
| $(kJ \, mol^{-1})$ | 1400 | 2860 | 4590 | 7480 | 9450 | 53 300 | 64 400 |

   a Explain why the successive ionisation energies increase.

   b Explain why there is a particularly large difference between the 5th and 6th ionisation energies of nitrogen.

# CHAPTER 2

# Atoms, molecules and stoichiometry (AS)

## By the end of this chapter you should be able to:

1 define the terms *relative atomic mass*, *relative isotopic mass*, *relative molecular mass* and *relative formula mass*, based on the $^{12}C$ scale;

2 describe the basic principles of the mass spectrometer;

3 outline the use of *mass spectrometry* in the determination of *relative isotopic mass*, *isotopic abundance* and *relative atomic mass*, and as a method for identifying elements;

4 interpret mass spectra in terms of isotopic abundances;

5 calculate the relative atomic mass of an element given the relative abundances of its isotopes, or its mass spectrum;

6 define the *mole* in terms of *Avogadro's constant* and *molar mass* as the mass of 1 mole of a substance;

7 define the terms *empirical formula* and *molecular formula*;

8 calculate empirical and molecular formulae, using composition by mass;

9 construct *balanced* chemical equations (full and ionic);

10 perform calculations involving reacting masses, volumes of gases and volumes and concentrations of solutions in simple acid–base *titrations,* and use those calculations to deduce *stoichiometric* relationships.

## Counting atoms and molecules

If you have ever had to sort and count coins, you will know that it is a very time-consuming business! Banks do not need to count sorted coins, as they can quickly check the amount by weighing. For example, as a 2p coin has twice the mass of a 1p coin, a bag containing £2.00 could contain one hundred 2p coins or two hundred 1p coins. Chemists are also able to count atoms and molecules by weighing them. This is possible because atoms of different elements also have different masses.

We rely on tables of relative atomic masses for this purpose. The **relative atomic mass**, $A_r$, of an element is the average mass of one atom of the element relative to the mass of carbon-12; one atom of this isotope (see chapter 1, page 7) is given a relative isotopic mass of exactly 12. The relative atomic masses, $A_r$, of the other elements are then found by comparing the average mass of their atoms with that of the carbon-12 isotope. Notice that we use the average mass of their atoms. This is because we take into account the abundance of their naturally occurring isotopes. Thus the precise relative atomic mass of hydrogen is 1.0079, whilst that of chlorine is 35.49. (Accepted relative atomic masses are shown on the Periodic Table on page 401.)

We use the term **relative isotopic mass** for the mass of an isotope of an element relative to carbon-12. For example, the relative isotopic mass of carbon-13 is 13.003. If the natural abundance of each isotope is known, together with their relative isotopic masses, we can calculate the relative atomic mass of the element as follows.

Chlorine, for example, occurs naturally as chlorine-35 and chlorine-37 with percentage natural abundances 75.5% and 24.5% respectively. So

$$\text{relative atomic mass} = \frac{(75.5 \times 35 + 24.5 \times 37)}{100}$$

$$= 35.5$$

### SAQ 2.1

Naturally occurring neon is 90.9% neon–20, 0.3% neon–21 and 8.8% neon–22. Use these figures to calculate the relative atomic mass of naturally occurring neon.

The masses of different molecules are compared in a similar fashion. The **relative molecular mass**, $M_r$, of a compound is the mass of a molecule of the compound relative to the mass of an atom of carbon-12, which is given a mass of exactly 12.

To find the relative molecular mass of a molecule, we add up the relative atomic masses of all the atoms present in the molecule. For example, the relative molecular mass of methane, $CH_4$, is $12 + (4 \times 1) = 16$.

Where compounds contain ions, we use the term **relative formula mass**. Relative molecular mass refers to compounds containing molecules.

### SAQ 2.2

Use the Periodic Table in the appendix (page 401) to calculate the relative formula mass of the following:

**a** magnesium chloride, $MgCl_2$;

**b** copper sulphate, $CuSO_4$;

**c** sodium carbonate, $Na_2CO_3 \cdot 10H_2O$ (10$H_2O$ means ten water molecules).

In the next section we shall see how we determine relative isotopic masses and isotopic abundances.

# Determination of $A_r$ from mass spectra

You may have wondered how tables of relative atomic masses have been obtained. An instrument called a mass spectrometer is used for this purpose; such instruments are too expensive to be found in most schools or colleges. Academic or industrial chemical laboratories may have one or two, depending on their needs and resources. Mass spectrometers have even been sent into space (*figure 2.1*).

In order to obtain the mass and the percentage abundance for the isotopes of an element, a method for separating atoms of different masses is required. The principles for this separation are relatively simple and are as follows:

■ Atoms are first converted into singly charged, positive ions. A vaporised sample of an element is bombarded with high-energy electrons. An ion forms when a high-energy electron collides with an atom of the element. Providing the electron has sufficient energy, the collision will

**The Viking space probe**

When the two *Viking* space probes were launched by NASA in 1975, they carried mass spectrometers. The purpose of these spectrometers was to look for traces of organic compounds on the surface of Mars. Scientists had put forward the hypothesis that living organisms would have left behind traces of organic compounds. However, the soil sampled on Mars showed no trace of organic compounds.

● **Figure 2.1** The surface of Mars, seen from the *Viking I* space probe.

remove an electron from the atom, forming a positive ion.

■ A beam of these positive ions is accelerated by using a positively charged electrode to repel it.

■ The beam of positive ions passes through a magnetic field where ions are deflected according to their masses.

■ As the magnetic field deflects lighter ions more than heavier ions, separation occurs.

■ A suitable detector measures the relative abundance of each isotope present. The charge on each ion produces a tiny electric current at the detector. The more ions there are of the same mass, the higher the current.

A simplified diagram of a mass spectrometer is shown in *figure 2.2*. In practice, mass spectrometers are very sophisticated pieces of equipment involving mechanical, electrical, electronic and computer engineering. A very low pressure is needed inside a mass spectrometer to avoid loss of ions by collision with air molecules. The results are displayed on a computer monitor as a chart of abundance against mass (see, for example, *figure 2.3*, the mass spectrum of zirconium).

Notice that the abundance is on the vertical axis. The horizontal axis displays the mass-to-charge ratio ($m/e$). Remember, the mass spectrometer sorts and detects positive ions. The ions almost always carry a single positive charge. Hence you often see this axis simply labelled mass because, numerically, mass/charge = mass.

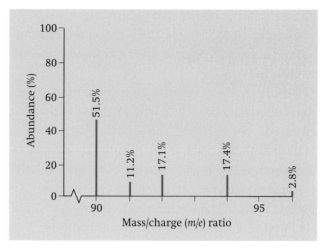

● **Figure 2.3** The mass spectrum of zirconium, Zr.

### SAQ 2.3

**a** List the isotopes present in zirconium.

**b** Use the percentage abundance of each isotope to calculate the relative atomic mass of zirconium.

Some modern mass spectrometers can be set up to determine isotopic masses to four or five decimal places. *Figure 2.4* shows a photograph of such a spectrometer.

# Counting chemical substances in bulk

## The mole and Avogadro's constant

When chemists write a formula for a compound, it tells us how many atoms of each element are present in the compound. For example, the formula of water is $H_2O$, and this tells us that two atoms of hydrogen are combined with one atom of oxygen. As the $A_r$ of hydrogen is 1 and the $A_r$ of oxygen is 16, the $M_r$ is 2 + 16 = 18 and the hydrogen and oxygen are combined in a mass ratio of 2:16. Although atoms are too small to be weighed individually, any mass of water will have hydrogen and oxygen in this ratio.

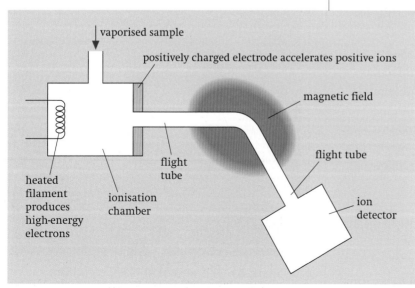

● **Figure 2.2** Simplified diagram of a mass spectrometer.

● **Figure 2.4** A high-resolution mass spectrometer, which may be used to determine accurately isotopic masses of elements.

For example, consider 18 g of water (2 + 16 = 18). This will actually contain 2 g of hydrogen and 16 g of oxygen. We can use any unit of mass as long as we keep to the same mass ratio. In 18 tonnes of water there will be 2 tonnes of hydrogen and 16 tonnes of oxygen. The actual number of atoms present will be very large indeed!

When we take the relative molecular mass or relative atomic mass of a substance in grams, we say that we have one mole of the substance. The mole is the chemist's unit of amount. A **mole** of substance is the mass of substance that has the same number of particles as there are atoms in exactly 12 g of carbon-12. The particles may be atoms, molecules, ions or even electrons.

The number of atoms or molecules in one mole is a constant known as **Avogadro's constant**. Avogadro's constant, $L$, is approximately $6 \times 10^{23} \, \text{mol}^{-1}$.

**Units used by chemists:**
  *Mass* is measured in g (kg in SI units).
  *Volume* is measured in $\text{cm}^3$ or $\text{dm}^3$
    ($1 \, \text{dm}^3 = 1000 \, \text{cm}^3 = 1 \, \text{litre}$).
  *Amount of substance* is measured in moles
    (abbreviation is mol).

You need to remember that *amount* has a specific meaning, as do *mass* and *volume*. Each has its own unit. SI is an abbreviation for the Système International d'Unités. In this internationally recognised system, kilogram, metre and mole are three of the seven base units from which all supplementary units are derived.

We often refer to the mass of one mole of a substance as the **molar mass**, $M$. The units of molar mass are $\text{g mol}^{-1}$.

In *figure 2.5* a mole of some elements may be compared.

Moles are particularly helpful when we need to measure out reactants or calculate the mass of product from a reaction. Such information is very important when manufacturing chemicals. For example, if the manufacture of a drug requires a particularly expensive reagent, it is important to mix it with the correct amounts of the other reagents to ensure that it all reacts and none is wasted. You will need to be able to write formulae in order to calculate amounts in moles. (See page 22 for some help with writing formulae.)

To find the amount of substance present in a given mass, we must divide that mass by the molar mass, $M$, of the substance. For example, for NaCl, $M = 23 + 35.5 = 58.5 \, \text{g mol}^{-1}$; so in 585 g of sodium chloride (NaCl) there are $585/58.5 \, \text{mol}$ of NaCl, i.e. 10 mol NaCl.

## SAQ 2.4
What amount of substance is there in:
**a**  35.5 g of chlorine *atoms*?
**b**  71 g of chlorine *molecules*, $Cl_2$?

● **Figure 2.5** From left to right, one mole of each of copper, bromine, carbon, mercury and lead.

## SAQ 2.5

Use Avogadro's constant to calculate the total number of atoms of chlorine in:
a  35.5 g of chlorine atoms.
b  71 g of chlorine molecules.

To find the mass of a given amount of substance, we multiply the number of moles of the substance by the molar mass.

## SAQ 2.6

Calculate the mass of the following:
a  0.1 mol of carbon dioxide.
b  10 mol of calcium carbonate, $CaCO_3$.

# Calculations involving reacting masses

If we are given the mass of a reactant, we can find out the mass of products formed in a chemical reaction. To do this, a balanced equation is used. (See page 23 for revision on balancing equations.)

Consider the formation of water from hydrogen and oxygen:

|  | $2H_2$ | + $O_2$ | $\rightarrow 2H_2O$ |
|---|---|---|---|
| this reads | 2 molecules hydrogen | + 1 molecule oxygen | $\rightarrow$ 2 molecules water |
| or | 2 moles hydrogen | + 1 mole oxygen | $\rightarrow$ 2 moles water |
| masses (g) | $2 \times 2 = 4$ | + 32 | $\rightarrow 2 \times (2 + 16) = 36$ |

If we mix 4 g of hydrogen with 32 g of oxygen we should produce 36 g of water on exploding the mixture. Notice that the number of moles of water does *not* equal the sum of the number of moles of hydrogen and oxygen, because they have chemically reacted to produce molecules with a different molecular mass.

Suppose we wish to calculate the mass of iron that can be obtained from a given mass of iron oxide, $Fe_2O_3$. When iron ore is reduced by carbon monoxide in a blast furnace (*figure 2.6*), the equation for the reaction is:

$$Fe_2O_3 + 3CO \rightarrow 2Fe + 3CO_2$$

The molar mass of $Fe_2O_3$ is $(2 \times 56) + (3 \times 16) = 160 \, g \, mol^{-1}$. One mole of $Fe_2O_3$ produces two moles of iron. Hence 160 g of $Fe_2O_3$ will produce $2 \times 56 = 112$ g iron; or

$$1000 \, g \text{ of } Fe_2O_3 \text{ will produce } 112 \times \frac{1000 \, g}{160} = 700 \, g \text{ iron.}$$

## SAQ 2.7

Hydrogen burns in chlorine to produce hydrogen chloride:
$H_2 + Cl_2 \rightarrow 2HCl$
a  Calculate the ratio of the masses of reactants.
b  What mass (in g) of hydrogen is needed to produce 36.5 g of hydrogen chloride?

## SAQ 2.8

Calculate the mass of iron produced from 1000 tonnes of $Fe_2O_3$. How many tonnes of $Fe_2O_3$ would be needed to produce 1 tonne of iron? If the iron ore contains 12% of $Fe_2O_3$, how many tonnes of ore are needed to produce 1 tonne of iron? (Note: 1 tonne = 1000 kg)

● **Figure 2.6** Workers taking the slag from the top of the molten iron in an open-hearth blast furnace.

# Calculation of empirical and molecular formulae

The **empirical formula** of a compound shows the simplest whole-number ratio of the elements present. For many simple compounds it is the same as the molecular formula. The **molecular formula** shows the total number of atoms of each element present in a molecule of the compound. Some examples are shown below:

| Compound | Empirical formula | Molecular formula |
|----------|-------------------|-------------------|
| water | $H_2O$ | $H_2O$ |
| methane | $CH_4$ | $CH_4$ |
| butane | $C_2H_5$ | $C_4H_{10}$ |
| benzene | $CH$ | $C_6H_6$ |

**SAQ 2.9**
Write down the empirical formulae of the following:
**a** hexane, $C_6H_{14}$; **b** hydrogen peroxide, $H_2O_2$.

The molecular formula is far more useful. It enables us to write balanced chemical equations and to calculate masses of compounds involved in a reaction. It is not possible to calculate the molecular formula from the percentage composition by mass of a compound. This information alone does not tell us how atoms are arranged in a molecule. However, the empirical formula can be found in this way. To find this, experimental methods that determine the mass of each element present in a compound are needed.

For example, if magnesium is burned in oxygen, magnesium oxide is formed. Suppose that a piece of magnesium of known mass is burned completely and the magnesium oxide produced is weighed. The weighings enable us to calculate the empirical formula of magnesium oxide.

In such an experiment, 0.240 g of magnesium ribbon produced 0.400 g of magnesium oxide:

| | Mg | O |
|---|-----|---|
| Mass (g) | 0.240 | 0.400 − 0.240 |
| | | = 0.160 |
| Amount (mol) | $=\dfrac{\text{mass}}{A_r}$ | $=\dfrac{\text{mass}}{A_r}$ |
| | $=\dfrac{0.240}{24}$ | $=\dfrac{0.160}{16}$ |
| | = 0.0100 | = 0.0100 |

Divide by the smallest amount to give whole numbers:

| Atoms (mol) | 1 | 1 |
|---|---|---|

Magnesium and oxygen atoms are present in the ratio 1 : 1. Hence the empirical formula of magnesium oxide is MgO. Notice that we convert the mass of each element to the amount in moles, as we need the ratio of the number of atoms of each element present.

**SAQ 2.10**
An oxide of copper has the following composition by mass: Cu, 0.635 g; O, 0.080 g. Calculate the empirical formula of the oxide.

## Combustion analysis

The composition by mass of organic compounds can be found by combustion analysis. This involves the complete combustion in oxygen of a sample of known mass. In combustion analysis, all the carbon is converted to carbon dioxide and all the hydrogen to water. The carbon dioxide and water produced are carefully collected by absorption and weighed. The apparatus is shown in *figure 2.7*. Calculation then gives the mass of carbon and hydrogen present. If oxygen is also present, its mass is found by subtraction (see example below). Other elements require further analytical determinations.

Let us consider an example. Suppose that 0.500 g of an organic compound X (containing only carbon, hydrogen and oxygen) produces

● **Figure 2.7** Modern microanalytical equipment used for routine determination of percentage of carbon and hydrogen in a compound.

0.733 g of carbon dioxide and 0.300 g of water on complete combustion. The mass spectrum of the compound shows it has a molecular mass of 60. How can we determine the molecular formula of the compound?

Remember that the $A_r$ of H = 1, C = 12, O = 16. The calculation goes as follows. As 12 g of carbon are present in 1 mol (= 44 g) $CO_2$,

$$\text{mass of carbon in } 0.733 \text{ g of } CO_2 = \frac{12}{44} \times 0.733 \text{ g}$$
$$= 0.200 \text{ g}$$
$$= \text{mass of carbon in X}$$

As 2 g of hydrogen are present in 1 mol (= 18 g) $H_2O$,

$$\text{mass of hydrogen in } 0.300 \text{ g of } H_2O = \frac{2}{18} \times 0.300 \text{ g}$$
$$= 0.033 \text{ g}$$
$$= \text{mass of hydrogen in X}$$

Hence

$$\text{mass of oxygen in X} = 0.500 - 0.200 - 0.033$$
$$= 0.267 \text{ g}$$

| | C | H | O |
|---|---|---|---|
| Mass (g) | 0.200 | 0.033 | 0.267 |
| Amount (mol) | 0.200/12 | 0.033/1 | 0.267/16 |
| | = 0.0167 | = 0.033 | = 0.0167 |

Divide by the smallest amount to give whole numbers:

| | | | |
|---|---|---|---|
| Atoms (mol) | 1 | 2 | 1 |

Hence the empirical formula is $CH_2O$. This has $M_r = 12 + 2 + 16 = 30$. As $M_r$ of X is 60, the molecular formula of the compound is $C_2H_4O_2$.

## SAQ 2.11

On complete combustion of 0.400 g of a hydrocarbon, 1.257 g of carbon dioxide and 0.514 g of water were produced.

a Calculate the empirical formula of the hydrocarbon.

b If the relative molecular mass of the hydrocarbon is 84, what is its molecular formula?

## Writing chemical formulae

By this point in your study of chemistry you will already know the formulae of some simple compounds. For advanced chemistry you will need to learn the formulae of a wide range of compounds. These formulae are determined by the electronic configurations of the elements involved and the ways in which they combine with other elements to form compounds. The chemical bonding of elements in compounds is studied in chapter 3. It will help if you learn some generalisations about the names and formulae of compounds.

In the formula of an ionic compound, the total number of positive charges in the compound must exactly equal the total number of negative charges. For magnesium oxide, magnesium (in Group II) forms $Mg^{2+}$ ions. Oxygen (in Group VI) forms $O^{2-}$ ions. Magnesium oxide is thus MgO (+2 − 2 = 0). Aluminium forms 3+ ions. Two $Al^{3+}$ ions and three $O^{2-}$ ions are needed in aluminium oxide (2 × (+3) + 3 × (−2) = 0). The formula is $Al_2O_3$. Note how the number of ions of each element in the formula is written as a small number following and below the element symbol.

Some compounds do not contain ions. These compounds contain covalent bonds. The formulae of simple covalent compounds may be deduced from the numbers of electrons required to complete the outer electron shell of each atom present. For example, in methane, carbon requires four more electrons to complete its second shell. Hydrogen requires one. This means that one carbon will combine with four hydrogen atoms to form $CH_4$ (methane). In chapter 3, you will see that each hydrogen forms one bond to carbon whilst the carbon forms four bonds to the four hydrogen atoms.

*Table 2.1* summarises the charges on some of the common ions that you need to learn. The position of the elements in the Periodic Table is helpful. In many instances, the Group in which an element lies indicates the charge on an ion of the element. Note that metals form positive ions, whilst non-metals form negative ions.

Metals do not usually change their names in compounds. However, non-metals change their name by becoming -ides. For example, chlorine becomes chloride in sodium chloride. Sodium has not changed its name, although its properties are now dramatically different! Many non-metals (and some metals) combine with other non-metals such as oxygen to form negative ions. These negative

| Charge | Examples |
|--------|----------|
| 1+ | $H^+$ and Group I, the alkali metal ions, e.g. $Li^+$, $Na^+$, $K^+$ |
| 2+ | Group II, the alkaline earth metal ions, e.g. $Mg^{2+}$, $Ca^{2+}$ |
| 3+ | $Al^{3+}$ |
| 1– | Group VII, the halogens, e.g. $F^-$, $Cl^-$, $Br^-$, $I^-$ |
|    | Nitrate, $NO_3^-$ |
| 2– | Group VI, $O^{2-}$ and $S^{2-}$ |
|    | Carbonate, $CO_3^{2-}$ |
|    | Sulphate, $SO_4^{2-}$ and sulphite, $SO_3^{2-}$ |
| 3– | Phosphate, $PO_4^{3-}$ |

● **Table 2.1** Charges on some common ions.

ions start with the name of the element and end in -ate (or sometimes -ite), e.g. sulphate (sulphite). Some of these ions are also included in *table 2.1*.

## SAQ 2.12

Write the molecular formula for each of the following compounds:

**a** magnesium bromide    **d** sodium sulphate
**b** hydrogen iodide    **e** potassium nitrate
**c** calcium sulphide    **f** nitrogen dioxide

## SAQ 2.13

Name each of the following compounds:

**a** $K_2CO_3$    **c** $LiNO_3$    **e** $SiO_2$
**b** $Al_2S_3$    **d** $Ca_3(PO_4)_2$

# Balancing chemical equations

Atoms are neither created nor destroyed in a chemical reaction. When we write a chemical equation we must, therefore, ensure we have the same number of atoms of each element on each side of the chemical equation. We do this by *balancing* the equation, as follows:

■ Write down the formulae of all the reactants and all the products. It may help you to write these in words first.

■ Now inspect the equation and count the atoms of each element on each side. As the elements present cannot be created or lost in the chemical reaction, we must balance the number of each element.

■ Decide what numbers must be placed in front of each formula to ensure that the same number of each atom is present on each side of the equation. It is most important that the formulae of the reactants and products are not altered; only the total number of each may be changed.

We shall now do an example. When iron(III) oxide is reduced to metallic iron by carbon monoxide, the carbon monoxide is oxidised to carbon dioxide. (The III in iron(III) oxide indicates that the iron has an oxidation state of +3. See page 94 for more on oxidation states.)

Iron(III) oxide + carbon monoxide
$$\rightarrow \text{iron + carbon dioxide}$$

The formulae are:

$$Fe_2O_3 + CO \rightarrow Fe + CO_2$$

On inspection we note that there are two iron atoms in the oxide on the left-hand side but only one on the right-hand side. We thus write

$$Fe_2O_3 + CO \rightarrow 2Fe + CO_2$$

Next we count the oxygen atoms: three in the oxide plus one in carbon monoxide, on the left-hand side. As there are only two on the right-hand side in carbon dioxide, we must double the number of $CO_2$ molecules in order to balance the number of oxygen atoms.

$$Fe_2O_3 + CO \rightarrow 2Fe + 2CO_2$$

On checking we see we have solved one problem but created a new one. There are now two carbon atoms on the right but only one on the left. Doubling the number of CO molecules balances the carbon atoms but unbalances the oxygen atoms again!

If we examine the equation again, we see that in the reaction between $Fe_2O_3$ and CO, each CO molecule requires only one oxygen atom to form $CO_2$. Thus three CO molecules combine with the three oxygen atoms lost from $Fe_2O_3$. Three $CO_2$ molecules will be formed:

$$Fe_2O_3 + 3CO \rightarrow 2Fe + 3CO_2$$

The equation is now balanced.

We often need to specify the physical states of chemicals in an equation. This can be important when, for example, calculating enthalpy changes (see chapter 5). The symbols used are: (s) for solid; (l) for liquid; (g) for gas. A solution in water is described as aqueous, so (aq) is used. Addition of the physical states to the equation for the reaction of iron(III) oxide with carbon monoxide produces:

$$Fe_2O_3(s) + 3CO(g) \rightarrow 2Fe(s) + 3CO_2(g)$$

### SAQ 2.14

Balance the equations for the following reactions.
a The thermite reaction (used for chemical welding of lengths of rail):
$$Al + Fe_2O_3 \rightarrow Al_2O_3 + Fe$$
b Petrol contains octane, $C_8H_{18}$. Complete combustion in oxygen produces only carbon dioxide and water.
c Lead nitrate, $Pb(NO_3)_2$, decomposes on heating to produce PbO, $NO_2$ and $O_2$.

# Balancing ionic equations

In some situations, chemists prefer to use ionic equations. Such equations are simpler than the corresponding full equation (which show the full formulae of all compounds present). For example, when a granule of zinc is placed in aqueous copper sulphate, copper metal is displaced, forming a red-brown deposit on the zinc. In the reaction, zinc dissolves to form zinc sulphate. The full equation for the reaction is:

$$Zn(s) + CuSO_4(aq) \rightarrow ZnSO_4(aq) + Cu(s)$$

During this reaction copper ions, $Cu^{2+}$, are converted to copper atoms, Cu, and zinc atoms, Zn, are converted to zinc ions, $Zn^{2+}$. The sulphate ion has remained unchanged. It is known as a spectator ion: it stays on the sidelines. The ionic equation does not show the ions that remain unchanged. It therefore provides a shorter equation which focusses our attention on the change taking place:

$$Zn(s) + Cu^{2+}(aq) \rightarrow Zn^{2+}(aq) + Cu(s)$$

In an ionic equation we must balance the overall charge on the ions on each side of the equation.

Notice that the charge on each side of this ionic equation is 2+. Ensure that the charges are balanced *before* balancing the number of atoms of each element.

The reaction of $Cu^{2+}(aq)$ with Zn(s) involves transfer of electrons. It is known as a **redox** reaction. You will learn more about such reactions in chapter 6 (see page 95). Ionic equations are frequently used for redox reactions. Chemists also prefer to use ionic equations for precipitation reactions. For example, when sodium hydroxide is added dropwise to copper sulphate a pale blue precipitate of copper(II) hydroxide, $Cu(OH)_2(s)$, is formed. The full equation is:

$$CuSO_4(aq) + 2NaOH(aq)$$
$$\rightarrow Cu(OH)_2(s) + Na_2SO_4(aq)$$

The ionic equation is:

$$Cu^{2+}(aq) + 2OH^-(aq) \rightarrow Cu(OH)_2(s)$$

Both sodium ions, $Na^+(aq)$, and sulphate ions, $SO_4^{2-}(aq)$, are spectator ions, meaning that they are unchanged, and can be omitted.

### SAQ 2.15

Try balancing the following ionic equations:
a $Cl_2(aq) + Br^-(aq) \rightarrow Cl^-(aq) + Br_2(aq)$
b $Fe^{3+}(aq) + OH^-(aq) \rightarrow Fe(OH)_3(s)$

# Calculations involving concentrations and gas volumes

## Concentrations of solutions

When one mole of a compound is dissolved in a solvent to make one cubic decimetre (1 $dm^3$) of solution, the concentration is 1 $mol\,dm^{-3}$. Usually the solvent is water and an aqueous solution is formed.

Traditionally, concentrations in $mol\,dm^{-3}$ have been expressed as molarities. For example, 2 $mol\,dm^{-3}$ aqueous sodium hydroxide is 2M aqueous sodium hydroxide, where M is the molarity of the solution. Although this is still a convenient method for labelling bottles, etc., it is better to use the units of $mol\,dm^{-3}$ in your calculations. Although you may have used $mol/dm^3$ or $mol/litre$

in the past, advanced chemistry requires you to use $mol\,dm^{-3}$.

An experimental technique in which it is essential to know the concentration of solutions is a titration. A titration (*figure 2.8*) is a way of measuring quantities of reactants, and can be very useful in determining an unknown concentration or following the progress of a reaction. In titrations there are five things you need to know:

- the balanced equation for the reaction showing the moles of the two reactants;
- the volume of the solution of the first reagent;
- the concentration of the solution of the first reagent;
- the volume of the solution of the second reagent;
- the concentration of the solution of the second reagent.

● **Figure 2.8** A titration enables the reacting volumes of two solutions to be accurately determined. One solution is measured with a graduated pipette into a conical flask, the other is added slowly from a burette. The point where complete reaction just occurs is usually shown using an indicator, which changes colour at this point (called the end-point).

If we know four of these, we can calculate the fifth. Remember that concentrations may be in $mol\,dm^{-3}$ or $g\,dm^{-3}$.

Many titration calculations start by finding the amount of a reagent (in moles) from a given concentration and volume. For example, what amount of sodium hydroxide is present in $24.0\,cm^3$ of an aqueous $0.010\,mol\,dm^{-3}$ solution?

Convert the volume to $dm^3$:

$$1\,dm^3 = 10 \times 10 \times 10\,cm^3 = 1000\,cm^3$$

$$24.0\,cm^3 = \frac{24.0}{1000}\,dm^3$$

$$\text{amount of NaOH in } 24.0\,cm^3 = \frac{24.0}{1000} \times 0.010\,mol$$
$$= 2.40 \times 10^{-4}\,mol$$

To check your calculations:

- Notice how the units multiply and cancel: $dm^3 \times mol\,dm^{-3} = mol$. Use this as a check.
- Ensure the units of the answer are those you would expect (e.g. mol for amount or $mol\,dm^{-3}$ for concentration).
- Think about the size of your answer (e.g. $24\,cm^3$ is much less than $1\,dm^3$, so we expect the quantity of sodium hydroxide in $24\,cm^3$ of $0.01\,mol\,dm^{-3}$ solution to be much less than $0.01\,mol$).

We also often need to find the concentration of a solution from the amount in a given volume. For example, what is the concentration of an aqueous solution containing $2 \times 10^{-4}\,mol$ of sulphuric acid in $10\,cm^3$?

As before, convert the volume to $dm^3$:

$$10\,cm^3 = \frac{10}{1000}\,dm^3 = 1 \times 10^{-2}\,dm^3$$

$$\text{concentration of sulphuric acid} = \frac{2 \times 10^{-4}}{1 \times 10^{-2}}\,mol\,dm^{-3}$$
$$= 2 \times 10^{-2}\,mol\,dm^{-3}$$

Again check by looking at the units:
$$\frac{mol}{dm^3} = mol\,dm^{-3}.$$

### SAQ 2.16

**a** Calculate the amount in moles of nitric acid in $25.0\,cm^3$ of a $0.1\,mol\,dm^{-3}$ aqueous solution.

**b** Calculate the concentration in $mol\,dm^{-3}$ of a solution comprising $0.125\,mol$ of nitric acid with water added, up to a volume of $50\,cm^3$.

Changing concentrations expressed in $mol\,dm^{-3}$ to $g\,dm^{-3}$ and vice versa is straightforward. We multiply by the molar mass $M$ to convert $mol\,dm^{-3}$ to $g\,dm^{-3}$. To convert $g\,dm^{-3}$ to $mol\,dm^{-3}$ we divide by $M$. Notice how the units cancel correctly.

### SAQ 2.17

a What is the concentration in $g\,dm^{-3}$ of $0.50\,mol\,dm^{-3}$ aqueous ethanoic acid ($CH_3CO_2H$)?

b What is the concentration in $mol\,dm^{-3}$ of an aqueous solution containing $4.00\,g\,dm^{-3}$ of sodium hydroxide?

A worked example follows of how such calculations are combined with a balanced chemical equation to interpret the result of a titration. Try to identify the 'five things to know' in this calculation. In the titration $20.0\,cm^3$ of $0.200\,mol\,dm^{-3}$ aqueous sodium hydroxide exactly neutralises a $25.0\,cm^3$ sample of sulphuric acid. What is the concentration of the sulphuric acid in **a** $mol\,dm^{-3}$, **b** $g\,dm^{-3}$?

The working goes as follows:

$$20.0\,cm^3 = \frac{20}{1000}\,dm^3 = 2.00 \times 10^{-2}\,dm^3$$

amount of sodium hydroxide
$$= 2.00 \times 10^{-2} \times 0.200\,mol$$
$$= 4.00 \times 10^{-3}\,mol$$

The balanced equation for the reaction is:

$$2NaOH(aq) + H_2SO_4(aq) \rightarrow Na_2SO_4(aq) + 2H_2O(l)$$

Exact neutralisation requires $2\,mol$ of NaOH to $1\,mol$ of $H_2SO_4$. So

amount of $H_2SO_4$ neutralised in the titration
$$= \tfrac{1}{2} \times \text{amount of NaOH}$$
$$= \tfrac{1}{2} \times 4.00 \times 10^{-3}\,mol$$
$$= 2.00 \times 10^{-3}\,mol$$

Volume of $H_2SO_4 = 25.0\,cm^3 = 25.0/1000\,dm^3$
$$= 2.5 \times 10^{-2}\,dm^3$$

a Concentration of $H_2SO_4$
$$= \frac{2.00 \times 10^{-3}}{2.5 \times 10^{-2}}\,mol\,dm^{-3}$$
$$= 0.080\,mol\,dm^{-3}$$

b As $M(H_2SO_4) = 2 + 32 + 4 \times 16 = 98\,g$
concentration of $H_2SO_4 = 98 \times 0.080\,g\,dm^{-3}$
$$= 7.84\,g\,dm^{-3}$$

### SAQ 2.18

$20.0\,cm^3$ of $0.100\,mol\,dm^{-3}$ potassium hydroxide exactly neutralises a $25.0\,cm^3$ sample of hydrochloric acid. What is the concentration of the hydrochloric acid in **a** $mol\,dm^{-3}$, **b** $g\,dm^{-3}$?

It is possible to use a titration result to arrive at the reacting mole ratio, called the **stoichiometric ratio**, and the balanced equation for a reaction.

The example that follows illustrates how this is done. A $25.0\,cm^3$ sample of $0.0400\,mol\,dm^{-3}$ aqueous metal hydroxide is titrated against $0.100\,mol\,dm^{-3}$ hydrochloric acid. $20.0\,cm^3$ of the acid were required for exact neutralisation of the alkali.

The working is as follows:

$$\text{amount of metal hydroxide} = \frac{25.0}{1000} \times 0.0400\,mol$$
$$= 1.00 \times 10^{-3}\,mol$$

$$\text{amount of hydrochloric acid} = \frac{20.0}{1000} \times 0.100\,mol$$
$$= 2.00 \times 10^{-3}\,mol$$

Hence the reacting (i.e. stoichiometric) mole ratio of metal hydroxide : hydrochloric acid is

$$1.00 \times 10^{-3} : 2.00 \times 10^{-3}$$
or $\qquad\qquad 1:2$

i.e. exactly one mole of the metal hydroxide neutralises exactly two moles of hydrochloric acid. One mole of HCl will neutralise one mole of hydroxide ions, so the metal hydroxide must contain two hydroxide ions in its formula. The balanced equation for the reaction is

$$M(OH)_2(aq) + 2HCl(aq) \rightarrow MCl_2(aq) + 2H_2O(l)$$

where M is the metal.

### SAQ 2.19

Determine the stoichiometric ratio, and hence the balanced equation, for the reaction of an insoluble iron hydroxide with dilute nitric acid, $HNO_3$. $4.00 \times 10^{-4}\,mol$ of the iron hydroxide is exactly neutralised by $24.0\,cm^3$ of $0.05\,mol\,dm^{-3}$ nitric acid.

## Gas volumes

In 1811, Avogadro discovered that equal volumes of all gases contain the same number of molecules. (Note that the volumes must be measured under the same conditions of temperature and pressure.) This provides an easy way of calculating the amount of gas present in a given volume. At room temperature and pressure, one mole of any gas occupies approximately 24.0 dm$^3$. For example, 24.0 dm$^3$ of carbon dioxide ($CO_2$) and 24.0 dm$^3$ of nitrogen ($N_2$) both contain one mole of molecules.

## SAQ 2.20

**a** Calculate the amount of helium present in a balloon with a volume of 2.4 dm$^3$. Assume that the pressure inside the balloon is the same as atmospheric pressure and that the balloon is at room temperature.

**b** Calculate the volume occupied by a mixture of 0.5 mol of propane and 1.5 mol of butane gases at room temperature and pressure.

We can use reacting volumes of gases to determine the stoichiometry of a reaction. The experiments must be carried out under the same conditions of temperature and pressure. We can then assume that equal volumes of gases contain the same number of moles. For example, measurements show that 20 cm$^3$ of hydrogen react with exactly 10 cm$^3$ of oxygen to form water. The ratio of reacting volumes of hydrogen : oxygen is 20 : 10 or 2 : 1. Hence the reacting mole ratio for hydrogen : oxygen (the stoichiometry of the reaction) is also 2 : 1, and so the balanced equation is:

$$2H_2(g) + O_2(g) \rightarrow 2H_2O(l)$$

The following example shows how we can find the formula of a hydrocarbon using measurements of reacting volumes.

10 cm$^3$ of a gaseous hydrocarbon X burned completely in exactly 50 cm$^3$ of oxygen to produce water and 30 cm$^3$ of carbon dioxide. All measurements were made at room temperature and pressure. We need to determine:

■ the formula of the hydrocarbon;
■ the balanced equation for the reaction.

We can present the calculations as follows:

| hydrocarbon X(g) + O$_2$(g) → CO$_2$(g) + H$_2$O(l) | | | |
|---|---|---|---|
| Gas volumes (cm$^3$) | 10 | 50 | 30 |
| Gas volume ratio | 1 | 5 | 3 |
| Gas mole ratio | 1 | 5 | 3 |

This tells us that 3 mol of carbon dioxide are obtained from 1 mol of the hydrocarbon, so each hydrocarbon molecule must contain 3 carbon atoms.

The 3 mol of carbon dioxide use up 3 out of the original 5 mol of oxygen.

Hence 2 mol of oxygen molecules, $O_2$(g), are left to combine with hydrogen atoms from the hydrocarbon, to form 4 mol of water. So there must be 4 × 2 = 8 hydrogen atoms present in the hydrocarbon. Therefore:

■ The formula of the hydrocarbon is $C_3H_8$.
■ The balanced equation for the reaction is:
    $C_3H_8(g) + 5O_2(g) \rightarrow 3CO_2(g) + 4H_2O(l)$

## SAQ 2.21

20 cm$^3$ of a gaseous hydrocarbon Y burned completely in exactly 60 cm$^3$ of oxygen to produce water and 40 cm$^3$ of carbon dioxide. All measurements were made at room temperature and pressure.

**a** What is the formula of the hydrocarbon?

**b** Write a balanced equation for the reaction.

# SUMMARY (AS)

◆ Definitions of atomic, isotopic and molecular masses are relative to carbon-12, which has a mass of exactly 12.

◆ One mole of a substance is the amount of substance that has the same number (called Avogadro's constant) of particles as there are atoms in exactly 12 g of carbon-12.

◆ A mass spectrometer enables ionised atoms to be accelerated into a beam of gaseous ions which are deflected in a magnetic field according to their mass.

◆ Mass spectra of elements enable isotopic abundances and relative atomic masses to be found.

◆ Empirical formulae show the simplest whole-number ratio of atoms in a compound whilst molecular formulae show the total number of atoms for each element present. Empirical formulae may be determined from the composition by mass of a compound. The molecular formula may then be found if the molecular mass is known.

◆ Molar masses enable calculations to be made using moles and balanced chemical equations involving reacting masses, volumes and concentrations of solutions and volumes of gases.

◆ Balanced chemical equations (which show the stoichiometry of a reaction) may also be derived by measuring reacting masses, volumes and concentrations of solutions or volumes of gases.

# Questions (AS)

1 Copper–nickel alloys are used to make some coins. The composition of coins may be checked by using mass spectrometry. The mass spectrum of the copper content of a coin is shown below:

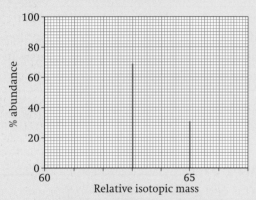

a State, for each of these isotopes of copper,
   (i) the number of protons and neutrons in the nucleus;
   (ii) the percentage abundance.
b Define the term **relative atomic mass**.
c Calculate the relative atomic mass of the copper in the coin.
d Pure nickel was not discovered until 1751 and it was named from the German word 'kupfernickel' meaning 'devil's copper'. A compound of nickel, A, was analysed and shown to have the following percentage composition by mass: Ni, 37.9%; S, 20.7%; O, 41.4%. Calculate the empirical formula of A.

2 Azides are compounds of metals with nitrogen, used mainly as detonators in explosives. However, sodium azide, $NaN_3$, decomposes non-explosively on heating to release nitrogen gas. This provides a convenient method of obtaining pure nitrogen in the laboratory:
$$2NaN_3(s) \rightarrow 2Na(l) + 3N_2(g)$$
a A student prepared $1.80\,dm^3$ of pure nitrogen in the laboratory by this method. This gas volume was measured at room temperature and pressure (r.t.p.).
   (i) How many moles of nitrogen, $N_2$, did the student prepare? [Assume that 1 mole of gas molecules occupies $24.0\,dm^3$ at r.t.p.]
   (ii) What mass of sodium azide did the student heat?
b After cooling, the student obtained $1.15\,g$ of solid sodium. She then carefully reacted this sodium with water to form $25.0\,cm^3$ of aqueous sodium hydroxide:
$$2Na(s) + 2H_2O(l) \rightarrow 2NaOH(aq) + H_2(g)$$
Calculate the concentration, in $mol\,dm^{-3}$, of the aqueous sodium hydroxide.

# CHAPTER 3

# Chemical bonding and structure (AS)

## By the end of this chapter you should be able to:

1 describe *ionic bonding* as the electrostatic attraction between two oppositely charged ions, including the use of *dot-and-cross* diagrams;

2 describe, in simple terms, the lattice structure of sodium chloride;

3 describe a covalent bond as a pair of electrons shared between two atoms;

4 describe, including the use of dot-and-cross diagrams, *covalent bonding* and *dative* covalent (coordinate) bonding;

5 appreciate that, between the extremes of ionic and covalent bonding, there is a gradual transition from one extreme to the other;

6 describe *electronegativity* as the ability of an atom to attract the bonding electrons in a covalent bond;

7 explain that bond polarity may arise when the atoms joined by a covalent bond have different electronegativities, and that *polarisation* may occur between cations of high charge density and anions of low charge density;

8 explain and predict the shapes of, and bond angles in, *molecules* and ions by using the qualitative model of *electron-pair repulsion* up to 4 electron pairs;

9 describe *metallic bonding*, present in a giant *metallic lattice* structure, as the attraction of a lattice of positive ions to a sea of *mobile electrons*;

10 describe *intermolecular forces* (van der Waals' forces), based on instantaneous and permanent *dipoles*;

11 describe, in simple terms, the *giant molecular structures* of graphite and diamond;

12 describe *hydrogen bonding* between molecules containing −OH and −NH groups, typified by water and ammonia;

13 describe and explain the anomalous properties of water resulting from hydrogen bonding;

14 describe, interpret and/or predict physical properties in terms of the types, motion and arrangement of particles (atoms, molecules and ions) and the forces between them, and the different types of bonding;

15 deduce the type of bonding present in a substance, given suitable information.

# Ionic bonding

Many familiar substances are ionic compounds. An example is common salt (sodium chloride). Sodium chloride and many other ionic compounds are present in sea-water. Crystals of salt are readily obtained by the partial evaporation of sea-water in a salt pan (*figure 3.1*).

We need to understand the bonding in compounds in order to explain their structure and physical properties. Ionic compounds:

■ are crystalline solids with high melting points;
■ conduct electricity, with decomposition at the electrodes, in aqueous solution or when they are molten;
■ are hard and brittle with crystals that cleave easily;
■ are often soluble in water.

**Ionic bonding** results from the electrostatic attraction between the oppositely charged ions. In sodium chloride, the ions are arranged in a crystal lattice, which determines the shape of the crystals grown from sea-water. Most other minerals are also found as well-formed crystals. The shapes of these crystals arise from the way in which the ions are packed together in the lattice. Some crystals are shown in *figure 3.2*.

Use is often made of the very high melting points of ionic compounds, e.g. aluminium oxide (melting point 2345 K, where K refers to the kelvin scale for temperature, 0 °C = 273 K). A fibrous form

● **Figure 3.2** A selection of minerals.

of aluminium oxide is used in tiles on the Space Shuttle for protection from the high temperatures experienced on re-entry into the atmosphere (*figure 3.3*) and in the lining of the portable gas forges of a modern 'high-tech' farrier.

Another important characteristic of ionic compounds is their ability to conduct electricity, with decomposition, when in aqueous solution or when they are molten. This process is called **electrolysis**. Electrolysis is used to produce chlorine from brine (concentrated aqueous

● **Figure 3.1** A salt mountain with a salt pan in the foreground, Sardinia.

● **Figure 3.3** The space shuttle *Columbia*, seen during the fitting of the thermal insulation tiles.

sodium chloride) (*figure 3.4*) and aluminium from molten aluminium oxide.

Ions are free to move through the aqueous solution or molten compound and are attracted to the oppositely charged electrode. Positive ions (cations) are attracted to the negative electrode (cathode), and negative ions (anions) to the positive electrode (anode). At the electrode, the ions discharge; e.g. chloride ions to chlorine or aluminium ions to aluminium metal. On being discharged, an ion will either gain or lose electrons. Electrons will be gained by **cations** (positively charged ions) and lost by **anions** (negatively charged ions). The number of electrons gained or lost will depend on the magnitude of the charge on the ion. A chloride ion will lose one electron; an aluminium ion will gain three electrons. These changes may be represented as follows:

at the positive electrode (anode): $Cl^- \rightarrow \frac{1}{2}Cl_2 + e^-$
at the negative electrode (cathode):

$$Al^{3+} + 3e^- \rightarrow Al$$

● **Figure 3.4** Industrial electrolysis: chlorine cell.

*SAQ 3.1*
Write similar equations, including electrons, for the discharge of copper and bromide ions during the electrolysis of copper bromide, $CuBr_2$, using carbon electrodes. Indicate the electrode at which each reaction will occur.

# Formation of ions from elements

Positive ions are formed when electrons are removed from atoms. This happens most easily with metallic elements. Atoms of non-metallic elements tend to gain electrons to form negative ions. Hence when metals combine with non-metals, electrons are transferred from the metal atoms to the non-metal atoms. Usually a metal atom will lose all of its outer-shell electrons and a non-metal atom will accept electrons to fill its outer shell. The net result of electron transfer from a metal atom to a non-metal atom is to produce filled outer shells similar to the noble-gas electronic configurations for both elements. The ionic bonding results from the electrostatic attraction between the oppositely charged ions.

Dot-and-cross diagrams are used to show the electronic configurations of elements and ions. The electrons of one element in the compound are shown by dots, those of the second element by crosses. *Table 3.1* shows some examples.

Usually when we draw a dot-and-cross diagram, the filled inner electron shells are omitted. A circle is drawn round the outer-shell electrons. In the case of a sodium ion $Na^+$, this shell no longer contains any electrons. The nucleus of the element is shown by the symbol for the element. The dot-and-cross diagram for an ion is placed in square brackets with the charge outside the brackets. Electrons are placed in pairs for clarity.

Often only the outer shell dot-and-cross diagram for the compound is needed. For sodium chloride this is:

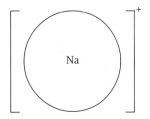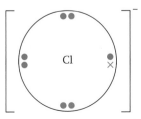

| Atom | Electronic configuration | Dot-and-cross diagram | Ion | Electronic configuration | Dot-and-cross diagram |
|------|-------------------------|----------------------|-----|-------------------------|----------------------|
| Na | 2,8,1 | | Na$^+$ | 2,8 | |
| Cl | 2,8,7 | | Cl$^-$ | 2,8,8 | |

● **Table 3.1** Examples of dot-and-cross diagrams.

## SAQ 3.2

Draw dot-and-cross diagrams for the following: **a** KF, **b** Na$_2$O, **c** MgO and **d** CaCl$_2$.

The typical properties of ionic compounds may be explained by the presence of ions, which are arranged in a giant ionic lattice. In the ionic lattice, positive and negative ions alternate in a three-dimensional arrangement. The way in which the ions are arranged depends on their relative sizes. Sodium chloride has a cubic ionic lattice.

Magnesium oxide has the same cubic structure with magnesium ions in place of sodium ions and oxide ions in place of chloride ions. In the lattice, the attraction between oppositely charged ions binds them together. These attractions greatly outweigh repulsions between similarly charged ions, as each ion is surrounded by six oppositely charged ions. Hence the melting points of ionic compounds are very high. The melting point usually increases as the charges on the ions increase. Sodium chloride with its singly charged ions has a melting point of 1074 K, and magnesium oxide with its doubly charged ions has a melting point of 3125 K.

Ionic compounds are hard and brittle. The cleavage of gemstones and other ionic crystals occurs between planes of ions in the ionic lattice. If an ionic crystal is tapped sharply in the direction of one of the crystal planes with a sharp-edged knife, it will split cleanly. As a plane of ions is displaced by the force of the knife, ions of similar charge come together and the repulsions between them cause the crystal to split apart. The natural shape of ionic crystals is the same as the arrangement of the ions in the lattice. This is because the crystal grows as ions are placed in the lattice and this basic shape continues to the edge of the crystal. Hence sodium chloride crystals are cubic. The smallest repeating unit in the lattice is known as the unit cell. The sodium chloride unit cell is shown in *figure 3.5*.

Gemstones and other semi-precious stones, such as emeralds, sapphires and rubies (*figure 3.6*), are ionic compounds valued for their colour and hardness. Gemstones are crystalline and are cut so that they sparkle in the light. They are cut by exploiting the cleavage planes between layers of ions in the crystal structure.

Ionic compounds may dissolve in water. As a general rule all metal nitrates and most metal chlorides are soluble, as are almost all of the salts of the Group I metals. Ionic compounds that carry

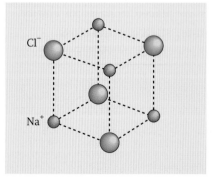

● **Figure 3.5** The sodium chloride (NaCl) unit cell.

● **Figure 3.6** Sapphires in the form of both rough crystals and cut gemstones.

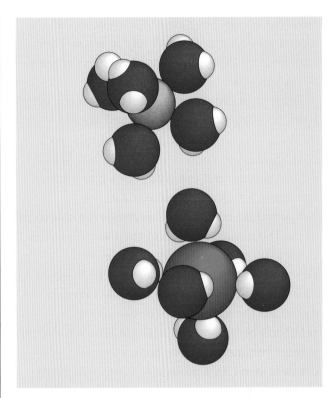

● **Figure 3.7** Hydrated sodium ion (grey) and chloride ion (green).

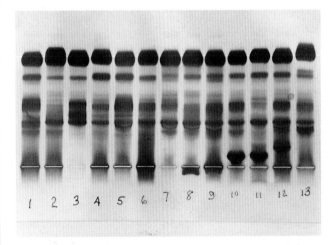

● **Figure 3.8** In this diagnostic test for leukaemia, negatively charged polypeptide ions (proteins) move towards a positive electrode (towards the top of the page).

higher charges on the ions tend to be less soluble or insoluble. For example, whilst Group I hydroxides are soluble, Group II and III hydroxides are sparingly soluble or insoluble in water (a sparingly soluble compound has only a very low solubility, e.g. calcium hydroxide as lime water). When ionic compounds dissolve, energy must be provided to overcome the strong attractive forces between the ions in the lattice. This energy is provided by the similarly strong attractive forces that occur in the hydrated ions. In a hydrated ion water molecules are attracted to an anion or cation by strong electrostatic forces. In the case of a cation, the oxygen atoms of the water molecules are attracted by the positive charge on the ion. Negative ions are attracted to the hydrogen end of the water molecule. This is possible as water molecules are polar (see page 44). *Figure 3.7* shows a hydrated sodium ion (grey) and a hydrated chloride ion (green). The water molecules are shown with oxygen = red and hydrogen = white.

In chapter 5, you will learn how to calculate the energy change when an ionic compound dissolves.

Electrolysis of ionic compounds can only occur when the ions are free to move. In the lattice the ions are in fixed positions, and ionic solids will thus not conduct electricity. On melting, or dissolving in water, the ions are no longer in fixed positions so they are free to move towards electrodes (*figure 3.8*).

# Covalent bonding

Many familiar compounds are liquids or gases or solids with low melting points, e.g. water, ammonia, methane, ethanol, sucrose and poly(ethene). Such compounds have very different properties to ionic compounds. They all contain **molecules** in which groups of atoms are held together by covalent bonds. They are non-conductors of electricity and may be insoluble in water. They may dissolve in organic solvents such as ethanol or cyclohexane.

Some crystalline covalent compounds are very hard, have high melting points and are more difficult to cleave than ionic compounds. Such compounds also contain covalent bonds, which extend throughout the crystal in a giant lattice structure, e.g. quartz crystals (*figure 3.9*).

In covalent compounds, electrons are shared in pairs. The negative charge of the electron-pair will attract the positively charged nuclei of the elements, and this holds the atoms together in a molecule. The electron-pair must lie between the nuclei for the attraction to outweigh the repulsion between the nuclei. Under such circumstances two atoms will be bound together by a covalent bond. In a molecule, atoms will share electrons, and, as a general rule, the number shared gives each atom filled outer shells similar to the electronic configuration of a noble gas. Covalent bonds are usually formed between pairs of non-metallic elements.

In a molecule the bonding electrons are now in molecular orbitals rather than atomic orbitals. The molecular orbitals may be considered to arise from the overlap of atomic orbitals. Molecular orbitals are given labels using Greek letters: σ, π, δ, etc. (pronounced sigma, pi, delta, respectively). These parallel the labels for atomic orbitals: s, p, d, etc. A single covalent bond consists of a σ orbital and is often called a σ bond. The σ bond in a hydrogen molecule is shown in *figure 3.10*. The π orbitals are found as π bonds. A double covalent bond consists of a σ bond and a π bond. You will find more on σ and π bonds on page 300.

Dot-and-cross diagrams for some examples of covalent compounds are shown in *figure 3.11*. Diagrams of molecules often show the covalent bonds as lines. A double line is used for a double bond. Such diagrams are called displayed formulae. Examples are shown with the dot-and-cross diagrams in *figure 3.11*. Remember that each covalent bond is a *shared* pair of electrons. Ionic compounds are held together by electrostatic attraction between oppositely charged *ions*.

## SAQ 3.3

**a** Draw dot–and–cross diagrams together with displayed formulae for each of the following: (i) $H_2$, (ii) HCl, (iii) $O_2$, (iv) $PCl_3$, (v) $BF_3$ and (vi) $SF_6$.

**b** How many electrons are present in the outer shell of boron in $BF_3$ and of sulphur in $SF_6$?

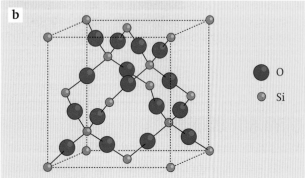

● **Figure 3.9**
**a** Quartz crystals.
**b** Model of the arrangement of atoms in a quartz lattice.

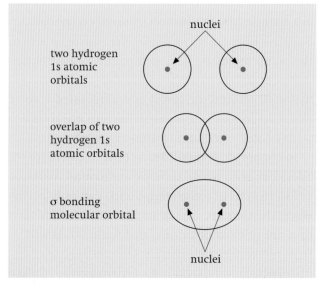

● **Figure 3.10** A σ bond in hydrogen, showing the overlap of 1s orbitals.

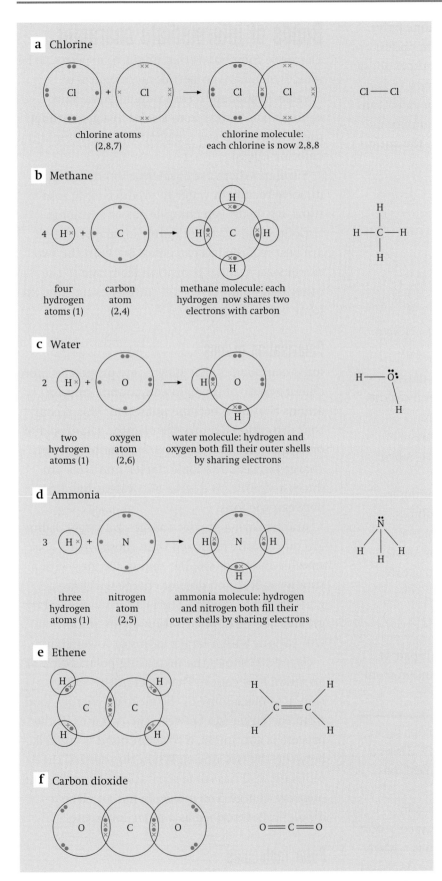

**a** Chlorine

chlorine atoms
(2,8,7)

chlorine molecule:
each chlorine is now 2,8,8

Cl — Cl

**b** Methane

four
hydrogen
atoms (1)

carbon
atom
(2,4)

methane molecule: each
hydrogen now shares two
electrons with carbon

**c** Water

two
hydrogen
atoms (1)

oxygen
atom
(2,6)

water molecule: hydrogen and
oxygen both fill their outer shells
by sharing electrons

**d** Ammonia

three
hydrogen
atoms (1)

nitrogen
atom
(2,5)

ammonia molecule: hydrogen
and nitrogen both fill their
outer shells by sharing electrons

**e** Ethene

**f** Carbon dioxide

O = C = O

● **Figure 3.11** Dot-and-cross diagrams for some covalent compounds:
**a** chlorine ($Cl_2$), **b** methane ($CH_4$), **c** water ($H_2O$), **d** ammonia ($NH_3$),
**e** ethene ($C_2H_4$) and **f** carbon dioxide ($CO_2$), also showing the
displayed formulae.

For example, $SF_6$ is now being used as an electrical insulator in large electrical transformers. It has largely replaced polychlorinated biphenyls (PCBs), which were found to cause environmental damage. $BF_3$ is an example of a molecule in which an atom does not achieve a noble-gas configuration in its outer shell. The sulphur atom in $SF_6$ has more electrons in its outermost shell than the next noble gas, argon. When chemists realised that it was possible for atoms to expand their outer shells in this way, it was suggested that noble gases, hitherto thought to be unreactive, might form compounds in the same way (*figure 3.12*).

## Lone-pairs

Atoms in molecules frequently have pairs of electrons in their outer shells that are not involved in covalent bonds. These

● **Figure 3.12** In compounds of noble gases, the outer electron shell expands beyond eight electrons. Xenon tetrafluoride ($XeF_4$) contains 12 outer-shell electrons. The photograph shows crystals of $XeF_4$.

non-bonding electron-pairs are called **lone-pairs**. In ammonia, nitrogen has one lone-pair, and in water, oxygen has two lone-pairs. Sometimes these lone-pairs are used to form a covalent bond to an atom that can accommodate two further electrons in its outer shell. An example is when ammonia and the hydrogen ion combine to form the ammonium ion, $NH_4^+$ (shown below):

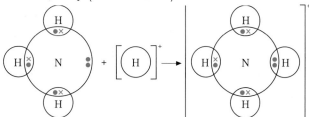

The covalent bond from the nitrogen atom to the $H^+$ ion is formed by sharing the nitrogen lone-pair. As both electrons come from the nitrogen atom, this is called a **dative covalent bond**. The word 'dative' derives from the Latin for 'give'. Dative covalent bonds are represented by arrows in displayed formulae of molecules. Dative covalent bonds are also called **coordinate bonds** in metal complexes.

A further example of coordinate bonding is found in aluminium chloride. When solid aluminium chloride is heated, it becomes a vapour at 180 °C. The vapour consists of $Al_2Cl_6$ molecules, which have the following structure:

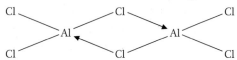

Two chlorine atoms each donate a lone-pair of electrons to a vacant orbital of an aluminium atom.

### SAQ 3.4

a Water molecules will hydrate the aqueous hydrogen ion to form the oxonium ion, $H_3O^+$. Draw a dot–and–cross diagram and the displayed formula of the oxonium ion.

b $BF_3$ forms a white solid when it reacts with gaseous ammonia. A bond forms between boron and nitrogen. The formula of the solid is $F_3BNH_3$. Draw a dot–and–cross diagram and the displayed formula of this product.

c Draw a dot–and–cross diagram and the displayed formula for carbon monoxide.

# Bonds of intermediate character

There are compounds that might be expected to be ionic which have properties more typical of covalent compounds. For example, some salts sublime (i.e. change from a solid to a gas without melting) at quite low temperatures, e.g. aluminium chloride ($AlCl_3$).

Similarly there are covalent compounds that dissolve readily in water to produce ionic solutions, e.g. hydrogen chloride gas or ammonia.

Compounds that are purely ionic or covalent are best regarded as extremes. Between the two extremes a gradual transition from one to the other takes place. We shall start by examining an ionic compound.

## Polarisation of ions

Ionic compounds that show some properties more characteristic of covalent compounds contain anions that have become **polarised**. This means that the cation distorts the electron charge-cloud on the anion. Polarisation brings more electron charge between the ionic nuclei, and thus produces a significant degree of covalent bonding between the ions.

Anions with a greater charge or a larger radius are more easily polarised than those with a smaller charge or smaller radius. Cations with a smaller radius or a greater charge will have a greater charge density. Such cations will exert a greater degree of polarisation on an anion than will cations with a larger radius or lower charge.

*Figure 3.13* shows the increasing polarisation of an anion by a cation. The effect of this polarisation is to place some of the electron charge-cloud from the larger ion between the two ions. If the process is continued, a covalent bond is created between the two nuclei. When this occurs, the molecule still has some separation of positive and negative charge. The molecule has an electric dipole; it is described as a **polar molecule**.

## Polar molecules

Covalent bonds in molecules are polar if there is a difference in electronegativity between the elements. **Electronegativity** is the ability of a bonded atom to attract electron charge.

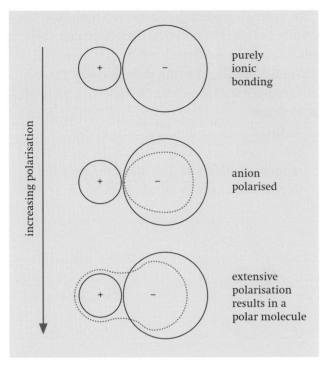

purely ionic bonding

anion polarised

extensive polarisation results in a polar molecule

increasing polarisation

● **Figure 3.13** Polarisation of an anion by a cation.

The electronegativity of the elements increases from Group I to Group VII across the Periodic Table. Electronegativity also increases up a Group of elements as the proton number decreases. Several attempts have been made to put numerical values on electronegativity. For our purposes, it is sufficient to recognise that electronegativities increase **a** moving from left to right across a Period in the Periodic Table and **b** vertically up Groups. The electronegativity of hydrogen is lower than that of most non-metallic elements. In the few cases where it is not lower, it is of a very similar magnitude to that of the non-metal.

increasing electronegativity

Cl < N < O < F

These electronegativity differences between atoms introduce a degree of polarity in covalent bonds between different atoms. A bigger difference in electronegativity will cause a greater degree of bond polarity. This accounts for the polarity of many simple diatomic molecules such as hydrogen chloride, HCl.

The situation is more complicated in polyatomic molecules, where the shape of the molecule must be taken into account. A symmetrical distribution of polar covalent bonds produces a non-polar molecule. The dipoles of the bonds exert equal and opposite effects on each other. An example is tetrachloromethane, $CCl_4$. This tetrahedral molecule has four polar C–Cl bonds. The four dipoles point towards the corners of the tetrahedral molecule, cancelling each other out. In the closely related trichloromethane, $CHCl_3$, the three C–Cl dipoles point in a similar direction. Their combined effect is not cancelled out by the C–H bond. (The C–H bond has a weak dipole, pointing towards the carbon atom.) Hence trichloromethane is a very polar molecule.

H——Cl
$\delta+$   $\delta-$

polar

H
$\delta+$
C▮▮▮-Cl
Cl
Cl
$\delta-$

polar

Cl
C▮▮▮-Cl
Cl
Cl

non-polar

*SAQ 3.5*

Predict the polarity of the following molecules: **a** $O_2$, **b** HF, **c** $CH_3Br$ and **d** $SCl_2$ (non-linear molecule).

Bond polarity can be a helpful indication of the reactivity of a molecule. This is clearly illustrated by a comparison of nitrogen and carbon monoxide. Both molecules contain triple bonds, which require a similar amount of energy to break them. (The CO bond actually requires more energy than the $N_2$ bond!) However, carbon monoxide is a very reactive molecule, whereas nitrogen is very unreactive. Non-polar nitrogen will only undergo reactions at high temperatures or in the presence of a catalyst. Carbon monoxide, which is a polar molecule, may be burned in air and it combines more strongly with the iron in haemoglobin than does oxygen. Many chemical reactions are started by a reagent attacking one of the electrically charged ends of a polar bond. Non-polar molecules are consequently much less reactive towards ionic or polar reagents. Other important polar molecules include water and ammonia.

As a knowledge of molecular shape is needed to predict the polarity of a polyatomic molecule, the next section shows how you can predict the shapes of simple molecules.

# Shapes of simple molecules

Molecules vary in shape, as shown by the six examples in *figure 3.14*.

## Electron-pair repulsion theory

As electrons are negatively charged, they exert a repulsion on each other. In chapter 1 (page 11), you saw that electrons may pair up with opposite spins in orbitals. This is also true in molecules. An electron-pair in the bonding (outermost) shell of the central atom in a simple molecule will exert a repulsion on the other electron-pairs. Each pair will repel each of the other pairs. The effect of these repulsions will cause the electron-pairs to move as far apart as possible within the confines of the bonds between the atoms in the molecule. This will determine the three-dimensional shape of the molecule.

The concept of **electron-pair repulsion** is a powerful theory, as it successfully predicts shapes, which are confirmed by modern experimental techniques.

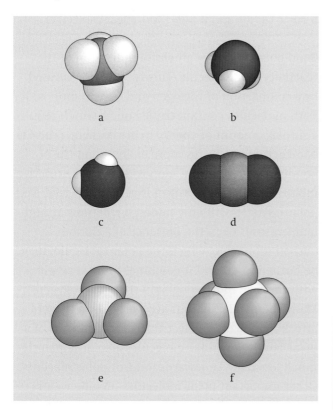

● **Figure 3.14** Shapes of molecules. These space-filling models show the molecular shapes of **a** methane ($CH_4$), **b** ammonia ($NH_3$), **c** water ($H_2O$), **d** carbon dioxide ($CO_2$), **e** boron trifluoride ($BF_3$) and **f** sulphur hexafluoride ($SF_6$).

In order to predict the shape of a molecule, the number of pairs of outer-shell electrons on the central atom is needed. It is best to start with a dot-and-cross diagram and then to count the electron-pairs, as shown in the following examples.

■ *Methane*

As there are four bonding pairs of electrons, these repel each other towards the corners of a regular tetrahedron. The molecule thus has a tetrahedral shape. A tetrahedron has four faces.

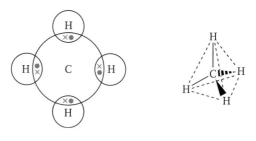

■ *Ammonia*

This has three bonding pairs and one lone-pair on the central atom, nitrogen. The four electron-pairs repel each other and occupy the corners of a tetrahedron as in methane. However, the nitrogen and three hydrogen atoms form a triangular pyramidal molecule.

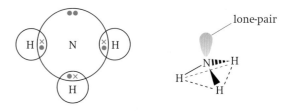

■ *Water*

There are two bonding pairs and two lone-pairs. Again, these repel each other towards the corners of a tetrahedron, leaving the oxygen and two hydrogen atoms as a non-linear (or bent) molecule.

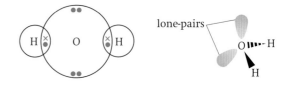

■ *Carbon dioxide*

This has two carbon–oxygen double bonds. Multiple bonds are best considered in the same way as single electron-pairs. If the two double bond pairs repel each other as far as possible, the molecule is predicted to be linear (i.e. the OCO angle is 180°):

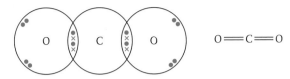

■ *Boron trifluoride*
This is an interesting molecule, as it only has six electrons in the bonding shell on boron, distributed between three bonding pairs. The three bonding pairs repel each other equally, forming a trigonal planar molecule with bond angles of 120°. Boron trifluoride is very reactive and will accept a non-bonding (lone) pair of electrons. For example, with ammonia $H_3N{\rightarrow}BF_3$ is formed (note the dative covalent bond indicated by the arrow).

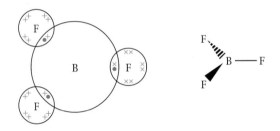

■ *Sulphur hexafluoride*
There are six bonding pairs and no lone-pairs. Repulsion between six electron-pairs produces the structure shown. All angles are 90°. The shape produced is an octahedron (i.e. eight faces).

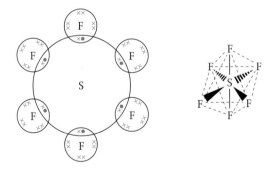

### SAQ 3.6

**a** Draw dot-and-cross diagrams for (i) $PCl_3$, (ii) $NH_4^+$, (iii) $H_2S$ and (iv) $SCl_2$.

**b** Consider the bonding and lone pairs you have drawn in **a**. Predict the shape of each molecule and illustrate each shape with a diagram.

## Lone-pairs, bonding pairs and bond angles

Lone-pairs of electrons are attracted by only one nucleus, unlike bonding pairs, which are shared between two nuclei. As a result, lone-pairs occupy a molecular orbital that is pulled closer to the nucleus than bonding pairs. The electron charge-cloud in a lone-pair has a greater width than a bonding pair. The diagram below shows the repulsions between lone-pairs (pink) and bonding pairs (white) in a water molecule.

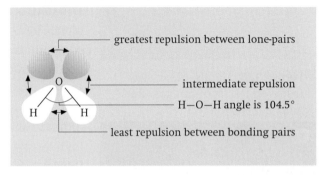

The repulsion between lone-pairs is thus greater than that between a lone-pair and a bonding pair. The repulsion between a lone-pair (LP) and a bonding pair (BP) is greater than that between two bonding pairs. To summarise:

LP–LP repulsion > LP–BP repulsion > BP–BP repulsion

This variation in repulsion produces small but measurable effects on the bond angles in molecules. In methane, all the HCH angles are the same at 109.5°. In ammonia, the slightly greater repulsion of the lone-pair pushes the bonding pairs slightly closer together and the angle reduces to 107°. In water, two lone-pairs reduce the HOH angle to 104.5°.

## Bond enthalpy and bond length

In general, double bonds are shorter than single bonds. In addition, the energy required to break a double bond is greater than that needed to break a single bond. The **bond enthalpy** is the energy required to break one mole of the given bond in the gaseous molecule (see also chapter 5, page 76). *Table 3.2* shows some examples of bond enthalpies and bond lengths.

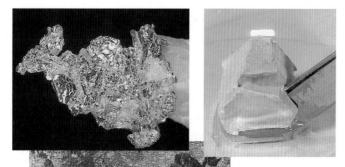

| Bond | Bond enthalpy (kJ mol⁻¹) | Bond length (nm) |
|------|--------------------------|-------------------|
| C–C | 347 | 0.154 |
| C=C | 612 | 0.134 |
| C–O | 358 | 0.143 |
| C=O | 805 | 0.116 |

● **Table 3.2** Some bond enthalpies and bond lengths. See page 73 for an explanation of enthalpy.

# Metallic bonding

Metals have very different properties to both ionic and covalent compounds. In appearance they are usually shiny (*figure 3.15*). They are good conductors of both heat and electricity (the latter in the solid state and without decomposition, unlike ionic compounds). They are easily worked and may be drawn into wires or hammered into a different shape, i.e. they are ductile and malleable. They often possess high tensile strengths and they are usually hard. *Table 3.3* provides information on some of the properties of aluminium, iron and copper, with the non-metal sulphur for comparison.

It is this range of properties that has led humans to use them to make tools, weapons and jewellery. Two major periods in our history are named after the metals in use at the time (*figure 3.16*). The change from bronze (an alloy of tin and copper) to iron reflected the discovery of methods for extracting different metals.

A simplified model of metallic bonding is adequate for our purposes. In a metallic lattice, the atoms lose their outer-shell electrons to become positive ions. The outer-shell electrons occupy new energy levels, which extend throughout the metal lattice. The bonding is often described as a 'sea' of mobile electrons surrounding a lattice of positive ions. This is shown in *figure 3.17*. The lattice is held together by the strong attractive forces between the mobile electrons and the positive ions.

The properties of metals can be explained in terms of this model of the bonding. Electrical conduction can take place in any direction, as electrons are free to move throughout the lattice. Conduction of heat occurs by vibration of the positive ions as well as via the mobile electrons.

a

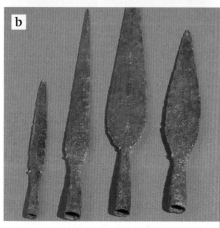

b

● **Figure 3.15** Metals. Clockwise from top left: sodium, gold and zinc.

● **Figure 3.16  a** Bronze age statue and  **b** Iron age spears.

|  | Density (g cm⁻³) | Tensile strength (10¹⁰ Pa) | Thermal conductivity (W m⁻¹ K⁻¹) | Electrical conductivity (10⁸ S m⁻¹) |
|--|------------------|----------------------------|-----------------------------------|--------------------------------------|
| Aluminium | 2.70 | 7.0 | 238 | 0.38 |
| Iron | 7.86 | 21.1 | 82 | 0.10 |
| Copper | 8.92 | 13.0 | 400 | 0.59 |
| Sulphur | 2.07 |  | 0.029 | 1 × 10⁻²³ |

● **Table 3.3** Properties of three metals and sulphur.

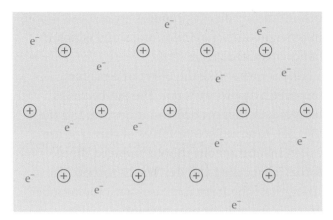

● **Figure 3.17** Metallic bonding. There are strong attractive forces between positively charged ions and a 'sea' of mobile electrons.

Metals are both ductile and malleable because the bonding in the metallic lattice is not broken when they are physically deformed. As a metal is hammered or drawn into a wire, the metal ions slide over each other to new lattice positions. The mobile electrons continue to hold the lattice together. Some metals will even flow under their own weight. Lead has a problem in this respect. It is often used on roofs where, over the years, it suffers from 'creep'. This is not only from thieves but also because the metal slowly flows under the influence of gravity.

The transition elements (see chapter 9, pages 200, 201) are metals that possess both hardness and high tensile strength. Hardness and high tensile strength are also due to the strong attractive forces between the metal ions and the mobile electrons in the lattice.

### SAQ 3.7

Use *table 3.3* to answer the following questions and give full explanations in terms of metallic bonding. (Assume steel and stainless steel have similar properties to iron.)
a  Why do some stainless steel saucepans have a copper base?
b  Aluminium with a steel core is used for overhead power cables in preference to copper. Why is aluminium preferred? What is the function of the steel core?
c  Apart from overhead power cables, copper is chosen for almost all other electrical uses. Suggest reasons for the choice of copper.

# Intermolecular forces

Before we discuss the attractive forces that exist between molecules, it may be helpful to review the kinetic theory of matter. Matter exists in solid, liquid and gaseous states. In the solid state, the particles are packed together in a regularly ordered way. This order breaks down when a substance melts. In the liquid state, there may be small groups of particles with some degree of order, but, overall in the liquid, particles are free to move past each other. In order to do this, many of the forces that bind the particles together must be overcome on melting. In the gaseous state, the particles are widely separated. They are free to move independently, and all the forces that bind the particles together in the solid or liquid have been overcome on vaporisation. In the gaseous state, the particles move randomly in any direction. As they do so, they exert a pressure (vapour pressure) on the walls of their container.

A multitude of biochemical compounds are involved in the enormous number of chemical reactions found in living organisms. They are also ultimately responsible for a seemingly infinite number of variations within a given species. All biochemical compounds rely significantly on weak attractive forces that exist between their molecules to produce this variety. These **intermolecular forces** (often called van der Waals' forces) are much weaker than ionic, covalent or metallic bonding forces.

The properties of all small molecules are dependent on intermolecular forces. It is the properties of these small molecules that provide evidence for the existence of intermolecular forces and help us to understand the nature of these forces. If a gas is able to condense to a liquid, which can then be frozen to a solid, there must be an attraction between the molecules of the gas. When a solid melts or a liquid boils, energy is needed to overcome this attraction. For example, water in a kettle will continue to boil only whilst the electricity is switched on. The temperature of the water is constant whilst the water is boiling, and the heating effect of energy from the electricity is separating the water molecules from each other to produce water vapour.

There are three types of intermolecular forces: instantaneous dipole–induced dipole forces, dipole–dipole forces and hydrogen bonds.

## Instantaneous dipole–induced dipole forces

Even noble-gas atoms must exert an attraction on each other. *Figure 3.18* shows the enthalpy change of vaporisation of the noble gases plotted against the number of electrons present. (Enthalpy change of vaporisation is the energy required to convert the liquid to a gas.) The trend in the enthalpy change of vaporisation shows an increase from helium to xenon as the number of electrons increases. Alkanes (chapter 16a) show a similar trend; their enthalpies of vaporisation also increase with increasing numbers of atoms in the molecules (and hence with increasing numbers of electrons). Both the noble gases and the alkanes have attractive forces between atoms and molecules, which are now known to depend on the number of electrons and protons present.

The forces arise because electrons in atoms or molecules are moving at very high speeds in orbitals. At any instant in time it is possible for more electrons to lie to one side of the atom or molecule than the other. When this happens, an instantaneous electric dipole occurs. The momentary imbalance of electrons provides the negative end of a dipole, with the atomic nucleus providing the positive end of the dipole. This

instantaneous dipole produces an induced dipole in a neighbouring atom or molecule, which is hence attracted (*figure 3.19*).

This is rather like the effect of a magnet (magnetic dipole) on a pin. The pin becomes temporarily magnetised and is attracted to the magnet. Intermolecular forces of this type are called **instantaneous dipole–induced dipole forces** (also called **van der Waals' forces**). The strength of the force increases with the number of electrons and protons present.

Instantaneous dipole–induced dipole forces are the weakest type of attractive force found between atoms or molecules. They are responsible for the slippery nature of graphite (*figure 3.20a*) in contrast to the great hardness of diamond (*figure 3.20b*), and for the volatility of bromine and iodine (*figure 3.21*).

A polymer is a molecule built up from a large number of small molecules (called monomers). Low-density poly(ethene), LDPE, and high-density poly(ethene), HDPE, have differing properties because of the way the polymer molecules are packed (*figure 3.22*). The HDPE molecules can pack much more closely as they are not branched. LDPE molecules are branched at intervals, which prevents them packing as closely. As a result, the instantaneous dipole–induced dipole forces are not as strong.

Teflon is poly(tetrafluoroethene), PTFE. A model of part of a PTFE molecule is shown in *figure 3.23* (page 44). The instantaneous dipole–induced dipole forces between oil or grease and PTFE are much weaker than those present in the oil or grease itself. This gives rise to the polymer's non-stick properties.

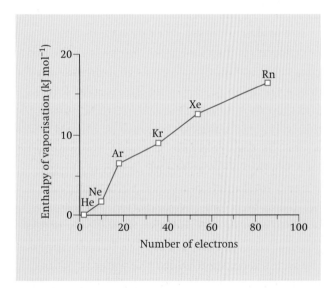

● **Figure 3.18** Enthalpy change of vaporisation of the noble gases plotted against the number of electrons present.

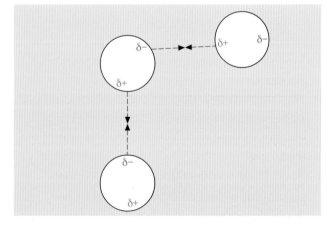

● **Figure 3.19** Induced dipole attractions.

● **Figure 3.20**

a The structure of graphite. In the planar sheets of carbon atoms, all the bonding electrons are involved in covalent bonds. The sheets are held together by much weaker instantaneous dipole–induced dipole forces. These forces are easily overcome, allowing the sheets to slide over each other (rather like a pack of cards). Graphite is often used as a lubricant.

b The structure of diamond. In contrast to graphite, each carbon atom forms four covalent bonds to four other carbon atoms. The resulting network of covalent bonds requires considerable energy to separate the atoms. The strength of the bonding in diamond is responsible for its great hardness.

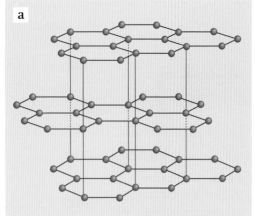
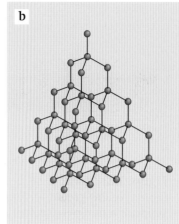

● **Figure 3.21** Bromine **a** and iodine **b** exist as covalent molecules. They are both volatile, as only very weak instantaneous dipole–induced dipole forces need to be overcome to achieve vaporisation.

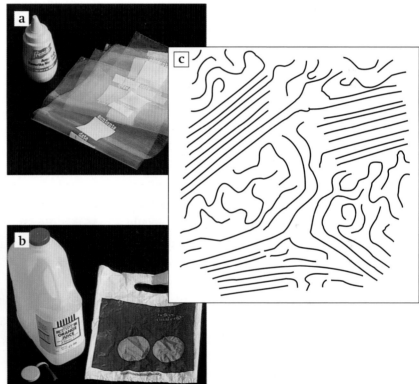

● **Figure 3.22** Low-density and high-density poly(ethene).

a LDPE is made under high pressure with a trace of oxygen as catalyst. The product consists primarily of a tangled mass of polymer chains with some regions where the chains have some alignment.

b HDPE is made using catalysts developed by the Swiss chemist Ziegler and the Italian chemist Natta. (They received a Nobel Prize for their discoveries.) In HDPE, the polymer chains are arranged in a much more regular fashion. This increases the density of the material and makes it more opaque to light. As the molecules are closer together in HDPE, the instantaneous dipole–induced dipole forces between the non-polar poly(ethene) molecules are greater and the tensile strength of the material is higher.

c Diagram of crystalline and non-crystalline regions in poly(ethene). LDPE has fewer of the crystalline regions than HDPE. In the crystalline regions, polymer chains (shown as lines in the diagram) lie parallel to each other.

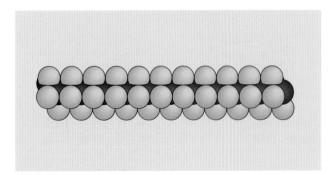

● **Figure 3.23** Model of PTFE. Note how the fluorine atoms (yellow-green) surround the carbon atoms to produce a non-polar polymer.

## Permanent dipole–dipole forces

A nylon rod may be given a charge of static electricity by rubbing it with a dry sheet of thin poly(ethene). If this is brought near a fine jet of water, the stream of water is attracted by the charge on the nylon rod. You can try this for yourself. Use a nylon comb and as fine a trickle of water from a tap as possible (see *figure 3.24*).

The water molecules are attracted to the charged nylon rod or comb because they have a permanent electric dipole. A force of this type is called a **dipole–dipole force**. The dipole of water arises because of the bent shape of the molecule and the greater electron charge around the oxygen atom. As we saw earlier in the case of the hydrogen chloride molecule, a molecule is often

polar if its atoms have different electronegativities. The diagram shows the lone-pairs and electric dipole of a water molecule (note that the arrow head shows the negative end of the dipole).

### SAQ 3.8

The nylon rod carries a positive charge. Which end of the water molecule is attracted to the rod? Why are no water molecules repelled by the rod? A poly(ethene) rod may be given a negative charge when rubbed with a nylon cloth. Will the charge on the poly(ethene) rod attract or repel a thin stream of water?

Many fabrics are made using poly(ester) fibres because of that polymer's strength. Production of poly(ester) fibres together with a section of a poly(ester) molecule are shown in *figure 3.25*.

● **Figure 3.24** Deflection of water by an electrically charged nylon comb.

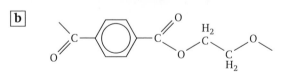

● **Figure 3.25**
**a** A photograph showing the production of poly(ester) fibre and
**b** a section of the poly(ester) chain. The strength of poly(ester) fibre is due to the strong dipole–dipole forces between ester groups of adjacent molecules.

## SAQ 3.9

Copy the section of the poly(ester) chain shown in *figure 3.25* and mark on your copy the polar groups, showing the δ+ and δ– charges. Draw a second section of poly(ester) chain alongside your first section and mark in the dipole–dipole forces with dotted lines.

## Water is peculiar

*Figure 3.26* shows the enthalpy changes of vaporisation of water and other hydrides of Group VI elements.

## SAQ 3.10

Explain the underlying increase in the enthalpy change of vaporisation with increasing atomic number. Estimate a value for water based on this trend. What is the cause of the much higher value observed for water?

The boiling point of water is also much higher than predicted by the trend in boiling points for other Group VI element hydrides. This trend would suggest that water should be a gas at room temperature and pressure. There are several more ways in which water behaves differently to most other liquids. For example, it has a very high surface tension and a high viscosity. Further, the density of ice is less than the density of water (*figure 3.27*). Most solids are denser than their liquids, as molecules usually pack closer in solids than in liquids.

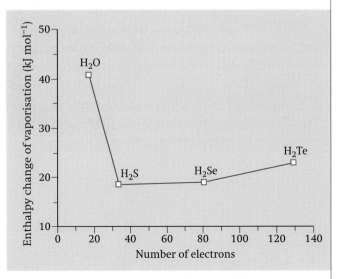

● **Figure 3.26** Enthalpy changes of vaporisation of Group VI hydrides, including water, plotted against number of electrons present.

● **Figure 3.27** Ice floats on water.

> **Surface tension of water**
> You can demonstrate the high surface tension of water for yourself by floating a needle on water. Rinse a bowl several times with water. Fill the bowl with water. Place a small piece of tissue paper on the surface of the water. Now place a needle on the tissue. Leave it undisturbed. The paper will sink, leaving the needle floating. Now carefully add a few drops of washing-up liquid (which lowers the surface tension of water) and observe the effect.

## Hydrogen bonds

The peculiar nature of water is explained by the presence of the strongest type of intermolecular force – the hydrogen bond (indicated on diagrams by dotted lines). Water is highly polar owing to the large difference in electronegativity between hydrogen and oxygen. The resulting intermolecular attraction between oxygen and hydrogen atoms on neighbouring water molecules is a very strong dipole–dipole attraction called a **hydrogen bond**. Each water molecule can form two hydrogen bonds to other water molecules. These form in the directions of the lone-pairs. In the liquid state, water molecules collect in groups. On boiling, the hydrogen bonds must be broken. This raises the boiling point significantly as the hydrogen bonds are stronger than the other intermolecular forces. Similarly the enthalpy change of vaporisation is much higher than it would be if no hydrogen bonds were present.

In ice, a three-dimensional hydrogen-bonded lattice is produced. In this lattice, each oxygen is surrounded by a tetrahedron of hydrogen atoms bonded to further oxygen atoms. The structure is shown in *figure 3.28*. The extensive network of hydrogen bonds raises the freezing point

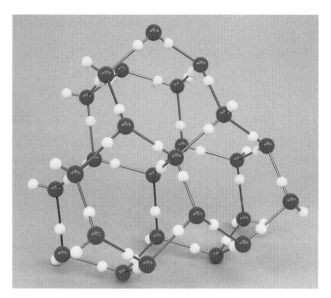

● **Figure 3.28** Model of ice. It is this hydrogen-bonded arrangement of molecules that makes ice less dense than water.

significantly above that predicted by the trend for other Group VI hydrides.

## SAQ 3.11

A diamond-type lattice is present in ice. The O····H hydrogen bond length is 0.159 nm and the O–H covalent bond length is 0.096 nm. When ice melts, some hydrogen bonds break and the density rises. Use *figure 3.28* and these values to explain why ice has a lower density than water.

The high surface tension of water is explained by the presence of a hydrogen-bonded network of water molecules at the surface. This network is sufficiently strong to enable a needle to be floated on the surface of water.

Within the bulk of water, small groups of molecules are attracted by hydrogen bonds. The hydrogen bonds are constantly breaking and re-forming at room temperature. As the temperature of water is raised towards the boiling point, the number of hydrogen bonds reduces. On boiling, the remaining hydrogen bonds are broken. Water vapour consists of widely separated water molecules.

## SAQ 3.12

Why does a needle floating on water sink on the addition of washing-up liquid to the water?

## SAQ 3.13

The boiling points for Group V element hydrides are as follows:

| Hydride | Boiling point (K) |
| --- | --- |
| ammonia, $NH_3$ | 240 |
| phosphine, $PH_3$ | 185 |
| arsine, $AsH_3$ | 218 |
| stibine, $SbH_3$ | 256 |
| bismuthine, $BiH_3$ | 295 |

Plot a graph of these boiling points against the relative molecular mass of the hydrides.
**a** Explain the steadily rising trend in the boiling points from phosphine to bismuthine.
**b** Explain why the boiling point of ammonia does not follow this trend.

## Nylon

This synthetic polymer is an example of a poly(amide). It is similar to poly(ester) with the –O– link replaced by –NH–. The structure of a section of the polymer chain of one type of nylon is shown in *figure 3.29*. The –CO–NH– link is called an amide link. Hence the name poly(amide).

Nylon fibres are produced in the same way as poly(ester) fibres. Their high tensile strength is due to strong hydrogen bonds forming between an –NH– hydrogen atom and a C=O oxygen atom on a neighbouring polymer chain.

## SAQ 3.14

**a** Ammonia is a gas which liquifies easily under pressure due to the formation of hydrogen bonds. Draw a diagram to show hydrogen bond formation between two adjacent molecules.
**b** Draw two parallel short sections of nylon-6,6 polymer chain and indicate where hydrogen bonds form between them.

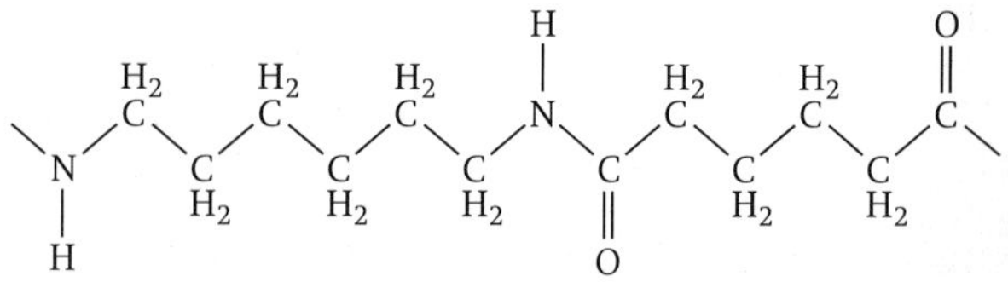

● **Figure 3.29** The structure of a section of nylon-6,6. Each building-block (monomer unit) contains six carbon atoms, hence the name nylon-6,6.

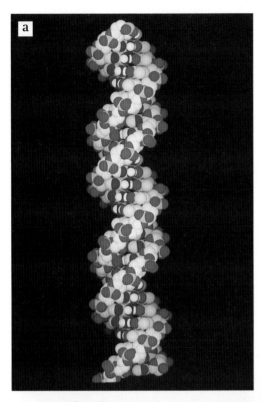

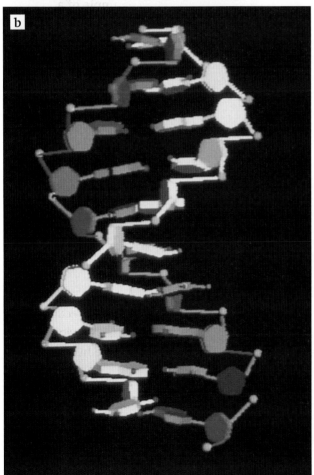

Not all the polymer chains lie close and parallel. When the fibres are stretched, the molecules straighten further but are held by the hydrogen bonds, which return the molecules to their original positions on release. The combination of strength and high elasticity are important properties in a climbing rope. If a climber falls, a nylon rope can stretch by up to half its length to stop the fall without injuring the climber.

Hydrogen bonds play a very important part in the structures and properties of biochemical polymers. For example, protein chains often produce a helical structure, and the ability of DNA molecules to replicate themselves depends primarily on the hydrogen bonds, which hold the two parts of the molecules together in a double helix (*figure 3.30*).

## Relative bond strengths

*Table 3.4* shows the relative strengths of intermolecular forces and other bonds. Note that all the intermolecular forces are much weaker than the forces of attraction found in typical covalent bonds or in ionic bonding. Instantaneous dipole–induced dipole forces are weaker than dipole–dipole forces. Hydrogen bonds are about twice as strong as the other intermolecular forces.

*Table 3.5* provides a summary of the pattern and variety of structures and bonding found among elements and compounds.

| | Energy (kJ mol$^{-1}$) |
|---|---|
| Instantaneous dipole–induced dipole, e.g. in xenon | 15 |
| Hydrogen bond, e.g. in water | 22 |
| O–H covalent bond in water | 464 |
| Ionic bonding, sodium chloride | 760 |

● **Table 3.4** Relative strengths of intermolecular forces and bonds.

● **Figure 3.30** Photographs of models of biochemical polymers: **a** the DNA helix formed by a protein molecule and **b** a section of the DNA molecule.

| | Type of structure | | | | | |
|---|---|---|---|---|---|---|
| | Giant lattices | | | Molecular | | |
| | Ionic | Covalent | Metallic | Macromolecular | Simple | Atomic |
| Where this type of structure is found | compounds formed between metals and non-metals | Group IV elements and some of their compounds | metals | polymers | some elements and some compounds formed between non-metals | noble gases |
| Some examples | sodium chloride, magnesium oxide | diamond, graphite, silicon(IV) oxide | aluminium, copper | nylon, DNA | hydrogen $H_2$, chlorine $Cl_2$, methane, ammonia | helium, neon |
| Particles present | ions | atoms | positive ions and electrons | long-chain molecules | small molecules | atoms |
| Attractions that hold particles together | between oppositely charged ions | electrons in covalent bonds attract nuclei | delocalised sea of electrons attracts positive ions | various intermolecular forces between molecules, covalent bonds within molecule | various intermolecular forces between molecules, covalent bonds within molecule | intermolecular forces between atoms: instantaneous dipole–induced dipole only |
| Common physical state(s) at room temperature and pressure | solid | solid | solid | solid | solids, liquids and gases | gases |
| Melting and boiling points, enthalpy change of vaporisation | high | very high | moderately high to high | moderate, may decompose | low | very low |
| Hardness | hard, brittle | very hard | hard, malleable | often soft, flexible | solids usually soft | |
| Electrical conductivity | conduct when molten or in aqueous solution | usually non-conductors | conduct when solid or molten | usually non-conductors | non-conductors | non-conductors |
| Solubility in water | many ionic compounds are soluble | insoluble ($SiO_2$ is very sparingly soluble) | insoluble, some react liberating hydrogen | mostly insoluble, natural polymers more likely to be soluble | usually insoluble unless very polar and capable of forming hydrogen bonds to water | sparingly soluble |

● **Table 3.5** Summary of structure and bonding.

# SUMMARY (AS)

◆ All bonding involves electrostatic attractive forces.

◆ In ionic bonding, the attractive forces are between oppositely charged ions.

◆ In a covalent bond (one electron from each atom) or a dative covalent bond (both electrons from one atom), the forces are between two atomic nuclei and pairs of electrons situated between them.

◆ Ionic and covalent bonds may be seen as extremes. Between the two, there is a gradual transition from one extreme to the other.

◆ In metallic bonding, the forces are between delocalised electrons and positive ions.

◆ Intermolecular attractive forces also involve electrostatic forces.

◆ Intermolecular forces (hydrogen bonds, dipole–dipole and instantaneous dipole–induced dipole forces) are much weaker than ionic, covalent or metallic bonding forces.

◆ Dot-and-cross diagrams enable ionic and covalent bonds to be described. Use of these diagrams with electron-pair repulsion theory enables molecular shapes to be predicted.

◆ In molecules, atomic orbitals combine to produce $\sigma$ and $\pi$ molecular orbitals.

◆ Physical properties and structures of elements and compounds may be explained in terms of kinetic theory and bonding (*table 3.5*).

# Questions (AS)

1 Hydrogen fluoride, HF, is one of the most important fluorine compounds. It can be prepared by reacting calcium fluoride, $CaF_2$, with sulphuric acid.
  a Showing outer-shell electrons only, draw 'dot-and-cross' diagrams of:
    (i) hydrogen fluoride;
    (ii) calcium fluoride.
  b Predict two differences between the physical properties of HF and $CaF_2$.

2 a Explain how the model of electron-pair repulsion can be used to explain the shape and bond angles of simple molecules using $CH_4$, $NH_3$ and $CO_2$ as examples.
  b Draw 'dot-and-cross' diagrams for the oxides of sulphur, $SO_3$ and $SO_2$, and predict the shape and bond angles of these molecules.

3 At room temperature, iodine, $I_2$, has a crystal lattice structure.
  a (i) What type of bond holds together the iodine atoms in an iodine molecule?
    (ii) What forces act between the iodine molecules in a crystal lattice of iodine?
  b When iodine is gently heated to $114\,^\circ C$, it turns directly from a solid into a gas without going through the liquid state. This unusual behaviour is called **sublimation**.
    (i) Explain, in terms of forces, the changes that occur to the structure of iodine as it sublimes.
    (ii) The diamond form of carbon sublimes at a much higher temperature than iodine. Suggest why this higher temperature is required.

# CHAPTER 4

# States of matter (AS)

## By the end of this chapter you should be able to:

1 describe, using a kinetic–molecular model, the solid, liquid and gaseous states, melting, vaporisation and vapour pressure;

2 state the basic assumptions of the kinetic theory as applied to an ideal gas;

3 explain qualitatively, in terms of intermolecular forces and molecular size,
(i) the conditions necessary for a gas to approach ideal behaviour, and
(ii) the limitations of ideality at very high pressures and very low temperatures;

4 state and use the ideal gas equation $PV = nRT$ in calculations, including the determination of the relative molecular mass of a volatile liquid;

5 describe in simple terms lattice structures of crystalline solids which are ionic, simple molecular, giant molecular, hydrogen-bonded or metallic;

6 outline the importance of hydrogen bonding to the physical properties of substances;

7 explain the properties and uses of ceramics in terms of their giant molecular structure;

8 describe and interpret the uses of aluminium, copper and their alloys in terms of their physical properties;

9 understand that materials are a finite resource and that recycling processes are important;

10 suggest from quoted physical data the type of structure and bonding present in a substance.

## The three states of matter

*Figure 4.1* shows the Grinnell glacier, at various times in the past. You can see just how much of the glacier has disappeared between 1914 and 1997. Many scientists believe that the increasing rate of melting of glacier ice, and ice at the polar ice caps, is a result of global warming. You may know that, if global warming continues, the sea level on Earth will gradually rise. Mainly the rise will be due to the expansion of sea-water with increasing temperature; but the melt water from glaciers and the polar ice caps will add to the increase as well. In fact, it has been estimated that, if all the ice over the Earth's land mass were to melt, sea level would rise by around 20 m. For many Europeans, the retreat of glaciers in mountainous regions and the end of reliable winter snow falls will be the end of skiing holidays. However, there are far more serious consequences world wide; for example, glaciers provide billions of gallons of water for drinking water and the irrigation of crops in lowland regions. In Africa, the end of glaciation will make vast tracts of land uninhabitable owing to the lack of melt water. It has been estimated that a rise of 4 °C in average air temperature will be enough to melt all the glaciers in Europe, and even the Himalayas.

• **Figure 4.1** Three photographs of the Grinnell glacier, Glacier National Park, USA, taken in **a** 1914, **b** 1938 and **c** 1997.

Studying the conditions that cause ice to form, and melt, and the change of water vapour into rain and snow, is part of chemistry. We know how and why water changes between its solid, liquid and gaseous forms; and this knowledge is important in predicting the results of global warming. However, the same processes are at work when any solid, liquid or gas changes from one form to another. This chapter will introduce you to the

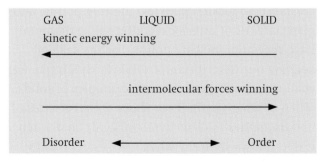

• **Figure 4.2** The relation between kinetic energy, disorder and intermolecular forces.

main factors that we believe are responsible for the different properties of gases, liquids and solids. However, as in all good stories, we should start at the beginning; and that means you need to know what we mean by states of matter.

The three states of matter are solid, liquid and gas. Whether a substance exists as a solid, liquid or gas mainly depends on two things:

1 *Kinetic energy* – which increases as a substance is heated.
2 *Intermolecular forces* – the forces between the molecules that make up the substance.

The kinetic energy of the molecules in a solid, liquid or gas is a measure of the amount of random movement of molecules. The more kinetic energy the molecules of a substance have, the greater is the tendency for its molecules to be jumbled up, i.e. to be more disordered. The most *disorderly* arrangement that molecules can achieve is in a gas. At the other extreme, the most orderly arrangement is in a solid. Liquids are somewhere in between. See *figure 4.2*.

Intermolecular forces tend to hold molecules together. There are intermolecular forces between all molecules; but between some they are very weak, and between others they are quite strong. When the forces are weak, the molecules are not likely to cling together to make a liquid or solid unless they have very little kinetic energy. The noble gases are excellent examples of this. For instance, helium will not liquefy until the temperature is almost as low as −269 °C, or 4 K. On the other hand, the intermolecular forces between water molecules are very strong – strong enough to hold them together up to 100 °C.

To summarise, we can say that:

> Intermolecular forces tend to bring order to the movements of molecules.
> Kinetic energy brings disorder, and leads in the direction of randomness or chaos.

Thus, at a given temperature, a substance will exist as a solid, liquid or gas depending on where the balance between these two opposing influences lies. An equilibrium can be set up when a substance changes state. This is discussed later in this chapter (page 57) and in chapter 7.

## How do we know that gases are disorderly?

One piece of evidence for this comes indirectly from the experiments first performed by Robert Brown in 1827. He observed the movement of pollen on the surface of water, which he found to be completely unpredictable. The random movements of the pollen, known as Brownian motion, were finally given a mathematical explanation by Albert Einstein (of relativity fame) in 1905. He showed that a grain of pollen went on a random walk. A random walk (*figure 4.3*) is the sort of walk that a very drunk person would go on if put out in an open space. If we assume that the drunk found it impossible to make a conscious choice, he (or she) would be as likely to walk in one direction as any other. The reason why the grains behave in this way is that they are being bombarded by molecules in the liquid, which are themselves moving in a random way.

Around 1908 Jean Perrin made observations of Brownian motion in gases. He showed that small particles, much larger than individual molecules but still very small (less than $10^{-6}$ m in diameter), also went on random walks. This could only be explained along the same lines as Brownian motion in liquids. The particles were being struck by the randomly moving gas molecules.

## How much order is there in a liquid?

The particles in a liquid group together, and it is just this tendency that produces some order in their arrangement (*figure 4.4*). However, the order is over a relatively short range, perhaps over a distance of $10^{-9}$ m (about 10 molecular diameters). Over greater distances, the degree of order

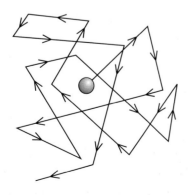

● **Figure 4.3** A random walk of a pollen grain.

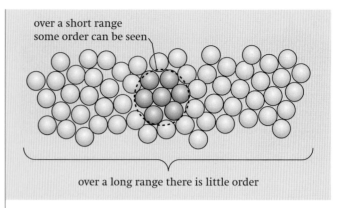

over a short range some order can be seen

over a long range there is little order

● **Figure 4.4** Order and disorder in a liquid.

diminishes, i.e. the groups themselves are randomly arranged. We can summarise the situation in this way:

> In a liquid there is short-range order, and long-range disorder.

However, as in a gas, the positions of the particles in a liquid are constantly changing; so membership of the groups is always changing.

## The arrangement of particles in a solid

First, a reminder: there are many types of solid, whose properties depend on the particles that they contain. For example, metal crystals consist of lattices of atoms, which are best viewed as positive ions existing in a 'sea' of electrons; ionic substances like sodium chloride have lattices built from positively and negatively charged ions ($Na^+$ and $Cl^-$); iodine crystals have a lattice of iodine molecules, $I_2$; graphite crystals contain layers of hexagonal rings of carbon atoms; and diamond is a giant lattice of carbon atoms all bonded in a tetrahedral arrangement. In general, metals and ionic substances have high melting points (although there are exceptions); molecular crystals (like iodine) have low melting points; and giant lattices of interlocked atoms (like diamond) have very high melting points. For the sake of keeping our description of solids fairly simple, we shall use metal crystals as our examples of solids. Much of what we shall say about the structures of metals applies to other types of solids (and when it doesn't, we shall say why).

When a liquid metal starts to crystallise, the atoms begin to fit together in regular patterns.

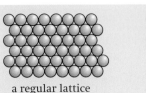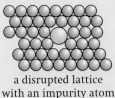

a regular lattice      a disrupted lattice
with an impurity atom

● **Figure 4.5** Disorder can appear even in very orderly solids.

A particularly simple pattern is shown in *figure 4.5*. It is clear that this is a very orderly arrangement. However, even at 0 K, the atoms are not completely still; they vibrate about the same average position. The very regular packing of particles in a solid extends over far greater distances than in a liquid. However, eventually the regularity breaks down. This can happen because of impurity atoms getting in the way, and blocking the normal pattern. It can also happen when crystals start to grow in several places and grow towards each other. Where the crystalline regions meet, the two lattices may not meet exactly. We can visualise such situations in the laboratory using bubble rafts, like that in *figure 4.6*. The study of order and disorder in metal crystals is of huge importance in industry. Variations in a metal lattice can lead to greater strength or, more worryingly, to metal fatigue (*figure 4.7*).

# Differences in properties of solids, liquids and gases

As we have seen, the particles in a gas are, on average, much further apart than they are in a liquid

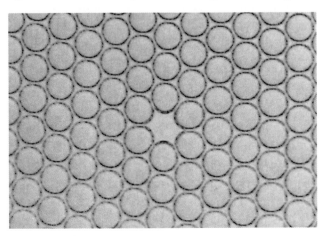

● **Figure 4.6** Bubble rafts can be used to show perfect order and imperfections.

● **Figure 4.7** Metal fatigue in the rails is likely to have contributed to the October 2000 train crash at Hatfield, UK.

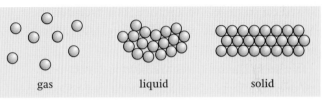

gas      liquid      solid

● **Figure 4.8** The arrangements of particles in a gas, a liquid and a solid.

or solid (*figure 4.8*). There is very little difference between the spacing of atoms in liquids and solids; that is why both liquids and solids are hard to compress. Also, the particles in a gas travel very much faster than those in a liquid. The differences in spacing, and in speed, are the main reason for the different properties of the three states of matter (*figure 4.9* and *table 4.1*). For example, notice that gases are not very good conductors of heat. For heat to be conducted by atoms or molecules, the movement energy of the molecules must be

● **Figure 4.9** Cloud, sea and iceberg – the three states of matter.

|  | **Solids** | **Liquids** | **Gases** |
|---|---|---|---|
| Amount of order of arrangement of particles | Very orderly | Short-range order, longer-range disorder | Almost complete disorder |
| Shape | Fixed | Takes shape of container | No shape |
| Position of particles | Fixed; no movement from place to place | Some movement from place to place | Always moving rapidly from place to place |
| Spacing of particles | Close ($\approx 10^{-10}$ m) | Close ($\approx 10^{-10}$ m) | Far apart ($\approx 10^{-8}$ m) |
| Compressibility | Very low | Very low | High |
| Conduction of heat | Metals and graphite very good; others poor | Metals very good; others poor | Very poor |

● **Table 4.1** Comparison of properties of the three states of matter.

passed on from one to another. This requires the molecules to collide, which happens less easily in a gas than in a liquid.

In a solid the particles are held in position by the overall effects of the attractions and repulsions of their neighbours. Even so, the particles do have some movement. They vibrate to and fro, although on average they keep the same position. As the temperature increases, they vibrate more violently, and they pass on the energy of their vibrations to their neighbours. However, the only solids that conduct heat very well are those that have electrons that can move from place to place. Especially, metals have many free electrons that can carry their movement energy with them even though the ions themselves are stuck in one place. That is, metals conduct heat well because of their free electrons, not as a result of vibrations of the particles.

Owing to the large amount of empty space in a gas, it is fairly easy to squeeze the molecules into a smaller volume; so gases are easily compressed. Liquids and solids have their molecules already very close together, so they are very difficult to compress.

# Comparing the melting and boiling points of substances

You will find some representative examples of melting and boiling points in *table 4.2*. A column showing the relative molecular masses ($M_r$) of the molecules has been included in the table. If you look carefully, you will see that there is a *general* rule that governs the values:

> The higher the relative molecular mass, the higher the melting point and the higher the boiling point.

One reason why melting and boiling points tend to increase with mass is that, the greater the mass of a molecule, the more electrons it possesses. It is one of the features of large molecules that their electron clouds are more spread out (diffuse), and it is just this type of molecule that has large forces between instantaneous dipoles. These forces are called **instantaneous dipole forces** (more correctly 'instantaneous dipole–induced dipole forces', and are also known as **van der Waals' forces**). Thus, as molecules get heavier, the instantaneous dipole forces become greater, and tend to keep the molecules together.

However, there are many exceptions to the general rule. In particular, you should know that:

> Where melting or boiling points are higher than expected, look for very strong intermolecular forces at work, especially hydrogen bonds.

There are two important examples that you should know about:

■ *Hydrogen fluoride*, HF, is rather like water in that its boiling point is far above those of the other hydrides of the halogens. The reason is, again, *hydrogen bonding*. Fluorine is the most electronegative of all the elements, and the hydrogen fluoride molecule is extremely polar. That is, the fluorine atom attracts the pair of electrons in the H–F bond towards itself. The bonding pair

| | Relative molecular mass, $M_r$ | Melting pt (°C) | Boiling pt (°C) | | Relative molecular mass, $M_r$ | Melting pt (°C) | Boiling pt (°C) |
|---|---|---|---|---|---|---|---|
| *Elements* | | | | *Compounds* | | | |
| Helium, He | 4 | | −269 | Methane, $CH_4$ | 16 | −182 | −161 |
| Neon, Ne | 20 | −249 | −249 | Ethane, $C_2H_6$ | 30 | −183 | −88 |
| Argon, Ar | 37 | −189 | −186 | Propane, $C_3H_8$ | 44 | −189 | −42 |
| Krypton, Kr | 84 | −157 | −152 | Butane, $C_4H_{10}$ | 58 | −138 | 0 |
| Fluorine, $F_2$ | 38 | −220 | −188 | Methanol, $CH_3OH$ | 32 | −98 | 65 |
| Chlorine, $Cl_2$ | 71 | −101 | −34 | Ethanol, $C_2H_5OH$ | 46 | −68 | 79 |
| Bromine, $Br_2$ | 160 | −7 | 58 | Propan-1-ol, $C_3H_7OH$ | 60 | −78 | 97 |
| Iodine, $I_2$ | 230 | 114 | 183 | Butan-1-ol, $C_4H_9OH$ | 74 | −89 | 118 |
| Carbon (diamond), C | 12 | 3550 | 4830 | Hydrogen fluoride, HF | 20 | −83 | 20 |
| Silicon, Si | 28 | 1410 | 2680 | Hydrogen chloride, HCl | 36.5 | −114 | −85 |
| Germanium, Ge | 73 | 940 | 2830 | Hydrogen bromide, HBr | 81 | −87 | −67 |
| Tin (white), Sn | 119 | 232 | 2690 | Hydrogen iodide, HI | 116 | −51 | −35 |
| Oxygen, $O_2$ | 32 | −219 | −183 | Water, $H_2O$ | 18 | 0 | 100 |
| Sulphur, S | 32 | 114.5 | 444.6 | Hydrogen sulphide, $H_2S$ | 34 | −85 | −60 |
| Selenium, Se | 79 | 217 | 685 | Hydrogen selenide, $H_2Se$ | 81 | −66 | −42 |
| Tellurium, Te | 128 | 450 | 1390 | Hydrogen telluride, $H_2Te$ | 130 | −49 | −2 |

● **Table 4.2** Melting points and boiling points of some elements and compounds. (Values have been measured at standard atmospheric pressure, 100 kPa.)

spend most of the time nearer the fluorine, thus giving the atom an excess of negative charge. The hydrogen atom has its nucleus (a single proton) only partially surrounded by electrons, and therefore it has an excess positive charge. We show the slight positive and negative charges by the symbols δ+ ('delta-plus') and δ− ('delta-minus'). The hydrogen bonds are the forces of attraction between the opposite charges and are shown by the dotted lines in *figure 4.10*.

■ *The Group VI hydrides*, especially water, $H_2O$. Compared to the other hydrides of Group VI,

the melting and boiling points of water are remarkably high. (The values are shown in *table 4.2*, and a graph of the data is included in *figure 4.11*.) The reason for this lies in hydrogen bonding (*figure 4.12*). In every one of its states,

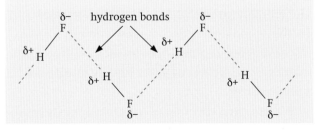

● **Figure 4.10** A representation of the structure of solid hydrogen fluoride, where the molecules take up a zig-zag shape. The molecules are held together by hydrogen bonds.

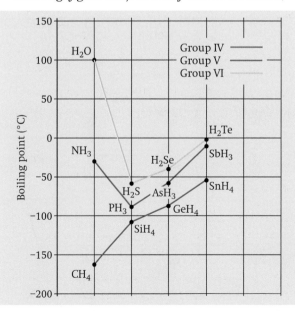

● **Figure 4.11** The boiling points of the Group IV, V and VI hydrides.

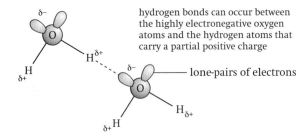

• **Figure 4.12** The origin of hydrogen bonding in water.

water molecules can hydrogen bond together. In ice the regular arrangement of the lattice leaves a large amount of free space. *Figure 4.13* illustrates the extent of the free space. Because the water molecules in ice are not so close together as in liquid water, ice is less dense than liquid water. In liquid water there is a tremendous amount of order compared to other liquids. Although the pattern of hydrogen bonding is always changing, water molecules are held together much more tightly than are molecules in most other liquids.

## SAQ 4.1

As shown in *figure 4.11*, water and ammonia have boiling points much higher than those of the other hydrides of the elements in their Groups. However, the boiling point of methane, $CH_4$, is lower than those of the other hydrides of Group IV. What is the reason for the difference?

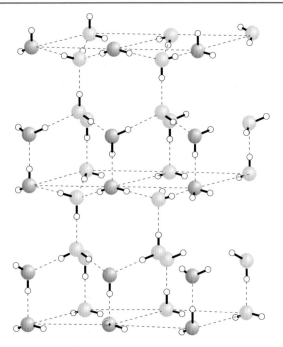

• **Figure 4.13** The structure of ice.

# Why gases liquefy, and solids melt

When two molecules are far apart, they move completely independently; neither will feel the presence of the other. However, if they come closer, then intermolecular forces get to work. The two molecules will attract one another. You will have learned about attractive intermolecular forces when you studied instantaneous dipole forces in chapter 3. Also, you should have come across hydrogen bonding and dipole–dipole interactions as intermolecular forces that tend to bring molecules together. However, think about molecules coming *very* close together. The 'outside' of a molecule is really a layer of negatively charged electrons: the electron cloud. When molecules approach closely, the electron clouds repel one another. It is the great strength of the repulsion that puts a limit on how close the atoms can get.

If two molecules collide with a great deal of energy, the negatively charged electron clouds get squeezed together and the resulting repulsion pushes them apart. Indeed, in a gas the force is so great that it overcomes the (attractive) intermolecular forces. Thus the molecules return to their life of rushing round at random in the body of the gas.

On the other hand, at lower temperatures the speeds of the molecules are lower and the force of collisions can be much less. There is a better chance of the intermolecular forces equalling, and indeed being greater than, the repulsive forces as the molecules collide. When this happens the molecules will not spring apart. Rather, they will remain close together and we see the gas turning to a liquid.

The molecules of different gases have their own characteristic intermolecular forces, and repulsive forces between their electron clouds. Therefore the temperature at which the forces between colliding molecules become low enough for the instantaneous dipole forces to win is different for every gas; i.e. different gases liquefy at different temperatures.

We can turn this line of argument on its head, and explain the change of liquid to gas by discussing the two opposing forces as the temperature of a liquid increases to its boiling point (see SAQ 4.2).

**a** Use your knowledge of intermolecular attractions and repulsions to explain why liquids turn into gases as the temperature increases.
**b** Why does every substance have its own particular boiling point?

## Explaining changes of state

Everyone is familiar with the change of liquid water to a vapour. This happens when water evaporates from a puddle, or when washing dries on a windy or sunny day, or when water boils in a kettle. Likewise, most people in industrialised countries convert liquid water into a solid, ice, by cooling water in a freezer. To understand why, and how, a substance changes state you need to know about intermolecular forces that attract molecules to each other, and the repulsions between the electron clouds when molecules get very close together. However, you also need to understand two further ideas: the first is that of *equilibrium,* and the second is the idea of *vapour pressure.*

We can bring these together by thinking about an experiment to measure the vapour pressure of a liquid, illustrated in *figure 4.14.* (You are not expected to know the details of the experiment for your examinations.) The idea is to introduce a small quantity of the liquid into a tube filled with mercury. (Owing to the high density of mercury, the liquid will float to the top.) Without the liquid, there would be a vacuum above the mercury, and, at standard conditions, the column of mercury would be 760 mm tall. With the liquid

present, some of the molecules escape into the space. Once in the vapour, they exert a pressure, and the mercury is pushed down slightly; i.e. the height of the mercury column is reduced. The difference between the heights (once some corrections are made for the presence of the liquid) is the vapour pressure of the liquid.

The molecules that escape from the surface of the liquid tend to have higher than average energies – that is why they escape. If a molecule has lower than, or about the same as, the average energy it is unlikely to escape the clutches of the other molecules – the intermolecular forces will hold it back. However, as more molecules escape into the space above the mercury, the chances of them bouncing back into the surface of the liquid increase. Eventually, the chance of a molecule leaving the surface equals the chance of a molecule in the vapour joining the liquid. At that time, **equilibrium** is reached (see chapter 7, page 120):

> At equilibrium, the rate at which molecules leave the liquid equals the rate at which molecules join the liquid.

At equilibrium, the space above the liquid has become saturated with the vapour – it contains the maximum amount of vapour possible at the given temperature. (If we were to increase the temperature of the apparatus, more vapour could exist in the space above the liquid, and the vapour pressure would increase.) Make sure you realise that equilibrium is a *dynamic* process: there is a great deal of change going on with molecules constantly leaving and joining the liquid. However, they do so at the same rate (many millions per second). *Figure 4.14* shows how evaporation of a liquid can take place under equilibrium conditions.

However, equilibrium will not always be achieved. For example, on a warm, windy day, wet clothes dry very quickly because the atmosphere is not saturated with water vapour as it would be on a cold, wet day. There are (relatively) so few water molecules in the atmosphere that they have little chance of going back on to the clothes once they

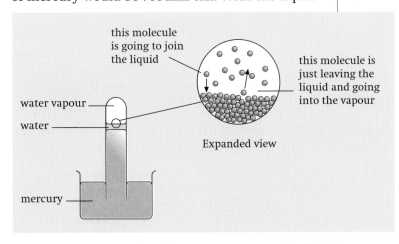

this molecule is going to join the liquid

this molecule is just leaving the liquid and going into the vapour

Expanded view

water vapour

water

mercury

● **Figure 4.14** Measuring the vapour pressure of a liquid (note that the diagram is not to scale).

have left the surface, or of water molecules already in the air sticking to the clothes. That is, wet clothes drying on a line will not reach equilibrium like the liquid in *figure 4.14*.

If we heat a liquid we give more energy to the molecules. This increases their chance of leaving the surface, and the liquid will evaporate more quickly. If we continue to heat the liquid, it will eventually boil (*figure 4.15*). We shall not prove it, but the condition for a liquid to boil is that:

> A liquid boils when its vapour pressure equals atmospheric pressure.

### SAQ 4.3

If you put a little alcohol (ethanol) or propanone on the back of your hand, the liquid will evaporate and you will feel the back of your hand get cold. Why does evaporation lead to cooling?

[*Hint:* Think about the range of energies the molecules possess, and why even the less energetic particles eventually evaporate.]

### SAQ 4.4

What are clouds made of? Briefly explain why clouds form, and why they often lead to rain falling.

● **Figure 4.15** Water boiling under reduced pressure. Water will even boil at room temperature if the pressure is low enough.

# Some remarkable substances

In this section we shall briefly consider some substances that are difficult to classify as a solid, liquid or gas.

## Liquid crystals

It seems a contradiction to call a crystal 'liquid'. We expect crystals to be solids, and certainly not liquids. Essentially, liquid crystals are liquids that have sufficient long-range order in them to make them behave like a solid. However, they will only behave like a solid over a certain range of temperatures. Usually a liquid crystal is made from molecules that are long, thin and not very symmetrical. You will find some examples in *figure 4.16*.

The intermolecular forces must be strong enough to hold the molecules together, but not so strong as to restrict their movement too much. The unsymmetrical nature of the molecules leads to an unsymmetrical packing of the molecules. The very useful property of liquid crystals is that the arrangement of the molecules can be upset by very slight changes in their surroundings. Especially, in the liquid crystals used in calculators, digital watches and computer displays (*figure 4.17*), the molecules rearrange themselves when the crystal is subjected to a small electric field. The rearrangement changes the way the crystal absorbs light.

## Glass

Glass is a most unusual material. For example, it allows light to pass through it very easily. Also, it melts over a range of temperatures and remains

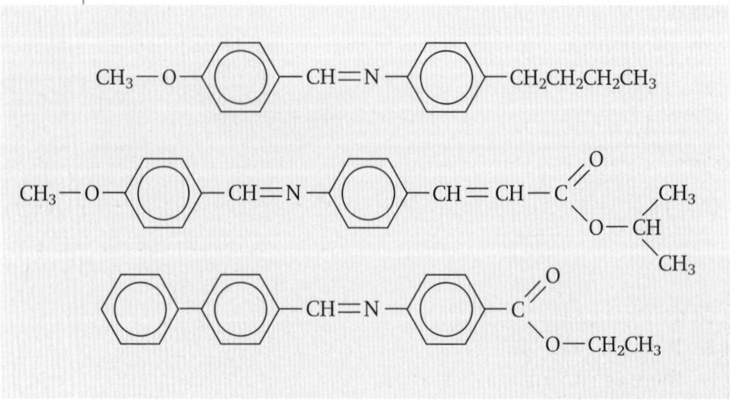

● **Figure 4.16** Examples of molecules that make liquid crystals.

viscous (rather like treacle). This allows glass to be 'blown into many different shapes (*figure 4.19*), or to be rolled into sheets for use in windows. The basic building block of ordinary glass is a tetrahedron built from a silicon atom with four oxygen atoms around it (*figure 4.18*). The tetrahedra join to give a three-dimensional interlocking structure that gives glass its high viscosity. However, unlike a normal solid, glass has no long-range order in its structure.

In 1880 the Irish physicist John Tyndall (who had a 'professional interest' in ice, as he was an extremely keen mountaineer) compared ice and glass in this way: "The ice is music, the glass is noise – the ice is order, the glass is confusion. In the glass, molecular forces constitute an inextricably entangled skein, in the ice they are woven to a symmetric web." (Quoted in W. H. Brock et al., *John Tyndall*, Royal Dublin Society, 1981, page 98.)

# Real and ideal gases

Now we shall consider the properties of gases in greater depth. To begin with, you need to know that gases show these properties:
1 They fill all the space open to them.
2 They expand when heated.
3 They exert a pressure on the walls of their containers.
4 The pressure changes as the temperature changes.

Shortly, we shall deal with each of these in more detail; but you will find that we shall spend only part of the time discussing the properties of real gases such as hydrogen, oxygen, methane and so on. Real gases are complicated things, and it can be helpful at first to use a simplified model of a gas. In fact, much of this chapter will be about 'gases' that do not exist in the real world – these are gases that we call *ideal gases*.

# The behaviour of ideal gases

Ideal gases have some, but not all, of the properties of real gases. A brief summary of the characteristics of an **ideal gas** is given in *box 4A*. An ideal gas is a gas in which there are no intermolecular forces, and in which the molecules don't take up any space themselves (we regard them as points). Also, we assume that the molecules do not change their total kinetic energy when they bump into each other; this is what we mean if we say that the collisions are 'perfectly elastic'. No real gas is ideal, although some come close to

---

**Box 4A Key assumptions about ideal gases**

*In an ideal gas:*
- the molecules have mass, but negligible size;
- there are no intermolecular forces;
- the collisions between the molecules are perfectly elastic.

---

● **Figure 4.17** A liquid crystal display.

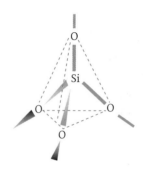

● **Figure 4.18** The tetrahedral group of a central silicon atom and four oxygen atoms that is the basis for the structure of glass.

● **Figure 4.19** A glass blower. Glass remains viscous over a large range of temperatures, which allows it to be blown into an amazing variety of shapes.

---

**Box 4B  The kinetic theory of gases**
*Main idea*:
■ Gases consist of molecules in a constant state of random motion.
*Related ideas*:
■ The pressure of a gas is due to the collisions of the molecules with the walls of the container.
■ The molecules travel in straight lines until they collide with one another, or with the walls of the container.
■ In these collisions, the total kinetic energy of the molecules does not change.

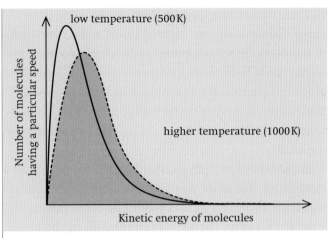

● **Figure 4.20** How the distribution of the kinetic energy of the molecules in a gas changes with temperature.

ideal behaviour, e.g. helium. You will find that we can compare real and ideal gases, and from their different characteristics we can learn a great deal about real gases. The key idea is to explain why real gases are different from ideal gases – but more of this later.

## The kinetic theory of gases

You will already know that the molecules in a gas are in a constant state of random motion. This feature of gases is one of the main foundations of the kinetic theory of gases. A statement of the main features of the kinetic theory of gases is given in *box 4B*. As far as we know, the kinetic theory of gases is extremely well-supported. There is a great deal of evidence to show that, to all intents and purposes, the motion of gas molecules is random. This means that in any gas, on average, there will be as many molecules moving in one direction as in any other direction.

You might like to know that the average speed of gas molecules is of the order of $500 \, m \, s^{-1}$ at room temperature. The lighter the molecule, the greater the average speed (and vice versa). For example, hydrogen molecules have an average speed somewhat above $1500 \, m \, s^{-1}$, and carbon dioxide molecules have an average speed nearer to $350 \, m \, s^{-1}$.

There is a wide range of energies among the molecules in a gas. Some move very rapidly, and much faster than the average, and some move very much more slowly than the average. When a gas is heated, *on average* all the molecules increase their kinetic energies (i.e. move faster); but this does not mean that they *all* increase. Always, some will pick up more energy than others. Indeed, during a collision between two molecules,

one of them may move off with a greater speed, and one with a lower speed than before. However, the majority move near to the average speed. The way the kinetic energy of the molecules varies with temperature is shown in *figure 4.20*. As the temperature goes up, the average energy of all the molecules increases, but the distribution of speeds, and therefore kinetic energies, spreads out. Especially, the proportion of molecules with high kinetic energies increases. If you look carefully at the shapes of the graphs, you will see that they are not quite symmetrical – the curve stretches out more at higher than at lower energies. (This is an important point when explaining how changes in temperature influence the rates of chemical reactions: see chapter 8, page 169.)

## SAQ 4.5

Use ideas from the kinetic theory of gases to answer these two questions:
**a** What happens to the average kinetic energy of the molecules in a gas as the temperature increases?
**b** What might happen to the kinetic energy of any individual molecule in a gas as the temperature increases?

## The pressure and volume of an ideal gas

The pressure of a gas is caused by the collisions of the molecules with the walls of its container. By doing some mathematics, it is possible to show that the pressure of an ideal gas depends on three factors:

1  the number of molecules per unit volume (i.e. the concentration of the gas);
2  the mass of the molecules;
3  their speed.

This should make sense to you because, if there are more molecules present in a given volume, there should be more collisions with the walls, so the pressure should increase. Likewise, if the molecules have a greater momentum (mass times speed), the harder they will bounce off the walls. Therefore, they exert a greater force on the walls, and cause the pressure to increase.

## SAQ 4.6

Look at *figure 4.21*. Two identical cylinders A and B fitted with pistons are kept in different rooms. Both contain the same number of molecules of gas, but the volume of one (A) is less than that of the other (B). What is the most likely reason for the difference in volume?

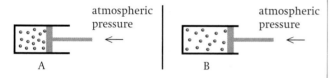

- **Figure 4.21** Both sets of cylinders and pistons A and B are subject to the same atmospheric pressure, and both contain the same number of molecules of gas.

# The ideal gas law

The behaviour of ideal gases is represented by the **ideal gas equation**:

$$PV = nRT$$

where $P$ is the pressure, measured in pascals, Pa; $V$ is the volume, measured in metre cubed, $m^3$; $T$ is the temperature on the Kelvin scale, measured in kelvin, K (notice that the degrees sign, °, is *not* put next to the K of a Kelvin temperature); $R$ is the gas constant, $8.314 \, J \, K^{-1} \, mol^{-1}$; and $n$ is the number of moles of gas.

If pairs of measurements of $V$ and $T$ taken around room temperature are plotted and the lines extended back, they meet at (almost) $-273 \, °C$.

At this temperature, the volume of the gases appears to reduce to zero. Clearly, this is impossible for real gases, but none the less the graphs show that the temperature is of great importance. We can use the $-273 \, °C$ point on the graph to define the zero of a new scale of temperature. This is the absolute scale or **Kelvin scale**. We can convert between degrees Celsius and kelvin by adding 273; e.g. $100 \, °C = (100 + 273) \, K = 373 \, K$. Similarly, we convert kelvin to degrees Celsius by subtracting 273; e.g. $127 \, K = (127 - 273) \, °C = -146 \, °C$.

When you use the equation, do be careful about the units. All the units given above are consistent; but sometimes you may have to use data that are given in other units. Especially, chemists often prefer to work in litres (more properly stated as $dm^3$) or in $cm^3$. Here is a way to change between these units:

$$1 \, m^3 = 1 \times 10^3 \, dm^3 = 1 \times 10^6 \, cm^3$$

Also, pressure is often quoted in kilopascals, kPa, where $1 \, kPa = 10^3 \, Pa$. An old unit of pressure is the atmosphere, where 1 atmosphere is approximately $100 \, kPa$. You may find that the volumes of gases are often quoted in litres or, more systematically, in $dm^3$. The relationship between the units of volume is as follows:

$$1 \text{ litre} = 1 \, dm^3 = 1000 \, cm^3 = 1 \times 10^{-3} \, m^3$$

## Worked example

What is the volume, given in $dm^3$, of 1 mol of an ideal gas at 20 °C and 100 kPa? (This combination of temperature and pressure is often called 'room temperature and pressure'.)

We have to convert the pressure to pascals and the temperature to kelvin: so we have $P = 100 \times 10^3 \, Pa$, $T = (20 + 273) \, K = 293 \, K$, $R = 8.314 \, J \, K^{-1} \, mol^{-1}$, and $n = 1 \, mol$. Putting these values into the ideal gas equation gives

$$100 \times 10^3 \, Pa \times V = 1 \, mol \times 8.314 \, J \, K \, mol^{-1} \times 293 \, K$$

$$V = \frac{1 \, mol \times 8.314 \, J \, K \, mol^{-1} \times 293 \, K}{100 \times 10^3 \, Pa}$$

$$V = 0.024 \, m^3$$

Converting this to $dm^3$ gives $V = 24.4 \, dm^3$. We usually make the approximation that 1 mol of gas occupies $24 \, dm^3$ at room temperature and pressure.

## SAQ 4.7

If a balloon contained 1 dm³ of helium at 20°C and 100 kPa pressure, how many moles of helium would be present?

## SAQ 4.8

A weather balloon (*figure 4.22*) may have an 'envelope' of material that may contain a total volume of, say, 1000 dm³ when it is fully expanded. However, the volume of helium put in the balloon when it is released into the atmosphere is only a fraction of this volume. Why is the balloon not fully inflated before it is released?

# The behaviour of real gases

One of the obvious ways that real gases differ from ideal gases is that they liquefy when the temperature is low enough and the pressure is high enough. Lowering the temperature of real gases allows the intermolecular forces to overcome the motion of the molecules. Squeezing the molecules together has a similar effect: bringing molecules closer together allows the intermolecular forces to be more effective (just as bringing the north and south poles of magnets close together increases the effects of their attractive forces).

● **Figure 4.22** A weather balloon being released.

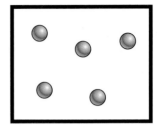

● **Figure 4.23** A *very* exaggerated impression of molecules taking up space – see text.

Only ideal gases would strictly obey the ideal gas equation. All real gases show deviations from ideal behaviour for two reasons:

1 The molecules in real gases take up space.
2 Real gases have intermolecular forces between the molecules.

We shall consider each of these factors in more detail now.

## Real molecules occupy space

In an ideal gas, it is assumed that the molecules do not occupy space (see *box 4A*, page 59), so the volume in which they exist is (literally) the volume of the container. However, for real gases, each molecule takes up a very small volume (of the order of $10^{-30}$ m³), which is then not available for another molecule to move in. There are so many molecules that the total volume they occupy cannot be ignored. *Figure 4.23* illustrates this idea.

As a very simple analogy, consider a box with a volume of 1000 cm³, in which there are five balls, with a volume of 20 cm³ each. Between them they take up 100 cm³, which is 10% of the total volume. Thus the volume open to them is at least 10% less than the volume of the container. The situation for molecules is just the same, although of a different scale. (Actually, calculating the real volume for the balls to move in is more complicated than we have assumed, but you don't have to know the details of why this is so.)

## SAQ 4.9

Assume that the effective volume of an oxygen molecule is $64 \times 10^{-30}$ m³.

**a** Estimate the volume occupied by 1 mol of oxygen molecules. Avagadro's number = $6.02 \times 10^{23}$ mol⁻¹

**b** What percentage of the volume of 1 mol of oxygen gas is this at room temperature and pressure?

## The influence of intermolecular forces

Intermolecular forces bring molecules together. These forces are always present in gases, even though a gas is only a gas because the intermolecular forces are not strong enough to prevent the molecules bouncing apart when they collide. Think about what happens if a molecule is moving out of the main body of a gas towards the walls of the container (see *figure 4.24*). The vast majority of molecules will be attracting it from behind, or from its sides. This tends to slow the molecule and prevent it colliding with the walls of the container with as much force as it would do if there were no intermolecular forces. In other words, the pressure exerted by a real gas is *less* than it would be if the gas were ideal.

## Summary table

|  | Molecules in an ideal gas | Molecules in a real gas | Effect in real gases |
|---|---|---|---|
| Occupation of space by molecules | None | Occupy space | Reduces volume from ideal value |
| Intermolecular forces | None | Present, and can be strong | Reduces pressure from ideal value |

● **Table 4.3** Summary of differences between real and ideal gases.

## Real gases can approach ideal behaviour

Remember that two of the conditions for ideal behaviour were that the molecules were of negligible size and that there were no intermolecular forces. We can sometimes come close to these conditions for real gases if:

1 we use gases that have very small intermolecular forces between the molecules;
2 we use gases at very low pressures.

Gases like hydrogen and helium fulfil the first condition; and by using very low pressures, the molecules of a gas spend a great deal of their time far apart from each other. This results in the intermolecular forces not having a chance to work effectively. It also means that because there are very few molecules in a given space at low

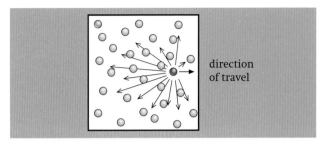

● **Figure 4.24** A molecule moving out of the main volume of the gas feels an overall force attracting it inwards.

pressures, the volume that the molecules do occupy is a very small proportion of the total; i.e. their own volume does become nearly negligible.

### SAQ 4.10

In your own words, explain why, at low pressures, real gases begin to behave more like ideal gases.

# Measuring the relative molecular mass of a volatile liquid

We shall now use the ideal gas equation to calculate the relative molecular mass of a volatile liquid. This may, at first sight, seem rather an odd statement given that the ideal gas equation plainly applies to gases and not to liquids. However, the key to the puzzle is that the method relies on turning the liquid into a gas. Before you go on, you should remind yourself about the mole as a measure of the quantity of matter in chemistry (see chapter 2, page 19).

### SAQ 4.11

What is the approximate volume of **a** 2 mol and **b** 0.25 mol of carbon dioxide at room temperature and pressure?

## The method

There are several ways of performing this experiment. The method we shall choose is to use the apparatus shown in *figure 4.25*.

The outline of the method is as follows:

1 Take a known mass of the volatile liquid.
2 Introduce the liquid into a gas syringe in an oven.
3 Turn the liquid to vapour and measure its volume.

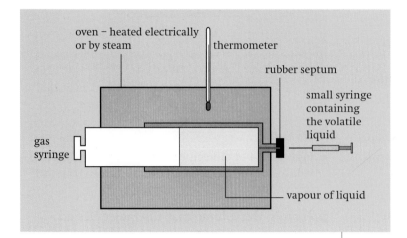

● **Figure 4.25** One method of measuring the volume of a volatile liquid using a gas syringe and an oven.

From these results we have

Mass of ethoxyethane
used = 0.224 g
Volume of vapour = 95.4 cm$^3$
= 95.4 × 10$^{-6}$ m$^3$

We can use the ideal gas equation to work out the number of moles, $n$, of ethoxyethane that this volume represents. We have

$$PV = nRT \quad \text{or} \quad n = \frac{PV}{RT}$$

$$n = \frac{100 \times 10^3 \, \text{Pa} \times 95.4 \times 10^{-6} \, \text{m}^3}{8.314 \, \text{J K}^{-1} \, \text{mol}^{-1} \times 372.6 \, \text{K}}$$

$$= 0.003 \, \text{mol}$$

$$\text{Relative molecular mass} = \frac{0.224 \, \text{g}}{0.003 \, \text{mol}}$$

$$= 74.7 \, \text{g mol}^{-1}$$

Knowing the gas volume and its temperature, we can use the ideal gas equation to work out how many moles of gas are present. Then, because we know the mass of this number of moles, we can work out the relative molecular mass of the gas, and hence of the liquid.

The nozzle of the gas syringe is covered with a rubber cap (a septum), and the gas syringe is put in the oven or steam jacket. Once the reading on the gas syringe shows no further change, the initial reading on the gas syringe is taken, and a sample of the liquid is taken up into a small syringe. Here, we shall assume that we are using ethoxyethane (ether) as the liquid. The small syringe is weighed and the ethoxyethane injected into the gas syringe. Then the small syringe is immediately reweighed. Once the ethoxyethane is in the gas syringe, the liquid quickly vaporises and the plunger is driven outwards. Eventually equilibrium is achieved and there is no further change in the volume recorded on the gas syringe. Provided the temperature of the steam jacket and the atmospheric pressure are known we can calculate the relative molecular mass.

## Some sample results

Here are some sample readings:

Mass of small syringe and ethoxyethane
before injection into gas syringe = 20.476 g
after injection into gas syringe = 20.252 g
Initial reading on gas syringe = 1.4 cm$^3$
Final reading on gas syringe = 96.8 cm$^3$
Temperature of steam jacket (oven) = 99.6 °C
= 372.6 K
Atmospheric pressure = 100 kPa

## Experimental error

The formula of ethoxyethane is $(C_2H_5)_2O$, so its true relative molecular mass is 74 g mol$^{-1}$. It is quite common for results in this experiment to over-estimate relative molecular masses. The most important reason for this is that, before the liquid can be injected into the gas syringe, some if it evaporates from the needle of the small syringe. This means that we over-estimate the mass of liquid that turns into gas in the gas syringe. For example, in our calculation above, the actual mass of liquid injected into the gas syringe may have been only 0.223 g. Then the relative molecular mass would have been calculated as 0.223 g/0.003 mol = 74.33 g mol$^{-1}$. (If the true mass injected were 0.222 g, the result would have been exactly 74 g mol$^{-1}$, the true relative molecular mass.)

### SAQ 4.12

The gas syringe experiment only works with liquids that are highly volatile, i.e. those which evaporate easily.
**a** Explain why the mass of liquid injected into the gas syringe is often *less* than that given by the weighings.
**b** How, and why, does this affect the calculation?

## SAQ 4.13

The volatile liquid propanone was used in an experiment to measure its relative molecular mass, like the one we have discussed above. The following data were collected:

Mass of syringe and propanone
before injection into gas syringe = 20.374 g

Mass of syringe and propanone
after injection into gas syringe = 20.193 g

Initial reading on gas syringe = 1.6 cm³

Final reading on gas syringe = 97.1 cm³

Temperature of steam jacket (oven) = 99.3 °C

Atmospheric pressure = 100.2 kPa

Calculate the relative molecular mass of propanone.

# Some lattice structures

Crystalline solids may be held together by a variety of bonds. The physical properties of solids reflect the nature of their bonding.

## Ionic lattices

As discussed in chapter 3, ionic bonding results from the electrostatic attractions between oppositely charged ions which are held in a giant ionic lattice. In such a lattice, there is a regular arrangement of anions and cations. The exact way in which the individual ions are arranged depends on their relative sizes and on the relative charges.

Sodium chloride (NaCl) and magnesium oxide (MgO) form a cubic lattice (see *figure 4.26*), in which each cation is surrounded by six anions and each anion is surrounded by six cations.

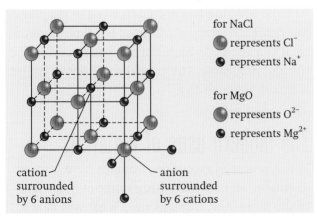

for NaCl
🔵 represents Cl⁻
⚫ represents Na⁺

for MgO
🔵 represents O²⁻
⚫ represents Mg²⁺

cation surrounded by 6 anions

anion surrounded by 6 cations

● **Figure 4.26** Lattice structures of sodium chloride and magnesium oxide.

In the ionic lattice there are strong electrostatic attractions throughout the lattice. This means that much energy is required to separate the ions and the melting point will be high. The liquid formed contains ions which will be attracted to oppositely charged ions present; thus the boiling point will also be high.

- For NaCl, the melting point is 808 °C and the boiling point is 1456 °C.
- For MgO, the melting point is 2853 °C and the boiling point is 3600 °C.

The very high melting point of magnesium oxide makes it very suitable for use as the lining of high temperature furnaces.

Ionic crystals are generally strong and hard, but may shatter when struck very hard. Solid ionic lattices do not conduct electricity, but molten ionic compounds will.

## Simple molecular lattices

Simple molecular lattices are often held together by instantaneous dipole–induced dipole forces (van der Waals' forces). As described in chapter 3, the strength of the force increases with the number of electrons present.

*Table 4.2* (page 55) shows that the melting points of the halogens (fluorine, chlorine, bromine and iodine) increase with increasing relative molecular mass. This is because the larger molecules have more electrons around them, which give rise to larger instantaneous dipole–induced dipole forces. Thus fluorine and chlorine are gases at room temperature, bromine is a liquid and iodine is a solid.

Solid iodine contains $I_2$ molecules in which there is a covalent bond *between* the atoms, but between the molecules there are much weaker instantaneous dipole–induced dipole forces. The crystal structure of solid iodine is shown in *figure 4.27*.

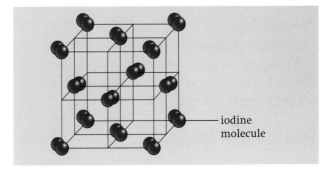

iodine molecule

● **Figure 4.27** The crystal structure of iodine.

When solid iodine is heated, the weaker instantaneous dipole–induced dipole forces are broken and individual $I_2$ molecules are set free from the lattice. In fact, the iodine sublimes (i.e. turns directly from the solid state to the vapour phase), producing a purple vapour of $I_2$ molecules.

Some simple molecular lattices are held together by permanent dipole–dipole forces. An example of this is hydrogen chloride (see chapter 3, page 37), in which chlorine is more electronegative than hydrogen:

$$\overset{\delta+}{H} - \overset{\delta-}{Cl}$$

When solid HCl is heated, the weaker permanent dipole–dipole forces break and HCl molecules leave the solid lattice.

Since instantaneous dipole–induced dipole forces and permanent dipole–dipole forces are relatively weak, simple molecular compounds containing them have low melting and boiling points. Simple molecular compounds do not conduct electricity when solid or liquid.

## Hydrogen-bonded lattices

As described earlier in the chapter (page 54), hydrogen bonding is another type of force which can exist between certain molecules, such as water. The structure of ice is given in *figure 4.13* and the origin of hydrogen bonding is shown in *figure 4.12* (see page 56).

As with other simple molecular solids, the weaker hydrogen bonds break when ice is melted, leaving covalent water molecules. The effect of hydrogen bonding on the physical properties of compounds is described in chapter 3 (see page 45).

Hydrogen bonds are stronger than dipole–dipole forces but much weaker than covalent bonds (see *table 3.4*, page 47).

## Giant molecular lattices

Giant molecular lattices are three-dimensional arrangements of atoms held together by strong

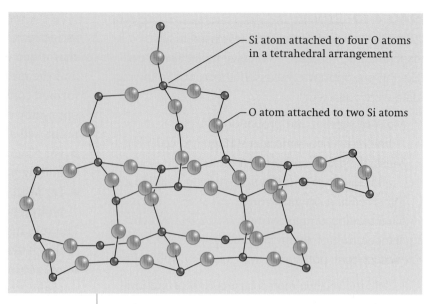

Si atom attached to four O atoms in a tetrahedral arrangement

O atom attached to two Si atoms

● **Figure 4.28** The structure of silicon(IV) oxide.

covalent bonds. Some giant molecular structures contain atoms of only one element. Examples of such structures are graphite and diamond; these are shown in *figure 3.20* (page 43).

Other lattices, such as that of silicon(IV) oxide, contain atoms of two different elements, again joined together by strong covalent bonds. The structure of silicon(IV) oxide is shown in *figure 4.28*.

When giant molecular substances are melted, large numbers of covalent bonds must be broken. Melting points are therefore high: silicon(IV) oxide (quartz) melts at 1610 °C and diamond melts at 3550 °C. With the exception of graphite, giant molecular substances do not conduct electricity in the solid or liquid states. Giant molecular substances are usually hard.

## Metallic lattices

Metallic bonding has been described in chapter 3 (see *figure 3.17*, page 41). Copper is a typical metal; i.e. it is a good conductor of electricity and is ductile and malleable. The crystal structure of copper is shown in *figure 4.29*.

# The modern uses of materials

In the course of evolution, humans have learned to employ an ever increasing range of materials. In the Stone Age, humans used what was near at hand and shaped it by their own efforts. By the Bronze Age, humans had learned to extract metals

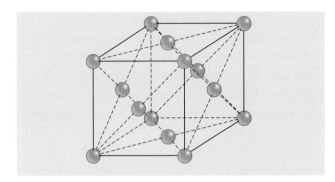

● **Figure 4.29** The face-centred cubic structure of copper.

such as copper, lead and tin from their ores. As the technology improved, the extraction process was extended to the smelting of iron (see *figure 3.16*, page 40). At the same time, objects made of pottery and, later, glass began to be produced.

Today, we have an enormous range of materials available: metals and their alloys, ceramics, glass, plastics and polymers.

## Metals

The major structural metal is iron, which has the great drawback of rusting.

Aluminium is widely used in transport for making the bodywork of aeroplanes, trains, buses, etc., in food packaging, and in overhead electrical power lines. Aluminium has a low density and does not readily corrode. It can be mixed with other metals, by melting them together, to form alloys which are light and strong.

Copper has high electrical and thermal conductivity, is malleable and ductile, and is resistant to corrosion. The pure metal is therefore widely used in electrical wiring, water pipes, central heating systems, roofing (*figure 4.30*) and kitchen utensils.

● **Figure 4.30** Copper used as a roofing material in the Duke of York's Headquarters, London.

Copper is also widely used in brass, an alloy with zinc which is fairly soft and easily worked into shape, and bronze, a stronger alloy with tin. Brass is used for screws, hinges and domestic objects; bronze is used in bearings and ships' propellers. The coinage of many nations has used copper alloys.

## Ceramics

The group of substances generally known as ceramics contains compounds that have giant structures. Ceramics are used in furnace linings, electrical insulators, glass and crockery.

Furnace linings must withstand high temperatures and compounds such as aluminium oxide (melting point 2040 °C) and magnesium oxide (melting point 2800 °C) are used.

The strong giant covalent lattices of the silicates (see *figure 4.18*, page 59) and similar compounds such as silicon(IV) carbide (SiC) and silicon(IV) nitride ($Si_3N_4$) give compounds that are strong, hard and rigid and are also electrical and thermal insulators. Such compounds find use as electrical insulators, as in overhead power lines, in glass and in crockery. They have the disadvantage of being brittle.

Tiles containing high-grade silicon(iv) oxide are used in the U.S. Space Shuttle as heat shields during re-entry to the Earth's atmosphere.

## Recycling

Raw materials extracted from the Earth cannot last for ever. Although some materials are more abundant than others, they are all finite resources.

Increasing demand for raw materials, coupled with ever growing problems of waste disposal, have led to considerable interest in recycling waste.

Recycling has a number of possible advantages:
■ it leads to reduced demand for new raw materials;
■ it leads to a reduction in environmental damage;
■ it reduces the demand for landfill sites to dump waste;
■ it reduces the cost of waste disposal;
■ it may reduce energy costs.

See also chapters 16 and 22.

# The effect of structure and bonding on physical properties

As shown in *table 3.5* (page 48), the nature of the bonding in a substance determines its physical properties. It is also possible to use knowledge of physical properties to predict the nature of bonding in an unknown substance.

Consider the following data:

| substance | $M_r$ | melting point (°C) | boiling point (°C) | electrical conductivity |
|---|---|---|---|---|
| A | 60 | 1610 | 2205 | none |
| B | 74.5 | 772 | 1407 | in liquid state |
| C | 86 | −95 | 69 | none |

Substances **A** and **B** both have high melting points, suggesting giant lattice structures. Substance **A** does not conduct at all, whereas substance **B** conducts when molten. Therefore, substance **B** is an ionic compound and substance **A** is a giant molecular compound. The very low melting and boiling points of substance **C** show that it must be simple molecular, which also agrees with its lack of electrical conductivity.

## SUMMARY (AS)

◆ The three states of matter are solid, liquid and gas. The state a substance exists in depends on the kinetic energy of the particles and the strength of the intermolecular forces between its particles.

◆ The particles in a solid have orderly arrangements; liquids have short-range order but long-range disorder; gases have completely disorderly arrangements of their particles.

◆ The space between gas particles is very much greater than the spaces between the particles in a solid or liquid. The spacing of particles in a liquid and solid is about the same.

◆ As the kinetic energy of particles increases, the temperature increases, intermolecular forces are overcome and solids tend to melt, and liquids turn to gas.

◆ Substances that have hydrogen bonds between their molecules often have unusually high melting and boiling points, e.g. $H_2O$, HF.

◆ Liquids have a characteristic vapour pressure at a given temperature and pressure. In a closed system, an equilibrium is set up such that the rate at which molecules leave the liquid equals the rate at which gaseous molecules return to the liquid.

◆ A liquid boils when its vapour pressure equals the atmospheric pressure.

◆ The key assumptions about ideal gases are:
  - The molecules have mass, but negligible size.
  - There are no intermolecular forces.

◆ The kinetic theory of gases claims that:
  - Gases consist of molecules in a constant state of random motion.
  - The pressure of a gas is due to the collisions of the molecules with the walls of the container.
  - The molecules travel in straight lines until they collide with one another, or with the walls of the container.
  - In these collisions the total kinetic energy of the molecules does not change.

◆ Ideal gases obey the ideal gas equation, $PV = nRT$.

◆ Real gases show deviations from ideal behaviour because:
  – the particles in a real gas occupy space;
  – real gases have intermolecular forces between their particles.

◆ Real gases approach ideal behaviour at (i) high temperature and (ii) low pressure.

◆ At low temperature and/or high pressure the intermolecular forces in real gases have a large effect and the behaviour of the gases are far from ideal.

◆ The relative molecular mass of a volatile liquid can be measured by: (i) weighing a sample; (ii) injecting the sample into a gas syringe held at a temperature greater than the liquid's boiling point; (iii) allowing equilibrium to be reached; (iv) measuring the temperature and volume of the vapour; and (v) using the ideal gas equation to calculate the number of moles of vapour present.

◆ Lattice structures may be ionic, simple molecular, giant molecular or metallic.

◆ Ionic lattices consist of a regular arrangement of cations and anions. Ionic compounds have high melting points and conduct electricity only when molten.

◆ Simple molecular lattices have weak intermolecular forces which result in low melting points. Simple molecular substances do not conduct in the liquid state.

◆ Hydrogen-bonded lattices, such as in water, consist of a giant structure of molecules held in place by hydrogen bonds. Because hydrogen bonds are stronger than van der Waals' forces, the melting points of hydrogen-bonded lattices are higher than expected.

◆ Giant molecular lattices contain strong covalent bonds throughout the structure. As a result, melting points are high. With the exception of graphite, giant molecular lattices are non-conductors in the solid or liquid states.

◆ Metal lattices consist of a lattice of cations in a 'sea' of mobile electrons. Metals conduct in the solid state, are malleable and ductile, and have fairly high melting points.

# Questions (AS)

1 *Table 4.2* and *figure 4.11* (page 55) provide information that you will need in order to answer this set of questions.
  a Why does carbon (as diamond) have such a high melting point?
  b What might be the reason for ammonia, $NH_3$, having an anomalous boiling point compared to other hydrides of Group V? [*Hint*: What is special about the structure of an ammonia molecule?]
  c What is the main type of bonding that holds the alkanes together in their solid or liquid states?
  d What is the main type of bonding that holds the alcohols together in their solid or liquid states?
  e How do the boiling points of the alkanes methane to butane compare with those of the corresponding alcohols methanol to butan-1-ol?

2 Use the data in *table 4.2* (page 55) to sketch a diagram showing how the boiling points of the Group VII hydrides (HF, HCl, HBr and HI) vary. Explain the trend that you observe.

**3** When water (or any liquid) boils, you can see bubbles appear in the liquid. What are the bubbles in boiling water?

**4** Check back: What is the connection between vapour pressure, atmospheric pressure and the boiling point of a liquid? Now explain why it takes longer to cook vegetables in water at high altitudes (e.g. on the side of a high mountain) than at sea level.

**5** Here is a question that will make you think about the repercussions of the idea that the particles in a gas are in a constant random motion. It will also bring home to you the relevance of the small scale of atoms and molecules compared to our everyday experience.

The diagram represents a container filled with nitrogen gas. The container is connected to a vacuum pump by a small tube fitted with a tap. Please remember that the diagram is not to scale!

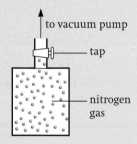

**a** What, if anything, is in the space between the nitrogen molecules?

**b** Suppose the tube connecting the container to the vacuum pump has a diameter of 1 cm. The diameter of a nitrogen molecule is approximately $4 \times 10^{-10}$ m. How many nitrogen molecules could fit across the diameter of the tube?

**c** Would a nitrogen molecule find it hard to find its way down the tube?

**d** Using a rough value, assume you are about 1 m wide. If the tube were of the same scale to you as it is to a nitrogen molecule, how wide would it be? How does this distance compare to, say, the diameter of the Earth (about $3 \times 10^{6}$ m)?

**e** Now imagine that the tap to the vacuum pump is opened very briefly so that some, but not all, of the nitrogen molecules escape. Draw a diagram like the one above to show what you think the arrangement of the molecules would be at the very instant the tap was closed.

**f** Briefly explain why some of the gas would go into the vacuum pump when the tap was opened.

**6** Trichloromethane (chloroform) has a boiling point of about 62 °C. On the face of it, this liquid should be a suitable candidate for using in the gas syringe experiment. Why might you expect its measured relative molecular mass not to be accurate? [*Hint*: Think about intermolecular forces.]

**7** At room temperature, iodine, $I_2$, has a crystal lattice structure.

**a** What type of bond holds together the iodine atoms in an iodine molecule?

**b** What forces act between the iodine molecules in a crystal lattice of iodine?

**c** When iodine is gently heated to 114 °C, it turns directly from solid into gas. No liquid state is formed. This process is called sublimation.

Explain, in terms of forces, the changes that occur to the structure of iodine as it sublimes.

**d** The diamond form of carbon sublimes at a much higher temperature than iodine. Suggest why this higher temperature is necessary.

*OCR, 1998*

# Chemical energetics (AS)

## By the end of this section you should be able to:

1 explain that some chemical reactions are accompanied by *enthalpy changes*, principally in the form of heat energy. The enthalpy changes can be *exothermic* ($\Delta H$ negative) or *endothermic* ($\Delta H$ positive);

2 recognise the importance of oxidation as an exothermic process, for example in the combustion of fuels and the oxidation of carbohydrates such as glucose in respiration;

3 recognise that endothermic processes require an input of heat energy;

4 construct a simple *enthalpy profile* diagram for a reaction to show the difference in enthalpy of the reactants compared with that of the products;

5 explain chemical reactions in terms of enthalpy changes associated with the breaking and making of chemical bonds;

6 explain and use the terms *enthalpy change of reaction*, *standard conditions* and *bond enthalpy*;

7 calculate enthalpy changes from appropriate experimental results, including the use of the relationship: energy change = $mc\Delta T$;

8 use Hess's law to construct *enthalpy cycles* and carry out calculations using such cycles and relevant enthalpy terms.

All chemical reactions involve change. In flames, for example, we can see the changes caused by very fast reactions between the chemicals in burning materials and oxygen from the atmosphere (*figure 5.1*). There are new substances, new colours and changes of state, but the most obvious changes in these reactions are the transfers of energy as light and heating of the surroundings. All life on Earth depends on the transfer of energy in chemical reactions. Plants need the energy from the Sun for the production of carbohydrates by photosynthesis; animals gain energy from the oxidation of their food chemicals.

● **Figure 5.1** The chemical reactions in this fire are releasing large quantities of energy.

## Energy transfer: exothermic and endothermic reactions

Most chemical reactions release energy to their surroundings. These reactions are described as **exothermic**. We recognise exothermic reactions most easily by detecting a rise in the temperature of the reaction mixture and the surroundings (the test-tube or beaker, the solvent, air, etc.). Examples of exothermic reactions include:

■ oxidation reactions such as:
the combustion of fuels, respiration in plants and animals (involving oxidation of carbohydrates such as glucose);

■ acids with metals,

■ water with 'quicklime' (calcium oxide) (see page 221).

Some chemical reactions occur only while energy is transferred to them *from* an external source. Reactions such as these which require a heat input are **endothermic** reactions. The energy input may come from a flame, electricity, sunlight or the surroundings. Examples of endothermic reactions include:

■ the decomposition of limestone by heating (*figure 5.2*):

$$CaCO_3(s) + energy \rightarrow CaO(s) + CO_2(g)$$

■ photosynthesis (*figure 5.3*). The energy is supplied to the reactions in the cells by sunlight:

$$CO_2(g) + H_2O(l) + energy$$
$$\rightarrow \text{carbohydrate in leaves} + O_2(g)$$

● **Figure 5.3** Photosynthesis in green leaves: the most essential chemical reaction of all.

■ dissolving ammonium chloride in water (*figure 5.4*). When the pack is kneaded, water and ammonium chloride crystals mix. As the crystals dissolve, energy is transferred from the surroundings, cooling the injury:

$$NH_4Cl(s) + H_2O(l) + energy \rightarrow NH_4^+(aq) + Cl^-(aq)$$

● **Figure 5.2** A modern lime kiln. Calcium carbonate, as limestone or chalk, has been converted to calcium oxide (quicklime) for centuries (see page 221), by strong heating in lime kilns. This is a gas-fired Maerz kiln belonging to Buxton Lime Industries.

● **Figure 5.4** The use of endothermic reactions to treat injuries.

## SAQ 5.1

Classify the following processes as exothermic or endothermic: evaporation; crystallisation; making magnesium oxide from magnesium and air; making copper oxide from copper carbonate.

# Energy is conserved

It is important to understand that energy is not being created by exothermic chemical reactions and it is not destroyed in endothermic reactions. Energy is transferred from the reacting chemicals to the surroundings or the other way around. The total energy of the whole system of reacting chemicals and the surroundings remains *constant*. This applies to any energy transfer and is summarised in the law of conservation of energy: energy can neither be created nor destroyed.

You may also hear this universal law called the first law of thermodynamics, as thermodynamics is the science of transfers of energy.

# Enthalpy, and enthalpy changes

Measurements of the energy transferred during chemical reactions must be made under controlled conditions. A special name is given to the energy exchange with the surroundings when it takes place at constant pressure. This name is enthalpy change.

**Enthalpy** is the total energy content of the reacting materials. It is given the symbol $H$. Enthalpy cannot be measured as such, but it is possible to measure the enthalpy change when energy is transferred to or from a reaction system and changes from one enthalpy to another.

Enthalpy change is given the symbol $\Delta H$ ($\Delta$ is the upper case of the Greek letter $\delta$, pronounced 'delta', and it is often used in mathematics as a symbol for change). So:

$$\Delta H = H_{products} - H_{reactants}$$

As $\Delta H$ is a measure of energy transferred to or from known amounts of reactants, the units are kilojoules per mole ($kJ\,mol^{-1}$).

We can illustrate enthalpy changes by **enthalpy profiles** (*figure 5.5*). An exothermic enthalpy

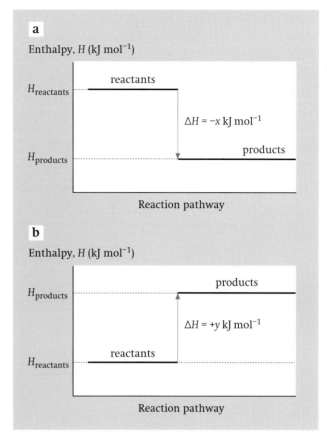

● **Figure 5.5** Enthalpy profiles for **a** an exothermic reaction and **b** an endothermic reaction.

change is always given a negative value, as the energy is lost from the system to the surroundings. It is shown in *figure 5.5a* as:

$$\Delta H = -x\,kJ\,mol^{-1}$$

For example, when methane burns:

$$CH_4(g) + 2O_2(g) \rightarrow CO_2(g) + 2H_2O(l);$$
$$\Delta H = -890.3\,kJ\,mol^{-1}$$

This means that when one mole of methane burns completely in oxygen, 890.3 kilojoules of energy are transferred to the surroundings (*figure 5.6a*).

An endothermic enthalpy change is always given a positive value, as the energy is gained by the system from the surroundings. It is shown in *figure 5.5b* as:

$$\Delta H = +y\,kJ\,mol^{-1}$$

For example, on heating calcium carbonate:

$$CaCO_3(s) \rightarrow CaO(s) + CO_2(g);$$
$$\Delta H = +572\,kJ\,mol^{-1}$$

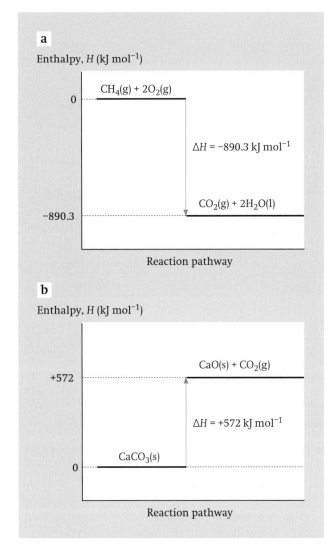

**a**

Enthalpy, $H$ (kJ mol$^{-1}$)

CH$_4$(g) + 2O$_2$(g)

0

$\Delta H = -890.3$ kJ mol$^{-1}$

CO$_2$(g) + 2H$_2$O(l)

−890.3

Reaction pathway

**b**

Enthalpy, $H$ (kJ mol$^{-1}$)

CaO(s) + CO$_2$(g)

+572

$\Delta H = +572$ kJ mol$^{-1}$

CaCO$_3$(s)

0

Reaction pathway

● **Figure 5.6** Enthalpy profiles for **a** the combustion of methane and **b** the decomposition of calcium carbonate.

This means that an input of 572 kilojoules of energy is needed to break down one mole of calcium carbonate to calcium oxide and carbon dioxide (*figure 5.6b*).

## Standard enthalpy changes: standard conditions

When we compare the enthalpy changes of various reactions we must use **standard conditions**, such as known temperatures, pressures, amounts and concentrations of reactants or products. This allows us to compare the standard enthalpy changes for reactions.

A standard enthalpy change for a reaction takes place under these standard conditions:

■ a pressure of 100 kilopascals (100 kPa);
■ a temperature of 298 K;

■ the reactants and products must be in the physical states (solid, liquid or gas) that are normal for these conditions;
■ any solutions have a concentration of 1.0 mol dm$^{-3}$.

The complete symbol for a standard enthalpy change of reaction may be written as, $\Delta H^{\ominus}_{\text{r},298}$, the meanings of the symbols being:

■ $\ominus$ means standard and assumes a pressure of 100 kPa;
■ r is a general symbol for reaction and is changed to f for formation reactions or c for combustion reactions;
■ 298 means all reactants and products are in their physical states at a temperature of 298 K, e.g. carbon dioxide is a gas at 298 K but water is a liquid.

Note that, as values for standard enthalpy changes are usually quoted at 298 K, it is common practice to omit 298 from the symbol.

## Standard enthalpy change of reaction $\Delta H^{\ominus}_{\text{r}}$

This is defined as: the **standard enthalpy change of reaction** is the enthalpy change when amounts of reactants, as shown in the reaction equation, react together under standard conditions to give products in their standard states.

It is necessary to make clear which reaction equation we are using when we quote a standard enthalpy change of reaction. For example, the equation for the reaction between hydrogen and oxygen can be written in two different ways and there are different values for $\Delta H^{\ominus}_{\text{r}}$ in each case.

equation (i)
2H$_2$(g) + O$_2$(g) → 2H$_2$O(l);

$\Delta H^{\ominus}_{\text{r}} = -572$ kJ mol$^{-1}$

equation (ii)
H$_2$(g) + $\frac{1}{2}$O$_2$(g) → H$_2$O(l);

$\Delta H^{\ominus}_{\text{r}} = -286$ kJ mol$^{-1}$

Note that the value of $\Delta H^{\ominus}_{\text{r}}$ in (ii) is half that of $\Delta H^{\ominus}_{\text{r}}$ in (i).

## Standard enthalpy change of formation $\Delta H^{\ominus}_{\text{f}}$

This is defined as: the **standard enthalpy change of formation** is the enthalpy change when one mole of a compound is formed from its elements under standard conditions; both compound and elements are in their standard states.

For example, water is formed in both equations (i) and (ii) above but only in equation (ii) is one mole of water formed. Thus equation (ii) shows that the value of $\Delta H_f^{\ominus}(H_2O) = -286\,kJ\,mol^{-1}$ (*figure 5.7*).

## SAQ 5.2

a Write balanced equations for the formation of (i) ethane ($C_2H_6$) and (ii) aluminium oxide ($Al_2O_3$). Use a data book to add values for $\Delta H_f^{\ominus}$ in each case.

b Draw the enthalpy profile for the enthalpy change of formation of ethane. Label your diagram fully.

## Standard enthalpy change of combustion $\Delta H_c^{\ominus}$

The **standard enthalpy change of combustion** is the enthalpy change when one mole of an element or compound reacts completely with oxygen under standard conditions.

For example, the standard enthalpy change of combustion of hydrogen is given by equation (ii) above:

$$H_2(g) + \tfrac{1}{2}O_2(g) \rightarrow H_2O(l);$$

$$\Delta H_c^{\ominus} = -286\,kJ\,mol^{-1}$$

Another example is shown in *figure 5.8*.

In practice it is not possible to achieve complete combustion under standard conditions. Measurements are taken under experimental conditions; then a value for the enthalpy change is determined and this is corrected to standard conditions through calculations.

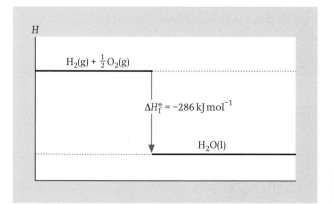

● **Figure 5.7** The standard enthalpy change of formation of water.

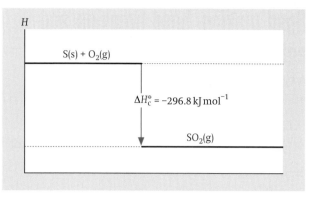

● **Figure 5.8** The standard enthalpy change of combustion of sulphur to form sulphur dioxide.

## SAQ 5.3

a Which of the labels $\Delta H_r^{\ominus}$, $\Delta H_f^{\ominus}$, $\Delta H_c^{\ominus}$ could be used for the enthalpy changes shown in *figure 5.6*?

b What are the reaction equations for the combustion of (i) octane ($C_8H_{18}$) and (ii) ethanol ($C_2H_5OH$), including the values for $\Delta H_c^{\ominus}$ (use a data book)?

c Why is the $\Delta H_f^{\ominus}$ of water the same as the $\Delta H_c^{\ominus}$ of hydrogen?

## Other standard enthalpy changes

We can define other standard enthalpy changes in a similar manner.

■ The **standard enthalpy change of hydration** is the enthalpy change when one mole of a gaseous ion dissolves in water to give an infinitely dilute solution.

■ The **standard enthalpy change of solution** is the enthalpy change when one mole of a solute dissolves in a solvent to give an infinitely dilute solution.

■ The **standard enthalpy change of neutralisation** is the enthalpy change when one mole of $H^+$ ions from an acid is completely neutralised by an alkali to give one mole of water.

■ The **standard enthalpy change of atomisation** of an element is the enthalpy change when one mole of gaseous atoms is formed from one mole of the element in its standard state.

# Bond making, bond breaking and enthalpy change

A typical combustion reaction, such as the burning of methane, is

$$CH_4(g) + 2O_2(g) \rightarrow CO_2(g) + 2H_2O(l);$$
$$\Delta H_c^{\ominus} = -890.3 \, kJ \, mol^{-1}$$

or, drawing the molecules to show the bonds:

For this reaction to occur, some bonds must break and others form:

- bonds breaking     $4 \times$ C–H and $2 \times$ O=O
- bonds forming     $2 \times$ C=O and $4 \times$ H–O

The basis of understanding energy transfers during chemical reactions is a fairly simple rule: When bonds break, energy is absorbed (endothermic process). When bonds form, energy is released (exothermic process).

If the energy released by the formation of some bonds is greater than the energy absorbed by the breaking of other bonds, there will be a surplus of energy transferred to the surroundings. The overall reaction will be exothermic.

If the energy released by bond formation is less than the energy absorbed by bond breaking then, overall, energy must be transferred from the surroundings. The reaction will be endothermic.

In the case of the combustion of methane, after all the bond breaking and bond formation, the surplus energy transferred to the surroundings is 890.3 kJ for each mole of methane.

## Bond enthalpy

Chemists find that it is useful to measure the amount of energy needed to break a covalent bond, as this indicates the strength of the bond. They call it the **bond enthalpy**. The values are always quoted as bond enthalpy per mole (of bonds broken).

Consider the example of oxygen gas, $O_2(g)$. The bond enthalpy of oxygen is the enthalpy change for the process:

$$O_2(g) \rightarrow 2O(g); \qquad \Delta H = +498 \, kJ \, mol^{-1}$$

The symbol $E$ is often used for bond enthalpy per mole. It is related to particular bonds as $E(X–Y)$, where X–Y is a molecule. Thus $E(X–Y)$ is the same as $\Delta H$ for the dissociation process

$$X–Y(g) \rightarrow X(g) + Y(g)$$

Typical values of bond enthalpies per mole are shown in *table 5.1*.

The values quoted in tables for bond enthalpies per mole satisfy the following four conditions.

- They are all positive, as the changes during breaking of bonds are endothermic (energy is absorbed). The same quantities of energy would be released in an exothermic change when the bonds form.
- They are average values. The actual value of the bond enthalpy for a particular bond depends upon which molecule the bond is in. For example, the C–C bond has slightly different strengths in ethane $C_2H_6$ and in propane $C_3H_8$, as it is affected by the other atoms and bonds in the molecules. The bond enthalpy quoted in data books for C–C is an average of the values from many different molecules.
- They are compared for bonds in gaseous compounds only.
- They are very difficult to measure directly. They are usually calculated using data from measurements of enthalpy changes of combustion of several compounds.

## SAQ 5.4

A book of data gives a value for the standard enthalpy change of combustion of hydrogen as $-285.8 \, kJ \, mol^{-1}$. A value for the enthalpy change of formation of water, calculated from bond energies, is $-283.1 \, kJ \, mol^{-1}$. Suggest why these values are slightly different.

| Bond | $E(X–Y)$ (kJ mol$^{-1}$) | Bond | $E(X–Y)$ (kJ mol$^{-1}$) |
|------|------|------|------|
| H–H | +436 | O=O | +498 |
| C–C | +347 | O–H | +464 |
| C=C | +612 | C–O | +358 |
| C–H | +413 | C=O | +805 |

● **Table 5.1** Some common bond enthalpies.

# Measuring energy transfers and enthalpy changes

Simple laboratory experiments can give us estimates of the energy transferred during some reactions. Enthalpy changes may then be calculated.

## Enthalpy changes of combustion

Measurements of $\Delta H_c^\ominus$ are important as they help to compare the energy available from the oxidation of different flammable liquids, which may be used as fuels.

The type of apparatus used for a simple laboratory method is shown in *figure 5.9*. A fuel, such as an alkane or an alcohol, burns at the wick. Measurements are made of:

- the mass of cold water in the metal calorimeter ($m$ g),
- the temperature rise of the water ($\Delta T$ K),
- the loss in mass of the fuel ($y$ g).

It is known that 4.2 J of energy are needed to raise the temperature of 1 g of water by 1 K. (This is called the specific heat capacity of water and equals $4.2\,\mathrm{J\,g^{-1}\,K^{-1}}$.)

The specific heat capacity of a liquid is given the general symbol $c$. The energy required to raise $m$ g of water by $\Delta T$ K is given by the general relationship:

energy transfer (as heating effect) = $mc\Delta T$ joules

Therefore, in the experiment, $m \times 4.2 \times \Delta T$ joules of energy are transferred during the burning of $y$ grams of the fuel. Therefore, if one mole of the fuel has a mass of $M$ grams, $m \times 4.2 \times \Delta T \times M/y$ joules of energy are transferred when one mole of the fuel burns. The answer will give an approximate value of the enthalpy change of combustion of the fuel in joules per mole ($\mathrm{J\,mol^{-1}}$). Divide this answer by 1000 to find the value for $\Delta H_c^\ominus$ in kilojoules per mole ($\mathrm{kJ\,mol^{-1}}$).

We shall now look at an example. In an experiment using the simple apparatus above to find the enthalpy change of combustion of propanol ($C_3H_7OH$), the following measurements were made:

| | |
|---|---|
| mass of water in the calorimeter ($m$) | = 100 g |
| temperature rise of the water ($\Delta T$) | = 21.5 K |
| loss in mass of propanol fuel ($y$) | = 0.28 g |

We are given: $A_r$ (H) = 1, $A_r$ (C) = 12, $A_r$ (O) = 16; and specific heat capacity of water $c = 4.2\,\mathrm{J\,g^{-1}\,K^{-1}}$

The energy transferred as heat from the burning propanol is

$$mc\Delta T = 100 \times 4.2 \times 21.5\,\mathrm{J}$$
$$= 9030\,\mathrm{J}$$

This is the energy transferred (heat produced) through burning 0.28 g of propanol. The mass of one mole of propanol is 60 g. Therefore energy transferred through burning one mole of propanol is

$$\Delta H_c^\ominus = 9030 \times 60/0.28\,\mathrm{J\,mol^{-1}}$$
$$= 1935\,000\,\mathrm{J\,mol^{-1}}$$
$$= 1935\,\mathrm{kJ\,mol^{-1}}$$

From this experiment, the value for $\Delta H_c^\ominus$ ($C_3H_7OH$) = $-1935\,\mathrm{kJ\,mol^{-1}}$.

### SAQ 5.5

The value for $\Delta H_c^\ominus$ ($C_3H_7OH$) in a book of data is given as $-2010\,\mathrm{kJ\,mol^{-1}}$. Suggest why the value calculated from the experimental results above is so much lower.

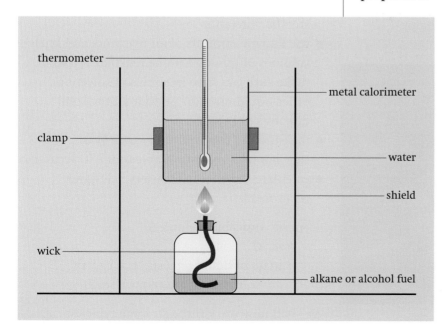

thermometer

metal calorimeter

clamp

water

shield

wick

alkane or alcohol fuel

● **Figure 5.9** Apparatus used for approximate measurements of energy transferred by burning known masses of flammable liquids.

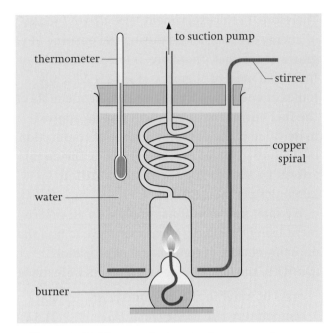

● **Figure 5.10** Flame calorimeter for measuring energy transfers during combustion of flammable liquids.

## An improved apparatus: the flame calorimeter

The simple apparatus shown in *figure 5.9* is not efficient because energy from burning of the fuel is lost in heating the apparatus and surroundings. A more effective apparatus is shown in *figure 5.10*.

In using this apparatus we need to know its heat capacity. This is the energy needed to raise the temperature of the whole apparatus by 1K. The heat capacity may be given by the manufacturer or calculated from measurements made using a fuel with known standard enthalpy change of combustion.

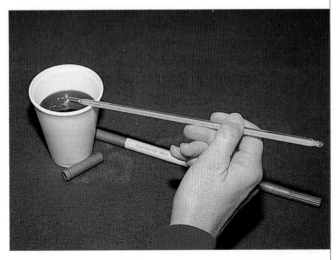

● **Figure 5.11** A simple apparatus used in school laboratories to measure enthalpy changes for reactions in aqueous solutions.

When the flame calorimeter is used, the energy transferred is found from:

energy transferred
$\quad$ = heat capacity of apparatus $\times \Delta T$

The 'unknown' $\Delta H_c^{\ominus}$ is calculated as shown in the previous example.

## Measuring enthalpy changes of other reactions

The experiments outlined above involved burning fuels. You may also undertake experiments in which the enthalpy changes are from reactions between chemicals in solutions. Here is an example.

We shall look at the enthalpy change of neutralisation in the reaction between an acid and an alkali:

e.g. hydrochloric acid plus sodium hydroxide solution:

$$HCl(aq) + NaOH(aq) \rightarrow Na^+(aq) + Cl^-(aq) + H_2O(l)$$

The reaction that produces the enthalpy change here is shown more simply as:

$$H^+(aq) + OH^-(aq) \rightarrow H_2O(l)$$

$Na^+(aq)$ and $Cl^-(aq)$ are **spectator ions** and take no part in the reaction producing the enthalpy change.

In such an experiment you would:
■ use a heat-insulated vessel, such as a vacuum flask or a thick polystyrene cup (*figure 5.11*), and stir the reactants;
■ use known amounts of all reactants and known volumes of liquids – if one reactant is a solid, make sure you have an excess of solvent or other liquid reactant, so that all the solid dissolves or reacts;
■ measure the temperature change by a thermometer reading to at least 0.2 °C accuracy;
■ calculate the energy transfers using the relationship

energy transferred (joules)
$\quad$ = $mc\Delta T$
$\quad$ = mass of liquid (g) $\times$ sp. heat cap. of aq. soln. ($J\,g^{-1}\,K^{-1}$) $\times$ temp. rise (K)

We shall now work through some typical results from an experiment. When 50 cm³ of HCl(aq) are added to 50 cm³ of NaOH(aq), both of concentration $1\,mol\,dm^{-3}$, in an insulated beaker, the temperature rises by 6.2 K. The acid and alkali are completely neutralised.

We may calculate the molar enthalpy change of neutralisation (for the reaction between hydrochloric acid and sodium hydroxide) as follows:

$$50\,cm^3\ HCl(aq) + 50\,cm^3\ NaOH(aq)$$
$$= 100\,cm^3\ solution$$
$$mass\ of\ this\ solution\ (m)\ \ = 100\,g$$
$$change\ in\ temperature\ (\Delta T) = 6.2\,K$$

We assume that the specific heat capacity ($c$) of the solution is the same as that for water ($4.2\,J\,g^{-1}\,K^{-1}$). Therefore the energy transferred (heat produced) by the reaction is

$$mc\Delta T = 100 \times 4.2 \times 6.2$$
$$= 2604\,J$$

$50\,cm^3$ of HCl(aq) or NaOH(aq) of concentration $1\,mol\,dm^{-3}$ contain $50/1000\,mol = 5 \times 10^{-2}\,mol$ of HCl or NaOH. So, the molar enthalpy change of neutralisation, for the reaction between 1 mol HCl and 1 mol NaOH to give 1 mol NaCl, is given by:

$$\Delta H_r^\ominus = -2604/5 \times 10^{-2}\,J\,mol^{-1}$$
$$= -52\,080\,J\,mol^{-1}$$
$$= -52.08\,kJ\,mol^{-1}$$

The data book value for the molar enthalpy change of neutralisation is $\Delta H_r^\ominus = -57.1\,kJ\,mol^{-1}$. In the above experiment, heat is lost to the surroundings. The result obtained is thus less exothermic than the data book value.

## SAQ 5.6

Suggest why the molar enthalpy changes of neutralisation for the reactions of acids such as hydrochloric, sulphuric, or nitric with alkalis such as aqueous sodium hydroxide or potassium hydroxide are all very similar in value, at about $-57.2\,kJ\,mol^{-1}$.

## The enthalpy change of solution of sodium hydroxide

In this experiment, the temperature is measured over time and a graph is plotted. Extrapolation of the curve obtained as the mixture cools allows correction to be made to the estimated

temperature rise. The corrected figure makes allowance for cooling losses to the surroundings.

### Method

1 Weigh a polystyrene cup of the kind shown in *figure 5.11.*

2 Weigh 100 g of distilled water into the polystyrene cup. (How could you work out roughly how much to add in advance?)

3 Measure the temperature of the water in the cup. Keep a check on it until the temperature is steady. Record this temperature.

4 Add a few pellets of solid sodium hydroxide straight from a previously sealed container. (Solid sodium hydroxide absorbs water from the air, so it gets heavier if you leave it standing. **Take care** – it is also very **corrosive**. Wash it off immediately with water if you get it on your skin, and report to your teacher.)

5 Stir the mixture immediately, and start a stopwatch. Keep stirring with the thermometer, and record the temperature every 30 seconds.

6 The temperature will reach a maximum, and then it will start to fall. When it has fallen for five minutes, you can stop taking readings.

7 Weigh the cup + solution to calculate the mass of sodium hydroxide you dissolved.

8 Plot a graph of temperature against time, and work out the maximum temperature the mixture might have reached (see graph in *figure 5.12*).

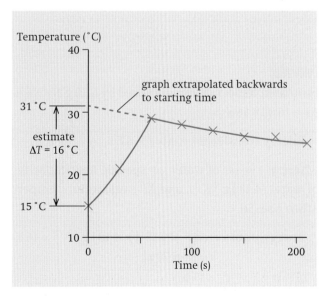

● **Figure 5.12** The results of the example experiment.

9  Calculate the amount of heat input to the solution, and calculate the amount of heat given out by the sodium hydroxide and water.

10  Scale the result to tell you how much heat energy would have been released on dissolving one mole (40 g) of sodium hydroxide to make the same strength of solution.

### A typical set of results

The example below will help you to understand the procedure and calculations:

| | | |
|---|---|---|
| Mass of polystyrene cup | = | 8.00 g |
| Mass of polystyrene cup + distilled water | = | 108.15 g |
| Mass of distilled water used | = | 100.15 g |
| Mass of cup + water + sodium hydroxide | = | 114.35 g |
| Mass of sodium hydroxide that dissolved | = | 6.20 g |
| Initial temperature of water in the cup | = | 15.0 °C |

Table showing temperature at fixed times after mixing:

| Time (s) | Temperature (°C) |
|---|---|
| 0 | 15.0 |
| 30 | 21.0 |
| 60 | 29.0 |
| 90 | 28.0 |
| 120 | 27.0 |
| 150 | 26.0 |
| 180 | 26.0 |
| 210 | 25.0 |

### Calculation

Estimated temperature rise caused by 6.20 g NaOH is $\Delta T = 16°C = 16 K$

$$\text{Energy transferred} = m \times c \times \Delta T$$

where $m$ = mass of water, $c$ = specific heat capacity of water ($4.18 \, \text{J} \, \text{g}^{-1} \text{K}^{-1}$), and $\Delta T$ = maximum temperature rise. So

$$\text{Energy transferred} = 100.15 \, \text{g} \times 4.18 \, \text{J} \, \text{g}^{-1} \text{K}^{-1} \times 16 \, \text{K}$$
$$= 6.70 \, \text{kJ}$$

6.20 g NaOH releases 6.28 kJ energy on dissolving it in water.

# Enthalpy changes by different routes: Hess's law

When we write a reaction equation, we usually show only the beginning and end, that is, the reactants and products. But there may be many different ways that the reaction actually occurs in between. The reaction may have different routes.

For example, consider a reaction system, with initial reactants A + B and final products C + D, in which two different routes (1 and 2) between A + B and C + D are possible (*figure 5.13*). What can be said about the enthalpy changes for the two different routes? Are they different too?

The answer to this question was first summarised in 1840 by Germain Hess and is now called **Hess's law**. A concise form is: The total enthalpy change for a chemical reaction is *independent* of the route by which the reaction takes place, provided the initial and final conditions are the same.

In the case of our example above, Hess's law tells us that the enthalpy change for route 1 would equal the total of the enthalpy changes for route 2; that is

$$\Delta H_1 = \Delta H_2 + \Delta H_3 + \Delta H_4$$

The overall enthalpy change is affected only by the initial reactants and the final products, not by what happens in between.

Hess's law seems fairly obvious in the light of the more universal first law of thermodynamics (law of conservation of energy – see page 73). If

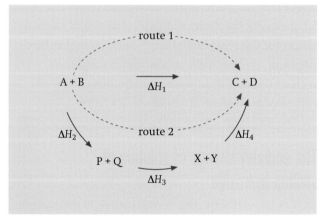

● **Figure 5.13** Two different routes between reactants and products. Hess's law tells us that $\Delta H_1 = \Delta H_2 + \Delta H_3 + \Delta H_4$.

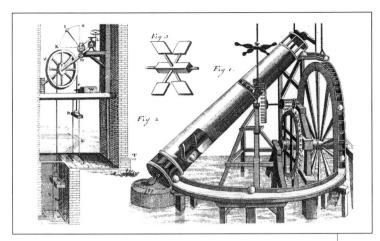

● **Figure 5.14** An attempt to design a mechanical perpetual motion machine. The heavy spheres cause the wheel to rotate. This operates the 'screw', which lifts the spheres back to the top of the wheel. Why does it not work?

different routes between the same reactants and products were able to transfer different amounts of energy, energy would be created or destroyed. We could make 'perpetual motion' machines (*figure 5.14*) and gain free energy for ever! Unfortunately, as in most aspects of life, you cannot get something for nothing.

## Using Hess's law: enthalpy cycles

Chemists often use an **enthalpy cycle** to calculate the enthalpy change for a reaction which cannot easily be measured directly. We shall look at three examples. The first example makes use of bond enthalpies; the second, enthalpy changes of formation and the third, enthalpy changes of combustion.

### Calculating $\Delta H_r^\ominus$ from bond enthalpy data

An important reaction which is covered in more detail in chapter 7 is the reaction for the Haber process (see page 133) for the synthesis of ammonia

$$N_2(g) + 3H_2(g) \rightarrow 2NH_3(g)$$

| Bond | Bond enthalpy (kJ mol$^{-1}$) |
|------|------------------------------|
| N≡N  | 945 |
| H–H  | 436 |
| N–H  | 391 |

● **Table 5.2** Bond enthalpies important for the Haber process.

Bond enthalpy data are shown in *table 5.2*.

When calculating $\Delta H_r^\ominus$ from bond enthalpy data, you will find it helpful to draw the enthalpy cycle showing the bonds present in the reactants and products. Remember that bond enthalpy is the enthalpy change for the formation of atoms from one mole of the bonds in the gaseous state.

The enthalpy cycle for the Haber process is shown in *figure 5.15*. Look at the equation for route 1. The following bonds are broken:

■ one N≡N triple bond;
■ three H–H single bonds;

and the following bonds are formed:

■ three N–H single bonds per molecule of ammonia – a total of six as two ammonia molecules are produced from one nitrogen and three hydrogen molecules.

Route 2 shows the input of enthalpy to break the bonds in the reactants, $E(N≡N) + 3 \times E(H–H)$ and the release of enthalpy when ammonia forms, $2 \times 3 \times E(N–H)$.

As, by Hess's Law, the enthalpy change for route 1 = total enthalpy change for route 2:

$\Delta H_r^\ominus$ = enthalpy change for bonds broken – enthalpy change for bonds formed
$= E(N≡N) + 3 \times E(H–H) - 6 \times E(N–H)$
$= 945 + (3 \times 436) - (6 \times 391)$
$= 2253 - 2346$
$= -93 \text{ kJ mol}^{-1}$

Remember that bond breaking is endothermic, bond formation is exothermic (hence the negative sign before $6 \times E(N–H)$).

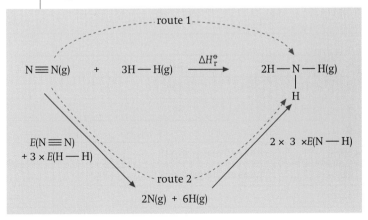

● **Figure 5.15** The enthalpy cycle for the production of ammonia by the Haber process.

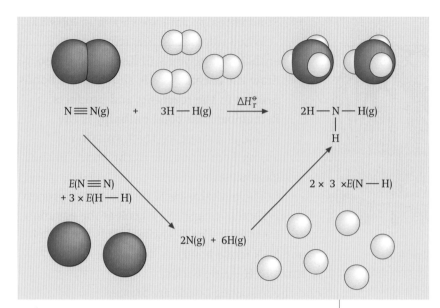

● **Figure 5.16** Bond breaking and bond formation in the enthalpy cycle for the Haber process.

*Figure 5.16* will help you to visualise which bonds are being broken and which formed with the help of molecular models.

Bond enthalpy calculations lend themselves to use of a spreadsheet on a computer. *Table 5.3* shows such a spreadsheet for the Haber process.

**SAQ 5.7**

A balanced chemical equation for the complete combustion of methane is:

$$CH_4(g) + 2O_2(g) \rightarrow CO_2(g) + 2H_2O(g)$$

a Re-write this equation to show the bonds present in each molecule.

b Using your equation, draw an enthalpy cycle showing bonds broken in the reactants, forming gaseous atoms, and bonds formed in the products from these gaseous atoms.

c Use the bond enthalpies given on page 76 to calculate the enthalpy change of combustion for methane (use a spreadsheet if possible).

d Compare the value for $\Delta H_c^\ominus$ with the experimentally determined value of $-890\,\text{kJ mol}^{-1}$. Which value is more accurate?

### Enthalpy change of reaction from enthalpy changes of formation

Enthalpy changes of formation of many compounds have been determined experimentally under carefully controlled conditions. Often these have been found indirectly from other experimental enthalpy

| | A | B | C | D | E | F |
|---|---|---|---|---|---|---|
| 1 | **Enthalpy of formation of ammonia from bond enthalpies** | | | | | |
| 2 | | | | | | |
| 3 | | | | | | |
| 4 | Bond | Bond enthalpy (kJ mol$^{-1}$) | Number of bonds broken | Enthalpy input (kJ mol$^{-1}$) | Number of bonds formed | Enthalpy output (kJ mol$^{-1}$) |
| 5 | | | | | | |
| 6 | N≡N | 945 | 1 | 945 | | 0 |
| 7 | H–H | 436 | 3 | 1308 | | 0 |
| 8 | N–H | 391 | | 0 | 6 | −2346 |
| 9 | | | | | | |
| 10 | | Total enthalpy input: | | 2253 | | |
| 11 | | Total enthalpy output: | | | | −2346 |
| 12 | | | | | | |
| 13 | | | | Enthalpy of reaction (kJ mol$^{-1}$): | | −93 |

● **Table 5.3** Bond enthalpy calculation for the Haber process.

changes such as enthalpy changes of combustion. Many data books provide detailed tables of enthalpy changes of formation. These enthalpy figures help chemists and chemical engineers to design a new chemical production plant. In such a plant, an exothermic process may release sufficient energy to cause a fire or explosion. Careful design of the plant allows the release of energy to be controlled and even re-used for heating or electricity generation.

Imagine that you are building a plant to make slaked lime from quicklime (see page 221). The equation for this exothermic reaction is:

$$CaO(s) + H_2O(l) \rightarrow Ca(OH)_2(s); \qquad \Delta H_r^\ominus = ?$$

The enthalpy changes of formation for each of the reactants and the product are

$$Ca(s) + \tfrac{1}{2}O_2(g) \rightarrow CaO(s);$$
$$\Delta H_f^\ominus [CaO(s)] = -635.1 \, kJ \, mol^{-1}$$
$$H_2(g) + \tfrac{1}{2}O_2(g) \rightarrow H_2O(l);$$
$$\Delta H_f^\ominus [H_2O(l)] = -285.8 \, kJ \, mol^{-1}$$
$$Ca(s) + H_2(g) + O_2(g) \rightarrow Ca(OH)_2(s);$$
$$\Delta H_f^\ominus [Ca(OH)_2(s)] = -986.1 \, kJ \, mol^{-1}$$

We can now draw the enthalpy cycle (*figure 5.17*).

■ As both $CaO(s)$ and $H_2O(l)$ appear in the top left-hand corner of the cycle, we must add the enthalpy changes of formation of each compound.

■ Route 1 contains the $\Delta H_r^\ominus$ which we wish to determine.

The total enthalpy change for route 1 is:

$$\Delta H_f^\ominus [CaO(s)] + \Delta H_f^\ominus [H_2O(l)] + \Delta H_r^\ominus$$
$$= (-635.1) + (-285.8) + \Delta H_r^\ominus \, kJ \, mol^{-1}$$

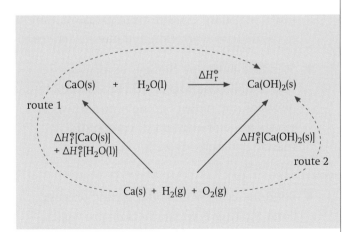

● **Figure 5.17** The enthalpy change for the reaction of quicklime with water.

and for route 2 is:

$$\Delta H_f^\ominus [Ca(OH)_2(s)] = -986.1 \, kJ \, mol^{-1}$$

By Hess's Law, the enthalpy change for route 1 = enthalpy change for route 2.

Thus:

$$(-635.1) + (-285.8) + \Delta H_r^\ominus = -986.1 \, kJ \, mol^{-1}$$

$$\text{or } \Delta H_r^\ominus = (-986.1) - [(-635.1) + (-285.8)] \, kJ \, mol^{-1}$$
$$= -65.2 \, kJ \, mol^{-1}$$

Notice the brackets inserted round each enthalpy change figure. These help ensure that you do not make a mistake over the signs!

## SAQ 5.8

The balanced equation for the decomposition of magnesium carbonate is:

$$MgCO_3(s) \rightarrow MgO(s) + CO_2(g)$$

a Draw an enthalpy cycle showing the formation of each of the reactants and products from their elements in their standard states.

b Use the following enthalpy changes of formation to calculate the enthalpy change for the decomposition of magnesium carbonate.

|  | $MgCO_3(s)$ | $MgO(s)$ | $CO_2(g)$ |
|---|---|---|---|
| $\Delta H_f^\ominus$ (kJ mol$^{-1}$) | −1096 | −602 | −394 |

### Enthalpy change of formation from enthalpy changes of combustion

Consider the formation of methane from carbon and hydrogen:

$$(a) \quad C(s) + 2H_2(g) \rightarrow CH_4(g); \qquad \Delta H_f^\ominus = ?$$

This could be a very useful reaction for making methane gas starting with a plentiful supply of carbon such as coal or wood charcoal. Scientists are trying to find ways of making it occur directly and need to know the value of the enthalpy change of formation of methane. The best way is to use different routes, from reactants to product, with reactions that are known to occur.

Carbon, hydrogen and methane all burn in oxygen and the enthalpy changes of combustion of each can be measured.

(b) $C(s) + O_2(g) \rightarrow CO_2(g)$;
$$\Delta H_c^{\ominus} = -393.5 \, kJ \, mol^{-1}$$

(c) $H_2(g) + \frac{1}{2}O_2(g) \rightarrow H_2O(l)$;
$$\Delta H_c^{\ominus} = -285.8 \, kJ \, mol^{-1}$$

(d) $CH_4(g) + 2O_2(g) \rightarrow CO_2(g) + 2H_2O(l)$;
$$\Delta H_c^{\ominus} = -890.3 \, kJ \, mol^{-1}$$

One helpful way to calculate the enthalpy change for reaction (a) above starts with an enthalpy cycle (*figure 5.18*):

- As in previous enthalpy cycles, the balanced equation for the enthalpy change we wish to calculate is written at the top of the cycle.

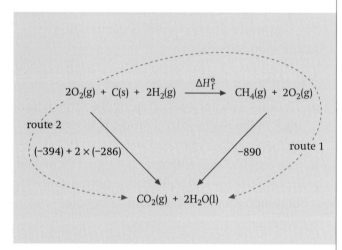

- Figure 5.18 An enthalpy cycle used to calculate the enthalpy change of formation of methane.

- In this example the common products of combustion are written at the bottom of the cycle. We add oxygen to both sides of the top equation to balance the equations for the downward pointing arrows. This does not alter the reaction in the top equation.

- Note that, in route 2, one mole of carbon is oxidised by combustion together with two moles of hydrogen.

The enthalpy change for route 1
$= \Delta H_f^{\ominus} + (-890) \, kJ \, mol^{-1}$
The enthalpy change for route 2
$= (-394) + 2 \times (-286) \, kJ \, mol^{-1}$

Applying Hess's Law:

$$\Delta H_f^{\ominus} + (-890) = (-394) + 2 \times (-286)$$

Hence:

$$\Delta H_f^{\ominus} = (-394) + 2 \times (-286) - (-890) = -76 \, kJ \, mol^{-1}$$

## SAQ 5.9

a Write the balanced chemical equation for the enthalpy change of formation of ethane, $C_2H_6(g)$.

b Using your equation, draw an enthalpy cycle, given the enthalpy change of combustion of ethane is $-1560 \, kJ \, mol^{-1}$.

c Using the enthalpy changes of combustion of carbon and hydrogen in the above example, calculate the enthalpy change of formation of ethane.

# SUMMARY (AS)

- Chemical reactions are often accompanied by transfers of energy to or from the surroundings, mainly as heat. In exothermic reactions, energy is transferred away from the reacting chemicals; in endothermic reactions, energy is gained by the reacting chemicals.

- Changes in energy of reacting chemicals at constant pressure are known as enthalpy changes ($\Delta H$). Exothermic enthalpy changes are shown as negative values (−) and endothermic enthalpy changes are shown as positive values (+).

- Standard enthalpy changes are compared under standard conditions of pressure, temperature, concentration and physical states.

- Standard enthalpy changes of formation $\Delta H_f^{\ominus}$ and of combustion $\Delta H_c^{\ominus}$ are defined in terms of one mole of compound formed or of one mole of element or compound reacting completely with oxygen; their units are $kJ \, mol^{-1}$.

- Bond breaking is an endothermic process; bond making is an exothermic process.

◆ Bond energy is a measure of the energy required to break a bond. The values quoted are usually average bond enthalpies, as the strength of a bond between two particular atoms is different in different molecules.

◆ Enthalpy changes may be calculated from measurements involving temperature change in a liquid, using the relationship:
enthalpy change = mass of liquid
  × specific heat capacity
    of liquid
  × temperature change.
$$\Delta H = mc\Delta T$$

◆ Hess's law states that 'the total enthalpy change for a chemical reaction is independent of the route by which the reaction takes place provided the inital and final conditions as the same'.

◆ The principle of Hess's law may be used to calculate enthalpy changes for reactions that do not occur directly or cannot be found by experiment. For example:
- the enthalpy change of reaction for the formation of ammonia may be calculated from the average bond enthalpies of the reactants ($N_2 + H_2$) and of the N–H bonds in ammonia, $NH_3$;
- the enthalpy change of reaction for the slaking of quicklime from the enthalpy changes of formation of the reactants, $CaO(s)$ and $H_2O(l)$, and product, $Ca(OH)_2(s)$;
- the enthalpy change of formation of methane from the enthalpy changes of combustion of carbon, hydrogen and methane.

# Questions (AS)

1  Considerable scientific research is taking place to develop hydrogen as a fuel for the future. Scientists are especially interested in developing hydrogen as a motor fuel because it burns more cleanly and more efficiently than petrol.

a  Suggest what is meant by the statement **hydrogen burns more cleanly than petrol.**

b  Fuel scientists use a term called the 'energy density' to compare fuels. Energy density is the energy produced from the combustion of **one gram** of a fuel. It can be calculated from the standard enthalpy change of combustion of a fuel.

(i)  Define the term standard enthalpy change of combustion.

(ii)  Calculate the energy density of hydrogen and of petrol. You may assume that petrol consists of the hydrocarbon $C_8H_{18}$.
[$\Delta H_c^\ominus$ ($H_2$): $-287\,kJ\,mol^{-1}$;
$\Delta H_c^\ominus$ ($C_8H_{18}$): $-5473\,kJ\,mol^{-1}$,
$A_r$: H, 1.00; C, 12.00.]

c  Suggest two reasons why petrol is the preferred fuel for motor vehicles even though hydrogen has a greater energy density.

**2** In an investigation to find the enthalpy change of combustion of ethanol, $C_2H_5OH$, a chemist found that 1.60 g of ethanol could heat 150 g of water from 22.0 °C to 71.0 °C.

**a** Explain what is meant by the enthalpy change of combustion of ethanol.

**b** Use the chemist's results to calculate a value for the enthalpy change of combustion of ethanol.

**c** Explain, with reasons, how you would expect this result to compare with the theoretical value of the standard enthalpy change of combustion of ethanol.

**3** Methane production as 'biogas' is growing rapidly as an alternative energy supply, particularly in some countries. Methane can be used as a fuel because of its exothermic reaction with oxygen.

$CH_4(g) + 2O_2(g) \rightarrow CO_2(g) + 2H_2O(l)$;
$\Delta H_c^{\ominus} (CH_4(g)) = -890.3 \text{ kJ mol}^{-1}$

**a** Explain what is meant by $\Delta H_c^{\ominus} (CH_4(g))$ $= -890.3 \text{ kJ mol}^{-1}$

**b** The enthalpy change of formation of methane, $\Delta H_f^{\ominus} (CH_4(g))$, cannot be measured directly.

(i) Using the data below, calculate the enthalpy change of formation of methane.

$$C(s) + 2H_2(g) \quad \rightarrow \quad CH_4(g)$$

| Compound | $\Delta H_c^{\ominus}$ (kJ mol$^{-1}$) |
|---|---|
| $CH_4(g)$ | −890.3 |
| $C(s)$ | −393.5 |
| $H_2(g)$ | −285.9 |

(ii) Suggest why the enthalpy change of formation of methane cannot be measured directly.

**c** A typical biogas plant in China, using the dung from five cows, can produce 3000 dm$^3$ of biogas in a day. The biogas produced contains 60% of methane by volume.

(i) Using the data in the table in part b(i), calculate the maximum heat energy that can be produced each day from the methane in this biogas. [Assume that 1 mole of methane occupies 24 dm$^3$ under these conditions.]

(ii) Suggest a practical difficulty of using biogas as a fuel on a large scale.

# Chemical energetics (A2)

## By the end of this section you should be able to:

9 explain the term *lattice enthalpy* of an ionic solid;

10 construct a *Born–Haber cycle* for an ionic solid;

11 name all the enthalpy changes in a Born–Haber cycle;

12 calculate lattice enthalpy from a Born–Haber cycle;

13 explain how the charge on an ion affects its lattice enthalpy;

14 explain how the size of an ion affects its lattice enthalpy;

15 state that magnesium oxide has a large lattice enthalpy and is used as a refractory lining;

16 describe the trend in the *decomposition temperatures* of the Group II carbonates ($MgCO_3$ to $BaCO_3$);

17 explain this trend by considering the effects of the charge density of the metal cations and the *polarisation* of the carbonate anion.

Ionic compounds are familiar to all of us, chemists as well as non-chemists, probably because three of them have been used throughout history – salt (NaCl), washing soda ($Na_2CO_3$) and caustic soda (NaOH).

■ Salt was used to pay Roman soldiers in AD 43 and the word 'salary' is derived from the Latin for salt, *salerium argentinium*. Nowadays we are cautious about taking too much salt in our diet because this has been linked to high blood pressure, but salt has always been recognised as necessary to life. One of the most famous of Gandhi's protests against British rule in India was the Salt March of 1930, when he and his followers marched on a salt factory as a protest against the Salt Tax that prevented them making their own salt. As the marchers moved forward in columns they were beaten to the ground, offering no resistance.

■ Washing soda has been used for centuries to soften water for bathing and washing, and it is still used as a common household chemical today.

■ Caustic soda is used in huge quantities in the paper and soap industries and many other industries too – for instance 17 million tonnes are used every year as part of the production process for aluminium.

You have already studied the ionic bonding and lattice structure of sodium chloride (see chapter 3). It is important to realise that solid ionic compounds do not form as a result of the transfer of electrons only – overall, forming the ions actually *requires* energy, as you can see if you look at the energy changes involved:

$$Na(g) \rightarrow Na^+(g) + e^- \qquad \Delta H^\ominus = +496 \, kJ \, mol^{-1}$$
$$\underline{Cl(g) + e^- \rightarrow Cl^-(g) \qquad\qquad \Delta H^\ominus = -349 \, kJ \, mol^{-1}}$$
$$Na(g) + Cl(g) \rightarrow Na^+(g) + Cl^-(g) \quad \Delta H^\ominus = +147 \, kJ \, mol^{-1}$$

Yet most ionic solids form easily from their elements. So if transferring electrons is not the reason why ionic compounds form, what is? It is the *huge release in energy* that occurs when the two ions of opposite charge combine to form a solid. This is the **lattice enthalpy**, $\Delta H_{latt}^{\ominus}$.

> The lattice enthalpy, $\Delta H_{latt}^{\ominus}$ is the enthalpy change when 1 mole of an ionic compound is formed from its gaseous ions under standard conditions (298 K, 100 kPa).

The *gaseous* ions are important here – the equation representing the lattice enthalpy of sodium chloride is

$$Na^+(g) + Cl^-(g) \rightarrow NaCl(s); \quad \Delta H_{latt}^{\ominus} = -787 \, kJ \, mol^{-1}$$

You can see that the process of bringing together the separate ions in the gaseous state and putting them together into a regular lattice structure releases a large amount of energy. This large exothermic value indicates that the sodium chloride lattice is very stable, and cannot easily be pulled apart again. Of course, to actually do this process *experimentally* is impossible – how can gaseous sodium ions and chloride ions be mixed together so that a solid forms?

The way in which we determine the lattice enthalpy is by using a **Born–Haber cycle**, which is a particular type of Hess's law enthalpy cycle (see page 80). In a Born–Haber cycle every step from the elements to the ionic compound can be measured experimentally, except the lattice enthalpy. The lattice enthalpy can therefore be calculated in the usual way in a Hess's law cycle.

The lattice enthalpy is an exothermic change and always has a negative value.

### SAQ 5.10

Explain what is meant by the terms:
a enthalpy change
b exothermic reaction
c endothermic reaction.

### SAQ 5.11

State Hess's law.

# The Born–Haber cycle

Let's go through the Born–Haber cycle for lithium fluoride step by step, as shown in *figure 5.19*.

We begin with the elements in their standard states, metallic lithium, Li(s) and gaseous diatomic fluorine, $F_2(g)$. From these we can follow two routes to obtain lithium fluoride, LiF(s).

- Route 1 is the direct combination of the elements to give LiF(s); this is the standard enthalpy change of formation, $\Delta H_f^{\ominus}$. You have used this enthalpy change earlier (page 74).
- Route 2 is the multi-step cycle which includes the lattice enthalpy and also gives LiF(s).

From Hess's law, we know that both paths have the same overall enthalpy change, so in route 1 $\Delta H_f^{\ominus}$ = sum of $\Delta H^{\ominus}$ for the steps in route 2.

Route 1 involves only one step, so is easily dealt with. This step is the *standard enthalpy change of formation of lithium fluoride*. The enthalpy change of formation is defined as the enthalpy change when 1 mole of a compound is formed from its elements in their standard states under standard conditions.

$$Li(s) + \tfrac{1}{2}F_2(g) \rightarrow LiF(s); \quad \Delta H_f^{\ominus} = -617 \, kJ \, mol^{-1}$$

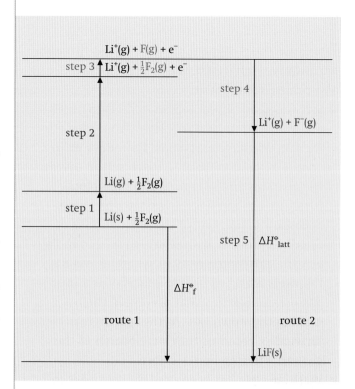

● **Figure 5.19** Born–Haber cycle for lithium fluoride.

The overall changes that take place in route 2 can be summarised as follows (see *figure 5.19*):

- the elements are converted to individual gaseous atoms (steps 1 and 3);
- these atoms are converted to gaseous ions (steps 2 and 4);
- the ions form the solid (step 5).

*Step 1* Converting solid lithium into separate gaseous lithium atoms is called the **standard enthalpy change of atomisation, $\Delta H_{at}^{\ominus}$**. This requires energy, so it is an endothermic change.

$$Li(s) \rightarrow Li(g); \quad \Delta H_{at}^{\ominus} = +161 \text{ kJ mol}^{-1}$$

> The **standard enthalpy change of atomisation** of an element is the enthalpy change when one mole of gaseous atoms are formed from the element in its standard state.

*Step 2* This step involves removing 1 mole of electrons from 1 mole of Li to form 1 mole of $Li^+$. Once again, this is an endothermic change. It is called the **ionisation energy, $\Delta H_{i1}^{\ominus}$**. (You met ionisation energies in chapter 1.)

$$Li(g) \rightarrow Li^+(g) + e^-; \quad \Delta H_{i1}^{\ominus} = +520 \text{ kJ mol}^{-1}$$

*Step 3* This is another enthalpy change of atomisation, but this time half a mole of fluorine *molecules*, $\frac{1}{2}F_2(g)$, are being converted into 1 mole of fluorine *atoms*, $F(g)$. This again is an endothermic change and it is equal to half the bond enthalpy of $F_2$. (You met bond enthalpies on page 76.)

$$\tfrac{1}{2}F_2(g) \rightarrow F(g); \quad \Delta H_{at}^{\ominus} = \tfrac{1}{2}(+159) = +79.5 \text{ kJ mol}^{-1}$$

*Step 4* Adding an electron to F to form $F^-$ is the **electron affinity, $\Delta H_{ea1}^{\ominus}$**. This is an exothermic change – the only exothermic change in this part of the Born–Haber cycle.

$$F(g) + e^- \rightarrow F^-(g); \quad \Delta H_{ea1}^{\ominus} = -328 \text{ kJ mol}^{-1}$$

> The **first electron affinity, $\Delta H_{ea1}^{\ominus}$**, is the enthalpy change when one electron is added to each gaseous atom in one mole, to form one mole of 1– gaseous ions:
>
> $$X(g) + e^- \rightarrow X^-(g)$$

> The **second electron affinity, $\Delta H_{ea2}^{\ominus}$**, is the enthalpy change when one electron is added to each 1– gaseous ion in one mole, to form one mole of gaseous 2– ions:
>
> $$X^-(g) + e^- \rightarrow X^{2-}(g)$$

*Step 5* This step represents the **lattice enthalpy**. The two gaseous ions come together to form the ionic solid, and this is an exothermic change.

$$Li^+(g) + F^-(g) \rightarrow LiF(s)$$

The enthalpy change for this step is usually unknown and has to be calculated.

## How to calculate the lattice enthalpy from a Born–Haber cycle

According to Hess's law,

$$\Delta H_f^{\ominus} = \Delta H_{at}^{\ominus}(Li(s) + \Delta H_{at}^{\ominus}(\tfrac{1}{2}F_2(g)) + \Delta H_{i1}^{\ominus} + \Delta H_{ea1}^{\ominus} + \Delta H_{latt}^{\ominus}$$

This can be rearranged;

> lattice enthalpy $= \Delta H_f^{\ominus} - \Delta H_{at}^{\ominus}(Li(s)) - \Delta H_{at}^{\ominus}(\tfrac{1}{2}F_2(g)) - \Delta H_{i1}^{\ominus} - \Delta H_{ea1}^{\ominus}$

In words, the formula is:

lattice enthalpy = heat of formation – heats of atomisation – ionisation energy – electron affinity

Putting in the figures:

$$\text{lattice enthalpy} = (-617) - (+161) - (+79.5) - (+520)$$
$$- (-328)$$
$$= -1049.5 \text{ kJ mol}^{-1}$$

### SAQ 5.12

Write equations to represent the following enthalpy changes:

- **a** the atomisation of oxygen gas;
- **b** the first ionisation energy of caesium;
- **c** the enthalpy change of formation of potassium chloride;
- **d** the first electron affinity of iodine;
- **e** the atomisation of barium.

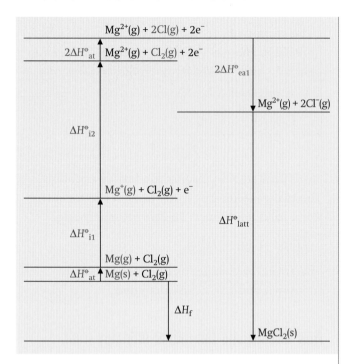

● **Figure 5.20** Born–Haber cycle for magnesium chloride.

## SAQ 5.13

**a** Draw a Born–Haber cycle for sodium chloride, naming each step.

**b** Calculate the lattice enthalpy for sodium chloride, given that

$$\Delta H_f^\ominus \text{ (NaCl)} = -411 \text{ kJ mol}^{-1}$$
$$\Delta H_{at}^\ominus \text{ (Na(g))} = +107 \text{ kJ mol}^{-1}$$
$$\Delta H_{at}^\ominus \text{ } (\tfrac{1}{2}Cl_2(g)) = +121 \text{ kJ mol}^{-1}$$
$$\Delta H_{i1}^\ominus \text{ (Na(g))} = +496 \text{ kJ mol}^{-1}$$
$$\Delta H_{ea1}^\ominus \text{ (Cl(g))} = -348 \text{ kJ mol}^{-1}$$

## The Born–Haber cycle for magnesium chloride

It is important that you know the Born–Haber cycle for sodium chloride, so make sure you have done *SAQ 5.13* and checked the answer. Another Born–Haber cycle you must know is the one shown for magnesium chloride (*figure 5.20*). It is essentially the same as before, with the same type of steps in each path. However, the magnesium ion is $Mg^{2+}$, so the gaseous magnesium atom is ionised *in two stages*:

$$Mg(g) \rightarrow Mg^+(g) + e^-$$

the first ionisation energy, $\Delta H_{i1}^\ominus$

$$Mg^+(g) \rightarrow Mg^{2+}(g) + e^-$$

the second ionisation energy, $\Delta H_{i2}^\ominus$

Whenever an ion is formed, it is done in stages, losing or gaining one electron at a time. So, to get to $Al^{3+}$, you will use three ionisation energies:

$$Al(g) \xrightarrow{\Delta H_{i1}^\ominus} Al^+(g) + e^- \xrightarrow{\Delta H_{i2}^\ominus} Al^{2+}(g) + 2e^- \xrightarrow{\Delta H_{i3}^\ominus} Al^{3+}(g) + 3e^-$$

The same principle applies to anions. To form $O^{2-}$, you will use two electron affinities:

$$O(g) + e^- \xrightarrow{\Delta H_{ea1}^\ominus} O^-(g); \qquad O^-(g) + e^- \xrightarrow{\Delta H_{ea2}^\ominus} O^{2-}(g)$$

One other difference to remember is that two $Cl^-$ ions are present in $MgCl_2$, hence both $2\Delta H_{at}^\ominus$ and $2\Delta H_{ea1}^\ominus$ are required in the Born–Haber cycle for $MgCl_2$.

## SAQ 5.14

Draw Born–Haber cycles for **a** MgO; **b** $Na_2O$.

# Trends in the lattice enthalpy

The lattice enthalpy is the result of electrostatic attractions between ions of opposite charge. The properties of the ions can therefore affect the value of the lattice enthalpy. We will look at two different ways that the lattice enthalpy is affected.

## Size of the ions

The lattice enthalpy becomes *less exothermic* as the size of the ion *increases*.

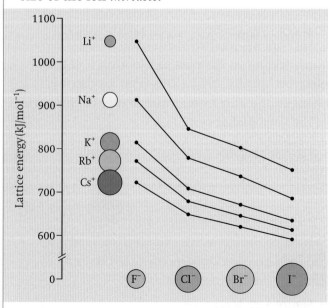

● **Figure 5.21** Lattice enthalpies of the Group I halides.

This applies to both cations and anions. The reason is that as the radius of the ion increases, the attraction between the ions decreases, so the lattice energy is less exothermic. You can see this in *figure 5.21*. The trends in the size of both the cations and the anions are shown, and you can see that the trend in lattice enthalpy is in the opposite direction.

## Charge of the ions

The lattice enthalpy becomes *more exothermic* as the charge on the ion *increases*.

The effect of the charge of the ion on lattice enthalpy can be seen by comparing LiF with MgO. Both solids have the same structure, the $Li^+$ ion is about the same size as the $Mg^{2+}$ ion, and the $F^-$ ion is about the same size as the $O^{2-}$ ion. The only difference between the two solids is the *charge* on the ions. Look at the lattice enthalpies for these two compounds:

LiF    $\Delta H^{\ominus}_{\text{latt}} = -1050 \text{ kJ mol}^{-1}$
MgO   $\Delta H^{\ominus}_{\text{latt}} = -3923 \text{ kJ mol}^{-1}$

They are very different. The lattice enthalpy for magnesium oxide is much more negative, which shows that doubly charged ions attract each other more strongly than singly charged ions.

This exceptionally high exothermic value for the lattice enthalpy of magnesium oxide means it is a very useful compound in certain situations. The lattice is so strong that it takes a great deal of heat to decompose it (the melting point is 2853 °C), and this means magnesium oxide is used to line furnaces – we say it is a refractory lining (*figure 5.22*).

● **Figure 5.22** Magnesium oxide is used as a lining in furnaces.

It is also used in high-temperature windows in furnaces, ceramics, wire coatings and flame-retardant particle boards. The strong lattice also means that magnesium oxide is used in anti-corrosion coatings in tankers which carry chemicals.

### SAQ 5.15

For each pair of compounds, suggest which will have the most exothermic lattice enthalpy.
**a** CaO and $CaCl_2$
**b** KCl and $K_2O$
**c** $BaI_2$ and $SrI_2$

### SAQ 5.16

Place the following compounds in order of increasingly exothermic lattice enthalpy.

$Li_2O$    LiF    MgO

Explain why you have placed them in this order.

# The stability of the Group II carbonates to heat

You may have already studied the Group II elements magnesium to barium (see chapter 10a) and you may have looked at
■ the reaction of magnesium carbonate with acids;
■ the thermal decomposition of calcium carbonate;
■ the formation of calcium carbonate when carbon dioxide gas is bubbled through lime water.
We will now look at the decomposition of the Group II carbonates when they are heated, and see what role the lattice enthalpy plays in determining the temperature at which this decomposition takes place.

The reaction showing the thermal decomposition of the Group II carbonates is

$MgCO_3(s) \rightarrow MgO(s) + CO_2(g)$

This reaction is the same for all the Group II metals.

*Figure 5.23* shows that the trend is increasing decomposition temperatures as the group is descended. $MgCO_3$ decomposes at 350 °C, $BaCO_3$ at 1450 °C. Let's think about this trend. What can we suggest about the lattice enthalpies of magnesium carbonate and barium carbonate?

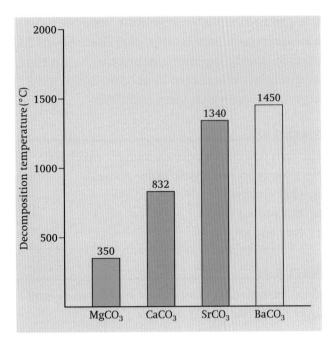

● **Figure 5.23** Decomposition temperatures of Group II carbonates.

■ MgCO₃ has the smallest cation and therefore the *most exothermic* lattice enthalpy (−3123 kJ mol⁻¹).

■ BaCO₃ has the largest cation and therefore the *least exothermic* lattice enthalpy (−2556 kJ mol⁻¹).

But these lattice enthalpies suggest that MgCO₃ has the strongest lattice and should therefore have the highest decomposition temperature.

Another factor must be considered – it is the effect of the cation's charge density on the large carbonate anion. The lattice structure of magnesium carbonate is weaker than the lattice structure of barium carbonate, and this is caused by the charge density of the cation **polarising** the anion. You have met this polarisation of the anion before in chapter 3. Let's go through the reasons for this again.

■ The small magnesium cation has a large charge density and so it has the greatest ability to polarise the carbonate ion. The cation pulls electron density from the O atoms of the $CO_3^{2-}$ ion towards it:

$\text{Mg}^{2+}$ $\text{CO}_3^{2-}$ small $Mg^{2+}$ ion polarises larger $CO_3^{2-}$ ion

■ The larger barium cation has a lower charge density so it polarises the carbonate anion to a lesser extent:

$\text{Ba}^{2+}$ $\text{CO}_3^{2-}$ ions same size – no polarisation

■ The greater the polarising power of the cation, the more distorted the $CO_3^{2-}$ ion becomes.
■ The distorted $CO_3^{2-}$ breaks up into $CO_2$ and $O^{2-}$ more readily.
■ As a result, the MgCO₃ lattice is less strong than the BaCO₃ lattice and decomposes at a lower temperature.

## SAQ 5.17

Explain why the decomposition temperature of calcium nitrate is higher than the decomposition temperature of magnesium nitrate.

## SUMMARY (A2)

◆ The lattice enthalpy of an ionic solid is the energy change when gaseous ions form a solid lattice.

◆ Lattice enthalpies are exothermic. A strong lattice has a more exothermic lattice enthalpy than a weak lattice.

◆ Lattice enthalpies can be calculated from a Born–Haber cycle, which is a type of Hess's law cycle.

◆ Each step of the Born–Haber cycle is a separate enthalpy change.

◆ The standard enthalpy change of atomisation of an element is the enthalpy change when one mole of gaseous atoms are formed from the element in its standard state.

◆ The value of the lattice enthalpy is affected by the size of the ions making up the lattice, and also by their charge.

◆ Magnesium oxide is an example of an ionic solid with a large exothermic lattice enthalpy, and therefore it has many uses.

◆ The Group II carbonates decompose at increasingly high temperatures as the group is descended.

◆ The reason for this trend can be explained by considering the charge density of the cation and the degree of polarisation of the anion.

# Questions (A2)

**4 a** In ionic compounds with certain metals, hydrogen exists as the hydride ion, $H^-$. Calculate the electron affinity of hydrogen ($\Delta H^\ominus$ for the reaction $H(g) + e^- \rightarrow H^-(g)$) by constructing a Born–Haber cycle for sodium hydride, NaH. Name each enthalpy change in the cycle.

$Na(s) \rightarrow Na(g)$
   $\Delta H^\ominus = +108 \text{ kJ mol}^{-1}$
$H_2(g) \rightarrow 2H(g)$
   $\Delta H^\ominus = +436 \text{ kJ mol}^{-1}$
$Na(g) \rightarrow Na^+(g) + e^-$
   $\Delta H^\ominus = +496 \text{ kJ mol}^{-1}$
$Na(s) + \frac{1}{2}H_2(g) \rightarrow NaH(s)$
   $\Delta H^\ominus = -57 \text{ kJ mol}^{-1}$
$Na^+(g) + H^-(g) \rightarrow NaH(s)$
   $\Delta H^\ominus = -812 \text{ kJ mol}^{-1}$ (lattice enthalpy)

**b** State and explain how the lattice enthalpies of KH and $MgH_2$ compare with the lattice enthalpy of NaH.

**5 a** Write an equation, including state symbols, showing the decomposition of barium carbonate.

**b** The decomposition temperature of barium carbonate is 1450°C. Estimate the decomposition temperature of magnesium carbonate.

**c** Explain why magnesium carbonate has a **more exothermic** lattice enthalpy than barium carbonate.

**d** Explain why magnesium carbonate has a **lower decomposition temperature** than barium carbonate.

**e** (i) Give one use of the compound magnesium oxide.
   (ii) Explain why it is suitable for this use.

# Electrochemistry (AS)

## By the end of this section you should be able to:

1 describe and explain redox processes in terms of electron transfer and/or of changes in oxidation state (oxidation number);

2 explain, including the electrode reactions, the industrial processes of:
- the electrolysis of brine, using a diaphragm cell,
- the extraction of aluminium from molten aluminium oxide/cryolite,
- the electrolytic purification of copper.

## Oxidation states

When you look at the formulae of many compounds you see that there are differences in the ratios of the atoms that combine with each other – MgO and $Al_2O_3$, for example. Chemists have devised various ways for comparing the 'combining ability' of individual elements. One term, much used in the past, but less so nowadays, is valency meaning 'strength'. The more useful measure is **oxidation state**. This is a numerical value associated with atoms of each element in a compound or ion. Some chemists prefer the term **oxidation number** (abbreviated ox. no.). The only difference between this and oxidation state is that we say an atom '*has* an oxidation number of +2' but 'is *in* an oxidation state of +2'.

There are rules for determining the values of oxidation states.

- Oxidation states are usually calculated as the number of electrons that atoms lose, gain or share when they form ionic or covalent bonds in compounds.
- The oxidation state of uncombined elements (that is, not in compounds) is always zero. For example, each atom in $H_2(g)$ or $O_2(g)$ or $Na(s)$ or $S_8(s)$ has an oxidation state of zero; otherwise, in a compound the numbers are always given a sign, + or −.
- For a monatomic ion, the oxidation state of the element is simply the same as the charge on the ion. For example:

| ion | $Na^+$ | $Ca^{2+}$ | $Cl^-$ | $O^{2-}$ |
|---|---|---|---|---|
| ox. state | +1 | +2 | −1 | −2 |

- In a chemical species (compound or ion), with atoms of more than one element, the most electronegative element is given the negative oxidation state. Other elements are given positive oxidation states. (For an explanation of the term 'electronegative', see chapter 3.) For example, in the compound disulphur dichloride, $S_2Cl_2$, chlorine is more electronegative than sulphur. The two chlorine atoms each have an oxidation state of −1, and thus the two sulphur atoms each have an oxidation state of +1.
- The oxidation state of hydrogen in compounds is +1, except in metal hydrides (e.g. NaH), when it is −1.
- The oxidation state of oxygen in compounds is −2, except in peroxides (e.g. $H_2O_2$), when it is −1, or in $OF_2$, when it is +2.
- The sum of all the oxidation states in a neutral compound is zero. In an ion, the sum equals the overall charge. For example, the sum of the oxidation states in $CaCl_2$ is 0; the sum of the oxidation states in $OH^-$ is −1.

Some examples of determining oxidation states will now be shown:

In $CO_2$     the ox. state of each O atom is −2, giving a total of −4
$CO_2$ is neutral
the ox. state of C is +4

In MgCl$_2$    the ox. state of Mg is +2
the ox. state of each Cl is −1

In NO$_3^-$    the ox. state of each O is −2
total for O$_3$ is −6
the overall charge on the ion is −1
therefore ox. state of N in NO$_3^-$ is +5

## SAQ 6.1

What is the oxidation state of: C in CO$_3^{2-}$; Al in Al$_2$Cl$_6$?

# Redox: oxidation and reduction

The term **redox** is used for the simultaneous processes of *reduction* and *oxidation*. Originally oxidation and reduction were related only to reactions of oxygen and hydrogen. They now include any reactions in which electrons are transferred.

For example, consider what happens when iron reacts with oxygen and with chlorine.

(i) with oxygen:
$$4Fe(s) + 3O_2(g) \rightarrow 2Fe_2O_3(s)$$

(ii) with chlorine:
$$2Fe(s) + 3Cl_2(g) \rightarrow 2FeCl_3(s)$$

In both of these reactions, each iron atom has lost three electrons and changed oxidation state from 0 in Fe(s) to +3 in Fe$_2$O$_3$(s) and FeCl$_3$(s).

$$Fe \rightarrow Fe^{3+} + 3e^-$$
ox. state      0      +3

This is **oxidation**. In all oxidation reactions, atoms of an element in a chemical species lose electrons and increase their oxidation states.

In reaction (i) above, the oxygen atoms each gain two electrons and change oxidation state from 0 in O$_2$(g) to −2 in Fe$_2$O$_3$(s).

$$O_2 + 4e^- \rightarrow 2O^{2-}$$
ox. state of atoms      0      −2

Similarly, in reaction (ii), chlorine atoms each gain one electron and change oxidation state from 0 to −1.

$$Cl_2 + 2e^- \rightarrow 2Cl^-$$
ox. state of atoms      0      −1

These are processes of **reduction**. In all reduction reactions, atoms of an element in a chemical species gain electrons and decrease their oxidation states.

We call reactions, such as (i) and (ii) above, redox reactions, as both oxidation and reduction take place at the same time. Any chemical system in which the oxidised and reduced forms of a chemical species exist is a redox system. The chemical that *gains* electrons acts as an oxidising agent; the chemical that *loses* electrons acts as a reducing agent.

# Electrolysis

Electrical conduction in a metal takes place by electrons moving through the metal lattice (see chapter 3). No chemical changes occur.

When an electric current (a d.c. supply) is passed through a solution of an ionic salt in water, the ions move through the solution and chemical changes occur at the electrodes. This process is called **electrolysis**. An example of electrolysis is passing a current through water containing a small amount of dilute sulphuric acid, using platinum electrodes, as shown in *figure 6.1*.

The ions present in the solution are H$^+$, OH$^-$ and a small quantity of SO$_4^{2-}$ ions. The anions are attracted to the positively charged **anode** and the cations are attracted to the negatively charged **cathode**.

At the anode, OH$^-$ ions lose electrons and are oxidised to oxygen. Water is also formed.

$$4OH^- \rightarrow O_2 + 2H_2O + 4e^-$$

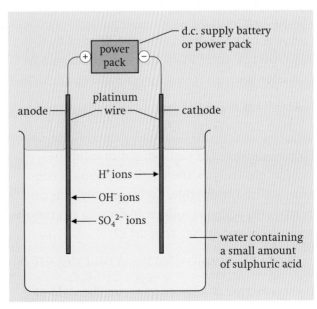

● **Figure 6.1** The movement of ions during electrolysis.

At the cathode, $H^+$ ions gain electrons and are reduced to hydrogen.

$$2H^+ + 2e^- \rightarrow H_2$$

The electrons released by $OH^-$ ions at the anode are driven round the external circuit by the power packs, so that they are available at the cathode.

Any sulphate ions will stay in solution. Since they contain sulphur in its highest oxidation state, they cannot be oxidised at the anode.

# The uses of electrolysis in industry

Electrolysis is widely used in industry. It can be used to bring about chemical decomposition with the formation of new compounds, as in the electrolysis of brine. Very reactive metals, such as magnesium and aluminium, are extracted from their molten compounds by electrolysis, which is also used to purify metals such as copper.

## The electrolysis of brine using a diaphragm cell

When brine, concentrated aqueous sodium chloride, is electrolysed, chlorine is given off at the anode and hydrogen is given off at the cathode. The solution that remains is sodium hydroxide.

At the anode, chlorine gas is formed from chloride ions.

$$2Cl^-(aq) \rightarrow Cl_2(g) + 2e^-$$

Sodium ions, $Na^+(aq)$, from the sodium chloride, remain in solution.

At the cathode, hydrogen ions, formed by the ionisation of water molecules, are discharged as hydrogen gas.

$$H_2O \rightleftharpoons H^+(aq) + OH^-(aq)$$
$$2H^+ + 2e^- \rightarrow H_2(g)$$

Hydroxide ions, $OH^-(aq)$, remain in solution.

After electrolysis, the resulting solution contains sodium hydroxide. Unfortunately, chlorine reacts with aqueous sodium hydroxide to produce sodium chlorate(I) (see chapter 12).

$$Cl_2(g) + 2NaOH(aq) \rightarrow NaClO(aq) + NaCl(aq) + H_2O(l)$$

If this reaction is allowed to occur, the yield of chlorine will be reduced and the cost of production of chlorine will be greater. To prevent this

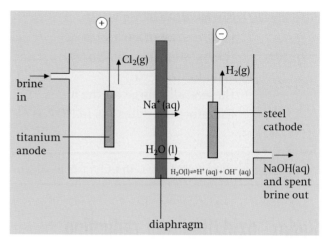

● **Figure 6.2** A diaphragm cell for the electrolysis of brine.

reaction from occurring, a diaphragm cell is used, which physically keeps the chlorine and the aqueous sodium hydroxide separate. This is shown in *figure 6.2* (see also *figure 3.4*).

In the diaphragm cell, a porous asbestos diaphragm separates the anode compartment from the cathode compartment. Brine is pumped into the anode compartment, which contains a titanium anode. The liquid in the anode compartment is kept at a higher level than in the cathode compartment, where there is a steel cathode.

In the anode compartment, chloride ions are discharged and chlorine gas produced. Sodium ions pass through the diaphragm to the cathode compartment. Here hydrogen ions are discharged, producing hydrogen gas and causing the equilibrium

$$H_2O(l) \rightleftharpoons H^+(aq) + OH^-(aq)$$

to produce $OH^-(aq)$ ions.

The liquid which leaves the cell contains sodium hydroxide, together with some unreacted sodium chloride. These are separated by causing the less soluble sodium chloride to crystallise out, leaving a solution of sodium hydroxide.

The three products of this process, sodium hydroxide, chlorine and hydrogen, are all industrially important (*figure 6.3*).

## The extraction of aluminium from molten aluminium ions

Aluminium is the third most abundant metal in the Earth's crust, occurring widely as the impure oxide, $Al_2O_3$. Bauxite is the major ore of

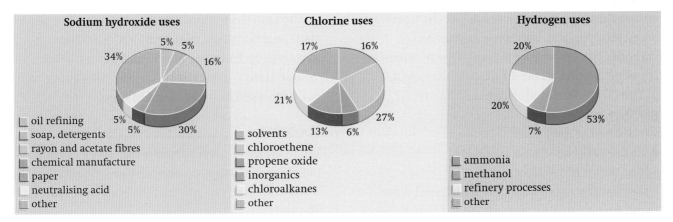

● **Figure 6.3** The industrial uses of the products of the electrolysis of brine.

aluminium and contains up to 60% of the oxide, with the common impurities being iron(III) oxide and silicon dioxide.

Early nineteenth century attempts to obtain aluminium from bauxite involved reducing the oxide with reactive metals such as sodium. Since sodium is obtained by electrolysis, it followed that electrolysis could also be used to obtain aluminium. In the modern industrial process, bauxite is first purified before electrolysis occurs. As bauxite has a very high melting point (2050 °C), it is dissolved in molten cryolite, $Na_3AlF_6$, at 950 °C. This solution is then electrolysed using carbon electrodes, as shown in *figure 6.4*.

Aluminium oxide is added to the top of the electrolytic cell, forming a solid crust which slowly dissolves in the molten cryolite.

At the graphite cathode lining the cell, aluminium ions are reduced.

$$Al^{3+} + 3e^- \rightarrow Al$$

The molten aluminium is removed from the bottom of the cell.

The reactions at the graphite anodes are complex and may be simplified as follows:

$$2O^{2-} \rightarrow O_2 + 4e^-$$

The oxygen reacts with the graphite anodes, forming carbon dioxide. The anodes will, therefore, wear away with time.

Aluminium is light, strong and resistant to corrosion. It is widely used in transport (aeroplanes, trains, coaches), food packaging and electricity power lines. Aluminium metal is easily recycled at low cost (see also chapter 4).

## The electrolytic purification of copper

Metallic copper obtained by smelting copper sulphide ores is 98–99% pure. For use in electrical wiring the impurities must be removed in order to increase the conductivity of the copper. This is

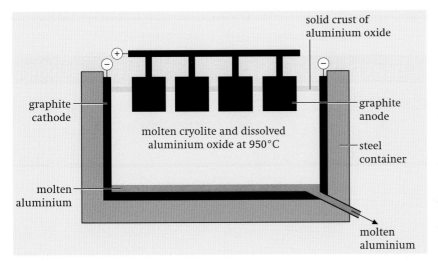

● **Figure 6.4** The extraction of aluminium by electrolysis. The photo shows an aluminium plant in Norway.

done by making the impure copper the anode of an electrolysis cell, with pure copper as the cathode. The electrolyte is a solution of aqueous copper(II) sulphate and dilute sulphuric acid.

The electrode reactions are as follows:

- at the anode

$$Cu(s) \rightarrow Cu^{2+}(aq) + 2e^-$$

- at the cathode

$$Cu^{2+}(aq) + 2e^- \rightarrow Cu(s)$$

Note that the anode reaction is different from those previously described. Instead of an anion being discharged with the loss of electrons, a cation is formed from a metal with the loss of electrons. Both of these processes are examples of oxidation.

The common impurities in copper are metals such as gold, silver, platinum and tin. These metals drop from the anode and form a solid 'anode sludge' beneath the anode. This is periodically removed and the elements recovered.

## SAQ 6.2

When aqueous silver nitrate is electrolysed using platinum electrodes, a colourless gas is produced at the anode. This gas will rekindle a glowing splint. The cathode increases in size.

Write half-equations for the reactions that occur:
a at the anode
b at the cathode.

# SUMMARY (AS)

- Oxidation Is Loss of electrons (OIL)
  Reduction Is Gain of electrons (RIG)
  This can be remembered as OILRIG

- Electrolysis only occurs in molten liquids and solutions. In an electrolytic cell the anode is positive and the cathode is negative. Anions migrate to the anode and cations migrate to the cathode.

- Electrons are released to the external circuit at the anode, e.g.

$$Cl^-(aq) \rightarrow \tfrac{1}{2}Cl_2(g) + e^-$$

or

$$Cu(s) \rightarrow Cu^{2+} + 2e^-$$

Oxidation therefore takes place at the anode.

- Electrons from the external circuit are used in the discharge of positive ions at the cathode. e.g.

$$Cu^{2+}(aq) + 2e^- \rightarrow Cu(s)$$

Reduction takes place at the cathode.

# Questions (AS)

1 a Draw and label the apparatus you would use to electrolyse molten lead bromide, $PbBr_2$.

b Write half-equations for the reactions which occur at the electrodes.

# Electrochemistry (A2)

## By the end of this section you should be able to:

3  define the terms:
- standard electrode (redox) potential;
- standard cell potential;

4  describe the standard hydrogen electrode;

5  describe methods used to measure the standard electrode potentials of:
- metals or non-metals in contact with their ions in aqueous solution;
- ions of the same element in different oxidation states;

6  calculate a standard cell potential by combining two standard electrode potentials;

7  use standard cell potentials to:
- explain/deduce the direction of electron flow from a simple cell;
- predict the feasibility of a reaction;

8  construct redox equations using the relevant half-equations;

9  predict qualitatively how the value of an electrode potential varies with the concentration of the aqueous ion;

10  state the possible advantages of developing other types of cell, e.g. the $H_2/O_2$ fuel cell and improved batteries (as in electric vehicles) in terms of smaller size, lower mass and higher voltage;

11  state the relationship, $F = Le$, between the Faraday constant, the Avogadro constant and the charge on the electron;

12  predict the identity of the substance liberated during electrolysis from the state of electrolyte (molten or aqueous), position in the redox series (electrode potential) and concentration;

13  calculate:
- the quantity of charge passed during electrolysis;
- the mass and/or volume of substance liberated during electrolysis, including those in the electrolysis of $H_2SO_4(aq)$ and $Na_2SO_4(aq)$;

14  describe the determination of a value of the Avogadro constant by an electrolytic method.

# Electrode potentials

Reduction reactions involve a substance gaining electrons. For example, metal ions can gain electrons in reactions and be reduced to metals, e.g.

$$Cu^{2+} + 2e^- \rightleftharpoons Cu$$

$$V^{2+} + 2e^- \rightleftharpoons V$$

Equations of this sort are called **half-equations**.

Some metals ions, such as $Cu^{2+}$ ions, are very easy to reduce like this, while other metal ions, such as $V^{2+}$ ions, are much harder. Fortunately for us, we can measure the ease with which the reduction takes place – we are not restricted to simple comparative words like 'easier' and 'harder'. The measured value is called the **electrode potential** for this reduction. It is measured in volts (V) and is a numerical indication of how favourable (or 'easy') the reduction is. Note that it is a convention that electrode potentials refer to the reduction reaction.

■ If the electrode potential is a more positive voltage the ion on the left is comparatively easy to reduce. For

$$Cu^{2+} + 2e^- \rightleftharpoons Cu$$

the voltage is +0.34 V.

■ If the electrode potential is a more negative voltage the ion on the left is comparatively hard to reduce. For

$$V^{2+} + 2e^- \rightleftharpoons V$$

the voltage is −1.20 V.

Therefore, it is easier to reduce $Cu^{2+}$ ions to Cu atoms than it is to reduce $V^{2+}$ ions to V atoms.

Remember the convention that electrode potentials refer to reduction reactions. In the reaction above, −1.20 V refers to

$$V^{2+} + 2e^- \rightleftharpoons V$$

the reduction reaction, and not to

$$V \rightleftharpoons V^{2+} + 2e^-$$

which would be an oxidation.

## How is the voltage for $Cu^{2+} + 2e^- \rightleftharpoons Cu$ measured?

In order to measure the electrode potential in volts for this reduction, a rod of pure copper must be placed in a 1.00 mol dm$^{-3}$ solution of $Cu^{2+}$ ions

copper rod

$Cu^{2+}$, 1 mol dm$^{-3}$
298 K

● **Figure 6.5** The $Cu^{2+}$/Cu half-cell.

(e.g. copper(II) sulphate solution) at a temperature of 25 °C (298 K) (*figure 6.5*). Unfortunately, the electrode potential cannot be measured using this set-up alone. The $Cu^{2+}$/Cu system described here cannot gain or lose electrons unless it is connected electrically to a similar system that will either provide or take up these electrons. The $Cu^{2+}$/Cu system is called a **half-cell**.

In order to work as required and give us a measure of how easy it is to reduce $Cu^{2+}$ ions to Cu atoms this half-cell *must* be connected to another half-cell. Connecting two half-cells together makes an **electrochemical cell**. An electrochemical cell has a voltage that can be measured and can be used to produce electrical energy and light a bulb. The sort of batteries that go in torches are simply cleverly packaged electrochemical cells. For convenience their wet ingredients are included in paste form, so they are called 'dry cells'.

# Standard electrode potentials

If the $Cu^{2+}$/Cu half-cell described above is connected electrically to another half-cell then a complete electrochemical cell has been created and the cell voltage can be measured. If the other half-cell consists of a 1.00 mol dm$^{-3}$ solution of $H^+$ ions in contact with hydrogen gas at 1 atmosphere pressure, all at a temperature of 298 K, then the voltage measured is called the **standard electrode potential** for the reaction

$$Cu^{2+} + 2e^- \rightleftharpoons Cu$$

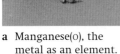

**a** Manganese(0), the metal as an element.  **b** Manganese(II), as a $Mn^{2+}$ solution.  **c** Manganese(III), as a $Mn^{3+}$ solution.  **d** Manganese(IV), as solid $MnO_2$.  **e** Manganese(VI), as the $MnO_4^{2-}$ ion.  **f** Manganese(VII), as the $MnO_4^-$ ion.

● **Figure 6.6** The various oxidation states of manganese.

The $H^+/H_2$ half-cell is called a **standard hydrogen electrode**.

A second half-cell of some kind is used because it is impossible to measure the voltage of the $Cu^{2+}/Cu$ half-cell on its own. A standard hydrogen electrode in particular is used as the second half-cell when measuring standard electrode potentials because this is what chemists have agreed upon. There is nothing particularly special about the $H^+/H_2$ half-cell, although the fact that it was chosen in this way gives it a special place in electrochemistry.

This seems like quite a fiddly way to collect data, but the data collected are *very* useful.

Manganese can form stable compounds in *five* different oxidation states (*figure 6.6*). Using standard electrode potential data it is possible to predict accurately which oxidation state of manganese forms in any particular reaction.

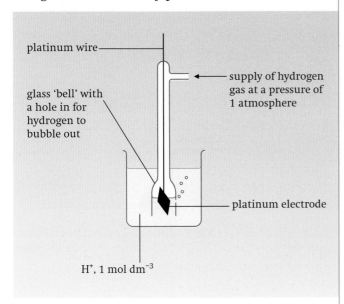

platinum wire

glass 'bell' with a hole in for hydrogen to bubble out

supply of hydrogen gas at a pressure of 1 atmosphere

platinum electrode

$H^+$, 1 mol dm$^{-3}$

● **Figure 6.7** The standard hydrogen electrode.

## The standard hydrogen electrode

A standard hydrogen electrode is shown in *figure 6.7*. Hydrogen gas is introduced into the standard hydrogen electrode at the top and bubbles out slowly from a hole in the glass bell. The platinum electrode allows electrical contact to be made. Platinum ensures good contact between $H^+$ ions and $H_2$ molecules so that electrode reactions occur quickly, but being an inert metal it does not take part in any reactions itself. The platinum electrode needs to be coated with finely divided platinum (known as platinum black).

The two possible electrode reactions here are

$$H^+ + e^- \rightarrow \tfrac{1}{2}H_2$$

if the other half-cell gives electrons to the standard hydrogen electrode, or

$$\tfrac{1}{2}H_2 \rightarrow H^+ + e^-$$

if the standard hydrogen electrode gives electrons to the other half-cell.

The standard hydrogen electrode is used as a **standard reference electrode** – if it is connected to another half-cell then the electrode potential of the other half-cell can be measured *relative* to the voltage of the standard hydrogen electrode. It is a lot like measuring the height of a mountain – the height is always given relative to sea level.

## Measuring a standard electrode potential

If all concentrations are 1.00 mol dm$^{-3}$, if the temperature is 298 K and if the pressures of any gases used are 1 atmosphere, then these conditions are

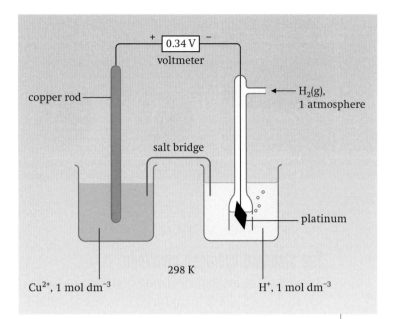

● **Figure 6.8** Measuring the standard electrode potential of a $Cu^{2+}/Cu$ half-cell.

called **standard conditions**. If an electrochemical cell is made up under standard conditions, using a standard hydrogen electrode as one half-cell and the half-cell under investigation as the second half-cell, then the voltage measured is the standard electrode potential of the half-cell under investigation (*figure 6.8*).

The **salt bridge** in *figure 6.8* is there to complete the electric circuit. A simple salt bridge can be made by soaking a piece of filter paper in potassium nitrate solution. The salt bridge completes the electric circuit by allowing movement of ions between the two half-cells. It does not allow the movement of electrons – these flow via the external circuit only.

The voltage of this electrochemical cell is 0.34 V, with the copper half-cell as the positive terminal and the hydrogen half-cell as the negative terminal. Since conditions are standard and the other half-cell is a standard hydrogen electrode, this means that +0.34 V is the standard electrode potential for the half-cell reaction

$$Cu^{2+} + 2e^- \rightleftharpoons Cu$$

This value of +0.34 V gives a numerical indication of the tendency of $Cu^{2+}$ ions to receive electrons, and of Cu atoms to lose electrons. It can be used to predict with accuracy which reactions $Cu^{2+}$ ions and Cu atoms will take part in.

The voltage of the electrochemical cell shown in *figure 6.9* is 0.76 V, with the zinc half-cell as the negative terminal and the hydrogen half-cell as the positive terminal. Since conditions are standard and the other half-cell is a standard hydrogen electrode, this means that −0.76 V is the standard electrode potential for the half-cell reaction

$$Zn^{2+} + 2e^- \rightleftharpoons Zn$$

(Remember the convention that half-equations are written as reductions.) This value of −0.76 V gives a numerical value of the tendency of $Zn^{2+}$ ions to receive electrons, and of Zn atoms to lose electrons. Since it is a more negative value than the value for $Cu^{2+}/Cu$ it means that $Zn^{2+}$ has a *lower* tendency to gain electrons than $Cu^{2+}$ has, and zinc has a *greater* tendency to lose electrons than copper has. This will be explained further in the section 'The meaning of $E^\ominus$ values' (page 105). The way in which standard electrode potential values can be used is explained further in the section 'Using $E^\ominus$ values to predict whether or not a reaction will occur' (page 108).

> The standard electrode potential for a half-cell reaction can therefore be defined as the voltage measured under standard conditions when the half-cell is incorporated into an electrochemical cell with the other half-cell being a standard hydrogen electrode.

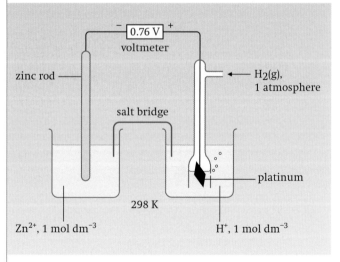

● **Figure 6.9** Measuring the standard electrode potential of a $Zn^{2+}/Zn$ half-cell.

The symbol for a standard electrode potential is $E^{\ominus}$, usually pronounced 'E nought' or 'E standard', with the $^{\ominus}$ sign representing standard conditions. We can therefore write:

$$Cu^{2+} + 2e^- \rightleftharpoons Cu; \qquad E^{\ominus} = +0.34\,V$$
$$Zn^{2+} + 2e^- \rightleftharpoons Zn; \qquad E^{\ominus} = -0.76\,V$$

### SAQ 6.3

Look at the electrochemical cells shown in *figure 6.10*.

**a** Write equations for the half-cell reactions in the half-cells on the left of each diagram (i.e. *not* the standard hydrogen electrode). Write each equation as a reduction (gain of electrons), e.g.

$$Zn^{2+} + 2e^- \rightleftharpoons Zn$$

**b** What are the standard electrode potentials for these half-cell reactions?

**c** List all necessary conditions in each cell.

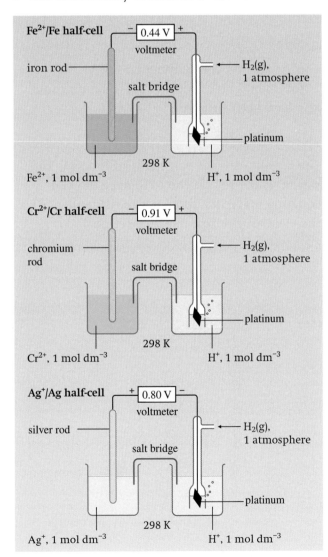

● **Figure 6.10**

The standard electrode potential for a half-cell reaction is the measured voltage of an electrochemical cell consisting of the half-cell and a standard hydrogen electrode. All conditions must be standard. The polarity of the half-cell within this electrochemical cell gives the sign of the standard electrode potential.

## Measuring standard electrode potentials involving two ions

We have considered how the standard electrode potential of a metal in contact with one of its ions can be measured. Standard electrode potentials can also be measured for reductions in which both the species involved are ions. For example:

$$Fe^{3+} + e^- \rightleftharpoons Fe^{2+}$$

The half-cell that is used here must contain *both* $Fe^{2+}$ ions and $Fe^{3+}$ ions, both at a concentration of $1.00\,mol\,dm^{-3}$. A platinum wire or platinum foil electrode is used to make electrical contact with the solution. The $Fe^{3+}/Fe^{2+}$ half-cell is then made into an electrochemical cell with a standard hydrogen electrode as the other half-cell. The measured voltage, the $E^{\ominus}$ value, is +0.77 V (*figure 6.11*).

Some reductions involve several ionic species. For example:

$$MnO_4^- + 8H^+ + 5e^- \rightleftharpoons Mn^{2+} + 4H_2O$$

The inclusion of $H^+$ ions here means that acid conditions are necessary for the reduction of $MnO_4^-$ ions (manganate(VII) ions) to $Mn^{2+}$ ions. In order to

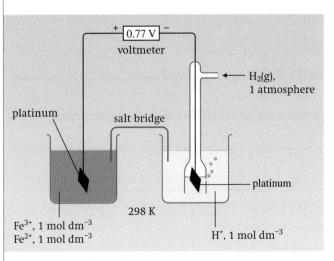

● **Figure 6.11** Measuring the standard electrode potential of an $Fe^{3+}/Fe^{2+}$ half-cell.

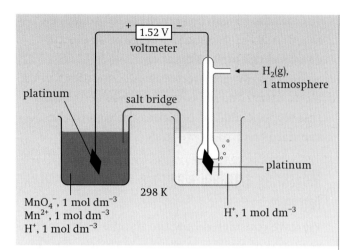

● **Figure 6.12** Measuring the standard electrode potential of an $MnO_4^-/Mn^{2+}$ half-cell.

measure the $E^\ominus$ value for this half-cell, the concentrations of $MnO_4^-$ ions, $H^+$ ions and $Mn^{2+}$ ions must all be $1.00\,mol\,dm^{-3}$. Once again electrical contact is made with a platinum wire or platinum foil electrode. If the voltage to be measured is to be the standard electrode potential for the $MnO_4^-/Mn^{2+}$ half-cell, then the other half-cell must be a standard hydrogen electrode and all conditions must be standard (*figure 6.12*).

## SAQ 6.4

What is the $E^\ominus$ value for the half-cell shown by this equation?

$$MnO_4^- + 8H^+ + 5e^- \rightleftharpoons Mn^{2+} + 4H_2O$$

## SAQ 6.5

What are standard conditions?

## SAQ 6.6

Why is platinum used in preference to other metals in half-cells where the reaction itself does not involve a metal element?

## SAQ 6.7

Show, with the aid of a diagram, how you would measure the $E^\ominus$ value for the half-cell shown by this equation:

$$VO^{2+} + 2H^+ + e^- \rightleftharpoons V^{3+} + H_2O$$

## Measuring standard electrode potentials involving non-metals

We can also measure the standard electrode potential for a non-metallic element in contact with a solution of its aqueous ions. As with measuring the standard electrode potential of two ions of the same element in different oxidation states, one difficulty here is how to make electrical contact. The answer again is to use a platinum wire.

The platinum wire must be in contact with both the element and the aqueous ions. The standard electrode potential is measured by connecting the half-cell to a standard hydrogen electrode and measuring the voltage produced under standard conditions.

The half-cell on the left of *figure 6.13* involves chlorine gas and chloride ions. The half-equation is therefore

$$\tfrac{1}{2}Cl_2 + e^- \rightleftharpoons Cl^-$$

The $E^\ominus$ value for this half-cell is $+1.36\,V$.

You should note that the half-equation could also have been written

$$Cl_2 + 2e^- \rightleftharpoons 2Cl^-$$

The $E^\ominus$ value for this half-cell is still $+1.36\,V$. The way in which you choose to balance the half-equation makes no difference to the tendency for the element chlorine to gain electrons!

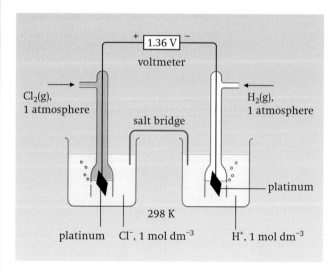

● **Figure 6.13** Measuring the standard electrode potential of a $Cl_2/Cl^-$ half-cell.

## SAQ 6.8

Look at the diagram in *figure 6.14* and write a half-equation for the half-cell on the left. What is the $E^\ominus$ value for this half-cell?

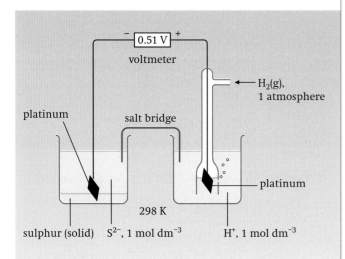

● **Figure 6.14** Measuring the standard electrode potential of an $S/S^{2-}$ half-cell.

## SAQ 6.9

Draw a diagram to show how you would measure the standard electrode potential for the half-cell

$$\tfrac{1}{2}I_2 + e^- \rightleftharpoons I^-$$

Include the actual $E^\ominus$ value of $+0.54\,V$ on your diagram.

If a cell is made using two identical half-cells, the voltage measured is always zero volts. This means that measuring the $E^\ominus$ for the half-cell

$$H^+ + e^- \rightleftharpoons \tfrac{1}{2}H_2$$

gives a value of $0.00\,V$. This value arises because of our choice of a standard hydrogen electrode as reference electrode, but it is still a relevant and useful piece of data.

# The meaning of $E^\ominus$ values

The previous section on measuring $E^\ominus$ values has explained how standard electrode potentials are measured using a half-cell, a standard hydrogen electrode, a salt bridge and a voltmeter. This section begins to explain how useful this data is to us.

$E^\ominus$ values give us a measure of how easy a reduction or oxidation is to carry out. (In this context 'easy' refers to the strength of oxidising or reducing agent required to make a change happen. If a species is 'easy' to oxidise it can be oxidised by a weaker oxidising agent.) This can be summarised in three ways.

■ The more positive a value of $E^\ominus$ is, the greater the tendency for this half-equation to proceed in a forward direction.

■ The more positive the value of $E^\ominus$, the easier it is to reduce the species on the left of the half-equation.

■ The less positive the value of $E^\ominus$, the easier it is to oxidise the species on the right of the half-equation.

Consider the following two half-equations as examples:

$$Cu^{2+} + 2e^- \rightleftharpoons Cu; \qquad\qquad E^\ominus = +0.34\,V$$
$$Zn^{2+} + 2e^- \rightleftharpoons Zn; \qquad\qquad E^\ominus = -0.76\,V$$

■ Comparing the two half-equations, $Cu^{2+}/Cu$ has a greater tendency to proceed in the forward direction, as its $E^\ominus$ value is more positive. $Zn^{2+}/Zn$ has a greater tendency to proceed in the backward direction, as its $E^\ominus$ value is more negative (*figure 6.15*).

■ The $Cu^{2+}/Cu$ half-equation has the more positive $E^\ominus$ value, so $Cu^{2+}$ is easier to reduce to Cu than $Zn^{2+}$ is to Zn. $Zn^{2+}$ ions *can* be reduced to Zn metal, but this requires a stronger reducing agent, with a more negative $E^\ominus$ value than the $E^\ominus$ value for $Zn^{2+}/Zn$.

■ The $Zn^{2+}/Zn$ half-equation has the less positive $E^\ominus$ value, so Zn is easier to oxidise to $Zn^{2+}$ than

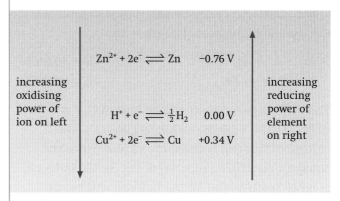

● **Figure 6.15** Comparing the oxidising power of ions and the reducing power of elements.

Cu is to $Cu^{2+}$. Cu metal *can* be oxidised to $Cu^{2+}$ ions, but it requires a stronger oxidising agent, with a more positive $E^{\ominus}$ value than the $E^{\ominus}$ value for $Cu^{2+}/Cu$.

## SAQ 6.10

Use the $E^{\ominus}$ data from page 107 to answer this question.

**a** Of the ions $Ag^+$, $Cr^{3+}$ and $Fe^{2+}$, which one needs the strongest reducing agent to reduce it to uncharged metal atoms?

**b** Of the atoms Ag, Cr and Fe, which one needs the strongest oxidising agent to oxidise it to an ion?

# Using $E^{\ominus}$ values to predict cell voltages

You have learnt how the $E^{\ominus}$ value of a half-cell can be measured and what the $E^{\ominus}$ value can tell us about how easy it is to oxidise or reduce a particular species. $E^{\ominus}$ values can also be used to calculate the voltage of an electrochemical cell made of two half-cells, and to predict whether or not a particular reaction occurs. This section deals with cell voltages.

To recap, if an electrochemical cell is made using two half-cells, standard conditions and a salt bridge, and if one of the half-cells is a standard hydrogen electrode then the voltage measured is the standard electrode potential of the other half-cell. However, if two half-cells are used, neither of which is a standard hydrogen electrode, then the voltage measured will be the *difference* in the $E^{\ominus}$ values of the two half-cells.

For the electrochemical cell shown in *figure 6.16*, the standard electrode potentials are:

$Ag^+ + e^- \rightleftharpoons Ag$;          $E^{\ominus} = +0.80\,V$
$Zn^{2+} + 2e^- \rightleftharpoons Zn$;          $E^{\ominus} = -0.76\,V$

The difference between $+0.80\,V$ and $-0.76\,V$ is $+1.56\,V$ ($+0.80 - (-0.76) = +1.56$) (*figure 6.17*). The voltage of this cell is therefore $+1.56\,V$. Since the standard electrode potential of the $Ag^+/Ag$ half-cell is more positive, the $Ag^+/Ag$ half-cell will be the positive pole and the $Zn^{2+}/Zn$ half-cell will be the negative pole of the cell.

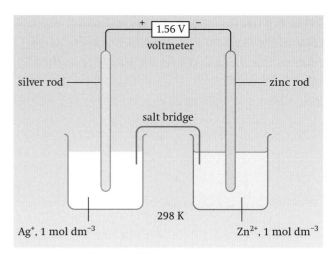

● **Figure 6.16** An $Ag^+/Ag$, $Zn^{2+}/Zn$ electrochemical cell.

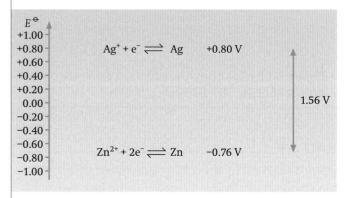

● **Figure 6.17** The difference between $+0.80\,V$ and $-0.76\,V$ is $1.56\,V$.

For the electrochemical cell shown in *figure 6.18*, the standard electrode potentials are:

$Fe^{3+} + e^- \rightleftharpoons Fe^{2+}$;          $E^{\ominus} = +0.77\,V$
$Cu^{2+} + 2e^- \rightleftharpoons Cu$;          $E^{\ominus} = +0.34\,V$

The difference between $+0.77\,V$ and $+0.34\,V$ is $+0.43\,V$ ($+0.77 - (+0.34) = 0.43$). The voltage of this

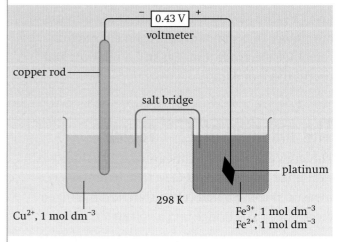

● **Figure 6.18** A $Cu^{2+}/Cu$, $Fe^{3+}/Fe^{2+}$ electrochemical cell.

cell is therefore 0.43 V. Since the standard electrode potential of the $Fe^{3+}/Fe^{2+}$ half-cell is more positive, the $Fe^{3+}/Fe^{2+}$ half-cell will be the positive pole, and the $Cu^{2+}/Cu$ half-cell will be the negative pole of the cell.

## SAQ 6.11

a  Draw a diagram of an electrochemical cell consisting of a $Cr^{3+}/Cr$ half-cell and a $Cl_2/Cl^-$ half-cell.
b  What will be the cell voltage?
c  Which half-cell will be the positive pole?
All necessary $E^\ominus$ values can be found below.

## $E^\ominus$ data

| Electrode reaction | $E^\ominus$(V) |
|---|---|
| $Ag^+ + e^- \rightleftharpoons Ag$ | +0.80 |
| $Br_2 + 2e^- \rightleftharpoons 2Br^-$ | +1.07 |
| $Ca^{2+} + 2e^- \rightleftharpoons Ca$ | -2.87 |
| $Cl_2 + 2e^- \rightleftharpoons 2Cl^-$ | +1.36 |
| $Cr^{3+} + 3e^- \rightleftharpoons Cr$ | -0.74 |
| $Cr_2O_7^{2-} + 14H^+ + 6e^- \rightleftharpoons 2Cr^{3+} + 7H_2O$ | +1.33 |
| $Cu^{2+} + 2e^- \rightleftharpoons Cu$ | +0.34 |
| $F_2 + 2e^- \rightleftharpoons 2F^-$ | +2.87 |
| $Fe^{2+} + 2e^- \rightleftharpoons Fe$ | -0.44 |
| $Fe^{3+} + e^- \rightleftharpoons Fe^{2+}$ | +0.77 |
| $2H^+ + 2e^- \rightleftharpoons H_2$ | 0.00 |
| $2H_2O + 2e^- \rightleftharpoons H_2 + 2OH^-$ | -0.83 |
| $H_2O_2 + 2H^+ + 2e^- \rightleftharpoons 2H_2O$ | +1.77 |
| $I_2 + 2e^- \rightleftharpoons 2I^-$ | +0.54 |
| $K^+ + e^- \rightleftharpoons K$ | -2.92 |
| $Mg^{2+} + 2e^- \rightleftharpoons Mg$ | -2.38 |
| $MnO_4^- + 8H^+ + 5e^- \rightleftharpoons Mn^{2+} + 4H_2O$ | +1.52 |
| $Na^+ + e^- \rightleftharpoons Na$ | -2.71 |
| $O_2 + 4H^+ + 4e^- \rightleftharpoons 2H_2O$ | +1.23 |
| $O_2 + 2H_2O + 4e^- \rightleftharpoons 4OH^-$ | +0.40 |
| $Pb^{2+} + 2e^- \rightleftharpoons Pb$ | -0.13 |
| $SO_4^{2-} + 4H^+ + 2e^- \rightleftharpoons SO_2 + 2H_2O$ | +0.17 |
| $Sn^{2+} + 2e^- \rightleftharpoons Sn$ | -0.14 |
| $Sn^{4+} + 2e^- \rightleftharpoons Sn^{2+}$ | +0.15 |
| $Zn^{2+} + 2e^- \rightleftharpoons Zn$ | -0.76 |

● **Table 6.1** $E^\ominus$ data in alphabetical order.

## SAQ 6.12

a  Draw a diagram of an electrochemical cell consisting of a $Mn^{2+}/Mn$ half-cell and a $Pb^{2+}/Pb$ half-cell.
b  What will be the cell voltage?
c  Which half-cell will be the positive pole?
All necessary $E^\ominus$ values can be found below.

# The chemical reaction taking place in an electrochemical cell

You will remember that an electrochemical cell is made of two half-cells joined by a salt bridge. When an electrochemical cell is working and producing a voltage, chemical energy is being

| Electrode reaction | $E^\ominus$(V) |
|---|---|
| $F_2 + 2e^- \rightleftharpoons 2F^-$ | +2.87 |
| $H_2O_2 + 2H^+ + 2e^- \rightleftharpoons 2H_2O$ | +1.77 |
| $MnO_4^- + 8H^+ + 5e^- \rightleftharpoons Mn^{2+} + 4H_2O$ | +1.52 |
| $Cl_2 + 2e^- \rightleftharpoons 2Cl^-$ | +1.36 |
| $Cr_2O_7^{2-} + 14H^+ + 6e^- \rightleftharpoons 2Cr^{3+} + 7H_2O$ | +1.33 |
| $O_2 + 4H^+ + 4e^- \rightleftharpoons 2H_2O$ | +1.23 |
| $Br_2 + 2e^- \rightleftharpoons 2Br^-$ | +1.07 |
| $Ag^+ + e^- \rightleftharpoons Ag$ | +0.80 |
| $Fe^{3+} + e^- \rightleftharpoons Fe^{2+}$ | +0.77 |
| $I_2 + 2e^- \rightleftharpoons 2I^-$ | +0.54 |
| $O_2 + 2H_2O + 4e^- \rightleftharpoons 4OH^-$ | +0.40 |
| $Cu^{2+} + 2e^- \rightleftharpoons Cu$ | +0.34 |
| $SO_4^{2-} + 4H^+ + 2e^- \rightleftharpoons SO_2 + 2H_2O$ | +0.17 |
| $Sn^{4+} + 2e^- \rightleftharpoons Sn^{2+}$ | +0.15 |
| $2H^+ + 2e^- \rightleftharpoons H_2$ | 0.00 |
| $Pb^{2+} + 2e^- \rightleftharpoons Pb$ | -0.13 |
| $Sn^{2+} + 2e^- \rightleftharpoons Sn$ | -0.14 |
| $Fe^{2+} + 2e^- \rightleftharpoons Fe$ | -0.44 |
| $Cr^{3+} + 3e^- \rightleftharpoons Cr$ | -0.74 |
| $Zn^{2+} + 2e^- \rightleftharpoons Zn$ | -0.76 |
| $2H_2O + 2e^- \rightleftharpoons H_2 + 2OH^-$ | -0.83 |
| $Mg^{2+} + 2e^- \rightleftharpoons Mg$ | -2.38 |
| $Na^+ + e^- \rightleftharpoons Na$ | -2.71 |
| $Ca^{2+} + 2e^- \rightleftharpoons Ca$ | -2.87 |
| $K^+ + e^- \rightleftharpoons K$ | -2.92 |

● **Table 6.2** $E^\ominus$ data in order of oxidising power.

converted into electrical energy. Therefore a chemical reaction is taking place, part of it in one half-cell and part of it in the other. When the reactants are used up in the cells that we put in torches etc., they stop working and we say they have run down or 'gone flat'.

The reaction that takes place is the one predicted by looking at the $E^\ominus$ values of the two half-cells. This reaction occurs just as successfully in the two separated half-cells as it does if the ingredients are put together in one beaker. The difference is that in the two separated half-cells the energy released by the reaction is in the form of electrical energy. When mixed in a beaker the reactants release this energy as heat.

In the example in *figure 6.19*, the half-equations are:

$$Ni^{2+} + 2e^- \rightleftharpoons Ni; \qquad E^\ominus = -0.25\,V$$
$$Fe^{3+} + e^- \rightleftharpoons Fe^{2+}; \qquad E^\ominus = +0.77\,V$$

The bottom half-equation, with its more positive $E^\ominus$ value, gains electrons and will proceed in a forward direction. The top half-equation, with its less positive $E^\ominus$ value, supplies electrons and will proceed in a backward direction. Therefore $Fe^{3+}$ is reduced to $Fe^{2+}$ and nickel atoms are oxidised to $Ni^{2+}$ ions. The overall chemical equation for the reaction that takes place in the cell is:

$$Ni + 2Fe^{3+} \rightarrow Ni^{2+} + 2Fe^{2+}$$

This means that in the nickel half-cell nickel metal is oxidised to $Ni^{2+}$ ions. In the iron half-cell $Fe^{3+}$ ions are reduced to $Fe^{2+}$ ions. The cell voltage

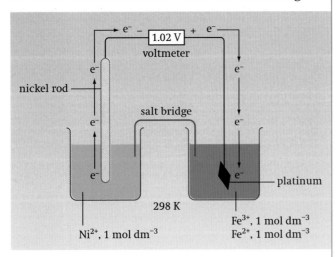

● **Figure 6.19** Electrons flow from the Ni/Ni$^{2+}$ half-cell to the Fe$^{3+}$/Fe$^{2+}$ half-cell.

is 1.02 V, with the iron half-cell as the positive pole. The electrons supplied by the $Ni^{2+}$/Ni half-cell flow to the $Fe^{3+}$/$Fe^{2+}$ half-cell through the external circuit. They don't flow through the salt bridge. This is shown in *figure 6.19*.

In order to write the equation:

$$Ni + 2Fe^{3+} \rightarrow Ni^{2+} + 2Fe^{2+}$$

the $Fe^{3+}$/$Fe^{2+}$ half-equation was doubled so that both half-equations would involve two electrons. This does not mean that the $E^\ominus$ value of +0.77 V had to be doubled when working out the cell voltage. Cell voltages are always correctly calculated using the $E^\ominus$ values as listed. In this case, +0.77 V − (−0.25 V) = 1.02 V.

### SAQ 6.13

Use the $E^\ominus$ values given on page 107 to predict the cell voltages and give the equations for the overall chemical reactions that take place in the following cells:

a  the Ag/Ag$^+$, Zn/Zn$^{2+}$ cell
b  the Fe$^{2+}$/Fe$^{3+}$, Cu/Cu$^{2+}$ cell
c  the cell in SAQ 6.11
d  the cell in SAQ 6.12.
e  Draw each electrochemical cell and show the direction of flow of electrons in the external circuit, as in *figure 6.19*.

# Using $E^\ominus$ values to predict whether or not a reaction will occur

An understanding of standard electrode potentials makes it possible to predict whether or not a particular oxidising agent can or cannot oxidise another named substance under standard conditions. It is also possible to predict whether or not a particular reducing agent can reduce another substance.

To find out whether or not a solution of Cu$^{2+}$ ions can oxidise zinc metal to Zn$^{2+}$ ions, first of all write down the half-equations with their standard electrode potential values:

$$Zn^{2+} + 2e^- \rightleftharpoons Zn; \qquad E^\ominus = -0.76\,V$$
$$Cu^{2+} + 2e^- \rightleftharpoons Cu; \qquad E^\ominus = +0.34\,V$$

The bottom half-equation has a more positive standard electrode potential value than the top one. This means that the bottom reaction can proceed in a forward direction (meaning $Cu^{2+}$ is reduced to copper) while the top reaction proceeds in a backward direction (meaning zinc is oxidised to $Zn^{2+}$). Therefore, $Cu^{2+}$ ions *can* oxidise zinc metal.

To write an equation for this reaction rewrite the two half-equations in the directions in which they will proceed:

$$Zn \rightarrow Zn^{2+} + 2e^-$$

(the zinc half-equation has been reversed)

$$Cu^{2+} + 2e^- \rightarrow Cu$$

(this half-equation has been left unchanged).

Adding the two half-equations gives:

$$Zn + Cu^{2+} + 2e^- \rightarrow Cu + Zn^{2+} + 2e^-$$

Cancelling the two electrons on each side gives:

$$Zn + Cu^{2+} \rightarrow Cu + Zn^{2+}$$

So, it is this reaction that takes place (*figure 6.20*) and not its opposite ($Zn^{2+} + Cu \rightarrow Cu^{2+} + Zn$). This may seem like a trivial example, involving a reaction you have been familiar with for some years, but it illustrates the predictive power of $E^{\ominus}$ values. Using $E^{\ominus}$ values enables you to predict whether or not a reaction takes place.

## Worked examples

### Can chlorine oxidise $Fe^{2+}$ ions to $Fe^{3+}$ ions?

First of all write down the half-equations with their standard electrode potential values:

$$Fe^{3+} + e^- \rightleftharpoons Fe^{2+}; \qquad E^{\ominus} = +0.77\,V$$
$$\tfrac{1}{2}Cl_2 + e^- \rightleftharpoons Cl^-; \qquad E^{\ominus} = +1.36\,V$$

The bottom half-equation, with its more positive standard electrode potential value, will proceed in a forward direction ($Cl_2$ is reduced to $Cl^-$ ions) while the top reaction proceeds in a backward direction ($Fe^{2+}$ is oxidised to $Fe^{3+}$). Therefore, chlorine *can* oxidise $Fe^{2+}$ ions. To write an equation for this reaction rewrite the two half-equations in the directions in which they will proceed:

$$\tfrac{1}{2}Cl_2 + e^- \rightarrow Cl^-$$
$$Fe^{2+} \rightarrow Fe^{3+} + e^-$$

Adding the two half-equations together and cancelling the electron on each side gives:

$$\tfrac{1}{2}Cl_2 + Fe^{2+} \rightarrow Cl^- + Fe^{3+}$$

### Can iodine oxidise $Fe^{2+}$ to $Fe^{3+}$?

The half-equations and $E^{\ominus}$ values are:

$$\tfrac{1}{2}I_2 + e^- \rightleftharpoons I^-; \qquad E^{\ominus} = +0.54\,V$$
$$Fe^{3+} + e^- \rightleftharpoons Fe^{2+}; \qquad E^{\ominus} = +0.77\,V$$

With a less positive $E^{\ominus}$ value the top reaction cannot proceed forward while the bottom reaction proceeds backward. Iodine *cannot* oxidise $Fe^{2+}$ to $Fe^{3+}$ under standard conditions.

The half-cell that gains electrons is always the one with the more positive $E^{\ominus}$ value. The half-cell that supplies electrons is always the one with the more negative $E^{\ominus}$ value. Remember: positive attracts electrons; negative repels electrons.

● **Figure 6.20** As predicted by the $E^{\ominus}$ values, zinc reacts with $Cu^{2+}$ ions but copper does not react with $Zn^{2+}$ ions.

## SAQ 6.14

Although iodine cannot oxidise $Fe^{2+}$ to $Fe^{3+}$, the half-equations predict that another reaction involving iodide ions and iron in a particular oxidation state *is* possible. Write an equation for this reaction.

The half-equations in the worked examples above both involve one electron only. This will not always be the case.

When using this method to find out whether or not a solution of $Ag^+$ can oxidise chromium metal to $Cr^{3+}$ the silver half-equation involves one electron, but the chromium half-equation involves three. Writing a balanced ionic equation for the reaction, if it occurs, will involve balancing the number of electrons involved.

Starting as before with the half-equations:

$$Cr^{3+} + 3e^- \rightleftharpoons Cr; \qquad E^\ominus = -0.74\,V$$
$$Ag^+ + e^- \rightleftharpoons Ag; \qquad E^\ominus = +0.80\,V$$

The bottom half-equation, with its more positive standard electrode potential value, will proceed in a forward direction while the top reaction proceeds in a backward direction. $Ag^+$ *can* oxidise chromium metal to $Cr^{3+}$ ions. Rewriting the half-equations in the directions in which they will proceed gives:

$$Cr \rightarrow Cr^{3+} + 3e^-$$
$$Ag^+ + e^- \rightarrow Ag$$

Before adding these together, the same number of electrons must be involved in each half-equation. In this case that means three electrons, so the bottom equation must be multiplied by three:

$$Cr \rightarrow Cr^{3+} + 3e^-$$
$$3Ag^+ + 3e^- \rightarrow 3Ag$$

Adding now gives:

$$Cr + 3Ag^+ + 3e^- \rightarrow Cr^{3+} + 3e^- + 3Ag$$

Cancelling the electrons gives:

$$Cr + 3Ag^+ \rightarrow Cr^{3+} + 3Ag$$

The final equation, therefore, says that one chromium atom can be oxidised to a $Cr^{3+}$ ion by three $Ag^+$ ions, which in turn are reduced to three silver atoms.

## SAQ 6.15

Use the $E^\ominus$ data in *tables 6.1* and *6.2* (page 107) to predict whether or not the following reactions occur. If a reaction does occur, write a balanced chemical equation for it.

**a** Can $MnO_4^-$ ions oxidise $Cl^-$ ions to chlorine in acid conditions?

- **Figure 6.21** If the $KMnO_4$(aq) is acidified, would it be safe to do this in an open lab or would chlorine gas be produced?

**b** Can $MnO_4^-$ ions oxidise $F^-$ ions to fluorine in acid conditions?
**c** Can $H^+$ ions oxidise $V^{2+}$ ions to $V^{3+}$ ions?
**d** Can $H^+$ ions oxidise $Fe^{2+}$ ions to $Fe^{3+}$ ions?

# Limitations of the standard electrode potential approach

As we have seen, standard electrode potentials are measured under standard conditions:
- a temperature of 298 K
- a pressure of one atmosphere
- all concentrations at $1.00\,mol\,dm^{-3}$.

The actual conditions for a reaction either in a lab or in industry are unlikely to be standard. Under such conditions the $E^\ominus$ values for the relevant half-equations are still a useful guide to what will or will not occur. If the $E^\ominus$ values of the two half-equations involved differ by more than 0.30 V then the reaction predicted by the $E^\ominus$ values will nearly always be the one that occurs, even under non-standard conditions of temperature, pressure or concentration.

Where the $E^\ominus$ values of the two half-equations are closer than 0.30 V, the actual conditions must be taken into account.

If a half-cell is constructed with non-standard concentrations, its electrode potential can be measured using a standard hydrogen electrode as the other half-cell. The voltage measured is now an $E$ value, not an $E^\ominus$ value. Increasing the concentration of a substance on the left of the half-equation will make the $E$ value more positive (or less negative) than $E^\ominus$. Increasing the concentration of a substance on the right of the half-equation will make the $E$ value less positive (or more negative) than $E^\ominus$. For example, under standard conditions

$$Fe^{3+} + e^- \rightleftharpoons Fe^{2+}; \qquad E^\ominus = +0.77\,V$$

- If $[Fe^{3+}]$ is more than $1.00\,mol\,dm^{-3}$, $E$ might be +0.85 V (i.e. greater than $E^\ominus$).
- If $[Fe^{3+}]$ is less than $1.00\,mol\,dm^{-3}$, $E$ might be +0.70 V.
- If $[Fe^{2+}]$ is more than $1.00\,mol\,dm^{-3}$, $E$ might be +0.70 V.
- If $[Fe^{2+}]$ is less than $1.00\,mol\,dm^{-3}$, $E$ might be +0.85 V.

## SAQ 6.16

The half-cell

$$Cr_2O_7{}^{2-} + 14H^+ + 6e^- \rightleftharpoons 2Cr^{3+} + 7H_2O$$

has an $E^\ominus$ value of +1.33 V. All concentrations in the solutions used to measure this value are, of course, $1.00\,mol\,dm^{-3}$.

**a** Suggest an $E$ value if:
  (i) $[Cr_2O_7{}^{2-}]$ were to be increased
  (ii) $[H^+]$ were to be decreased
  (iii) $[Cr^{3+}]$ were to be increased.
**b** What effect would each of these concentration changes have on the strength of the $Cr_2O_7{}^{2-}$ solution as an oxidising agent?
**c** What conditions would you use to make a solution of $Cr_2O_7{}^{2-}$ as strong an oxidising agent as possible?
**d** Use Le Chatelier's principle to explain your answer to part **c**.

0.30 V is given here as a *rough guide* figure only. If $E^\ominus$ values differ by over 0.30 V then the reaction predicted by the $E^\ominus$ value is *nearly always* the one that occurs. If $E^\ominus$ values differ by less than 0.30 V, non-standard conditions *may well* result in an unexpected outcome. If this leaves you desiring a bit more precision, you will have to find out about the Nernst equation!

A well-known example of the effect of non-standard conditions is the reaction of $MnO_2$ with concentrated HCl to make chlorine. This reaction involves $MnO_2$ being reduced to $Mn^{2+}$ under acid conditions while $Cl^-$ ions are oxidised to $Cl_2$. The relevant half-equations are:

$$MnO_2 + 4H^+ + 2e^- \rightleftharpoons Mn^{2+} + 2H_2O; \qquad E^\ominus = +1.23\,V$$
$$\tfrac{1}{2}Cl_2 + e^- \rightleftharpoons Cl^-; \qquad E^\ominus = +1.36\,V$$

The $E^\ominus$ values predict that $MnO_2$ *cannot* oxidise $Cl^-$ ions to $Cl_2$ under standard conditions (in fact, chlorine should be able to oxidise $Mn^{2+}$ to $MnO_2$). However, the $E^\ominus$ values are close enough for non-standard concentrations to make a difference. If concentrated HCl is used, the concentrations of $H^+$ and $Cl^-$ will be well over $1.00\,mol\,dm^{-3}$. Under these conditions the $E$ values might be:

$$\tfrac{1}{2}Cl_2 + e^- \rightleftharpoons Cl^-; \qquad E = +1.30\,V$$
$$MnO_2 + 4H^+ + 2e^- \rightleftharpoons Mn^{2+} + 2H_2O; \qquad E = +1.40\,V$$

This predicts that under such conditions $MnO_2$ will oxidise $Cl^-$ ions to chlorine, which is what is observed.

# Reaction rate has a role to play too

The rate of a particular reaction may also lead to a prediction based on $E^\ominus$ values proving unsatisfactory. Standard electrode potentials can tell you whether or not a particular redox reaction will take place but *not* whether or not it takes place at a useful rate. If predicted to happen, the reaction may happen at an unacceptably slow rate. The $E^\ominus$ values can tell us nothing about the rate of the reaction.

One example of this is the lack of a reaction between zinc metal and water. Water contains $H^+$ ions. The relevant half-equations are :

$$Zn^{2+} + 2e^- \rightleftharpoons Zn; \qquad E^\ominus = -0.76\,V$$
$$H^+ + e^- \rightleftharpoons \tfrac{1}{2}H_2; \qquad E^\ominus = 0.00\,V$$

The concentration of $H^+$ ions in water is well below $1.00\,mol\,dm^{-3}$, but even when this is taken into account, these $E^{\ominus}$ values predict that the reaction

$$Zn + 2H^+ \rightarrow Zn^{2+} + H_2$$

should occur. Any reaction that does take place, however, is too slow to be observed. Although $E^{\ominus}$ values predict that zinc should react with water at $298\,K$ to give $Zn^{2+}$ ions and hydrogen gas, $E^{\ominus}$ values cannot predict whether or not this reaction occurs at a reasonable rate. It doesn't! The reaction between zinc and water is very slow indeed.

### SAQ 6.17

Summarise briefly the two limitations to using $E^{\ominus}$ values to predict the feasibility of a reaction.

### SAQ 6.18

If an industrial process relied on a reaction that was impractically slow under normal conditions how might the chemical engineers in charge try to solve the problem? You should use your knowledge of reaction rates to suggest several different approaches.

# Commercial electrochemical cells

International concerns about the 'greenhouse effect' (see chapter 16) have led to renewed interest in obtaining energy from electrochemical cells in order to reduce the combustion of hydrocarbon fuels with the resulting production of carbon dioxide.

Electrochemical cells – usually termed batteries, which are really combinations of such cells – are widely used in vehicles, radios, watches, mobile telephones, etc. Some batteries cannot be recharged and the used chemicals are thrown away. Rechargeable batteries need a source of electricity to recharge them, but in vehicles this is achieved by driving a dynamo or alternator from the internal combustion engine.

## The dry cell

Probably the most common battery is the zinc–carbon dry cell. Each cell has a maximum

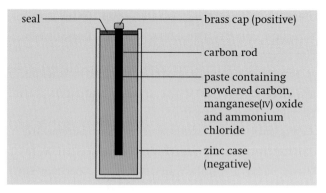

● **Figure 6.22** A zinc–carbon dry cell.

cell voltage of $1.5\,V$ and may be combined to give batteries with voltages of $3.0\,V$, $4.5\,V$, etc.

The dry cell is not strictly *dry*, as the chemicals inside are made into a paste with water before the cell is sealed. *Figure 6.22* shows a typical dry cell.

The electrode reactions are as follows:
at the positive carbon rod

$$2NH_4^+(aq) + 2e^- \rightarrow 2NH_3(aq) + H_2(g)$$

at the negative zinc case

$$Zn(s) \rightarrow Zn^{2+}(aq) + 2e^-$$

When the cell is working, hydrogen bubbles form on the central carbon rod and prevent more $NH_4^+$ ions from being discharged. In order to prevent this, manganese(IV) oxide is present to oxidise the hydrogen formed to water. Eventually the zinc case may dissolve and the cell may split. Since the hydrogen formed at the carbon electrode is removed as water, the cell reaction cannot be reversed. This cell is therefore not rechargeable.

## The lead–acid battery

The lead–acid battery is usually made up of six cells, each of which produces $2\,V$, giving an overall output of $12\,V$. Each cell consists of two lead plates in a moderately concentrated solution of sulphuric acid. Before use, the battery is charged. This results in one plate (the positive) being covered with lead(IV) oxide and the other plate (the negative) being covered with lead metal.

During discharge, the following reactions take place:
positive terminal

$$PbO_2(s) + 4H^+(aq) + SO_4^{2-}(aq) + 2e^-$$
$$\rightarrow PbSO_4(s) + 2H_2O(l)$$

negative terminal

$$Pb(s) + SO_4^{2-}(aq) \rightarrow PbSO_4(s) + 2e^-$$

Unlike the dry cell, the lead–acid battery can be recharged.

The lead–acid battery has the disadvantage of being very heavy, which makes its use as an alternative to the internal combustion engine rather limited. Consequently, much research is being done into lighter cells. One such involves sodium and sulphur, with both being molten when the cell is working.

## The fuel cell

A fuel cell produces electricity directly from the fuel used without the need for boilers or dynamos.

The most common type of fuel cell produces electricity from hydrogen and oxygen (*figure 6.23*). Water is the other product. Consequently, hydrogen–oxygen fuel cells have been widely used in manned spaceflights.

In a hydrogen–oxygen fuel cell, hydrogen and oxygen are bubbled over electrodes containing nickel as a catalyst. The electrodes are in contact with aqueous potassium hydroxide. The electrode reactions, which are the reverse of the electrolysis of water, are as follows:

at the negative electrode

$$\tfrac{1}{2}H_2(g) + OH^-(aq) \rightarrow H_2O(l) + e^-$$

at the positive electrode

$$\tfrac{1}{2}O_2(g) + H_2O(l) + 2e^- \rightarrow 2OH^-(aq)$$

Overall, the reaction is

$$H_2(g) + \tfrac{1}{2}O_2(g) \rightarrow H_2O(l)$$

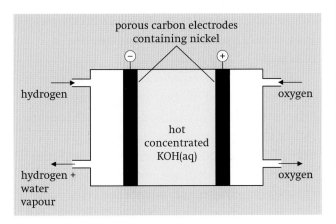

● **Figure 6.23** A hydrogen–oxygen fuel cell.

### SAQ 6.19

Use *tables 6.1* and *6.2* (page 107) to find $E^\circ$ values for each half-equation in the fuel cell described above and calculate the cell voltage.

While fuel cells are clearly less polluting than the internal combustion engine, there are considerable problems in their development. Firstly, hydrogen is very difficult to store safely, particularly in a vehicle. Secondly, large amounts of hydrogen are not readily available. One possible solution to the latter problem is to obtain hydrogen by the electrolysis of water using electricity from photovoltaic cells, which convert sunlight into electrical energy.

## Michael Faraday and electrolysis

Michael Faraday (1791–1867) investigated electrolysis quantitatively by measuring the amount of chemical change brought about by a known current for a known time. Faraday's laws of electrolysis may be written in a modern chemical style as follows.

1 The mass of substances liberated during electrolysis is directly proportional to the amount of electricity passed.

2 In order to liberate one mole of a substance during electrolysis, an integral number of moles (1, 2, 3, etc.) of electrons must be used.

The quantity of electricity passed is measured in coulombs (C). One coulomb of electricity is the electric charge passed when a current of one ampere (A) flows for one second (s).

number of coulombs = current (in A) × time (in s)

An electron has a charge of $1.60 \times 10^{-19}$ C. The charge on one mole of electrons is this charge (*e*) multiplied by the number of electrons in one mole (the Avogadro number, *L*). The charge on one mole of electrons is called the Faraday constant (*F*).

$$F = Le$$
$$= 6.02 \times 10^{23} \times 1.60 \times 10^{-19}$$
$$\approx 96\,500\,C$$

# Determination of the Avogadro constant (*L*)

The relationship $F = Le$ can be used to obtain a value for the Avogadro constant. An electrolytic cell containing aqueous silver nitrate with silver electrodes is set up and a known constant current passed for a known time.

The cathode reaction is:

$$Ag^+(aq) + e^- \rightarrow Ag(s)$$

The increase in mass of the cathode is measured and the number of coulombs required to produce an increase in mass of 108 g (one mole) of silver calculated. Since one mole of electrons is required to produce one mole of silver, use of the equation $F = Le$ will provide a value for $L$.

$$L = \frac{\text{no. of C required to deposit 1 mol of Ag}}{\text{charge on the electron}}$$

# What is liberated during electrolysis?

When molten salts, such as NaCl(l), are electrolysed, the ions present in the salt will be discharged. This is because they are the only ions present. E.g.

$$NaCl(l) \rightarrow Na(l) + \tfrac{1}{2}Cl_2(g)$$

This is how many reactive metals such as potassium, sodium, magnesium and aluminium are produced.

When more than one cation or anion is present during electrolysis, only one substance will be liberated at each electrode. For example, a solution containing copper(II) chloride and sodium iodide will give copper at the cathode and iodine at the anode, with sodium ions and chloride ions remaining in solution.

Cations and anions can be arranged in order of their relative ease of discharge at a cathode or anode, as appropriate. *Table 6.3* shows lists of cations and anions in order of ease of discharge. Such a list is known as the **electrochemical series**.

In order to deduce which ions will be discharged during the electrolysis of a solution containing a mixture of ions, it is necessary to read up from the bottom of each series. The lowest ion in the list will be discharged first.

| Cations | | Anions | |
|---|---|---|---|
| $K^+$ | | $SO_4^{2-}$ | |
| $Ca^{2+}$ | | $Cl^-$ | |
| $Na^+$ | | $Br^-$ | ease of |
| $Mg^{2+}$ | ease of | $I^-$ | discharge of anion increases |
| $Zn^{2+}$ | discharge of cation increases | $OH^-$ | |
| $Fe^{2+}$ | | | |
| $Sn^{2+}$ | | | |
| $Pb^{2+}$ | | | |
| $H^+$ | | | |
| $Cu^{2+}$ | | | |
| $Ag^+$ | | | |

● **Table 6.3** The electrochemical series for the discharge of ions during electrolysis.

The electrochemical series is clearly linked to $E^\ominus$ values (see *table 6.2*). In order to discharge a metal ion, the following half-equation must occur.

$$M^{n+}(aq) + ne^- \rightarrow M(s)$$

The ease of this reaction is the reverse of the ease of formation of the cation. $E^\ominus$ values are a measure of the ease of formation of the cation.

There are, however, occasions when use of the electrochemical series does not explain what occurs during electrolysis. For example, in the diaphragm cell electrolysis of brine, hydrogen ions are discharged at the cathode but hydroxide ions are *not* discharged at the anode.

The brine used is at least $1.0 \, mol \, dm^{-3}$ aqueous sodium chloride. Thus, in the solution, the chloride ion concentration is $1.0 \, mol \, dm^{-3}$, while the hydroxide ion concentration is only $1.0 \times 10^{-7} \, mol \, dm^{-3}$ (see page 146). In this case, the concentration of chloride ions is so much greater than that of hydroxide ions that chlorine is liberated.

Changing the electrodes may alter the product. An earlier method of obtaining chlorine from brine used a mercury cathode, at which sodium rather than hydrogen was discharged. The chemistry of this cathode reaction is very complicated. Mercury cathode cells are now being replaced by cheaper diaphragm and membrane cells. Such cells are free from the environmental problems associated with mercury compounds.

## SAQ 6.20

When aqueous copper sulphate is electrolysed between platinum electrodes, a colourless gas is evolved at the anode, no gas is evolved at the cathode and the solution gradually loses its colour.

**a** Write half-equations which explain *both* observations.

When electrolysis continues after the solution has become colourless, a gas is evolved at the cathode.

**b** Write a half-equation for this cathode reaction.

# How much change occurs during electrolysis?

Faraday's laws of electrolysis may be used to determine how much change occurs during electrolysis. If a circuit were set up as in *figure 6.24*, where two electrolytic cells are in series, the same current will flow through both cells.

In the silver cell, the electrode reactions are as follows:

anode     $Ag(s) \rightarrow Ag^+(aq) + e^-$
cathode    $Ag^+(aq) + e^- \rightarrow Ag(s)$

In the zinc cell, similar reactions will take place.

anode     $Zn(s) \rightarrow Zn^{2+}(aq) + 2e^-$
cathode    $Zn^{2+}(aq) + 2e^- \rightarrow Zn(s)$

In order to deposit one mole of silver on the silver cathode, one mole of electrons must pass through the circuit. This would also cause one mole of silver atoms to dissolve at the silver anode. This is

the change brought about by one faraday (96 500 C).

In the zinc cell, the passage of one mole of electrons would cause 0.5 mol of zinc atoms to dissolve and 0.5 mol of zinc ions to be discharged. This too is the change caused by 96 500 C.

If a current of 2.0 A were passed through the cells in *figure 6.24* for 30 minutes, how much silver and how much zinc would be deposited on the respective cathodes?

quantity of electricity passed (C)
= current (A) × time (s)
= 2.0 × 30 × 60
= 3600 C

In the silver cell:

96 500 C will deposit 108 g of silver

3600 C will deposit $\dfrac{108 \times 3600}{96\,500}$ = 4.03 g of silver

In the zinc cell:

96 500 C will deposit $\dfrac{65.4}{2}$ g of zinc

3600 C will deposit $\dfrac{65.4}{2} \times \dfrac{3600}{96\,500}$ = 1.22 g of zinc

We can also use Faraday's laws to deduce how much gas is produced when a gas such as hydrogen or oxygen is a product of electrolysis.

If water, containing a small amount of sulphuric acid, is electrolysed (see *figure 6.1*, page 95), hydrogen and oxygen are formed. The electrode reactions are as follows:

anode     $4OH^-(aq) \rightarrow O_2(g) + 2H_2O(l) + 4e^-$
cathode    $2H^+(aq) + 2e^- \rightarrow H_2(g)$

From these half-equations, it can be seen that in order to produce one mole of oxygen, $O_2(g)$, 4 × 96 500 C are needed. To produce one mole of hydrogen, $H_2(g)$, 2 × 96 500 C are needed. Thus, when 4 × 96 500 C of electricity pass through the cell, one mole of oxygen and two moles of hydrogen will be formed.

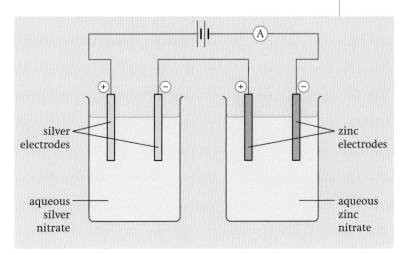

● **Figure 6.24** Two electrolytic cells in series.

If a current of 1.6 A were passed through a cell, for 10 minutes, what volumes of gas would be formed?

quantity of electricity passed = $1.6 \times 10 \times 60$
$$= 960 \, C$$

$4 \times 96\,500 \, C$ will produce 1 mol of oxygen

$960 \, C$ will produce $\dfrac{1}{4} \times \dfrac{960}{96\,500}$

$= 2.49 \times 10^{-3} \, mol$ of oxygen

$= 59.7 \, cm^3$ at room temperature and pressure

The volume of hydrogen will be $2 \times 59.7 \, cm^3$
$= 119.4 \, cm^3$ at room temperature and pressure

# SUMMARY (A2)

◆ A half-cell can contain either an element electrode in contact with its aqueous ions, or two different aqueous ions of the same element in two different oxidation states using platinum as the electrode.

◆ The standard electrode potential of a half-cell, $E^{\ominus}$ is defined as the voltage of the half-cell compared with a standard hydrogen electrode.

◆ The standard electrode potential of a half-cell is a measure in volts of the ease with which one oxidation state in the half-cell can be converted into the other oxidation state.

◆ Standard conditions are necessary when measuring an $E^{\ominus}$ value.

◆ Two half-cells put together form an electrochemical cell. The cell voltage of an electrochemical cell can be calculated by finding the difference between the standard electrode potentials of the two half-cells.

◆ A particular redox reaction will occur if the standard electrode potential of the half-equation involving the species being reduced is more positive than the standard electrode potential of the half-equation involving the species being oxidised.

◆ Balanced equations can be written for the reaction taking place in an electrochemical cell.

◆ Under non-standard concentrations a different reaction from the one predicted by standard electrode potentials may take place.

◆ Although a reaction predicted by standard electrode potentials will occur spontaneously it may be very slow.

◆ The ions that are discharged during electrolysis are those that require least energy and are shown by the electrochemical series.

◆ The amount of substance liberated during electrolysis depends on the quantity of electricity (A × s) flowing through the cell and on the charge on the ion being discharged.

# Questions (A2)

**2** The $E^\ominus$ value for the $Mn^{3+}/Mn^{2+}$ half-cell is +1.49 V.

**a** Write a half-equation for the $Mn^{3+}/Mn^{2+}$ half-cell.

**b** Draw a fully labelled diagram of the electrochemical cell you would set up to measure the $E^\ominus$ value of the $Mn^{3+}/Mn^{2+}$ half-cell. Include all essential conditions.

**c** Write a chemical equation for the reaction that takes place in this electrochemical cell.

**3** This question is about the 2+ and 3+ aqueous ions of manganese, iron and cobalt. The relevant $E^\ominus$ values are:

$Mn^{3+} + e^- \rightleftharpoons Mn^{2+}$;      $E^\ominus = +1.49$ V
$Fe^{3+} + e^- \rightleftharpoons Fe^{2+}$;      $E^\ominus = +0.77$ V
$Co^{3+} + e^- \rightleftharpoons Co^{2+}$;      $E^\ominus = -0.28$ V

**a** Which is the strongest oxidising agent out of $Mn^{3+}$, $Fe^{3+}$ and $Co^{3+}$? Which is the weakest?

**b** Which is the strongest reducing agent out of $Mn^{2+}$, $Fe^{2+}$ and $Co^{2+}$? Which is the weakest?

**c** Which ion can oxidise $Fe^{2+}$ to $Fe^{3+}$?

**d** Which ion can reduce $Fe^{3+}$ to $Fe^{2+}$?

**e** If $Mn^{3+}/Mn^{2+}$, $Fe^{3+}/Fe^{2+}$ and $Co^{3+}/Co^{2+}$ half-cells were made, which two of these together would give an electrochemical cell with the largest cell voltage? What would that voltage be? What would be the positive pole of the cell? Write an equation for the cell reaction that would take place.

**4** Look at the electrochemical cell illustrated in *figure 6.25*.

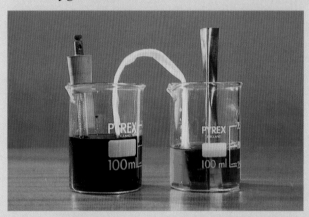

● **Figure 6.25**

The two half-cells are:

$MnO_4^- + 8H^+ + 5e^- \rightleftharpoons Mn^{2+} + 4H_2O$;
                                    $E^\ominus = +1.52$ V
$Cu^{2+} + 2e^- \rightleftharpoons Cu$;      $E^\ominus = +0.34$ V

**a** What is the cell voltage?

**b** Which half-cell is the positive pole of the cell?

**c** Does this mean:

(i) $Cu^{2+}$ ions can oxidise $Mn^{2+}$ ions to $MnO_4^-$ ions *or*

(ii) $MnO_4^-$ ions in acid solution can oxidise Cu atoms to $Cu^{2+}$ ions?

**d** Write a balanced equation for the overall chemical reaction that takes place in the cell.

5 Since $Mn^{3+}$ may be reduced to $Mn^{2+}$ and $Mn^{2+}$ may be oxidised to $Mn^{3+}$, the half-equation can be written as a reversible reaction:

$$Mn^{3+} + e^- \rightleftharpoons Mn^{2+}; \qquad E^\ominus = +1.49\,V$$

Changing the concentration of either ion shifts the position of equilibrium. This means the tendency for the reaction to go forwards or backwards is changed. This causes the $E$ value to change.

a Suggest an $E$ value for a $Mn^{3+}/Mn^{2+}$ half-cell if $[Mn^{3+}]$ is $2.00\,mol\,dm^{-3}$ and $[Mn^{2+}]$ is $0.500\,mol\,dm^{-3}$.

b Suggest an $E$ value for a $Mn^{3+}/Mn^{2+}$ half-cell if $[Mn^{3+}]$ is $0.500\,mol\,dm^{-3}$ and $[Mn^{2+}]$ is $2.00\,mol\,dm^{-3}$.

c Use Le Chatelier's principle to explain your answers.

6 An electric current is passed through three electrolytic cells in series. Each cell has platinum electrodes. The electrolytes are $AgNO_3(aq)$, $CuSO_4(aq)$ and dilute $H_2SO_4$. If $0.242\,g$ of silver are deposited on the cathode of the first cell, calculate:

a the number of coulombs passed through the circuit;

b the mass of copper deposited on the cathode in the second ecell;

c the volume of hydrogen evolved at the cathode of the third cell.

# Equilibria (AS)

## By the end of this section you should be able to:

1 explain the features of a *dynamic equilibrium*;

2 state *Le Chatelier's principle* and apply it to deduce qualitatively (from appropriate information) the effect of a change in temperature, concentration or pressure on a homogeneous system in equilibrium;

3 deduce that, for an equilibrium system, changes in concentration and pressure and the presence of a catalyst have no effect on the magnitude of the equilibrium constant and an increase in temperature decreases the value of $K_c$ or $K_p$ for an exothermic reaction and increases the value of $K_c$ or $K_p$ for an endothermic reaction;

4 deduce, for *homogeneous reactions*, expressions for the *equilibrium constants* $K_c$, in terms of concentrations, and $K_p$, in terms of partial pressures;

5 calculate the values of the equilibrium constants $K_c$ or $K_p$, including determination of units, given appropriate data;

6 calculate a concentration or partial pressure present at *equilibrium*, given appropriate data;

7 describe and explain the conditions used in the *Haber process* and the *Contact process* as examples of the importance of a compromise between chemical equilibrium and reaction rate in the chemical industry;

8 describe and use the *Brønsted–Lowry theory* of acids and bases, to include conjugate acid–base pairs;

9 explain qualitatively, in terms of dissociation, the differences between *strong* and *weak acids* and between *strong and weak bases* in terms of the extent of dissociation.

## Reversible reactions

You will be familiar with a number of reversible physical processes. For example, if you decrease the temperature of water below 0 °C, ice forms. Allow the ice to warm to room temperature and it soon melts. The process can be represented as follows:

$$H_2O(s) \rightleftharpoons H_2O(l)$$

The $\rightleftharpoons$ sign in this equation is used to indicate that the process is reversible.

Another reversible physical process is the dissolving of carbon dioxide in water. You will have met aqueous carbon dioxide in the form of fizzy drinks such as cola. Carbon dioxide is dissolved in the drink under pressure. When the drink is poured, the carbon dioxide escapes as bubbles of gas producing a pleasant sensation when the cola is consumed. An equation for this reversible change is:

$$CO_2(aq) \rightleftharpoons CO_2(g)$$

The solubility of carbon dioxide in water is enhanced by chemical reaction with water, producing hydrogen ions, $H^+(aq)$, and hydrogen carbonate ions, $HCO_3^-(aq)$:

$$H_2O(l) + CO_2(aq) \rightleftharpoons H^+(aq) + HCO_3^-(aq)$$

This reaction is also easily reversed. Boiling the water will decompose the hydrogencarbonate ions and drive off carbon dioxide.

Many other chemical reactions are reversible. An environmentally important reversible reaction is the formation of ozone, $O_3(g)$, from oxygen. Ultraviolet light is needed to form ozone; chlorine atoms (from CFCs) have the overall effect of reversing the reaction, causing damage to the ozone layer:

$$3O_2(g) \underset{CFCs}{\overset{UV \text{ light}}{\rightleftharpoons}} 2O_3(g)$$

In this chapter we shall explore the nature of reversible reactions in more detail.

## Equilibrium – a state of balanced change

The notion of a system being in **equilibrium** is a familiar one. You can stir salt into water until no more will dissolve. At this point the solution is described as a saturated solution and is in equilibrium with the undissolved solid. Although the concentration of the saturated solution stays the same, the ions and molecules are in a constant state of motion. We describe this as a **dynamic equilibrium**. Ions in the crystal lattice of the undissolved solid continue to go into solution. However, they are immediately replaced elsewhere in the lattice by the same numbers and kinds of ion. The dynamic nature of the equilibrium is only observable at the ionic or molecular level. The situation is one of continued but balanced change (*figure 7.1a*).

A similar situation exists when you close the tap on a cylinder of butane gas, in a camping gas stove for example. Evaporation and condensation go on until the liquid and gas phases are in equilibrium with one another. Again the equilibrium is dynamic. At equilibrium some of the molecules of liquid butane are evaporating, but only at the same rate as molecules of gaseous butane are condensing (*figure 7.1b*).

In general, in a dynamic equilibrium, the rate of reaction in the *forwards* direction equals the rate of reaction in the *reverse* direction.

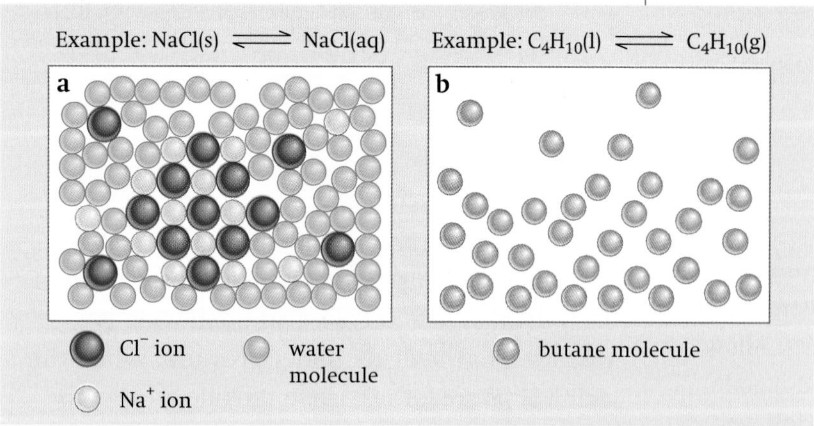

## Equilibrium and chemical change

If you heat calcium carbonate it decomposes, forming calcium oxide and carbon dioxide:

$$CaCO_3(s) \rightarrow CaO(s) + CO_2(g)$$

On the other hand, if you leave calcium oxide in an atmosphere of carbon dioxide, the reverse reaction occurs, and calcium carbonate forms:

$$CaO(s) + CO_2(g) \rightarrow CaCO_3(s)$$

If these substances are put in a sealed container at a high temperature (say 700 K) and left to get on with it, an equilibrium is set up. Both of the above reactions occur until a balance is reached. At this point the rate of formation of calcium carbonate equals its rate of decomposition.

All chemical reactions can reach equilibrium, a situation where the reactants are in equilibrium with the products. Again, these are dynamic equilibria: reagents are constantly being converted to products, and vice versa. At equilibrium the rate of the forward process is the same as that of the backward one. The idea that *all*

Example: $NaCl(s) \rightleftharpoons NaCl(aq)$    Example: $C_4H_{10}(l) \rightleftharpoons C_4H_{10}(g)$

a

b

Cl⁻ ion    water molecule    butane molecule

Na⁺ ion

● **Figure 7.1** Two physical equilibria. In both situations there is a constant interchange of particles, which maintains a steady balance. In **a** ions leave a crystal structure, while others join it. In **b** molecules escape from the crush in a liquid to relative isolation in a gas, while others leave the gas to join the liquid.

chemical reactions can reach equilibrium seems to conflict with experience, e.g. the burning of magnesium in air. In many cases the degree of conversion of reactants to products is so large that, at the conclusion of the reaction, no reactants can be detected by normal analytical means. At other times two reagents, e.g. the nitrogen and oxygen in the air, do not seem to react at all. Such reactions are often considered to be irreversible one-way reactions under those conditions.

Suppose, for example, we mix an equal number of molecules of hydrogen with either chlorine or bromine. The green colour of the chlorine or the orange colour of the bromine disappears, and we are left with hydrogen chloride or hydrogen bromide. The reverse reaction is so minimal that both reactions go to apparent completion as indicated by these equations:

$$H_2(g) + Cl_2(g) \rightarrow 2HCl(g)$$
$$H_2(g) + Br_2(g) \rightarrow 2HBr(g)$$

When we mix hydrogen gas and iodine vapour, however, we find that the violet colour of the iodine persists. There is an equilibrium set up between the three components in which all three are present in significant amounts, as shown in the equation below and in *figure 7.2*:

$$H_2(g) + I_2(g) \rightleftharpoons 2HI(g)$$

The equation tells us that when a molecule of hydrogen reacts with a molecule of iodine, two molecules of hydrogen iodide are formed. It also enables us to examine the reaction in reverse. If

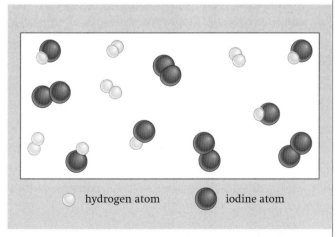

○ hydrogen atom ● iodine atom

● **Figure 7.2** A snapshot of the dynamic equilibrium between hydrogen gas, iodine gas and hydrogen iodide gas.

two molecules of hydrogen iodide dissociate (i.e. split apart), then a molecule each of hydrogen and iodine are formed.

When you cook on a camping gas stove, butane gas is released and burned. The liquid butane will evaporate to maintain the gas supply. However, equilibrium will not be restored in the cylinder unless the gas is turned off at the tap. We must have a **closed system** to achieve a dynamic equilibrium.

## SAQ 7.1

A beaker contains saturated aqueous sodium chloride in contact with undissolved solid sodium chloride. Is this a closed system? Explain your answer.

When we view a system at equilibrium, we are not aware that constant change is taking place. From our viewpoint the system looks static because all the dynamic change is occurring at the molecular or ionic level. The properties that we can see or measure remain constant. We call these macroscopic properties. In a camping gas cylinder with the tap closed, the volume of liquid and the pressure do not change once dynamic equilibrium is achieved. The concentration of salt in a saturated solution is also constant at equilibrium. The temperature of both systems must also be constant. Another feature of a dynamic equilibrium is this constancy of macroscopic properties.

In summary the characteristic features of an equilibrium are:
■ It is dynamic at the molecular or ionic level.
■ Both forward and reverse processes occur at equal rates.
■ A closed system is required.
■ Macroscopic properties remain constant.

# Changing conditions: Le Chatelier's principle

Now that we have established the characteristic features of an equilibrium, we can ask the question "What happens to the equilibrium if we change the conditions in some way?" We could, for example, alter the temperature or change the concentration of a reactant.

Suppose we add more water to the equilibrium mixture of solid sodium chloride and saturated aqueous sodium chloride we saw in *figure 7.1*. The mixture will no longer be in equilibrium. However, more of the solid will dissolve and, providing there is sufficient solid, the solution will again become saturated. The system readjusts to restore equilibrium.

Raising the temperature of our sealed container of calcium carbonate in equilibrium with calcium oxide and carbon dioxide provides the energy that allows more calcium carbonate to decompose. Again, the system adjusts to restore equilibrium. Intially, more calcium oxide and carbon dioxide is formed. Equilibrium is restored when the rate of formation of the calcium oxide and carbon dioxide is the same as the rate of the reverse reaction to form calcium carbonate.

Observations of this type led the French chemist Henri Louis Le Chatelier in 1884 to put forward an important principle. The essence of **Le Chatelier's principle** is that:

> when any of the conditions affecting the position of a dynamic equilibrium are changed, then the position of that equilibrium will shift to minimise that change.

Next we will consider how we can qualitatively predict the effect of changing temperature, pressure or concentration on the equilibrium position using Le Chatelier's principle.

## The effect of temperature on the position of equilibrium

We know that calcium carbonate decomposes to calcium oxide and carbon dioxide at a high temperature. At room temperature, no change is seen. The white cliffs of Dover are still calcium carbonate, as they were when first seen by Julius Caesar!

When calcium carbonate is heated in a closed system (see page 221), an equilibrium mixture containing both reactant and products results. The reaction is endothermic and, on raising the temperature, the position of the equilibrium shifts towards the formation of calcium oxide and carbon dioxide. In the closed system, the higher the temperature, the greater is the proportion of products at equilibrium.

The dissociation of hydrogen iodide is an example of a homogeneous endothermic reaction:

$$2HI(g) \rightleftharpoons H_2(g) + I_2(g)$$

The effect of different temperatures on the equilibrium concentration of hydrogen can be seen in *table 7.1* and *figure 7.3*. As the temperature rises, the equilibrium concentration of hydrogen rises. The position of equilibrium in this gas phase reaction shifts towards the formation of hydrogen and iodine at higher temperature.

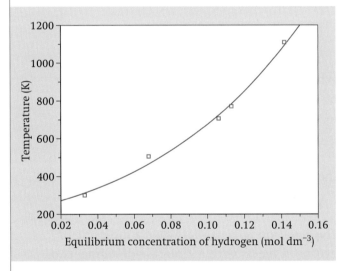

● **Figure 7.3** In an endothermic reaction such as the dissociation of hydrogen iodide, as the temperature is increased the equilibrium concentration of the products increases. The graph shows the increase in concentration of hydrogen with increasing temperature.

| Temperature (K) | Equilibrium concentration of hydrogen iodide (mol dm$^{-3}$) | Equilibrium concentration of hydrogen (or iodine) (mol dm$^{-3}$) |
|---|---|---|
| 298 | 0.934 | 0.033 |
| 500 | 0.864 | 0.068 |
| 700 | 0.786 | 0.107 |
| 764 | 0.773 | 0.114 |
| 1100 | 0.714 | 0.143 |

● **Table 7.1** The dissociation of hydrogen iodide, HI(g), at various temperatures.

When we raise the temperature of an endothermic reaction, there is an increase in the enthalpy in the system. According to Le Chatelier's principle, the equilibrium position should shift towards the products in order to compensate for the additional enthalpy input.

Suppose we consider an increase in temperature for an exothermic reaction. The reverse reaction will be endothermic, so Le Chatelier's principle tells us that the equilibrium will shift towards the reactants to compensate for the extra enthalpy input.

*Table 7.2* summarises the effects of temperature changes on the equilbrium position for exothermic and endothermic reactions.

## The effect of changes in concentration on the equilibrium position

We will consider the formation of an ester, such as ethyl ethanoate. When ethanol is warmed with ethanoic acid in the presence of a few drops of concentrated sulphuric acid, ethyl ethanoate is formed (see pages 187 and 337).

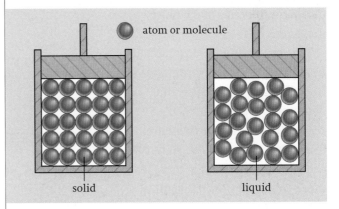

$$H_3C - C\overset{O}{\underset{O-H}{\big\|}} + \overset{H}{\underset{O-CH_2-CH_3}{}} \rightleftharpoons H_3C - C\overset{O}{\underset{O-CH_2-CH_3}{\big\|}} + H_2O$$

ethanoic acid      ethanol      ethyl ethanoate      water

The sulphuric acid catalyses this reaction. An equilibrium is soon established in the reaction mixture with significant concentrations of both products and reactants present. Suppose we increase the concentration of ethanol in the mixture. The position of equilibrium is disturbed. Applying Le Chatelier's principle, more ethyl ethanoate and water will form and the concentration of ethanol and ethanoic acid will fall until a new position of equilibrium is established. The position of equilibrium moves towards the products.

**SAQ 7.2** _____

**SAQ 7.2** _____

Consider the equilibrium involved in the formation of ethyl ethanoate.

**a** Use Le Chatelier's principle to predict how the position of equilibrium would change on adding more water to the mixture.

**b** Ethyl ethanoate is a useful solvent. It is used, for example, in nail varnish remover. Suggest how a chemical company might optimise the conversion of ethanol and ethanoic acid to ethyl ethanoate.

## The effect of pressure on equilibria

Pressure has virtually no effect on the chemistry of solids and liquids. As shown in *figure 7.4*, pressure does not affect the concentration of solids and liquids – the molecules concerned are already in contact and it is difficult to push them closer together.

Pressure does have significant effects on the chemistry of reacting gases. As *figure 7.5* shows, the concentrations of gases increase with an increase in pressure, and decrease with a decrease in pressure. Since chemical equilibria are influenced by concentration changes, pressure changes also have an effect on equilibria where one or more of the reagents is a gas.

atom or molecule

solid          liquid

● **Figure 7.4** Pressure has little, if any, effect on the concentrations of solids and liquids.

● **Table 7.2** The effect of temperature change on the equilibrium positions of reactions involving gases.

| Example | Endothermic reaction, $2HI(g) \rightleftharpoons H_2(g) + I_2(g)$ | Exothermic reaction, $2SO_2(g) + O_2(g) \rightleftharpoons 2SO_3(g)$ |
|---|---|---|
| Temperature increase | equilibrium position shifts towards products: more hydrogen and iodine form | equilibrium position shifts towards reactants: more sulphur dioxide and oxygen form |
| Temperature decrease | equilibrium position shifts towards reactant: more hydrogen iodide forms | equilibrium position shifts towards product: more sulphur trioxide forms |

Again we can apply Le Chatelier's principle to predict how pressure change will affect an equilibrium. Imagine a reaction in the gaseous phase where two molecules, A and B, combine to form a single molecule, C:

$$A(g) + B(g) \rightleftharpoons C(g)$$

The situation is illustrated in *figure 7.6*.

It helps to remember that the pressure of a gas depends on the number of molecules in a given volume of the gas. The greater the number of molecules, the greater the number of collisions per second, and hence the greater the pressure of the gas. In the reaction above, when the pressure is increased *the equilibrium shifts to minimise this increase*, that is, to reduce the pressure overall. Therefore, there must be fewer molecules present than before. This can only happen if A and B molecules react to make more molecules of C.

This reasoning is summarised in *table 7.3*, which summarises the effects of increasing and decreasing the pressure on reactions in which **a** there are fewer molecules on the right of the equilibrium, and **b** there are more molecules on the right of the equilibrium.

## SAQ 7.3
Predict the effect on the equilibrium position of increasing the pressure on the following reactions
**a** $2HI(g) \rightleftharpoons H_2(g) + I_2(g)$
**b** $N_2(g) + 3H_2(g) \rightleftharpoons 2NH_3(g)$

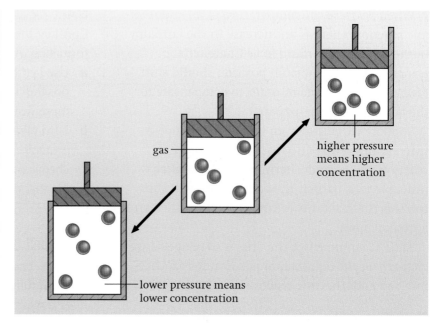

● **Figure 7.5** Pressure has a considerable effect on the concentrations of gases.

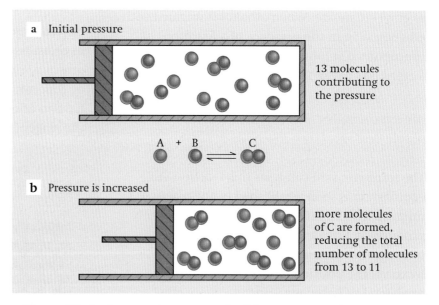

● **Figure 7.6** An increase in pressure in this case causes the equilibrium to shift to the right, to produce more molecules of C than before, but fewer molecules in the reaction vessel overall.

| Example | Fewer molecules on right $2SO_2(g) + O_2(g) \rightleftharpoons 2SO_3(g)$ | More molecules on right $N_2O_4(g) \rightleftharpoons 2NO_2(g)$ |
|---|---|---|
| Pressure increase | equilibrium position shifts towards products: more $SO_3$ forms | equilibrium position shifts towards reactants: more $N_2O_4$ forms |
| Pressure decrease | equilibrium position shifts towards reactants: more $SO_2$ and $O_2$ form | equilibrium position shifts towards products: more $NO_2$ forms |

● **Table 7.3** The effect of pressure change on the equilibrium position of reactions involving gases.

## The effect of catalysts on equilibria

As you know, a catalyst reduces the activation energy of a reaction, and hence speeds it up. A catalyst affects the rate of reaction, but does not feature in the overall equation for the reaction. More catalyst could mean a faster reaction, one in which an equilibrium was established more quickly, *but does not change the equilibrium concentration of reactants or products.*

# Crocodiles, blood and carbon dioxide

An equilibrium reaction that you studied on page 119 is the one that exists in a can of fizzy drink. You will be very familiar with the observation of bubbles of carbon dioxide being released when the drink is poured into a glass. The equilibrium involved is represented by the following equation:

$$CO_2(g) \rightleftharpoons CO_2(aq)$$

Remember the $\rightleftharpoons$ sign indicates that the reaction is reversible. In the can, carbon dioxide gas dissolves in the drink under pressure. An equilibrium exists between undissolved carbon dioxide gas and the carbon dioxide dissolved in the drink. Within the sealed can, the rate at which the carbon dioxide is dissolving equals the rate at which the gas is escaping from the drink. We describe the equilibrium as a dynamic equilibrium.

Provided that the temperature is constant and the can is not opened, the equilibrium concentration of the carbon dioxide in the drink is constant. Equilibria are only reached in closed systems such as in the sealed can or where all reactants and products are in the same aqueous solution. A further characteristic of a dynamic equilibrium is the constancy of macroscopic properties such as concentration (see *box 7A*).

### Box 7A Dynamic equilibrium

When we view a system at equilibrium, we are not aware that constant change is taking place at the microscopic level of molecules and ions. Properties we can see or measure easily remain constant. We call these macroscopic properties. Once dynamic equilibrium is achieved, the macroscopic properties such as concentration, pressure, temperature, mass or volume remain constant.

In summary, the characteristic features of a dynamic equilibrium are that

- it is dynamic at the molecular or ionic level;
- the position of equilibrium can be approached from either side of the chemical equation;
- both forward and reverse processes occur at equal rates;
- a closed system is required;
- macroscopic properties remain constant.

So where do crocodiles and blood fit into all this? Crocodiles kill their prey by diving under water once their prey is firmly between their powerful jaws (*figure 7.7*). Crocodiles can survive under water for much longer than their prey, which dies from drowning long before the crocodile needs to surface for air.

As carbon dioxide builds up in body tissues it is converted to hydrogencarbonate ions, $HCO_3^-(aq)$, as shown in the following equilibrium equation:

$$CO_2(aq) + H_2O(l) \rightleftharpoons H^+(aq) + HCO_3^-(aq) \qquad (7.1)$$

Haemoglobin (Hb) and oxygen are also in equilibrium in the blood. This equilibrium can be represented by an equilibrium equation:

$$Hb(aq) + O_2(aq) \rightleftharpoons HbO_2(aq) \qquad (7.2)$$

The secret of a crocodile's ability to stay under water whilst its prey drowns lies in a difference in its haemoglobin. This difference allows an increase in $[HCO_3^-(aq)]$, resulting from the increase in $[CO_2(aq)]$, to release more of the oxygen carried by the crocodile haemoglobin, enabling the crocodile to survive. Meanwhile, the prey's haemoglobin is incapable of a similar response, so the prey dies.

● **Figure 7.7** A crocodile drowns its prey under water. Why does the crocodile not drown like its prey?

## SAQ 7.4

**a** Explain, in terms of the equilibrium shown in *reaction 7.1*, why $[HCO_3^-]$ increases as the crocodile drowns its prey.

**b** (i) Describe and explain the changes in equilibrium concentrations which take place in *reaction 7.2* in the crocodile's blood as the crocodile drowns its prey.

(ii) In which direction does the position of equilibrium change?

Scientists in the UK and USA are applying knowledge and understanding of the behavior of haemoglobin from several animal sources and of the basic structure-function relationships to the development of recombinant human haemoglobin. Recombinant human haemoglobin, produced by genetically modified bacteria, may one day significantly reduce the need for blood donors for blood transfusion. *Figure 7.8* shows a chromatography column loaded with recombinant human haemoglobin.

The genetic coding responsible for the behaviour of both crocodile haemoglobin and that of certain fish has now been identified and introduced into the bacterium used to make artificial human haemoglobin. Artificial haemoglobin which behaves as crocodile or fish haemoglobin might allow humans to stay under water for longer periods. Such haemoglobin could be useful to divers. More importantly, it might also be helpful to those people with diseases which cause breathing difficulties.

● **Figure 7.8** Recombinant human haemoglobin being purified from bacteria at Baxter Haemoglobin Therapeutics, USA.

Many other reactions in living organisms involve chemical equilibia. A study of chemical equilibria leads us to a better understanding of such processes.

# Equilibria in organic reactions

Like many biochemical reactions, many of the organic reactions that you will meet elsewhere in this book also involve equilibria.

One example of an organic equilibrium reaction is the hydrolysis of the ester ethyl ethanoate, $CH_3COOCH_2CH_3$ (see chapter 20a). This ester hydrolyses slowly, forming ethanoic acid and ethanol when mixed with water and an acid catalyst such as sulphuric or hydrochloric acid. The equation for the reaction is as follows.

$$CH_3COOCH_2CH_3(l) + H_2O(l) \rightleftharpoons CH_3COOH(l) + CH_3CH_2OH(l)$$

*Table 7.4* shows the equilibrium concentrations for four experiments. The mixtures were prepared by mixing together known masses of ester and water. The mixtures were placed in stoppered flasks and $1.0\,cm^3$ of concentrated sulphuric acid was added to each flask. The flasks were then left undisturbed for one week at room temperature. One week is necessary for the mixtures to reach equilibrium, even though a catalyst is used! After one week, the flasks were opened and the contents analysed by titration with standardised sodium hydroxide. A separate titration was also carried out to determine the volume of sodium hydroxide required to neutralise the sulphuric acid. The data in *table 7.4* were calculated from these titration results and the initial weighings. The last column of the table contains the symbol $K_c$, which is known as the **equilibrium constant**. The small subscript '$c$' refers to concentration. You will see that the val-

| Experiment | Concentration (mol dm⁻³) | | | | $K_c$ |
|---|---|---|---|---|---|
| | $CH_3COOCH_2CH_3$ | $H_2O$ | $CH_3COOH$ | $CH_3CH_2OH$ | |
| 1 | 7.22 | 2.47 | 2.03 | 2.03 | |
| 2 | 6.38 | 3.69 | 2.56 | 2.56 | 0.278 |
| 3 | 4.69 | 8.16 | 3.28 | 3.28 | 0.281 |
| 4 | 2.81 | 16.6 | 3.56 | 3.56 | |

● **Table 7.4** Data for the hydrolysis of ethyl ethanoate.

ues of $K_c$ for the data in experiments 2 and 3 are in close agreement. How is this constant calculated from the data? First of all we write the equation for the reaction:

$$CH_3COOCH_2CH_3(l) + H_2O(l)$$
$$\rightleftharpoons CH_3COOH(l) + CH_3CH_2OH(l)$$

Now we can write the equilibrium constant, $K_c$, as the ratio of the product concentrations (multiplied together) divided by the reactant concentrations (multiplied together), as follows:

$$K_c = \frac{[CH_3COOH][CH_3CH_2OH]}{[CH_3COOCH_2CH_3][H_2O]}$$

### SAQ 7.5

Try substituting the data for experiment 2 in the above expression for $K_c$. Check your answer with the value in *table 7.4*.

Calculate the missing values of $K_c$. Remember the results are experimental, so not all values of $K_c$ will be as close as those for experiments 2 and 3.

# Finding the balance

Iodine gas is purple. The more there is, the deeper the shade of purple. A colorimeter can be used to measure this intensity, and hence the concentration of iodine in a reaction vessel.

The equilibrium

$$H_2(g) + I_2(g) \rightleftharpoons 2HI(g)$$

can be approached from either side:
- by using a mixture of hydrogen gas and iodine gas (purple), which reacts to form colourless hydrogen iodide, or
- by using pure hydrogen iodide, which dissociates to form hydrogen and iodine.

The equation for the reaction is

$$H_2(g) + I_2(g) \rightleftharpoons 2HI(g)$$

*Figure 7.9* illustrates what happens when 5.00 moles of each of hydrogen molecules and iodine molecules react at 500 K. As time passes, the purple colour of the iodine fades until a steady state is reached. Analysis shows that the final amount of the iodine is 0.68 moles. There must also be 0.68 moles of hydrogen left, as the equation shows. The remaining 4.32 moles of each gas have been converted to 8.64 moles of hydrogen iodide molecules.

### SAQ 7.6

The same equilibrium can be achieved starting with 10 moles of hydrogen iodide molecules (*figure 7.10*). Describe what happens and satisfy yourself that, if 0.68 moles of iodine molecules are found to be in the final mixture, then there must be 8.64 moles of hydrogen iodide molecules present.

We can find the concentrations of the three components in any equilibrium by analysing the amount of iodine present in the equilibrium mixture, knowing the amount of hydrogen and iodine we had to start with. *Table 7.5* shows some values obtained. The fourth column shows the value of $[HI]^2/[H_2][I_2]$, which, as you can see, is constant (allowing for experimental error). It is called the equilibrium constant, $K_c$, for the reaction, and in this case it is given by the square of the equilibrium concentration of the hydrogen iodide, divided by the product of the equilibrium concentrations of the hydrogen and the iodine.

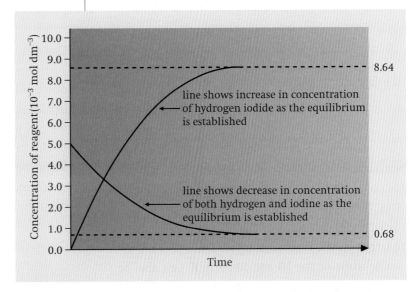

● **Figure 7.9** The changes in the concentrations of reagents as 5.00 moles of each of hydrogen and iodine react to form an equilibrium with hydrogen iodide in a vessel of volume 1 m³.

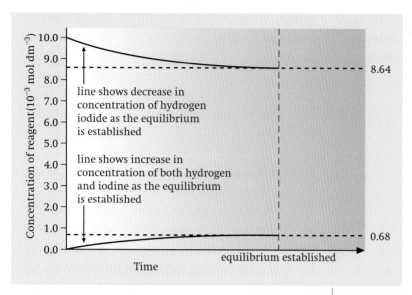

● **Figure 7.10** The changes in the concentrations of reagents as 10 moles of hydrogen iodide react to form an equilibrium with hydrogen and iodine gases in a vessel of $1\,m^3$.

| $[H_2](mol\,dm^{-3})$ | $[I_2](mol\,dm^{-3})$ | $[HI](mol\,dm^{-3})$ | $\dfrac{[HI]^2}{[H_2][I_2]}$ |
|---|---|---|---|
| $0.68 \times 10^{-3}$ | $0.68 \times 10^{-3}$ | $8.64 \times 10^{-3}$ | 161 |
| $0.50 \times 10^{-3}$ | $0.50 \times 10^{-3}$ | $6.30 \times 10^{-3}$ | 159 |
| $1.10 \times 10^{-3}$ | $1.10 \times 10^{-3}$ | $13.9 \times 10^{-3}$ | 160 |
| $1.10 \times 10^{-3}$ | $2.00 \times 10^{-3}$ | $18.8 \times 10^{-3}$ | 161 |
| $2.50 \times 10^{-3}$ | $0.65 \times 10^{-3}$ | $16.1 \times 10^{-3}$ | 160 |

● **Table 7.5** Equilibrium concentrations of hydrogen, $H_2(g)$, iodine, $I_2(g)$, and hydrogen iodide, $HI(g)$, at 500 K.

From *table 7.5*, $K_c$ can be found:

$$K_c = \frac{[HI][HI]}{[H_2][I_2]}$$

$$= \frac{[HI]^2}{[H_2][I_2]}$$

Notice that the 2HI in the reaction equation becomes $[HI]^2$ in the equilibrium constant expression. As a general rule, each concentration is raised to the number of moles of the relevant reactant in the balanced equation.

The units of the HI equilibrium $K_c$ can also be found:

$$= \frac{(\text{mol\,dm}^{-3})^2}{(\text{mol\,dm}^{-3}) \times (\text{mol\,dm}^{-3})}$$

As the units in this expression cancel, this $K_c$ has no units. However, each equilibrium constant must be considered individually. $K_c$ will not have units whenever the equilibrium is homogeneous and the total number of molecules on each side of the balanced equation is the same.

Consider the equilibrium for the Contact process for the manufacture of sulphuric acid. In this process, a key stage involves the oxidation of sulphur dioxide to sulphur trioxide by oxygen. The equation and equilibrium constant for this reaction are:

$$2SO_2(g) + O_2(g) \rightleftharpoons 2SO_3(g)$$

$$K_c = \frac{[SO_3]^2}{[SO_2]^2 \times [O_2]}$$

$$\text{units of } K_c = \frac{(\text{mol\,dm}^{-3})^2}{(\text{mol\,dm}^{-3})^2 \times (\text{mol\,dm}^{-3})}$$

$$= \frac{1}{(\text{mol\,dm}^{-3})} = dm^3\,mol^{-1}$$

### SAQ 7.7

Write the formula for $K_c$ for each of the following reactions, and work out the units for $K_c$ assuming the concentrations of the gases are measured in $mol\,dm^{-3}$.

**a** $\quad 2NO_2(g) \rightleftharpoons N_2O_4(g)$

**b** $\quad 2NO(g) + O_2(g) \rightleftharpoons 2NO_2(g)$

**c** $\quad N_2(g) + 3H_2(g) \rightleftharpoons 2NH_3(g)$

Use of the equilibrium constant expression has an additional advantage in that, if we can determine one equilibrium concentration and we know the initial concentrations of other compounds present, we can determine the equilibrium concentrations of the other chemical species present. From this information, we can calculate a value for $K_c$.

For example, propanone reacts with hydrogen cyanide as follows (see chapter 19, page 353):

$$H_3C-\overset{\overset{\displaystyle O}{\|}}{C}-CH_3 \;+\; HCN \;\rightleftharpoons\; H_3C-\overset{\overset{\displaystyle OH}{|}}{\underset{\underset{\displaystyle CN}{|}}{C}}-CH_3$$

A mixture initially containing $0.0500\,mol\,dm^{-3}$ propanone and $0.0500\,mol\,dm^{-3}$ hydrogen cyanide in ethanol is left to reach equilibrium at room temperature. At equilibrium the concentration of the product is 0.0233 mol dm$^{-3}$. Calculate the equilibrium constant for this reaction under these conditions.

A helpful approach is shown below.

*Step 1* Write out the equation with the initial data underneath. Notice how the chemical formulae for the compounds enable the information to be tabulated.

*Step 2* The equilibrium concentration of the only product is 0.0233 mol dm$^{-3}$. As 1 mole of each reactant produces 1 mole of product, the concentration of each of the reactants decreases by 0.0233 mol dm$^{-3}$. Hence the equilibrium concentration of each reactant is now 0.0500 – 0.0233 mol dm$^{-3}$ = 0.0267 mol dm$^{-3}$.

| | $H_3C-\overset{\overset{O}{\|}}{C}-CH_3$ | + | HCN | $\rightleftharpoons$ | $H_3C-\overset{\overset{OH}{\|}}{\underset{\underset{CN}{\|}}{C}}-CH_3$ |
|---|---|---|---|---|---|
| Initial concentrations (mol dm$^{-3}$) | 0.0500 | | 0.0500 | | 0 |
| Equilibrium concentrations (mol dm$^{-3}$) | 0.0500 – 0.0233 = 0.0267 | | 0.0500 – 0.0233 = 0.0267 | | 0.0233 |

*Step 3* Write the equilibrium constant for this reaction in terms of concentrations.

$$K_c = \frac{[\text{product}]}{[\text{propanone}][\text{hydrogen cyanide}]} \, \text{dm}^3 \, \text{mol}^{-1}$$

Note that the units are

$$\frac{\text{mol dm}^{-3}}{\text{mol dm}^{-3} \times \text{mol dm}^{-3}} = \frac{1}{\text{mol dm}^{-3}} = \text{dm}^3 \, \text{mol}^{-1}$$

*Step 4* The equilibrium concentrations can now be used to calculate $K_c$.

$$K_c = \frac{0.0233}{0.0267 \times 0.0267} \, \text{dm}^3 \, \text{mol}^{-1}$$

$$= 32.7 \, \text{dm}^3 \, \text{mol}^{-1}$$

*SAQ 7.8*

Calculate the equilibrium constant for the following reaction.

$$H_2(g) + CO_2(g) \rightleftharpoons CO(g) + H_2O(g)$$

The initial concentration of hydrogen is 10.00 mol dm$^{-3}$ and of carbon dioxide is 90.00 mol dm$^{-3}$. At equilibrium 9.47 mol dm$^{-3}$ of carbon monoxide are formed.

# $K_c$ and Le Chatelier's principle

On pages 122–4 you saw how Le Chatelier's principle can be used to predict the effects of changes in concentration, pressure or temperature on the position of an equilibrium. For example, increasing the concentration of a reactant will lead to an increase in the concentrations of the products at a new position of equilibrium.

Predictions using Le Chatelier's principle of the effects of temperature changes are summarised, with examples, in *table 7.6*.

## $K_c$ and temperature changes

A consequence of the effects shown in *table 7.6* of changing the temperature of a reaction is that the equilibrium constant $K_c$ must also change. We can now understand why we must carry out experiments to determine values of $K_c$ at a constant temperature.

For example, the information in *table 7.6* states that an increase in temperature for an endothermic reaction, such as the decomposition of hydrogen iodide, causes more hydrogen and iodine to form. For this reaction:

$$K_c = \frac{[H_2][I_2]}{[HI]^2}$$

We can see that, if the concentrations of products increase, the concentration of HI must fall and $K_c$

● **Table 7.6** The effect of temperature change on equilibria.

| Example | Endothermic reaction, $2HI(g) \rightleftharpoons H_2(g) + I_2(g)$ | Exothermic reaction, $2SO_2(g) + O_2(g) \rightleftharpoons 2SO_3(g)$ |
|---|---|---|
| Temperature increase | equilibrium position shifts towards products: more hydrogen and iodine form | equilibrium position shifts towards reactants: more sulphur dioxide and oxygen form |
| Temperature decrease | equilibrium position shifts towards reactant: more hydrogen iodide forms | equilibrium position shifts towards product: more sulphur trioxide forms |

| Reaction | Temperature (K) | $K_c$ |
|---|---|---|
| $2HI(g) \rightleftharpoons H_2(g) + I_2(g)$ | 300 | $1.26 \times 10^{-3}$ |
| | 500 | $6.25 \times 10^{-3}$ |
| | 1000 | $18.5 \times 10^{-3}$ |

● **Table 7.7** Equilibrium constants and their variation at different temperatures for the decomposition of hydrogen iodide.

must increase. *Table 7.7* shows some values for the equilibrium constant for the decomposition of hydrogen iodide at different temperatures.

### SAQ 7.9

Deduce the effect of an increase in temperature on $K_c$ for the oxidation of $SO_2$, shown in *table 7.6*.

For the oxidation of $SO_2$ shown in *table 7.6*, an increase in temperature produces less of the product, $SO_3$. The concentrations of the reactants will rise and $K_c$ will decrease. This reaction is the key stage in the manufacture of concentrated sulphuric acid in which temperatures of 700 to 800 K are used. Despite these temperatures, a very high percentage conversion (over 99.5%) is achieved by passing the reactants through a total of four beds of the catalyst, vanadium(V) oxide $(V_2O_5)$.

The effects of temperature changes on $K_c$ are summarised in *table 7.8*.

The equilibrium constant expression can be also be used to predict the outcome of changes in concentration or pressure. However, unlike temperature changes, concentration or pressure changes do not affect the magnitude of $K_c$.

### $K_c$ and concentration changes

Consider again the decomposition of hydrogen iodide:

$$2HI(g) \rightleftharpoons H_2(g) + I_2(g)$$

| | Endothermic reaction, $\Delta H$ positive | Exothermic reaction, $\Delta H$ negative |
|---|---|---|
| temperature increase | equilibrium constant increases | equilibrium constant decreases |
| temperature decrease | equilibrium constant decreases | equilibrium constant increases |

● **Table 7.8** The effect of temperature changes on equilibrium constants.

The equilibrium constant, at 500 K, is:

$$K_c = \frac{[H_2][I_2]}{[HI]^2} = 6.25 \times 10^{-3}$$

Suppose more hydrogen iodide is introduced into the equilibrium mixture, whilst maintaining a constant volume and a temperature of 500 K. [HI] will increase and the mixture will no longer be in a state of equilibrium. To restore equilibrium, both $[H_2]$ and $[I_2]$ must increase whilst [HI] decreases. Equilibrium will be restored when the values of these concentrations, when entered in the equilibrium constant expression, once again equal the value of $K_c$ at 500 K ($6.25 \times 10^{-3}$).

## Equilibrium constants and pressure changes

So far we have expressed equilibrium constants in terms of $K_c$, where the small subscript 'c' indicates concentration. Where gases are involved in the reactions, chemists prefer to use pressures rather than concentrations. The **equilibrium constant** in terms of pressures has the symbol $K_p$, where the subscript 'p' indicates pressure.

For the decomposition of hydrogen iodide, the equilibrium constant in terms of partial pressures is:

$$K_p = \frac{p(H_2) \times p(I_2)}{p(HI)^2}$$

The term $p(H_2)$ indicates the equilibrium partial pressure of hydrogen in a closed system containing the equilibrium mixture at a constant temperature.

In a closed container, the **partial pressure** of a gas in a mixture of gases is the pressure exerted by that gas *alone* whilst disregarding the presence of the other gases. In the Haber process to form ammonia from hydrogen and nitrogen, the partial pressures of hydrogen, nitrogen and ammonia are required. The total pressure of these gases in any mixture is the sum of the partial pressures (*figure 7.11*).

### Calculating partial pressures

We can calculate the partial pressure of each gas present if we know both the

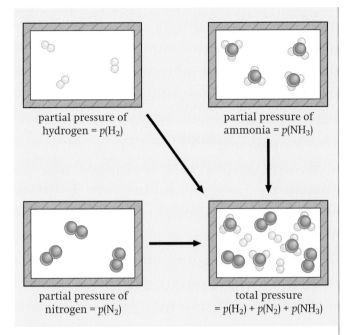

● **Figure 7.11** Each gas (hydrogen, nitrogen and ammonia) contributes its partial pressure to the total pressure.

total pressure and the number of moles of each gas present.

For example, a sample of air at 500 kPa pressure contains 1 mole of oxygen and 4 moles of nitrogen. Calculate the partial pressure of each.

*Step 1* Calculate the **mole fraction** of each gas. In total there is 1 mole of oxygen plus 4 moles of nitrogen, so the total number of moles is 5.

mole fraction of oxygen = $\frac{1}{5}$ = 0.200

mole fraction of nitrogen = $\frac{4}{5}$ = 0.800

Check: the sum of the mole fractions should add up to 1.00.

*Step 2* The next step is to calculate the partial pressure of each gas by multipling the mole fraction by the total pressure.

partial pressure oxygen = $p(O_2)$ = 0.200 × 500 kPa
= 100 kPa;

partial pressure nitrogen = $p(N_2)$
= 0.800 × 500 kPa
= 400 kPa.

*Step 3* Make a final check – does the sum of the partial pressures equal the total pressure?

100 + 400 = 500 kPa, so we can have confidence in our calculation.

# The Haber process and calculating $K_p$

The Haber process for the production of ammonia from nitrogen and hydrogen is described later in this chapter (see *figures 7.13, 7.14* and *7.15*).

The conditions used for this process are a compromise between a sufficiently fast rate without too much reduction in yield. The reaction is exothermic so increasing the temperature decreases the yield of ammonia whilst increasing the reaction rate.

The equation for the Haber process reaction is as follows:

$$N_2(g) + 3H_2(g) \rightleftharpoons 2NH_3(g)$$

The conditions used in a modern plant are as follows:

■ a pressure between 2.5 and 15 MPa;
1 MPa = 1 × $10^6$ Pa

■ a temperature of between about 670 and 770 K.

In terms of the partial pressures of nitrogen, hydrogen and ammonia, the equilibrium constant expression is:

$$K_p = \frac{p(NH_3)^2}{p(N_2) \times p(H_2)^3}$$

## SAQ 7.10

Write down the expression and units for $K_p$ in the following equilibria:
**a** $N_2(g) + O_2(g) \rightleftharpoons 2NO(g)$
**b** $C_2H_4(g) + H_2O(g) \rightleftharpoons C_2H_5OH(g)$

## SAQ 7.11

At a temperature of 670 K and 5 MPa pressure, an equilibrium mixture in the Haber process was found to contain 0.925 mol nitrogen, 2.775 mol hydrogen and 0.150 mol ammonia.
**a** (i) Use the above data to calculate the mole fraction of each of the gases in the mixture.
   (ii) Hence calculate the partial pressure of each gas.
**b** (i) Use the equilibrium constant expression above, together with your answer from a(ii), to calculate a value for the equilibrium constant, $K_p$, for the Haber process reaction.
   (ii) Determine the units for your value of $K_p$.

# Using $K_c$ and $K_p$

You should try to develop a 'feel' for values of $K_c$ and $K_p$, so that when you look at an equilibrium and the values for the equilibrium constants you can begin to imagine the extent of the formation of product from reactant. High values of $K_c$ or $K_p$ indicate a high percentage of products compared to reactants.

Another way is to tackle problems involving equilibrium constants – something expected of you in A-level examinations. Some examples are given below.

## Question

Write the equation for the equilibrium established in the reaction between nitrogen and oxygen to produce nitrogen monoxide, NO. Write the expression for the equilibrium constant $K_p$ for this reaction. What are the units for $K_p$?

## Answer

Equation is

$$N_2(g) + O_2(g) \rightleftharpoons 2NO(g)$$

$$K_p = \frac{p(NO)^2}{p(N_2)\,p(O_2)} \quad \text{units:} \quad \frac{(Pa)^2}{Pa \times Pa}$$

The units all cancel, i.e. $K_p$ is a number – it has no units.

## Question

The value of the equilibrium constant for the above reaction at 293 K and 100 kPa pressure is $4.0 \times 10^{-31}$. What does this value tell you about the equilibrium?

---

## Box 7B Pollution and the equilibrium $N_2(g) + O_2(g) \rightleftharpoons 2NO(g)$

At 1100 K the value of $K_c$ increases to $4 \times 10^{-8}$, still very small. However, calculations show that in $1\,cm^3$ of air at this temperature there would be around $2 \times 10^{15}$ molecules of nitrogen oxide in an equilibrium – a small fraction of the total but enough to pose a pollution threat. Vehicle engines are a significant source of nitrogen oxide molecules. They contribute to a complex series of reactions with other molecules such as carbon monoxide, sulphur dioxide and hydrocarbons. Light energy plays its part, and the result can be a 'photochemical smog' of the form experienced in cities (figure 7.12). The irritating chemicals produced include low-level ozone, $O_3$, and peroxyacetyl nitrates (PAN: $RCO \cdot O_2 \cdot NO_2$), which make your eyes water. Both of these are implicated in triggering asthma attacks.

In chapter 8, you can see how the work of chemists contributed to the development of catalytic converters for use in cars. However, whilst these converters remove NO, CO and unburnt hydrocarbons, they are only really a stopgap solution. Vehicles that burn hydrocarbons contribute large quantities of $CO_2$ to the atmosphere. This $CO_2$ is now accepted as making a major contribution to global warming by the greenhouse effect. Also, the metals in the catalytic converters, such as platinum, are gradually lost from catalytic converters. Measurable quantities of platinum have been found in road dust. This loss is a problem as these metals are very expensive and many people have an adverse reaction to platinum and its compounds. The supplies of fossil fuels such as oil are limited and scientists are seeking alternatives. However, even these alternatives may have environmental consequences. A car burning hydrogen as a fuel will produce NO if the combustion temperature is high.

In view of such problems we should be questioning our reliance on individual motorised transport and seeking major improvements in public transport in order to reduce the number of sources of pollutants.

Some photochemical smog occurs naturally. The haze of the Smoky Mountains in the USA seems to be caused by the reactions between oils from the pine forests and citrus groves with naturally occurring ozone. Atmospheric chemistry is both fascinating and complex: there will always be a need for research in this area.

● **Figure 7.12** Photochemical smog caused by light reacting with pollutant molecules.

## Answer

The extremely low value indicates that at 293 K and 100 kPa the equilibrium is very much to the left-hand side, i.e. the reaction hardly occurs at all. (This is just as well – we live in a nitrogen/oxygen atmosphere, which would fuel this reaction!)

## Question

$\Delta H^{\ominus}$ is positive for the above equilibrium between nitrogen and oxygen. How would you expect $K_p$ to change with temperature?

## Answer

If $\Delta H$ is positive, the reaction is endothermic, i.e. heat is required to move the equilibrium to the right. If the temperature of the reaction is raised, the system would have to absorb more energy. Le Chatelier's principle predicts that the equilibrium would respond to minimise this effect. The additional energy could be used to create more nitrogen oxide, i.e. move the equilibrium to the right. (See box 7B.)

You have now been introduced to the quantitative approaches that chemists use for a chemical equilibrium. In the A2 material in this chapter, we will apply this quantitative approach to understand how acids, bases and buffers work.

# An equilibrium of importance: the Haber process

We will now gather together these ideas using a reaction that is important from the theoretical, the practical and the industrial points of view. It is the Haber process for the 'fixation' of atmospheric nitrogen. We need large amounts of nitrogen compounds, particularly for fertilisers. Air is 80% nitrogen, so atmospheric nitrogen is the most plentiful and readily available source. At the same time, it cannot be used directly in the gaseous form; it needs to be 'fixed' into a chemically combined form to make a useful compound. One possible conversion might be to ammonia. Unlike nitrogen, ammonia is a reactive gas readily soluble in water, is readily convertible to ammonium salts, and can be converted to nitric acid by the Ostwald process of oxidation.

The equation for the reaction to form ammonia is as follows:

$$N_2(g) + 3H_2(g) \rightleftharpoons 2NH_3(g); \qquad \Delta H = -93\,\text{kJ mol}^{-1}$$

$\Delta H$ refers to the enthalpy change of reaction (see chapter 5). The unreactive nature of nitrogen is, of course, a problem. Although the reaction is exothermic, the triple bond within nitrogen molecules lends them great strength, so the reaction has a high activation energy. How may the equilibrium be influenced to give a good yield of ammonia? This problem was solved in the early 1900s by the German chemist Fritz Haber, and the process that he developed is essentially that which is still in use today.

The obvious thing to do would seem to be to increase the temperature. However, by using Le Chatelier's principle, since the reaction is exothermic, increasing the temperature will drive the equilibrium to the left (table 7.2). This effect is quite dramatic (table 7.9); at 373 K and 25 atm the percentage of ammonia resulting from an initial mixture of 1 volume of nitrogen and 3 volumes of hydrogen is 91.7%: at 973 K this percentage drops to 0.9%.

Pressure is another variable. We can reason that an increase of pressure will drive the equilibrium to the right. From Avogadro's hypothesis, we know that equal volumes of all gases under the same conditions of temperature and pressure contain the same number of molecules. One mole of any gas therefore occupies the same volume, at standard temperature, 298 K, and pressure, 1 atm = 101 kPa. From this we can deduce the proportions by volume of the gases as follows:

$$N_2(g) + 3H_2(g) \rightleftharpoons 2NH_3(g);$$

1 volume   3 volumes   2 volumes     $\Delta H = -93\,\text{kJ mol}^{-1}$

According to Le Chatelier's principle, an increase in pressure should drive the equilibrium to the right, since this will result in a decrease in volume. This is found in practice, and table 7.9 gives the relevant figures.

Imagine you were asked to design a chemical production plant for the manufacture of ammonia. From our discussion we might consider using the highest possible pressure with a suitably low temperature, for example about 50 MPa and 300 K.

However, such a choice would create difficulties. The high activation enthalpy means that the rate of reaction is effectively zero at 300 K. Very high pressures increase the rate of reaction but dramatically increase the cost of the plant. The cost of labour for running the plant also increases as the type of pumps required for maintaining high pressure require more maintenance.

The problem of the very low rate of reaction can be partially overcome by the choice of a suitable catalyst (see page 188) such as porous iron (figure 7.13). Small amounts of the oxides of potassium, magnesium, aluminium and silicon improve the efficiency of the catalyst. The catalyst enables the reaction to proceed by a different route with a lower activation energy (see page 171). The rate can also be increased by raising the temperature and accepting a reduced equilibrium percentage of ammonia in the mixture. Modern plants operate at much lower pressures than older plants despite the reduction in the equilibrium percentage of ammonia. Such compromises reduce the overall production costs sufficiently to justify replacing an old plant.

There are two more ways in which the efficiency of an ammonia plant may be improved:

■ Ammonia is removed as it is formed so that the reaction mixture is not left to reach equilibrium. This means that the reaction rate stays reasonably high. If the reaction is allowed to approach equilibrium, the reaction rate

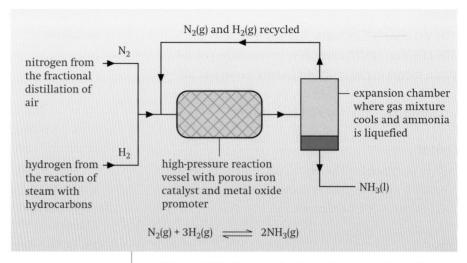

$$N_2(g) + 3H_2(g) \rightleftharpoons 2NH_3(g)$$

● **Figure 7.13** The production of ammonia by the Haber process.

decreases as concentrations of the reactants decrease.

■ The plant operates continuously and, after passing through the reaction vessel, the reaction mixture is passed into an expansion chamber where rapid expansion cools the mixture and allows ammonia to liquefy (figure 7.13). The liquefied ammonia is run off to pressurised storage vessels and the unreacted nitrogen and hydrogen is recirculated over the catalyst in the reaction vessel.

Modern Haber process plants (figure 7.14):

■ are highly efficient in conversion of nitrogen and hydrogen to ammonia;

| | Percentage of ammonia at equilibrium | | | |
|---|---|---|---|---|
| Temperature (K) | 25 atm | 50 atm | 100 atm | 200 atm |
| 373 | 91.7 | 94.5 | 96.7 | 98.4 |
| 573 | 27.4 | 39.6 | 53.1 | 66.7 |
| 773 | 2.9 | 5.6 | 10.5 | 18.3 |
| 973 | 0.9 | 1.2 | 3.4 | 8.7 |

● **Table 7.9** Percentage of ammonia in the equilibrium mixture at various temperatures and pressures.

● **Figure 7.14** This modern ammonia plant is based on the chemical reaction devised by Fritz Haber in the early 1900s.

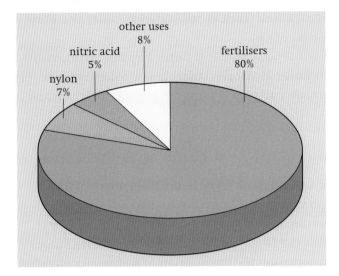

nylon 7%

nitric acid 5%

other uses 8%

fertilisers 80%

● **Figure 7.15** The uses of ammonia.

■ have a low energy consumption (around 35 MJ per kg of nitrogen converted to ammonia);
■ are smaller, so they are less expensive to build;
■ have less environmental impact;
■ may be sited where they are needed, reducing transport costs.

The conditions used in modern plant are:
■ a pressure between 2.5 and 15 MPa;
■ a temperature between 670 and 770 K;
■ a finely divided or porous iron catalyst with metal oxide promoters.

80% of ammonia production goes into making fertilisers such as ammonium sulphate. It has been claimed that without the invention of the Haber process, a much higher proportion of the World's population would have died of starvation. The increasing human population requires ever more intensive agricultural production techniques. In order to grow crops repeatedly in the same soil, artificial fertilisers are added to maintain fertility.

Much smaller proportions of ammonia production are used for making nitric acid (which in turn is used to make explosives) and polymers such as nylon. These proportions are shown in *figure 7.15*.

# A second equilibrium of importance: the Contact process

The Contact process for the manufacture of sulphuric acid from sulphur involves three main reactions:

■ the burning of sulphur in air at about 1000 °C to produce sulphur dioxide

$$S(g) + O_2(g) \rightarrow SO_2(g)$$

■ the reaction between sulphur dioxide and more air, in the presence of a vanadium(V) oxide, $V_2O_5$, catalyst, to produce sulphur trioxide

$$2SO_2(g) + O_2(g) \rightleftharpoons 2SO_3(g); \Delta H = -197 \, kJ \, mol^{-1}$$

■ the absorption of sulphur trioxide in concentrated sulphuric acid to form oleum, $H_2S_2O_7$, which is then diluted to give sulphuric acid of the required concentration.

$$SO_3(g) + H_2SO_4(l) \rightarrow H_2S_2O_7(l)$$
$$H_2S_2O_7(l) + H_2O(l) \rightarrow 2H_2SO_4(aq)$$

The conversion of sulphur dioxide into sulphur trioxide is an equilibrium reaction which is exothermic (see *tables 7.2* and *7.3*). The conditions used in a modern plant are as follows:
■ a vanadium(V) oxide catalyst;
■ a temperature of 400 °C to 600 °C;
■ a pressure that is just above atmospheric pressure.

As with the Haber process, the conditions used for the conversion of sulphur dioxide into sulphur trioxide are a compromise.

Higher yields of sulphur trioxide are obtained by using a considerable excess of air, thus, according to Le Chatelier's principle, forcing the equilibrium to the right-hand side.

Le Chatelier's principle also predicts higher yields when low temperatures and high pressures are used. In practice, a temperature of at least 400 °C must be used because the catalyst is ineffective below this temperature. The catalyst and the higher temperature each increase the rate of conversion of sulphur dioxide into sulphur trioxide.

High pressures are uneconomic and in the Contact process a pressure is used that is high enough to pump the gases around the chemical plant.

There are two further aspects of the process that improve its efficiency.

■ A three- or four-stage process is used for the actual conversion of sulphur dioxide into sulphur trioxide. After each exothermic stage, the gas mixture is cooled back to 400 °C before passing it over another bed of vanadium(v) oxide. This gives an overall conversion of sulphur dioxide into sulphur trioxide of 99.5%.

■ Waste heat produced by the combustion of sulphur and the conversion of sulphur dioxide into sulphur trioxide is used as a source of energy elsewhere in the chemical works.

Water cannot be used to absorb the sulphur trioxide because when the two compounds are mixed a mist of sulphuric acid is formed, which will not readily condense as a liquid. Such a mist would be a major pollution hazard.

The small amount of sulphur dioxide remaining, which would cause acid rain, is removed before the nitrogen present is released into the atmosphere.

Sulphuric acid is used in a wide variety of industries. The main uses are:

■ the manufacture of paints;
■ the manufacture of detergents and soaps;
■ the manufacture of phosphate fertilisers;
■ the manufacture of dyestuffs.

# Acids and their reactions

You will have learnt to recognise an **acid** by its behaviour. For example, an acid:

■ turns blue litmus red;
■ has a pH of less than 7;
■ produces carbon dioxide when added to a carbonate, such as magnesium carbonate;

■ is neutralised by an **alkali** (such as sodium hydroxide) or a **base** (such as magnesium oxide).

Hydrochloric acid is a typical acid. It is formed by dissolving hydrogen chloride gas in water. Hydrogen chloride is a polar covalent molecule which ionises completely in water, producing $H^+(aq)$ and $Cl^-(aq)$ ions:

$$HCl(g) \xrightarrow{\text{water}} H^+(aq) + Cl^-(aq)$$

We call the aqueous solution of $H^+(aq)$ and $Cl^-(aq)$, hydrochloric acid. $H^+(aq)$ is a hydrated proton (a hydrogen *atom* consists of a proton and an electron; a hydrogen *ion* is simply a proton). We sometimes represent the $H^+(aq)$ ion as the oxonium ion $H_3O^+(aq)$. We can rewrite the equation for the reaction of hydrogen chloride gas with water as follows:

$$HCl(g) + H_2O(l) \rightarrow H_3O^+(aq) + Cl^-(aq)$$

Equations like this, which show the presence of ions, are called ionic equations (see also page 24). Chemists find ionic equations useful when discussing reactions of acids. Ionic equations are also useful when discussing other reactions involving ions, such as redox reactions (see page 95).

Chemists often define an acid as having the ability to transfer a proton to another molecule or ion. In *figure 7.16* hydrogen chloride has donated a proton to a water molecule. Hence we can define hydrogen chloride as an acid. Some of the reactions of a typical acid are summarised in *table 7.10*.

## Salt formation by acids

### The reaction of hydrogen chloride with ammonia

Hydrogen chloride gas will also react with ammonia gas. You may have seen the experiment shown in *figure 7.17*.

The pieces of cotton wool soaked in concentrated hydrochloric acid and in concentrated ammonia readily give off fumes of the

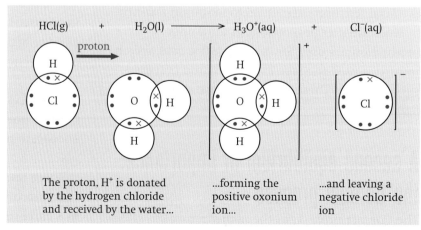

The proton, $H^+$ is donated by the hydrogen chloride and received by the water...

...forming the positive oxonium ion...

...and leaving a negative chloride ion

● **Figure 7.16** An acid is a proton donor. Hydrogen chloride is the acid in this reaction.

| Type of reactant | Example | Equation |
|---|---|---|
| metal | zinc | $Zn(s) + 2H^+(aq) \rightarrow Zn^{2+}(aq) + H_2(g)$ |
| base | copper(II) oxide | $2H^+(aq) + CuO(s) \rightarrow Cu^{2+}(aq) + H_2O(l)$ |
| carbonate | sodium carbonate | $2H^+(aq) + Na_2CO_3(s) \rightarrow 2Na^+(aq) + CO_2(g) + H_2O(l)$ |
| alkali | aqueous potassium hydroxide | $H^+(aq) + OH^-(aq) \rightarrow H_2O(l)$ |

● **Table 7.10** Some reactions of a typical acid. With hydrochloric acid, the chloride salt of the metal is formed.

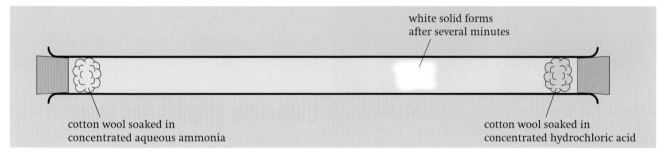

● **Figure 7.17** An experiment to show that hydrogen chloride gas (an acid) and ammonia gas (a base) react to form solid ammonium chloride.

two gases. These fumes diffuse along the glass tube. At the point where they meet, a reaction occurs producing ammonium chloride as a white solid. This appears about a third of the way along the tube from the concentrated hydrochloric acid end. This is because $NH_3$ molecules are lighter and smaller than HCl molecules, so they diffuse faster. An equation for this reaction is

$$HCl(g) + NH_3(g) \rightarrow NH_4Cl(s)$$

Ammonium chloride is a salt containing ammonium ions, $NH_4^+$, and chloride ions, $Cl^-$. We could rewrite the equation as:

$$HCl(g) + NH_3(g) \rightarrow NH_4^+(s) + Cl^-(s)$$

Again, by our definition, hydrogen chloride has behaved as an acid, in this reaction donating a proton to an ammonia molecule. By neutralising the acid, the ammonia molecule is behaving as a base.

### The production of a fertiliser salt

The reaction of ammonia with dilute sulphuric acid is a particularly important reaction as the product is the fertiliser ammonium sulphate, $(NH_4)_2SO_4$. The full equation for the reaction of ammonia with dilute sulphuric acid is:

$$2NH_3(aq) + H_2SO_4(aq) \rightarrow (NH_4)_2SO_4(aq)$$

The sulphuric acid has donated protons to ammonia molecules to form $NH_4^+(aq)$. As with hydrochloric acid, ammonia is behaving as a base by neutralising the acid. The ionic equation is:

$$2NH_3(aq) + 2H^+(aq) + SO_4^{2-}(aq) \\ \rightarrow 2NH_4^+(aq) + SO_4^{2-}(aq)$$

The sulphate ions are unchanged during the reaction and the equation may be simplified to:

$$NH_3(aq) + H^+(aq) \rightarrow NH_4^+(aq)$$

We describe ions which are unchanged in a reaction as **spectator ions**. They are present to balance the charges of oppositely charged ions in the reaction mixture.

### The formation of salts with metals, metal oxides and metal carbonates

The reactions of hydrochloric acid with magnesium, magnesium oxide or magnesium carbonate are described on page 220. In each case a salt (magnesium chloride, $MgCl_2$) is formed. Such behaviour is typical of all acids. For example, black copper(II) oxide dissolves in dilute sulphuric acid on warming to give a blue solution of copper sulphate (*figure 7.18a*). With hydrochloric acid, copper(II) oxide forms a green solution of copper(II) chloride (*figure 7.18b*). Metal oxides which dissolve in an acid are termed bases as the oxide ions accept protons.

● **Figure 7.18** Small beakers of black copper(II) oxide dissolving in **a** sulphuric acid and **b** hydrochloric acid.

The ionic equation for the reaction of copper(II) oxide with hydrochloric acid is:

$$2H^+(aq) + 2Cl^-(aq) + CuO(s)$$
$$\rightarrow Cu^{2+}(aq) + 2Cl^-(aq) + H_2O(l)$$

$2Cl^-(aq)$ appears on both sides of the equation. It is unchanged, so we can simplify the equation to:

$$2H^+(aq) + CuO(s) \rightarrow Cu^{2+}(aq) + H_2O(l)$$

In this reaction two protons from hydrochloric acid have been donated to an oxide ion, $O^{2-}$, in copper(II) oxide to form a water molecule. Like the sulphate ions in the production of ammonium sulphate fertiliser, the chloride ions are also spectator ions.

### SAQ 7.12

**a** Write balanced ionic equations for the reaction of hydrochloric acid with (i) calcium, (ii) strontium oxide, SrO(s), and (iii) barium carbonate, $BaCO_3(s)$.

**b** Name and give the formula of the salt formed for each reaction in part **a**.

### Strong and weak acids

Hydrochloric acid is described as a **strong acid**. Molecules of strong acids, such as hydrogen chloride, are fully dissociated to ions in aqueous solution. Nitric and sulphuric acids are also strong acids.

Many organic acids are described as **weak acids**. This term signifies that their molecules are only partially ionised in aqueous solution. An equilibrium exists between the undissociated molecules and the ions. For example, ethanoic acid is a weak acid; the equilibrium equation can be written as:

$$CH_3COOH(aq) \rightleftharpoons CH_3COO^-(aq) + H^+(aq)$$

In water, approximately one in a thousand molecules of ethanoic acid are dissociated into ions.

# Definitions of acids and bases

In 1923, the Danish chemist J. N. Brønsted and the English chemist T. M. Lowry made the suggestion that an acid may be defined as a proton donor, and a base as a proton acceptor. A proton is a positive hydrogen ion, $H^+$. This is a long way from the first definitions you may have used for acids and bases (see *box 7C*).

Modern definitions are more precise than those which define an acid as something with a sour taste that turns blue litmus red, and a base as something that tastes bitter, feels soapy and turns red litmus blue (*figure 7.19*). Such statements have some validity, but are limited and arbitrary. Health and safety legislation prevents us using taste to identify acids or bases in the laboratory.

● **Figure 7.19**
**a** The sour taste of lemons is due to citric acid and that of vinegar is due to ethanoic (acetic) acid.
**b** A solution of washing soda feels soapy. Washing soda is used to soften water prior to washing clothes.

## Box 7C Acids and bases

Here are some definitions of acids and bases. (An alkali is a water-soluble base.)
Chemists tend to use the Brønsted–Lowry definition, as we will in this book.

| Definition of acid | Definition of base | Advantage of definition |
|---|---|---|
| Tastes sharp or sour, like lemon | Tastes bitter, feels soapy or greasy | Is there any? |
| Turns purple cabbage juice red | Turns purple cabbage juice green or yellow | You can make your own indicator to test liquids |
| Turns blue litmus red | Turns red litmus blue | You can use test papers |
| Turns universal indicator red, orange or yellow | Turns universal indicator green, blue or purple | You can compare strengths of various acids and alkalis |
| Produces an excess of hydrogen ions, $H^+$(aq), in aqueous solution (Arrhenius 1884) | Produces an excess of hydroxide ions, $OH^-$(aq), in aqueous solution (Arrhenius 1884) | Enables acid–base reactions, e.g. neutralisation, to be explained as a reaction: $H^+$(aq) + $OH^-$(aq) → $H_2O$(l) |
| Donates protons during a chemical reaction (Brønsted and Lowry 1923) | Accepts protons during a chemical reaction (Brønsted and Lowry 1923) | Explains the role of water and why (for example) HCl(aq) is acidic but dry HCl(g) is not |

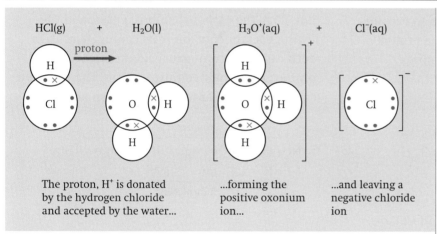

HCl(g) + H₂O(l)      H₃O⁺(aq) + Cl⁻(aq)

The proton, $H^+$ is donated by the hydrogen chloride and accepted by the water...

...forming the positive oxonium ion...

...and leaving a negative chloride ion

● **Figure 7.20** An acid is a proton donor. Hydrogen chloride is the acid in this reaction. A base is a proton acceptor. Water is the base in this reaction. Remember that a proton is a hydrogen ion, $H^+$.

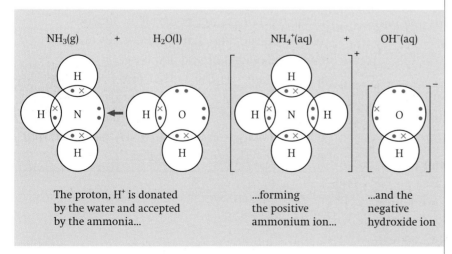

NH₃(g) + H₂O(l)      NH₄⁺(aq) + OH⁻(aq)

The proton, $H^+$ is donated by the water and accepted by the ammonia...

...forming the positive ammonium ion...

...and the negative hydroxide ion

● **Figure 7.21** Water is the proton donor (it is the acid); ammonia is the proton acceptor (it is the base).

Nor do such statements help to explain what is going on when acids and bases take part in chemical reactions.

The **Brønsted–Lowry definition** is particularly appropriate when considering the chemistry of aqueous solutions. We will start with the formation of one of the most familiar acids of all – hydrochloric acid. It is made when hydrogen chloride, a gas, dissolves and reacts in water.

In aqueous solution, hydrogen chloride donates a proton to water to form the oxonium ion, $H_3O^+$(aq), as shown in *figure 7.20*.

In contrast, a base will accept a proton to give the hydroxide ion, $OH^-$(aq), as shown for ammonia in *figure 7.21*. Note that water behaves as a base in the hydrogen chloride solution, and as an acid in the ammonia solution. Substances which can act as an acid or a base are described as **amphoteric**. Aluminium oxide, $Al_2O_3$, is another example of an amphoteric compound.

In both cases we have omitted an important fact: the reactions should, strictly speaking, be written as equilibria. So for the first case we write

$$HCl(g) + H_2O(l) \rightleftharpoons H_3O^+(aq) + Cl^-(aq)$$

When we think about the forward reaction, HCl(g) is an acid because it donates a proton, $H^+$. Water is a base because it receives this proton. On page 138, hydrochloric acid was described as a strong acid. Strong acids are fully dissociated into ions, so this equilibrium lies well to the right of the above reaction equation.

Now consider the reverse reaction:

$$H_3O^+(aq) + Cl^-(aq) \rightleftharpoons HCl(g) + H_2O(l)$$

The proton is donated to the chloride ion to form hydrogen chloride. (The oxonium ion, $H_3O^+$, a proton donor, is an acid.) At the same time the chloride ion, $Cl^-(aq)$, accepts a proton to become hydrogen chloride. The chloride ion, a proton acceptor, is therefore a base. This can be summarised as shown:

conjugate pair

$$HCl(g) + H_2O(l) \rightleftharpoons H_3O^+(aq) + Cl^-(aq)$$

B–L acid    B–L base    B–L acid    B–L base

conjugate pair

Look at the relationship between the species. The chlorine-containing species, HCl(g) and $Cl^-(aq)$, form a pair. They are acid and base respectively, with the acid the richer in protons. We call this couple a **conjugate pair** (B–L is Brønsted–Lowry).

Consider the equilibrium between ammonia and water. The conjugate pairs of acids and bases are shown in the following equation.

conjugate pair

$$NH_3(aq) + H_2O(l) \rightleftharpoons NH_4^+(aq) + OH^-(aq)$$

B–L base    B–L acid    B–L acid    B–L base

conjugate pair

An ammonia molecule accepts a proton from water. Ammonia is thus behaving as a Brønsted–Lowry base in forming an ammonium ion, its conjugate pair acid. Water, meanwhile, has donated a proton to an ammonia molecule. Water is behaving as a Brønsted–Lowry acid in forming a hydroxide ion, its conjugate pair base.

## How to spot an acid or a base

Know these definitions:

- A Brønsted–Lowry acid is a proton (or $H^+$) donor.
- A Brønsted–Lowry base is a proton acceptor.

The Brønsted–Lowry definition applies to chemical changes in which protons, $H^+$, are transferred. Examine the change, and find the donors and acceptors.

We shall now look at the following example. Which are the conjugate pairs of acid and base in this reaction?

$$NH_4^+(aq) + CO_3^{2-}(aq) \rightleftharpoons HCO_3^-(aq) + NH_3(aq)$$

We can see that the ammonium ion donates a proton to the carbonate ion, and forms ammonia. Thus the ammonium ion is an acid, and the ammonia is its conjugate base. The carbonate ion accepts a proton, forming a hydrogencarbonate ion. Thus the carbonate ion is a base, and the hydrogencarbonate ion is its conjugate acid. In both cases the conjugate acids are richer in protons than their conjugate bases. The equation can therefore be annotated as shown below:

conjugate pair

$$NH_4^+(aq) + CO_3^{2-}(aq) \rightleftharpoons HCO_3^-(aq) + NH_3(g)$$

B–L acid    B–L base    B–L acid    B–L base

conjugate pair

### SAQ 7.13

Use the Brønsted–Lowry definition of acid and base to identify the acids and bases in these equilibria and their conjugate bases and acids. Note that one of the reactions is not occurring in aqueous solution, a situation that could not be covered by earlier definitions of acid and base.

**a** $H_2SO_4(aq) + H_2O(l) \rightleftharpoons H_3O^+(aq) + HSO_4^-(aq)$

**b** $CH_3COOH(aq) + H_2O(l) \rightleftharpoons CH_3COO^-(aq) + H_3O^+(aq)$

**c** $CH_3NH_2(aq) + H_2O(l) \rightleftharpoons CH_3NH_3^+(aq) + OH^-(aq)$

**d** $NH_3(g) + HCl(g) \rightleftharpoons NH_4^+Cl^-(s)$

# The role of water

Water seems a familiar, almost benign substance, not one to be involved when acids react with bases, e.g. in the formation of common salt from sodium hydroxide and hydrochloric acid. It seems to sit on the sidelines:

$$NaOH(aq) + HCl(aq) \rightleftharpoons NaCl(aq) + H_2O(l)$$

Don't be misled. Water is not an innocent by-stander in acid–base reactions. Water plays a crucial part. It helps to understand this if you know more about pure water itself.

## Water: facts and models

It is a fact that pure water conducts electricity, even if ever so slightly. It is quite unlike liquid helium, for example, or cyclohexane, which do not conduct electricity at all. Unlike these two sub-stances, water contains ions that can carry charge – indeed pure water can be electrolysed by a direct current. The conductivity of pure water is very low.

### SAQ 7.14

What does the low conductivity of water tell you about the number of ions available for carrying a direct current?

We can imagine a model for the formation of ions from water molecules, in terms of proton transfer. Suppose every now and then one water molecule could react with another to form ions. It could be as shown in *figure 7.22*. Protons leave one molecule of water for another, ions are formed, and these ions can transfer electrons during electrolysis.

This reaction can be summarised as

$$2H_2O(l) \rightleftharpoons H_3O^+(aq) + OH^-(aq)$$

or more simply as

$$H_2O(l) \rightleftharpoons H^+(aq) + OH^-(aq)$$

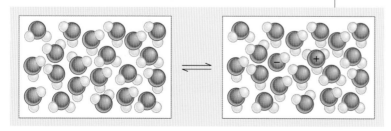

● **Figure 7.22** A proton is transferred from one water molecule to another, so that a positive ion, $H_3O^+$, is formed and a negative ion, $OH^-$, is left behind.

### SAQ 7.15

Experimental evidence tells us that the equilibrium constant for this reaction is very, very small. At 298 K it is $1 \times 10^{-14} \, mol^2 \, dm^{-6}$. What does this tell you about the relative proportions of water molecules, protons and hydroxide ions? Does this fit in with your knowledge of the electrical conductivity of pure water?

# Base behaviour and neutralisation

Acids react with bases and are said to neutralise each other. It is interesting to look at what neutralises what. Consider what is present in two separate solutions of hydrochloric acid and sodium hydroxide.

■ In the acid   $H^+(aq)$, $Cl^-(aq)$ and $H_2O(l)$
■ In the base   $Na^+(aq)$, $OH^-(aq)$ and $H_2O(l)$

When this soup of ions is mixed, the protons and hydroxide ions meet and react as follows:

$$H^+(aq) + OH^-(aq) \rightleftharpoons H_2O(l);$$
$$\Delta H^\ominus = -57 \, kJ \, mol^{-1}$$

As we saw above, the reaction favours the forma-tion of water molecules – the equilibrium is well to the right. Hardly any of the protons and hydrox-ide ions remain. The vast majority neutralise each other to form water. This is what neutralisation is – the formation of water by the exothermic for-ward reaction shown above. The ions remaining, $Na^+$ and $Cl^-$, stay dissolved in that water – and would form salt crystals if the water was allowed to evaporate.

All reactions between acids and alkalis are like this. However, not all reagents release their protons and hydroxide ions in large numbers as do the so-called strong acids hydrochloric acid and the strong bases such as sodium hydroxide. We need to consider the relative strengths of acids and bases, and what this means for neutralisation.

## Acids and bases of varying strength

Strong acids and bases are those which are totally ionised when dissolved in water. The strong acids include hydrogen halides and strong bases include the

Group I metal hydroxides. Consider what happens when examples of these dissolve in water and then react.

For every mole of these solutes, a mole of each positive and negative ion is produced in solution:

$$LiOH(s) \xrightarrow{\text{water}} Li^+(aq) + OH^-(aq)$$

$$HCl(g) \xrightarrow{\text{water}} H^+(aq) + Cl^-(aq)$$

If a mole of protons mixes with a mole of hydroxide ions they combine to form a mole of water molecules.

Weak acids and weak bases do not ionise totally when they dissolve in water; in fact, they may hardly ionise at all. When it comes to donating protons, weak acids are very limited. Ethanoic acid is a good example. Hardly any protons are liberated when it reacts in water, so that the concentration of protons is low. In the reaction shown below, the equilibrium is very much to the left:

$$CH_3COOH(l) \rightleftharpoons H^+(aq) + CH_3COO^-(aq)$$

Organic acids such as ethanoic acid (the sharp-tasting liquid in vinegar), and citric acid (the mouth-watering stuff of lemons) are typical weak acids. As proton donors go, they are pretty feeble. Weak bases are similarly feeble when it comes to accepting protons. They include the conjugate bases of strong acids, such as chloride and sulphate ions.

Table 7.11 shows some examples of conjugate acid–base pairs, together with their relative strengths.

As you will see, the relative strengths of acids and bases need to be known in order to monitor reactions between them. You need to understand the arithmetic behind measuring their relative strengths.

| | Acid | | | | Base | |
|---|---|---|---|---|---|---|
| strongest acid | hydrochloric | HCl | $\rightleftharpoons$ | $H^+ + Cl^-$ | chloride | weakest base |
| | benzoic | $C_6H_5COOH$ | $\rightleftharpoons$ | $H^+ + C_6H_5COO^-$ | benzoate | |
| | ethanoic | $CH_3COOH$ | $\rightleftharpoons$ | $H^+ + CH_3COO^-$ | ethanoate | |
| | ammonium | $NH_4^+$ | $\rightleftharpoons$ | $H^+ + NH_3$ | ammonia | |
| | phenol | $C_6H_5OH$ | $\rightleftharpoons$ | $H^+ + C_6H_5O^-$ | phenoxide | |
| | hydrogen-carbonate | $HCO_3^-$ | $\rightleftharpoons$ | $H^+ + CO_3^{2-}$ | carbonate | strongest base |
| weakest acid | water | $H_2O$ | $\rightleftharpoons$ | $H^+ + OH^-$ | hydroxide | |

(left arrow) Increasing acid strength    (right arrow) Increasing base strength

● **Table 7.11** Relative acid and base strength of some conjugate acid–base pairs.

# SUMMARY (AS)

◆ A reversible reaction is a reaction that may proceed in either direction (forward or reverse), depending on the applied conditions.

◆ Dynamic equilibrium occurs when the rate for the forward reaction is equal to the rate of the reverse reaction, so that products are formed at the same rate as they are decomposed. The equilibrium is dynamic because it is maintained despite continual changes occurring between molecules.

◆ A closed system is needed for equilibrium to be established in a chemical reaction. Equilibria are characterised by the constancy of macroscopic properties such as concentration.

◆ Le Chatelier's principle states that the equilibrium will shift so as to minimise the effect of a change in concentration, pressure or temperature.

◆ A catalyst may accelerate the rate at which the reaction achieves equilibrium.

- The conditions used in the Haber process for the production of ammonia are a compromise between ideal reaction conditions and the expense involved in producing those conditions. The key requirement is to produce the most yield for the least cost.

- Large quantities of ammonia are used for producing fertilisers such as ammonium sulphate.

- Acids are proton donors. Acids form salts and hydrogen with many metals. Acids are neutralised by: basic metal oxides to form salts and water; metal carbonates to form salts, water and carbon dioxide; alkalis to form salts and water. Ammonia behaves as a base as it is neutralised by sulphuric acid to form the salt ammonium sulphate.

- Strong acids, such as hydrochloric acid, are fully dissociated into ions. Weak acids, such as ethanoic acid, are only partially dissociated into ions. An equilibrium exists between the weak acid molecules and ions.

- The mole fraction of one gas in a mixture of gases is the number of moles of the particular gas divided by the total number of moles of all the gases present in a given volume.

- The partial pressure of a gas in a mixture of gases is the mole fraction × the total pressure.

- An equilibrium constant, $K_c$ (for concentrations) may be written using a balanced chemical equation for the reaction. For example, in the reaction
$N_2(g) + 3H_2(g) \rightleftharpoons 2NH_3(g)$
$$K_c = \frac{[NH_3]^2}{[N_2][H_2]^3} \, dm^6 \, mol^{-2}$$
The concentration (in square brackets) is raised to the power of the number of moles shown in the equation. Units must be worked out for each equilibrium constant. This may be done by placing them in the equation and cancelling out, as appropriate.

- For gas-phase reactions an alternative equilibrium constant, $K_p$ (for partial pressures), is often used. For the reaction above to produce ammonia
$$K_p = \frac{p(NH_3)^2}{p(N_2) \times p(H_2)^3} \, MPa^{-2}$$

- For an equilibrium system, changes in pressure or concentration have no effect on the value of the equilibrium constant. However, an **increase** in **temperature** for an **exo**thermic reaction **decreases** the value of the equilibrium constant and for an **endo**thermic reaction **increases** the value of the equilibrium constant.

- Large values for equilibrium constants indicate high theoretical yields of product (and vice versa). Most organic reactions achieve an equilibrium with appreciable amounts of both reactants and products present.

- The Brønsted–Lowry definition of an acid is a proton donor; a base is a proton acceptor.

- Weak acids are only partially ionised in solution; strong acids are almost fully dissociated in solution.

# Questions (AS)

1   The dissociation of hydrogen iodide can be represented by the equation below:

$$2HI(g) \rightleftharpoons H_2(g) + I_2(g); \Delta H^\circ = -53\,kJ\,mol^{-1}$$

  **a** Using this reaction as an example, explain what is meant by

    (i) a reversible reaction;

    (ii) a dynamic equilibrium.

  **b** Explain, giving a reason, the effect on the equilibrium above of:

    (i) increasing the temperature whilst keeping the pressure constant;

    (ii) increasing the pressure whilst keeping the temperature constant.

  **c** State the effect on the equilibrium above of adding a catalyst whilst keeping pressure and temperature constant.

2   Ammonia is made by the Haber process from nitrogen and hydrogen. The conditions used are a compromise to obtain a reasonable yield at a satisfactory rate. Typically, a temperature between 650 and 720 K is chosen with an iron catalyst containing promoters such as potassium hydroxide. In the most up-to-date Haber process plant, the pressure used is 11 MPa. These conditions typically produce about 15% conversion to ammonia.

The equation and enthalpy change for the reaction are as follows.

$$N_2(g) + 3H_2(g) \rightleftharpoons 2NH_3(g);$$
$$\Delta H^\circ = -92\,kJ\,mol^{-1}$$

  **a** (i) State Le Chatelier's principle.

    (ii) Use Le Chatelier's principle and the equation for the Haber process reaction to explain why a pressure of 11 MPa is used rather than a lower pressure.

    (iii) When a temperature lower than 650 K is used, a higher percentage conversion is achieved. Use Le Chatelier's principle and the enthalpy change for the Haber process to explain this effect.

    (iv) Explain why a temperature in the range 650–720 K is used even though a lower temperature produces a higher percentage conversion of ammonia.

  **b** Large quantities of ammonia are converted into ammonium sulphate by reaction of ammonia with sulphuric acid.

    (i) Write a balanced equation for this reaction.

    (ii) Suggest a use for the large quantities of ammonium sulphate produced in this way.

3   An acid, such as hydrochloric acid, will dissolve metals, carbonates, bases and alkalis to form salts.

  **a** (i) Describe what is meant by an acid, using hydrochloric acid as an example.

    (ii) Hydrochloric acid is a strong acid; many organic acids are weak acids. Explain the difference between a strong acid and a weak acid.

  **b** Write balanced equations for the following reactions:

    (i) The reaction of magnesium with hydrochloric acid to form magnesium chloride and hydrogen;

    (ii) The reaction of magnesium carbonate with hydrochloric acid to form magnesium chloride, carbon dioxide and water.

  **c** One of the two reactions in **b** is a redox reaction. Use oxidation states to identify which reaction is the redox reaction. Identify which element is oxidised and which is reduced. Give your reasons.

4 The key step in the Contact process for the manufacture of sulphuric acid involves the oxidation of sulphur dioxide to sulphur trioxide over a vanadium(v) oxide catalyst. The equation for this oxidation is shown below.

$2SO_2(g) + O_2(g) \rightleftharpoons 2SO_3(g)$ $\Delta H^\ominus = -197\,kJ\,mol^{-1}$

The industrial conditions chosen for this reaction are a temperature of 700 K and a pressure of $5 \times 10^5\,Pa$.

a Suggest reasons for this choice of temperature and pressure.

b Under the above conditions of temperature and pressure, 20.0 mol of sulphur dioxide and 10.0 mol of oxygen produced an equilibrium mixture in which 90% of the sulphur dioxide had been oxidised.

(i) Determine the amount in moles of sulphur dioxide present at equilibrium.

(ii) Hence calculate the amounts of oxygen and sulphur trioxide at equilibrium.

(iii) Calculate the mole fraction of each gas at equilibrium when the total pressure is $5 \times 10^5\,Pa$.

(iv) Hence calculate the partial pressure of each gas at equilibrium.

c (i) Write the equilibrium constant expression for this reaction in terms of partial pressures.

(ii) Using your data from part b, calculate a value for this equilibrium constant and state the units.

CHAPTER 7b

# Equilibria (A2)

**By the end of this section you should be able to:**

**10** define the terms pH, $K_w$, $K_a$ and $pK_a$;

**11** calculate pH from $[H^+(aq)]$ and $[H^+(aq)]$ from pH for strong acids and bases and for weak acids;

**12** explain the choice of suitable indicators for acid–base titrations, given the pH range of the indicator;

**13** describe acid–base titration *pH curves* for strong and weak acids and bases, recognise their shapes and explain these changes in terms of the strengths of acids and bases;

**14** explain what is meant by a *buffer solution* (as a system that minimises pH changes on addition of an acid or a base);

**15** explain the role of each component in a buffer solution in the control of pH;

**16** state the importance of buffer solutions for controlling pH in blood and shampoos;

**17** calculate the pH of a buffer solution, for example from the $K_a$ value of a weak acid and the equilibrium concentrations of the conjugate acid–base pair;

**18** explain and apply the concept of *solubility product,* $K_{sp}$;

**19** calculate $K_{sp}$ from concentrations and vice versa;

**20** explain the *common ion effect.*

## Introducing $K_w$, the ionic product of water

As shown already, pure water dissociates according to this equation:

$$H_2O(l) \rightleftharpoons H^+(aq) + OH^-(aq); \qquad \Delta H^\ominus = -57\,kJ\,mol^{-1}$$

The equilibrium constant expression is:

$$K_c = \frac{[H^+][OH^-]}{[H_2O]}$$

As $[H_2O]$ is effectively constant, we can write:

$$K_W = [H^+][OH^-]$$

The product, $[H^+][OH^-]$, is called the **ionic product of water**, $K_W$. At 298 K, $K_W = 1.00 \times 10^{-14}\,mol^2\,dm^{-6}$.

From the equation

$$H_2O(l) \rightleftharpoons H^+(aq) + OH^-(aq)$$

we can see that the concentration of protons equals the concentration of hydroxide ions.

We have defined $K_w$:

$$K_W = [H^+][OH^-] = 1 \times 10^{-14}\,mol^2\,dm^{-6} \text{ (at 298 K)}$$

This means that the concentration of each species, $[H^+]$ and $[OH^-]$, is $1 \times 10^{-7}\,mol\,dm^{-3}$ $(1 \times 10^{-7} \times 1 \times 10^{-7} = 1 \times 10^{-14})$.

# Introducing pH

The concentration of protons and hydroxide ions in pure water is clearly very small. Because it is awkward to fiddle about with tiny amounts like $1.0 \times 10^{-7}$ (0.000 000 1, a tenth of a millionth), chemists revert to using logarithmic scales. They do the same for large numbers too – see *box 7D*.

Chemists define **pH** as $-\log[H^+]$, i.e. the negative logarithm to the base ten of the concentration of the hydrogen ion. (The negative part helps us to cope with very small numbers, actually negative powers of ten.) Now you can appreciate why a neutral aqueous solution has a pH of 7:

$$pH = -\log_{10}[H^+]$$

With a scientific calculator you need to learn how to use the log button. For some calculators, the calculation is as follows:

- *Step 1*: Enter the concentration
$$10^{-7} \text{ or } 0.0000001$$
- *Step 2*: Press the log button      Ans: −7

- *Step 3*: Change the sign from − to +      Ans: +7
Be careful to use the $\log_{10}$ (or $\lg_{10}$) button and *not* the ln button (which is $\log_e$)!
- You should ensure that you know how to carry out this calculation on *your* scientific calculator.

## SAQ 7.16

Use the same process to calculate the pH of these solutions:

a  An aqueous solution with $[H^+] = 3 \times 10^{-4}\,mol\,dm^{-3}$ (e.g. a cola drink).

b  An aqueous solution with $[H^+] = 1 \times 10^{-2}\,mol\,dm^{-3}$ (stomach contents!).

c  An aqueous solution with $[H^+] = 4 \times 10^{-8}\,mol\,dm^{-3}$ (blood).

You can use the reverse process to calculate the concentration of protons, $[H^+(aq)]$. For example, calculate the concentration of protons in an aqueous solution with pH = 3.2.

- *Step 1* Enter the pH value      3.2

---

### Box 7D  Little numbers, large numbers and logs

Chemists deal with little and large. Miniscule molecules of water in enormous numbers are found in a sip of lemonade. To cope with this number range, we use powers of ten, as shown below:

| | | |
|---|---|---|
| Number of molecules of water in a sip of lemonade | 300 000 000 000 000 000 000 000 | $3 \times 10^{23}$ |
| Distance between the atoms in a molecule of water | 0.000 000 000 111 metres | $1.11 \times 10^{-10}\,m$ |

Other numbers that chemists might come across include the mass of the Earth $(5.97 \times 10^{24}\,kg)$ and the mass of a hydrogen atom $(1.67 \times 10^{-27}\,kg)$.

Ten to the power of 3 $(10^3$ or 1000) is ten times bigger than ten to the power of 2 $(10^2$ or 100). Powers of ten represent tenfold jumps in size and are called logarithms. Because we count in tens (unlike computers, which count in twos), we call these powers 'logarithms to the base ten', and write them as $\log_{10}$. In general, when we write 'number' $= 1 \times 10^x$, the value of $x$ is $\log_{10}$ ('number').

*Table 7.12* shows how $\log_{10}$ is used to represent the range of numbers we might use.

| Example | Number | | $\log_{10}$ |
|---|---|---|---|
| Molecules of ozone in $1\,cm^3$ of air on a good day | 100 000 000 000 000 | $= 10^{14}$ | 14.0 |
| Speed of light $(m\,s^{-1})$ | 300 000 000 | $= 3 \times 10^8$ | 8.5 |
| Solubility of $Ca(OH)_2\,(mol\,dm^{-3})$ | 0.015 3 | $= 1.53 \times 10^{-2}$ | −1.8 |
| Concentration of protons in pure water at 298 K $(mol\,dm^{-3})$ | 0.000 000 1 | $= 1 \times 10^{-7}$ | −7.0 |
| Concentration of protons in $0.1\,mol\,dm^{-3}$ NaOH(aq) $(mol\,dm^{-3})$ | 0.000 000 000 000 1 | $= 1 \times 10^{-13}$ | −13.0 |

- **Table 7.12** You will come across the term 'negative log' or '$-\log_{10}$'. This is not to complicate matters. It is simply a way of getting rid of the minus sign of the log of a small number. If $\log_{10}$('number') = −3, then −log10 ('number') = −1 × −3 = 3.

- *Step 2* Change the sign                                        −3.2
- *Step 3* Press the inverse log button or press the $10^x$ button                                 0.00063 or $6.3 \times 10^{-4}$
- *Step 4* Remember the units:

$$[H^+(aq)] = 6.3 \times 10^{-4}\,mol\,dm^{-3}$$

The pH values of some aqueous solutions with which you might be familiar are shown in *table 7.13*.

## Calculating the pH of strong acids and strong bases

Strong acids dissociate completely. This means that we know, from the initial concentration of the strong acid, just how many protons are present in a solution. If one mole of a monobasic acid, which has one replaceable proton, such as hydrochloric acid is present in a decimetre cube of solution, then the concentration of protons is $1\,mol\,dm^{-3}$. You can see this from the equation:

$$\overset{\text{water}}{HCl(g) \rightleftharpoons H^+(aq) + Cl^-(aq)}$$
$$\quad\; 1\text{mol} \qquad 1\text{mol} \qquad 1\text{mol}$$

| Solution | pH |
|---|---|
| hydrochloric acid ($1\,mol\,dm^{-3}$) | 0.0 |
| hydrochloric acid ($0.1\,mol\,dm^{-3}$) | 1.0 |
| hydrochloric acid ($0.01\,mol\,dm^{-3}$) | 2.0 |
| stomach 'juices' (contain HCl(aq)) | 1.0–2.0 |
| lemon juice | 2.3 |
| vinegar | 3 |
| coffee | around 5 |
| rain-water (normal) | 5.7 |
| saliva | 6.3–6.8 |
| urine | 6.0–7.4 |
| fresh milk | around 6.5 |
| pure water | 7.0 |
| blood | 7.4 |
| pancreatic juices | 7.1–8.2 |
| sea-water | around 8.5 |
| baking soda in water | around 9 |
| milk of magnesia | 10 |
| soapy water (cheap soap!) | 11 |
| bench sodium hydroxide ($0.1\,mol\,dm^{-3}$) | 13 |
| bench sodium hydroxide ($1\,mol\,dm^{-3}$) | 14 |

- **Table 7.13** pH values of some familiar aqueous solutions.

The pH of a $1\,mol\,dm^{-3}$ solution of hydrochloric acid is therefore $-\log_{10}[H^+] = -\log_{10}(1.0)$, i.e. zero.

Strong bases also contain stoichiometric amounts of protons in solution, although it is much less obvious. We tend to think of strong bases as producers of hydroxide ions, but of course there are protons present too – only in very small quantities. Follow the calculation below, for the pH of a $0.05\,mol\,dm^{-3}$ solution of sodium hydroxide.

Sodium hydroxide ionises completely:

$$\overset{\text{water}}{NaOH(s) \longrightarrow Na^+(aq) + OH^-(aq)}$$
$$\quad 1\text{mol} \qquad\quad 1\text{mol} \qquad 1\text{mol}$$
$$\quad 0.05\text{mol} \qquad 0.05\text{mol} \quad 0.05\text{mol}$$

The concentration of hydroxide ions in a $0.05\,mol\,dm^{-3}$ NaOH solution is clearly $0.05\,mol\,dm^{-3}$. Now the ionic product of water, $K_w$, is constant and (at 298 K) equals $1 \times 10^{-14}\,mol^2\,dm^{-6}$. This means we can write

$$K_w = [H^+][OH^-] = 1 \times 10^{-14}\,mol^2\,dm^{-6}$$

so

$$[H^+] = \frac{1 \times 10^{-14}\,mol^2\,dm^{-6}}{[OH^-]\,mol\,dm^{-3}} = \frac{1 \times 10^{-14}}{0.05}\,mol\,dm^{-3}$$
$$= 2 \times 10^{-13}\,mol\,dm^{-3}$$

so

$$pH = -\log_{10}[H^+] = -\log_{10}(2 \times 10^{-13}) = 12.7$$

There is a quicker way of getting the same answer: find $-\log_{10}[OH^-]$ and subtract it from 14. (This works because $-\log_{10}[H^+] - \log_{10}[OH^-] = 14$.)

### SAQ 7.17

Find the pH of the following strong acids and strong bases given that $K_w = 1.0 \times 10^{-14}\,mol^2\,dm^{-6}$ at 298 K.

a   $1\,mol\,dm^{-3}$ nitric acid, $HNO_3(aq)$.

b   $0.5\,mol\,dm^{-3}$ nitric acid, $HNO_3(aq)$.

c   An aqueous solution containing 3 g of hydrogen chloride, HCl, per $dm^3$.

d   A $0.001\,mol\,dm^{-3}$ potassium hydroxide solution, KOH(aq).

e   An aqueous solution containing 0.2 g of sodium hydroxide, NaOH, per $dm^3$.

# Ionic equilibria: the definition of $K_a$ and p$K_a$

The following single equation summarises all strong acid–strong base neutralisations:

$$H^+(aq) + OH^-(aq) \rightleftharpoons H_2O(l); \qquad \Delta H^\ominus = -57\,kJ\,mol^{-1}$$

In keeping with this, the same enthalpy change of reaction is observed whatever strong acid–strong base combination is involved (provided the solution is sufficiently dilute that the other ions do not interact), so that the reaction above goes to completion.

Most acids are weak. They do not react completely with water. A good example is ethanoic acid, of which vinegar is a dilute solution. Here the ethanoic acid will donate a proton to water, so it is indeed an acid, but the backward reaction, the acceptance of a proton by the ethanoate anion, must also be taken into account. When the two reactions are proceeding at the same rate, an equilibrium is set up:

$$CH_3COOH(aq) \rightleftharpoons H^+(aq) + CH_3COO^-(aq)$$

The equilibrium constant $K_a$ can now be written:

$$K_a = \frac{[H^+][CH_3COO^-]}{[CH_3COOH]}\,mol\,dm^{-3}$$

This constant, $K_a$, is called the **acid dissociation constant**, and at 298 K for ethanoic acid its value is $1.7 \times 10^{-5}\,mol\,dm^{-3}$. Its value gives us a feel for the strength of the acid, and of course the extent to which it ionises in water. Chemists often write the general formula HA for a monobasic acid. Using this formula, the balanced equation for the ionisation of a weak acid becomes:

$$HA(aq) \rightleftharpoons H^+(aq) + A^-(aq)$$

so

$$K_a = \frac{[H^+][A^-]}{[HA]}\,mol\,dm^{-3}$$

If the acid dissociates to a large extent, $[H^+]$ and $[A^-]$ are relatively large, and $[HA]$ is smaller. Both effects would make $K_a$ comparatively big. You can see this in *table 7.14*. Yet again we can be dealing with a large range of values, some of them very small. Just as pH was invented for hydrogen ion concentration, **p$K_a$** has been invented to deal with the dissociation of acids.

$$pK_a = -\log_{10}[K_a]$$

| Acid or ion | Equilibrium in aqueous solution | $K_a$ (mol dm$^{-3}$) | p$K_a$ |
|---|---|---|---|
| nitric | $HNO_3 \rightleftharpoons H^+ + NO_3^-$ | About 40 | −1.4 |
| sulphurous | $H_2SO_3 \rightleftharpoons H^+ + HSO_3^-$ | $1.5 \times 10^{-2}$ | 1.8 |
| hydrated Fe$^{3+}$ ion | $[Fe(H_2O)_6]^{3+} \rightleftharpoons H^+ + [Fe(H_2O)_5(OH)]^{2+}$ | $6.0 \times 10^{-3}$ | 2.2 |
| hydrofluoric | $HF \rightleftharpoons H^+ + F^-$ | $5.6 \times 10^{-4}$ | 3.3 |
| nitrous | $HNO_2 \rightleftharpoons H^+ + NO_2^-$ | $4.7 \times 10^{-4}$ | 3.3 |
| methanoic | $HCOOH \rightleftharpoons H^+ + HCOO^-$ | $1.6 \times 10^{-4}$ | 3.8 |
| benzoic | $C_6H_5COOH \rightleftharpoons H^+ + C_6H_5COO^-$ | $6.3 \times 10^{-5}$ | 4.2 |
| ethanoic | $CH_3COOH \rightleftharpoons H^+ + CH_3COO^-$ | $1.7 \times 10^{-5}$ | 4.8 |
| propanoic | $CH_3CH_2COOH \rightleftharpoons H^+ + CH_3CH_2COO^-$ | $1.3 \times 10^{-5}$ | 4.9 |
| hydrated Al$^{3+}$ ion | $[Al(H_2O)_6]^{3+} \rightleftharpoons H^+ + [Al(H_2O)_5(OH)]^{2+}$ | $1.0 \times 10^{-5}$ | 5.0 |
| carbonic | $CO_2 + H_2O \rightleftharpoons H^+ + HCO_3^-$ | $4.5 \times 10^{-7}$ | 6.35 |
| silicic | $SiO_2 + H_2O \rightleftharpoons H^+ + HSiO_3^-$ | $1.3 \times 10^{-10}$ | 9.9 |
| hydrogencarbonate ion | $HCO_3^- \rightleftharpoons H^+ + CO_3^{2-}$ | $4.8 \times 10^{-11}$ | 10.3 |
| hydrogensilicate ion | $HSiO_3^- \rightleftharpoons H^+ + SiO_3^{2-}$ | $1.3 \times 10^{-12}$ | 11.9 |
| water | $H_2O \rightleftharpoons H^+ + OH^-$ | $1.0 \times 10^{-14}$ | 14.0 |

● **Table 7.14** Acid dissociation constants, $K_a$, for a range of acids, for aqueous solutions in the region of 0.0–0.01 mol dm$^{-3}$.

**SAQ 7.18**

Look at *table 7.14*. Work out which species are Brønsted–Lowry acids, and which are conjugate bases.

# Calculating the pH of a weak acid

The pH of a weak acid may be calculated from the acid dissociation constant, $K_a$, the equilibrium constant expression and the concentration of the acid solution.

Unless we wish to determine pH to more than two decimal places, we make two assumptions to simplify the calculation.

- We assume that $[H^+] = [A^-]$.
- [HA] is approximately equal to the concentration of the acid, making the assumption that none has dissociated.

The first of these assumptions may not seem to be an approximation until we remember that some water will have dissociated to form hydrogen ions. As very few water molecules will have dissociated in this way, this approximation will not affect a pH calculated to two decimal places. Using this assumption, the expression for $K_a$ simplifies to

$$K_a = \frac{[H^+][A^-]}{[HA]} = \frac{[H^+]^2}{[HA]} \text{ mol dm}^{-3}$$

The second assumption relies on the fact that we are dealing with a weak acid. Clearly, some molecules will dissociate but the proportion is such that the pH value calculated will not be significantly affected until we reach the third decimal place.

Having accepted that, for our puposes, these assumptions are sound, we can proceed to do a calculation. Suppose we wish to calculate the pH of $0.100 \text{ mol dm}^{-3}$ ethanoic acid ($K_a = 1.7 \times 10^{-5} \text{ mol dm}^{-3}$).

Ethanoic acid dissociates as shown:

$$CH_3COOH(aq) \rightleftharpoons H^+(aq) + CH_3COO^-(aq)$$

Using our simplified expression for $K_a$

$$[HA] = [CH_3COOH(aq)]$$
$$[H^+] = [H^+(aq)] \text{ and}$$
$$[A^-] = [CH_3COO^-(aq)]$$

So we can write

$$K_a = \frac{[H^+]^2}{[HA]} \text{ mol dm}^{-3}$$

Putting numbers in we have

$$1.7 \times 10^{-5} = \frac{[H^+]^2}{0.100} \text{ mol dm}^{-3}$$

Rearranging this equation

$$[H^+]^2 = 1.7 \times 10^{-5} \times 0.100 = 1.7 \times 10^{-6}$$

Taking square roots

$$[H^+] = 1.304 \times 10^{-3} \text{ mol dm}^{-3}$$

Now we can calculate pH.

$$pH = -\log_{10}(1.304 \times 10^{-3}) = 2.9$$

Check that you arrive at the same value by keying the data into your calculator. Use the square root key to find the square root of $1.7 \times 10^{-6}$; remember to use $\log_{10}$ and to enter the powers of ten using the 'exp' key (remembering the minus sign for this as well as the minus in front of the $\log_{10}$).

**SAQ 7.19**

Using the data from *table 7.14* work out
a the pH of a solution containing $0.02 \text{ mol dm}^{-3}$ of benzoic acid in water;
b the pH of an aqueous solution containing $0.01 \text{ mol dm}^{-3}$ of aluminium ions;
c the pH of a solution of $0.1 \text{ mol dm}^{-3}$ methanoic acid in water.

# Measuring pH

Many dyes are susceptible to acids and alkalis. Their molecular structure can be modified by changes in pH so that they change colour (*figure 7.23*).

pH affects the colour of some dyes in quite dramatic ways. The dyes are used in the laboratory, sometimes as mixtures, to monitor the pH of chemical changes; when used in this way, they are called indicators. They usually change over a pH range of between 1 and 2 'units', with a recognised end-point somewhere in the middle. The end-point is the point where the indicator is most clearly seen to be between the two extremes of its colour.

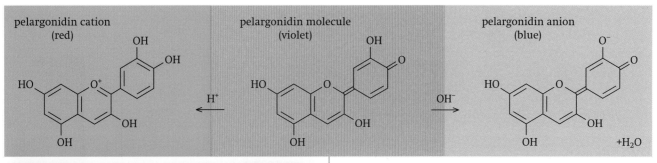

pelargonidin cation (red)  → H⁺ → pelargonidin molecule (violet)  → OH⁻ → pelargonidin anion (blue) +H₂O

- **Figure 7.23** The red petals of geraniums contain the dye pelargonidin. Hydrogen or hydroxide ions can tweak its molecular structure to produce different colours.

For example, bromothymol blue is yellow in acidic solutions and blue in alkaline solutions. The colour change takes place from pH 6.0 to pH 7.6 and the end-point occurs when the pH is 7.0. The colours, ranges and end-points of indicators vary considerably, as can be seen in *table 7.15*. For example, phenolphthalein is colourless in solutions with pH less than 8.2 and does not reach its final red colour until the pH is 10. Hydrogen or hydroxide ions have a considerable effect on the molecular structure, as shown in *figure 7.24*.

Universal indicator is actually a choice mixture of dyes whose combined colours can create a range of hues, each corresponding to a pH unit – or even fraction of a unit. Indicators can be designed to incorporate a wide pH range, e.g. 1–11, or for specific tasks a smaller range, e.g. pH 4–6 in intervals of 0.2 of a pH 'unit'.

Any measurement made using dyes must be subjective and far from accurate. There can also be problems with coloured solutions such as beer (where pH measurement is routine). For the accurate measurements required for research, particularly in biological and biochemical areas, pH measurement is done electrically. Great accuracy can be achieved with modern pH meters.

# Acids with alkalis: monitoring change

Measuring the concentration of acid and alkaline solutions is a routine task. A traditional method involves titration, i.e. measuring just how much of a reagent of known concentration is needed to react with all of another. *Figure 7.25* shows a familiar example, the titration of a strong acid against a strong base. Bear in mind that neutralisation means the reaction between equal amounts of hydrogen and hydroxide ions to form water (page 141).

| Name of dye | Colour at low pH | pH range | End-point | Colour at higher pH |
|---|---|---|---|---|
| Methyl violet | yellow | 0.0–1.6 | 0.8 | blue |
| Methyl yellow | red | 2.9–4.0 | 3.5 | yellow |
| Methyl orange | red | 3.2–4.4 | 3.7 | yellow |
| Bromophenol blue | yellow | 2.8–4.6 | 4.0 | blue |
| Bromocresol green | yellow | 3.8–5.4 | 4.7 | blue |
| Methyl red | red | 4.2–6.3 | 5.1 | yellow |
| Bromothymol blue | yellow | 6.0–7.6 | 7.0 | blue |
| Phenolphthalein | colourless | 8.2–10.0 | 9.3 | pink/violet |
| Alizarin yellow | yellow | 10.1–13.0 | 12.5 | orange/red |

- **Table 7.15** Some of the chemical indicators used to monitor pH, with their pH ranges of use and pH of end-point.

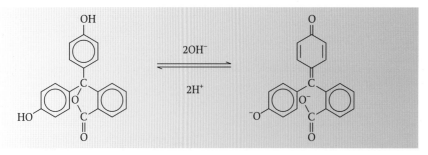

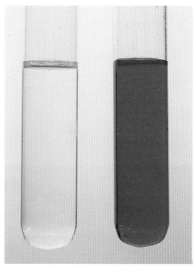

● **Figure 7.24** Colour change in phenolphthalein. At a pH of less than 8.2, the molecular structure isolates three benzene rings, each with its own delocalised electrons in a different plane from the other two. In more alkaline solutions, the structure changes: a planar ion is formed (a flat ion!) and delocalised electrons extend over virtually the entire structure. This extended electron system absorbs most, but not all, of the light in the visible spectrum, so that the solution is pink.

## Strong acids with strong bases

*Figure 7.25* shows a strong acid being titrated 'against' a strong base. The acid is delivered slowly from the burette into the alkali in the flask, with constant stirring. The pH of the mixture is monitored using a pH meter, and values recorded manually or by a data logger. The graph shows how the pH changes as drop after drop is added. Note the sharp fall in the graph. In this region, tiny additional amounts of hydrogen ions from the acid have a drastic effect on pH. The midpoint

of this steep slope corresponds to a pH of 7. An indicator such as bromothymol blue, which changes from blue to yellow over the range 6.0–7.6, would register this change. Note, however, that the slope is steep over the range pH = 3.5 to pH = 10.5. Other indicators would also mark this sudden change. Phenolphthalein, effective in the pH range 8.2 to 10.0, could also be used (*figure 7.26*), although it can be difficult to judge when a colour just disappears.

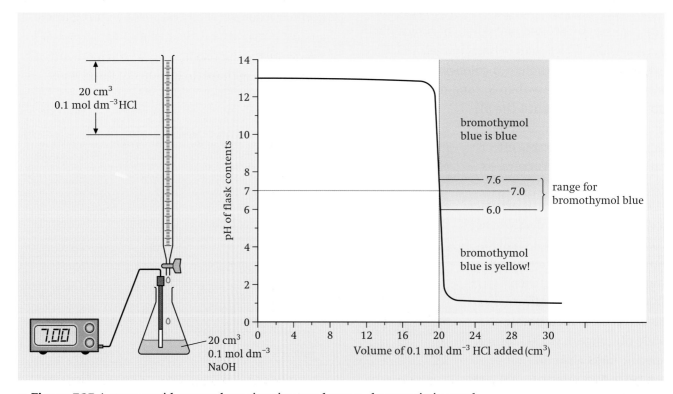

● **Figure 7.25** A strong acid–strong base titration produces a characteristic graph.

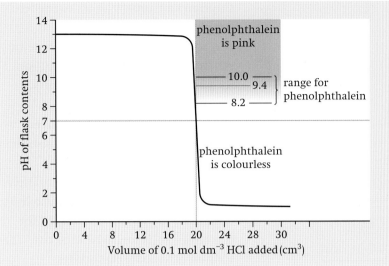

**Figure 7.26** A strong acid–strong base titration with phenolphthalein as the indicator.

## SAQ 7.20

Use *table 7.15* to identify those indicators which could used for a strong acid–strong base titration like this, and those which could not.

## Strong acids with weak bases

A strong acid such as $0.1 \text{ mol dm}^{-3}$ nitric acid reacts with a weak base like ammonium hydroxide as shown in *figure 7.27*. Which part of the graph corresponds to the graph in *figure 7.26*? Methyl orange would be a suitable indicator, as the sudden decrease of pH occurs in the range in which methyl orange changes colour, i.e. 3.2–4.4.

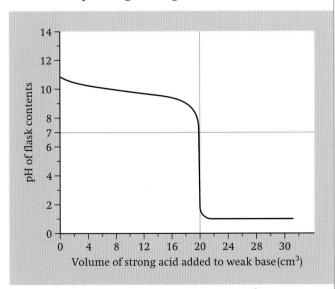

**Figure 7.27** A typical strong acid–weak base titration.

## SAQ 7.21

Use *table 7.15* to find those indicators which could be used for a strong acid–weak base titration, and those which could not.

## Weak acids with strong bases

The change in pH for the reaction of a weak acid such as benzoic acid with a strong base such as potassium hydroxide is shown in *figure 7.28*.

## SAQ 7.22

Compare *figure 7.28* to *figures 7.26* and *7.27*, noticing similarities and differences. Phenolphthalein, with its colour change at 9.3, is a suitable indicator for the end-point in *figure 7.28*. Why would methyl orange be unsuitable?

## Weak acids with weak bases

As *figure 7.29* shows, there is no significant pH range in which the addition of a small amount of one reagent produces a sharp change. In circumstances like this, none of the indicators in *table 7.15* would be effective. In the example shown, bromothymol blue would start to change colour when $19.5 \text{ cm}^3$ of acid had been added, and would finish changing after another $1 \text{ cm}^3$ had been added. Such a large range is unacceptable in situations when an accuracy of $0.05 \text{ cm}^3$ is desirable.

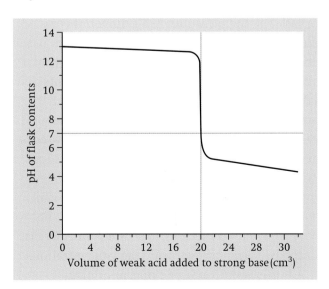

**Figure 7.28** A typical weak acid–strong base titration.

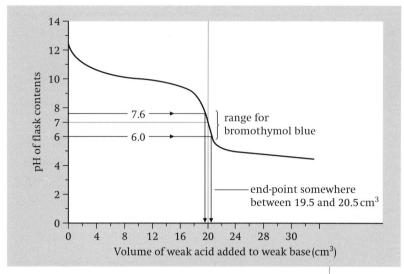

pH of flask contents

7.6
6.0
range for bromothymol blue

end-point somewhere between 19.5 and 20.5 cm$^3$

Volume of weak acid added to weak base (cm$^3$)

● **Figure 7.29** A typical weak acid–weak base titration.

## SAQ 7.23

Suggest a suitable indicator to find the end-points of the reactions between:

**a** 0.05 mol dm$^{-3}$ nitric acid and 0.05 mol dm$^{-3}$ aqueous ammonia;

**b** 2 mol dm$^{-3}$ sodium hydroxide solution and 1 mol dm$^{-3}$ sulphuric acid;

**c** 0.005 mol dm$^{-3}$ potassium hydroxide and aspirin (2-ethanoyloxybenzoic acid), which has a $K_a$ of $3 \times 10^{-4}$ mol dm$^{-3}$.

# Buffer solutions

In *table 7.13* the pH values of a number of commonly occurring solutions were given. Often it does not matter if these pH values vary slightly, but for biological solutions (stomach contents and saliva, for example), and for many industrial processes, it is important to maintain a steady pH value. It can be vital. If your blood pH increases or decreases by 0.5, you will lose consciousness and drift into a coma. Your blood has to have some sort of control system to cope with increases in hydrogen or hydroxide ion concentration. It has to have a buffer – something to soak up any increase in the hydrogen or hydroxide ion concentrations.

A **buffer solution** is one that minimises changes in pH, even when moderate amounts of acid or base are added to it. However, no buffer solution can cope with an excessive supply of acid or alkali.

A solution of sodium ethanoate in ethanoic acid is just such a solution. It operates because the equilibria involved respond to increases in hydrogen or hydroxide ion concentration in such a way as to minimise the increase – another practical application of Le Chatelier's principle.

Note that ethanoic acid and sodium ethanoate must both be present for the buffer solution to be effective. The sodium ethanoate dissociates completely to produce ethanoate ions:

$$CH_3COONa(aq) \rightarrow Na^+(aq) + CH_3COO^-(aq)$$

This complete dissociation influences the dissociation of ethanoic acid, which reaches an equilibrium:

$$CH_3COOH(aq) \rightleftharpoons H^+(aq) + CH_3COO^-(aq)$$

The result is that there are large reservoirs of the acid, $CH_3COOH$, and its conjugate base, $CH_3COO^-$.

An increase in hydrogen ion concentration would rapidly lower the pH of water. However, in this buffer solution it shifts the following equilibrium to the right.

$$CH_3COO^-(aq) + H^+(aq) \rightleftharpoons CH_3COOH(aq)$$
(mainly from sodium ethanoate)

Hydrogen ions are transferred to the ethanoate ions (of which there are plenty) so that ethanoic acid is formed. A moderate input of hydrogen ions therefore has a marginal effect on the overall pH.

The effect of an alkali, which in water would rapidly increase the pH, is minimised in a similar way. The following equilibrium shifts to the right as hydroxide ions remove protons from ethanoic acid molecules to form ethanoate ions and water.

$$CH_3COOH(aq) + OH^-(aq) \rightleftharpoons CH_3COO^-(aq) + H_2O(l)$$

In general, a buffer solution can be made from a conjugate acid and its base where either the acid or the base is weak. An example of a buffer solution involving a weak base is a solution containing both ammonia and ammonium chloride.

There is an alternative explanation for the way in which this buffer solution copes with an increase of hydroxide ions. The explanation suggests that the hydroxide ions first neutralise any hydrogen ions present, which are then replaced by the dissociation of more ethanoic acid. The fact is that we don't know which mechanism actually operates – so keep it simple. Remember the two components – the weak acid, which counters the addition of hydroxide ions, and the salt of the weak acid, which counters the addition of hydrogen ions.

## SAQ 7.24

Ammonia dissociates in water as follows

$$NH_3(aq) + H_2O(l) \rightleftharpoons NH_4^+(aq) + OH^-(aq)$$

whilst the ammonium chloride is fully ionised

$$NH_4Cl(aq) \rightarrow NH_4^+(aq) + Cl^-(aq)$$

**a** Using the above equations, identify the conjugate acid–base pair in a buffer solution containing ammonia and ammonium chloride.

**b** Explain how the ammonia/ammonium chloride buffer solution minimises changes in pH on adding dilute aqueous solutions of

(i) hydrochloric acid

(ii) sodium hydroxide

## 'Bicarb' and pH control

On page 125 you were introduced to the reason why crocodiles survive longer than their prey under water. This is because more of the oxygen carried by the haemoglobin in the blood of the crocodile can be utilised than from the blood of its prey.

Oxygen from the air diffuses into your bloodstream in the lungs, and reacts with haemoglobin, Hb. This 'organo-metallic' compound, the first protein ever to be obtained as a crystalline solid, contains iron – hence its red colour. It reacts with oxygen as shown:

$$Hb + O_2 \rightleftharpoons HbO_2$$

This reaction is easily reversed in tissues all over the body, releasing oxygen for the energy-generating process called aerobic respiration. For example, glucose oxidises in an exothermic reaction, producing water, carbon dioxide and heat. The equation below is a gross over-simplification of the many reactions that it summarises.

$$C_6H_{12}O_6(aq) + 6O_2(g) \rightarrow 6CO_2(aq) + 6H_2O(aq);$$
$$\Delta H^\ominus = -2802\,kJ\,mol^{-1}$$

Your blood is now left with a waste-disposal problem, which is potentially poisonous. The problem, and part of the solution, lies in the equation below. The rates of both the forward and backward reactions in the equilibrium are rapid, thanks to the enzyme carbonic anhydrase.

$$H_2O(aq) + CO_2(aq) \underset{\text{anhydrase}}{\overset{\text{carbonic}}{\rightleftharpoons}} H^+(aq) + HCO_3^-(aq)$$

The generation of hydrogen ions, if unchecked, would lead to a lowering of blood pH and you would slip into a coma. Your blood needs a buffer.

In fact, it has at least *three*, the most important by far being the buffering action of hydrogencarbonate ion, $HCO_3^-(aq)$. Haemoglobin and plasma, both proteins, also act as buffers, but play much smaller parts.

Hydrogen ions in the blood are mopped up by hydrogencarbonate ions, the equation being the one above in which the equilibrium is well to the left. The carbon dioxide produced is carried to the lungs and breathed out. Lung infections that inhibit breathing can hinder this extraction process, leading to acidosis – i.e. decrease in blood pH.

The chemistry of pH control in the body is more complex than this section suggests, involving many other ions, particularly when acidosis is severe. The kidneys also play a crucial part. Understanding pH control is vital when treating certain diseases, e.g. coronary thrombosis. Anaesthetists constantly monitor blood pH in long operations that involve heart–lung machines, and may inject controlled amounts of sodium hydrogencarbonate – 'bicarb' – to cater for a pH fall.

## Calculating the pH of a buffer solution

We can calculate the pH of a buffer solution given the following data:

■ $K_a$ of the weak acid;

■ the equilibrium concentrations of the conjugate acid–base pair.

For example, a buffer solution could be made containing $0.600\,mol\,dm^{-3}$ propanoic acid and $0.800\,mol\,dm^{-3}$ sodium propanoate. The equilibrium constant, $K_a$, for propanoic acid is $1.3 \times 10^{-5}\,\text{mol dm}^{-3}$.

The equation for the equilibrium reaction is

$$C_2H_5COOH(aq) \rightleftharpoons H^+(aq) + C_2H_5COO^-(aq)$$

from which we can write the equilibrium constant expression

$$K_a = \frac{[H^+][C_2H_5COO^-]}{[C_2H_5COOH]}$$

Rearranging this equation gives

$$[H^+] = K_a \times \frac{[C_2H_5COOH]}{[C_2H_5COO^-]}\,\text{mol dm}^{-3}$$

Substituting the data given produces

$$[H^+] = 1.3 \times 10^{-5} \times \frac{0.600}{0.800}\,\text{mol dm}^{-3}$$

$$= 9.75 \times 10^{-6}\,\text{mol dm}^{-3}$$

so

$$pH = -\log_{10}(9.75 \times 10^{-6})$$
$$= -(-5.01) = 5.01$$

### SAQ 7.25

Practise this calculation by doing the calculations below. Use *table 7.14* on page 149 for the values of $K_a$.

Calculate the pH of a solution containing
a   $0.0500\,\text{mol dm}^{-3}$ methanoic acid and $0.100\,\text{mol dm}^{-3}$ sodium methanoate
b   $0.0100\,\text{mol dm}^{-3}$ benzoic acid and $0.0400\,\text{mol dm}^{-3}$ sodium benzoate.

Of course, there is a limit to the efficiency of buffers, as we have indicated above. Rain-water has a pH of 5.7 in unpolluted regions, because it dissolves carbon dioxide, which in solution forms a dilute solution of the weak acid carbonic acid, $H_2CO_3(aq)$, with a $pK_a$ of 6.4. This buffer solution will accommodate small additions of acid and alkali. But in highly polluted industrial regions, or in rural areas that lie down-wind of such contamination, the pH of rain-water is around 4, so-called 'acid rain'. Here the atmospheric pollutant gases are sulphur dioxide and sulphur trioxide, arising from the combustion of fossil fuels containing sulphur, and nitrogen monoxide and nitrogen

dioxide, due mainly to nitrogen oxidation in internal combustion engines. These gases dissolve in rain-water and overwhelm the buffering effect.

## Determining $pK_a$ from a pH titration curve

This is a neat way of finding $pK_a$.

Consider the addition of $0.500\,\text{mol dm}^{-3}$ sodium hydroxide to $20.0\,\text{cm}^3$ of $0.500\,\text{mol dm}^{-3}$ ethanoic acid (*figure 7.30*). The pH of the solution rises steeply at first but then less steeply as the concentration of ethanoate ions increases. The pH rises less steeply as the mixture of the conjugate acid–base pair (ethanoic acid and ethanoate ion) is a buffer solution. As the end-point is neared, the pH rises more steeply producing the stepped shape of a pH titration curve.

The equation for the ionisation of ethanoic acid is

$$CH_3COOH(aq) \rightleftharpoons H^+(aq) + CH_3COO^-(aq)$$

The acid dissociation constant is

$$K_a = \frac{[H^+][CH_3COO^-]}{[CH_3COOH]}$$

Rearranging this equation

$$[H^+] = K_a \times \frac{[CH_3COOH]}{[CH_3COO^-]}\,\text{mol dm}^{-3}$$

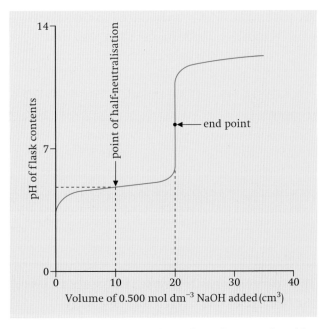

● **Figure 7.30** Determination of $pK_a$ for a weak acid. Sodium hydroxide ($0.500\,\text{mol dm}^{-3}$) is added from a burette to a $20.0\,\text{cm}^3$ sample of $0.500\,\text{mol dm}^{-3}$ ethanoic acid. At the point of half-neutralisation pH = $pK_a$.

At the mid-point between the start of the titration and the end point

$$[CH_3COOH] = [CH_3COO^-]$$

(This mid-point can be called 'the point of half-neutralisation'.)

These equal values enable the equation above to be simplified as follows:

$$[H^+] = K_a \times \frac{[\cancel{CH_3COOH}]}{[\cancel{CH_3COO^-}]} \, mol \, dm^{-3}$$

so

$$[H^+] = K_a \, mol \, dm^{-3}$$

or

$$pH = pK_a$$

We can simply read off the pH from the graph and we have determined $pK_a$.

### SAQ 7.26

An acid is found to have $pK_a = 6.35$

a  Calculate $K_a$ for this acid.

b  Refer to *table 7.14* on page 149 to identify the acid.

c  Write the formula of the conjugate base of this weak acid.

## Buffers in the bathroom and beyond

Tucked away on bathroom shelves and cabinets are all sorts of products whose acidity or alkalinity has to be controlled. From antacids and eye-drops to skin creams and baby lotion, buffers are used to maintain an appropriate pH. Safety is most important – the pH control system must be harmless. Non-toxic buffers have to be used.

Citric acid is a weak acid found in many products for the consumer, from fizzy lemonade to shampoos. The structure of citric acid is shown below.

$$
\begin{array}{c}
CH_2COOH \\
| \\
HO - C - COOH \\
| \\
CH_2COOH
\end{array}
$$

citric acid

Note the presence of three carboxylic acid groups. For most purposes, we can assume that only one

of these groups ionises in aqueous solution. We can thus represent the ionisation of citric acid as shown.

$$HA(aq) \rightleftharpoons H^+(aq) + A^-(aq)$$

Citric acid is added to shampoos as a 'pH adjuster' Sodium hydroxide is also added. This will partly neutralise the citric acid to produce the citrate ion, $A^-(aq)$. The resulting buffer solution will counteract the alkalinity of the soaps and detergents present in the shampoo. With no citric acid present, the alkaline shampoo may irritate skin and eyes. The pH may be adjusted to be close to that of skin, which is about pH 5.5.

Baby lotion is buffered – 'pH balanced' as the adverts claim – to minimise nappy rash (*figure 7.31*). This skin irritation is caused by ammonia. Dirty nappies contain just the right ingredients for making ammonia – urine and faeces. The latter contains a bacterium, *Bacillus ammoniagenes*, which lives in the baby's colon. Urine contains water and urea. An enzyme from the bacterium reacts with water and urea, forming ammonia in reactions summarised by this equation:

$$\underset{\text{urea}}{CO(NH_2)_2(aq)} + H_2O(l) \rightarrow \underset{\text{ammonia}}{2NH_3(aq)} + CO_2(aq)$$

These bacteria multiply well in the pH range 7–9, but not at all at pH 6. Consequently, baby lotion is buffered to keep the pH about 6 – around the pH of the skin itself. The offending bacteria do not multiply and ammonia production is limited.

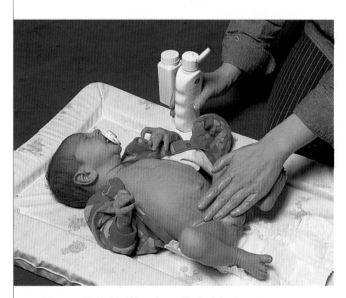

● **Figure 7.31** Buffers benefit babies!

Nappies should be washed well to kill these bacteria. A hot water wash at 60 °C does this.

Washing powders include buffers. Without them the high alkalinity of the detergent present would damage skin – they would not be kind to your hands! Buffers are also used in washing powders containing enzymes, to let them operate at the optimum conditions. For example, protease, an enzyme that breaks down proteins, operates best at pH from 9 to 10. Interestingly, this enzyme is produced by the bacterium *Bacillus licheniformis*, which would itself be digested by protease at this pH. The biotechnologists who produce this enzyme use buffers to keep their fermenters at pH 7 to stop this.

Drugs must be manufactured with an eye to pH control. Most drugs are a mixture of substances, and some ingredients could affect the optimum pH without the use of buffers.

# Solubility product and solubility

Salts which are termed 'insoluble' do dissolve to a small extent. In a saturated solution of a salt such as silver chloride, an equilibrium exists between undissolved salt and dissolved ions.

$$AgCl(s) \rightleftharpoons Ag^+(aq) + Cl^-(aq)$$

We can write the following expression for $K_c$ for this equilibrium.

$$K_c = \frac{[Ag^+(aq)]\,[Cl^-(aq)]}{[AgCl(s)]}$$

At a given temperature, $[AgCl(s)]$ is constant and the expression may be rewritten by combining $K_c$ and $[AgCl(s)]$ in a new constant $K_{sp}$ where

$$K_{sp} = [Ag^+(aq)]\,[Cl^-(aq)]$$

$K_{sp}$ is the **solubility product** and is defined as the product of the ionic concentrations in a saturated solution of a sparingly soluble salt at a constant temperature.

For salts which are not 1 : 1 compounds, the $K_{sp}$ expression must reflect the ratio of ions present. For example:

for silver carbonate, $Ag_2CO_3$

$$K_{sp} = [Ag^+(aq)]^2\,[CO_3^{2-}(aq)]$$

| Compound | Solubility product |
|---|---|
| barium sulphate | $1.0 \times 10^{-10}$ |
| calcium carbonate | $5.0 \times 10^{-9}$ |
| calcium fluoride | $4.0 \times 10^{-11}$ |
| calcium sulphate | $2.0 \times 10^{-5}$ |
| lead(II) bromide | $3.9 \times 10^{-5}$ |
| lead(II) chloride | $2.0 \times 10^{-5}$ |
| lead(II) iodide | $7.1 \times 10^{-9}$ |
| lead(II) sulphate | $1.6 \times 10^{-8}$ |
| silver bromide | $5.0 \times 10^{-13}$ |
| silver carbonate | $6.3 \times 10^{-12}$ |
| silver chloride | $2.0 \times 10^{-10}$ |
| silver iodide | $8.0 \times 10^{-17}$ |
| strontium sulphate | $5.1 \times 10^{-7}$ |

● **Table 7.16** The solubility products of some common compounds, at 25 °C.

and for calcium fluoride, $CaF_2$

$$K_{sp} = [Ca^{2+}(aq)]\,[F^-(aq)]^2$$

Values of $K_{sp}$ for a number of salts are given in *table 7.16*.

The solubility of a salt may be given in different units, such as grams of solute in $1\,dm^3$ of solution or amount of solute (in moles) in $1\,dm^3$ of solution. The following examples show the relationship between solubility and solubility product.

## Calculating solubility product from solubility

The solubility of silver carbonate, $Ag_2CO_3$, is $0.032\,g\,dm^{-3}$ at 25 °C. What is the value of the solubility product at this temperature?

$$\text{solubility of } Ag_2CO_3 = 0.032\,g\,dm^{-3}$$
$$= \frac{0.032}{276}\,mol\,dm^{-3}$$
$$= 1.16 \times 10^{-4}\,mol\,dm^{-3}$$
$$[CO_3^{2-}] = 1.16 \times 10^{-4}\,mol\,dm^{-3}$$
$$[Ag^+] = 2 \times 1.16 \times 10^{-4}\,mol\,dm^{-3}$$
$$K_{sp} = [Ag^+]^2\,[CO_3^{2-}]$$
$$= (2 \times 1.16 \times 10^{-4})^2 \times (1.16 \times 10^{-4})$$
$$= 6.3 \times 10^{-12}$$

## SAQ 7.27

The solubility of lead chloride at 20 °C is 0.70 g per 100 cm³ of solution. What is the solubility product at this temperature?

## Calculating solubility from solubility product

The solubility product of lead(II) sulphate, $PbSO_4$, is $1.6 \times 10^{-8}$ at 25 °C. What is the solubility at this temperature?

$$K_{sp} = [Pb^{2+}][SO_4^{2-}]$$

Since this is a 1 : 1 salt, $[Pb^{2+}] = [SO_4^{2-}]$

so $K_{sp} = [Pb^{2+}]^2$

$[Pb^{2+}] = \sqrt{K_{sp}} = \sqrt{1.6 \times 10^{-8}} = 1.26 \times 10^{-4}$

Each mole of $PbSO_4$ that dissolves produces one mole of $Pb^{2+}$ in solution.

$[PbSO_4] = [Pb^{2+}] = 1.26 \times 10^{-4}$

solubility of $PbSO_4 = 1.26 \times 10^{-4} \times 303$

$= 0.038 \, g \, dm^{-3}$

## SAQ 7.28

The solubility product of silver chromate, $Ag_2CrO_4$, at 25 °C is $1.00 \times 10^{-12}$. Calculate the solubility of silver chromate in $mol \, dm^{-3}$ at this temperature.

# The common ion effect

In a saturated solution of a salt such as silver chloride, a dynamic equilibrium exists between the solid and the ions in solution.

$$AgCl(s) \rightleftharpoons Ag^+(aq) + Cl^-(aq)$$

If more chloride ions are added to the saturated solution, for example by adding some aqueous sodium chloride, the equilibrium will move to the left forming more solid silver chloride. This is in accordance with Le Chatelier's principle.

If we consider this change in terms of $K_{sp}$, when the aqueous sodium chloride is added, $[Cl^-]$ is increased. This means that

$$[Ag^+][Cl^-] > K_{sp}$$

Precipitation will therefore occur until

$$[Ag^+][Cl^-] = K_{sp}$$

When this happens, the two ionic concentrations will no longer be equal.

For a saturated solution of AgCl at 25 °C,
$K_{sp} = 2.0 \times 10^{-10}$

$$[Ag^+] = [Cl^-] = 1.4 \times 10^{-5} \, mol \, dm^{-3}$$

If a saturated solution of silver chloride is mixed with an equal volume of $0.2 \, mol \, dm^{-3}$ sodium chloride solution, the concentration of each compound is halved.

After mixing:

$$[Cl^-] = 0.1 + 0.7 \times 10^{-5} = 0.100007 \approx 0.1 \, mol \, dm^{-3}$$

$$\text{new } [Ag^+] = \frac{K_{sp}}{[Cl^-]} = \frac{2.0 \times 10^{-10}}{0.1} = 2.0 \times 10^{-9} \, mol \, dm^{-3}$$

the change in $[Ag^+] = 1.4 \times 10^{-5} - 2.0 \times 10^{-9}$

$= 1.3998 \times 10^{-5} \, mol$

the amount of AgCl precipitated
$= 1.3998 \times 10^{-5} \, mol$

This means that almost all of the silver chloride present in the saturated solution has been precipitated.

The precipitation of a salt by the addition of another compound with an ion common to itself and the salt is called the common ion effect. (See also the salting out of soap in chapter 20.)

# SUMMARY (A2)

◆ $K_w$ is the ionic product of water:
At 298 K, $K_w = [H^+][OH^-] = 1.0 \times 10^{-14} \, mol^2 \, dm^{-6}$

◆ pH is a measure of $[H^+(aq)]$, it is defined as:
$pH = -\log_{10}[H^+]$

◆ $K_a$ is the dissociation constant for an acid. It is the equilibrium constant for the dissociation of a weak acid, HA:
$HA(aq) \rightleftharpoons H^+(aq) + A^-(aq)$
$$K_a = \frac{[H^+][A^-]}{[HA]} \, mol \, dm^{-3}$$
Chemists often use a more convenient scale for comparing acid strengths by using $pK_a$:
$pK_a = -\log_{10}K_a$

◆ pH titration curves enable end-points for acid–base titrations to be found. The end-point of a titration is when the quantity of acid is sufficient to exactly neutralise the base present. The curves may also be used to suggest appropriate indicators for a particular acid–base titration. At the point of half-neutralisation $pH = pK_a$

◆ A buffer solution minimises pH changes on addition of an acid or a base. A buffer solution consists of a conjugate acid and its base where one of the pair is weak.

◆ Buffer solutions are important in controlling the pH of many fluids in living organisms, for example in blood. Commercial products may also contain buffer solutions to control pH, for example in shampoos.

◆ The solubility product, $K_{sp}$, of a salt is the product of the ionic concentrations in a saturated solution of the salt at a constant temperature.

◆ Solubility products are only used with sparingly soluble salts.

◆ Addition of a common ion, cation or anion, causes precipitation of a sparingly soluble salt.

# Questions (A2)

5 Shampoos frequently contain citric acid as a 'pH adjuster'. Some sodium hydroxide may also be added. The sodium hydroxide would neutralise some of the citric acid to produce sodium citrate. The presence of both citric acid and sodium citrate controls the pH of the shampoo by acting as a buffer solution. The structure of citric acid is shown below.

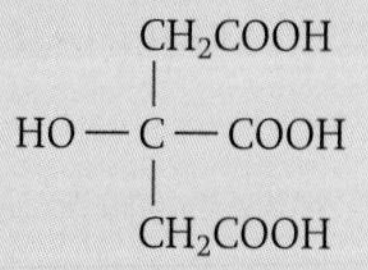

$$CH_2COOH$$
$$|$$
$$HO-C-COOH$$
$$|$$
$$CH_2COOH$$

citric acid

a Write a balanced equation to show the neutralisation of 1 mole of citric acid by 1 mole of sodium hydroxide. (You may assume that only the –COOH on the second carbon atom is neutralised.)

b (i) Define pH.
  (ii) Citric acid and a citrate ion are a **conjugate acid–base pair**. Explain what is meant by this term.
  (iii) Citric acid is a weak acid. What is meant by the term **weak acid**?
  (iv) Describe how an aqueous solution of a weak acid and its salt acts as a buffer solution.

c (i) Write an expression for the $K_a$ of citric acid. You may represent citric acid as HA.
  (ii) Calculate the pH of a solution containing $0.200 \, mol \, dm^{-3}$ of citric acid and $0.100 \, mol \, dm^{-3}$ sodium citrate. For citric acid $K_a = 7.24 \times 10^{-4} \, mol \, dm^{-3}$.

d Suggest a reason for the presence of a buffer solution containing citric acid in a shampoo.

# Reaction kinetics (AS)

## By the end of this section you should be able to:

1 describe qualitatively, in terms of *collision theory*, the effect of concentration changes on the rate of a reaction;

2 explain why an increase in the pressure of a gas, increasing its concentration, may increase the rate of a reaction involving gases;

3 explain qualitatively, using the Boltzmann distribution and enthalpy profile diagrams, what is meant by the term *activation energy*;

4 describe qualitatively, using the Boltzmann distribution and enthalpy profile diagrams, the effect of temperature changes on the rate of a reaction;

5 explain what is meant by a *catalyst*;

6 explain that, in the presence of a catalyst, a reaction proceeds via a different route, i.e. one of lower activation energy, giving rise to an increased reaction rate;

7 interpret catalytic behaviour in terms of the Boltzmann distribution and enthalpy profile diagrams;

8 describe enzymes as biological catalysts (proteins) which may have specific activity.

## Speed, rates and reactions

In a race, the fastest car, horse or runner is the winner. The winner needs to cover the given distance in the shortest possible time. We measure the speed of the winner by measuring the distance travelled in one hour. For example, in the 2003 Malaysian Grand Prix, Kimi Raikonnen completed the 308.6 kilometre race in 1 hour, 32 minutes and 22.195 seconds. Raikonnen's average speed was $200.5\,km\,h^{-1}$, the distance travelled divided by the time taken.

The speed of the winner of a car race is much higher than that of the winning horse or runner in their respective races. Different chemical reactions also proceed at very different speeds. Some reactions can be very fast whilst others may be very slow (*figure 8.1*). Reactions also proceed at different speeds when conditions are changed. For example, glucose will burn rapidly in air, but

when used as an energy source in our bodies, it is oxidised much more slowly. In both cases the products are the same (carbon dioxide and water).

For chemical reactions we use the term rate instead of speed to describe how fast a reaction proceeds. The rate of a reaction is found by measuring the amount in moles of a reactant which is used up in a given time. The study of rates of reactions is referred to as chemical kinetics.

In the 2003 Malaysian Grand Prix, Raikonnen's speed on timed sections of the course varied from $100\,km\,h^{-1}$ to $300\,km\,h^{-1}$. His speed built up at the start of the race, was higher in clear straight sections, and lower on bends or corners. The rate of a chemical reaction also varies throughout a reaction but in a very different way. Unlike Raikonnen's speed, a reaction rate starts high and then decreases throughout the reaction. When all the reactants have been used up, the rate has dropped to zero. Raikonnen, however, was still driving very fast as he passed the chequered flag!

# Rates of reaction – why bother?

There are many reasons why chemists study reaction rates, for example to:

- improve the rate of production of a chemical;
- help understand the processes going on in our bodies or in the environment;
- gain an insight into the mechanism of a reaction.

During the manufacture of a chemical such as a fertiliser or a medicine, the reaction rate is one of the factors which determine the overall rate of production. In the next chapter, you will see how an understanding of how fast a reaction proceeds helps chemists and chemical engineers to choose the conditions used in the manufacture of a particular chemical.

The consequences of improving a reaction rate

● **Figure 8.1** **a** A variety of rapid combustion reactions take place following the ignition of fireworks. **b** Fortunately, rusting is a very slow reaction.

may have far-reaching consequences on chemical manufacture. For example, before the Second World War, it took about a week to make nitroglycerine, a high explosive, in commercial quantities. During the war, research by an ICI chemist increased the rate by about seven times – very useful at the time.

The rate of formation of ozone in the stratosphere is dependent on the intensity of ultraviolet (UV) radiation reaching the Earth from the Sun. In chapters 16 and 17 you will cover, you learnt how ozone depletion has been caused by chlorine free radicals. The ozone layer normally helps to filter out UV radiation from sunlight, but its destruction leads to high levels of UV radiation reaching the Earth's surface where it causes problems such as skin cancer. The chlorine free radicals are formed by the action of UV radiation on chlorofluorocarbons (see page 332). A knowledge of the rates of these various reactions has enabled chemists to contribute much to an understanding of this environmental problem, highlighting the urgent need to control the use of chlorofluorocarbons.

Also in chapters 16 and 17 you will cover several reaction mechanisms. Many of these mechanisms have been discovered by a study of reaction rates. It is the slowest step in a mechanism which determines the overall rate of reaction. The slowest step in a reaction mechanism is called the **rate-determining step**. In the formation of ozone in the stratosphere, the slowest step involves the photodissociation (breakdown by light) of oxygen molecules by high-energy ultraviolet radiation into oxygen atoms. Environmental chemists have studied the rates of many of the reactions which take place in the atmosphere. Such research has contributed much to our understanding of these reactions and of the effects of pollutant gases. It is this work which has both demonstrated the need for the control of man-made pollutants and led to the development of more environmentally friendly products.

## Factors that affect the rate of a reaction

Factors that may affect the rate of a chemical reaction are:

1 *Concentration of reactants*, for example increasing the concentration of hydrochloric acid in the

reaction of magnesium with the acid (see page 220), will cause the reaction rate to increase. This will be seen in the more vigorous evolution of hydrogen gas. For reactions involving gases, an increase in pressure will increase the reaction rate, as pressure is proportional to concentration. The Haber process is operated under high pressure in order to increase the rate of reaction (see page 134).

2 *Temperature.* A catalytic converter only functions properly when it is hot as the rate of the reactions on the surface of the catalyst are negligible when the converter is cold. Nearly all reactions show an increase in rate as the temperature is increased. In general, an increase of 10 kelvin causes the rate of many reactions to approximately double.

3 If the *surface area* of a solid or liquid reactant is increased, the reaction rate will be increased. For example, powdered magnesium produces hydrogen more rapidly than magnesium ribbon when treated with hydrochloric acid.

4 Some reactions require visible or ultraviolet radiation for reaction to occur. An increase in the *intensity of the radiation* will increase the reaction rate, for example in the free radical sub-stitution of methane by chlorine (see page 295).

5 *Catalysts* are well known for their ability to speed up reactions (see page 170), for example nickel in the hydrogenation of vegetable oils to make margarine (see page 302).

## Methods of following rates of reaction

We can measure reaction rates in a variety of ways to study the factors which affect chemical reaction rates. Each of these factors is a variable which we could investigate. However, as there are several variables which affect the rate of a reaction, experiments need to be designed with care if the measurements made are to be of value. For example, if we wish to study how an increase in temperature affects the rate of a reaction, we must keep other variables, such as the concentra-tions of reactants, the same for each experiment we carry out over the range of temperatures chosen. A fair test is required.

We must also be certain of the stoichiometry (see page 26) of the reaction. In other words, we need to know the mole ratios of reactants and products as shown by the balanced chemical equation. We must be sure that there are no side reactions taking place, as these will affect our measurements.

Armed with the above information, we can now decide which variable to investigate and which others will need to be controlled. If the reaction is taking place in a solution, concentrations of reactants can be controlled by ensuring that a large excess of each is present with the exception of the reactant under investigation.

Lastly we must decide how we can monitor the progress of the reaction. This might involve following the change in concentration of a reactant or of a product. There are two types of method accessible to us:

■ A destructive method based on chemical analysis (for example, a titration). As this takes time, the reaction mixture must be quenched to slow down or stop the reaction. Quenching by cooling in ice might be sufficient. Alternatively, a reagent might be removed by a rapid reaction – an acid catalyst could be neutralised using a base.

■ Non-destructive methods using a variety of physical techniques (measuring, for example, a decrease in mass of a reaction mixture, the volume of a gas evolved, change in colour intensity, change in pH or change in electrical conductivity). As these changes do not involve interfering with the progress of the reaction, there is no need to quench the reaction mixture.

An outline follows of some of these methods for monitoring reaction rates.

## Monitoring reaction rate using mass loss

When a gas is evolved during a reaction, monitor-ing mass loss may provide a suitable method of measuring the reaction rate. There needs to be sufficient loss in mass to be followed with reason-able accuracy on the balance available. For exam-ple, 2.00 g of small marble chips will give a satisfactory loss in mass when treated with $150 \, cm^3$ of $2 \, mol \, dm^{-3}$ hydrochloric acid. *Figure 8.2* illustrates the equipment in use. Ideally, the mass loss can be monitored using a computer.

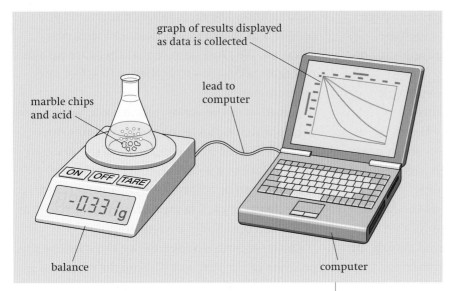

● **Figure 8.2** The apparatus used to measure the mass loss during the reaction of marble chips with hydrochloric acid.

## SAQ 8.1

The equation for the reaction of marble (calcium carbonate, $CaCO_3$) with hydrochloric acid is:

$$CaCO_3(s) + 2HCl(aq) \rightarrow CaCl_2(aq) + CO_2(g) + H_2O(l)$$

a Calculate the amounts, in moles, of calcium carbonate (marble chips) and hydrochloric acid used in this experiment.

b Which reagent is present in excess?

c By how much is it present in excess?

d Explain why a reagent is present in excess.

*Figure 8.3* shows some results obtained with 1.0, 2.0 and 4.0 mol dm⁻³ solutions of hydrochloric acid at room temperature.

● **Figure 8.3** Graphs showing results obtained for the loss in mass when marble chips react with hydrochloric acid. The rate of reaction can be found by measuring the mass lost in a given time. The steeper the curve the faster the rate of reaction. When no more gas is evolved, the reaction rate is zero and the line on the graph becomes horizontal.

## SAQ 8.2

a Determine the mass lost after 300 seconds from the graph shown in *figure 8.3* for the 1.0 and 2.0 mol dm⁻³ solutions of hydrochloric acid.

b These two masses are a measure of the relative reaction rates over 300 seconds. How has the reaction rate changed on doubling the acid concentration from 1.0 to 2.0 mol dm⁻³?

c Suggest a mathematical relationship between the reaction rate and the acid concentration.

## Monitoring reaction rate using volume of gas evolved

The reaction of calcium carbonate with hydrochloric acid may also be monitored by collecting the carbon dioxide evolved. The gas may be collected in a gas syringe or in an inverted, water-filled burette (*figure 8.4*). The volume of carbon dioxide produced over a period of time is proportional to the reaction rate.

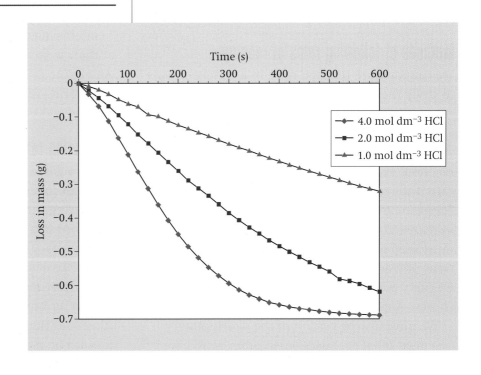

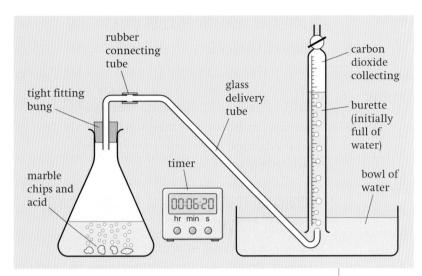

● **Figure 8.4** Cross section of the apparatus used to monitor reaction rate by measuring volume of gas evolved.

## Monitoring reaction rate using colour intensity

*Figure 8.5* shows three glasses of juice diluted with water. Can you tell in which glass the concentration is greatest? Could you rank them in order of concentration? Could you tell how much juice is in each glass?

The answer to the first two questions should be 'yes'. The answer to the third cannot be found without getting an idea of what the colour actu-

● **Figure 8.5** Juice drinks of different concentrations.

● **Figure 8.6** 'Standard' juice solutions with an unknown alongside. Try to estimate the concentration of the unknown.

ally means in terms of concentration.

It would be possible to hazard a good guess. You could prepare calibration solutions like these:

a $2.0\,cm^3$ juice in $10\,cm^3$ solution
b $1.6\,cm^3$ juice in $10\,cm^3$ solution
c $1.2\,cm^3$ juice in $10\,cm^3$ solution
d $0.8\,cm^3$ juice in $10\,cm^3$ solution
e $0.4\,cm^3$ juice in $10\,cm^3$ solution

You could put them in specimen tubes like the ones shown in *figure 8.6*. They must all be filled to the same level.

You could take a sample of juice from one of the glasses and put it into an identical tube, to exactly the same depth. It may be better to look down from above to distinguish the colours. This increases the amount of liquid that the light passes through, so that faint colours show up better. It also helps to standardise how far away from the samples your eyes are.

This method could be used to estimate the concentration of copper ions in the experiment shown in *figure 8.8*. You could have a range of coloured solutions, each representing a concentration from (say) 1 to $0.1\,mol\,dm^{-3}$. There might be better methods of course, and scientists spend much of their time inventing improved methods and equipment. For example, a simple **colorimeter** for measuring the concentration of chlorine is shown in *figure 8.7*. The colorimeter measures the

● **Figure 8.7** A colorimeter is used to analyse the concentration of chlorine in drinking water.

amount of light of a specific colour that passes through a sample.

A spectrophotometer is often used to measure colour concentration. The word 'spectrophotometer' means 'light-measurer making use of part of the spectrum'. In practice the spectrophotometer measures how much light of a particular wavelength can pass through a sample, liquid or gas.

The beaker in *figure 8.8a* contains $1\,dm^3$ of $1.00\,mol\,dm^{-3}$ aqueous copper sulphate, so it contains one mole of copper ions ($63.5\,g$ of them). Iron wool reacts with the copper ions in solution, displacing them and changing the colour of the solution as a result.

$$Cu^{2+}(aq) + Fe(s) \longrightarrow Fe^{2+}(aq) + Cu(s)$$

Solutions appear coloured because they absorb radiation in the visible region of the spectrum. Aqueous copper sulphate, $CuSO_4(aq)$, absorbs radiation in the yellow, orange and red regions. Blue light passes through the solution, so the solution appears blue.

A colorimeter measures the absorbance of radiation over a selected narrow range of wavelengths. The wavelength range is selected by choosing a filter which transmits light over the range absorbed by the compound under study. Hence a yellow, orange or red filter would be appropriate for measurements of absorption by aqueous copper sulphate.

● **Figure 8.8** Copper ions replacing atoms of iron. After several minutes the blue colour of the solution (**a**) has become paler and a red-brown deposit has formed on the iron wool (**b**).

## Monitoring reaction rates of gases using pressure changes

Measurements of pressure change at a given temperature can be used to calculate concentration change as a reaction proceeds. For example, this method can be used to monitor the production of carbon dioxide from limestone in a sealed container (*figure 8.9*).

## Monitoring reaction rates of solutions using chemical analysis

If there is a change in acidity or basicity as a reaction proceeds, suitable titrations can be made to follow the rate. The rate of formation of sulphurous acid, $H_2SO_3$ (a component of acid rain formed by the reaction of sulphur dioxide with water), could be followed by measuring the increase in concentration of hydrogen ions produced. This is monitored by titrating samples of the increasingly acidic solution against a basic solution of known concentration, for example $0.001\,mol\,dm^{-3}$ aqueous sodium hydroxide. The more sodium hydroxide that is needed to neutralise the sample, the more sulphurous acid is present.

# The collision theory of reactivity

Collisions occur between billiard balls in a game of snooker. There are a few stories from the second half of the nineteenth century of explosions occurring when two billiard balls collided with exceptional force. One story describes how such an

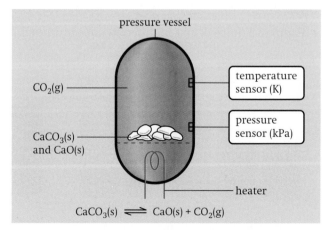

● **Figure 8.9** A notional system to investigate the effect of heat on the decomposition of limestone.

explosion set off a gunfight in a Colorado saloon.

Why should billiard balls explode? At the time billiard balls were made from celluloid (a mixture of nitrocellulose and camphor). Sometimes the balls were varnished with a nitrocellulose paint. If two such billiard balls collided with sufficient energy they might conceivably explode. As modern billiard balls are no longer made of celluloid, this is not something we are likely to experience, however many hours we spend watching snooker on television!

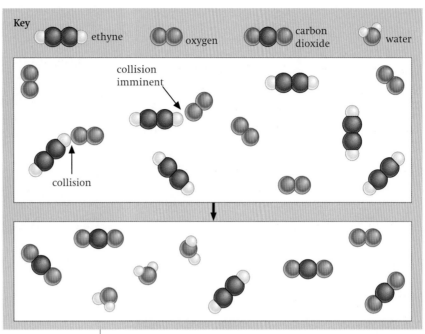

The 'exploding billiard balls' story enables us to visualise the collision theory of reactivity. Collision theory helps to provide explanations for the following experimental observations, made by measuring rates of reaction. The measurements show that the rate of reaction can be increased by:

- increasing the concentration of a reactant;
- increasing the pressure of a gaseous reactant;
- increasing the temperature;
- using a catalyst.

An example of a reaction, well known to welders, is the combustion of ethyne in oxygen when using an oxyacetylene torch. (Acetylene is a more traditional name for ethyne. This gas is an example of an alkyne. Alkynes contain a C≡C triple bond.) This gaseous reaction involving two reactants is shown in *figures 8.10* and *8.11*. The reactant molecules are moving around and occasionally, random collisions will occur.

### SAQ 8.3

Write the balanced equation for the reaction in *figure 8.10*.

It is not hard to imagine that, like the exploding billiard balls, collision of an ethyne and an oxygen molecule can result in a reaction. However, again like our nineteenth century billiard balls, only a few of these collisions result in a reaction. Not all the collisions are effective. A collision is not necessarily followed by a reaction. Effective

● **Figure 8.10** Molecules of ethyne, $C_2H_2(g)$, and oxygen, $O_2(g)$, can collide. If the collision is big enough, chemical bonds are broken. They are re-formed when the fragments combine to make new molecules: carbon dioxide, $CO_2(g)$, and steam, $H_2O(g)$.

collisions occur when the kinetic energy of the colliding molecules provides sufficient energy for reaction. We shall explore this aspect later (see page 169). However, a reaction certainly *cannot* occur if the molecules don't collide.

This simple notion is the basis of the collision theory of reactivity. When there are more balls on a billiard table, more collisions are likely to occur. If we increase the pressure of a gas, the molecules are closer together and more collisions will occur. Increasing the number of collisions will increase the number of effective collisions and so the reaction proceeds at a faster rate (*figure 8.12*).

The theory also generally applies to reactions in solutions. The reactants in solution behave rather like those in a gas – in each case the reactants are separated from each other. An increase in pressure increases the number of gas molecules in a given volume, which means the concentration is increased. When we increase the concentration of reagents in solution, the rate of reaction also increases.

In studying the influence of concentration on rate, we have to be careful to keep temperature constant, because a change in temperature will

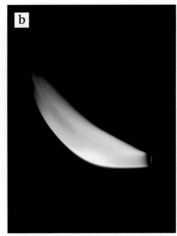

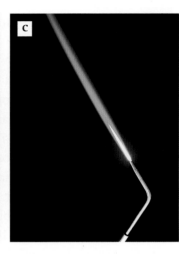

● **Figure 8.11**
a Ethyne, mixed with oxygen, is used in an oxyacetylene torch. Here the gas is not ignited, and you can see it bubbling through water.
b The ethyne is now ignited, but is not completely combusting because the yellow flame indicates the presence of carbon: the temperature of the flame is relatively low.
c The ethyne is now being completely converted into carbon dioxide and water: the temperature of the flame is much higher.

alter the reaction rate. The qualitative influence is for an increase in temperature to increase reaction rate, and using the simple collision theory model it is not hard to see why. There will be a wide distribution of energies (and therefore speeds) of molecules, but increasing the temperature will certainly increase the average speed of the molecules. Indeed, an increase in temperature is the same thing as an increase in the random kinetic energies, and hence the speeds, of the molecules. The increased speeds of molecules will lead to more molecules gaining sufficient energy to react on collision.

We can summarise all this as follows:
■ Molecules will react only if they collide with each other.
■ Reactions will occur only if there is enough energy in the collison.
■ Increased concentration of molecules increases the likelihood of collision, which increases reaction rate.
■ Increased temperature increases the proportion of molecules with sufficient energy to react which increases reaction rate.

## The Boltzmann distribution

In any mixture of moving molecules, the energy of each molecule varies enormously. Like bumper cars at a fairground, some are belting along at high speeds while others are virtually at a standstill. The situation changes moment by moment: a car (or particle) travelling at a fairly gentle pace can get a shunt from behind and speed off

● **Figure 8.12** The larger number of molecules in **a** than in **b** leads to more collisions between molecules and a faster reaction rate.

with much greater energy than before; the fast car (or particle) that caused the collision will slow down during the collision.

The **Boltzmann distribution** represents the numbers of cars (or particles) with particular energies. It does not work too well for bumper cars, but it does with samples of gas, where there are billions and billions of molecules in constant random motion. A few are almost motionless. A minority have momentary speeds far in excess of the average. The majority have speeds around an average value. This is illustrated by the graph shown in *figure 8.13*.

This average value will increase if the temperature of the entire collection of molecules is increased. Some molecules will still be almost immobile, but at any one time there is a greater number at a higher speed than before. The new distribution is shown in *figure*

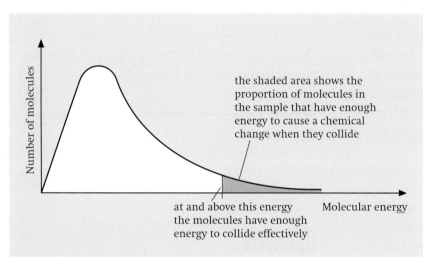

● **Figure 8.13** The Boltzmann distribution for molecular energies in a sample of gas. Since the mass of each molecule is the same, the difference in energies is due to a difference in speed. Note the asymmetric shape of the curve.

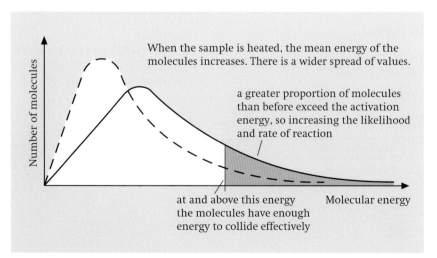

● **Figure 8.14** Note how the Boltzmann distribution flattens and shifts to the right at the higher temperature. The areas under both curves are the same – they represent the total number of molecules in the sample, and this should not change before a reaction occurs.

*8.14.* The effect of this shift in the distribution is to increase the proportion of molecules with sufficient energy to react. This energy value is called the **activation energy**. The collision energy of the exploding billiard balls mentioned earlier must have exceeded the activation energy for reaction.

## Activation energy

Just as two cars with effective bumpers may collide at low speed with no real damage being done (apart from frayed tempers), so low-energy collisions will not result in reaction. The molecules will bounce apart unchanged (*figure 8.15*). On the other hand, a high speed collision between one car and another will result in permanent damage, and the configuration of each vehicle will be drastically altered (and the same may go for the drivers). In the same sort of way, molecules have to collide with a certain minimum energy $E_a$ for there to be a chance of reaction. $E_a$ is referred to as the **activation energy** for the reaction. Like other energy changes, activation energy has units of kJ mol$^{-1}$.

But why should we have to surmount this energy barrier $E_a$ to bring about reaction? After all, as we saw in chapter 5, if a reaction is exothermic the sum of the bond energies in the product molecules is less than the sum of the bond energies in the reactant molecules. Why doesn't a reaction, such as the combustion of methane in oxygen, flow spontaneously downhill to give carbon dioxide and water (a less energetic, more stable, state) as

● **Figure 8.15** These collisions, frequent as they are, are not effective. They do not, we hope, result in permanent damage – chemical change.

illustrated in *figure 8.16*? Before we consider the answer to this question, it must be pointed out that such a situation would be inconvenient, if not catastrophic. Methane (or other hydrocarbons) would ignite spontaneously on contact with air! The equation for the complete combustion of methane is:

$$CH_4(g) + 2O_2(g) \rightarrow CO_2(g) + 2H_2O(l)$$

We have to ignite the methane; that is, we must give it sufficient energy for the reaction to get started. There is no reaction between the two gases (methane and oxygen) before ignition, and without this boost they sit together quite contentedly for an indefinite length of time. This is because, as the methane and oxygen molecules approach one another, the outer electrons of one molecule repel the outer electrons of the other. It's only if this repulsion can be overcome by a substantial input of energy that bonds can be broken and the attractive forces (between the electrons of one molecule and the positive nuclear charge of the other) can take over. The redistribution of electrons that occurs results in the bond-breaking and bond-making processes – it sets off a molecular reaction. Once the reaction has started, enough heat energy is produced to keep the reaction going (it is self-sustained).

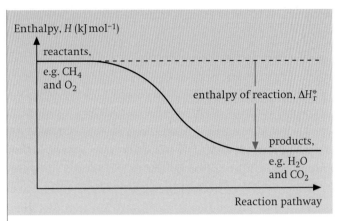

● **Figure 8.16** A 'down-hill-all-the-way' reaction. Fortunately, it does not happen for methane and oxygen at normal temperatures and pressures. For an explanation of enthalpy, see page 73.

*Figure 8.17* shows the situation diagrammatically. Overall the reaction pathway (or coordinate) lies downhill, but initially the path lies uphill.

## SAQ 8.4

In the case of the reaction between methane and oxygen, where could the activation energy come from?

# Catalysis

A catalyst is something added to a reaction that increases its rate, but does not itself change in concentration: the same amount remains after the reaction as before. However, it is not true to say that the catalyst is unchanged.

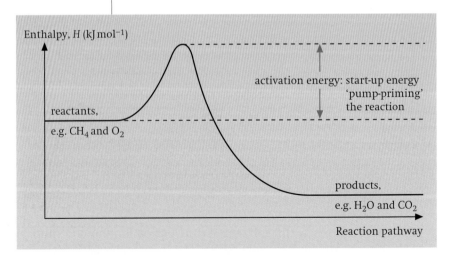

● **Figure 8.17** A reaction pathway diagram, showing the activation energy. This is an exothermic reaction.

## Why should endothermic reactions go at all?

If we have a reaction that is exothermic, it is obvious why the reaction should proceed to give the more stable products, so long as it is provided with a boost to enable it to surmount its particular activation barrier. But why ever should we be able to get an endothermic reaction to go?

Not only do we have the activation barrier to get over, but even when we do this, the energy of the product molecules is greater than the energy of the reactant molecules (*figure 8.18*). We have an apparent decrease in stability – the reaction has 'gone uphill'. We can only say that this is a very legitimate question to which the answer is that there is another factor that influences the relative stability of a system. It is called entropy. Entropy is a measure of the disorder or randomness of a system. The greater the degree of disorder, the greater the stability; and thus the total free energy of a system is the sum of the enthalpy and the entropy.

At this stage we can say no more, but if you proceed beyond this level with your studies of physics and chemistry, you will hear a lot more about entropy. It is a fascinating and essential idea in understanding the chemical changes in our environment.

## SAQ 8.5

Examples of ordered instability and disordered stability are shown in *figure 8.19*. Which has the lower entropy? Which has the higher entropy and with it the greater stability?

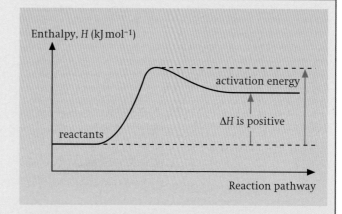

● **Figure 8.18** An enthalpy pathway diagram for an endothermic reaction. $\Delta H$ is the enthalpy change of the reaction.

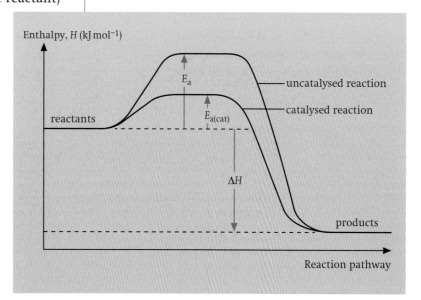

● **Figure 8.19** Entropy at work.

Catalysts work by providing a different reaction pathway (route or mechanism) for the reaction. A reactant (in some case more than one reactant) will combine weakly with the catalyst to form an activated complex. This activated complex will undergo further reaction to form the products, releasing the catalyst for re-use. The catalyst takes part in the reaction but is restored at the end of the reaction.

The reaction rate increases because the catalysed reaction pathway has a lower activation energy than that of the uncatalysed reaction. This is shown in *figure 8.20*. The Boltzmann distribution in *figure 8.21* shows how the lower activation energy for the catalysed reaction increases the number of molecules that will react on collision.

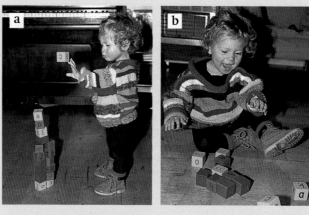

● **Figure 8.20** The catalysed reaction follows a different route (pathway) with a lower activation energy, $E_{a(cat)}$.

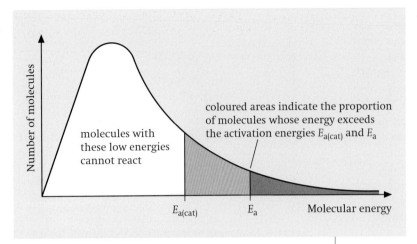

● **Figure 8.21** The route with the lower activation energy does not alter the Boltzmann distribution; however, it does increase the number of molecules with energies above the activation energy.

# Enzymes

**Enzymes** are proteins that act as biological catalysts. Without them, the reactions that make life possible would be too slow for life to exist. Enzymes:

■ show great specificity, only catalysing reactions involving a particular molecule or class of molecule;

■ control the specificity of a reaction in such a way as to produce 'clean' reactions with very few side-products;

■ are extremely sensitive to changes in conditions such as temperature and pH;

■ are extremely sensitive to the presence of certain molecules known as inhibitors and cofactors;

■ are far more efficient than the inorganic catalysts used in the chemical industry.

## The 'lock and key' model

In 1894, Emil Fischer proposed a model of enzyme activity that explained the specificity of enzymes. He suggested that substrates bind to enzymes in a similar way to a key fitting into a lock (*figure 8.22*).

Only one substrate will fit the active site, just as only one key fits a lock. This model has become known as the 'lock and key' model.

The energy profile shown in *figure 8.23* shows how the formation of the enzyme–substrate complex reduces the energy requirement for the reaction to proceed. A similar energy profile for an exothermic reaction is shown in *figure 8.17*.

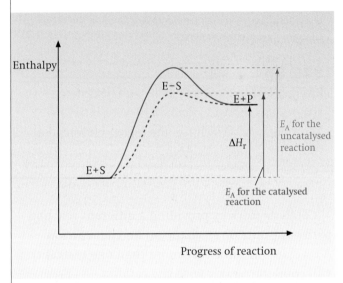

● **Figure 8.23** Energy profile for an enzyme-catalysed endothermic reaction, compared to the same reaction without a catalyst. As for inorganic catalysts, the enzyme provides a different reaction pathway with a lower activation energy ($E_A$) but the overall enthalpy change ($\Delta H_r$) is unaffected.

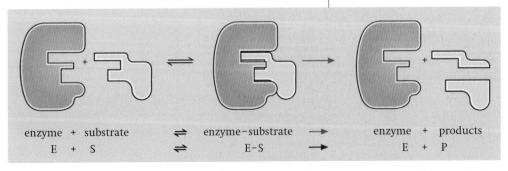

● **Figure 8.22** The 'lock and key' model of enzyme action. The substrate fits precisely into the active site of the enzyme. The enzyme then catalyses the breakdown of the substrate into the products, which can then leave the active site of the enzyme.

## SUMMARY (AS)

- The rate of a chemical reaction is measured by the amount (in moles) of a reactant used up in a given time. Chemical kinetics is the study of rates of chemical reactions.

- Chemists study rates of reaction to:
  - improve the rate of production of a chemical;
  - help understand the processes going on in our bodies or in the environment;
  - gain an insight into the mechanism of a reaction.

- The factors that affect the rate of a chemical reaction are:
  - concentration (or pressure of gases);
  - temperature;
  - surface area or intensity of radiation;
  - catalysts.

  The progress of a chemical reaction may involve sampling, followed by quenching to slow or stop the reaction prior to chemical analysis by, for example, titration. Alternatively a physical method, such as following mass loss, volume of produced, absorbance of light by coloured solution, pH or conductivity may be used.

- The increase in rate of a chemical reaction when there is an increase in concentration (or pressure) of a reactant may be explained using collision theory. At higher concentration (or pressure), more collisions occur between reactant molecules. The proportion of these collisions which are effective also increases. Effective collisions are those where the molecules have sufficient energy for reaction to occur.

- The activation energy of a reaction is the minimum energy required for reaction to occur. Enthalpy profile diagrams show how the activation energy provides a barrier to reaction.

- The Boltzmann distribution represents the numbers of molecules in a sample with particular energies. The change in the Boltzmann distribution as temperature is increased shows how more molecules have kinetic energy which is above the activation energy. This, in turn, leads to an increase in reaction rate.

- A catalyst increases the rate of a reaction by providing an alternative reaction pathway with a lower activation energy. More molecules have sufficient energy to react, so the rate of reaction is increased.

- Enzymes are proteins that act as biological catalysts.

## Questions (AS)

1 Catalysts are widely used in industry to alter the rate of a chemical reaction. Describe how catalysts carry out this function. Your answer should contain reference to activation energy, homogeneous catalysis and heterogeneous catalysis. Include diagrams and appropriate examples.

2 In the Haber process, ammonia is produced from nitrogen and hydrogen as shown in the equation below.
$$N_2(g) + 3H_2(g) \rightarrow 2NH_3(g)$$

a Describe, using the Boltzmann distribution, the effect of an increase in temperature on the rate of this reaction.

b The rate of formation of ammonia in the Haber process is increased by using an iron catalyst. This is an example of heterogeneous catalysis.

   Explain what is meant by the term heterogeneous catalysis.

# Reaction kinetics (A2)

## By the end of this section you should be able to:

9 explain and use the terms: *rate of reaction*, *order*, *rate constant*, *half-life*, *rate-determining step*;

10 deduce, from a concentration–time graph, the rate of a reaction and the half-life of a first-order reaction;

11 recall that the half-life of a first-order reaction is independent of the concentration and use the half-life of a first-order reaction in calculations;

12 deduce, from a rate–concentration graph, the order (0, 1 or 2) with respect to a reactant;

13 calculate, using the *initial-rates method*, the order (0, 1 or 2) with respect to a reactant;

14 construct a *rate equation* of the form: rate $= k[A]^m[B]^n$, for which $m$ and $n$ are 0, 1 or 2;

15 calculate a rate constant from a rate equation;

16 explain qualitatively, the effect of temperature change on a rate constant and hence the rate of a reaction;

17 for a multi-step reaction, predict an expression for the rate equation, given the rate-determining step, know that a rate equation enables a rate-determining step to be proposed, and use a rate equation and the balanced equation for a reaction to suggest possible steps in a *reaction mechanism*;

18 state what is meant by *homogeneous catalysis* and *heterogeneous catalysis*;

19 outline, as an example of homogeneous catalysis, how gaseous chlorine free radicals, formed by the action of ultraviolet radiation on CFCs, catalyse the breakdown of the gaseous ozone layer into oxygen;

20 describe catalysts as having great economic importance, for example in fertiliser production;

21 for carbon monoxide, oxides of nitrogen and unburnt hydrocarbons, describe their presence in and/or formation from the internal combustion engine and state their environmental consequences;

22 outline, as an example of heterogeneous catalysis, how a catalytic converter removes carbon monoxide and nitrogen monoxide emissions from internal combustion engines;

23 outline the catalytic role of atmospheric oxides of nitrogen in the oxidation of atmospheric sulphur dioxide;

24 outline the catalytic role of $Fe^{2+}$ or $Fe^{3+}$ in the $I^-/S_2O_8^{2-}$ reaction.

# More about reaction rates

Earlier in this chapter you were introduced to the more qualitative aspects of reaction rates. For example, you saw how collision theory can be used to explain the effect of changing concentration, pressure or temperature on reaction rate. Quantitative aspects were limited to making measurements during rate experiments and using activation energy to explain the effect of temperature changes or catalysts on reaction rate.

A knowledge and understanding of the rate of a reaction for the production of a chemical is essential before work begins on the design of a manufacturing plant. Previously, you saw how the work of Haber led to the process for making ammonia that bears his name.

Over the past 25 years, the study of atmospheric chemistry has developed. There are many different chemical species naturally present in the atmosphere. Many more chemical species are present due to the activities of humans. Studies of the atmosphere have shown that the variety of reactions between these species is very large indeed. Many of these reactions require ultraviolet radiation. Some are only possible in the upper atmos-

phere (figure 8.24); others occur under the different conditions present close to the surface of the Earth.

Where the reaction rates are particularly fast, the study of these reactions has required new techniques. Ronald Norrish and George Porter won the 1967 Nobel Prize in Chemistry for their work in Cambridge on the development of a technique to follow fast reactions. Their technique, known as 'flash-photolysis' used a flashlight to 'freeze' reactions and observe intermediates with lifetimes of $10^{-6}$ to $10^{-3}$ s. Porter (figure 8.25) subsequently refined the technique and developed the use of a laser to study reactions. The reaction is started by a very short, intense flash from the laser. This is very quickly followed by a second flash which allows the composition of the mixture to be studied spectroscopically.

The 1986 Nobel Prize for Chemistry went to Dudley Herschbach, Yuan Lee and John Polanyi, who used a crossed molecular beam technique to enable even faster reactions, with lifetimes of intermediates in picoseconds (ps, $10^{-12}$ s), to be studied. More recently, the Egyptian chemist Ahmed Zewail won the 1999 Nobel Prize for measurements of even faster reactions taking place in femtoseconds (fs, $10^{-15}$ s). Zewail's technique allows chemists to follow vibrations of individual bonds, which last 10–100 fs, for reactions which are complete in less than 200 fs.

● **Figure 8.24** The Northern Lights (aurora borealis) are the result of many complex reactions taking place in the upper atmosphere. A knowledge of reaction rates is needed to understand the natural reactions involved and how these might be disturbed by artificial emissions.

● **Figure 8.25** George Porter, who, with Ronald Norrish, won a Nobel Prize in 1967 for their work on measuring fast reaction rates.

## SAQ 8.6

**a** Which region of the electromagnetic spectrum would enable the vibrations of individual bonds to be identified?

**b** Write 200 fs in seconds using standard form.

In this chapter you will find out about the quantitative aspects of reaction rates. In particular, you will meet the rate equation for a reaction and learn how to determine rate equations from measurements made whilst following a reaction.

You will also, like the Nobel Prizewinners mentioned above, find out how a study of reaction rates leads to ideas for the intermediates present in reaction mechanisms. However, the reactions that you will study take place over several minutes rather than in split seconds!

# The rate equation

A simple example of a **rate equation** is provided by the isomerisation of cyclopropane to propene.

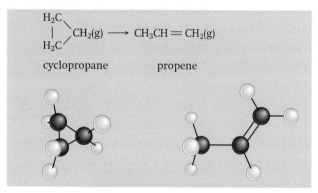

*Table 8.1* shows the change in concentration of cyclopropane at 500 °C. As temperature affects the rate of reaction, the measurements in *table 8.1* were all made at the same temperature. *Figure 8.26* shows a plot of the cyclopropane concentration against time, using the data from *table 8.1*. Note the square brackets round 'cyclopropane'. These square brackets are the symbols that chemists use to indicate concentration, in this case of cyclo-

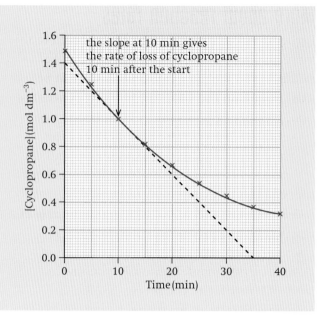

- **Figure 8.26** The rate of decrease of cyclopropane concentration over time as isomerisation proceeds. The rate of reaction at a given time can be found by drawing a tangent and measuring its gradient.

propane. More usually, the brackets will be round the formula of the chemical species, but sometimes it is more helpful to write the name of the compound.

The rate of a chemical reaction can be found by dividing the change in concentration by time. (Remember speed is distance travelled divided by time taken.) For the cyclopropane reaction, writing $\Delta[\text{cyclopropane}]$ for a change in concentration over a time interval $\Delta t$, the rate of reaction is shown by the following expression:

$$\text{rate of decrease of cyclopropane concentration} = \frac{\Delta[\text{cyclopropane}]}{\Delta t}$$

*Figure 8.26* shows a method for measuring the reaction rate for the cyclopropane isomerisation. A tangent is drawn at a chosen point on the graph. This is drawn so as to *just touch* the curve of the concentration against time plot. The two angles between the straight line and the curve

| Time (min) | 0 | 5 | 10 | 15 | 20 | 25 | 30 | 35 | 40 |
|---|---|---|---|---|---|---|---|---|---|
| [cyclopropane](mol dm⁻³) | 1.50 | 1.23 | 1.00 | 0.82 | 0.67 | 0.55 | 0.45 | 0.37 | 0.33 |
| [propene](mol dm⁻³) | 0.00 | 0.27 | 0.49 | 0.68 | 0.83 | 0.95 | 1.08 | 1.13 | 1.20 |

- **Table 8.1** Concentrations of reactant (cyclopropane) and product (propene) at 5 min intervals (temperature = 500 °C (773 K)).

should look very similar. Note that the tangent is then extended to meet the axes of the graph. By extending the tangent to the axes, we reduce the error in the measurements made from the graph. The slope of the tangent is a measure of the rate of reaction.

Ten minutes after the start of the reaction, the slope of the tangent is:

$$\text{slope} = \frac{1.4 - 0.0\,\text{mol dm}^{-3}}{35 \times 60\,\text{s}}$$

$$= 6.67 \times 10^{-4}\,\text{mol dm}^{-3}\,\text{s}^{-1}$$

$$= \text{rate of decrease of cyclopropane concentration.}$$

Notice the units for rate of reaction are (change in) concentration per second; compare them to the typical units for the speed of a runner, metres per second ($\text{m s}^{-1}$).

Take another look at *figure 8.26*. Notice that, as time passes, the concentration of cyclopropane falls – hardly surprising. The question to ask is: 'In what way does it fall?' Does it fall in a predictable way? Is there a mathematical way of describing it?

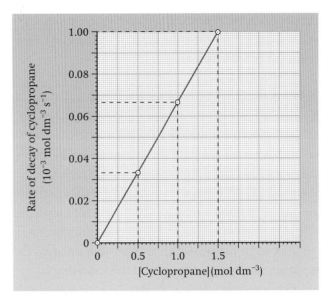

● **Figure 8.28** The rate of decay of cyclopropane. Note how the gradient (rate/concentration) is constant.

*Figure 8.27* supplies some answers. We will use it to calculate the rate of reaction at different concentrations: $1.5\,\text{mol dm}^{-3}$, $1.0\,\text{mol dm}^{-3}$, and $0.5\,\text{mol dm}^{-3}$. (Again, we can measure the rate at any point on a graph by drawing the tangent to the curve and measuring its slope at that point.)

The three measurements are shown in *table 8.2* and are represented by the graph in *figure 8.28*.

The data and *figure 8.28* show that the rate of the reaction does depend directly upon the concentration of cyclopropane as we predicted. If the concentration of cyclopropane drops to two thirds, so does its reaction rate.

## SAQ 8.7

Consider the cyclopropane reaction described above. What would happen to the reaction rate if the concentration of cyclopropane was halved?

The third line in *table 8.2* shows that rate/concentration is a number that is pretty well constant ($6.7 \times 10^{-4}\,\text{s}^{-1}$). This can be expressed mathematically:

$$\text{rate of reaction} = k \times [\text{cyclopropane}]$$

The proportionality constant, $k$, is called the **rate constant**. For the

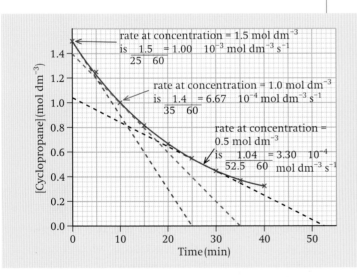

● **Figure 8.27** Calculations of the rate of decay of cyclopropane, made at regular intervals.

| concentration $(\text{mol dm}^{-3})$ | 1.5 | 1.0 | 0.5 |
|---|---|---|---|
| rate $(\text{mol dm}^{-3}\,\text{s}^{-1})$ | $1.00 \times 10^{-3}$ | $6.67 \times 10^{-4}$ | $3.30 \times 10^{-4}$ |
| $\dfrac{\text{rate}}{\text{concentration}}\,(\text{s}^{-1})$ | $6.7 \times 10^{-4}$ | $6.7 \times 10^{-4}$ | $6.6 \times 10^{-4}$ |

● **Table 8.2** Rates of decay for cyclopropane at different concentrations, calculated from *figure 8.27*.

reaction above, it has the units of rate divided by concentration, $s^{-1}$. For the data of *table 8.2* the rate constant is $6.7 \times 10^{-4}\,s^{-1}$.

## SAQ 8.8

**b** Plot the data in *table 8.1* for yourself. Measure the rate after 10 minutes by drawing a tangent which is about 5 cm in length and not extended to the axes. Mark the horizontal and vertical measurements on your graph and calculate a value for the rate of reaction. Compare your value with the value given in *table 8.2*. Which value do you consider to be more reliable? Explain your answer.

**b** Draw two further tangents at the following cyclopropane concentrations: 1.25 and $0.75\,mol\,dm^{-3}$. Extend these tangents to meet both axes. Use the data from these measurements, together with the data in *figure 8.27* to plot your own version of *figure 8.28*. Your data should also lie on, or close to, the straight line.

## More rate equations

We already have a rate equation for the decomposition of cyclopropane:

rate = $k$ [cyclopropane]

This rate equation was found by experiment – not by theoretical calculation.

The reaction between hydrogen gas and nitrogen monoxide, NO, at 800 °C produces water and nitrogen gas:

$2H_2(g) + 2NO(g) \rightarrow 2H_2O(g) + N_2(g)$

Experiment shows that doubling the concentration of hydrogen doubles the rate of reaction, tripling $[H_2]$ triples the rate, and so on. So

rate $\propto [H_2]$     or     rate = $k_1 \times [H_2]$

Further experiment shows that doubling the concentration of nitrogen monoxide quadruples the rate of reaction ($2^2$), tripling [NO] increases it

by a factor of nine ($3^2$), and so on. Therefore

rate $\propto [NO]^2$     or     rate = $k_2 \times [NO]^2$

The two equations can be combined as follows:

rate of reaction $\propto [H_2][NO]^2$

or     rate of reaction = $k_1 \times k_2 \times [H_2] \times [NO]^2$
$= k \times [H_2] \times [NO]^2$

(where $k_1 \times k_2 = k$), which can be written as

rate of reaction = $k[H_2][NO]^2$

More rate equations are shown in *table 8.3*. They were all found by experiment. They cannot be predicted from the equation – so don't assume they can. The units for $k$ may be different for each reaction; they must be worked out for each reaction. For example:

$k[H_2][NO]^2$ = rate of reaction in $mol\,dm^{-3}\,s^{-1}$

so $k$ is in $\dfrac{(mol\,dm^{-3}\,s^{-1})}{(mol\,dm^{-3}) \times (mol\,dm^{-3})^2}$

i.e. $k$'s units are $dm^6\,mol^{-2}\,s^{-1}$.

## Order of reaction

The order of a reaction gives us an idea of how the concentration of a reagent affects the reaction rate. It is defined as follows: the **order of a reaction** is the power to which we have to raise the concentration to fit the rate equation.

The easiest way to explain order is to use an example.

- Chemical equation:
  $2NO(g) + O_2(g) \rightarrow 2NO_2(g)$
- Experimental rate equation:
  rate of reaction = $k[NO]^2[O_2]^1 = k[NO]^2[O_2]$

The order of the reaction as far as nitrogen monoxide (NO) is concerned is 2. It is the power of 2 in $[NO]^2$. We say the reaction is 'second order with respect to nitrogen monoxide'.

The order of reaction as far as oxygen is concerned is 1. We say the reaction is 'first order with respect to oxygen'.

Overall, the order of reaction is $2 + 1 = 3$. Note how careful you should be when you talk about reaction orders. Always ask yourself the question: 'Order with respect to *what*?'

| Equation for the reaction | Rate equation | Units for $k$ |
|---|---|---|
| $2H_2(g) + 2NO(g) \rightarrow 2H_2O(g) + N_2(g)$ | rate = $k[H_2][NO]^2$ | $dm^6\,mol^{-2}\,s^{-1}$ |
| $H_2(g) + I_2(g) \rightarrow 2HI(g)$ | rate = $k[H_2][I_2]$ | $dm^3\,mol^{-1}\,s^{-1}$ |
| $NO(g) + CO(g) + O_2(g) \rightarrow NO_2(g) + CO_2(g)$ | rate = $k[NO]^2$ | $dm^3\,mol^{-1}\,s^{-1}$ |

● **Table 8.3** Rate equations for some reactions.

## SAQ 8.9

What is the order of reaction for the decomposition of cyclopropane to propene? The rate equation is

rate of reaction = $k$[cyclopropane]

## Zero-order reactions

Ammonia gas decomposes on a hot tungsten wire.

$$2NH_3(g) \xrightarrow{W} N_2(g) + 3H_2(g)$$

The rate of decomposition does not depend upon the concentration of ammonia gas. The rate of reaction is fixed. Doubling and tripling the concentration of ammonia makes no difference to the rate at which the ammonia decomposes. Thus

rate of reaction = $k$

which can be written as

rate of reaction = $k[NH_3]^0$

(since anything to the power 0 equals 1). When a graph of rate of reaction against concentration is plotted for a zero-order reaction, a horizontal straight line is obtained as shown in *figure 8.29*.

## First-order reactions

The gas dinitrogen oxide, $N_2O$, decomposes on a heated gold surface:

$$2N_2O(g) \xrightarrow{Au} 2N_2(g) + O_2(g)$$

The rate of reaction depends directly upon the concentration of $N_2O$. If its concentration is doubled, its reaction rate doubles. Thus

rate of reaction = $k[N_2O]$

which can be written as

rate of reaction = $k[N_2O]^1$

(since anything to the power 1 is unchanged). When a graph of rate of reaction against concentration is plotted for a first-order reaction, an inclined straight line is obtained as shown in *figure 8.29*.

## Second-order reactions

Ethanal vapour ($CH_3CHO$) decomposes at 800 K:

$$CH_3CHO(g) \rightarrow CH_4(g) + CO(g)$$

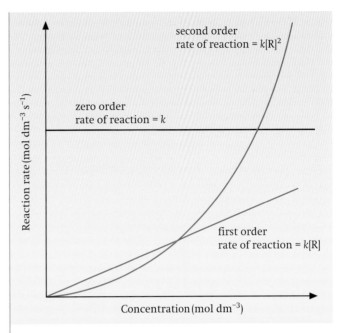

● **Figure 8.29** Zero-, first- and second-order reactions: how changes in the concentration of a reactant affect the reaction rate.

The rate of reaction depends directly upon the square of the concentration of $CH_3CHO$. If its concentration is doubled, its rate of reaction quadruples. Thus

rate of reaction = $k[CH_3CHO]^2$

When a graph of rate of reaction against concentration is plotted for a second-order reaction, a curved line is obtained as shown in *figure 8.29*.

An alternative method of distinguishing between these three types is shown in *figure 8.30*.

*Figure 8.30* shows the differences between the concentration against time graphs for zero-, first- and second-order reactions. The zero-order data is immediately recognisable as it is a straight line. However, both the first- and second-order data produce a curve. In the next section you will see how we can distinguish between these curves, so we can identify a first-order reaction.

A generalised form of the rate equation for the reaction

A + B → products

is

rate of reaction = $k[A]^m[B]^n$

The powers $m$ and $n$ show the order of the reaction with respect to reactants A, B.

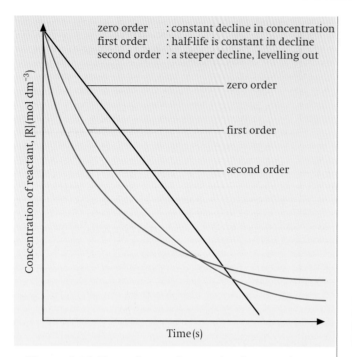

- **Figure 8.30** Zero-, first-and second-order reactions: how changes in the concentration of a reactant affect the time taken for a reaction to proceed.

# Half-life and reaction rates

In chemical reactions **half-life** ($t_{\frac{1}{2}}$) refers to concentrations of reactants – it is the time taken for the concentration of a reactant to fall to half its original value.

A feature of a first-order reaction is that the half-life is independent of concentration. This is not true for zero- or second-order reactions. As you have just seen, a graph of concentration against time for a zero-order reaction produces a straight line, whereas such graphs for first- and second-order reactions are curves.

To distinguish between first-order and second-order reactions, measurement of two (or more) half-lives is made from the graph. *Figure 8.31* and *table 8.4* show such measurements for the cyclopropane isomerisation reaction.

The three figures for the half-lives in *table 8.4* are quite close, producing a mean half-life for this reaction of 17.0 min. A second-order reaction shows significant increases when half-lives are measured in this way. A zero-order reaction shows significant decreases in half-lives. As this book deals only with orders of 0, 1 or 2 with respect to an individual reagent, you may assume that a concentration–time curve with a half-life which

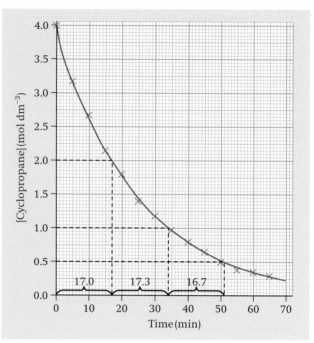

- **Figure 8.31** Measurement of half-life for cyclopropane isomerisation.

increases with decreasing concentration is a second-order reaction. In general, this is not a satisfactory way of identifying a second-order reaction as orders of reaction other than 0, 1 or 2 do exist. For example, orders of −1 or fractional orders are known. Much less common are third-order reactions. Concentration against time graphs for these other orders may also be curves.

You will only be expected to identify orders of 0, 1 or 2 from rate measurements.

For a first-order reaction, the half-life, $t_{\frac{1}{2}}$, is related to the rate constant, $k$, by the following equation:

$$t_{\frac{1}{2}} = \frac{0.693}{k}$$

Thus if the half-life is known, the value of $k$ can be easily calculated.

For a first-order reaction, the half-life is independent of the concentration. The units of $t_{\frac{1}{2}}$ will be $s^{-1}$ or $min^{-1}$.

| Δ[cyclopropane] (mol dm$^{-3}$) | Half-life (min) |
|---|---|
| 4.0 to 2.0 | 17.0 |
| 2.0 to 1.0 | 34.3 − 17.0 = 17.3 |
| 1.0 to 0.5 | 51.0 − 34.3 = 16.7 |

- **Table 8.4**

# Finding the order of reaction using raw data

We are now going to proceed to a more complex example. Keep clear in your mind the meanings of the terms 'rate of reaction', 'rate constant', and 'order of reaction'. It helps also to keep an eye on the units you will use.

We can identify a sequence of steps in the processing of the experimental results:

- summarising the raw data in a table;
- plotting a graph of raw data;
- finding the rate at a particular concentration;
- tabulating rate data;
- plotting a graph of rate/concentration data.

Table 8.5 gives rate and concentration data for the reaction of methanol with aqueous hydrochloric acid to give chloromethane and water at 298K:

$$CH_3OH(aq) + HCl(aq) \rightarrow CH_3Cl(aq) + H_2O(l)$$

## SAQ 8.10

The data in table 8.5 could have been obtained by titrating small samples of the reaction mixture with a standard strong base. What would have been found like this? How else might the reaction have been monitored?

| Time (min) | [HCl] (mol dm⁻³) | [CH₃OH] (mol dm⁻³) |
|---|---|---|
| 0 | 1.84 | 1.84 |
| 200 | 1.45 | 1.45 |
| 400 | 1.22 | 1.22 |
| 600 | 1.04 | 1.04 |
| 800 | 0.91 | 0.91 |
| 1000 | 0.81 | 0.81 |
| 1200 | 0.72 | 0.72 |
| 1400 | 0.66 | 0.66 |
| 1600 | 0.60 | 0.60 |
| 1800 | 0.56 | 0.56 |
| 2000 | 0.54 | 0.54 |

● **Table 8.5** Data for the reaction between methanol and hydrochloric acid.

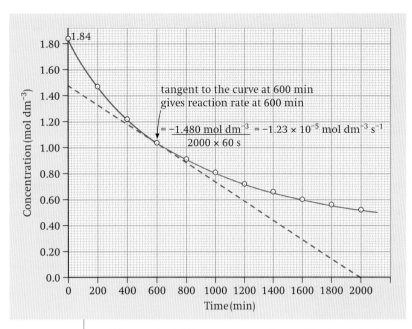

● **Figure 8.32** The concentrations of hydrochloric acid and methanol fall at the same rate as time elapses.

Figure 8.32 shows a graph of these data, and the beginnings of an exploration of the data.

First look to see if there is a consistent half-life for this reaction. Half of the initial amount of each reagent is $1.84/2 \, \text{mol dm}^{-3} = 0.92 \, \text{mol dm}^{-3}$. The half-life is 780 min. However, this amount, $0.92 \, \text{mol dm}^{-3}$, does not halve again in another 780 min. The second half-life (from 0.92 to $0.46 \, \text{mol dm}^{-3}$) is off the graph at around 1400–1500 min. The concentration–time graph has a long 'tail' at low concentration which is typical of a second-order graph. The half-life increases – so the overall order of reaction is likely to be 2.

As with the previous reaction, we can draw tangents to the curve to derive approximate rates at different times. This is shown for $t = 600$ min in figure 8.32. Other values have been calculated from these data and are shown in table 8.6. You can draw your own graph using the data in table 8.5 to find out what results you obtain – they should vary a bit owing to the difficulty of drawing an accurate tangent by eye.

By examining the data in table 8.6 you can see that the rate of reaction diminishes with time – unlike a zero-order reaction. A graph (figure 8.33, overleaf) shows that it most closely resembles a second-order plot (see figure 8.29, page 179).

| Time (min) | Concentration (mol dm$^{-3}$) | Rate from graph (mol dm$^{-3}$ min$^{-1}$) | Rate from graph (mol dm$^{-3}$ s$^{-1}$) |
|---|---|---|---|
| 0 | 1.84 | $2.30 \times 10^{-3}$ | $3.83 \times 10^{-5}$ |
| 200 | 1.45 | $1.46 \times 10^{-3}$ | $2.43 \times 10^{-5}$ |
| 400 | 1.22 | $1.05 \times 10^{-3}$ | $1.75 \times 10^{-5}$ |
| 600 | 1.04 | $0.74 \times 10^{-3}$ | $1.23 \times 10^{-5}$ |
| 800 | 0.91 | $0.54 \times 10^{-3}$ | $0.90 \times 10^{-5}$ |

● **Table 8.6** Values calculated for the reaction between methanol and hydrochloric acid.

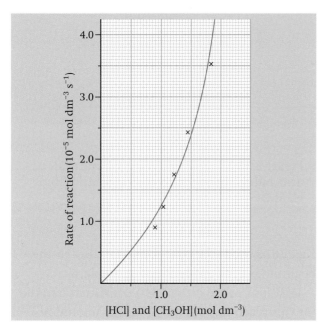

● **Figure 8.33** A graph showing how concentration changes of hydrochloric acid or methanol affect reaction rate. The curve show that the reaction is likely to be second order.

| Time (min) | Rate constant $k$ ($10^{-5}$ dm$^3$ mol$^{-1}$ s$^{-1}$) |
|---|---|
| 0 | 1.13 |
| 200 | 1.16 |
| 400 | 1.18 |
| 600 | 1.14 |
| 800 | 1.09 |

● **Table 8.7** Calculations for the rate constant $k$ assuming that the reaction is first order with respect to each of the starting reagents.

The results in *table 8.7* show that over a range of times during the reaction, $k$ is constant. (Although the figures are not exactly equal, they are fairly close considering that tangents were estimated from a graph.)

# The initial-rates method

We have seen that the rate of a reaction changes as the reactants are used up. For some reactions, measuring these changes over time may not be the best method for determining the rate equation. For instance, if the rate is quite slow, then obtaining a useful set of measurements would take an inconvenient amount of time. However, we usually know the initial concentrations of the reactants that we mix together in the reaction flask, and we can measure the **initial rate** of reaction. (For example, look again at the graph in *figure 8.27*, page 177: the rate we calculated at the concentration of 1.5 mol dm$^{-3}$ is the initial rate.) If we carry out several experiments with different initial concentrations of reactants, and we measure the initial rates of these experiments, then we can determine the rate equation. The best way to illustrate this is with an example.

Dinitrogen pentoxide decomposes to nitrogen dioxide and oxygen:

$$2N_2O_5(g) \rightarrow 4NO_2(g) + O_2(g)$$

## SAQ 8.11

**a** Look again at the raw data in *table 8.5* (previous page). Notice that the concentrations of both CH$_3$OH and HCl are changing.
  (i) Are both reactants affecting the rate or is only one reactant responsible for the data in *table 8.5*?
  (ii) Suggest how the experiment might be re-designed to obtain data that would provide evidence for the effect of changing the HCl concentration whilst controlling the CH$_3$OH concentration.

**b** Further experiments have shown that the rate of this reaction is first order with respect to each of methanol, hydrogen ions and chloride ions. Suggest how these experiments could be carried out.

| Initial concentration $[N_2O_5]$ (mol dm$^{-3}$) | Initial rate $(10^{-5}$ mol dm$^{-3}$ s$^{-1})$ |
| --- | --- |
| 3.00 | 3.15 |
| 1.50 | 1.55 |
| 0.75 | 0.80 |

● **Table 8.8** Data for the decomposition of dinitrogen pentoxide.

| Exp. | [HCl] (mol dm$^{-3}$) | [propanone] (mol dm$^{-3}$) | [iodine] $(10^{-3}$ mol dm$^{-3})$ | Initial rate $(10^{-6}$ mol dm$^{-3}$ s$^{-1})$ |
| --- | --- | --- | --- | --- |
| 1 | 1.25 | 0.5 | 1.25 | 10.9 |
| 2 | 0.625 | 0.5 | 1.25 | 4.7 |
| 3 | 1.25 | 0.25 | 1.25 | 5.1 |
| 4 | 1.25 | 0.5 | 0.625 | 10.7 |

● **Table 8.9** Experimental results for the reaction of propanone with iodine at varying aqueous concentrations.

*Table 8.8* gives the values of the initial rate as it varies with the concentration of dinitrogen pentoxide. A graph of the data (*figure 8.34*) shows that the initial rate of reaction is directly proportional to the initial concentration:

$$\text{Rate of reaction} \propto [N_2O_5]$$
$$= k[N_2O_5]$$

**SAQ 8.12**

**a**  What is the order of reaction for the decomposition of dinitrogen pentoxide?

**b**  Use the data for 3.00 mol dm$^{-3}$ $N_2O_5$ to calculate a value for the rate constant for this decomposition.

Another example of the use of initial rates is provided by data from experiments to follow the acid-catalysed reaction of iodine with propanone.

$$CH_3COCH_3 + I_2 \rightarrow CH_3COCH_2I + HI$$
propanone

This reaction is readily followed using a colorimeter. The yellow colour of the iodine fades as the reaction progresses.

*Table 8.9* shows data obtained at 20 °C from four separate experiments to measure the initial rates of reaction. The data are from real experiments so we must bear in mind experimental errors. Note that in each experiment the initial concentration of just one reagent has been changed from that in experiment 1.

Compare experiments 1 and 2. You will see that the concentration of H$^+$(aq) in experiment 2 is half the value of that in experiment 1. The initial rate has also been approximately halved. From this information we can deduce that the reaction is first order with respect to the acid catalyst.

Now compare experiments 1 and 3. The propanone concentration in experiment 3 is half that in experiment 1. Again the initial rate has been halved. We deduce that the reaction is first order with respect to propanone.

Finally, compare experiments 1 and 4. The iodine concentration has been halved but the initial rate stays approximately the same. We deduce that the reaction is zero order with respect to iodine.

**SAQ 8.13**

**a**  Write the rate equation for the acid-catalysed reaction of iodine with propanone using the above deductions.

**b**  Calculate the rate constant for this reaction.

**c**  Deduce the units of the rate constant.

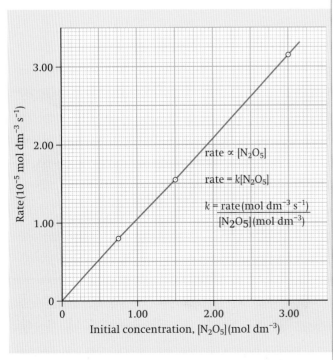

● **Figure 8.34** The initial rate of decomposition of dinitrogen pentoxide is directly proportional to the initial concentration.

| Temperature (K) | Rate constant (dm$^3$ mol$^{-1}$ s$^{-1}$) |
| --- | --- |
| 500 | $4.3 \times 10^{-7}$ |
| 600 | $4.4 \times 10^{-4}$ |
| 700 | $6.3 \times 10^{-2}$ |
| 800 | 2.6 |

● **Table 8.10** Rate constants for the reaction of hydrogen and iodine over a range of temperatures.

# Rate constants and temperature changes

An increase in the temperature of a reaction mixture by 10 °C approximately doubles the rate of reaction. How can this increase in rate be explained by the rate equation? A general form of the rate equation for reaction of A and B to form products is

rate of reaction = $k[A]^m[B]^n$

As temperature will not change the concentrations of A or B, the rate constant, $k$, must change if the reaction rate is to increase. We can predict that an increase in temperature will increase the value of $k$. An example of the rate constants for a reaction over a range of temperatures confirms our prediction.

*Table 8.10* shows the rate constants for the reaction of hydrogen and iodine at different temperatures. The equation for this reaction is

$H_2(g) + I_2(g) \rightarrow 2HI(g)$

The rate equation is:

rate of reaction = $k[H_2(g)][I_2(g)]$

From the above examples we can make some important deductions about the kinetics of chemical processes. As we stressed earlier in this chapter, the first step in a kinetic investigation is to establish the stoichiometry of the reaction, so we must analyse all the reaction products. The stoichiometry for a reaction shows the mole ratio of reactants and products in the balanced equation for the reaction. However, there is no correspondence between the stoichiometric equation for the reaction and the rate equation. We certainly cannot predict one from the other.

# Rate equations – the pay-off

Chemists are particularly interested in the mechanisms of chemical reactions – which chemical bonds are broken, which are made and in what order. Such an understanding helps chemists to design the synthesis of new compounds (see *figure 8.35*). For example, an understanding of the mechanism of stereoregular polymerisation (see chapter 22) has led to new catalysts for the polymerisation of ethene or propene. The polymers produced by the new catalysts (called metallocenes) are stronger and more tear-resistant than other polymers. They can be used for food packaging as they are very impermeable to air and moisture.

By using the rate equation, sometimes along with other items of information, we can deduce something about the separate bond-making and bond-breaking processes that go to make up the overall reaction.

Some reactions may consist of a single step. For example, when aqueous sodium hydroxide is mixed with dilute hydrochloric acid, the reaction is simply one in which hydrogen ions pair up with hydroxide ions to form water. The other ions do not participate in the reaction – they are called spectator ions and just get left alongside each other in solution:

$Na^+(aq) + OH^-(aq) + H^+(aq) + Cl^-(aq)$
$$\rightarrow H_2O(l) + Na^+(aq) + Cl^-(aq)$$

● **Figure 8.35** A very thin film of polymer produced using a metallocene catalyst. The strength and puncture resistance are being tested using a ball point pen.

Very frequently, a reaction is made up of a number of sequential steps. Each step will have a rate associated with it, but to find the overall rate of reaction, all we need to know is the rate of the *slowest* step (also called the **rate-determining step**). This is the case when all other steps are much faster. Fast steps, like selecting items off shelves in a supermarket, become insignificant when compared to the slow step, like queuing at the checkout.

We use the following principle, by which we can use the rate equation to construct the reaction mechanism: *If the concentration of a reactant appears in the rate equation, then that reactant or something derived from it takes part in the slow step of the reaction. If it does not appear in the rate equation, then neither the reactant nor anything derived from it participates in the slow step.*

This is the key to the interpretation of rate equations in terms of mechanisms of reactions. We can now consider some of the reactions we have looked at above, in terms of what their kinetic character, and other data, may tell us of their mechanism.

## Reaction mechanisms

We look again at the reaction for the decomposition of dinitrogen pentoxide:

$$2N_2O_5(g) \rightarrow 4NO_2(g) + O_2(g)$$

You may have been surprised that this did not turn out to be a second-order reaction. The stoichiometry is bimolecular – we need two molecules of dinitrogen pentoxide to balance the equation. So we can imagine that the reaction might start by two $N_2O_5$ molecules colliding and breaking up as suggested in the equation shown in *figure 8.36*.

But the rate equation tells us something different.

$$\text{rate of reaction} = k[N_2O_5]$$

The rate equation tells us that the slow step of the reaction involves *one* molecule of dinitrogen pentoxide decomposing (to nitrogen dioxide and nitrogen trioxide). This is the first step. The subsequent steps are comparatively fast. (*Fast* and *slow* are not absolute terms, so when we speak of fast and slow steps within the context of a given reaction, we mean relative to one another.) The actual mechanism of this reaction is shown in *figure 8.37* (overleaf). The first step of the reaction is the slow step.

Now let's look at the acid-catalysed reaction of propanone with iodine:

$$CH_3COCH_3(aq) + I_2(aq) \xrightarrow{\ H^+(aq)\ } CH_3COCH_2I(aq) + HI(aq)$$

It appears that hydrogen ions from the acid are not directly involved. Either they are not used up or they are regenerated with the products, at the same rate as they are used up. In either case the hydrogen ions behave as a catalyst.

The rate equation sheds some light on this (also see page 183). It is

$$\text{rate of reaction} = k[CH_3COCH_3]^1[H^+]^1[I_2]^0$$

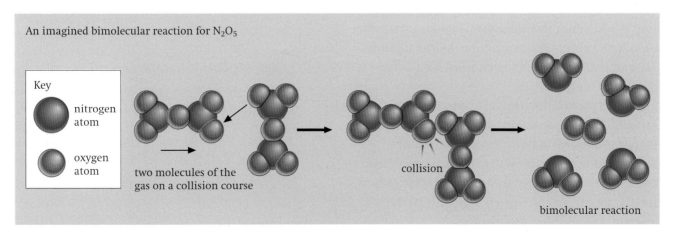

An imagined bimolecular reaction for $N_2O_5$

Key

- nitrogen atom
- oxygen atom

two molecules of the gas on a collision course

collision

bimolecular reaction

● **Figure 8.36** The equation for the decomposition of dinitrogen pentoxide suggests that a reaction between two molecules occurs (a bimolecular reaction). The rate equation tells us otherwise.

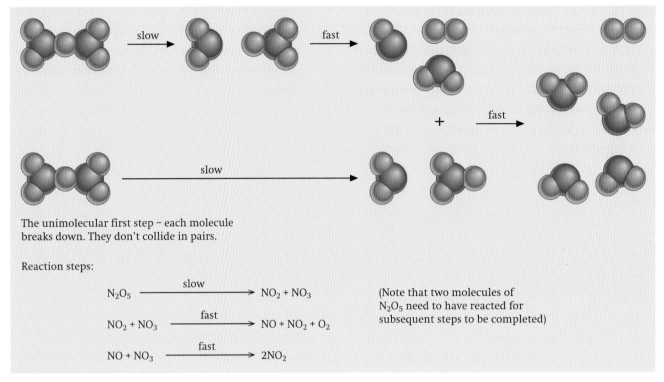

The unimolecular first step – each molecule breaks down. They don't collide in pairs.

Reaction steps:

$$N_2O_5 \xrightarrow{\text{slow}} NO_2 + NO_3$$

$$NO_2 + NO_3 \xrightarrow{\text{fast}} NO + NO_2 + O_2$$

$$NO + NO_3 \xrightarrow{\text{fast}} 2NO_2$$

(Note that two molecules of $N_2O_5$ need to have reacted for subsequent steps to be completed)

● **Figure 8.37** The rate equation tells us that the decomposition of individual molecules of dinitrogen pentoxide is the rate-determining step. The subsequent reactions are much faster by comparison, and do not have much influence on the overall rate. Try to match the equations with the illustrations to get a picture of what is happening.

Therefore, the rate-determining step must involve propanone and hydrogen ions. The concentration of iodine does not need to be included in the rate equation as iodine does not participate in the rate determining step – the reaction is zero order with respect to iodine, which means that the reaction proceeds until all the iodine is used up.

A mechanism consistent with the rate equation is given in *figure 8.38*. Notice that the slow step does not involve either propanone or hydrogen ions directly, but *something more rapidly derived from them both*, protonated propanone. Iodine intrudes later in the sequence, in what must be a subsequent fast step.

We can picture the reaction sequence as follows. The propanone exists in equilibrium with its protonated form (see chapter 7b for more about acid–base equilibria). Every now and then one of these protonated molecules decomposes to lose H⁺, not from the oxygen atom but from carbon, to yield the intermediate

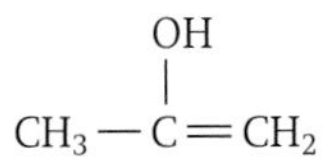

$$\underset{\displaystyle CH_3 - C = CH_2}{\overset{\displaystyle OH}{\vert}}$$

We could not have deduced this reaction scheme precisely from the rate equation, but it does fit in with that equation. Confirmatory evidence is given by the fact that if we carry out the reaction not with iodine, but with heavy water, $D_2O$, a deuterium atom, D (a hydrogen atom with a neutron as well as a proton in the nucleus) is taken up by

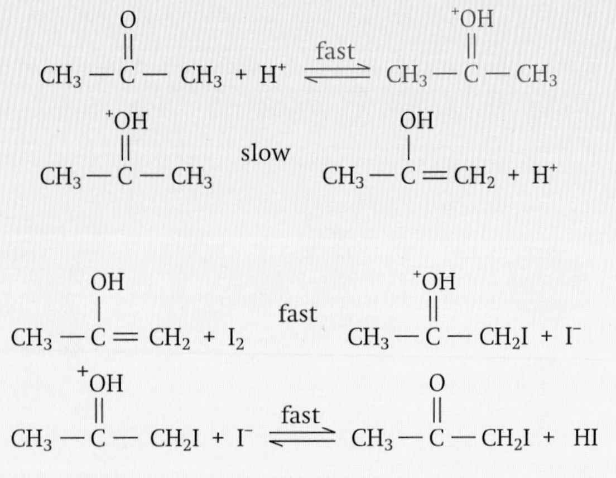

● **Figure 8.38** Propanone rapidly accepts hydrogen ions to form an intermediate. This intermediate slowly forms propen-2-ol, which reacts rapidly in two stages to form $CH_3COCH_2I$.

the methyl group of the propanone at exactly the same rate as iodine is in the first reaction. The two reactions have the same rate-determining steps.

## A reaction revisited

The rate equation for the reaction between methanol and hydrochloric acid:

$$CH_3OH(aq) + HCl(aq) \rightarrow CH_3Cl(aq) + H_2O(l)$$

as established by experiment (see page 181) is

rate of reaction = $k[CH_3OH][HCl]$

Extra information can help us to formulate a reaction mechanism. The rate equation suggests that a simple readjustment of bonds in a single-step reaction is involved (figure 8.39).

However, experiments show that the rate can be increased by the addition of a strong acid, $H^+$ ions, to the reaction mixture as well as by the addition of sodium chloride or a similar source of chloride ions, $Cl^-$. It is clear that the rate equation does not cater for the separate effects of varying concentrations of hydrogen ions and chloride ions. The new rate equation that is correct for hydrochloric acid, but also accounts for the separate effects of hydrogen ions and chloride ions, is

rate = $k[CH_3OH][H^+][Cl^-]$

Now let us re-examine the proposed mechanism for this reaction in the light of the more general rate equation. The first stage consists of a protonation equilibrium:

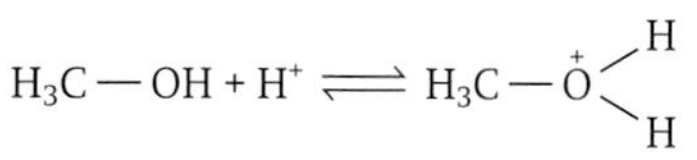

This is followed by an attack by the chloride ion.

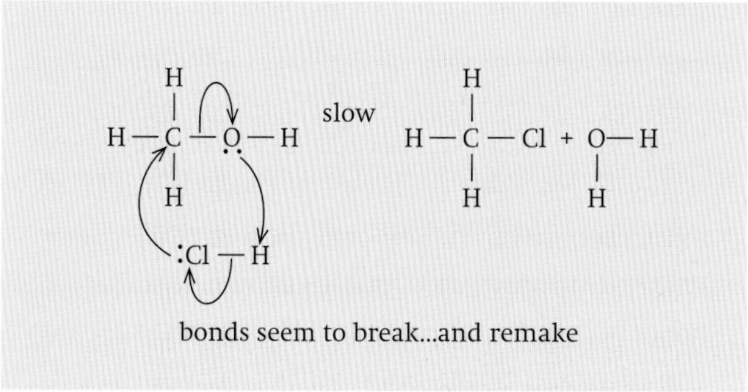

bonds seem to break...and remake

● **Figure 8.39** An apparent mechanism for the reaction between methanol and hydrochloric acid.

## SAQ 8.14

Write the second stage of the reaction between methanol and hydrochloric acid so that it fits the rate equation based upon the supplementary facts we know about the reaction.

# Catalysis

There are two forms of catalysis:
- **homogeneous catalysis**, the catalyst and reactants are present in the same phase (solid, liquid or gas), often in aqueous solution;
- **heterogeneous catalysis**, the catalyst is present in a different phase to the reactants, for example gaseous reactants with a solid catalyst.

A good example of a reaction that involves homogeneous catalysis is the esterification of ethanol (see page 337). The products of this reaction are ethyl ethanoate and water:

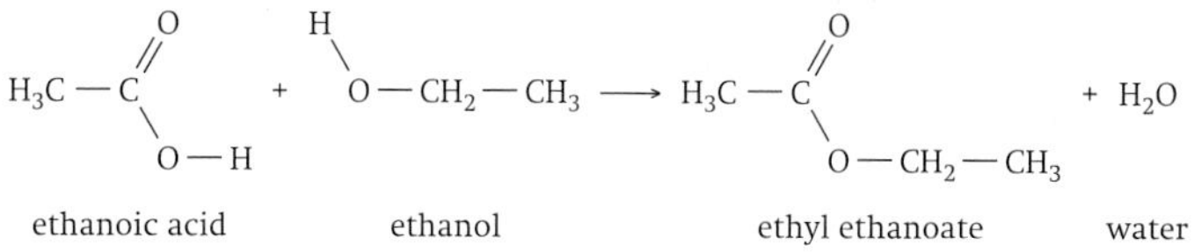

ethanoic acid     ethanol     ethyl ethanoate     water

This reaction is catalysed by an acid. For example, concentrated sulphuric acid is usually added to a mixture of ethanol and ethanoic acid. The catalyst and the two reactants are all in the same liquid phase. The rate of formation of the products is increased by the presence of the acid. Although hydrogen ions from the catalyst take part in the reaction mechanism, the concentration of acid at the end of the reaction is the same as it was when the reagents were mixed.

A second example of homogeneous catalysis is the loss of ozone from the stratosphere as a result of the use of CFCs (see page 332). In this gas phase reaction, chlorine free radicals catalyse the decomposition of ozone into oxygen. When CFCs, such as $CCl_2F_2$, reach the stratosphere, ultraviolet light breaks carbon–chlorine bonds, generating chlorine free radicals, $Cl\cdot$.

Overall, this reaction is:

$$2O_3(g) \rightarrow 3O_2(g)$$

The two steps in the mechanism which involve the chlorine free radical are as follows:

$$Cl\cdot + O_3 \rightarrow ClO\cdot + O_2$$
$$ClO\cdot + O \rightarrow Cl\cdot + O_2$$

The chlorine free radicals regenerated in the second step are available for further reaction with ozone molecules. The reaction rate is fast and a few chlorine free radicals rapidly destroy many ozone molecules. It has been estimated that, during its lifetime, one chlorine free radical could destroy up to 100 000 ozone molecules.

The oxygen free radicals, O in the second equation, are formed continuously in the stratosphere. Ultraviolet light produces oxygen free radicals from oxygen molecules, $O_2$, or ozone molecules, $O_3$.

The role of the intermediate $ClO\cdot$ free radical was conclusively proved in 1987. A high-altitude plane carrying an American-led international team of scientists was flown into the ozone hole from the tip of South America. Concentrations of ozone and the $ClO\cdot$ free radical were measured as the plane flew south. The dramatic measurements they recorded are shown in *figure 8.40*. The concentration of ozone fell as the concentration

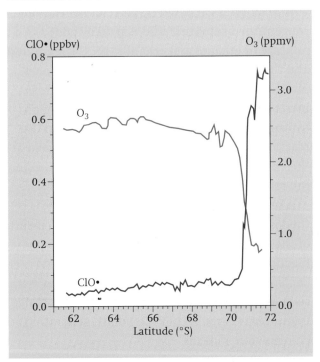

● **Figure 8.40** Chlorine oxide and ozone concentrations over Antarctica at 18 km altitude, 21 September, 1987, as measured on aircraft. ppbv = parts per billion by volume; ppmv = parts per million by volume.

of $ClO\cdot$ free radicals soared. The measurements the scientists obtained provided convincing evidence for the role of chlorine free radicals in the loss of ozone from the stratosphere.

Many economically important industrial processes involve the use of heterogeneous catalysts. For example:

1 the cracking, isomerisation and re-forming reactions which provide us with appropriate blends of petrol for our cars (see page 311);
2 hydrogenation of vegetable oils to produce margarine using a nickel catalyst (see page 302). An unsaturated fat is converted to a saturated fat by the addition of a hydrogen molecule to each of the carbon–carbon double bonds in the fat:

$$-CH=CH- + H_2 \xrightarrow{\text{nickel}} -CH_2-CH_2-$$

The nickel catalyst must be finely divided to provide a large surface area for reaction.
3 the production of ammonia by the Haber process. Before the German chemist Fritz Haber developed this process, much nitrogen was converted to ammonia using an expensive electrical discharge process. The Haber process uses a gas-phase reaction between nitrogen and hydrogen:

$$N_2(g) + 3H_2(g) \rightarrow 2NH_3(g)$$

The major part of the ammonia produced is used to manufacture fertilisers for increasing the yield of food crops. It is often said that, without such fertilisers, a far greater proportion of the world's human population would have suffered starvation during the twentieth century. Fritz Haber's discovery gained him the 1918 Nobel Prize for Chemistry.

The Haber process reaction is catalysed by contact with a finely divided iron catalyst. Without a catalyst, the activation energy needed to break the very strong N≡N triple bond is extremely high. In the presence of the iron catalyst, molecules of nitrogen are weakly adsorbed on to iron atoms. This process weakens the nitrogen triple bond sufficiently for reaction to take place (*figure 8.41*). We will look further at the Haber process later in this chapter.

*SAQ 8.15*

Why is the iron catalyst finely divided?

Chemists are engaged in studying the surfaces of catalysts to find out just how they work, with the aim of developing new catalysts or improving existing ones. Improving the rates of large scale chemical processes leads to savings in energy and other costs such as that of the chemical plant. In recent years progress has been more rapid due to new techniques such as scanning probe microscopy (SPM). This technique enables the positions of gaseous molecules or atoms to be seen on a metal surface and provides support for models of heterogeneous catalysts such as that in *figure 8.41*. SPM provides powerful evidence to support reaction pathways such as adsorption of reactants, breaking of covalent bonds in reactant molecules and the presence of atoms on catalyst surfaces (*figure 8.42*).

## Catalytic converters

Another area where chemists have contributed to an improvement in air quality is the development of catalytic converters. It is now a legal requirement for the exhausts of all new cars sold in many

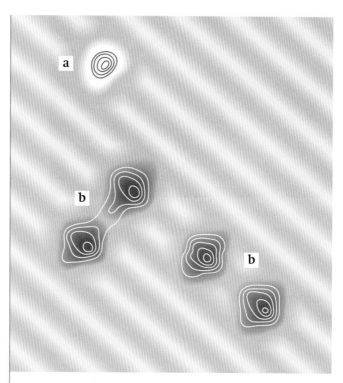

● **Figure 8.42** A scanning probe microscope (SPM) picture of oxygen on a copper surface. The diagonal rows coloured orange are copper atoms. **a** is an oxygen molecule, $O_2$, adsorbed on the surface. **b** are four $O^-$ ions. The distance between these is about 0.80 nm, which is large enough to show they are not bonded together.

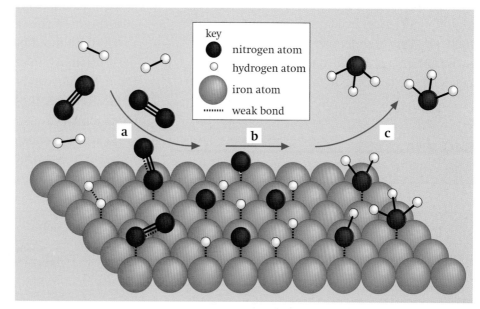

● **Figure 8.41** A possible model for the reaction pathway for the formation of ammonia from nitrogen and hydrogen by the Haber process. Heterogeneous catalysts bond to reactants which are **adsorbed** onto the catalyst atoms. Covalent bonds in the reactants are weakened and broken. New bonds form to give the product molecules which are **desorbed** from the catalyst.

**a** Adsorption of nitrogen and hydrogen molecules onto iron catalyst surface. Each molecule bonds weakly to iron atoms, causing bonds in the molecules to weaken.

**b** Nitrogen and hydrogen molecules dissociate into atoms as covalent bonds break on the surface of the catalyst. Nitrogen and hydrogen atoms bond to iron atoms.

**c** Nitrogen and hydrogen atoms combine in steps to form ammonia molecules. Desorption of ammonia molecules readily occurs as weak bonds to iron break.

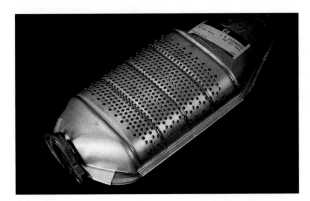

● **Figure 8.43** A three–way catalytic converter is designed to remove carbon monoxide, oxides of nitrogen and unburnt hydrocarbons from an engine's exhaust gases.

countries to be fitted with a catalytic converter. *Figure 8.43* shows a modern catalytic converter.

These pollutant gases are present in the gaseous mixture produced following the combustion of petrol in the engine of the car (see *table 8.11*). Carbon monoxide is formed by the incomplete combustion of fuel. This will occur when there is insufficient air mixed with the fuel. An equation for the incomplete combustion of octane is:

$$C_8H_{18} + 8\tfrac{1}{2}O_2 \rightarrow 8CO + 9H_2O$$

Nitrogen(II) oxide (monoxide) forms at the very high temperatures inside the engine (around 1000 °C). This high temperature provides sufficient energy for nitrogen and oxygen molecules to combine to form nitrogen(II) oxide:

$$N_2(g) + O_2(g) \rightarrow 2NO(g)$$

## SAQ 8.16

What is the source of nitrogen in the engine?

Nitrogen(II) oxide is oxidised when it mixes with air:

$$2NO(g) + O_2(g) \rightarrow 2NO_2(g)$$

The product, nitrogen(IV) oxide, $NO_2(g)$, is a brown gas; nitrogen(II) oxide, $NO(g)$, is colourless.

The catalytic converter helps to promote the following reactions:

■ The oxidation of carbon monoxide to carbon dioxide:

$$2CO(g) + O_2(g) \rightarrow 2CO_2(g)$$

■ The reduction of nitrogen monoxide back to nitrogen:

$$2NO(g) + 2CO(g) \rightarrow N_2(g) + 2CO_2(g)$$

■ The oxidation of hydrocarbons to water and oxygen. For example:

$$C_6H_6(g) + 7\tfrac{1}{2}O_2(g) \rightarrow 6CO_2(g) + 3H_2O(l)$$

The catalyst can be expensive, as it is made of an alloy of platinum, rhodium and palladium. Research to reduce costs has led to oxides of transition metals like chromium being used instead. As with other examples of heterogeneous catalysis, the above reactions will involve adsorption of the reactants on the surface of the catalyst, followed by chemical reaction and then desorption of the products as gaseous molecules. Catalytic converters must be hot to start working (typically 150–240 °C). They are not effective on short journeys.

If carbon monoxide, nitrogen(II) oxide and unburnt hydrocarbons are not removed from the car exhaust, they can lead to the formation of

| Name of gas | Formula | Origin | Effect |
|---|---|---|---|
| Carbon monoxide | CO | Incomplete combustion of hydrocarbons in petrol | Poisonous gas that combines with oxygen-carrying haemoglobin in the blood, and prevents oxygen from being carried |
| Nitrogen dioxide | $NO_2$ | Atmospheric nitrogen and oxygen combine under the high-temperature conditions of the engine to form nitrogen monoxide. This is oxidised in the atmosphere to form nitrogen dioxide | Nitrogen dioxide is involved in the formation of photochemical smog and low level ozone |
| Hydrocarbons | $C_xH_y$ | Some hydrocarbons in petrol may not be combusted at all | Some hydrocarbons (for example benzene) are toxic and may cause cancer |

● **Table 8.11** Pollutants in vehicle exhaust fumes.

photochemical smog. Such smog has become a major source of irritation to humans, and to animals and plants. For photochemical smog to occur, bright sunlight and the still air conditions present in a temperature inversion are also required. Under these conditions, low-level ozone is formed from nitrogen(IV) oxide. Energy from the bright sunlight breaks down the nitrogen(IV) oxide into nitrogen(II) oxide and oxygen atoms:

$$NO_2(g) \rightarrow NO(g) + O(g)$$

Oxygen atoms combine with oxygen molecules to form ozone:

$$O(g) + O_2(g) \rightarrow O_3(g)$$

> **Temperature inversion**
> Close to the Earth's surface, air temperature normally decreases with height above ground level. In a temperature inversion, a layer of cool air becomes trapped under less dense warmer air. In this still air, pollutants from car exhausts build up.

High level ozone in the stratosphere is beneficial as it protects us from the harmful effects of high energy ultraviolet radiation. However, close to ground level, ozone is harmful to humans and affects the growth of plants. In still conditions, the gaseous cocktail of ozone and other pollutant gases from car exhausts produces a variety of compounds such as aldehydes and peroxyacetyl nitrate (PAN) by many different reactions. Ozone and PAN are particularly irritating to the eyes, nose and throat.

● **Figure 8.44** Photochemical smog caused by light reacting with pollutant molecules.

The steadily increasing reliance of the world's population on cars is the key factor in the formation of photochemical smog. In addition, whilst the work of chemists and other scientists has enabled catalytic converters to be developed, there are still many older vehicles in use without them. We can expect to see scenes such as the one shown in *figure 8.44* for some time into the 21st century unless we take action to curb the use of private cars.

# Acid rain

The carbon dioxide, oxides of nitrogen and oxides of sulphur which occur naturally in an unpolluted atmosphere would be expected to give rain-water a pH of about 5.6–5.0. 'Acid rain' is the term used to describe rain-water with a lower pH than the natural value. In much of the industrialised world, the pH of rain-water can be as low as 4.5 Globally, the natural and industrial emissions of acidic gases are similar, but in the Northern Hemisphere over 90% of all sulphur dioxide emissions occur as a result of industrial activity.

It is thought that oxides of nitrogen from car exhausts may oxidise sulphur dioxide to sulphur trioxide in the following catalytic cycle:

$$SO_2(g) + NO_2(g) \rightarrow SO_3(g) + NO(g)$$
$$NO(g) + \tfrac{1}{2}O_2(g) \rightarrow NO_2(g)$$

The sulphur trioxide then forms sulphuric acid:

$$SO_3(g) + H_2O(l) \rightarrow H_2SO_4(l)$$

Acid rain washes nutrients from soils and lowers the pH of rivers and lakes. It also damages limestone and marble in buildings.

To minimise the effects of acid rain it is necessary to:
- remove sulphur dioxide from the exhaust gases of power stations where fossil fuels, particularly coal, are burned;
- remove sulphur from petrol and diesel fuel at the oil refinery so that less sulphur dioxide is emitted from vehicle exhausts;
- use catalytic converters on car exhausts systems, reducing the emissions of oxides of nitrogen and hence the formation of sulphur trioxide by the catalytic cycle shown above.

# The oxidation of $I^-$ by $S_2O_8^{2-}$

The ability of transition metals to vary their oxidation state (see chapter 13) is the key factor in their efficiency as homogeneous catalysts. The oxidation of $I^-$ ions by $S_2O_8^{2-}$ ions is an example of such behaviour.

The redox reaction

$$2I^-(aq) + S_2O_8^{2-}(aq) \rightarrow I_2(aq) + 2SO_4^{2-}(aq)$$

is catalysed by a number of transition metal ions, such as $Fe^{2+}$ or $Fe^{3+}$.

The following redox potentials (see chapter 6) are relevant:

step 1: $S_2O_8^{2-} + 2e^- \rightleftharpoons 2SO_4^{2-}$;     $E^\ominus = +2.01\,V$

step 2: $Fe^{3+} + e^- \rightleftharpoons Fe^{2+}$;     $E^\ominus = +0.77\,V$

step 3: $I_2 + 2e^- \rightleftharpoons 2I^-$;     $E^\ominus = +0.54\,V$

The uncatalysed reaction (steps 1 and 3) is slow but, as suggested by the $E^\ominus$ values, is able to go to completion. The $E^\ominus$ values, however, give no indication of the rate of the reaction. In this case, the reaction is between two negatively charged ions, which naturally repel each other.

In the presence of $Fe^{2+}$ ions, the rate of reaction is increased. A possible alternative mechanism is:

$$S_2O_8^{2-}(aq) + 2Fe^{2+}(aq) \rightarrow 2SO_4^{2-}(aq) + 2Fe^{3+}(aq)$$

followed by

$$2I^-(aq) + 2Fe^{3+}(aq) \rightarrow I_2(aq) + 2Fe^{2+}(aq)$$

Reference to $E^\ominus$ values shows each of these reactions to be feasible. Since they both involve reactions between oppositely charged ions, it is likely that the activation energies are lower. When $Fe^{3+}$ ions are added, these are reduced to $Fe^{2+}$ ions by $I^-$ ions.

# SUMMARY (A2)

◆ The rate of reaction is a measure of the rate of use of reactants and the rate of production of products. It is measured in units of concentration per unit time ($mol\,dm^{-3}\,s^{-1}$).

◆ The rate of reaction is related to the concentrations of the reactants by the rate equation, which (for two reactants A and B) is of the form:
rate of reaction = $k[A]^m[B]^n$

where $k$ is the rate constant, [A] and [B] are the concentrations of the reactants, $m$ is the order of reaction with respect to A and $n$ is the order of reaction with respect to B.

◆ The rate equation cannot be predicted from the stoichiometric equation.

◆ The overall order of reaction is the sum of the individual orders of the reactants. For the example above:
overall order = $m + n$

◆ The order of reaction may be determined by the initial-rates method, in which the initial rate is measured for several experiments using different concentrations of reactants. One concentration is changed whilst the others are fixed, so that a clear and systematic set of results is obtained.

◆ The order of reaction may also be determined from a single experiment, in which a concentration–time graph is recorded over a period of time. Tangents taken from several points on the graph give a measure of how the reaction rate changes with time. The rate of reaction at a particular point is the gradient of the graph at that point.

◆ The half-life of a first-order reaction is the time taken for the initial concentration of a reactant to halve, and it is independent of the concentration(s) of reactant(s).

◆ The increase in rate of a reaction with increasing temperature is accompanied by an increase in the value of the rate constant, $k$, for the reaction.

◆ The order of reaction with respect to a particular reactant indicates how many molecules of that reactant participate in the slow step (rate-determining step) of a reaction mechanism. This slow step determines the overall rate of reaction.

◆ Determination of the slow step provides evidence for the mechanism of a reaction.

◆ The rate equation for a reaction may be deduced given its slowest step.

◆ In homogeneous catalysis, both reactants and catalyst are in the same phase. Examples include: the acid catalysed formation of an ester from an alcohol and a carboxylic acid;  the destruction of ozone by chlorine free radicals in the stratosphere.

◆ In heterogeneous catalysis, the reactants are in the liquid or gas phase with the catalyst in the solid phase. Examples include: the cracking, isomerisation and reforming reactions for modern petrol; the hydrogenation of vegetable oil to make margarine; the production of ammonia by the Haber process; catalytic converters for removing pollutants from car exhaust gases.

◆ The pollutants in car exhaust gases are carbon monoxide, nitrogen(II) oxide and unburnt hydrocarbons. If these gases are not removed by catalytic converters, they lead to the formation of low level ozone and photochemical smog. Both low level ozone and photochemical smog can be harmful to humans, animals and plants.

# Questions (A2)

3 Nitrogen(II) oxide is formed at high temperature in car engines which run on petrol. When this gas is released from the car exhaust into the atmosphere it oxidises to nitrogen(IV) oxide. The following equation shows one reaction in which NO is oxidised to $NO_2$ in air.

$2NO(g) + O_2(g) \rightarrow 2NO_2(g)$

The following table shows data obtained from four experiments to investigate the effect of changing concentrations of NO and $O_2$ on the rate of this reaction at a temperature of 20 °C.

| Experiment | Initial [NO] $(10^{-2}\,mol\,dm^{-3})$ | Initial $[O_2]$ $(10^{-2}\,mol\,dm^{-3})$ | Initial rate of formation of $NO_2$ $(10^{-4}\,mol\,dm^{-3}\,s^{-1})$ |
|---|---|---|---|
| 1 | 1.0 | 1.0 | 0.7 |
| 2 | 2.0 | 1.0 | 2.8 |
| 3 | 1.0 | 2.0 | 1.4 |
| 4 | 3.0 | 2.0 | 12.6 |

a (i) Using the results for experiments 1 to 3, deduce the order of reaction with respect to each of NO and $O_2$. Explain your reasoning.

(ii) Use the orders of reaction that you have deduced in part (i) to explain the numerical value of the rate of reaction in experiment 4.

b (i) Write the expression for the rate equation for this reaction.

(ii) Use the results for experiment 2 together with your rate equation to calculate the rate constant for this reaction. Give the units of this rate constant.

(iii) The overall order for this reaction is unusual. State the overall order and suggest a reason why this order of reaction is unusual.

4 Ethyl ethanoate, $CH_3COOCH_2CH_3$, hydrolyses very slowly in water. The reaction is catalysed by the addition of an acid such as sulphuric acid. The equation for this hydrolysis reaction is:

$CH_3COOCH_2CH_3(l) + H_2O(l)$
$\rightleftharpoons CH_3COOH(l) + CH_3CH_2OH(l)$

Data obtained for this reaction at a temperature of 50°C is shown in the table below.

| $[CH_3COOCH_2CH_3]$ $(mol\,dm^{-3})$ | 0.50 | 0.39 | 0.31 | 0.17 | 0.13 | 0.09 |
|---|---|---|---|---|---|---|
| time $(10^4\,s)$ | 0.00 | 0.20 | 0.40 | 0.90 | 1.10 | 1.40 |

a Using these results, deduce the order of this reaction with respect to ethyl ethanoate. Explain your reasoning.

b Outline further experiments you would need to carry out in order to establish the rate equation for the reaction.

A student investigated the rate of the reaction of methanoic acid, HCOOH, with aqueous bromine and obtained the results shown in the table. She used a large excess of methanoic acid and maintained the reaction mixture at a constant temperature whilst making her measurements. The equation for the reaction is shown below.

$HCOOH(aq) + Br_2(aq)$
$\rightarrow CO_2(g) + 2H^+(aq) + 2Br^-(aq)$

| $[Br_2]$ $(10^{-3}\,mol\,dm^{-3})$ | Rate $(10^{-5}\,mol\,dm^{-3}\,s^{-1})$ |
|---|---|
| 10.0 | – |
| 9.2 | 3.2 |
| 8.4 | 2.9 |
| 7.0 | 2.4 |
| 5.0 | 1.7 |
| 2.5 | 0.9 |
| 1.2 | 0.4 |

a (i) Explain why she used a large excess of HCOOH.

(ii) Suggest two methods the student might have chosen to follow this reaction.

**b** (i) Describe how she would have obtained the rate figures from a graph that she plotted of concentration of bromine against time.

(ii) Using the data in the table and an appropriate graph, deduce the order of reaction with respect to bromine.

(iii) Using your answer to **b**(ii), state the rate equation under these conditions.

(iv) Calculate a value of the rate constant when $[Br_2] = 7.0 \times 10^{-3} \, mol \, dm^{-3}$.

**6** A good example of the effect of a catalyst is the decomposition of hydrogen peroxide to oxygen:

$$2H_2O_2(aq) \rightarrow 2H_2O(l) + O_2(g)$$

This occurs slowly at room temperatures. The reaction is accelerated by the addition of a small amount of water-soluble iodide. The reaction mechanism is as follows:

$$H_2O_2(aq) + I^-(aq) \rightarrow IO^-(aq) + H_2O(l) \quad (slow)$$
$$H_2O_2(aq) + IO^-(aq) \rightarrow H_2O(l) + O_2(g) + I^-(aq) \quad (fast)$$

Deduce the rate equation from this reaction mechanism.

**7** The rate equation for the hydrolysis of 2-bromo-2-methylpropane by water is

rate of reaction
$= k[\text{2-bromo-2-methylpropane}]$.
Suggest a mechanism for this hydrolysis.

**8** The atmospheric pollutant $NO_2$ is present in car exhaust gases. State two environmental consequences of nitrogen oxides and outline their catalytic removal from car exhaust gases.

**9** In the stratosphere, ozone, $O_3(g)$, is formed by the action of ultraviolet radiation on oxygen, $O_2(g)$. At the same time it is being lost by reactions such as the one shown in equation 1.

Equation 1: $O_3(g) + O(g) \rightarrow 2O_2(g)$;
$\Delta H^\ominus = -390 \, kJ \, mol^{-1}$

**a** Use collision theory to explain why, when the concentration of oxygen atoms, $O(g)$, is increased, the rate of the reaction shown shown in equation 1 is also increased.

**b** The reaction shown in equation 1 is catalysed by gaseous chlorine free radicals. The chlorine free radicals are formed by the action of ultraviolet radiation on CFCs.

(i) Write equations which show the two steps involved when chlorine acts as a catalyst for this reaction.

(ii) Catalysts act by providing a different reaction route with a lower activation enthalpy. What is meant by the term **activation energy**?

(iii) Draw a labelled enthalpy profile to illustrate the effect of a catalyst on the activation energy for the reaction shown in equation 1.

# CHAPTER 9

# Chemical periodicity (AS)

## By the end of this chapter you should be able to:

1 describe the Periodic Table in terms of the arrangement of elements by increasing atomic number, in Periods showing repeating physical and chemical properties, and in Groups having similar physical and chemical properties;

2 classify the elements into s, p and d blocks;

3 describe qualitatively (and indicate the periodicity in) the variations in atomic radius, ionic radius, melting point and electrical conductivity of the elements (see the Data Booklet);

4 explain qualitatively the variation in atomic radius and ionic radius;

5 interpret the variation in melting point and in electrical conductivity in terms of the presence of simple molecular, giant molecular or metallic bonding in the elements;

6 explain the variation in first ionisation energy;

7 describe the reactions, if any, of the elements with oxygen, with chlorine and with water;

8 state and explain the variation in oxidation number of the oxides and chlorides;

9 describe the reactions of the oxides with water;

10 describe and explain the acid–base behaviour of oxides and hydroxides, including, where relevant, amphoteric behaviour in reaction with sodium hydroxide and acids;

11 describe and explain the reactions of the chlorides with water;

12 interpret the variations and trends in points 8, 9, 10 and 11 in terms of bonding and electronegativity;

13 suggest the types of chemical bonding present in chlorides and oxides from observations of their chemical and physical properties;

14 predict the characteristic properties of an element in a given Group by using knowledge of chemical periodicity;

15 deduce the nature, possible position in the Periodic Table, and identity of unknown elements from given information of physical and chemical properties.

# Introduction to periodicity

## Patterns of chemical properties and atomic masses

If you were given samples of all the elements (some are shown in *figure 9.1*) and the time to observe their properties, you would probably find many ways of arranging them. You could classify them by their states at a particular temperature (solids, liquids or gases) or as metals and non-metals; you might find patterns in their reactions with oxygen or water or other chemicals. Would you consider trying to link these properties to the relative atomic masses of the elements?

If you have studied the metallic elements lithium, sodium and potassium, you will know that they have similar reactions with oxygen, water and chlorine, and form similar compounds. The rates of their reactions show that sodium comes between lithium and potas-sium in reactivity. Now look at their relative atomic masses:

| Li | Na | K |
|------|------|------|
| 6.9 | 23 | 39.1 |

The relative atomic mass of sodium is the mean of the relative atomic masses of lithium and potassium. There is a pattern here which is also shown by other groups of elements in threes – chlorine, bromine and iodine, for example. The 'middle' element has the mean relative atomic mass and other properties inbetween those of the other two. This pattern was first recorded by the German chemist Johann Döbereiner (1780–1849) as his 'Law of Triads' (*figure 9.2*). At the time, however, it was little more than a curiosity, as too few elements were known and values for atomic masses were uncertain.

Later in the century, more elements were known and atomic masses could be measured more accurately. A British chemist, John Newlands (1837–98), suggested that, when the elements were arranged in order of increasing atomic mass, 'the eighth element, starting from a given one, is a kind of repetition of the first, like the eighth note in an octave of music'.

Newlands presented his ideas for a 'Law of Octaves' to a meeting of the Chemical Society in 1866 (*figure 9.3*). They were not well received. Unfortunately, his 'octaves' only seemed to apply to the first 16 elements. He had not allowed space in his table for the possibility of new elements to be discovered.

Despite the Chemical Society's sceptical reception of Newlands'

● **Figure 9.1** A few of the 115 known elements.

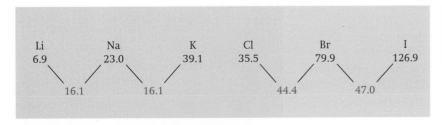

| Li | Na | K | Cl | Br | I |
|------|------|------|------|------|------|
| 6.9 | 23.0 | 39.1 | 35.5 | 79.9 | 126.9 |
| | 16.1 | 16.1 | | 44.4 | 47.0 |

● **Figure 9.2** Two of Döbereiner's 'triads'.

CHEMICAL NEWS,}
March 9, 1866.}

Table II.—Elements arranged in Octaves.

| No. | No. | No. | No. | No. | No. | No. | No. |
|---|---|---|---|---|---|---|---|
| H 1 | F 8 | Cl 15 | Co & Ni 22 | Br 29 | Pd 36 | I 42 | Pt & Ir 50 |
| Li 2 | Na 9 | K 16 | Cu 23 | Rb 30 | Ag 37 | Cs 44 | Os 51 |
| G 3 | Mg 10 | Ca 17 | Zn 24 | Sr 31 | Cd 38 | Ba & V 45 | Hg 52 |
| Bo 4 | Al 11 | Cr 19 | Y 25 | Ce & La 33 | U 40 | Ta 46 | Tl 53 |
| C 5 | Si 12 | Ti 18 | In 26 | Zr 32 | Sn 39 | W 47 | Pb 54 |
| N 6 | P 13 | Mn 20 | As 27 | Di & Mo 34 | Sb 41 | Nb 48 | Bi 55 |
| O 7 | S 14 | Fe 21 | Se 28 | Ro & Ru 35 | Te 43 | Au 49 | Th 56 |

● Figure 9.3

a John Newlands.

b This is the table Newlands presented to the Chemical Society in 1866 in a paper entitled 'The Law of Octaves, and the Causes of Numerical Relations among the Atomic Weights'. Note that some elements have symbols that we do not use today, e.g. G and Bo. What are these elements?

ideas, we now know that he had found the important pattern of periodicity. This means that the properties of elements have a regularly recurring or 'periodic' relationship with their relative atomic masses.

## Mendeleev's periodic table

The greatest credit for producing chemistry's most famous organisation of elements – 'the Periodic Table' – is always given to Dmitri Mendeleev (1834–1907) from Russia.

Mendeleev arranged the elements, just as Newlands had, in order of increasing relative atomic mass (figure 9.4). At the time (late 1860s) over 60 elements were known, and he saw that there was some form of regularly repeating pattern of properties.

Mendeleev made several crucial decisions that ensured the success of his first periodic table. The most important decisions were the following.

a **Ueber die Beziehungen der Eigenschaften zu den Atomgewichten der Elemente. Von D. Mendelejeff.** — Ordnet man Elemente nach zunehmenden Atomgewichten in verticale Reihen so, dass die Horizontalreihen analoge Elemente enthalten, wieder nach zunehmendem Atomgewicht geordnet, so erhält man folgende Zusammenstellung, aus der sich einige allgemeinere Folgerungen ableiten lassen.

$$
\begin{array}{llllll}
 & & & Ti=50 & Zr=90 & ?=180 \\
 & & & V=51 & Nb=94 & Ta=182 \\
 & & & Cr=52 & Mo=96 & W=186 \\
 & & & Mn=55 & Rh=104,4 & Pt=197,4 \\
 & & & Fe=56 & Ru=104,4 & Ir=198 \\
 & & Ni=Co=59 & Pd=106,6 & Os=199 \\
 & H=1 & & Cu=63,4 & Ag=108 & Hg=200 \\
 & Be=9,4 & Mg=24 & Zn=65,2 & Cd=112 \\
 & B=11 & Al=27,4 & ?=68 & Ur=116 & Au=197? \\
 & C=12 & Si=28 & ?=70 & Sn=118 \\
 & N=14 & P=31 & As=75 & Sb=122 & Bi=210? \\
 & O=16 & S=32 & Se=79,4 & Te=128? \\
 & F=19 & Cl=35,5 & Br=80 & J=127 \\
Li=7 & Na=23 & K=39 & Rb=85,4 & Cs=133 & Tl=204 \\
 & & Ca=40 & Sr=87,6 & Ba=137 & Pb=207 \\
 & & ?=45 & Ce=92 \\
 & & ?Er=56 & La=94 \\
 & & ?Yt=60 & !Di=95 \\
 & & ?In=75,6] & Th=118?
\end{array}
$$

● Figure 9.4

a Mendeleev's first published periodic table in the *Zeitschrift für Chemie* in 1869. Note that the elements with similar properties (e.g. Li, Na, K) are in horizontal rows in this table.

b This photograph shows a late version of Mendeleev's periodic table on the building where he worked in St Petersburg. Elements with similar properties are now arranged vertically in groups.

| Property | Mendeleev's predictions for 'eka-silicon' | Germanium |
|---|---|---|
| Appearance | light-grey solid | dark-grey solid |
| Atomic mass | 72 | 72.59 |
| Density (g cm$^{-3}$) | 5.5 | 5.35 |
| Oxide formula | eka-SiO$_2$ | GeO$_2$ |
| Oxide density (g cm$^{-3}$) | 4.7 | 4.2 |
| Chloride density (g cm$^{-3}$) | 1.9 (liquid) | 1.84 (liquid) |
| Chloride b.p. (°C) | <100 | 84 |

● **Table 9.1** Comparison of Mendeleev's predictions for eka-silicon with known properties of germanium.

■ He left spaces in the table so that similar elements could always appear in the same Group.
■ He said that the spaces would be filled by elements not then known. Furthermore, he predicted what the properties of these elements might be, based on the properties of known elements in the same Group. He made predictions, for example, about the element between silicon and tin in Group IV. This element was only discovered about 15 years later. Mendeleev had called it 'eka-silicon'; it is now known as germanium (*table 9.1*).

## SAQ 9.1
From *table 9.1*, how well do you think Mendeleev's predicted properties for eka–silicon compare with the known properties of germanium?

A theory or model is most valuable when it is used to explain and predict. Mendeleev's periodic table was immensely successful. By linking the observed periodicity in the properties of elements with the atomic theory of matter, the table helped to organise and unify the science of chemistry and led to much further research. It has been greatly admired ever since. It was even able to cope with the discovery of a whole new group of elements, now called 'the noble gases' (helium to radon), though these had not been predicted by Mendeleev.

### Atomic structure and periodicity
In 1913 the British scientist Henry Moseley was able to show that the real sequence in the Periodic

Table is not the order of relative atomic masses. The sequence is the order of atomic numbers – the numbers of protons in the nuclei of atoms of the elements (see chapter 1). This sequence of elements by atomic numbers is close to the sequence by relative atomic masses, but not exactly the same.

## SAQ 9.2
a What is the relationship between atomic numbers and relative atomic masses?
b Why are the relative atomic mass values for tellurium (Te) and iodine (I; J in Mendeleev's table) the 'wrong' way around in the Periodic Table, whereas their atomic numbers fit the Table?

Moseley's work was about the nature of the nucleus and led to the correct sequence of elements. It did not, however, answer questions about the periodic variations in physical and chemical properties. This is because these properties depend much more upon the numbers and distributions of electrons in atoms.

# Versions of the Periodic Table
Chemists have enjoyed displaying the Periodic Table in many different ways (for two versions, see *figure 9.5*). You may be able to invent some new versions.

The Periodic Table most often seen is shown in *figure 9.6* (and also in the appendix, page 401). Its main features are:
■ the vertical Groups of elements, labelled I, II, III, up to VII; the noble gases are not called Group VIII but Group 0;
■ the horizontal Periods labelled 1, 2, 3, etc.

### Blocks of elements in the Periodic Table
Chemists find it helpful to identify 'blocks' of elements by the type of electron orbital most affecting the properties. These are shown on the Periodic Table in *figure 9.6*.
■ Groups I and II elements are in the s-block.

● **Figure 9.5** Two rather unusual versions of the Periodic Table:
**a** the elements according to relative abundance and
**b** a three-dimensional, four-vaned model.

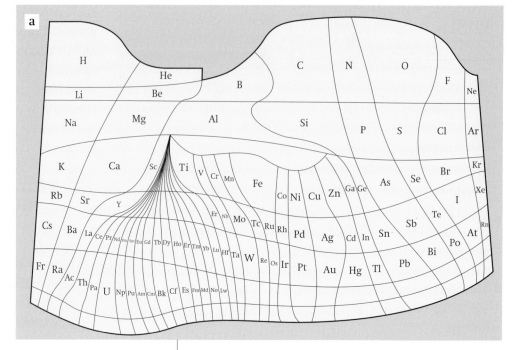

- Groups III to VII and Group 0 (except He) are in the p-block.
- The transition elements are included in the d-block.
- The lanthanide and actinide elements are included in the f-block.

# Periodic patterns of physical properties of elements

We shall now look in more detail at the physical properties of elements and their relationships with the electronic configurations of atoms.

## Summary of structure and bonding of the first 36 elements

*Figure 9.7* shows details of the structures and bonding of elements 1 to 36, hydrogen (H) to krypton (Kr).

## Periodic patterns of electronic configurations

Magnesium and calcium are both s-block elements in Group II. Their electronic configurations are:

Mg   $1s^2\,2s^2\,2p^6\,3s^2$
Ca   $1s^2\,2s^2\,2p^6\,3s^2\,3p^6\,4s^2$

Notice that they have the same outer-shell configuration, $s^2$. All the Group II elements have an outer-shell configuration of $s^2$.

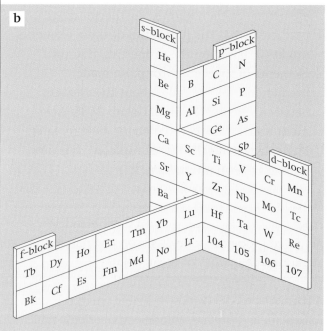

### SAQ 9.3

Carbon and silicon are both p-block elements and in Group IV.

**a** Write down the electronic configurations of carbon and silicon.

**b** What do you notice about their outer-shell configurations?

**c** Suggest, giving a reason, the outer-shell configuration for germanium.

● **Figure 9.6** The Periodic Table of the elements.

In general:

■ in the s-block, the outermost electrons are in an s orbital. In the p-block, the outermost electrons are in p orbitals;

■ elements in the same Group have the same number of electrons in their outer shell;

■ for the elements in Groups I to VII, the number of outer-shell electrons is the same as the Group number. For example, chlorine in Group VII has seven outer-shell electrons: $1s^2\,2s^2\,2p^6\,3s^2\,3p^5$, a total of seven electrons in the third shell;

■ Group 0 elements, the noble gases, have a full outer shell of eight electrons: $s^2\,p^6$. For example, neon has the electronic configuration $1s^2\,2s^2\,2p^6$.

## Periodic patterns of atomic radii

The size of an atom cannot be measured precisely as their electron shells do not define a clear outer limit. However, one measure of the size of an atom is its 'atomic radius'. This can be either the 'covalent radius' or the 'metallic radius' (*figure 9.8*). **Covalent radius** is half the distance between the nuclei of neighbouring atoms in molecules.

● **Figure 9.7** Structures of elements 1 (hydrogen, H) to 36 (krypton, Kr).

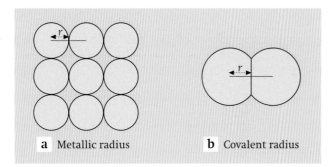

a Metallic radius     b Covalent radius

● **Figure 9.8** Metallic and covalent radii.

**Metallic radius** is half the distance between the nuclei of neighbouring atoms in metallic crystals. The covalent radius can be measured for most elements and is usually what is meant when we use the term **atomic radius**.

Atomic radii of elements 1 to 36 are shown in *figure 9.9*. When atomic (covalent) radii are plotted against proton numbers for the first 36 elements, the graph appears as in *figure 9.10*. The noble gases are not included as they do not have covalent radii.

## SAQ 9.4

Why do the noble gases not have any measured covalent radii?

Note the relative positions of the elements in any one Group, such as Group I (alkali metals) or Group VII (halogens), and across the Periods 2 and 3. The trends (*figure 9.11*) show that atomic radii:

■ increase down a Group;
■ decrease across a Period;
■ after some decrease, are relatively constant across the transition elements, titanium to copper.

Note that the trends in atomic radii are generally in the opposite direction to the trends in first ionisation energies. As atomic radii become larger, first ionisation energies become smaller. In any one atom, both trends are due to the same combined effects of:

■ the size of the nuclear charge;

| H<br>0.037 | | | | | | | | | | | | | | | | | He<br>– |
|---|---|---|---|---|---|---|---|---|---|---|---|---|---|---|---|---|---|
| Li<br>0.123 | Be<br>0.089 | | | | | | | | | | | B<br>0.080 | C<br>0.077 | N<br>0.074 | O<br>0.074 | F<br>0.072 | Ne<br>– |
| Na<br>0.157 | Mg<br>0.136 | | | | | | | | | | | Al<br>0.125 | Si<br>0.117 | P<br>0.110 | S<br>0.104 | Cl<br>0.099 | Ar<br>– |
| K<br>0.203 | Ca<br>0.174 | Sc<br>0.144 | Ti<br>0.132 | V<br>0.122 | Cr<br>0.117 | Mn<br>0.117 | Fe<br>0.116 | Co<br>0.116 | Ni<br>0.115 | Cu<br>0.117 | Zn<br>0.125 | Ga<br>0.125 | Ge<br>0.122 | As<br>0.121 | Se<br>0.117 | Br<br>0.114 | Kr<br>– |

● **Figure 9.9** The atomic (covalent) radii of elements 1 to 36, measured in nanometres (nm).

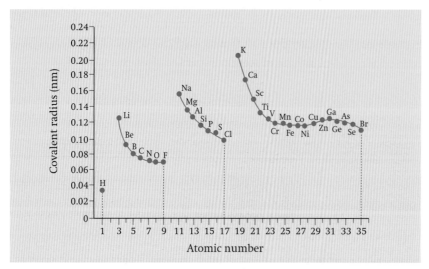

● **Figure 9.10** Plot of atomic (covalent) radii against atomic number of elements. The noble gases (He–Kr) are not included.

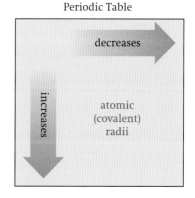

● **Figure 9.11** Trends of atomic (covalent) radii.

- the distance of the outer electron shell from the nucleus;
- the shielding effect of filled inner electron shells upon the outer shell.

*Down any one Group*, the nuclear charges increase, but the distance and shielding effects increase even more, as extra electron shells are added. The overall result is an increase in atomic radii.

*Across Periods 2 and 3*, the nuclear charges increase from element to element. The distance and shielding effects remain fairly constant, because electrons are added to the same outer shell. As the increasing attraction pulls the electrons closer to the nuclei, the radii of the atoms decrease.

## Periodic patterns of ionic radii

The radii of ions also decrease across a Period, but it must be remembered that elements on the left form cations and elements on the right form anions.

Ionic radii for elements in Period 3 are shown in *table 9.2*. The radii of cations $Na^+$ to $Si^{4+}$ are smaller than the radii of the corresponding atoms. The radii of the anions $P^{3-}$ to $Cl^-$ are larger than the corresponding atoms. The radii of the cations and of the anions decrease from left to right.

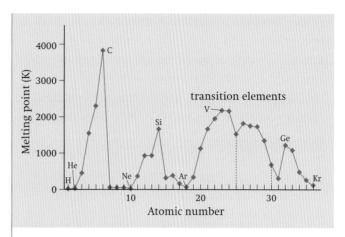

● **Figure 9.13** Plot of melting points of elements 1 to 36 against atomic numbers.

## Periodic patterns of melting points for elements 1 to 36

The variation in melting points is shown in *figures 9.12 and 9.13*. In any melting solid, particles are entering the liquid phase in large numbers. If the forces of attraction between the particles in the solid are strong, the melting point is high; if the forces are weak, the melting point is low.

Note that the 'peaks' of the graph are occupied by elements from the same Group – carbon and silicon from Group IV. Their high melting points are due to the strong covalent bonds between atoms of these elements, which exist in the giant molecular lattice structure. These bonds are broken when the elements melt.

The 'troughs' are occupied by elements that consist of diatomic molecules ($H_2$, $N_2$, $O_2$, $F_2$, $Cl_2$, $Br_2$) or single atoms (He, Ne, Ar,

|  | Cations | | | | Anions | | |
|---|---|---|---|---|---|---|---|
| ion | $Na^+$ | $Mg^{2+}$ | $Al^{3+}$ | $Si^{4+}$ | $P^{3-}$ | $S^{2-}$ | $Cl^-$ |
| ionic radius (nm) | 0.098 | 0.065 | 0.045 | 0.038 | 0.212 | 0.190 | 0.181 |

● **Table 9.2** Ionic radii for Period 3 cations and anions.

| H 14 | | | | | | | | | | | | | | | | | He 4 |
|---|---|---|---|---|---|---|---|---|---|---|---|---|---|---|---|---|---|
| Li 454 | Be 1556 | | | | | | | | | | | B 2300 | C 3823 | N 63 | O 54 | F 53 | Ne 25 |
| Na 371 | Mg 923 | | | | | | | | | | | Al 932 | Si 1683 | P 317 | S 392 | Cl 172 | Ar 84 |
| K 336 | Ca 1123 | Sc 1673 | Ti 1950 | V 2190 | Cr 2176 | Mn 1517 | Fe 1812 | Co 1768 | Ni 1728 | Cu 1356 | Zn 693 | Ga 303 | Ge 1210 | As 1090 | Se 490 | Br 266 | Kr 116 |

● **Figure 9.12** Melting points of elements 1 to 36, measured in kelvin (K).

Kr). The forces of attraction between the particles are very weak and are readily broken. The diatomic molecules or atoms are easily separated from each other as the temperature rises.

Elements in Groups I, II and III occupy similar positions on the rising parts of the curve. Most of the elements in these Groups are metals. The metallic bonding is stronger on moving from Group I to Group II to Group III, as there are more outer-shell electrons available to be mobile and take part in the bonding.

## SAQ 9.5

Why do both phosphorus ($P_4$) and sulphur ($S_8$) occupy low positions on the melting-point curve but have higher boiling points than chlorine?

## SAQ 9.6

*Figure 9.13* shows the melting points of elements 1 to 36.

Explain the following in terms of structure and bonding of the elements:

**a** the increase in the melting points between sodium and aluminium;

**b** the very high melting point of silicon;

**c** the low melting points of sulphur to argon.

## Periodic patterns of electrical conductivities

Electrical conductivities are measured in units called 'siemens per metre' ($S\,m^{-1}$). Siemens are the reciprocal of the units of electrical resistance (ohms, $\Omega$), $S = \Omega^{-1}$. *Figure 9.14* shows the known values of electrical conductivities, in units of $10^8\,S\,m^{-1}$, for elements up to bromine. Conductivity values give an indication of how easily electrons move through the element. Metallic elements thus have higher electrical conductivities than molecular elements.

## SAQ 9.7

**a** Why do electrical conductivities increase from Group I to Group III elements in Period 3?

**b** Why are the electrical conductivities of d-block transition elements relatively high, compared with most p-block elements?

# Periodic patterns of first ionisation energies

The first ionisation energies of the first 36 elements in the Periodic Table are shown in *figure 9.15*. Their variation with atomic number is displayed in *figure 9.16*. The most significant features of the graph are:

- The 'peaks' are all occupied by elements of the same Group (Group 0, the noble gases) and the 'troughs' by the Group I elements (the alkali metals).
- There is a general increase in ionisation energy across a Period, from the Group I elements to the Group 0 elements, but the trend is uneven.
- The first ionisation energies of the elements 21 (scandium) to 29 (copper) (the d-block elements of Period 4) vary much less than other series of elements.

| H | | | | | | | | | | | | | | | | | He |
|---|---|---|---|---|---|---|---|---|---|---|---|---|---|---|---|---|---|
| – | | | | | | | | | | | | | | | | | – |
| Li | Be | | | | | | | | | | | B | C (graphite) | N | O | F | Ne |
| 0.108 | 0.25 | | | | | | | | | | | $10^{-12}$ | $7\times10^{-4}$ | – | – | – | – |
| Na | Mg | | | | | | | | | | | Al | Si | P | S | Cl | Ar |
| 0.218 | 0.224 | | | | | | | | | | | 0.382 | $2\times10^{-10}$ | $10^{-17}$ | $10^{-23}$ | – | – |
| K | Ca | Sc | Ti | V | Cr | Mn | Fe | Co | Ni | Cu | Zn | Ga | Ge | As | Se | Br | Kr |
| 0.143 | 0.218 | 0.015 | 0.024 | 0.04 | 0.078 | 0.054 | 0.010 | 0.16 | 0.145 | 0.593 | 0.167 | 0.058 | $2.2\times10^{-8}$ | 0.029 | 0.08 | $10^{-18}$ | – |

● **Figure 9.14** Electrical conductivities of elements 1 to 36, measured in $10^8$ siemens per metre ($10^8\,S\,m^{-1}$, or $10^{-8}\,\Omega^{-1}\,m^{-1}$).

| H 1310 | | | | | | | | | | | | | | | | | He 2370 |
|---|---|---|---|---|---|---|---|---|---|---|---|---|---|---|---|---|---|
| Li 519 | Be 900 | | | | | | | | | | | B 799 | C 1090 | N 1400 | O 1310 | F 1680 | Ne 2080 |
| Na 494 | Mg 736 | | | | | | | | | | | Al 577 | Si 786 | P 1060 | S 1000 | Cl 1260 | Ar 1520 |
| K 418 | Ca 590 | Sc 632 | Ti 661 | V 648 | Cr 653 | Mn 716 | Fe 762 | Co 757 | Ni 736 | Cu 745 | Zn 908 | Ga 577 | Ge 762 | As 966 | Se 941 | Br 1140 | Kr 1350 |

● **Figure 9.15** The first ionisation energies of elements 1 to 36, measured in kilojoules per mole (kJ mol$^{-1}$).

How are these periodic variations in first ionisation energies to be explained in terms of the model of atomic structure and electronic configurations outlined in chapter 1?

Consider some examples:

fluorine, element 9, has the configuration
$1s^2 2s^2 2p^5$
neon, element 10, has the configuration
$1s^2 2s^2 2p^6$
sodium, element 11, has the configuration
$1s^2 2s^2 2p^6 3s^1$

As you see in *figure 9.16*, the ionisation energy of neon is higher than that of fluorine; sodium's ionisation energy is much lower. The main differences in the atoms of these elements are:

■ the numbers of protons in their nuclei, and hence their positive nuclear charges, are different;

■ the outer occupied orbital in both fluorine and neon is in the 2p subshell but sodium has an electron in the next shell, in its 3s orbital;

■ neon has a completely filled outer shell, fluorine has one electron fewer than a complete shell and sodium has one electron more than a complete shell.

These differences between the atoms may be explained by the factors that influence their first ionisation energies (see chapter 1):

■ An increase in positive nuclear charge will tend to cause an increase in first ionisation energies.

■ The forces of attraction between the positive nuclear charge and the negatively charged electrons decreases as the quantum number of the shells increases. The further the shell is from the nucleus the lower the first ionisation energy is.

■ Filled inner electron shells shield outer electrons. The outer electrons are repelled by the electrons in the filled inner shells so the first ionisation energy falls.

We shall now apply these ideas to the three elements, 9, 10, and 11 – fluorine, neon and sodium.

The outer electrons in both fluorine and neon atoms are in the 2p orbitals. This means that the 'distance' effect and the 'shielding' effect are similar. However, the nuclear charge in a neon atom is larger and attracts the 2p electrons more strongly. This causes the first ionisation energy of neon to be higher than that of fluorine.

The outer electron of sodium is in the 3s orbital, as the 2p orbitals are full. The ionisation energy of sodium is much lower than that of neon, even though a sodium atom has a larger nuclear charge. This shows how the combined

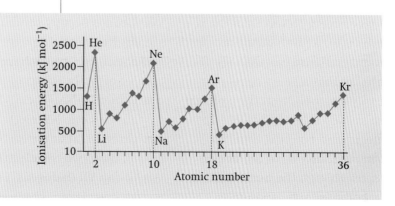

● **Figure 9.16** The first ionisation energies of elements 1 to 36, plotted against atomic number.

effects, of increased distance and of shielding, reduce the effective nuclear charge. The 3s electron in a sodium atom is further from the nucleus than any 2p electrons. It is also shielded from the attractions of the nuclear charge by two complete inner shells ($n = 1$ and $n = 2$). The electrons in shell $n = 2$ are shielded only by the electrons in one shell ($n = 1$).

## First ionisation energies across a Period

From *figure 9.16* you will see that there is a general trend of increasing ionisation energies across a Period. However, the trend is uneven. Look, for example, at elements 3, 4 and 5, lithium ($1s^2\ 2s^1$), beryllium ($1s^2\ 2s^2$) and boron ($1s^2\ 2s^2\ 2p^1$). We might have predicted that boron would have the highest ionisation energy of the three; in fact, it is beryllium. Experimental evidence such as this leads to a further assumption about electronic configurations: it is easier to remove electrons from p orbitals than from s orbitals in the same shell. Our modern theories for electronic structure show that the p orbitals are higher energy levels than the s orbital for a given quantum number. Hence our theories predict that an electron is more easily removed from the p orbital than the s orbital. Thus the 2p electron in boron is easier to remove than one of the 2s electrons. Though the nuclear charge in boron is larger than in beryllium, boron has the lower first ionisation energy.

Now look at the other elements in Period 2:

|  | *Carbon* | *Nitrogen* | *Oxygen* |
|---|---|---|---|
| atomic number | 6 | 7 | 8 |
| electronic config. | $1s^2\ 2s^2\ 2p^2$ | $1s^2\ 2s^2\ 2p^3$ | $1s^2\ 2s^2\ 2p^4$ |
| box config. for 2p | ↑ ↑ ☐ | ↑ ↑ ↑ | ↑↓ ↑ ↑ |

|  | *Fluorine* | *Neon* |
|---|---|---|
| atomic number | 9 | 10 |
| electronic config. | $1s^2\ 2s^2\ 2p^5$ | $1s^2\ 2s^2\ 2p^6$ |
| box config. for 2p | ↑↓ ↑↓ ↑ | ↑↓ ↑↓ ↑↓ |

In the general trend across the Period, we might expect the ionisation energy of oxygen to be higher than that of nitrogen. In fact, the ionisation energy of nitrogen is the higher of the two. Nitrogen has three electrons in the p orbitals, each of them unpaired; oxygen has four electrons, with two of them paired. The repulsion between the electrons in the pair increases the energy and makes it easier to remove one of them and to ionise an atom of oxygen, even though the nuclear charge is larger than in an atom of nitrogen.

The general trend, of increasing ionisation energies across a Period, is re-established in atoms of fluorine and neon, by the effect of larger nuclear charge.

A similar pattern exists for the elements in Period 3, see *figure 9.16*.

## SAQ 9.8

In terms of their electronic configurations, explain the relative first ionisation energies of:

**a** sodium, magnesium and aluminium;

**b** silicon, phosphorus and sulphur.

## First ionisation energies in Groups

Elements are placed in Groups in the Periodic Table, as they show many similar physical and chemical properties. Note how elements in Groups occupy similar positions on the plot of first ionisation energy against atomic number (*figure 9.16*). This is evidence that the elements in Groups have similar electronic configurations in their outer orbitals. For example:

- Group I (alkali metals, Li–Cs)
  all have one (s1) electron in their outer orbitals
- Group II (alkaline-earth metals, Be–Ba)
  all have two (s2) electrons in their outer orbitals
- Group VII (halogens, F–At)
  all have seven (s2 p5) electrons in their outer orbitals

The first ionisation energies generally decrease down a vertical Group, with increasing atomic number. This shows the combined result of several factors. With increasing proton number, in any Group:

- the positive nuclear charge increases;
- the atomic radius increases so the distance of the outer electrons from the nucleus also increases with each new shell;
- the shielding effect of the filled inner electron shells increases as the number of inner shells grows.

The distance and shielding effects together reduce the effect of the increasing nuclear charges from element to element down any Group.

## SAQ 9.9

Helium has the highest first ionisation energy in the Periodic Table. Suggest which element is likely to have the lowest first ionisation energy and why.

## First ionisation energies and reactivity of elements

Ionisation energies give a measure of the energy required to remove electrons from atoms and form positive ions. The lower the first ionisation energy of an element, the more easily the element forms positive ions during reactions:

$$M(g) \rightarrow M^+(g) + e^-$$

This is the main reason for the metallic nature of the elements on the 'left' of the Periodic Table (Groups I, II and III) and increasingly metallic nature of elements down all Groups.

- In elements with low first ionisation energies, one or more electrons are relatively free to move from atom to atom in the metallic bonding of the structure.
- The characteristic chemical properties of metallic elements include the formation of positive ions. In the reactions of metals with oxygen, chlorine or water, for example, formation of positive ions is one of several stages involving enthalpy changes. The elements with low first ionisation energies usually do react more quickly and vigorously. In any Period, the Group I elements (alkali metals) have the lowest first ionisation energies and are the most reactive metals. They also have lower first ionisation energies going

'down' the Group, with increasing atomic number, and become much more reactive. The factors that affect the values of ionisation energies thus also influence the reactivities of many elements. We shall examine the effect of ionisation energies on reactivity for Group II metals in the next chapter (see page 219).

## Successive ionisation energies and the Periodic Table

Successive ionisation may be interpreted in terms of the position of an element in the Periodic Table. In chapter 1, the pattern of successive ionisation energies for an element was used to:

- provide evidence for the general pattern of electron shells;
- predict the simple electronic configuration of an element;
- confirm the position of an element in the Periodic Table.

For any one element, successive ionisation energies steadily increase as electrons are removed. A large increase occurs between two successive ionisation energies when the next electron is removed from a lower electron shell.

For example, carbon has the following successive ionisation energies:

1090, 2350, 4610, 6220, 37 800, 47 300 kJ mol$^{-1}$.

The first four values show a steady increase followed by a very large increase at the fifth value. Hence, a total of four electrons are removed from the outer shell of carbon. Carbon has the simple electronic configuration 2,4 which also confirms the position of carbon in Group IV.

## SAQ 9.10

a Phosphorus is in Group V. Between which of the first eight ionisation energies will there be a large rise in ionisation energy?

b In which Group of the Periodic Table would you place the element with the following successive ionisation energies?
1680, 3370, 6040, 8410, 11 000, 15 200, 17 900, 92 000, 106 000 kJ mol$^{-1}$.

# Reactions of the Period 3 elements

Recurring patterns occur everywhere in the natural world, from the beat of the heart to the movement of the planets. You have already looked at the periodic variation of properties such as metallic character and ionisation energies of elements. Now you will see how some compounds of Period 3 elements also show periodic variations. The compounds you will study are predominantly the oxides and the chlorides. Chemists have studied these compounds extensively because they are usually easy to prepare and they show how the structure and bonding of a compound affect its reactions. Some of them are important in ways most people find unexpected.

In chapter 10 you can see that magnesium oxide is a very useful substance because it has such a high melting point and can withstand corrosive chemicals. Another important use of magnesium oxide is as an additive to cattle feed, as without magnesium as a trace element cattle rapidly become ill.

Aluminium oxide is also important, but in quite a different way – aluminium is a very reactive metal so when it is exposed to air a layer of aluminium oxide rapidly forms on the surface of the metal. This layer prevents the rest of the metal reacting, which means that aluminium foil is safe to use next to food, aluminium cans do not dissolve into the drink they contain and aeroplanes will not dissolve in water when they fly through a rain cloud (*figure 9.17*). This oxide layer is so important that it is sometimes made thicker by a process called anodising. Without it, aluminium would not be the widely used metal it is today.

Another very useful oxide is the gas sulphur dioxide, $SO_2$. It is a vital part of the Contact process, producing sulphuric acid. Sulphuric acid is not just a useful laboratory chemical, but it is used in huge quantities and so it is produced in huge quantities. Without it we would not have many of the paints, pigments, fertilisers, plastics, fibres and other products we enjoy today.

Sodium chloride needs no introduction; as salt it is both well known and well used. What about other chlorides of Period 3? Magnesium chloride is the source of magnesium metal – it is electrolysed to give magnesium and chlorine gas. Carbon tetrachloride, $CCl_4$, was previously used as a dry-cleaning fluid because it dissolves grease so well, but this use has been discontinued as it has toxic fumes. Silicon(IV) chloride, $SiCl_4$, is used to produce pure silicon for integrated circuits, one of the purest materials used routinely, without which the computer industry could not function.

So these oxides and chlorides have a variety of uses, but chemically we will be looking at the trends in properties which they show. You will not study all the oxides and chlorides of the Period 3 elements – you need to know just those which are covered in this chapter.

● **Figure 9.17** Uses of aluminium, made possible by the layer of aluminium oxide on the surface of the object.

# Preparation of Period 3 oxides

The elements of Period 3 form oxides by direct combination with oxygen. We are only interested here in six of these oxides: sodium oxide, magnesium oxide, aluminium oxide, phosphorus(v) oxide, sulphur dioxide and sulphur trioxide.

- **Sodium oxide**

  Sodium combines vigorously with oxygen. Freshly cut sodium metal tarnishes rapidly on exposure to air and sodium burns readily in air or oxygen with a brilliant yellow flame.

  $$4Na(s) + O_2(g) \rightarrow 2Na_2O(s)$$

  Sodium oxide is a white solid.

- **Magnesium oxide** (see also chapter 10)

  Magnesium burns very vigorously (once the reaction has started) with a bright white flame, producing a white solid which is magnesium oxide.

  $$2Mg(s) + O_2(g) \rightarrow 2MgO(s)$$

- **Aluminium oxide**

  Aluminium oxide forms easily at room temperature, as mentioned earlier, and is a useful protection for the metal underneath. Powdered aluminium can catch fire and burn, but solid lumps of aluminium will not do this. Aluminium oxide, like magnesium oxide, is a white solid.

  $$4Al(s) + 3O_2(g) \rightarrow 2Al_2O_3(s)$$

- **Phosphorus(v) oxide**

  Phosphorus burns readily in air or oxygen. When an excess of air or oxygen is used, the solid white oxide $P_4O_{10}$ is formed.

  $$P_4(s) + 5O_2(g) \rightarrow P_4O_{10}(s)$$

- **Sulphur dioxide** and **sulphur trioxide**

  Solid sulphur burns easily with a blue flame and produces sulphur dioxide gas. Sulphur dioxide can be made to react with more oxygen in the presence of a heated vanadium pentoxide, $V_2O_5$, catalyst to give sulphur trioxide, which is a solid with a melting point of 17 °C.

  $$S(s) + O_2(g) \rightarrow SO_2(g)$$

  $$2SO_2(g) \xrightarrow[V_2O_5]{heat} 2SO_3(g) + O_2(g)$$

## SAQ 9.11

Suggest what observations you would make if a piece of calcium was burnt in air. Construct an equation for this reaction.

## SAQ 9.12

As part of the industrial preparation of sulphuric acid, sulphur is burnt in air to form sulphur dioxide. When the sulphur dioxide is passed over a heated $V_2O_5$ catalyst, further reaction occurs. Write an equation showing the overall reaction.

# Preparation of Period 3 chlorides

The elements of Period 3 form chlorides by direct combination with chlorine. We are only interested here in six of these chlorides: sodium chloride, magnesium chloride, aluminium chloride, silicon(iv) chloride, phosphorus(iii) chloride and phosphorus(v) chloride.

- **Sodium chloride**

  Sodium burns in chlorine gas to give white sodium chloride.

  $$2Na(s) + Cl_2(g) \rightarrow 2NaCl(s)$$

- **Magnesium chloride**

  Like sodium, magnesium burns in chlorine gas to give white magnesium chloride.

  $$Mg(s) + Cl_2(g) \rightarrow MgCl_2(s)$$

- **Aluminium chloride**

  When aluminium is heated in a stream of chlorine gas the volatile white solid aluminium chloride is formed.

  $$2Al(s) + 3Cl_2(g) \rightarrow 2AlCl_3(s)$$

  In the vapour phase, aluminium chloride exists as the dimer $Al_2Cl_6$ (see pages 36 and 211).

- **Silicon(iv) chloride**

  Silicon(iv) chloride is a volatile liquid, which is produced by heating silicon in chlorine gas.

  $$Si(s) + 2Cl_2(g) \rightarrow SiCl_4(l)$$

- **Phosphorus(iii) chloride** and **phosphorus(v) chloride**

  Phosphorus(iii) chloride is a volatile colourless liquid which is made by exposing phosphorus to chlorine gas – no heating is required. If excess chlorine is present then the phosphorus(iii) chloride reacts with chlorine to give phosphorus(v) chloride, which is a pale yellow solid.

  $$P_4(s) + 6Cl_2(g) \rightarrow 4PCl_3(l)$$

  followed, in excess chlorine, by

  $$PCl_3(l) + Cl_2(g) \rightarrow PCl_5(s)$$

Construct an equation for the reaction between chlorine and calcium.

What observation would you make if chlorine was passed over solid phosphorus?

# The reactions of sodium and magnesium with water

The reactions of sodium and magnesium with water are redox reactions, in which the metal is oxidised and hydrogen gas is produced. The remaining solution is an alkali.

When a piece of sodium is placed onto the surface of water it floats and fizzes about. If it gets stuck in one place it can become so hot that it catches fire, burning with an orange flame.

$$2Na(s) + 2H_2O(l) \rightarrow 2NaOH(aq) + H_2(g)$$

The solution of sodium hydroxide remaining has a high pH of 12–14. Because sodium hydroxide is very soluble, there is a high concentration of $OH^-(aq)$ ions present in solution.

When a piece of magnesium is placed into water it sinks and at first nothing appears to happen. However, if an inverted test-tube full of water is placed over the magnesium and left, after a few days you can see a gas has collected – this is hydrogen. So magnesium does react with water in the cold, but the reaction is very slow. Magnesium hydroxide is not as soluble as sodium hydroxide so the pH of the resulting solution is lower, around 9–11. As you may predict, magnesium reacts faster with steam, but the product here is magnesium oxide.

$$Mg(s) + 2H_2O(l) \rightarrow Mg(OH)_2(aq) + H_2(g)$$
$$Mg(s) + H_2O(g) \rightarrow MgO(s) + H_2(g)$$

We can see that sodium and magnesium react with water to give *alkaline solutions*, but there are two differences in these reactions.

- Sodium is more reactive with water than magnesium is.
- Aqueous sodium hydroxide is a stronger alkali

than aqueous magnesium hydroxide because NaOH is more soluble in water.

Show, by writing equations, the different products obtained when magnesium reacts with
**a** steam;
**b** cold water.

# The variations in oxidation number of the oxides and chlorides of Period 3

Across Period 3, the oxidation numbers of the oxides and chlorides increase. In the highest oxidation state the elements usually have oxidation numbers that correspond to the number of electrons in their outer shell.

## Structure and bonding of the oxides, and their reactions with water

Sodium and magnesium oxides have *giant ionic lattice structures* with *ionic bonding*.

When sodium oxide reacts with water it produces a solution of the alkali sodium hydroxide.

$$Na_2O(s) + H_2O(l) \rightarrow 2NaOH(aq)$$

Since sodium hydroxide is very soluble in water, the pH of this solution is about 11–14.

When magnesium oxide reacts with water it produces the alkali magnesium hydroxide in aqueous solution, but this product is not highly soluble, so the pH is around 9–11.

$$MgO(s) + H_2O(l) \rightarrow Mg(OH)_2(aq)$$

Aluminium oxide has a *giant ionic lattice structure* with a significant amount of *covalent bonding*. It is described as having *intermediate bonding*. It does not react with water – it is insoluble.

Phosphorus(v) oxide has *covalent bonding*. It reacts vigorously with water to give a solution of phosphoric(v) acid. The pH of this solution is about 2–4.

$$P_4O_{10}(s) + 6H_2O(l) \rightarrow 4H_3PO_4(aq)$$

Both sulphur dioxide and sulphur trioxide have *simple molecular structures* with *covalent bonding*. In solid sulphur trioxide van der Waals' forces operate between the molecules; in sulphur dioxide gas there are no forces between the molecules (as molecules in a gas are widely separated). Both these oxides react with water to give acids.

$$SO_2(g) + H_2O(l) \rightarrow H_2SO_3(aq)$$

and

$$SO_3(g) + H_2O(l) \rightarrow H_2SO_4(aq)$$

We can see certain trends emerging here (*figure 9.18*).

■ Metal oxides (on the left of the Periodic Table) have giant ionic lattice structures with ionic bonding and react with water to give alkalis. They are basic oxides and react with acids to give salts, for example:

$$MgO(s) + H_2SO_4(aq) \rightarrow MgSO_4(aq) + H_2O(l)$$

■ Non-metal oxides (on the right of the Periodic Table) have simple molecular structures with covalent bonding and react with water to give acids. They are acidic oxides and react with bases to give salts, for example:

$$SO_3(g) + MgO(s) \rightarrow MgSO_4(s)$$

■ Oxides in the centre of the Periodic Table have intermediate properties. They are amphoteric oxides and react with both acids and bases, for example:

$$Al_2O_3(s) + 6HCl(aq) \rightarrow 2AlCl_3(aq) + 3H_2O(l)$$

$$Al_2O_3(s) + 6NaOH(aq) + 3H_2O(l)$$
$$\rightarrow 2Na_3Al(OH)_6(aq)$$

*SAQ 9.16*

Predict the structure of:

**a** barium oxide;

**b** nitrogen dioxide;

**c** lithium oxide.

## Structure and bonding of the chlorides, and their reactions with water

Sodium chloride and magnesium chloride have *giant ionic lattice structures* with *ionic bonding*. Sodium chloride simply dissolves in water to give a *neutral* solution, pH 7. Magnesium chloride also dissolves in water but the solution here is *very slightly acidic*, pH 6.5.

Aluminium chloride exists as the dimeric covalent molecule $Al_2Cl_6$. In each molecule there are two co-ordinate bonds.

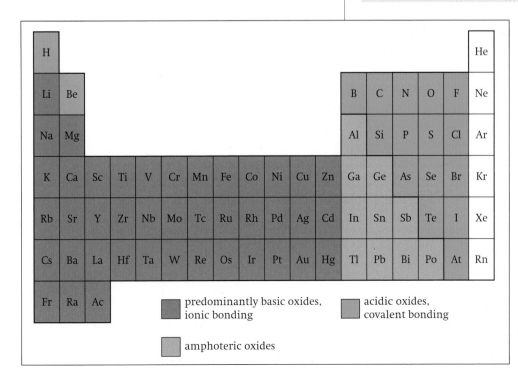

● **Figure 9.18** The Periodic Table and types of oxides.

The arrangement around each aluminium atom is tetrahedral.

Solid aluminium chloride dissolves in water with the formation of an ionic solution which is acidic.

$$Al_2Cl_6(s) + 12H_2O(l) \rightarrow 2[Al(H_2O)_6]^{3+}(aq) + 6Cl^-(aq)$$

The liquids silicon(IV) chloride and phosphorus(III) chloride have *simple molecular structures* with *covalent bonding*. $PCl_5$ in the gaseous state is a covalent molecule. These chlorides react vigorously with water in an exothermic reaction giving off white fumes of hydrogen chloride gas. This is called a **hydrolysis** reaction, and the solution remaining is *acidic*, pH 2.

- **Hydrolysis of silicon(IV) chloride**
  The reaction is

  $$SiCl_4(l) + 2H_2O(l) \rightarrow SiO_2(s) + 4HCl(g)$$

- **Hydrolysis of phosphorus(V) chloride**

  $$PCl_5(l) + 4H_2O(l) \rightarrow H_3PO_4(aq) + 5HCl(g)$$

  $H_3PO_4$ is known as phosphoric(V) acid.

Again, as with the oxides, we can see certain trends emerging here (*figure 9.19*).

- Metal chlorides (on the left of the Periodic Table) have giant ionic lattice structures with ionic bonding and react with water to give neutral (or slightly acidic) solutions. They are neutral chlorides.
- Non-metal chlorides (on the right of the Periodic Table) have simple molecular structures with covalent bonding and react with water to give acids. They are acidic chlorides.

## SAQ 9.17
Predict the pH value of a solution formed by dissolving lithium chloride in water.

## SAQ 9.18
Carbon tetrachloride does not mix or react with water, but silicon tetrachloride, $SiCl_4$, reacts violently.
a State what type of reaction this is.
b Write an equation showing this reaction.
c Give three observations you would make watching this reaction.

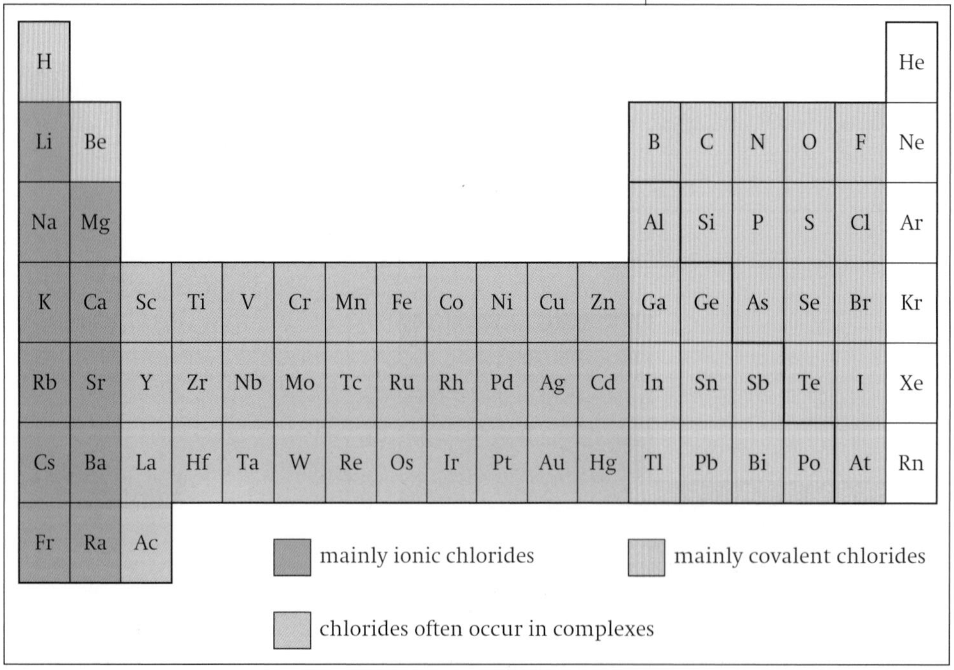

| H | | | | | | | | | | | | | | | | | He |
|---|---|---|---|---|---|---|---|---|---|---|---|---|---|---|---|---|---|
| Li | Be | | | | | | | | | | | B | C | N | O | F | Ne |
| Na | Mg | | | | | | | | | | | Al | Si | P | S | Cl | Ar |
| K | Ca | Sc | Ti | V | Cr | Mn | Fe | Co | Ni | Cu | Zn | Ga | Ge | As | Se | Br | Kr |
| Rb | Sr | Y | Zr | Nb | Mo | Tc | Ru | Rh | Pd | Ag | Cd | In | Sn | Sb | Te | I | Xe |
| Cs | Ba | La | Hf | Ta | W | Re | Os | Ir | Pt | Au | Hg | Tl | Pb | Bi | Po | At | Rn |
| Fr | Ra | Ac | | | | | | | | | | | | | | | |

mainly ionic chlorides   mainly covalent chlorides

chlorides often occur in complexes

● **Figure 9.19** The Periodic Table and types of chlorides.

# SUMMARY (AS)

- Early periodic patterns (regularly repeating variations) in the properties of elements were based on the elements in order of their relative atomic masses. The modern Periodic Tables are based on the elements in order of their atomic numbers.

- A Group in the Periodic Table contains elements with the same outer-shell electronic configuration but very different atomic numbers; the elements and their compounds have many similar chemical properties.

- The elements in a Block have their outer-most electrons in the same type of subshell. For example, s-block elements have their outermost electrons in an s subshell.

- Periods in the Periodic Table are sequences of elements, differing by one proton and one electron, from Group I to Group 0.

- Periodic variations may be observed across Periods in physical properties such as ionisation energies, electron configurations, atomic radii, boiling points, melting points and electrical conductivities.

- The main influences on ionisation energies and atomic radii are: the size of the positive nuclear charge; the distance of the electron from the nucleus; the shielding effect on outer electrons by electrons in filled inner shells.

- Ionisation energies decrease down a Group and tend to increase across a Period; atomic radii increase down a Group (effect of increasing shielding) and decrease across a Period (effect of increasing nuclear charge).

- The uneven trend of ionisation energies across a Period is explained by: a change from s to p subshells with a drop in first ionisation energy between Groups II and III; the commencement of electron pairing in a Group VI p orbital resulting from increased energy from electron-pair repulsion and a consequent fall in first ionisation energy between Groups V and VI.

- Across a Period (left to right, from Group I to Group VII), the structures of the elements change from giant metallic, through giant molecular to simple molecular. Group 0 elements consist of individual atoms.

- Successive ionisation energy data of an element may be interpreted in terms of the position of the element within the Periodic Table.

- Data on electronic configurations, atomic radii, electrical conductivity, melting points and boiling points may be interpreted to demonstrate periodicity.

- Chemically, the elements change from reactive metals, through less reactive metals and less reactive non-metals to reactive non-metals. Group 0 contains the extremely unreactive noble gases.

- The elements of Period 3 react directly with oxygen to give oxides, and with chlorine to give chlorides.

- Metal oxides have giant ionic lattice structures and ionic bonding. They are basic oxides that react with water to give hydroxides, which are basic.

- Non-metal oxides have simple molecular structures and covalent bonding. They are acidic oxides with a pH value in aqueous solution of around 1–2.

◆ Metal chlorides have giant ionic lattice structures and ionic bonding. They are neutral with a pH value in aqueous solution of 7 (or slightly higher).

◆ Non-metal chlorides have simple molecular structures with covalent bonding. They are acidic with a pH value in aqueous solution of around 2.

◆ Sodium and magnesium react with water to give the aqueous hydroxides. Sodium reacts more vigorously than magnesium.

◆ Aqueous sodium hydroxide has a pH of 12–14, aqueous magnesium hydroxide has a pH of 9–11. Aqueous magnesium hydroxide is a weaker alkali than aqueous sodium hydroxide because it is less soluble in water.

# Questions (AS)

1 Patterns in data have enabled chemists to gain a better understanding of many physical properties of elements. Look at the following figure, which gives the boiling points of the elements in Period 3 of the Periodic Table.

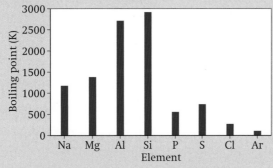

a Explain, in terms of their structures, why:
  (i) the boiling point of phosphorus is different from that of silicon;
  (ii) the boiling point of aluminium is different from that of magnesium.
b Explain why the pattern in the figure is described as being **periodic**.

2 In the Periodic Table there are trends in physical properties of the elements across periods and down groups. Describe and explain:
a the trend in electrical conductivity for Period 3;
b the trend in atomic radii down Group II.

3 The Periodic Table is divided into blocks labelled s, p, d and f.
a Give the full electron configurations of:
  (i) calcium;    (ii) silicon;
  (iii) selenium;   (iv) nickel.
b Give the Periodic Table block in which the elements in **a** may be found.
c Explain, in terms of electronic configurations, what the elements in the p-block have in common.

4 Describe the acid–base nature of the solutions obtained when the following compounds are added to water. Use equations to illustrate your answer.
a NaCl           b $SO_3$
c $Na_2O$          d $PCl_5$.

5 a (i) Write an equation to show the reaction of magnesium with water.
  (ii) Predict and explain the pH of the resulting solution.
b When magnesium is added to water, the reaction is very slow. In contrast, phosphorus trichloride reacts vigorously with water.
  (i) Write an equation, including state symbols, showing the reaction of phosphorus trichloride with water.
  (ii) Predict the pH of the solution obtained.
  (iii) State one observation a student watching the reaction would make.

# Group II (AS)

## By the end of this section you should be able to:

1 describe and explain the trends in electronic configurations, atomic radii and ionisation energies of the Group II elements (Mg to Ba);

2 interpret and make predictions from the chemical and physical properties of the Group II elements and their compounds;

3 show awareness of the importance and use of Group II elements and their compounds, with appropriate chemical explanations;

4 describe oxidation and reduction in terms of electron transfer and changes in oxidation state;

5 describe the redox reactions of the elements Mg to Ba with oxygen and water and explain the trend in reactivity in terms of ionisation energies;

6 describe the reactions of Mg, MgO and $MgCO_3$ with hydrochloric acid;

7 describe the behaviour of the Group II oxides with water;

8 describe the thermal decomposition of the nitrates and carbonates of Group II elements;

9 describe the thermal decomposition of $CaCO_3$ to form CaO (lime) and the subsequent formation of $Ca(OH)_2$ (slaked lime) with water;

10 describe lime water as an aqueous solution of $Ca(OH)_2$ and state its approximate pH;

11 describe the reaction of lime water with carbon dioxide forming $CaCO_3(s)$, and with excess carbon dioxide, forming $Ca(HCO_3)_2(aq)$, as in hard water.

## Introduction

The elements of Group II are often called the alkaline earth metals. They are:

| | | |
|---|---|---|
| beryllium | Be | $[He]2s^2$ |
| magnesium | Mg | $[Ne]3s^2$ |
| calcium | Ca | $[Ar]4s^2$ |
| strontium | Sr | $[Kr]5s^2$ |
| barium | Ba | $[Xe]6s^2$ |
| radium | Ra | $[Rn]7s^2$ |

Beryllium is markedly different from the other members of the Group, and so we shall not consider it here. We also shall not consider radium (the element discovered and isolated by Marie Curie – *box 10A*), as all its isotopes are radioactive.

The alkaline earth metals from magnesium to barium are white metals, with low melting and boiling points compared to transition metals like iron. They are good conductors of heat and electricity. The white colour is an oxide film – the metals themselves are shiny but react quickly with air, and the oxide film prevents further reaction. These metals burn in air with characteristic flame colours – magnesium white, calcium brick red, strontium red and barium green. Their physical properties are listed in *table 10.1*.

The metals of Group II all have two electrons in their outer s subshell, and these are lost when the metal reacts. This means that they always form an ion of oxidation number +2 in their compounds, such as $Mg^{2+}$ and $Ca^{2+}$. It also means that they are less reactive than Group I metals, because they have to lose two outer-shell electrons, whereas Group I metals lose only one.

## SAQ 10.1

a Using *table 10.1*, describe, for magnesium to barium, the trend in: (i) their metallic radii and (ii) their first ionisation energies.

b Explain the trends that you have described in **a**.

c Predict and explain the trend in electronegativity of the Group II elements.

# General properties of the Group II elements

The general properties of the Group II elements magnesium to barium are as follows:

- They are all metals.
- They are good conductors of heat and electricity.
- Their compounds are all white or colourless.
- In all their compounds they have an oxidation number +2.
- Their compounds are ionic.
- They are called alkaline earth metals because their oxides and hydroxides are basic.
- They react with acids to give hydrogen.

Compared with the metals of Group I:

- They are harder and denser.

### Box 10A Marie Curie

Marie Curie, *née* Marja Skłodowska, was born in Poland in 1867. Her first job was as a governess, which she took to pay for her sister's medical training in France. After her sister qualified Marie also went to Paris to study at the Sorbonne, where she obtained the highest marks in physics. She also met and married Pierre Curie, who was a research scientist.

Marie Curie suspected that in the uranium ore called pitchblende there was another radioactive substance as well as uranium. She treated tonnes of pitchblende and eventually isolated a small quantity of radium chloride – radium was unknown before this. Pierre Curie helped her in this work, which was remarkable in its detective work, as 10 tonnes of pitchblende contain about 1g of radium. The Curies were awarded the Nobel Prize in 1903 (along with Becquerel, who discovered radioactivity in 1896) for this work.

In 1906 Pierre, by then Professor of Physics at the Sorbonne, was killed by a horse-drawn carriage and Marie took over his post. She was the first woman to hold this position. In 1911 she was awarded a second Nobel Prize for her discovery of radium and polonium (which she named after Poland). The Curies' daughter Irene, with her husband Frederic Joliot, was also awarded a Nobel Prize for chemistry in 1935.

● **Figure 10.1** Marie Curie.

|  | Mg | Ca | Sr | Ba |
|---|---|---|---|---|
| Atomic number | 12 | 20 | 38 | 56 |
| Metallic radius (nm) | 0.160 | 0.197 | 0.215 | 0.224 |
| Ionic radius (nm) | 0.072 | 0.100 | 0.113 | 0.136 |
| First ionisation energy (kJ mol$^{-1}$) | 738 | 590 | 550 | 503 |
| Second ionisation energy (kJ mol$^{-1}$) | 1451 | 1145 | 1064 | 965 |
| Third ionisation energy (kJ mol$^{-1}$) | 7733 | 4912 | 4210 |  |
| Melting point (°C) | 649 | 839 | 769 | 725 |
| Boiling point (°C) | 1107 | 1484 | 1384 | 1640 |

● **Table 10.1** Physical properties of Group II elements.

- They have higher melting points.
- They exhibit stronger metallic bonding (because they have two outer-shell electrons instead of one).

# Uses

The elements of Group II and their compounds are widely used in commerce and industry.

*Magnesium* burns with a bright white light, and is used in flares, incendiary bombs and tracer bullets. It was once used in photographic flash bulbs.

Magnesium has such a strong reducing power that it is widely used to protect steel objects such as ships, outboard motors and bridges from corrosion. Its strong reducing power also means that it can be used to extract less electropositive (the ease with which elements lose electrons) metals such as titanium in the Kroll process, which takes place at 1250 K under an argon atmosphere:

$$2Mg(s) + TiCl_4(g) \rightarrow Ti(s) + 2MgCl_2(l)$$

Magnesium is also found in chlorophyll, the substance in plants which performs photosynthesis.

*Magnesium hydroxide* is a weak alkali and is used in indigestion remedies and in toothpastes, where it helps to neutralise acids in the mouth which encourage tooth decay. Representing acid as $H^+(aq)$, the following reaction occurs:

$$Mg(OH)_2(s) + 2H^+(aq) \rightarrow Mg^{2+}(aq) + 2H_2O(l)$$

*Magnesium oxide* is a refractory material, which means that it is resistant to heat (its melting point is over 3000 K). Its main use is for the lining of furnaces.

*Magnesium fluoride* is used to coat the surface of camera lenses, to reduce the amount of reflected light. It is responsible for the violet colour on the surface of the lens.

*Calcium carbonate* is an important compound as it is used in making cement – see *box 10B*.

*Lime* or *quicklime*, which is *calcium oxide*, was used in cement, mortar (*figure 10.2*) and plaster manufacture. It still has a very important role in purifying iron, as it reacts with impurities in the ore to form a molten slag:

$$\underset{\substack{\text{basic} \\ \text{oxide}}}{CaO(s)} + \underset{\substack{\text{acidic} \\ \text{oxide}}}{SiO_2(s)} \rightarrow CaSiO_3(l)$$

---

## Box 10B Cement

Calcium carbonate occurs in vast quantities in sedimentary rocks, such as limestone, chalk and dolomite. Marble is also a form of calcium carbonate, in which the marbling effect is caused by the presence of iron oxides. However, the largest use of calcium carbonate is in the manufacture of cement.

Cement is made by heating a finely ground mixture of limestone with clay (aluminosilicate) at 1750 K in a rotary kiln. This process results in clinker, which is reground and mixed with about 3% gypsum (calcium sulphate). This is a complex process, and the final formula of cement can be regarded as

$$2Ca_3SiO_5 + Ca_3Al_2O_6$$

The setting of cement is also a complex process – the cement reacts with water and carbon dioxide from the air.

The annual production of cement worldwide is about 1 billion tonnes.

● **Figure 10.2**
a Calcium oxide was used in lime mortar before the introduction of cement mortar.
b Addition of water to dry calcium oxide causes the solid to crumble, in an exothermic reaction producing calcium hydroxide.

Calcium oxide is the origin of the theatrical term 'limelight', because it glows with a bright white light when strongly heated and was originally used in stage lighting.

*Solid calcium hydroxide* is also used on acidic soil, to reduce the acidity of the soil. This increases crop yields. Representing acid as $H^+(aq)$, the following reaction occurs:

$$Ca(OH)_2(s) + 2H^+(aq) \rightarrow Ca^{2+}(aq) + 2H_2O(l)$$

Compare this reaction to that of magnesium hydroxide in indigestion remedies, above.

Lime mortar, which is prepared by mixing sand and calcium oxide with water, was widely used in bricklaying until the beginning of the 20th century.

*Plaster of Paris*, used to set broken bones and for modelling, is an insoluble form of *calcium sulphate*, $2CaSO_4.H_2O$. When it is mixed with water, it hydrates to $CaSO_4.2H_2O$ and sets hard.

The *hydrogencarbonates of calcium and magnesium* are responsible for the hardness of water – the metal ions are originally picked up when rain-water trickles over limestone and other similar rocks.

*Barium sulphate* is insoluble and, in suspension, is given to patients as a 'barium meal'. The barium ions coat the walls of the stomach and digestive tract and, as they are opaque to X-rays, they make any imperfections visible by X-ray photography. Soluble barium compounds are toxic, but barium sulphate is safe to use because its solubility is so low – for this reason, the presence of a barium sulphate precipitate is also used as a laboratory test for the sulphate ion.

*Strontium* has few uses. However, the isotope $^{90}_{38}Sr$ has been well studied, as it is produced in many nuclear reactions.

---

**Names of calcium compounds**
Several calcium compounds have common names based on the word 'lime', derived from limestone, which is one of the most widespread types of rock:

| | | |
|---|---|---|
| limestone | calcium carbonate | $CaCO_3$ |
| quicklime | calcium oxide | $CaO$ |
| slaked lime | solid calcium hydroxide | $Ca(OH)_2(s)$ |
| lime water | a solution of calcium hydroxide (only sparingly soluble) | $Ca(OH)_2(aq)$ |

# Reactions of Group II elements

These elements are powerful reducing agents. See chapter 6 (pages 94 and 95) for an explanation of reduction, oxidation, oxidation states and redox reactions.

## The reactions of the Group II metals with water

All the Group II metals from magnesium to barium reduce water to hydrogen. Magnesium reacts very slowly with cold water. A little hydrogen and magnesium hydroxide are formed over a few days.

$$Mg(s) + 2H_2O(l) \rightarrow Mg(OH)_2(s) + H_2(g)$$

The aqueous solution is weakly alkaline as magnesium hydroxide is very sparingly soluble. When water, as steam, is passed over heated magnesium, there is a rapid reaction (*figure 10.3a*). Hydrogen is released and magnesium oxide remains.

$$Mg(s) + H_2O(g) \rightarrow MgO(s) + H_2(g)$$

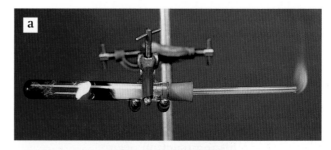

● **Figure 10.3**
**a** Apparatus to show the reaction of magnesium with steam. The steam is generated by heating material soaked in water at the left-hand end of the test-tube.
**b** Barium reacts readily with cold water, producing a rapid stream of bubbles of hydrogen.

The reactivity of the elements with water increases down the Group from magnesium to barium (*figure 10.3b*). Unlike magnesium, the metals calcium to barium all react readily with cold water to form a cloudy white precipitate of the hydroxide (which is sparingly soluble). During the reaction with water, the metal atoms lose electrons which are transferred to hydrogen atoms in water molecules. For example:

$$Ca(s) + 2H_2O(l) \rightarrow Ca(OH)_2(s) + H_2(g)$$

Ox. states   Ca: 0   H: +1   Ca: +2   H: 0
                    O: −2    O: −2
                                  H: +1

In this example, each calcium atom loses two electrons and changes oxidation state from 0 in $Ca(s)$ to +2 in $Ca(OH)_2(s)$. This is oxidation.

Meanwhile, two hydrogen atoms gain one electron each and change oxidation state from +1 in $H_2O(l)$ to 0 in $H_2(g)$. This is reduction. Notice that two water molecules are required for each calcium atom. Only one of the two hydrogen atoms in a water molecule is reduced, the oxidation state of the second hydrogen atom is unchanged at +1 in $Ca(OH)_2(s)$.

● **Figure 10.4** Magnesium ribbon burning in air. The reaction was used in the first photographic flash, and is still used in fireworks and flares.

Two electrons are lost from each metal atom in the reaction. Down the Group, the first two ionisation energies decrease from magnesium to barium. Consequently, the reactivity of the metals increase down the Group as less energy is required to remove the two electrons. A similar trend in reactivity is found when the Group II metals react with oxygen.

## The reactions of the Group II metals with oxygen

The reactions of these metals with oxygen, once started, are vigorous.

Magnesium metal is normally covered with a layer of its oxide. It burns rapidly in air or oxygen with a brilliant whitish flame (*figure 10.4*). This reaction is much used in fireworks and warning flares. White, crystalline magnesium oxide is formed.

$$2Mg(s) + O_2(g) \rightarrow 2MgO(s)$$

### SAQ 10.2

Some magnesium ribbon (0.2 g) was heated in a crucible until it began to burn. When the burning finished, a white powder remained in the crucible. What is this white powder? Calculate the mass of powder you would expect to find.

### SAQ 10.3

a Write an equation, including state symbols, for the burning of strontium in oxygen.

b Describe what you might observe during this reaction.

c Identify the element which is oxidised and the element which is reduced. Explain your answer in terms of electron transfer and oxidation states.

d Explain the increasing reactivity of the Group II metals.

## Formation of salts with hydrochloric acid

The salts of Group II elements are all white, crystalline compounds. They are easily prepared by reaction of the metal, metal oxide or metal carbonate with an acid. For example, magnesium, magnesium oxide or magnesium carbonate all dissolve in hydrochloric acid to form colourless solutions containing aqueous magnesium chloride, $MgCl_2$(aq). This salt may be obtained as a white crystalline compound by partial evaporation of the solution to the point where a good crop of crystals form on cooling. The crystals may be separated by filtration and dried in air (*figure 10.5*).

- Reaction of magnesium with hydrochloric acid:
  Magnesium ribbon dissolves rapidly in cold dilute hydrochloric acid with rapid evolution of hydrogen gas:
  $Mg(s) + 2HCl(aq) \rightarrow MgCl_2(aq) + H_2(g)$

- Reaction of magnesium oxide with hydrochloric acid:
  Magnesium oxide dissolves slowly in cold dilute hydrochloric acid. The reaction proceeds more rapidly on warming:
  $MgO(s) + 2HCl(aq) \rightarrow MgCl_2(aq) + H_2O(l)$

- Reaction of magnesium carbonate with hydrochloric acid:
  Magnesium carbonate dissolves rapidly in cold dilute hydrochloric acid with the evolution of carbon dioxide:
  $MgCO_3(s) + 2HCl(aq) \rightarrow MgCl_2(aq) + H_2O(l) + CO_2(g)$

## SAQ 10.4

**a** Predict what you might observe when calcium carbonate is added to dilute hydrochloric acid. Write a balanced equation, including state symbols, for any reaction that you have predicted.

**b** Explain why calcium hydroxide might be added to acidic soil.

**c** Magnesium hydroxide is used in antacid tablets. They relieve excessive acidity in the stomach by neutralising some of the hydrochloric acid present. Write a balanced equation, including state symbols, for the reaction of magnesium hydroxide with hydrochloric acid.

● **Figure 10.5** Magnesium chloride crystals after they have been separated from solution and dried in air.

## The reactions of the oxides with water

The metal oxides are all basic and each reacts with water, forming a solution of the hydroxide which is alkaline, for example:

$MgO(s) + H_2O(l) \rightarrow Mg(OH)_2(aq)$
$BaO(s) + H_2O(l) \rightarrow Ba(OH)_2(aq)$

The reaction of magnesium oxide with water is slow; the other oxides react readily with water.

The solubilities of the hydroxides formed increase down the Group (see *table 10.2*) and the solutions become more alkaline.

| Hydroxide | Solubility at 298 K (mol per 100 g of water) |
|---|---|
| $Mg(OH)_2$ | $2.0 \times 10^{-5}$ |
| $Ca(OH)_2$ | $1.5 \times 10^{-3}$ |
| $Sr(OH)_2$ | $3.4 \times 10^{-3}$ |
| $Ba(OH)_2$ | $1.5 \times 10^{-2}$ |

● **Table 10.2** Solubilities of Group II hydroxides at 298 K.

## The thermal decomposition of Group II nitrates and carbonates

The nitrates all decompose on heating to form the corresponding metal oxide, nitrogen dioxide and oxygen, for example:

$2Mg(NO_3)_2(s) \rightarrow 2MgO(s) + 4NO_2(g) + O_2(g)$

The carbonates all decompose on heating to form the corresponding oxide and carbon dioxide, for example:

$BaCO_3(s) \rightarrow BaO(s) + CO_2(g)$

For both the nitrates and the carbonates, the decomposition temperature increases down the Group.

## Chalk and lime chemistry

The white cliffs of Dover are composed of chalk. The cliffs are the sedimentary remains of marine invertebrates. Chemically, they are composed of calcium carbonate, $CaCO_3$. Limestone is a similar sedimentary deposit which also contains calcium carbonate (*figure 10.6*). Limestone and chalk are used in large quantities to manufacture quicklime (calcium oxide) and cement.

● **Figure 10.6** These limestone cliffs are sedimentary deposits that contain calcium carbonate.

Strong heating of calcium carbonate produces calcium oxide, CaO, and carbon dioxide.

$$CaCO_3(s) \rightarrow CaO(s) + CO_2(g)$$

This type of reaction, where a compound is broken down by heat, is known as a **thermal decomposition** (see also page 72).

Traditionally, chalk or limestone were heated in a lime kiln using fuels such as wood or coal (*figure 10.7*).

Calcium oxide reacts vigorously with water (see page 217) to produce calcium hydroxide, $Ca(OH)_2$ (slaked lime).

$$CaO(s) + H_2O(l) \rightarrow Ca(OH)_2(s)$$

The name 'quicklime' for CaO derives from the vigour of this reaction. Here, 'quick' is used in the sense of 'alive'. During the Black Death, corpses were buried under a layer of quicklime. The quick-

lime reacted with moisture from the corpses, helping to control the spread of disease. In more recent times, quicklime has also been used in this way, for example following the tragic earthquake in Turkey in 1999.

Further addition of water to calcium hydroxide produces the saturated aqueous solution that we call 'lime water'. Calcium hydroxide is only slightly soluble in water, the saturated solution has a concentration of approximately $1.5 \times 10^{-2}\,mol\,dm^{-3}$. Chemists often describe compounds which are slightly soluble as being 'sparingly soluble'. As the concentration of calcium hydroxide in lime water is low, the solution has a low concentration of hydroxide ion, $OH^-$. The pH of lime water is about 9–10.

You will probably be familiar with lime water as the reagent used to identify carbon dioxide gas. When a sample of carbon dioxide is bubbled through lime water, a cloudy white precipitate forms. The precipitate is solid calcium carbonate.

$$Ca(OH)_2(aq) + CO_2(g) \rightarrow CaCO_3(s) + H_2O(l)$$

*Figure 10.8* shows a straightforward method for performing the lime water test for carbon dioxide.

If we continue to bubble carbon dioxide through lime water after the white precipitate has formed, eventually the mixture turns clear again. The white precipitate of calcium carbonate reacts with water and aqueous carbon dioxide to form a solution of aqueous calcium hydrogen carbonate, $Ca(HCO_3)_2(aq)$.

$$CaCO_3(s) + H_2O(l) + CO_2(aq) \rightarrow Ca(HCO_3)_2(aq)$$

● **Figure 10.7** Old lime kilns near Agrigento in Sicily.

> **Precipitates and suspensions**
> These words have different meanings, although each is used to describe a mixture of a solid with a solvent such as water. A precipitate of calcium carbonate will look very similar to a suspension of calcium carbonate. The difference lies in the way each has been formed. A *suspension* is formed when a finely powdered insoluble solid is shaken with water. A *precipitate* forms following reaction between two soluble compounds.

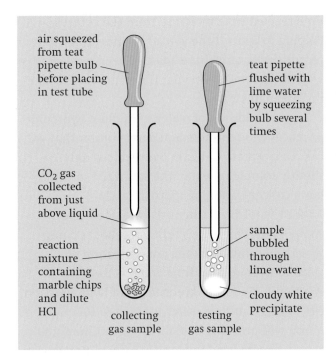

air squeezed
from teat
pipette bulb
before placing
in test tube

teat pipette
flushed with
lime water
by squeezing
bulb several
times

$CO_2$ gas
collected
from just
above liquid

reaction
mixture
containing
marble chips
and dilute
HCl

sample
bubbled
through
lime water

cloudy white
precipitate

collecting
gas sample

testing
gas sample

● **Figure 10.8** The lime water test for carbon dioxide.

● **Figure 10.9** The limestone hillside has slowly been eroded by the acidity of rain-water.

## Hard water

Hard water contains dissolved calcium (or magnesium) ions. The calcium (or magnesium) ions in hard water produce a scum with soap. Hard water is formed by the action of water and carbon dioxide on calcium carbonate (as in the above equation). Rain dissolves carbon dioxide from the air. When such rain falls on rocks containing chalk or limestone, the calcium carbonate slowly dissolves forming very dilute aqueous calcium hydrogen carbonate. Over many years, fissures and eventually large caves may be created (*figure 10.9*).

## Flue gas desulphurisation (FGD)

Calcium carbonate is used to remove sulphur dioxide from the flue gases produced when coal is burnt in power stations. The flue gases are passed through a suspension of calcium carbonate and calcium sulphate is formed.

$$CaCO_3(s) + SO_2(g) \rightarrow CaSO_3(s) + CO_2(g)$$

$$CaSO_3(s) + \tfrac{1}{2}O_2(g) \rightarrow CaSO_4(s)$$

The calcium sulphate is recovered and sold to make plaster.

## SUMMARY (AS)

◆ The Group II elements magnesium to barium are typical metals with high melting points and good conductivity of heat and electricity;

◆ Progressing down Group II from magnesium to barium, the atomic radius increases. This is due to the addition of an extra shell of electrons for each element as the Group is descended.

◆ Many of the compounds of Group II elements are commercially important. For example, slaked lime (calcium hydroxide) is used to neutralise acid soil. Magnesium hydroxide is used in antacid tablets to neutralise excess acid in the stomach.

◆ Reactivity of the elements with oxygen or water increases down Group II as the first and second ionisation energies decrease.

- The reactions of Group II elements are redox reactions. The elements are powerful reducing agents. Redox reactions may be explained in terms of electron transfer (oxidation is loss of electrons, reduction is gain of electrons) or change of oxidation states (oxidation increases oxidation state; reduction decreases oxidation state).

- The Group II elements magnesium to barium react with water to produce hydrogen gas and the sparingly soluble metal hydroxide. As the hydroxide solutions have a pH of 8 or higher, they are called the alkaline earth elements.

- The Group II elements magnesium to barium burn in air with characteristic flame colours to form the oxide as a white solid. Flame colours are magnesium white; calcium brick red; strontium red; barium green.

- Salts of these metals are readily prepared by reaction of the metal, metal oxide or metal carbonate with an acid. For example, dilute hydrochloric acid reacts with magnesium metal, magnesium oxide or magnesium carbonate to produce magnesium chloride.

- Calcium carbonate (as chalk or limestone) may be decomposed by heat to form calcium oxide (quicklime) which reacts violently with water to form calcium hydroxide (slaked lime). Calcium hydroxide is sparingly soluble in water forming lime water.

- Lime water produces a milky precipitate with carbon dioxide. This precipitate is calcium carbonate, which will dissolve in excess carbon dioxide to form calcium hydrogencarbonate. It is this reaction which is responsible for the formation of hard water.

## Questions (AS)

1   The Group II metals magnesium to barium and their compounds are widely used.
    a   (i)   State the trend in the reactivity of these metals with water.
        (ii)  Write an equation for the reaction of one of these metals with water.
    b   Suggest one use for each of these:
        (i)   magnesium oxide;
        (ii)  calcium hydroxide.

2   Water was gradually added to a Group II metal oxide and a white solid **X** was formed. **X** is slightly soluble in water and is used in agriculture.
    a   Identify **X**.
    b   Predict the pH of a solution of **X** in water.
    c   Explain why **X** is used in agriculture.

3   Chalk and limestone provide important sources of calcium carbonate. Calcium carbonate is used to make lime (calcium oxide, CaO) from which hydrated lime (calcium hydroxide, $Ca(OH)_2$) is made. Write balanced equations, including state symbols, for:

    a   the conversion of calcium carbonate to calcium oxide;
    b   the formation of calcium hydroxide from calcium oxide.

4   The Group II elements all burn fiercely in oxygen.
    a   (i)   Describe the trend in reactivity down Group II when the elements burn in oxygen.
        (ii)  Explain the observed trend in reactivity in terms of ionisation energies.
    b   (i)   Write a balanced equation for the reaction when magnesium burns in oxygen.
        (ii)  Using your equation from (i) and oxidation states, identify the oxidation state changes which take place in this reaction. Identify which element is oxidised and which is reduced. Give your reasons.

# Group II (A2)

**By the end of this section you should be able to:**

**12** interpret and explain qualitatively the trend in the thermal stability of the nitrates and carbonates in terms of the charge density of the cation and the polarisability of the large anion;

**13** interpret and explain qualitatively the variation in solubility of the sulphates in terms of the relative magnitudes of the enthalpy change of hydration and the corresponding lattice enthalpy.

## The decomposition of the nitrates and carbonates

The nitrates and carbonates of Group II elements undergo thermal decomposition.

- Nitrates form the metal oxide, nitrogen dioxide and oxygen, for example:

    $$2Mg(NO_3)_2(s) \rightarrow 2MgO(s) + 4NO_2(g) + O_2(g)$$

- Carbonates form the metal oxide and carbon dioxide, for example:

    $$CaCO_3(s) \rightarrow CaO(s) + CO_2(g)$$

In each case, the salt consists of the large nitrate ion or carbonate ion and a smaller metal cation. The smaller cation polarises and distorts the larger anion, which breaks up when heated.

Down Group II, the decomposition temperature increases, as shown in *table 10.3*.

The increase in decomposition temperature down the Group may be explained in terms of the increased size of the cations from $Mg^{2+}$ to $Ba^{2+}$ and the corresponding reduction in polarising power. For a fuller explanation of this trend see chapter 5, page 92.

## The solubilities of Group II sulphates

The solubilities of the sulphates of Group II elements decrease down the Group, as shown in *table 10.4*. Magnesium sulphate is very soluble, while barium sulphate is one of the most insoluble substances known.

This trend in solubilities can be simply explained in a similar way to the trend in decomposition temperatures, but involving lattice energy and the enthalpy change of hydration of the ions in the salt.

The sulphates consist of a large $SO_4^{2-}$ ion and a smaller $M^{2+}$ ion. As Group II is descended, the size of the $M^{2+}$ ion increases. This means that down the Group the lattice enthalpy decreases but, because the sulphate ion is large and dominant, the change is relatively small (*table 10.5*).

| Carbonate | Decomposition temperature (°C) |
|-----------|-------------------------------|
| $MgCO_3$ | 350 |
| $CaCO_3$ | 832 |
| $SrCO_3$ | 1340 |
| $BaCO_3$ | 1450 |

● **Table 10.3** Decomposition temperatures of Group II carbonates.

| Sulphate | Solubility (mol per 100 g of water) |
|----------|-------------------------------------|
| $MgSO_4$ | $1.83 \times 10^{-1}$ |
| $CaSO_4$ | $4.66 \times 10^{-3}$ |
| $SrSO_4$ | $7.11 \times 10^{-5}$ |
| $BaSO_4$ | $9.43 \times 10^{-7}$ |

● **Table 10.4** Solubilities of Group II sulphates at 298 K.

| Sulphate | Lattice enthalpy $(kJ\,mol^{-1})$ | Enthalpy change of solution $(kJ\,mol^{-1})$ |
|---|---|---|
| $MgSO_4$ | −2959 | −91 |
| $CaSO_4$ | −2704 | −18 |
| $SrSO_4$ | −2572 | −2 |
| $BaSO_4$ | −2459 | +26 |

● **Table 10.5** Lattice enthalpies and enthalpy changes of solution for Group II sulphates.

| Ion | Ionic radius (nm) | Enthalpy change of hydration $(kJ\,mol^{-1})$ |
|---|---|---|
| $Mg^{2+}$ | 0.065 | −1890 |
| $Ca^{2+}$ | 0.099 | −1562 |
| $Sr^{2+}$ | 0.113 | −1414 |
| $Ba^{2+}$ | 0.135 | −1273 |
| $SO_4^{2-}$ | | −1160 |

● **Table 10.6** Ionic radii and enthalpy changes of hydration for Group II cations and the sulphate anion.

On the other hand, the enthalpy change of hydration for the reaction:

$$M^{2+}(g) + aq \rightarrow M^{2+}(aq)$$

decreases considerably down the Group due to the increasing size of $M^{2+}$ (*table 10.6*).

For the salt to dissolve readily, the enthalpy change of hydration must be greater than the lattice enthalpy. For $MgSO_4$ this is the case. As the Group is descended, the greater decrease in the enthalpy change of hydration compared with the decrease in the lattice enthalpy means that the process of solvation becomes less exothermic and the solubility decreases – see *figure 10.10*.

It must be stressed that this is a simplified argument, which is perfectly acceptable at this level. A more detailed argument must involve entropy change (see chapter 8, page 171).

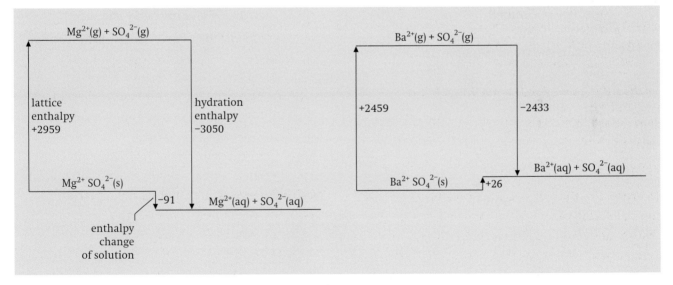

● **Figure 10.10** Principal enthalpy changes (in $kJ\,mol^{-1}$) for the dissolving of Group II sulphates.

## SUMMARY (A2)

- The thermal stabilities for the Group II nitrates and carbonates increase down the Group.

- This trend can be explained in terms of the increased size and reduction in the charge density of the cation and the resulting degree of polarisation of the anion.

- The solubilities of the Group II sulphates decrease down the Group.

- This trend can be explained in terms of the decrease in enthalpy change of hydration from $Mg^{2+}$ to $Ba^{2+}$ being greater than the decrease in lattice enthalpy from $MgSO_4$ to $BaSO_4$.

## Questions (A2)

5  a  Describe the change in cation size from $Mg^{2+}$ to $Ba^{2+}$.

  b  Explain how this change affects the polarising power of the cation.

  c  Describe the trend observed in the decomposition temperature of the nitrates of Group II.

  d  Use your answers to parts **a** and **b** to explain the trend you have described in part **c**.

6  a  Explain what is meant by the terms *lattice enthalpy* and *enthalpy change of hydration*.

  b  Describe the trend in the solubilities of Group II sulphates.

  c  Explain this trend in terms of lattice enthalpy and enthalpy change of hydration.

# CHAPTER 11

# Group IV (A2)

**By the end of this chapter you should be able to:**

1 outline the variations in melting point and in electrical conductivity of the elements and interpret them in terms of structure and bonding;

2 describe and explain the bonding in, molecular shape and volatility of the tetrachlorides;

3 describe and explain the reactions of the tetrachlorides with water in terms of structure and bonding;

4 describe and explain the bonding, acid–base nature and thermal stability of the oxides of oxidation states II and IV;

5 describe and explain the relative stability of higher and lower oxidation states of the elements in their oxides and aqueous cations, including, where relevant, $E^{\ominus}$ values;

6 recognise the properties and uses of ceramics based on silicon(IV) oxide.

## Introduction

The elements of Group IV with their respective electronic configurations are:

| | | |
|---|---|---|
| carbon | C | [He]2s$^2$ 2p$^2$ |
| silicon | Si | [Ne]3s$^2$ 3p$^2$ |
| germanium | Ge | [Ar]3d$^{10}$ 4s$^2$ 4p$^2$ |
| tin | Sn | [Kr]4d$^{10}$ 5s$^2$ 5p$^2$ |
| lead | Pb | [Xe]4f$^{14}$ 5d$^{10}$ 6s$^2$ 6p$^2$ |

Group IV is the most interesting Group in the Periodic Table in the way that trends and patterns in properties of the elements occur. Generally, in other Groups, the elements all have similar chemical and physical properties, and certain trends in these properties are apparent. But in Group IV the elements are very different from one another. The most striking difference is the change from non-metallic carbon at the top of the Group to metallic tin and lead at the bottom. Down the Group the physical and chemical properties change dramatically. Between non-metallic carbon and metallic tin and metallic lead are silicon and germanium. These two elements are known as

metalloids because their properties fall between those of non-metals and those of metals.

● **Figure 11.1** Two Group IV elements: carbon and lead.

Compare the appearances of carbon and lead. Do they reflect the change in character going down the Group?

Carbon exists as **allotropes**, which are different crystalline or molecular forms of a substance. Graphite and diamond are well known allotropes of carbon, and it is difficult to imagine two substances made of the same atom that are so different. Graphite is black, diamond is colourless; graphite conducts electricity, diamond does not conduct electricity; graphite is soft and 'greasy', diamond is extremely hard. Graphite is the standard state of carbon, as it is the more stable at ordinary temperatures and pressures. Not many people realise that diamond changes to graphite under normal conditions, but fortunately for jewellery owners this occurs at a negligible rate!

In the late 1980s another allotrope of carbon was discovered, called buckminsterfullerene (also known as 'bucky balls'). This allotrope consists of balls of carbon atoms, $C_{60}$ (figure 11.2). The evidence for this allotrope, present in tiny amounts, was by mass spectroscopy of samples of soot. In 1990 scientists learned how to prepare multigram samples of $C_{60}$, and this has led to the manufacture of a number of new materials.

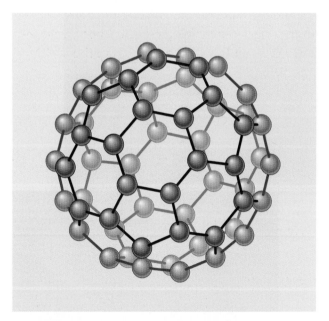

● **Figure 11.2** $C_{60}$ has now been found in geological samples formed by the meteor impact that occurred around the time that dinosaurs became extinct.

# Bonding and expansion of the octet

The elements of Group IV all have four electrons in their outermost electron shell. They have outermost electron configurations of $ns^2\,np^2$ – two electrons in the s subshell and two electrons in the p subshell. In covalent compounds each of these electrons forms a pair with an electron from an atom of the other element so that four covalent bonds are formed. The resulting molecule is tetrahedral in shape, but is only a perfect tetrahedron if all four atoms joined to carbon are equivalent (figure 11.3). For more about the valence shell electron pair repulsion theory, see chapter 3.

However, all the Group IV elements except carbon can make more than four bonds. This is because a set of d orbitals is available to use in bonding. These d orbitals are the empty d orbitals of the outer shell – the 3d orbitals for silicon, the 4d orbitals for germanium and so on. The empty d orbitals are close in energy to the full orbitals occupied by the covalent bonds formed by the four outermost electrons, and so can accommodate electrons. This allows the element to hold more than eight electrons in its bonding shell. This is called *expansion of the octet*. Expansion of the octet cannot happen in carbon, because there is no 2d orbital, but it can occur in other elements in Period 3 and below.

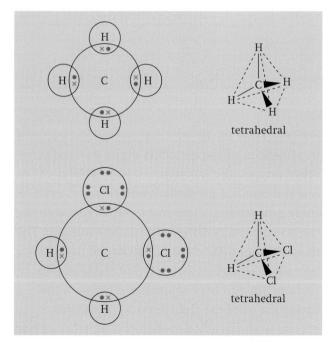

● **Figure 11.3** Dot-and-cross diagrams of $CH_4$ and $CH_2Cl_2$.

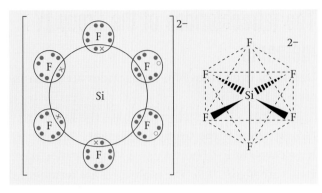

● **Figure 11.4** The $SiF_6^{2-}$ ion.

## SAQ 11.2

Phosphorus forms two compounds with chlorine, $PCl_3$ and $PCl_5$.

**a** Draw a dot-and-cross diagram for each compound.

**b** Explain how each compound is formed in terms of electron structure.

---

The complex ion $SiF_6^{2-}$, shown in *figure 11.4*, illustrates this point. There are 12 electrons (6 pairs) around the silicon atom. Silicon provides four bonding electrons for four fluorine atoms, but it is also possible for two fluoride ions to bond as well. These fluoride ions have dative bonds that occupy the silicon 3d orbital. The two fluoride ions also provide two 'extra' electrons, which gives the complex an overall charge of 2−.

## SAQ 11.3

The hydrides of the Group IV elements are tetrahedral. Give an explanation for this shape in terms of electron-pair repulsion theory.

---

# Melting points and electrical conductivities

The trends in these two physical properties clearly show the change in character of the elements in Group IV. Both these trends can be explained by considering the type of structure and bonding of each element.

■ The melting points generally *decrease* on descending the Group (*table 11.1*).

At the top of the Group, carbon has a giant covalent structure; all the electrons are fixed in position in bonding **orbitals** as covalent bonds. This means that the melting point is very high, as the atoms are held firmly so cannot pass on heat energy vibrations easily. The large decrease in melting point between carbon and silicon is due to longer, weaker bonds in the silicon covalent structure – the larger the atoms the weaker the bond. Germanium again has larger atoms, weaker covalent bonds and a lower melting point. Tin and lead have metallic bonding, which is easier to break down with heat energy than covalent bonding.

■ The electrical conductivities *increase* on descending the Group (*table 11.2*).

In diamond, all the electrons are used in bonding, so there are no free electrons and no electrical conductivity. In graphite, one electron per carbon atom is not used for bonding and joins a delocalised cloud, and this means that graphite is a conductor.

| Element | C | | Si | Ge | Sn | Pb |
|---|---|---|---|---|---|---|
| | diamond | graphite | | | | |
| Atomic radius (nm) | 0.077 | 0.077 | 0.117 | 0.122 | 0.162 | 0.175 |
| Melting point (°C) | 3550 | 3627 | 1410 | 940 | 232 | 328 |
| Bonding | giant covalent | giant covalent | giant covalent | giant covalent | metallic | metallic |

● **Table 11.1** Melting points of the Group IV elements.

| Element | C | | Si | Ge | Sn | Pb |
|---|---|---|---|---|---|---|
| | diamond | graphite | | | | |
| Electrical conductivity | poor | good | semiconductor | semiconductor | good | good |

● **Table 11.2** Electrical conductivities of the Group IV elements.

At the bottom of the Group, tin and lead each have a giant metallic structure. The outer electrons are held less tightly as the distance from the nucleus and shielding are both increased, so a delocalised sea of electrons forms in conduction bands. The electrical conductivity is good, as you would expect for a typical metallic structure with mobile electrons free to move throughout the conduction bands.

Silicon and germanium are semiconductors – they conduct electricity only under certain circumstances. This property arises because of the relative positions of the bonding orbitals and the conduction bands. In insulators, the energy difference between the bonding orbitals and the first conduction band is large – we say the band gap is large. In semiconductors the band gap is small enough to make the conduction band accessible, even though it is not usually occupied. Semiconductors do not normally conduct electricity but can be made to conduct if they are doped with a suitable element. Doping means adding a small quantity of a similar sized atom to the semiconductor, such that the doping atoms fit neatly into the semiconductor structure.

**Semiconductors**
- Germanium can be doped with arsenic. An arsenic atom has one extra electron than a germanium atom. This electron occupies a conduction band. This means that when a potential difference is applied across the doped germanium it can conduct – this is called an n-type conductor ('n' for negative electrons).
- Germanium can also be doped with gallium. A gallium atom has one less electron than a germanium atom, so the doped germanium has fewer electrons overall. We say that gallium introduces positive 'holes', which enable the electrons to move through the solid more easily and so conduct. This is a p-type conductor ('p' for positive holes).

# The tetrachlorides of the Group IV elements

Details of the Group IV tetrachlorides are given in *table 11.3*.

The Group IV tetrachlorides have the formula $ECl_4$, where E is the Group IV element. They all have covalent E–Cl bonds and a simple molecular structure (*figure 11.5*). The molecules are tetrahedral in shape, as predicted by valence shell electron-pair repulsion theory (see chapter 3, page 38).

The Group IV tetrachlorides are volatile liquids at room temperature (lead(IV) chloride is an oily liquid which decomposes into lead(II) chloride and chlorine when gently heated). They have low melting and boiling points because the $ECl_4$ molecule is non-polar. The only intermolecular attractions are van der Waals' forces, which are small because the molecules are non-linear.

It is worth thinking carefully about the non-polar nature of the Group IV tetrachloride molecules. Look at the diagram of $CCl_4$. Each C–Cl bond is polar, because C and Cl have different electronegativity values (see page 36). However, the molecule *as a whole* is non-polar because it has a symmetrical shape.

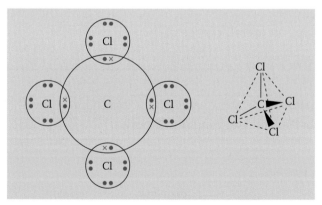

● **Figure 11.5** The shape of $CCl_4$ molecules.

| | CCl₄ | SiCl₄ | GeCl₄ | SnCl₄ | PbCl₄ |
|---|---|---|---|---|---|
| Boiling point (°C) | 77 | 58 | 87 | 114 | 105 (explodes) |
| Bonding | ←———————————————— covalent ————————————————→ | | | | |
| Structure | ←———————————————— molecular ————————————————→ | | | | |
| Shape | ←———————————————— tetrahedral ————————————————→ | | | | |
| Reaction with water | none | ←———————— hydrolysed ————————→ | | | |

● **Table 11.3** Group IV tetrachlorides.

## Reactions of the tetrachlorides with water

All the Group IV tetrachlorides, except carbon tetrachloride, are readily hydolysed forming HCl, for example:

$$SiCl_4(l) + 2H_2O(l) \rightarrow SiO_2(s) + 4HCl(aq)$$
$$\text{silica}$$

These reactions can be spectacular to observe, as they are strongly exothermic and produce white fumes. The mechanism for this reaction is shown in *figure 11.6*. The lone pair on the oxygen is attracted to the silicon atom, which has a partial positive charge because the more electronegative chlorine atoms withdraw electron density. For a short while, the silicon atom has five bonds round it. The extra bond occupies the 3d orbital – this illustrates expansion of the octet. The reaction can be regarded to take place in stages:

$$SiCl_4 + H_2O \rightarrow Si(OH)Cl_3 + HCl$$
$$Si(OH)Cl_3 + H_2O \rightarrow Si(OH)_2Cl_2 + HCl$$
$$Si(OH)_2Cl_2 + H_2O \rightarrow Si(OH)_3Cl + HCl$$
$$Si(OH)_3Cl + H_2O \rightarrow Si(OH)_4 + HCl$$
$$Si(OH)_4 \rightarrow SiO_2 + 2H_2O$$

overall

$$SiCl_4 + 2H_2O \rightarrow SiO_2 + 4HCl$$

Why is $CCl_4$ unaffected by water? There are two reasons for this.

■ Reactions of carbon cannot involve expansion of the octet, but reactions of the other Group IV elements can. A bond has to be formed between the O atom on $H_2O$ and the C atom in $CCl_4$ if a reaction is to occur, and there is no d orbital available for this bond to occupy.

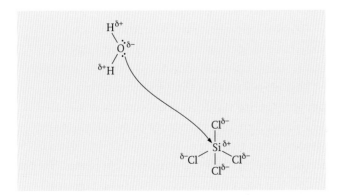

● **Figure 11.6** The mechanism for the $SiCl_4/H_2O$ reaction.

■ $CCl_4$ is a smaller molecule than the other Group IV tetrachloride molecules because the carbon atom is the smallest in the Group and the C–Cl bond is the shortest. This means that the $H_2O$ molecule cannot get close enough to the carbon atom in the centre of $CCl_4$ to react with it.

### SAQ 11.4
The hydrides of the Group IV elements become less stable on descending the Group. Explain why this is.

# Oxides of the Group IV elements

There are two types of Group IV oxides:
■ dioxides, with oxidation state +4 and general formula $EO_2$;
■ monoxides, with oxidation state +2 and general formula $EO$.

## Group IV dioxides

*Table 11.4* shows the properties and reactions of the Group IV dioxides.

The +4 oxidation state gets less stable as the Group is descended, so all the dioxides except $PbO_2$ are thermally stable. $PbO_2$ decomposes as follows:

$$2PbO_2(s) \rightarrow 2PbO(s) + O_2(g)$$

The ionic character of the bonding increases as the atomic size increases. Carbon dioxide is a gas and so is a simple molecule, whereas all the others have giant structures.

The acid–base character of the Group IV dioxides changes as the Group is descended. The dioxides become less acidic.

■ $CO_2$ is acidic and dissolves in water to give a weak acidic solution.

$$CO_2(g) + H_2O(l) \rightarrow H^+(aq) + HCO_3^-(aq)$$

■ $SiO_2$ is acidic. It is insoluble in water but dissolves in concentrated alkali.

$$SiO_2(s) + 2OH^-(aq) \rightarrow SiO_3^{2-}(aq) + H_2O(l)$$
$$\text{conc}$$

| | $CO_2$ | $SiO_2$ | $GeO_2$ | $SnO_2$ | $PbO_2$ |
|---|---|---|---|---|---|
| Melting point (°C) | −56 | 1610 | 1116 | 1127 | decomposes at 300 |
| Thermal stability | ◄──────── stable to high temperatures ────────► decomposes | | | | |
| Bonding | ◄──── covalent ────► ◄──── increasingly ionic ────► | | | | |
| Structure | molecular (gas) ◄──────────── giant ────────────► | | | | |
| Acid–base nature | ◄──── acidic ────► ◄──── amphoteric ────► | | | | |
| Solubility in water | slightly soluble ◄──────── insoluble ────────► | | | | |

● **Table 11.4** The Group IV dioxides

■ $GeO_2$ is amphoteric. It dissolves in acid and in alkali.

$GeO_2(s) + 4HCl(aq) \rightarrow GeCl_4(aq) + 2H_2O(l)$
$GeO_2(s) + 2OH^-(aq) + 2H_2O(l) \rightarrow [Ge(OH)_6]^{2-}(aq)$

■ $SnO_2$ and $PbO_2$ are also amphoteric, and have similar reactions to $GeO_2$.

## Group IV monoxides

The Group IV monoxides are CO, GeO, SnO and PbO (SiO does exist, but only at high temperatures). Carbon monoxide, CO, is the 'odd one out', as it has a simple molecular structure:

$$C \rightleftharpoons O$$

It is a neutral gas which is insoluble in water.

Carbon monoxide is a powerful reducing agent, as we have already seen (see page 23). The monoxides of Ge, Sn and Pb are solids and are amphoteric in nature. Lead(II) oxide is commonly known as litharge. It is a yellow-orange solid that is easily reduced, and the crystal structure has a considerable amount of covalent character. Typical reactions are as follows:

reaction with acid
$PbO(s) + 2HCl(aq) \rightarrow PbCl_2(aq) + H_2O(l)$

reaction with alkali
$PbO(s) + 2OH^-(aq) \rightarrow PbO_2^{2-}(aq) + H_2O(l)$

Both PbO and SnO are thermally stable, as expected for a compound in a stable oxidation state.

### SAQ 11.5
If you wanted to make a solution of lead(II) oxide, which acid would you choose, and why?

**Red lead**
A third oxide of lead, $Pb_3O_4$, may be obtained by heating PbO in air at 450°C.

$6PbO(s) + O_2(g) \rightarrow 2Pb_3O_4(s)$

The $Pb_3O_4$ formed has a brilliant red colour and is known as 'red lead'. It is a mixed oxide, containing both PbO and $PbO_2$, and has the reactions of both oxides.

It is used in red lead paint to protect iron from rusting.

### SAQ 11.6
Lead(IV) oxide reacts with sulphur dioxide in the following way.

$PbO_2(s) + SO_2(g) \rightarrow PbSO_4(s)$

Is this a redox reaction? If it is, identify the species that are oxidised and reduced.

## Oxidation states

All the Group IV elements form compounds in which they have oxidation number +4, such as $CCl_4$ (tetrachloromethane) and $SiO_2$ (silicon dioxide or silica – the main component of sand). In these compounds all four outer-shell electrons, $ns^2$ and $np^2$, take part in the bonding.

Tin and lead also form compounds in which they have oxidation number +2. Examples are $SnCl_2$, tin(II) chloride, and $PbSO_4$, lead(II) sulphate.

This shows us that the lower oxidation state becomes more stable as the Group is descended. The reason for this is that there is an increasing tendency for the two s electrons not to take part in the bonding as the atomic size increases. This is called the inert pair effect. The two p electrons only are lost to form a +2 ion and give the bonding characteristics of a metal.

## The inert pair effect

The inert pair effect arises because of variations in ionisation enthalpies, lattice enthalpies and covalent bond enthalpies. The bond energy of the $MX_2$ compounds become smaller down the Group and cannot compensate for the energy required to promote the Group IV element from the +2 to the +4 oxidation state.

No satisfactory simple way of explaining the inert pair effect is available, so in this book, as in many others, it is used as a useful description and not a full explanation.

This trend in oxidation states is also shown in the following standard electrode potential values.

$$Sn^{4+}(aq) + 2e^- \rightleftharpoons Sn^{2+}(aq); E^\ominus = +0.15\,V$$
$$Pb^{4+}(aq) + 2e^- \rightleftharpoons Pb^{2+}(aq); E^\ominus = +1.69\,V$$

The $E^\ominus$ value for the reduction of lead(IV) is very positive, so it is a favourable reaction. Lead(IV) oxide is therefore a powerful oxidising agent. The $E^\ominus$ value for the reduction of tin(IV) is also positive.

Metals are generally good reducing agents, and the reducing powers of tin(II) and lead(II) can be seen from the following standard electrode potential values. Tin(II) is a good reducing agent.

$$Sn^{2+}(aq) + 2e^- \rightleftharpoons Sn(s); E^\ominus = -0.14\,V$$
$$Pb^{2+}(aq) + 2e^- \rightleftharpoons Pb(s); E^\ominus = -0.13\,V$$

Both values are negative, which means that both tin and lead can displace hydrogen from acids. This could lead you to believe that lead is unsuitable as a building material that would be exposed to rain, as rain is slightly acidic. However, an oxide coating forms on lead. As this coating is insoluble it protects the lead from reacting with rain-water.

### SAQ 11.7

Can lead displace tin from aqueous tin(II) chloride?

What are the consequences of the different stabilities of the two oxidation states? The following equations give some examples. They show that, at the top of the Group, a compound with oxidation state +2 can be a good reducing agent because it will tend to gain electrons and become oxidised to +4. At the bottom of the Group a compound with oxidation state +4 will be a good oxidising agent because it will tend to lose electrons and be reduced to +2.

- CO is a powerful reducing agent

$$CO(g) + \tfrac{1}{2}O_2(g) \rightarrow CO_2(g)$$
$$3CO(g) + Fe_2O_3(s) \rightarrow 2Fe(s) + 3CO_2(g)$$

- $PbO_2$ is a powerful oxidising agent
$$PbO_2(s) + 4HCl(aq) \rightarrow PbCl_2(aq) + 2H_2O(l) + Cl_2(g)$$

Another consequence of the different stabilities of the two oxidation states is that $PbCl_4$ is thermally unstable, giving $PbCl_2$, the compound with the more stable oxidation state.

$$PbCl_4(l) \rightarrow PbCl_2(s) + Cl_2(g)$$

# Some uses of Group IV elements and compounds

Carbon is found in all living things because of its ability to catenate, or form long chains of carbon atoms. This is the basis of organic chemistry. Carbon in the form of diamond is used in jewellery but also in industry because diamond is so hard – for example, diamonds form the tips of bits used for drilling oil. Diamonds for industrial use are made artificially by heating graphite at high pressures and temperatures.

Carbon fibres are a form of graphite used to strengthen polymers in lightweight turbine blades, in racing car brakes and the hulls of speed boats. Graphite is also used as an industrial lubricant, and as a 'moderator' for slowing down neutrons in nuclear reactors.

In 1990 scientists learned how to prepare multi-gram samples of $C_{60}$ and related compounds with enclosed metal atoms, called fullerenes. This led to the manufacture of a number of new materials such as fullerene films, which have exceptional lubricating properties.

Graphite can be rolled into tubes only a few nanometres in diameter – these are called 'nanotubes'. Nanotube technology is a fast-growing area, as nanotubes can be used to make threads and cables of extreme strength, called nanofibres. The University of Illinois is famous for filling nanotubes with buckyballs, forming a 'nano-peapod'. There are also nanohorns, which are cone-shaped and have remarkable adsorptive and catalytic properties, and may be used in a

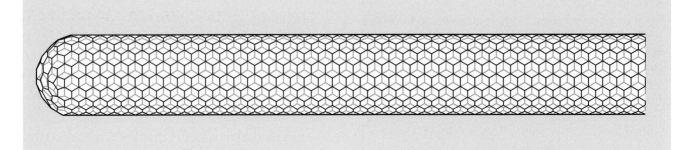

**Figure 11.7** A nanotube.

new generation of fuel cells. Lastly, there are nano-test-tubes, which are nanotubes filled with different materials, such as biological molecules. *Figure 11.7* shows one of these structures.

Silicon is unique because huge quantities of it are refined to a higher purity than any other substance ever has been. Some people say that the defining technical wonder of this age is that we can make large quantities of super-pure silicon, and then slice it into wafers and etch it into micro-circuits. Certainly our lives would be very different without computer technology.

Germanium is a lot like silicon, as it is a semiconductor used to build complex electronic circuits. It is much more expensive than silicon and not as widely used. Germanium is opaque to visible light, but can transmit X-rays and infrared light. It is therefore used as an X-ray lens to focus X-rays, and in heat-sensing cameras where it blocks the visible light and only allows infrared light through.

Tin is a perfect metal for casting because it melts at a fairly low temperature so simple moulds can be used – even moulds made of rubber. It is non-toxic (unlike lead) and does not tarnish.

Lead is used as a screen against radiation in hospitals and in industry, and for the storage of radioactive isotopes, because X-rays and gamma-rays cannot pass through it. Lead is also a useful roofing material.

Lead has been known since ancient times – its Latin name *plumbum* gave water supply workers their name 'plumber'. Lead pipes for carrying water from the Roman empire can still be used today. However, we now know that lead is a cumulative poison that collects in the brain and impairs its function, so lead levels in water and air are kept as low as possible – very few vehicles now use leaded petrol. There is a theory that the Roman Empire fell into decline because the acidic wine the Romans drank dissolved lead as lead acetate, which poisoned them!

## Ceramics based on silicon(IV) oxide, $SiO_2$

A ceramic is a non-metallic, non-polymeric solid that has been hardened by heating to high temperatures. There are many types of ceramics. Silicates are ceramics based on silica, $SiO_2$, and they are useful because they:
- are good electrical insulators
- are good thermal insulators
- have great rigidity
- are hard.

Some uses for silicate ceramics (see chapter 4) are:
- furnace linings
- power line insulators
- parts of turbines
- glasses for solar panels.

The silicate building unit is the orthosilicate group, $SiO_4^{4-}$. This consists of a central Si atom with 4 O atoms arranged tetrahedrally around it (*figure 11.8*). The $SiO_4$ tetrahedra are linked by

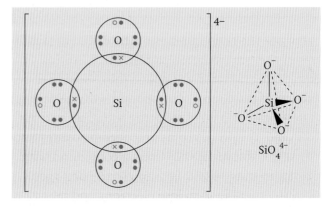

● **Figure 11.8** The orthosilicate group.

### Silicones

Silicones have properties of both plastics and minerals. The simplest silicones are built up of units of $(CH_3)_2Si(OH)_2$ in long chains; the length of the chain is controlled by a chain terminating unit. The organic groups give silicones flexibility and low intermolecular forces between chains, while the O–Si–O backbone gives them thermal stability and non-flammability. These compounds are unreactive, and that means they have many uses, including anti-foam agents in cooking oil for chips, in theatre make-up, contact lenses, plastic surgery and reconstructive surgery.

sharing oxygen atoms. A sample of pure quartz, which contains $SiO_4$ tetrahedra joined in a three-dimensional network, has the overall formula of $SiO_2$.

Several well-known minerals such as beryl and zircon contain $SiO_4{}^{4-}$ ions. In silicates the –Si–O– group repeats itself endlessly (*figure 11.9*), much like the –C–C– group in organic polymer chains. Silicates are the most important minerals on the planet because they are the dominant form of matter in the non-living world.

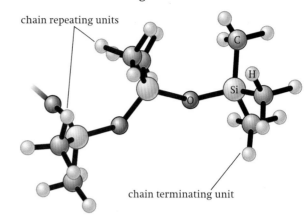

chain repeating units

chain terminating unit

● **Figure 11.9** Silicone chain.

# SUMMARY (A2)

◆ The Group IV elements differ considerably from one another. The most striking difference is the change in character from non-metals at the top of the Group to metals at the bottom.

◆ All the elements, except carbon, can expand their octet of outer-shell electrons and form complex ions with more than eight electrons in the outer shell.

◆ The melting points of the elements decrease and the electrical conductivities increase as the Group is descended. These trends are linked to the structure and bonding of the elements.

◆ The tetrachlorides are volatile liquids. The molecules have a regular tetrahedral shape.

◆ All the tetrachlorides, except carbon tetrachloride, are readily hydrolysed. This mechanism involves expansion of the octet of outer-shell electrons.

◆ As the Group is descended, the +2 oxidation state becomes more stable than the +4 oxidation state. This may be explained by the inert-pair effect.

◆ The dioxides go from acidic to amphoteric on descending the Group. The monoxides go from neutral to amphoteric.

◆ Graphite is the basis of nanotube technology. Silicon and germanium are semiconductors with multiple uses in computer technology.

# Questions (A2)

**1** The melting points of lead(II) chloride and lead(IV) chloride are 327 °C, 498 °C and −15 °C respectively. Explain the differences in the melting points of these substances in terms of the bonding in each of them.

**2** The boiling points of Group IV tetrachlorides are given in the table.

| | $CCl_4$ | $SiCl_4$ | $GeCl_4$ | $SnCl_4$ | $PbCl_4$ |
|---|---|---|---|---|---|
| Boiling point (°C) | 77 | 58 | 84 | 114 | – |

**a** (i) Comment on, and explain as far as you are able, the trend in the boiling points of these compounds on descending the Group.

(ii) Explain, with the aid of an equation, why there is no value for the boiling point of lead(IV) chloride.

**b** The melting points and boiling points of the dichlorides of tin and lead are given below.

| | $SnCl_2$ | $PbCl_2$ |
|---|---|---|
| Melting point (°C) | 246 | 498 |
| Boiling point (°C) | 652 | 950 |

Explain the difference in bonding between the dichlorides and tetrachlorides, using the data in this question to support your answer.

*UCLES, 1994*

**3 a** Compare and contrast the properties of the Group IV chlorides by copying and completing the table below.

| | $CCl_4$ | $SiCl_4$ | $PbCl_2$ |
|---|---|---|---|
| Physical state at room temperature | | | |
| Electrical conductivity when liquid | | | |
| Effect of adding water at room temperature | | | |
| Type of bonding | | | |

**b** (i) Write an equation for **one** of the Group IV oxides reacting with a base.

(ii) Write an equation for **one** of the Group IV oxides reacting with an acid.

*UCLES, 1994*

# CHAPTER 12

# Group VII (AS)

## By the end of this chapter you should be able to:

1 explain the trend in the volatilities of chlorine, bromine and iodine in terms of van der Waals' forces;

2 describe the relative reactivity of the elements $Cl_2$, $Br_2$ and $I_2$ in displacement reactions and explain this trend in terms of oxidising power, i.e. the relative ease with which an electron can be captured;

3 describe and explain the reactions of the elements with hydrogen;

4 describe and explain the relative thermal stabilities of the hydrides and interpret these in terms of bond enthalpies;

5 describe the characteristic reactions of the ions $Cl^-$, $Br^-$ and $I^-$ with aqueous silver ions followed by aqueous ammonia;

6 describe and explain the reactions of halide ions with concentrated sulphuric acid;

7 describe and interpret, in terms of changes in oxidation state, the reactions of chlorine with cold, dilute aqueous sodium hydroxide to form bleach and with hot aqueous sodium hydroxide;

8 explain the use of chlorine in water purification;

9 recognise the industrial importance and environmental significance of the halogens and their compounds.

## Introduction

The elements of Group VII are called the **halogens**:

| | | |
|---|---|---|
| fluorine | F | $[He]2s^2\,2p^5$ |
| chlorine | Cl | $[Ne]3s^2\,3p^5$ |
| bromine | Br | $[Ar]3d^{10}\,4s^2\,4p^5$ |
| iodine | I | $[Kr]4d^{10}\,5s^2\,5p^5$ |
| astatine | At | $[Xe]4f^{14}\,5d^{10}\,6s^2\,6p^5$ |

All the isotopes of astatine are radioactive and so this element will not be considered here. Also, we shall not include fluorine in *all* the discussions on Group VII, because its small size and high electronegativity give it some anomalous properties.

The name 'halogen' is derived from the Greek and means 'salt producing'. It was first used at the beginning of the nineteenth century because chlorine, bromine and iodine are all found in the sea as salts. Nowadays we still use the term, because the halogens are very reactive and readily react with metals to form salts.

The halogens are a family of non-metallic elements with some very similar chemical properties, although there are also clear differences between each element. Their reactivity decreases going down the Group. Their chemical characteristics are caused by the outermost seven electrons – two electrons in the s subshell and five electrons in the p subshell. Therefore only one more electron is needed to complete the outer shell of electrons. As a result the most common oxidation state for the halogens is −1, although other oxidation states do exist, especially for chlorine, which exhibits a range of oxidation states from −1 to +7. In compounds a halogen atom increases its share of electrons from seven to

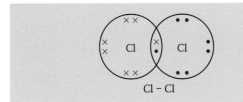

● **Figure 12.1** A dot-and-cross diagram of the covalent bonding in chlorine gas, $Cl_2(g)$.

eight (a full outer shell) by either (a) gaining an electron to form a halide ($Cl^-$, $Br^-$, $I^-$) in ionic compounds, or (b) sharing an electron from another atom in a covalent compound.

The halogen elements form covalent diatomic molecules. The atoms are joined by a single covalent bond (*figure 12.1*).

Fluorine, chlorine and bromine are poisonous. Their melting and boiling points increase with increasing atomic number: fluorine and chlorine are gases at room temperature; bromine is a liquid; and iodine is a solid. This decrease in volatility is the result of increasingly strong van der Waals' forces as the number of electrons present in a molecule increases. Halogens form diatomic non-polar molecules, so only instantaneous dipole–induced dipole attractions (see page 42) are present between molecules.

The colour of the elements deepens with increasing atomic number: fluorine is a pale yellow gas; chlorine is a greenish yellow gas; bromine is a dark red liquid giving off a dense red vapour; iodine is a shiny, grey-black crystalline solid which sublimes (changes directly from a solid to a gas) to a purple vapour.

The halogens are all oxidising agents, and fluorine is the strongest. The oxidising ability is reflected by the reactivity – fluorine is the most reactive halogen. It is also reflected by the electronegativities – fluorine is the most electronegative element, chlorine the third. Look at *table 12.1* for a summary of the physical properties.

### SAQ 12.1

What is the oxidation number of chlorine in $Cl_2$, $CaCl_2$, $Cl_2O_7$ and $ClO_2$?

# General properties of the Group VII elements

The general properties of the Group VII elements chlorine, bromine and iodine are as follows:

■ They behave chemically in a similar way.
■ They are non-metals.
■ They all exist as diatomic molecules at room temperature.
■ Their melting and boiling points increase with increasing atomic number.
■ The colour of the elements deepens with increasing atomic number.
■ They are very reactive and readily form salts.
■ In compounds a halogen atom increases its share of electrons from seven to eight by ionic or covalent bonding.
■ The reactivity of the elements decreases on descending the Group.
■ They exhibit a range of oxidation states.
■ The electronegativity of the elements decreases on descending the Group.
■ Their oxidising ability decreases on descending the Group.

### SAQ 12.2

Draw dot-and-cross diagrams of NaCl, showing the ionic bond; and of HCl, showing the covalent bond.

Note for A2 students:
The relative reactivity of the halogens as oxidising agents can be deduced from values of standard electrode potentials, $E^\ominus$ – see chapter 6, page 107.

|  | F | Cl | Br | I |
|---|---|---|---|---|
| Atomic radius (nm) | 0.071 | 0.099 | 0.114 | 0.133 |
| Ionic radius (nm) | 0.133 | 0.180 | 0.195 | 0.215 |
| Electronegativity | 4.0 | 3.0 | 2.8 | 2.5 |
| Electron affinity (kJ mol$^{-1}$) | −328 | −349 | −325 | −295 |
| Melting point (°C) | −220 | −101 | −7 | 114 |
| Boiling point (°C) | −188 | −35 | 59 | 184 |

● **Table 12.1** Physical properties of Group VII elements.
(The electron affinity is the enthalpy change for the process $X(g) + e^- \rightarrow X^-(g)$, where X is the halogen.)

# The reactivity of the halogens: displacement reactions

The electron affinity of the halogens is shown in *table 12.1*. The more negative the electron affinity, the greater the ease with which a halogen can capture an electron and the greater the oxidising power of the halogen. Electron affinity becomes less negative from chlorine to iodine so oxidising power of the elements decreases down Group VII.

In most of their oxidising reactions the halogens react as $X_2$ molecules (X represents a halogen) and form hydrated halide ions, $X^-(aq)$. As the oxidising ability decreases from chlorine to iodine, any halogen can displace another lower in the Group. This means that, if each halogen is reacted with a halide ion in aqueous solution, a series of **displacement reactions** occurs.

- Chlorine displaces bromine and iodine:
  $$Cl_2(aq) + 2Br^-(aq) \rightarrow 2Cl^-(aq) + Br_2(aq)$$
  $$Cl_2(aq) + 2I^-(aq) \rightarrow 2Cl^-(aq) + I_2(aq)$$
- Bromine displaces iodine:
  $$Br_2(aq) + 2I^-(aq) \rightarrow 2Br^-(aq) + I_2(aq)$$
- Iodine does not displace either chlorine or bromine.

One of the problems with doing these displacement reactions is being able to see if a reaction has taken place – the halide ion solutions are all colourless and very dilute solutions of the halogens can also appear colourless. To avoid this problem, an organic solvent such as cyclohexane is added to the mixture, which forms a separate layer. The halogens are more soluble in organic solvents than in aqueous solution, so they are taken up by the cyclohexane and the colour is much more apparent (*figure 12.2*). For instance, bromine is a strong orange-yellow colour in cyclohexane, and iodine is purple. So if aqueous bromine is mixed with cyclohexane, the bromine dissolves in the cyclohexane,

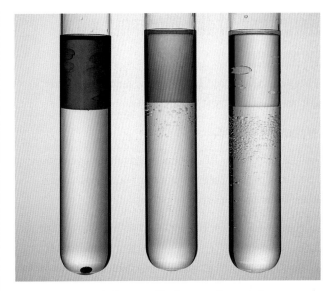

● **Figure 12.2** Colours of halogens in cyclohexane (upper layer) and water (lower layer).

which turns orange. Then if aqueous potassium iodide is added, the cyclohexane turns purple, which shows us that bromine has become bromide ion and displaced iodine from solution (*table 12.2*).

## SAQ 12.3
From your knowledge of the structure and bonding of the halogens, explain why they are more soluble in organic solvents than in aqueous solution.

## SAQ 12.4
Bromine water (aqueous bromine, $Br_2$) was shaken with a small volume of cyclohexane, and then the following aqueous solutions were added to separate portions:
a  aqueous sodium iodide,
b  aqueous chlorine,
c  aqueous sodium astatide, NaAt.
Each mixture was shaken again. Describe what you would expect to see. Write equations for any reactions that would occur.

| | Halide ion | | |
|---|---|---|---|
| **Halogen** | **Chloride, $Cl^-$** | **Bromide, $Br^-$** | **Iodide, $I^-$** |
| Chlorine, $Cl_2$ | | orange-yellow bromine released | purple iodine released |
| Bromine, $Br_2$ | no reaction | | purple iodine released |
| Iodine, $I_2$ | no reaction | no reaction | |

● **Table 12.2** Displacement reactions of halogens in aqueous solution (the colours refer to the colours of the halogens in cyclohexane, see *figure 12.2*).

# Reactions of the elements with hydrogen

The halogens react with hydrogen to give the corresponding hydrogen halide:

$$H_2 + X_2 \rightarrow 2HX$$

As the reactivity of the halogens decreases down the Group, the ease of reaction with hydrogen also decreases down the Group.

$H_2(g) + Cl_2(g) \rightarrow 2HCl(g)$    explosive when exposed to ultraviolet light

$H_2(g) + Br_2(l) \rightarrow 2HBr(g)$    reaction occurs slowly on heating

$H_2(g) + I_2(s) \rightarrow 2HI(g)$    incomplete reaction on heating

This trend is clearly shown in the values of the standard enthalpy changes of formation of the hydrogen halide, $\Delta H_f^{\ominus}$, given in *table 12.3*.

The hydrogen halides formed are all simple molecular compounds which are gaseous at room temperature. As the size of the halogen atom increases down the Group, the H–X bond length also increases. Consequently, the H–X bond enthalpy decreases down the Group, as shown in *table 12.3*.

The decrease in bond enthalpies means that the stabilities of the hydrogen halides decrease down the Group:

- hydrogen chloride is stable at 1500 °C;
- hydrogen bromide decomposes appreciably at 800 °C;
- hydrogen iodide decomposes appreciably at 500 °C – if a red hot glass rod is placed in a gas jar containing hydrogen iodide, purple fumes of iodine are seen.

Hydrogen iodide is thus the least stable of these three hydrogen halides and can act as a strong reducing agent.

|  | HCl | HBr | HI |
|---|---|---|---|
| $\Delta H_f^{\ominus}$ (kJ mol$^{-1}$) | −92 | −36 | +26 |
| bond enthalpy (kJ mol$^{-1}$) | +431 | +366 | +299 |

● **Table 12.3** Standard heats of formation and bond enthalpy values for hydrogen halides.

# Which halide?

Halides (ions of Group VII elements) are extremely common, so a test to identify which halide is present is very useful. This test is based on the colour of silver halides and the different solubilities of the silver halides in ammonia solution.

- Acidify the unknown halide solution with dilute nitric acid.
- Add aqueous silver nitrate
  caution: silver nitrate is poisonous
  - a white precipitate of silver chloride forms if $Cl^-(aq)$ is present
  - a cream precipitate of silver bromide forms if $Br^-(aq)$ is present
  - a yellow precipitate of silver iodide forms if $I^-(aq)$ is present.
- Identification by colour is not completely reliable, so aqueous ammonia is added:
  - white silver chloride dissolves in dilute aqueous ammonia forming a colourless solution;
  - cream silver bromide dissolves in concentrated aqueous ammonia forming a colourless solution;
  - yellow silver iodide does not dissolve in concentrated aqueous ammonia.

When the precipitate of silver chloride or silver bromide dissolves, the silver ion forms a complex ion (see chapter 13, pages 251–2).

$$AgCl(s) + 2NH_3(aq) \rightleftharpoons [Ag(NH_3)_2]^+(aq) + Cl^-(aq)$$

The colours of the silver halide precipitates are shown in *figure 12.3*.

The equation for the precipitation of silver chloride is:

$$Ag^+(aq) + Cl^-(aq) \rightarrow AgCl(s)$$

● **Figure 12.3** Colours of silver halide precipitates.

Another test which can be used to distinguish between halides is their reaction with concentrated sulphuric acid – <u>caution</u>: concentrated sulphuric acid is corrosive.

Halide ions react with concentrated sulphuric acid to produce the corresponding hydrogen halide.

$$NaX(s) + H_2SO_4(l) \rightarrow NaHSO_4(s) + HX(g)$$

For example, white fumes of hydrogen chloride are formed when concentrated sulphuric acid is added to sodium chloride.

$$NaCl(s) + H_2SO_4(l) \rightarrow NaHSO_4(s) + HCl(g)$$

However, concentrated sulphuric acid is an oxidising agent and can oxidise hydrogen bromide to bromine and hydrogen iodide to iodine. Therefore, when concentrated sulphuric acid is added to sodium bromide or sodium iodide, the characteristic colours of bromine or iodine can be seen.

With sodium bromide, the sulphuric acid is reduced to sulphur dioxide.

$$NaBr(s) + H_2SO_4(l) \rightarrow NaHSO_4(s) + HBr(g)$$
$$2HBr(g) + H_2SO_4(l) \rightarrow 2H_2O(l) + Br_2(g) + SO_2(g)$$
$$\text{orange vapour}$$

When sodium iodide is reacted with concentrated sulphuric acid, the hydrogen iodide produced reduces the sulphuric acid to sulphur dioxide, sulphur and hydrogen sulphide.

$$NaI(s) + H_2SO_4(l) \rightarrow NaHSO_4(s) + HI(g)$$
$$2HI(g) + H_2SO_4(l) \rightarrow 2H_2O(l) + I_2(g) + SO_2(g)$$
$$6HI(g) + H_2SO_4(l) \rightarrow 4H_2O(l) + 3I_2(g) + S(s)$$
$$8HI(g) + H_2SO_4(l) \rightarrow 4H_2O(l) + 4I_2(g) + H_2S(g)$$

The reaction is exothermic and some purple iodine vapour will be seen in the test-tube and the foul smell of hydrogen sulphide detected.

From these reactions we can see that:
■ hydrogen chloride is not oxidised by concentrated sulphuric acid;
■ hydrogen bromide is oxidised by concentrated sulphuric acid, reducing it to sulphur dioxide;
■ hydrogen iodide is a stronger reducing agent than hydrogen bromide and reduces concentrated sulphuric acid to hydrogen sulphide.

# Disproportionation reactions of chlorine

## The reactions of chlorine with sodium hydroxide

The way in which chlorine reacts with aqueous sodium hydroxide depends on the temperature.

With *cold* (15 °C) dilute aqueous sodium hydroxide a mixture of halide ($Cl^-$) and halate(I) ($ClO^-$) ions is formed:

$$Cl_2(g) + 2NaOH(aq)$$
$$\rightarrow NaCl(aq) + NaClO(aq) + H_2O(l)$$

This is an interesting reaction because it demonstrates **disproportionation** – a particular type of redox reaction in which one species is oxidised and reduced at the same time. This happens to the chlorine – the ionic equation shows that the oxidation state of chlorine in the products of the reaction are both lower and higher than chlorine itself:

$$Cl_2 + 2OH^- \rightarrow Cl^- + ClO^- + H_2O$$
oxidation state of Cl   0        −1    +1
reduction
oxidation

This reaction is used commercially to produce bleach, which is known as HClO, chloric(I) acid or hypochlorous acid. You can see this name on some bleach products. Household bleach is an aqueous solution of sodium chloride and sodium chlorate(I), NaClO, in a one-to-one mole ratio.

■ With hot concentrated aqueous sodium hydroxide another disproportionation reaction occurs and a mixture of chloride ($Cl^-$) and chlorate(V) ($ClO_3^-$) ions is formed.

$$3Cl_2(g) + 6NaOH(aq)$$
$$\rightarrow 5NaCl(aq) + NaClO_3(aq) + 3H_2O(l)$$

The sodium chlorate(V) produced is used as a weed killer.

## The purification of drinking water

When chlorine is used to purify drinking water, disproportionation again occurs to form hydrochloric acid and chloric(I) acid:

$$Cl_2 + H_2O \rightarrow HCl + HClO$$
oxidation state of Cl        0           −1    +1

The bacteria in water are killed by reactive oxygen atoms which are produced by a slow decomposition of the chloric(I) acid:

$$HClO \rightarrow HCl + O$$

# Uses

The oxidising ability of the halogens means that they are useful in many ways. Chlorine and its aqueous solution, known as chlorine water, are often used as oxidising agents (chlorine water contains chlorine and chloric(I) acid, HClO). Chlorine is also used in industry as a bleach; it oxidises large organic molecules to colourless compounds. In recent years controversy has arisen over the use of chlorine for bleaching paper – although very white paper pulp can be produced, the process results in the formation of dioxins, which are poisonous and can accumulate in living organisms, as dioxins do not break down easily. Nowadays ozone is often used to bleach paper that does not have to be pure white, such as tissues, nappies and toilet paper.

The strong oxidising ability of chlorine is also used by the water industry to treat drinking water. Chlorine is added to water from reservoirs to kill any bacteria, and small amounts of chlorine remain in the water piped to consumers to prevent bacterial contamination. Chlorine is also used to keep water in swimming pools free from contamination.

Fluorine is rarely used as an oxidising reagent as it is difficult to handle.

*Chlorine* is used in vast quantities for many different processes – twenty-nine million tonnes of chlorine are used worldwide annually. Its main uses are in water purification, as a bleach and in the manufacture of various chemicals such as chloroethene, which is used to make PVC.

One of the classes of organic chemicals made using chlorine is CFCs (*chlorofluorocarbons*). CFCs have been used as aerosol propellants, refrigerants and as foaming agents in polymers. They are currently being withdrawn from many applications because they are pollutants which contribute to the destruction of the ozone layer. However, they are useful in at least two ways – they are used in fire extinguishers because they are inert and non-

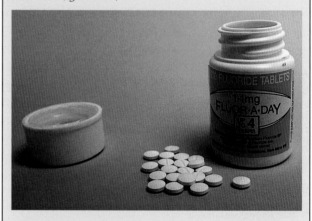
flammable, and they are vital constituents of artificial blood.

Solvents containing chlorine, such as *di-chloromethane*, $CH_2Cl_2$, are widely used to dissolve fats and oils.

*Chlorine* is a good germicide, and is used to kill bacteria in drinking water and swimming pools. Some environmental campaigners are trying to have chlorine banned due to worries over traces of organo-chlorine compounds in water. The danger of this was demonstrated when Peru banned its use in drinking water in 1993. Over a million Peruvians contracted cholera, with 10 000 deaths.

Chlorine and some of its compounds are used as domestic and commercial bleaches. In the First World War chlorine and mustard gas ($ClCH_2CH_2SCH_2CH_2Cl$) were used with devastating effect as poison gases. Chlorine is produced by the electrolysis of brine (see pages 30–1).

*Fluorine* is used, like chlorine, in CFCs. It is also used to make PTFE (polytetrafluoroethene), which is used as a lubricant, as a coating for non-stick cooking pans, as electrical insulation and in waterproof clothing.

*Fluoride* ions help to prevent tooth decay. Some children are given fluoride tablets (*box 12A*); many toothpastes contain tin fluoride ($SnF_2$); and some water supplies are fluoridated with sodium fluoride.

*Hydrofluoric acid* (HF) is used to etch glass.

*Bromochlorodifluoromethane* ($CClBrF_2$) is used in fire extinguishers.

*Silver bromide* is used in photographic film.

*Iodine* is an essential part of our diet, and an imbalance can cause thyroid problems.

A solution of *iodine in alcohol* is sometimes used as an antiseptic.

# SUMMARY (AS)

- The halogens chlorine, bromine and iodine are covalent diatomic molecules at room temperature. They become increasingly less volatile and more deeply coloured on descending Group VII. The volatility decreases as van der Waals' forces increase.

- The halogens have many characteristics in common. They are all reactive, and this reactivity decreases on descending the Group.

- All the halogens are good oxidising agents. Chlorine is the strongest oxidising agent of the three halogens studied.

- The order of reactivity can be determined by displacement reactions. A halogen can displace another which has a less negative electron affinity.

- The hydrogen halides can be formed by reacting the halogen with hydrogen. The ease of reaction and the stability of the hydride decrease down the Group.

- The identification of a halide ion in solution is made after adding silver nitrate solution and then aqueous ammonia.

- All halides react with concentrated sulphuric acid. The hydrogen halide is formed at first but hydrogen bromide and hydrogen iodide are oxidised to bromine and iodine respectively.

- Chlorine reacts with cold hydroxide ions in a disproportionation reaction. This reaction produces commercial bleach.

- Chlorine reacts with hot concentrated hydroxide ions in another disproportionation reaction, forming sodium chlorate(v) and sodium chloride.

- The halogens all have important industrial uses, especially chlorine, which is used in the manufacture of many other useful products. Possibly the most important use of chlorine is in the prevention of disease by chlorination of water supplies.

# Questions (AS)

1 Sodium chlorate(I), found in bleach, decomposes slowly, releasing oxygen, $O_2(g)$.
   a Write the equation for this decomposition.
   b Identify which element has been oxidised and which has been reduced.

2 The relative reactivities of the halogens can be shown by displacement reactions.
   a Copy and complete the table below to show the products of the reaction of each halogen with halide ions. If the reagents do not react, write *no reaction*.
   b Write an equation for the reaction between chlorine and aqueous sodium astatide, NaAt.

| Reagents | Aqueous sodium chloride, NaCl(aq) | Aqueous sodium bromide, NaBr(aq) | Aqueous sodium iodide, NaI(aq) |
|---|---|---|---|
| Chlorine, $Cl_2$ | | | |
| Bromine, $Br_2$ | | | |
| Iodine, $I_2$ | | | |

● Table for Question 2a

3 The colours of silver halides and their reactions with aqueous ammonia may be used to identify aqueous halide ions. Describe tests which use this information to identify an unknown solution that contains either sodium chloride or sodium bromide or sodium iodide.

4 Chlorine is used in the manufacture of bleach, which is widely used as a disinfectant. Bleach is produced by passing chlorine gas up a tower, down which aqueous sodium hydroxide is flowing. The equation for the reaction which takes place in the tower is as follows:
$Cl_2(g) + 2NaOH(aq)$
$\rightarrow NaClO(aq) + NaCl(aq) + H_2O(l)$
Using oxidation states, identify the oxidation state changes which take place in this reaction. Identify which element is oxidised and which is reduced. Give your reasons.

# CHAPTER 13

# The transition elements (A2)

## By the end of this chapter you should be able to:

1 give a description of a *transition element*;

2 work out the *electronic configuration* of the first row transition element atoms and ions;

3 state that the atomic radii, ionic radii and first ionisation energies of the transition elements are relatively invariant;

4 contrast, qualitatively, the melting point, density, atomic radius, ionic radius, first ionisation energy and conductivity of the transition elements with those of calcium as a typical s-block element;

5 use iron and copper to explain the *variable oxidation states* of transition elements in compounds, the formation of coloured ions and why transition elements are good catalysts;

6 predict from a given electronic configuration the likely oxidation states of a transition element;

7 describe the reactions of aqueous $Fe^{2+}$, $Fe^{3+}$ and $Cu^{2+}$ with aqueous sodium hydroxide;

8 explain the terms *complex ion* and *ligand*;

9 predict the shape of a complex from its formula;

10 describe *ligand substitution* of $H_2O$ in $[Cu(H_2O)_6]^{2+}$ by the chloride ion and by ammonia;

11 describe ligand substitution of $H_2O$ in $[Fe(H_2O)_6]^{3+}$ by the thiocyanate ion;

12 explain qualitatively $CO/O_2$ ligand exchange in haemoglobin;

13 describe how you would determine the formula of a complex using *colorimetry*;

14 predict the colour of a complex from its *visible spectrum*;

15 construct *redox equations* involving transition metals or ions using half-equations;

16 describe *redox titrations* involving transition metal ions and perform calculations with data obtained from such titrations;

17 predict, using $E^{\ominus}$ values, the likelihood of redox reactions.

Transition elements are a popular area of experimental chemistry because their compounds are coloured, and so experiments involve blue, yellow, pink and green solutions (*figure 13.1*). This property means compounds of these elements are used in pigments for many applications such as traffic lane paints (*figure 13.2*), ceramic glazes and oil paints.

**Transition elements** are metals, and include the metals which most people recognise because they are used so frequently – gold and silver jewellery, copper wiring, chromium car bumpers, iron pipes (*figure 13.3*). Iron is also well known for the role of its ions in haemoglobin.

Other transition metals are not as well known but also have very important uses. Most light bulbs have tungsten filaments. Drill bits are made from tungsten carbide. A mixture of platinum, rhodium and palladium is used in catalytic converters on car exhausts. Zirconium is used in nuclear reactors.

Many transition elements are important in the diets of living organisms as trace elements – only needed in small quantities, but necessary for life. In humans, vanadium ions are needed in fat metabolism, chromium for glucose utilisation, manganese and copper for cell respiration as well as the iron we all know is necessary as part of the haemoglobin in blood. An interesting trace element is zinc, part of the enzyme alcohol dehydrogenase, which metabolises ethanol. People with low levels of zinc ions get drunk on very little alcohol because their bodies cannot metabolise the alcohol away.

● **Figure 13.2** Yellow road markings contain pigments made from the transition element chromium.

Transition metals are so important to mankind that most reserves will be used up within the next fifty years or so. This means that other sources of transition metals must be found, and one source which may be used is on the ocean floor. Here nodules have been found over large areas, some a few millimetres and some a few metres in diameter, containing mostly manganese and iron oxides but also many other transition metal oxides in smaller quantities. Altogether there are billions of tonnes of these nodules on the ocean floors, but there are two problems linked with using them. The first problem is the technical expertise required to mine from such an inhospitable place. The second problem is that, legally, the ocean floors are international property, so ownership of the nodules and the wealth associated with them must be carefully worked out.

Did you know that the d-block metal mercury, the only liquid metal at room temperature and

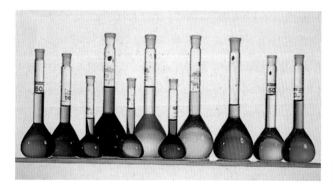

● **Figure 13.1** From left to right, the strongly coloured solutions of the following transition elements: $Ti^{3+}$, $V^{3+}$, $VO^{2+}$, $Cr^{3+}$, $Cr_2O_7^{2-}$, $Mn^{2+}$, $MnO_4^-$, $Fe^{3+}$, $Co^{2+}$, $Ni^{2+}$ and $Cu^{2+}$.

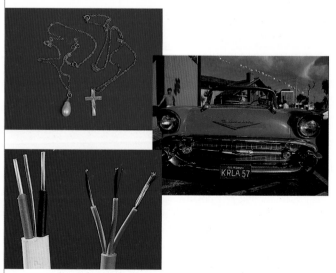

● **Figure 13.3** Transition elements have many uses.

pressure, is responsible for one of literature's most famous characters – the Mad Hatter in *Alice in Wonderland*? A hatter made hats from felt, and felt was made from animal hair by a process involving mercury compounds. These compounds are toxic, so people who made felt and inhaled the dust of the mercury compounds suffered personality disorders and shaking. This was called 'hatter's shakes', and gives us a rather sinister explanation of the zany personality of the Mad Hatter.

This chapter deals with the chemistry of the first row of the transition elements, which are found in the d-block of the Periodic Table, located between Groups II and III. There is a precise definition of a transition element:

> A transition element is an element that forms at least one ion with a partly filled d orbital.

The transition elements have certain common *physical properties*:

- they have high densities;
- they are metals with high melting points;
- they are hard and rigid, and so are useful as construction materials;
- they are good conductors of electricity.

They also have certain common *chemical properties*:

- they can show several different oxidation states in their compounds;
- they are good catalysts;
- they form coloured compounds;
- they form **complexes** with **ligands** (these terms may be new to you – they are explained on page 251).

The physical properties of the transition elements can all be explained by the strong metallic bonding that exists in these elements (see chapter 3). There are more electrons in the outer shell of atoms of transition elements than in the outer shell of Group I and Group II metals, so the delocalised sea of electrons typical of metallic bonding produces a strong force holding the positive ions together. The melting points of the transition elements are high because it takes a lot of energy to disrupt this strong metallic bonding. This bonding also explains the good electrical conductivity, as there are many mobile electrons present. The hardness of the transition elements is caused by the atoms being held firmly in place by the metallic bonding.

# Electronic structures

The electronic structures of the d-block elements dictate their chemistry, and so are extremely important.

> Remember the shorthand chemists have to show the full subshells in electronic configurations – they use the symbol of the noble gas with the full subshells in square brackets, like this: $[Ar]3d^0 4s^0$.

| | | |
|---|---|---|
| scandium | Sc | $[Ar]3d^1 4s^2$ |
| titanium | Ti | $[Ar]3d^2 4s^2$ |
| vanadium | V | $[Ar]3d^3 4s^2$ |
| chromium | Cr | $[Ar]3d^5 4s^1$ |
| manganese | Mn | $[Ar]3d^5 4s^2$ |
| iron | Fe | $[Ar]3d^6 4s^2$ |
| cobalt | Co | $[Ar]3d^7 4s^2$ |
| nickel | Ni | $[Ar]3d^8 4s^2$ |
| copper | Cu | $[Ar]3d^{10} 4s^1$ |
| zinc | Zn | $[Ar]3d^{10} 4s^2$ |

Where [Ar] is $1s^2 2s^2 2p^6 3s^2 3p^6$

If you look at these electronic configurations, you will see that the d subshell is being filled as we move from scandium to zinc, hence the term 'd-block' – scandium has one d electron, and zinc has ten, a full d subshell. The 4s level is filled before the 3d level but the two levels remain very close in energy. We see this closeness illustrated in chromium and copper. Chromium, instead of having a $[Ar]3d^4 4s^2$ structure, has $[Ar]3d^5 4s^1$; it has two half-filled subshells, which gives it greater stability. This exchange is made possible by the closeness of the two subshells. Similarly, copper has a full d subshell and a half-filled 4s shell: $[Ar]3d^{10} 4s^1$.

As the transition elements are metals they all form *positive* ions, so electrons are *lost* from a transition metal atom when an ion is formed. So the electronic configuration of $Fe^{2+}$ is two electrons less than the electronic configuration of Fe. These electrons are lost from the 4s orbital first, and then the 3d orbital, which means the electronic configuration of $Fe^{2+}$ is $1s^2\,2s^2\,2p^6\,3s^2\,3p^6\,3d^6$.

As you will see in the next section, transition metals can form several different ions, and iron can form $Fe^{3+}$ as well as $Fe^{2+}$. The electronic configuration of $Fe^{3+}$ is $1s^2\,2s^2\,2p^6\,3s^2\,3p^6\,3d^5$.

### SAQ 13.1

Write down the electronic configurations of
**a** Cr  **b** $Cr^{3+}$  **c** Cu  **d** $Cu^{2+}$  **e** Mn  **f** $Mn^{2+}$.

Take a look at the electronic configurations of the first element, scandium, and the last d-block element, zinc. For scandium the only observed oxidation state is +3, so the ion is $Sc^{3+}$, with the electronic configuration $1s^2\,2s^2\,2p^6\,3s^2\,3p^6$. This ion has no d electrons, so does not satisfy the definition of a transition element – scandium is a d-block element but is not a transition element. Now look at zinc. The only observed oxidation state is $Zn^{2+}$, with the electronic configuration $1s^2\,2s^2\,2p^6\,3s^2\,3p^6\,3d^{10}$. This ion has a completely filled, not a partially filled, d subshell – so zinc is not a transition element. This is the reason why the compounds of zinc and scandium are white, and not coloured like those of transition elements (see page 250).

## Properties of the elements

### Atomic and ionic radii

In chapter 9, periodic patterns of atomic radii were discussed. *Figures 9.9* and *9.10* (page 202) show the changes in atomic radii with atomic number. Across each period, there is an overall decrease in atomic radius. For the transition elements, however, there is very little change, although scandium and zinc do not readily fit into this pattern.

For ionic radii too, the changes from scandium to zinc are relatively small. Details are given in *table 13.1*. These ions are all smaller than the $Ca^{2+}$ ion, which has an ionic radius of 0.094 nm.

### Ionisation energies

Periodic patterns of first ionisation energies were discussed in chapter 9 – see *figures 9.15* and *9.16* (page 205).

Across each period, lithium to neon, sodium to argon, etc., there is a general increase in first

| Ion | Ionic radius (nm) |
| --- | --- |
| $Sc^{3+}$ | 0.081 |
| $Ti^{2+}$ | 0.090 |
| $V^{3+}$ | 0.074 |
| $Cr^{3+}$ | 0.069 |
| $Mn^{2+}$ | 0.080 |
| $Fe^{2+}$ | 0.076 |
| $Fe^{3+}$ | 0.064 |
| $Co^{2+}$ | 0.078 |
| $Ni^{2+}$ | 0.078 |
| $Cu^{2+}$ | 0.069 |
| $Zn^{2+}$ | 0.074 |

● **Table 13.1** Ionic radii of transition element cations.

ionisation energies. For transition elements, the first ionisation energy increases across the d-block, but much less than for complete periods.

The first ionisation energy of a transition element involves the removal of a 4s electron which is partly shielded from the nucleus by inner 3d electrons. Across the block, nuclear charge increases but the additional 3d electrons reduce its effect so that 4s electrons experience a relatively small extra attraction from scandium to zinc.

### Melting points

Compared to calcium and other s-block elements, the melting points of transition elements are high, suggesting that the metallic bonding in these elements is strong. This may be explained by both 3d and 4s electrons being delocalised in the metal lattice.

### Density

The transition elements have a close-packed structure and are much denser than s-block elements. The close packing and small atomic size make the metallic bonding stronger, resulting in high densities – see *table 13.2*.

### Conductivity

The transition elements all conduct electricity – see *figure 9.14* (page 204). With the notable exception of copper, they are all less good conductors than calcium.

| Element | Density ($g\,cm^{-3}$) |
|---|---|
| calcium | 1.55 |
| scandium | 2.99 |
| titanium | 4.50 |
| vanadium | 5.96 |
| chromium | 7.20 |
| manganese | 7.20 |
| iron | 7.86 |
| cobalt | 8.90 |
| nickel | 8.90 |
| copper | 8.92 |
| zinc | 7.14 |

● **Table 13.2** Densities of calcium and transition elements scandium to zinc.

# Variable oxidation states

Transition elements occur in multiple **oxidation states**. The most common oxidation state is +2, which occurs when the two 4s electrons are lost (for example $Fe^{2+}$ and $Cu^{2+}$). But because the 3d electrons are very close in energy to the 4s electrons they can quite easily be lost too, so one element can form several different ions by losing different numbers of electrons, and all the ions will be almost equally stable. This closeness in energy between the 3d and 4s electrons also explains why the transition elements have such similar properties to each other.

*Table 13.3* shows the main oxidation states of the first row of the d-block elements. The commonly

| Element | | Oxidation states | | | | |
|---|---|---|---|---|---|---|
| Sc | | +3 | | | | |
| Ti | | +2 | +3 | +4 | | |
| V | | +2 | +3 | +4 | +5 | |
| Cr | | +2 | +3 | +4 | +5 | +6 |
| Mn | | +2 | +3 | +4 | +5 | +6 | +7 |
| Fe | | +2 | +3 | +4 | +5 | +6 |
| Co | | +2 | +3 | +4 | +5 |
| Ni | | +2 | +3 | +4 |
| Cu | +1 | +2 | +3 |
| Zn | | +2 |

● **Table 13.3** Main oxidation states of the first row d-block elements.

occurring oxidation states are highlighted. It is worth noting that the highest oxidation state for the first five elements is the same as the total number of 4s and 3d electrons for the element; and for the second five elements, a common oxidation state is +2. It is important that you know the oxidation states of iron and copper in particular, and be able to give the electronic configurations of all their ions. *Box 13A* shows you how to determine oxidation numbers.

In transition element chemistry, the changes in oxidation state of the ions are often shown by changes in the colour of the solutions. For example, potassium dichromate(VI) is often used in titrations:

$$Cr_2O_7^{2-}(aq) + 14H^+(aq) + 6e^- \rightarrow 2Cr^{3+}(aq) + 7H_2O(l)$$

orange                 green

---

**Box 13A How to determine oxidation states**

- Oxidation states are usually calculated as the number of electrons that atoms have to lose, gain or share, when they form ionic or covalent bonds in compounds.
- The oxidation state of uncombined elements is always zero. For example, each atom in $H_2(g)$ or $O_2(g)$ or $Na(s)$ or $S_8(s)$ has an oxidation state of zero; otherwise, the states are always given a sign, + or −.
- For a monatomic ion, the oxidation state of the element is simply the same as the charge on the ion. For example:

  | ion | $Na^+$ | $Ca^{2+}$ | $Cl^-$ | $O^{2-}$ |
  |---|---|---|---|---|
  | ox. state | +1 | +2 | −1 | −2 |

- In a chemical species (compound or ion), with atoms of more than one element, the most electronegative element is given the negative oxidation state. Other elements are given positive oxidation states. For example, in the compound disulphur dichloride, $S_2Cl_2$, chlorine is more electronegative than sulphur. The two chlorine atoms each have an oxidation state of −1, and thus the two sulphur atoms each have the oxidation state of +1.
- The oxidation state of hydrogen in compounds is always +1, except in metal hydrides (e.g. NaH), when it is −1.
- The oxidation state of oxygen in compounds is always −2, except in peroxides (e.g. $H_2O_2$), when it is −1, or in $OF_2$, when it is +2.
- The sum of all the oxidation states in a neutral compound is zero. In an ion, the sum equals the overall charge. For example, the sum of the oxidation states in $CaCl_2$ is 0; the sum of the oxidation states in $OH^-$ is −1.

The lower oxidation states are usually found in ionic compounds. Typical cations in such compounds are $Cr^{3+}$, $Mn^{2+}$, $Fe^{2+}$, $Fe^{3+}$, $Cu^+$ and $Cu^{2+}$. Higher oxidation states occur in complex ions such as $CrO_4^{2-}$, $Cr_2O_7^{2-}$ and $MnO_4^-$.

### SAQ 13.2

What is the oxidation state of chromium in
**a** $Cr_2O_7^{2-}$ and **b** $Cr^{3+}$?

# Transition elements as catalysts

A catalyst is a substance that speeds up a chemical reaction, without itself being permanently changed in a chemical way (see chapter 8). Many transition elements are effective catalysts, and are used in reactions both in the laboratory and in industry.

In the laboratory, you may have seen the decomposition of hydrogen peroxide to water and oxygen:

$$2H_2O_2(l) \rightarrow 2H_2O(l) + O_2(g)$$

At room temperature this reaction is very slow. However, if manganese(IV) oxide is added it acts as a catalyst, and the reaction becomes very rapid.

In industry, one of the best-known reactions that depends on a catalyst is the Haber process, in which nitrogen and hydrogen react to give ammonia (see chapter 8).

$$N_2(g) + 3H_2(g) \rightleftharpoons 2NH_3(g)$$

The catalyst used in this reaction is finely divided *iron*.

Transition elements make efficient catalysts for two reasons.
■ They can have several different oxidation states, so they can easily transfer electrons. This provides an alternative route for a reaction in a way that lowers the activation energy and so speeds up the reaction.
■ They provide sites at which reactions can take place. Transition elements can bond to a wide range of ions and molecules, and can have different numbers of bonds, so the reacting molecules can be held in place while the reaction occurs (see chapter 8).

# Coloured compounds

Transition metal ions in aqueous solution are frequently coloured; some examples are

| | | | |
|---|---|---|---|
| $Fe^{2+}$ | green | $Co^{2+}$ | pink |
| $Fe^{3+}$ | yellow | $Ti^{3+}$ | purple |
| $Cu^{2+}$ | blue | $Cr^{3+}$ | violet |
| $Ni^{2+}$ | green | $Mn^{2+}$ | pink |

This colour is related to the presence of partly filled d orbitals; for this reason, an ion with a *full* d orbital will not be coloured. So compounds of zinc, where zinc is in the form $Zn^{2+}$ with an electronic configuration $1s^2\,2s^2\,2p^6\,3s^2\,3p^6\,3d^{10}$ are white. Similarly, compounds with an empty d orbital, such as $TiO_2$, are also white. Here the titanium has an oxidation state of +4 so its electronic configuration is $1s^2\,2s^2\,2p^6\,3s^2\,3p^6\,3d^0\,4s^0$.

## Visible spectroscopy of transition metal ions

Transition metal ions are coloured because they absorb radiation in the visible region of the electromagnetic spectrum. The spectrum produced shows us the colour of the transition metal ion. If you study the *Transition Elements* option you will study this phenomenom more closely.

Visible spectroscopy is also called absorption spectroscopy. *Figure 13.4* shows the absorption spectrum of the hydrated $Cu^{2+}$ ion in aqueous solution (it has the formula $[Cu(H_2O)_6]^{2+}$ as it is a complex, see next page). The solution is a blue colour. The spectrum shows us that incoming yellow and red light are absorbed. We see the

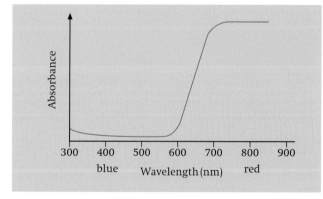

● **Figure 13.4** The visible spectrum of $[Cu(H_2O)_6]^{2+}(aq)$, showing that incoming yellow and red light are absorbed and other wavelengths are transmitted.

| Absorbed colour | λ (nm) | Observed colour | λ (nm) |
|---|---|---|---|
| violet | 400 | green-yellow | 560 |
| blue | 450 | yellow | 600 |
| blue-green | 490 | red | 620 |
| yellow-green | 570 | violet | 410 |
| yellow | 580 | dark blue | 430 |
| orange | 600 | blue | 450 |
| red | 650 | green | 520 |

● **Table 13.4** The relation between absorbed and observed colours.

colour that is transmitted, which is blue. *Table 13.4* provides information on wavelength, absorbed colour and observed colour.

### SAQ 13.3

*Figure 13.5* shows the visible spectrum of a transition metal ion in aqueous solution.

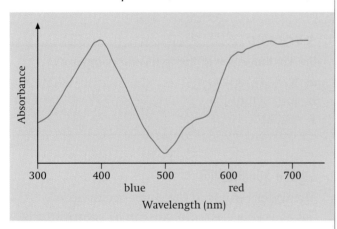

● **Figure 13.5**

**a** Make a copy of the spectrum, and write the colours of the visible spectrum underneath the appropriate wavelengths.
**b** Deduce the colour of the solution.
**c** Suggest the identity of the transition metal ion.

## Precipitating transition metal hydroxides

When aqueous sodium hydroxide is added to a solution of a transition metal ion, a precipitate of the transition metal hydroxide is formed. These precipitates resemble a jelly so are called

**gelatinous** and their colour can identify the transition metal ion.

$$Cu^{2+}(aq) + 2OH^-(aq) \rightarrow Cu(OH)_2(s) \quad \text{pale blue}$$
$$Fe^{2+}(aq) + 2OH^-(aq) \rightarrow Fe(OH)_2(s) \quad \text{green}$$
$$Fe^{3+}(aq) + 3OH^-(aq) \rightarrow Fe(OH)_3(s) \quad \text{rust}$$
$$Mn^{2+}(aq) + 2OH^-(aq) \rightarrow Mn(OH)_2(s) \quad \text{cream}$$
$$Cr^{3+}(aq) + 3OH^-(aq) \rightarrow Cr(OH)_3(s) \quad \text{grey-green}$$

Note that gelatinous precipitates can also be formed when ammonia solution is added to the aqueous transition element ion. This is because ammonia is a weak base that exists in equilibrium with the hydroxide ion in aqueous solution:

$$NH_3(aq) + H_2O(l) \rightleftharpoons NH_4^+(aq) + OH^-(aq)$$

This means that aqueous ammonia is a source of hydroxide ions. For example, aqueous ammonia added to $Mn^{2+}(aq)$ gives a cream precipitate of $Mn(OH)_2$.

### SAQ 13.4

Write equations to predict the reactions between aqueous sodium hydroxide and aqueous solutions of **a** $Ni^{2+}$ **b** $Ti^{3+}$.

## Complexes

Transition elements form complexes, or coordination compounds, with ligands. Ligands are electron-pair donors and they form *dative* or *coordinate* covalent bonds with a central transition element ion or atom. Ligands can be either anions or neutral molecules. *Figure 13.6* shows the complex formed between $Cu^{2+}$ ions and water ligands.

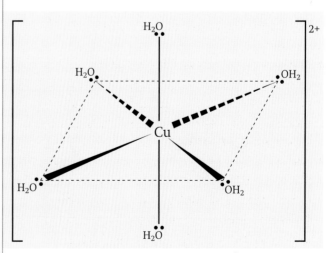

● **Figure 13.6** The shape of $[Cu(H_2O)_6]^{2+}(aq)$.

The formula of a complex is always written with the central transition element ion first, followed by the ligands (*table 13.5*), and with the overall charge of the ion at the end, for example $[Ni(CN)_4]^{2-}$ and $[Cr(H_2O)_4Cl_2]^+$. Note the use of square brackets. The overall charge on the complex is simply the individual charges of the transition element ion and the ligands added together. In these two examples, we know that the ligands must be $CN^-$, $Cl^-$ and $H_2O$, so we can work out that the transition element ions are $Ni^{2+}$ and $Cr^{3+}$.

### SAQ 13.5

State the formulae and charges of the complexes made from:

**a** one iron(III) ion and four chloride ions;

**b** one titanium(III) ion and six water molecules.

### Shapes of complexes

There are two main shapes adopted by transition element complexes – octahedral and tetrahedral (*figure 13.7*). These names show the shape of the outside 'surfaces' of the complex.

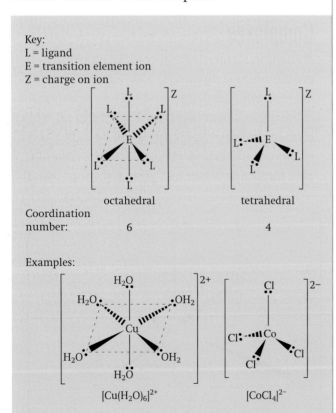

Key:
L = ligand
E = transition element ion
Z = charge on ion

| | |
|---|---|
| octahedral | tetrahedral |

Coordination number: 6 — 4

Examples:

$[Cu(H_2O)_6]^{2+}$  —  $[CoCl_4]^{2-}$

● **Figure 13.7** The shapes of transition element complexes.

| Type of ligand | Formula | Name |
|---|---|---|
| monodentate | $H_2O$ | water |
| | $NH_3$ | ammonia |
| | $Cl^-$ | chloride ion |
| | $CN^-$ | cyanide ion |
| | $SCN^-$ | thiocyanate ion |

● **Table 13.5** Some of the more common ligands.

- An octahedral complex has a *six* ligands surrounding the metal.
- A tetrahedral complex has *four* ligands surrounding the metal.

One of the best-known complexes is formed in a solution of copper(II) sulphate, $CuSO_4$. In aqueous solution the copper ion is not isolated, but forms a complex with six water molecules. The complex has an octahedral shape, as shown in *figures 13.6* and *13.7*. This complex is responsible for the blue colour associated with a copper sulphate solution.

### SAQ 13.6

Predict the shape of the following complexes:

**a** $[Co(NH_3)_5Cl]^{2+}$

**b** $[Cr(H_2O)_4Cl_2]^+$

**c** $[FeCl_4]^-$

### Ligand substitution

The water ligands in the copper complex of aqueous copper(II) sulphate can be substituted by other ligands to form a more stable complex. When concentrated hydrochloric acid is added drop by drop, the solution turns yellow as a new complex is formed – the water ligands are substituted by four chloride ion ligands to give $[CuCl_4]^{2-}$:

$$[Cu(H_2O)_6]^{2+}(aq) + 4Cl^-(aq) \rightarrow [CuCl_4]^{2-}(aq) + 6H_2O(l)$$

Sodium chloride can also be used as a source of chloride ions in this reaction.

The chloride ion ligands are similarly replaced by ammonia ligands when concentrated ammonia solution is added, producing a deep-blue solution:

$$[CuCl_4]^{2-}(aq) + 4NH_3(aq) + 2H_2O(l)$$
$$\rightarrow [Cu(NH_3)_4(H_2O)_2]^{2+}(aq) + 4Cl^-(aq)$$

Of course, if the ammonia solution is added dropwise and you watch the solution carefully, you will

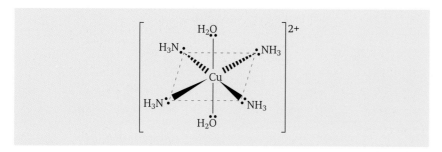

● **Figure 13.8** The structure of $[Cu(NH_3)_4(H_2O)_2]^{2+}$.

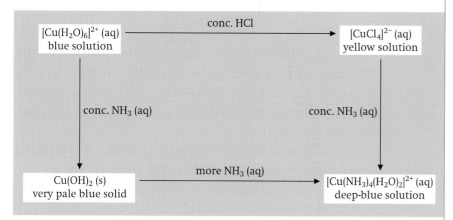

● **Figure 13.9** Ligand substitution reactions of various copper complexes.

| Complex | | |
|---|---|---|
| $[Cu(H_2O)_6]^{2+}$ | | |
| $[CuCl_4]^{2-}$ | | increasing |
| $[Cu(NH_3)_4(H_2O)_2]^{2+}$ | | stability |

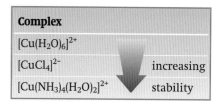

● **Table 13.6** The stability of copper complexes.

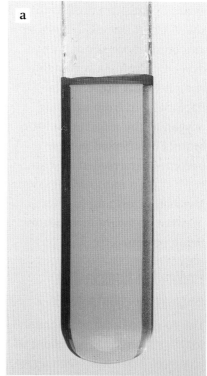

see a pale blue precipitate of $Cu(OH)_2$ appear first and then this will dissolve as the deep-blue complex between $Cu^{2+}$ and $NH_3$ is formed. *Figure 13.8* shows the structure of the octahedral complex.

*Figure 13.9* summarises this series of reactions. This sequence of ligand replacement means that we can list the complexes in order according to their stability (*table 13.6*).

Another striking colour change that can be seen when one ligand substitutes for another is the reaction of aqueous $Fe^{2+}$ ions with thiocyanate ions, $SCN^-$. Here one $H_2O$ ligand in each complex ion is replaced by an $SCN^-$ ligand, and the colour changes from yellow to deep blood-red (*figure 13.10*).

$[Fe(H_2O)_6]^{3+}(aq) + SCN^- (aq) \rightarrow [Fe(H_2O)_5SCN]^{2+}(aq) + H_2O(l)$
  yellow                          blood-red

## SAQ 13.7

The $[Ni(H_2O)_6]^{2+}$ ion is *green* in aqueous solution. Concentrated ammonia was added dropwise to this solution, which turned *dark blue*. Suggest an explanation for these observations.

## Carbon monoxide poisoning

Another complex which contains iron is haemoglobin. An adult human body contains about 3 g of iron in the form of haemoglobin, which is an extremely complicated molecule – see *figure 13.11*. The iron(II) ion in haemoglobin has a coordination number of 6. Five of

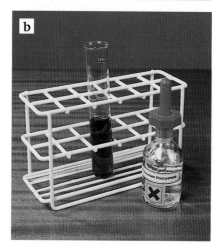

● **Figure 13.10**
**a** A yellow solution of $[Fe(H_2O)_6]^{3+}(aq)$.
**b** Addition of potassium thiocyanate turns the solution red. One $H_2O$ ligand is substituted by a $SCN^-$ ligand to form $[Fe(H_2O)_5SCN]^{2+}(aq)$.

the sites around the iron ion are occupied by nitrogen atoms, four in a ring system and the fifth from a protein molecule.

Oxygen molecules can be reversibly bonded to haemoglobin at the sixth site, allowing haemoglobin to carry oxygen to muscles where it is needed. Other ligands can bind to this site. Carbon monoxide does so and binds more strongly than oxygen, forming a very stable complex. This prevents the haemoglobin from carrying oxygen to the muscles and the brain. The affected person becomes paralysed at first and, since carbon monoxide is odourless, colourless and tasteless, may not be aware he or she is being poisoned.

## Finding the formula of a complex by colorimetry

The colour of a transition metal ion can change as the ligand is changed, as we have seen above. We can use this change in colour to find the ratio of ligand to metal in a complex, using a colorimeter. In a colorimeter a narrow beam of light passes through the solution under test towards a sensitive photocell (*figure 13.12*). The wavelength of this light can be selected by using an appropriate filter. The current generated in the photocell is proportional to the

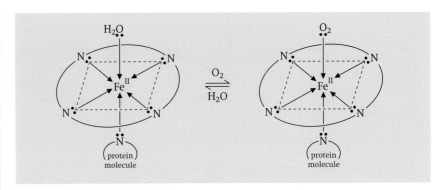

● **Figure 13.11** Haemoglobin (simplified).

amount of light transmitted by the solution, which depends on the colour of the solution. The colorimeter is usually calibrated to show the fraction of light absorbed by the solution – the most intensely coloured solution absorbs the most light, and the faintest coloured solution absorbs the least light.

Let's use an example to see how this method works. A solution of $Fe^{3+}$ ions, such as aqueous $FeCl_3$, is yellow. The complex ion is actually $[Fe(H_2O)_6]^{3+}$. When aqueous sodium thiocyanate, NaSCN, is added the complex turns blood-red as the thiocyanate ligands ($SCN^-$) displace the water ligands. How do we work out the formula of the $Fe^{3+}/SCN^-$ complex? Ten tubes are prepared which contain different amounts of $Fe^{3+}$ and $SCN^-$. The tube with the most intense colour, as read by the colorimeter, contains the maximum amount of ligand molecules to metal ions. *Table 13.7* contains details of one method you can follow. The principles of the method are always the same, although the volumes and concentrations of the metal ion and ligand solutions can change. What is extremely important is to use the *same volume of solution* in each tube.

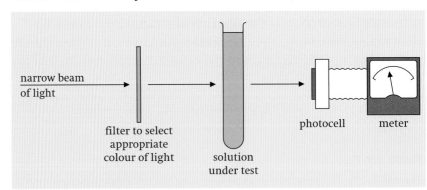

● **Figure 13.12** Using a colorimeter.

| Tube | 1 | 2 | 3 | 4 | 5 | 6 | 7 | 8 | 9 | 10 |
|---|---|---|---|---|---|---|---|---|---|---|
| vol. in $cm^3$ of $0.1\,mol\,dm^{-3}$ $Fe^{3+}$(aq) | 10 | 10 | 10 | 10 | 10 | 10 | 10 | 10 | 10 | 10 |
| vol. in $cm^3$ of $0.1\,mol\,dm^{-3}$ $SCN^-$(aq) | 2 | 4 | 6 | 8 | 10 | 12 | 14 | 16 | 18 | 20 |
| vol. in $cm^3$ of $H_2O$ added to make final volume $40\,cm^3$ | 28 | 26 | 24 | 22 | 20 | 18 | 16 | 14 | 12 | 10 |

● **Table 13.7** Mixtures of $Fe^{3+}$(aq), $SCN^-$(aq) and $H_2O$ for a colorimetry experiment.

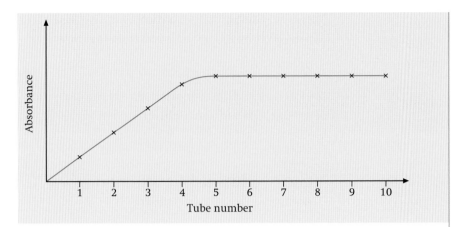

● **Figure 13.13** Experimental results.

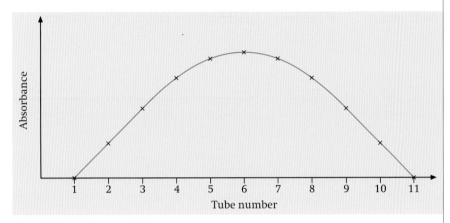

● **Figure 13.14** Colorimetry experiment results.

The $Fe^{3+}$ and $SCN^-$ solutions are measured as accurately as possible into the tubes. The final solution from each tube in turn is then placed in a test-tube or cuvette and placed in the colorimeter. The complex is red so it absorbs in the blue region of the spectrum, so a blue filter is used, showing that the complementary colour to the complex is used in the filter. The absorbance reading is taken. The results are shown in *figure 13.13*.

As you can see, the absorbance readings taken on the colorimeter go up as the red colour gets more intense, and finally the readings level out. The point where the horizontal line is reached shows the number of moles of $Fe^{3+}$ and $SCN^-$ which form the complex. In this case it is at tube 5. In this experiment, this solution contains $10 \, cm^3$ of $0.1 \, mol \, dm^{-3}$ $Fe^{3+}$ and $10 \, cm^3$ of $0.1 \, mol \, dm^{-3}$ $SCN^-(aq)$. From these values you can work out the amount in moles of each species:

$0.001 \, mol \, Fe^{3+}$ and $0.001 \, mol \, SCN^-$
So the ratio is $1 \, Fe^{3+} : 1 SCN^-$

The formula of the complex is therefore $[Fe(H_2O)_5(SCN)]^{2+}$.

**SAQ 13.8**
In the colorimetry experiment described above, what pieces of apparatus are used for measuring out
**a** the $Fe^{3+}$ solution
**b** the $SCN^-$ solution?

**SAQ 13.9**
The results in *figure 13.14* were obtained from a colorimetry experiment to find the formula of a $Ni^{2+}$ complex with the ligand known as edta. *Table 13.8* shows the details of the solutions. Show that the ratio of $Ni^{2+}$ to ligand in this complex is 1 : 1.

# Redox behaviour

Transition metals have a variety of different oxidation states and so they can be readily oxidised or reduced. Their redox reactions are an important part of their chemistry, especially as they are used in titrations for many different types of analysis.

| Test-tube number | Vol of $0.1 \, mol \, dm^{-3}$ $Ni^{2+}$ solution ($cm^3$) | Vol of $0.1 \, mol \, dm^{-3}$ edta solution ($cm^3$) |
|---|---|---|
| 1 | 0.0 | 5.0 |
| 2 | 0.5 | 4.5 |
| 3 | 1.0 | 4.0 |
| 4 | 1.5 | 3.5 |
| 5 | 2.0 | 3.0 |
| 6 | 2.5 | 2.5 |
| 7 | 3.0 | 2.0 |
| 8 | 3.5 | 1.5 |
| 9 | 4.0 | 1.0 |
| 10 | 4.5 | 0.5 |
| 11 | 5.0 | 0.0 |

● **Table 13.8** Mixtures of $Ni^{2+}(aq)$ and edta(aq) for a colorimetry experiment.

## Redox reactions

[Note: in this section state symbols have not been put into the equations, to make the species involved stand out more clearly.]

There are many redox reactions involving transition metal ions. One which you must know is the reaction between iron(II) ions ($Fe^{2+}$) and manganate(VII) ions ($MnO_4^-$) in acidified aqueous solution. Here is the equation for this reaction:

$$5Fe^{2+} + MnO_4^- + 8H^+ \rightarrow Mn^{2+} + 5Fe^{3+} + 4H_2O$$

purple             pink

The colour change, as you can see, is from purple aqueous $MnO_4^-$ to pale pink aqueous $Mn^{2+}$, but this pale pink is usually so faint that the solution simply appears to be decolorised. (You may wonder why the $Fe^{3+}$ does not colour the solution yellow. Again, it is such a faint colour that it usually cannot be noticed. The green colour of $Fe^{2+}$ is masked by the strong purple colour of $MnO_4^-$.) This colour change is often used as an indicator in a redox titration (see below).

This type of redox equation can be constructed from two half-equations:

■ the half-equation showing oxidation of Fe(II) in $Fe^{2+}$ to Fe(III) in $Fe^{3+}$:
$$Fe^{2+} \rightarrow Fe^{3+} + e^-$$

■ the half-equation showing reduction of Mn(VII) in $MnO_4^-$ to Mn(II) in $Mn^{2+}$ in the presence of acid:
$$MnO_4^- + 8H^+ + 5e^- \rightarrow Mn^{2+} + 4H_2O$$

To construct the final equation, write the two half-equations so that the number of electrons in each is the same. This means the first half-equation is multiplied by 5. Then the half-equations can be added together and the electrons on each side of the arrow cancel:

$$5Fe^{2+} \rightarrow 5Fe^{3+} + 5e^-$$
$$\underline{MnO_4^- + 8H^+ + 5e^- \rightarrow Mn^{2+} + 4H_2O}$$
$$5Fe^{2+} + MnO_4^- + 8H^+ \rightarrow 5Fe^{3+} + Mn^{2+} + 4H_2O$$

This method can be used for finding the redox equation between any two half-equations. Another example is the reaction between aqueous $Fe^{2+}$ ions and hydrogen peroxide, $H_2O_2$. The $Fe^{2+}$ ions are oxidised to $Fe^{3+}$ ions, and the hydrogen peroxide is reduced to water.

$$Fe^{2+} \rightarrow Fe^{3+} + e^-$$
$$H_2O_2 + 2H^+ + 2e^- \rightarrow 2H_2O$$

This time the top half-equation is multiplied throughout by 2. The final redox equation is:

$$2Fe^{2+} + H_2O_2 + 2H^+ \rightarrow 2Fe^{3+} + 2H_2O$$

Another useful half-equation shows the reduction of orange Cr(VI) in the dichromate ion, $Cr_2O_7^{2-}$, to blue-green Cr(III) in $Cr^{3+}$. This is another reaction that requires acid:

$$Cr_2O_7^{2-} + 14H^+ + 6e^- \rightarrow 2Cr^{3+} + 7H_2O$$

orange               green

This is the reaction that occurs when primary and secondary alcohols are oxidised to aldehydes and ketones respectively (see chapter 19). Aqueous potassium dichromate(VI) is a common oxidising agent in organic chemistry.

### SAQ 13.10

Construct the redox equation showing the reaction between dichromate(VI) ions and Fe(II) ions in aqueous solution, given:

$$Fe^{2+} \rightarrow Fe^{3+} + e^-$$

and

$$Cr_2O_7^{2-} + 14H^+ + 6e^- \rightarrow 2Cr^{3+} + 7H_2O$$

## Redox titrations

The colour changes of redox reactions involving transition metal ions in aqueous solutions can be used to show when a titration has reached the end-point. A good example of this is the redox titration between $Fe^{2+}$ and $MnO_4^-$ in aqueous acid solution:

$$5Fe^{2+} + MnO_4^- + 8H^+ \rightarrow 5Fe^{3+} + Mn^{2+} + 4H_2O$$

The purple aqueous $MnO_4^-$ is added from the burette into the acidified aqueous $Fe^{2+}$, and immediately turns pale pink or colourless as it reacts. The end-point of the titration is when all the $Fe^{2+}$ has reacted and a permanent pink colour can be seen.

■ This redox titration can be used for calculating how much $Fe^{2+}$ is contained in an iron tablet.

■ It can also be used for standardising a solution of aqueous $KMnO_4$. It is not possible to weigh out solid $KMnO_4$ to make up into a solution of accurate concentration because the solid

KMnO$_4$ is not pure. However, it is possible to find the mass of a piece of pure iron and then to use this reaction to calculate the concentration of the aqueous KMnO$_4$.

*Example*

A piece of iron wire with a mass of 0.14 g was converted into Fe$^{2+}$ by reaction with acid, and titrated against aqueous KMnO$_4$. The titre obtained was 26.2 cm$^3$. Calculate the concentration of the aqueous KMnO$_4$.

$$\text{Amount of Fe} = \frac{0.14\,\text{g}}{56\,\text{g mol}^{-1}}$$
$$= 0.0025\,\text{mol}$$

$$\text{Amount of Fe}^{2+} = \text{Amount of Fe}$$
$$= 0.0025\,\text{mol}$$

From the equation, 5 moles of Fe$^{2+}$ react with 1 mole of MnO$_4^-$

$$5Fe^{2+} + MnO_4^- + 8H^+ \rightarrow 5Fe^{3+} + Mn^{2+} + 4H_2O$$

So amount of KMnO$_4$ in the titre $= \dfrac{0.0025}{5}$
$$= 0.0005\,\text{mol}$$

$$\text{Concentration of KMnO}_4(aq) = \frac{0.0005\,\text{mol}}{26.2 \times 10^{-3}\,\text{dm}^3}$$
$$= 0.019\,\text{mol dm}^{-3}$$

### SAQ 13.11

A piece of iron ore was treated with acid so that the iron was oxidised to aqueous Fe$^{2+}$ ions, and then titrated against 0.040 mol dm$^{-3}$ aqueous potassium manganate(VII). The titre was found to be 25.0 cm$^3$.

**a** Calculate the mass of iron in the sample.

**b** If the mass of the iron ore was 0.42 g, calculate the percentage mass of iron in the iron ore.

Whether a reaction will occur is determined by the standard electrode potentials, $E^\ominus$, of the relevant half-equations – see chapter 6. For example, both MnO$_4^-$ ions and Cr$_2$O$_7^{2-}$ ions will oxidise Fe$^{2+}$ ions in acid solution to form Fe$^{3+}$ ions.

## Oxidation with MnO$_4^-$ ions in acid solution

The $E^\ominus$ values are:

$$MnO_4^- + 8H^+ + 5e^- \rightleftharpoons Mn^{2+} + 4H_2O; \quad E^\ominus = +1.52\,V$$
$$Fe^{3+} + e^- \rightleftharpoons Fe^{2+}; \qquad\qquad\qquad E^\ominus = +0.77\,V$$

The MnO$_4^-$/Mn$^{2+}$ half-equation has the more positive $E^\ominus$ value and will proceed in the forward direction, while the Fe$^{3+}$/Fe$^{2+}$ half-equation proceeds in the backward direction.

The cell potential is given by:

$$E^\ominus_{cell} = +1.52 - (+0.77) = +0.75\,V$$

indicating that the reaction will occur readily.

## Oxidation with Cr$_2$O$_7^{2-}$ ions in acid solution

The $E^\ominus$ values are:

$$Cr_2O_7^{2-} + 14H^+ \rightleftharpoons 2Cr^{3+} + 7H_2O; \quad E^\ominus = +1.33\,V$$
$$Fe^{3+} + e^- \rightleftharpoons Fe^{2+}; \qquad\qquad\qquad E^\ominus = +0.77\,V$$

As in the previous example, the Fe$^{3+}$/Fe$^{2+}$ half-equation has a less positive value, indicating that Fe$^{2+}$ ions should be oxidised by Cr$_2$O$_7^{2-}$ ions in acid solution.

The cell potential is given by:

$$E^\ominus_{cell} = +1.33 - (+0.77) = +0.56\,V$$

which is still sufficiently large for the reaction to occur readily.

### SAQ 13.12

**a** Can MnO$_4^-$ ions oxidise Cl$^-$ ions in acid solution?

**b** Can Cr$_2$O$_7^{2-}$ ions oxidise Cl$^-$ ions in acid solution?

For the half-cell

$$Cl_2 + 2e^- \rightleftharpoons 2Cl^-; \qquad E^\ominus = +1.36\,V$$

# SUMMARY (A2)

- The transition elements are metals with similar physical and chemical properties.

- The electronic configurations of the elements includes electrons in the 3d subshell.

- A transition element is defined as having a partly filled 3d subshell in at least one of its ions.

- When a transition element is oxidised, it loses electrons from the 4s subshell first and then the 3d subshell.

- Transition elements can exist in several oxidation states.

- Transition elements are good catalysts because they can transfer electrons easily and provide a site for the reaction to take place.

- Transition metal compounds are often coloured, The colour can be recorded by visible spectroscopy.

- Transition elements react with aqueous hydroxide ions to give precipitates. The colour of the precipitate depends on the transition metal ion.

- Transition elements form complexes by combining with ligands. A strong ligand can displace a weak ligand in a complex. This can result in a change of colour.

- The formula of a complex can be found by colorimetry.

- Many reactions involving transition elements are redox reactions. Some redox reactions are used in titrations to determine concentrations.

# Questions (A2)

1 A student investigated ligand substitution in complexes experimentally. He divided a solution of aqueous copper sulphate into two portions. He then added concentrated hydrochloric acid to one portion and concentrated ammonia solution to the other.

   a Explain the meaning of the terms **ligand** and **complex**.

   b Describe any observations the student made and explain them in terms of ligand substitution.

   c Use these reactions to discuss different shapes of transition metal complexes.

2 a Copy and complete the electronic configuration of $Cu^{2+}$:
$1s^2 2s^2 2p^6 3s^2 3p^6$

   b Transition metals are frequently used as catalysts in industrial reactions.

     (i) Give one example of such a catalyst.

    (ii) Explain why transition metals are good catalysts.

   c Transition metal compounds are also found as waste products in industry. To test if the chromate ion, $CrO_4^{2-}$, is present in waste water from a chrome-plating plant, sodium dithionite, $Na_2S_2O_4$, is used:

$$3S_2O_4^{2-}(aq) + 2CrO_4^{2-}(aq) + 2H_2O(l) + 2OH^-(aq) \rightarrow 6SO_3^{2-}(aq) + 2Cr(OH)_3(s)$$

In this test, $22\,cm^3$ of waste water reacted exactly with $50\,cm^3$ of standard $0.2\,mol\,dm^{-3}$ aqueous sodium dithionite. Calculate

   (i) the amount of sodium dithionite used in the reaction;

  (ii) the amount of chromate ion used in the reaction;

 (iii) the concentration of chromate ions in the waste water;

 (iv) the oxidation number of S in $S_2O_4^{2-}$ and $SO_3^{2-}$.

# CHAPTER 14

# Nitrogen and sulphur (AS)

**By the end of this chapter you should be able to:**

**1** explain the lack of reactivity of nitrogen;

**2** describe the displacement of ammonia from its salts;

**3** outline the industrial importance of ammonia and of nitrogen compounds derived from ammonia;

**4** explain the environmental consequences of the uncontrolled use of nitrate fertilisers;

**5** explain why atmospheric oxides of nitrogen are pollutants, including their use in the oxidation of atmospheric sulphur dioxide;

**6** describe the formation of atmospheric sulphur dioxide from the combustion of sulphur-contaminated carbonaceous fuels;

**7** describe the role of sulphur dioxide in the formation of acid rain and the environmental consequences of acid rain;

**8** describe the main details of the Contact process and outline the industrial importance of sulphuric acid;

**9** describe the use of sulphur dioxide in food preservation.

## Introduction

The element nitrogen, $N_2$, the nitrogen oxides nitrogen(II) oxide, NO, and nitrogen(IV) oxide, $NO_2$, and sulphur dioxide, $SO_2$, are all gases in the Earth's atmosphere.

Nitrogen is the most common element in the Earth's atmosphere, making up about 78% of the atmosphere. Unlike oxygen, the other main component of the atmosphere, nitrogen is particularly unreactive. Oxides of nitrogen are, however, produced under certain conditions in combustion reactions – see chapter 8, page 190. Sulphur dioxide is formed when fossil fuels containing sulphur are burned – see chapter 16, page 314. Together, the oxides of nitrogen and sulphur dioxide are atmospheric pollutants and are also responsible for acid rain – see *figure 16.27* (page 314).

## Nitrogen

Nitrogen exists as the molecule $N_2$. Each nitrogen atom in the molecule has five electrons in the bonding shell and completes its octet of electrons by sharing *three pairs* of electrons with the other nitrogen atom.

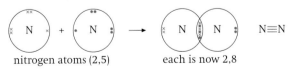

nitrogen atoms (2,5)          each is now 2,8

The bond formed between the two nitrogen atoms is a triple bond of great strength. The bond enthalpy (see chapter 3, page 39) is $945\,kJ\,mol^{-1}$, which makes breaking the triple bond very difficult. As a result, nitrogen has few reactions, most of which involve high temperatures or high energy in order to overcome the high bond

● **Figure 14.1** Elemental nitrogen reacts here.

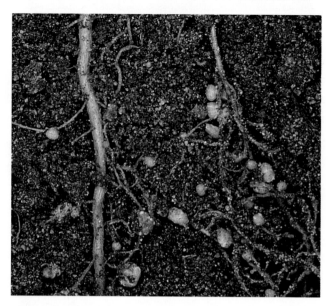

**Figure 14.2** Elemental nitrogen also reacts here.

strength of the $N_2$ molecule. Typical of these are the reactions between nitrogen and oxygen:

- in the upper atmosphere during a thunderstorm (*figure 14.1*);
- in an internal combustion engine.

$$N_2(g) + O_2(g) \rightarrow 2NO(g)$$

followed by

$$2NO(g) + O_2(g) \rightarrow 2NO_2(g)$$

### SAQ 14.1

Why will nitrogen react with oxygen:
**a** in a thunderstorm,
**b** in a car engine?

Nitrogen is also converted into ammonia, $NH_3$, in the Haber process – see chapter 7, page 133. This is an equilibrium reaction which requires particular conditions of temperature and pressure, uses a catalyst and gives a low yield.

$$N_2(g) + 3H_2(g) \rightleftharpoons 2NH_3(g)$$

Atmospheric nitrogen is 'fixed' as nitrate ions by bacteria in the roots of certain plants such as peas, beans and clover (leguminous plants).

### SAQ 14.2

How can bacteria in the root nodules of some plants enable nitrogen to form nitrates and other nitrogen compounds?

## Ammonia and ammonium compounds

Ammonia, $NH_3$, is a base, readily forming ammonium ions.

$$NH_3(g) + H^+(aq) \rightleftharpoons NH_4^+(aq)$$

The formation and structure of the ammonium ion were discussed in chapter 3, page 36. Ammonium compounds, such as ammonium sulphate, $(NH_4)_2SO_4$, are ionic salts that are usually soluble in water. When heated with a base, they give off ammonia.

$$(NH_4)_2SO_4(s) + 2NaOH(s)$$
$$\rightarrow Na_2SO_4(s) + 2H_2O(l) + 2NH_3(g)$$

$$2NH_4Cl(s) + CaO(s) \rightarrow CaCl_2(s) + H_2O(l) + 2NH_3(g)$$

## The industrial importance of ammonia and other compounds of nitrogen

Nitrogen extracted from liquefied air is used to make ammonia in the Haber process. Nitrogen is also used as an inert atmosphere in food storage and during some metalworking processes when oxidation must be prevented.

The production of ammonia is an extremely important manufacturing process, primarily for fertiliser production – see chapter 7, *figure 7.15* (page 135). The continual growth of the world's population means that each year more food must be produced. This can only be achieved by using synthetic fertilisers.

Ammonia itself can be used as a fertiliser on acidic soils by pumping it directly into the ground. Ammonia can also be converted into ammonium sulphate, $(NH_4)_2SO_4$, ammonium nitrate, $NH_4NO_3$, or urea, $CO(NH_2)_2$, each of which is used as a fertiliser. Each is made by an acid–base reaction, for example:

$$NH_3(g) + HNO_3(aq) \xrightarrow{heat} NH_4NO_3(aq)$$

$$2NH_3(g) + CO_2(g) \xrightarrow{heat} CO(NH_2)_2(s) + H_2O(l)$$

### SAQ 14.3

Why is the formation of urea from ammonia and carbon dioxide an acid–base reaction?

## Nitric acid manufacture

Another important industrial use of ammonia is the manufacture of nitric acid, $HNO_3$, by catalytic oxidation by air using a platinum/rhodium catalyst at about 900 °C. There is a series of reactions involving the gases NO and $NO_2$ and dissolving the product in water. The overall reaction is:

$$NH_3(g) + 2O_2(g) \rightarrow HNO_3(l) + H_2O(l)$$

Nitric acid is an important industrial compound, used to make ammonium nitrate (fertiliser and explosive), nylon, 2,4,6-trinitrotoluene (TNT, see *figure 16.40*, page 323) and other explosives.

## The use of nitrate fertilisers

For plants to grow well they need soils which contain compounds of nitrogen, phosphorus and potassium, as well as trace elements. Each element must be available in a suitable form if it is to be a plant nutrient.

Nitrogen is absorbed by plants through their roots in the form of nitrate ions, $NO_3^-$. The nitrate ions are converted by bacteria into ammonia and eventually plant protein. When plants die and rot away, the nitrogen in the plant protein is returned to the soil in the form of $NH_4^+$ ions which can be used by new plants. The $NH_4^+$ ions will be oxidised by soil bacteria to $NO_3^-$ ions before they are taken up by new plants.

If, however, plants are harvested and removed from the land for food, the nitrogen is lost and

● **Figure 14.3** Spreading fertiliser on farmland.

must be replaced. This can be achieved by using either natural animal manure or plant compost, or by using synthetic fertilisers. Unfortunately, natural manures and composts contain only small amounts of plant nutrients, typically less than 1% as nitrogen compounds. Synthetic fertilisers are therefore used by many growers because they contain larger amounts of active ingredients, typically about 10% as nitrogen compounds. Synthetic fertilisers are often mixtures of compounds that contain nitrogen, phosphorus and potassium. A common compound fertiliser contains ammonium nitrate, ammonium phosphate and potassium chloride.

## Environmental consequences of the use of fertilisers

When fertilisers are applied to the soil, the nitrates and other plant nutrients dissolve in water and are taken up by plants. If too much fertiliser is used, or if it is applied shortly before heavy rainfall, the nitrates and other nutrients are leached from the soil and enter water courses and drain into rivers and lakes. Increased concentrations of nitrates in rivers and lakes cause the plants and algae present in the waterways to grow rapidly. The algae soon cover the surface of the water, restricting the amount of light available to aquatic plants growing on the bottom. This reduction in photosynthesis causes a reduction in the concentration of dissolved oxygen in the water. When the algae die and decay, dissolved oxygen is used up, with the result that fish die. This process is called *eutrophication* (*figure 14.4*).

● **Figure 14.4** A river suffering from eutrophication.

Nitrates are very difficult to remove from drinking water supplies because, unlike phosphates, they cannot be precipitated out. High nitrate concentrations, greater than 100 ppm (parts per million), may affect small babies. The oxygen-carrying capacity of their blood may be reduced, giving rise to 'blue baby' syndrome.

## Nitrogen oxides in the atmosphere

The high temperatures and pressures of petrol and diesel engines enable nitrogen and oxygen in the air to combine to form oxides of nitrogen – see chapter 8, page 190. The exhaust gases from motor vehicles contain a mixture of products, including carbon monoxide, carbon particles and unburned hydrocarbons resulting from incomplete combustion of the fuel. Nitrogen oxides and sulphur dioxide are also present (*table 14.1*).

### SAQ 14.4

How is sulphur dioxide produced in the exhaust gases of motor vehicles?

Catalytic converters (see *figure 8.43*, page 190) are used in modern car engines to remove carbon monoxide, oxides of nitrogen and hydrocarbons from the exhaust gases. If these compounds are not removed they can lead to the formation of a photochemical smog – see chapter 8, page 191 and *figure 8.44*.

# Sulphur

## Sulphur dioxide in the atmosphere

The Earth's atmosphere contains carbon dioxide, oxides of nitrogen and sulphur dioxide from natural sources. Rain falling from an unpolluted atmosphere would have a pH of about 5.5 to 6.0. However, in much of the industrialised world, rain has a significantly lower pH, as low as 4.0 in places. Such rain is called acid rain.

Sulphur dioxide and the oxides of nitrogen contribute to acid rain, which is essentially a mixture of nitric and sulphuric acids.

The reactions that lead to the formation of acid rain are complex and thought to involve the following sequence:

$$SO_2(g) + NO_2(g) \rightarrow SO_3(g) + NO(g)$$
$$2NO(g) + O_2 \rightarrow 2NO_2(g)$$

The sulphur trioxide dissolves in water as sulphuric acid.

$$SO_3(g) + H_2O(l) \rightarrow H_2SO_4(l)$$

The nitrogen(IV) oxide ($NO_2$) dissolves with oxygen in water to form nitric acid.

$$2NO_2(g) + H_2O(l) + \tfrac{1}{2}O_2(g) \rightarrow 2HNO_3(l)$$

### SAQ 14.5

Nitrogen(II) oxide, NO, is often described as a catalyst in the formation of acid rain. Explain why this can be considered to be correct.

Acid rain is corrosive and will attack buildings made of limestone or marble (*figure 14.5*). It also corrodes metals. In addition, when acid rain falls on soil, it causes aluminium ions and heavy metal ions present in soil to dissolve and enter water courses. Aluminium ions are toxic to many forms of aquatic life, while heavy metal ions are believed to cause damage to trees.

| Fuel | Carbon monoxide | Hydrocarbons | Nitrogen oxides | Sulphur dioxide | Black smoke |
|---|---|---|---|---|---|
| petrol | 236 | 25 | 29 | 0.9 | 0.6 |
| diesel | 10 | 17 | 59 | 3.8 | 18.0 |

● **Table 14.1** Emission levels for motor vehicles, measured in grams of pollutant produced per kilogram of fuel.

● **Figure 14.5** These buildings have been damaged by acid rain.

A reduction in acid rain can be brought about by reducing $SO_2$ emissions. Natural gas and crude oil, which contain varying amounts of sulphur, are treated to remove much of the sulphur present as the element. This sulphur is then used to make sulphuric acid (*figure 14.6*).

Power stations that burn coal have their exhaust gases passed through calcium oxide or calcium carbonate to remove $SO_2$ as calcium sulphate. The calcium sulphate is sold as gypsum for making plaster.

## The Contact process

Sulphuric acid is manufactured in the Contact process. Like the Haber process (chapter 7, page 133) it includes an equilibrium reaction where theoretical and economic considerations are used to give an overall efficient and cost-effective process by using a compromise set of operating conditions.

There are three essential reactions in the Contact process.

1 Sulphur is burned in air to give sulphur dioxide.

$$S(g) + O_2(g) \rightarrow SO_2(g)$$

The sulphur used comes from naturally occurring sulphur deposits or has been recovered from natural gas or crude oil.

Sulphur dioxide may also be obtained by roasting sulphide ores during metal extraction. Metal oxides are also formed which are then reduced to the metal, for example:

$$2ZnS(s) + 3O_2(g) \rightarrow 2ZnO(s) + 2SO_2(g)$$

2 Sulphur dioxide and air are passed over a vanadium(V) oxide, $V_2O_5$, catalyst to form sulphur trioxide, $SO_3$.

$$2SO_2(g) + O_2(g) \rightleftharpoons 2SO_3(g);$$
$$\Delta H = -96 \, \text{kJ mol}^{-1}$$

This is an equilibrium reaction which is exothermic and has fewer molecules on the right-hand side than on the left-hand side. Application of Le Chatelier's principle suggests that a low temperature and a high pressure would give a greater yield of sulphur trioxide. In practice, however, because the catalyst is ineffective below 400 °C, the process is operated at 400–600 °C. The pressure used is just above atmospheric pressure and is large enough to enable the gases to be pumped through the plant.

In order to increase the yield of $SO_3$, an excess of air is used to drive the equilibrium to the right-hand side. The process also involves

● **Figure 14.6** This chemical plant produces sulphuric acid.

the use of four beds of $V_2O_5$ catalyst used in succession. The exothermic reaction that occurs on each catalyst bed raises the temperature of the gaseous mixture. Before the gases are passed through the next catalyst bed they are cooled, again driving the equilibrium to the right-hand side.

3  The final stage of the process involves the conversion of the sulphur trioxide into sulphuric acid. This is NOT done by passing $SO_3$ gas directly into water because the reaction is dangerously exothermic. Instead, the $SO_3$ is passed into 98% $H_2SO_4$ where the $SO_3$ dissolves. Water is added to the product to keep the concentration at 98%. The sulphuric acid produced is removed regularly and when more dilute acid is required it is carefully diluted with water.

The main uses of sulphuric acid are in the manufacture of:

- paints and pigments
- detergents
- fertilisers
- dyestuffs.

Sulphuric acid is also used in smaller amounts in a wide variety of industrial and manufacturing processes.

## Sulphur dioxide in food preservation

When present in the atmosphere, $SO_2$ can cause respiratory problems to humans – especially babies, the elderly and those who suffer from asthma and bronchitis.

Sulphur dioxide is, however, used in food preservation either as the gas itself or as a sulphite, i.e. aqueous $SO_2$.

$$SO_2(g) + H_2O(l) \rightarrow H_2SO_3(aq)$$

Sulphur dioxide and sulphites inhibit the growth of moulds, yeasts and aerobic bacteria. They are also reducing agents and retard the oxidation of foodstuffs.

Sulphur dioxide and sulphites are used to prevent the spoilage of dried fruit, dehydrated vegetables, fruit juices and sausages.

# SUMMARY (AS)

- The high bond strength of the $N \equiv N$ bond makes nitrogen very unreactive. Reactions of nitrogen only occur under conditions of high temperature and/or high pressure – such as in thunderstorms or in a car engine.

- Ammonia, a base, readily forms salts. It may be displaced from its salts by heating them with a base such as NaOH(s).

- Ammonia and nitric acid are important industrial compounds of nitrogen. Ammonia is used to manufacture nitric acid and fertilisers such as ammonium nitrate or ammonium sulphate. Nitric acid is used to manufacture fertilisers, nylon and explosives.

- Oxides of nitrogen present in the atmosphere from internal combustion engines are atmospheric pollutants. Sulphur dioxide becomes an atmospheric pollutant when many carbon-containing fuels are burned. In the presence of oxides of nitrogen in the upper atmosphere it produces acid rain.

- Sulphuric acid is manufactured by the Contact process. In this process, the conditions are adjusted to give the optimum yield of $SO_3$ prior to its conversion to sulphuric acid.

- Sulphur dioxide is used in food preservation.

# Questions (AS)

**1** **a** Magnesium reacts with nitrogen only at a very high temperature, producing a yellow solid **D**. **D** contains 72% of magnesium by mass.

   (i) Suggest why a high temperature is required for this reaction.

   (ii) Calculate the empirical formula of **D**.

**b** When water is added to the yellow solid **D**, a white suspension forms and ammonia is liberated.

   Identify the white suspension and write an equation for the action of water on **D**.

*CIE, 1993*

**2** A coal-fired power station (which generates electricity) is fitted with a Flue Gas Desulphurisation (FGD) plant, which removes some of the sulphur dioxide from waste gases.

   In the FGD plant, the waste gases are treated with powdered limestone, $CaCO_3$, producing calcium sulphite, $CaSO_3$. This oxidised by air to form solid calcium sulphate, $CaSO_4$.

   The diagram below shows the amounts of substances used, and produced, by such a coal-fired power station with an FGD plant in one year.

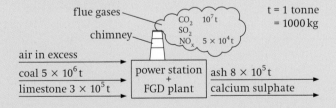

**a** (i) What process provides the energy used in the power station?

   (ii) Which gas, not listed in the diagram, is the chief component of the flue gases?

   (iii) Explain why oxides of nitrogen ($NO_x$) are present in the flue gases?

**b** Write a balanced equation in each case to show how

   (i) limestone reacts with sulphur dioxide,

   (ii) air oxidises calcium sulphite.

**c** (i) Use the equation in **b i** to determine the maximum mass of sulphur dioxide which could be removed by $3 \times 10^5$ t of limestone in the FGD plant.
   (t = tonne = 1000 kg)

   (ii) Use the equations in **b** to determine the maximum mass of calcium sulphate which would be produced from the $3 \times 10^5$ t of limestone.

**d** The FGD plant removes 90% of the sulphur dioxide from the waste gases.

   Using your answer to **c i**, calculate the mass of sulphur dioxide which is released into the atmosphere each year by this power station when $5 \times 10^6$ t of coal is burnt.

**e** Which other substance, as well as calcium sulphate, will be formed by the limestone acting on the flue gases?

**f** Suggest **two** possible disadvantages of the use of an FGD plant.

*CIE, 1994*

# CHAPTER 15

# Introduction to organic chemistry (AS)

## By the end of this chapter you should be able to:

1 interpret and use the terms nomenclature, molecular formula, general formula, structural formula, displayed formula, skeletal formula, homologous series and functional group;

2 use IUPAC rules for naming organic compounds;

3 perform calculations, involving use of the mole concept and reacting quantities, to determine the percentage yield of a reaction;

4 describe and explain *structural isomerism* in compounds with the same molecular formula but different structural formulae;

5 interpret and use the term *stereoisomerism* in terms of *cis–trans* and optical isomerism;

6 describe and explain *cis–trans isomerism* in alkenes, in terms of restricted rotation about a double bond;

7 determine the possible structural and/or *cis–trans* isomers of an organic molecule of given molecular formula;

8 explain the term *chiral centre* and identify any chiral centres in a molecule of given structural formula (for example, amino acids and 2-hydroxypropanoic acid (lactic acid));

9 understand that chiral molecules prepared synthetically in the laboratory may contain a mixture of optical isomers, whereas molecules of the same compound produced naturally in living systems will often be present as one optical isomer only (for example L-amino acids).

Organic chemistry includes the study of compounds containing carbon and hydrogen *only* (that is, hydrocarbons) and of compounds containing other elements *in addition* to carbon and hydrogen. Such compounds were originally described as organic as they were all believed to be derived from living organisms. Although this idea was dispelled by the synthesis of urea from an inorganic compound, ammonium cyanate, (by the German chemist Friedrich Wöhler in 1828, *figure 15.1*) we still use the term 'organic'.

Organic chemistry is a large subject, mainly because one of its 'essential ingredients', carbon, forms a much greater number and variety of compounds than any other element. Over 90% of known compounds contain carbon, despite the existence of several elements with much greater natural abundance.

Reasons for the greater number and variety of carbon compounds include the following:

■ Carbon readily bonds to itself and to most other elements, including metals.

● **Figure 15.1** Friedrich Wöhler made the organic compound urea from an inorganic source. This dispelled the theory that all organic compounds originated from living organisms.

■ Carbon can bond in a variety of ways giving rise to chains, rings and even cages of carbon atoms. Compounds that contain only carbon and hydrogen atoms are known as hydrocarbons (*figure 15.2*). Organic chemistry includes the study of hydrocarbons and of compounds containing other elements as well as carbon and hydrogen. As single carbon–carbon and carbon–hydrogen bonds are relatively unreactive, the reactions of these compounds are typically those involving particular functional groups (*table 15.2*, page 270).

Organic compounds are also classified as either aliphatic or aromatic. **Aromatic** compounds contain one or more arene rings (see page 270). They are called aromatic compounds as they have distinctive, usually pleasant, smells. All other organic compounds are **aliphatic**. Hence alkanes and alkenes are aliphatic compounds, whilst benzene is an aromatic compound.

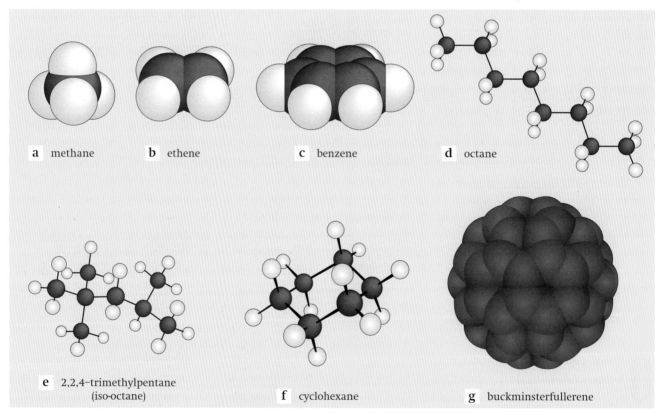

**a** methane   **b** ethene   **c** benzene   **d** octane

**e** 2,2,4–trimethylpentane (iso-octane)   **f** cyclohexane   **g** buckminsterfullerene

● **Figure 15.2** Examples of the variety of hydrocarbons and one other carbon-containing molecule. Chemists use various types of models for different purposes. The colours used in modelling of molecules are shown in *table 15.1*.

**a-c** These hydrocarbons are shown as space-filling models. Such models show the region of space occupied by the atoms and the surrounding electrons.

**d-f** These hydrocarbons are shown as ball-and-stick models, which enable bonds between atoms to be clearly seen.

**g** Buckminsterfullerene is not a hydrocarbon but an allotrope of carbon (diamond and graphite are other allotropes), a spherical $C_{60}$ molecule named after the architect who designed geodesic domes.

| Colour | Atom/electron cloud |
|---|---|
| white | hydrogen |
| dark grey | carbon |
| red | oxygen |
| blue | nitrogen |
| yellow-green | fluorine |
| green | chlorine |
| orange-brown | bromine |
| brown | phosphorus |
| violet | iodine |
| pale yellow | sulphur |
| yellow ochre | boron |
| pink | lone-pair electron clouds |
| green | $\pi$-bond electron clouds |

● **Table 15.1** Colours used in molecular modelling in this text.

# Types of formulae

As well as using different types of models to help visualise molecules, chemists also use different formulae. These include the following.

■ *Molecular formula*

A **molecular formula** simply shows the number of atoms of each element present in the molecule, e.g. the molecular formula of hexane is $C_6H_{14}$.

■ *General formula*

A **general formula** may be written for each

series of compounds. For example, the general formula for the alkanes is $C_nH_{2n+2}$ (where $n$ is the number of carbon atoms present).

■ *Structural formula*

This shows how the atoms are joined together in a molecule. The **structural formula** of hexane is $CH_3CH_2CH_2CH_2CH_2CH_3$. More information is conveyed. Hexane is seen to consist of a chain of six carbon atoms; the carbon atoms at each end are joined to one carbon and three hydrogen atoms; the carbon atoms between the two ends are joined to two hydrogen and two carbon atoms.

■ *Displayed formula*

This shows all the bonds and all the atoms. The **displayed formula** of hexane is:

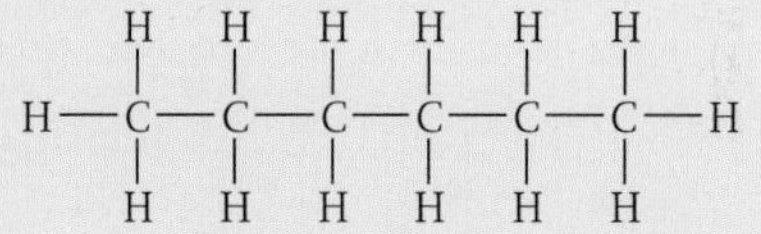

Displayed formulae are also called full structural formulae. One of their disadvantages is that they are a two-dimensional representation of molecules which are three-dimensional. Compare the displayed formula for hexane with the model in *figure 15.6a* (page 271).

■ *Skeletal formula*

This shows the carbon skeleton only. Hydrogen atoms on the carbon atoms are omitted. Carbon atoms are not labelled. Other types of atom are shown as in a structural formula. **Skeletal formulae** are frequently used to show the structures of cyclic hydrocarbons. The skeletal formula of hexane is:

■ *Three-dimensional formula*

A **three-dimensional formula** gives the best representation of the shape of a molecule. Examples of the different types of formulae for the amino acid phenylalanine are shown in *figure 15.3*. Phenylalanine is a common, naturally occurring amino acid.

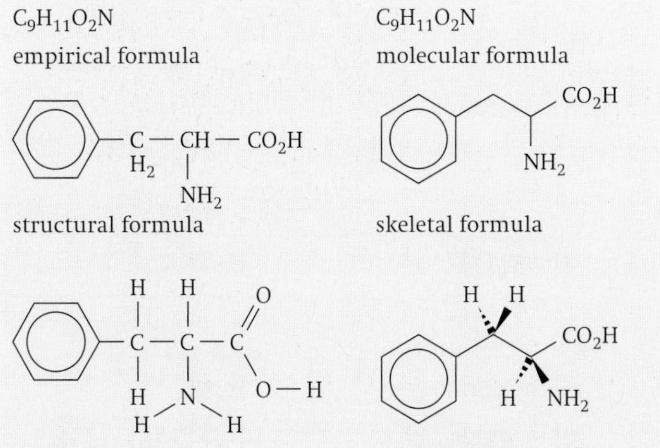

● **Figure 15.3** Different types of formulae for phenylalanine. Note that the skeletal form of the phenyl ring ($-C_6H_5$) is acceptable in all of these formulae.

# Functional groups

Organic chemistry can be studied in a particularly structured and systematic manner because each different group of atoms that becomes attached to carbon has its own characteristic set of reactions.

Chemists refer to these different groups of atoms as **functional groups**. The functional groups that you will meet in the following chapters are shown in *table 15.2*.

*Table 15.2* provides you with the classes and structures of these functional groups. An example is also provided of a simple molecule containing each functional group. Each functional group gives rise to a **homologous series** (molecules with the same functional group but different length carbon chains). For example, the alcohol functional group gives rise to the homologous series of alcohols. The first four of these are methanol ($CH_3OH$), ethanol ($CH_3CH_2OH$), propan-1-ol ($CH_3CH_2CH_2OH$) and butan-1-ol ($CH_3CH_2CH_2CH_2OH$). The members of a homologous series all have similar chemical properties.

A **general formula** may be written for each homologous series. For example, the general formula of the aliphatic alcohols is $C_nH_{2n+1}OH$ (where $n$ is the number of carbon atoms present).

## Molecular modelling

*Figure 15.4* shows a range of naturally occurring molecules. They are computer-produced images of ball-and-stick molecular models. In such models, atoms are shown as spheres with radii propor-

| Class of functional group | Structure of functional group | Names of example(s) | Structural formula(e) of example(s) |
|---|---|---|---|
| alkenes | 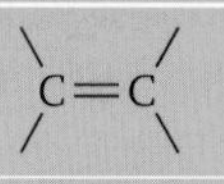 $\backslash$C$=$C$/$ | ethene | $CH_2{=}CH_2$ |
| arenes | 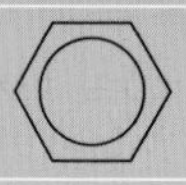 (benzene ring) | benzene | 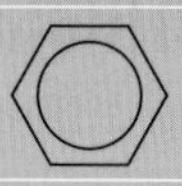 (benzene ring) |
| halogenoalkanes | $-X$, where X = F, Cl, Br, I | chloromethane | $CH_3Cl$ |
| alcohols and phenols | $-OH$ | methanol, phenol | $CH_3OH$, $C_6H_5OH$ |
| aldehydes | 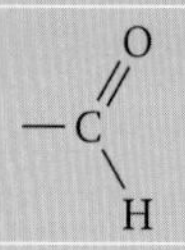 $-C{\,}^{O}_{H}$ | ethanal | $CH_3CHO$ |
| ketones | 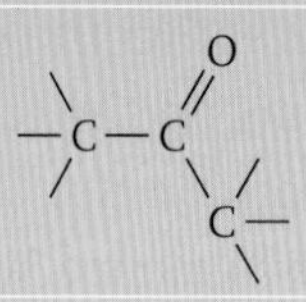 $-C-C{\,}^{O}_{C-}$ | propanone | $CH_3COCH_3$ |
| carboxylic acids | 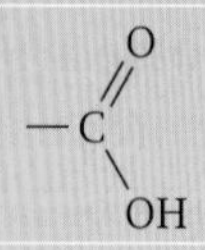 $-C{\,}^{O}_{OH}$ | ethanoic acid | $CH_3COOH$ |
| esters | 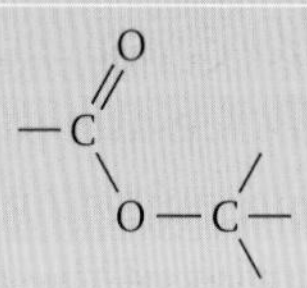 $-C{\,}^{O}_{O-C-}$ | ethyl ethanoate | $CH_3COOC_2H_5$ |
| acyl chlorides | 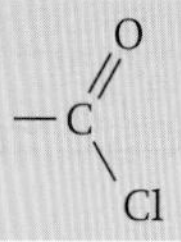 $-C{\,}^{O}_{Cl}$ | ethanoyl chloride | $CH_3COCl$ |
| amines | $-NH_2$ | methylamine | $CH_3NH_2$ |
| amides | 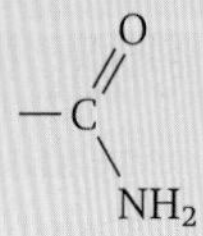 $-C{\,}^{O}_{NH_2}$ | ethanamide | $CH_3CONH_2$ |
| nitriles | $-C{\equiv}N$ | ethanenitrile | $CH_3CN$ |

● **Table 15.2** Functional groups you will meet in the following chapters.

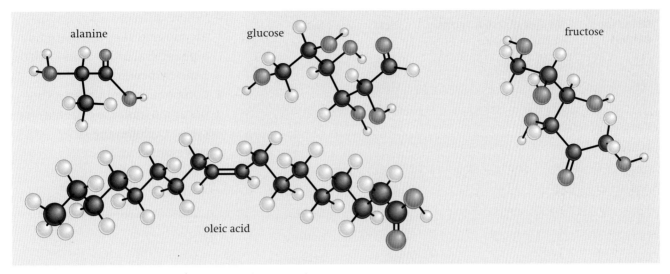

alanine     glucose     fructose

oleic acid

● **Figure 15.4** Ball-and-stick models of some naturally occurring molecules.

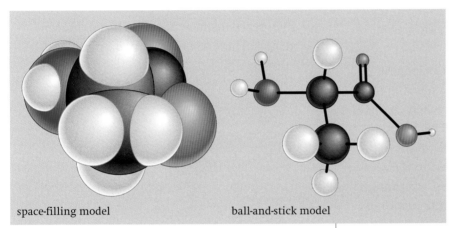

space-filling model     ball-and-stick model

● **Figure 15.5** Different model types for alanine.

tional to the atomic radii of the elements involved. A single bond is represented by a rod and a double bond by two rods. Different elements are distinguished by colour, as shown in *table 15.1*.

### SAQ 15.1

Draw the structural formulae for the molecules shown in *figure 15.4*. Identify and label the functional groups present.

Various computer-produced images of molecular models will be used where appropriate throughout this book. Another type that will be used is a space-filling model. In space-filling models, atoms are shown including the space occupied by their electron orbitals. As

their orbitals overlap significantly, a very different image to the ball-and-stick image results. *Figure 15.5* shows these two types of model for alanine.

# Naming organic compounds

The names given in *figure 15.6* are the **systematic names** for the **structural isomers** of hexane (see later in this chapter for more about isomerism). Such names precisely describe the structure of a molecule and enable chemists to communicate clearly. International rules have been agreed for the systematic naming

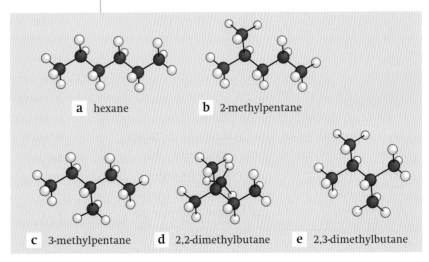

**a** hexane     **b** 2-methylpentane

**c** 3-methylpentane     **d** 2,2-dimethylbutane     **e** 2,3-dimethylbutane

● **Figure 15.6** Models and systematic names of $C_6H_{14}$.

| Molecular formula | Number of carbon atoms in longest chain | Stem | Name |
|---|---|---|---|
| $CH_4$ | 1 | meth- | methane |
| $C_2H_6$ | 2 | eth- | ethane |
| $C_3H_8$ | 3 | prop- | propane |
| $C_4H_{10}$ | 4 | but- | butane |
| $C_5H_{12}$ | 5 | pent- | pentane |
| $C_6H_{14}$ | 6 | hex- | hexane |
| $C_7H_{16}$ | 7 | hept- | heptane |
| $C_8H_{18}$ | 8 | oct- | octane |
| $C_9H_{20}$ | 9 | non- | nonane |
| $C_{10}H_{22}$ | 10 | dec- | decane |
| $C_{20}H_{42}$ | 20 | eicos- | eicosane |

● **Table 15.3** Naming simple alkanes.

of most compounds. The basic rules for naming hydrocarbons are as follows:

1 The number of carbon atoms in the longest chain provides the stem of the name. Simple alkanes consist entirely of unbranched chains of carbon atoms. They are named by adding -ane to this stem, as shown in *table 15.3*.

2 Branched-chain alkanes are named in the same way. The name given to the longest continuous carbon chain is then prefixed by the names of the shorter side-chains. The same stems are used with the suffix -yl. Hence $CH_3-$ is methyl (often called a methyl group). In general, such groups are called alkyl groups. The position of an alkyl group is indicated by a number. The carbon atoms in the longest carbon chain are numbered from one end of the chain. Numbering starts from the end that produces the lowest possible numbers for the side-chains. For example

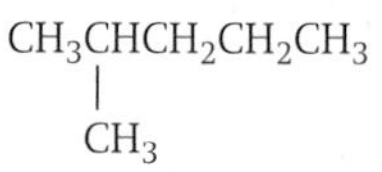

$$CH_3CHCH_2CH_2CH_3$$
$$|$$
$$CH_3$$

is 2-methylpentane, not 4-methylpentane.

3 Each side-chain must be included in the name. If there are several identical side-chains, the name is prefixed by di-, tri-, etc. For example 2,2,3-trimethyl- indicates that there are three methyl groups, two on the second and one on the third carbon atom of the longest chain. Note that numbers are separated by commas, whilst a number and a letter are separated by a hyphen.

4 Where different alkyl groups are present, they are placed in alphabetical order as in 3-ethyl-2-methylpentane.

5 Compounds containing a ring of carbon atoms are prefixed by cyclo-. Cyclohexane is represented as:

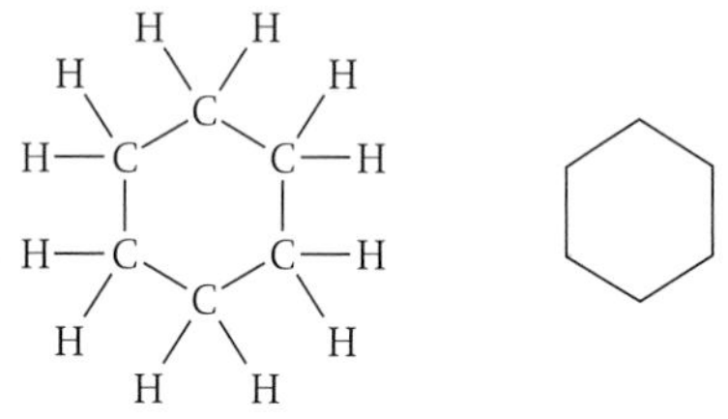

displayed formula    skeletal formula

6 Hydrocarbons may contain alkene or arene groups. These are represented as follows:

alkene: ethene

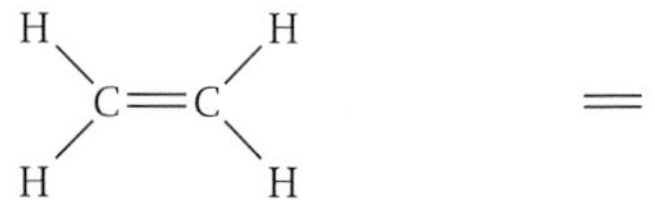

arene: benzene

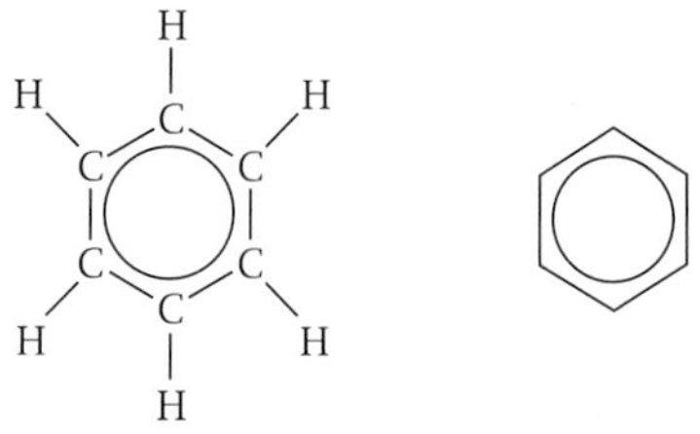

displayed formulae    skeletal formulae

Hydrocarbons containing one double bond are called alkenes. The same stems are used but are followed by -ene. The position of an alkene double bond is indicated by the lower number of the two carbon atoms involved. This number is placed between the stem and -ene. Hence $CH_3CH=CHCH_3$ is but-2-ene.

7 The simplest arene is benzene. When one alkyl group is attached to a benzene ring, a number is not needed because all the carbon atoms are equivalent. Two or more groups will require a number. For example:

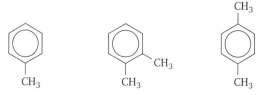

methylbenzene    1,2-dimethylbenzene    1,4-dimethylbenzene

8 Halogeno compounds are named in the same way as alkyl-substituted alkanes or arenes:

9 Aliphatic alcohols and ketones are named in a similar way to alkenes:

CH₃CH₂CHBrCH₃

2-bromobutane          1,3-dichlorobenzene

10 Aliphatic aldehyde and carboxylic acid groups are at the end of a carbon chain, so they do

CH₃CH₂CH₂OH          CH₃CH₂COCH₂CH₃

propan-1-ol          pentan-3-one

not need a number. There is only one possible butanoic acid, $CH_3CH_2CH_2COOH$, or butanal, $CH_3CH_2CH_2CHO$. The names of ketones, aldehydes and carboxylic acids include the carbon atom in the functional group in the stem. Hence $CH_3COOH$ is ethanoic acid.

11 Amines are named using the alkyl- or aryl-prefix followed by -amine. Hence $CH_3CH_2NH_2$ is ethylamine.

## SAQ 15.2

**a** Name the following compounds:

A          CH₃CH₂CH₂CH₂CH₂CH₂CH₃

B           C

D 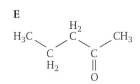          E

F 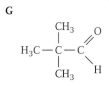          G

**b** Draw structural formulae for the following compounds: (i) propanal; (ii) propan-2-ol; (iii) 2-methylpentan-3-one; (iv) propylamine.

## SAQ 15.3

Represent the compound 2-chloro-2-methylpropane by means of the following types of formulae:
**a** displayed, **b** structural, **c** skeletal, **d** molecular, **e** three-dimensional.

## SAQ 15.4

Draw displayed formulae for the following compounds:
**a** 2,2,3-trimethylbutane; **b** cyclobutane;
**c** 3-ethylpent-2-ene; **d** ethylbenzene.

# Determination of empirical formulae of organic compounds

The determination of the empirical formula of an organic compound involves combustion analysis. A known mass of the compound is burned completely in an excess of oxygen. The carbon dioxide and water produced are collected by absorption onto suitable solids, and the masses of these products are measured. From these results we can determine the masses of carbon and of hydrogen in the known mass of the compound. If oxygen is present this is found by subtracting the masses of the other elements present.

If the compound contains nitrogen, a second sample of known mass is reduced using a mixture of reducing agents. Subsequent treatments drive the nitrogen off as ammonia, the quantity of which is determined by titration with acid. This method was named after Kjeldahl (pronounced Keldale) who used it in 1883 for the analysis of the grain for Carlsberg lager (*figure 15.7*).

● **Figure 15.7** Fermentation vessels in the Carlsberg brewery.

Let us now look at how the empirical formula of an amino acid is determined. We shall assume, for example, that 0.10000 g of an amino acid produced 0.11710 g of carbon dioxide and 0.05992 g of water, and that in a Kjeldahl determination of nitrogen, a second 0.10000 g of the amino acid produced 0.02264 g of ammonia. To determine the empirical formula of the amino acid, we first calculate the masses of carbon, hydrogen and nitrogen in 0.10000 g of the amino acid:

As 12 g of carbon are present in 1 mol (= 44 g) $CO_2$,

$$\text{mass of carbon in } 0.11710 \text{ g of } CO_2 = \frac{12}{44} \times 0.11710 \text{ g}$$
$$= 0.03194 \text{ g}$$
$$= \text{mass of carbon in the amino acid}$$

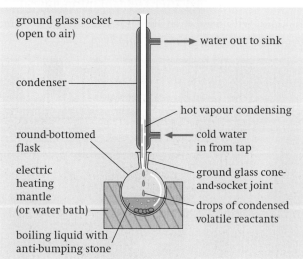

• **Figure 15.8** The apparatus for carrying out a reaction under reflux.

ground glass socket (open to air)

water out to sink

condenser

hot vapour condensing

round-bottomed flask

cold water in from tap

electric heating mantle (or water bath)

ground glass cone-and-socket joint

drops of condensed volatile reactants

boiling liquid with anti-bumping stone

As 2 g of hydrogen are present in 1 mol (= 18 g) $H_2O$,

$$\text{mass of hydrogen in } 0.05992 \text{ g of } H_2O = \frac{2}{18} \times 0.05992 \text{ g}$$
$$= 0.00666 \text{ g}$$
$$= \text{mass of hydrogen in the amino acid}$$

As 14 g of nitrogen are present in 1 mol (= 17 g) $NH_3$,

$$\text{mass of nitrogen in } 0.02264 \text{ g of } NH_3 = \frac{14}{17} \times 0.02264 \text{ g}$$
$$= 0.01864 \text{ g}$$

The remaining mass of the amino acid must consist of oxygen. Hence:

$$\text{mass of oxygen in the amino acid}$$
$$= (0.10000 - 0.03194 - 0.00666 - 0.01864) \text{ g}$$
$$= 0.04276 \text{ g}$$

| | C | H | O | N |
|---|---|---|---|---|
| Mass (g) | 0.03194 | 0.00666 | 0.04276 | 0.01864 |
| Amount (mol) | 0.03194/12 $= 2.66 \times 10^{-3}$ | 0.00666/1 $= 6.66 \times 10^{-3}$ | 0.04276/16 $= 2.67 \times 10^{-3}$ | 0.01864/14 $= 1.33 \times 10^{-3}$ |

Divide by the smallest amount to give whole numbers:

| Atoms (mol) | 2 | 5 | 2 | 1 |
|---|---|---|---|---|

Hence the empirical formula is $C_2H_5O_2N$.

### SAQ 15.5

A 0.2000 g sample of an organic compound, **W**, was analysed by combustion analysis. 0.4800 g of carbon dioxide and 0.1636 g of water were obtained. A second 0.2000 g sample of **W** produced 0.0618 g of ammonia in a Kjeldahl analysis. Use this data to show that **W** contains only carbon, hydrogen and nitrogen and calculate the empirical formula of **W**.

## Practical techniques

Many organic reactions proceed slowly. They often require heating for a period of time. As the reaction mixtures required often contain volatile reactants or solvent, the heating must be carried out under reflux: a condenser is placed in the neck of the reaction flask so that the volatile components are condensed and returned to the flask. *Figure 15.8* illustrates the arrangement together with a cross-section diagram (of the type you might reproduce in an examination answer). Note that the water flows into the condenser at the lower (hotter end). This provides the most rapid cooling of the vapour back to liquid. The liquid which is returned to the flask is still close to its boiling point.

The time required for the reflux period will depend on the rate of the reaction. Many reactions require a short period of reflux (perhaps 10 to 30 minutes). Some reactions may require as long as 24 hours. The use of thermostatically controlled heating mantles (shown in the cross-section diagram in *figure 15.8*) allows long refluxes to be carried out safely overnight.

After reflux, the reaction mixture is likely to consist of an equilibrium mixture containing both reactant and product molecules. These may usually be separated by a simple distillation. A photograph of distillation apparatus appears in *figure 15.9*. Compare the water flow with the flow for the reflux apparatus. For distillation, although the cold water enters at the lower end of the condenser (as with reflux), this entry point is further from the flask. The water not only condenses the vapour, but also cools the liquid to bring it close to room temperature.

After distillation, further purification may require washing the impure product with water in a separating funnel (*figure 15.10*). This enables the separation of immiscible liquids. After washing in a separating funnel, the liquid may require drying. It is placed in a stoppered flask together

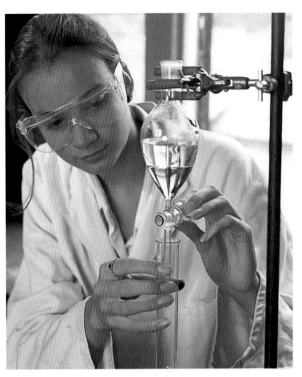

● **Figure 15.10** A separating funnel enables the pink organic layer to be separated from the aqueous layer.

with an anhydrous (containing no water) salt such as calcium chloride. This absorbs excess water. After drying, the liquid will require filtering and redistilling.

Where the product is a solid, distillation is inappropriate. Solid products may crystallise in the reaction flask or may be precipitated on pouring the reaction mixture into water. Rapid separation of the solid is achieved by vacuum filtration (*figure 15.11*).

After separation, the solid is purified by recrystallisation from a suitable solvent. The aim of recrystallisation is to use just enough hot solvent to completely dissolve all the solid. On cooling, the product crystallises, leaving impurities in solution. The purity of a compound may be checked by finding its melting point. A pure compound will usually have a sharp melting point (that is, the point from where it begins to soften to where it is completely liquid is a narrow range of temperature (1 or 2 °C)), whereas an impure compound will melt over a larger range of temperature. The melting-point apparatus shown in *figure 15.12* enables the melting of individual crystals to be seen.

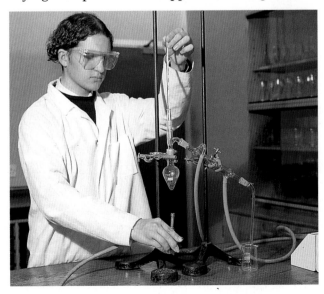

● **Figure 15.9** The apparatus for a distillation.

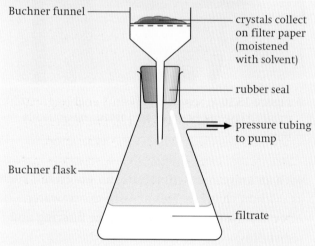

● **Figure 15.11** The apparatus required for a vacuum filtration.

## Criteria for checking purity

Determination of the melting point of a solid is one method for checking the purity of a product. The boiling point of a liquid may also give some indication of purity. In addition, there are many modern techniques for establishing purity. Amongst these methods, the techniques of thin-layer chromatography, gas–liquid chromatography and high-performance liquid chromatography are widely used. Paper chromatography and electrophoresis are also used.

Many of these methods are coupled to spectro-scopic techniques. Gas–liquid chromatography is often followed by mass spectrometry of the separated components. High-performance liquid chromatography and electrophoresis may be followed by ultraviolet or visible spectroscopy of each component. A capillary electrophoresis apparatus is shown in *figure 15.13*, together with a sample print of results showing the spectra of the components using a three-dimensional graph.

## Calculation of percentage yields

Organic reactions often give yields much less than 100%. This is hardly surprising when the product is subjected to recrystallisation or distillation. Material is lost each time the product is trans-ferred from one piece of equipment to another. In

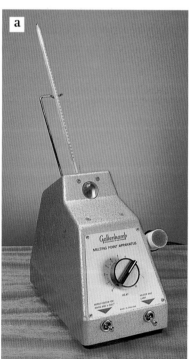

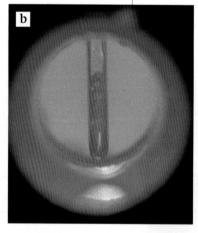

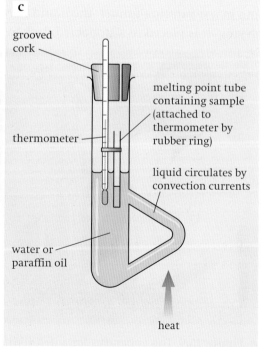

● **Figure 15.12**
a A simple apparatus used to determine melting point.
b Close-up of crystals melting in the apparatus.
c Diagram of a Thiele tube apparatus, also used to determine melting point.

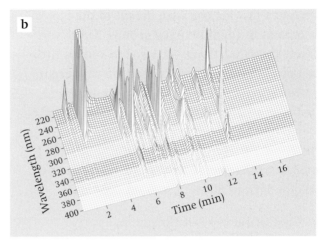

● **Figure 15.13**
**a** Capillary electrophoresis equipment.
**b** Capillary electrophoresis enables the separation of organic molecules to take place under the influence of a high voltage. This electrophoretogram shows the retention times for compounds in a mixture; different compounds pass through the capillary tube at different rates. As each compound emerges from the capillary tube, its ultraviolet spectrum is also recorded. The vertical axis shows the absorption of ultraviolet radiation for each compound at certain wavelengths.

addition to this problem, many reactions produce equilibrium mixtures.

In order to find the yield of the product, you first calculate the maximum mass of product that you could obtain from the starting material. This may involve a preliminary calculation to decide if one or more of the reagents is in excess. If a reagent is in excess, the other reagent will limit the maximum yield of product. We will use the synthesis of aspirin as an example.

2.0 g of 2-hydroxybenzoic acid is refluxed with 5.5 g of ethanoic anhydride. The products are aspirin and ethanoic acid. The aspirin is easily separated as a solid. The equation for the reaction, together with the relative molecular masses of the compounds, is:

$$\underset{\substack{\text{2-hydroxybenzoic acid}\\M_r=138}}{\ce{C6H4(CO2H)(OH)}} + \underset{\substack{\text{ethanoic}\\\text{anhydride}\\M_r=102}}{(CH_3CO)_2O} \longrightarrow \underset{\substack{\text{aspirin}\\M_r=180}}{\ce{aspirin}} + CH_3CO_2H$$

$$\text{Amount of 2-hydroxybenzoic acid used} = \frac{2.0}{138}$$
$$= 0.0145\,\text{mol}$$

$$\text{Amount of ethanoic anhydride used} = \frac{5.5}{102}$$
$$= 0.054\,\text{mol}$$

As 0.0145 mol of 2-hydroxybenzoic acid requires only 0.0145 mol of ethanoic anhydride, a large excess of ethanoic anhydride has been used.

The reaction equation shows us that one mole of 2-hydroxybenzoic acid produces one mole of aspirin.

Hence maximum yield of aspirin

$$= \frac{180}{138} \times 2.0 = 2.6\,\text{g}$$

A student making aspirin whilst studying this module prepared 1.2g of recrystallised aspirin. His percentage yield was thus

$$\frac{1.2}{2.6} \times 100 = 46\%$$

## SAQ 15.6

A student prepared a sample of 1-bromobutane, $C_4H_9Br$, from 10.0 g of butan-1-ol, $C_4H_9OH$. After purification she found she had made 12.0 g of 1-bromobutane. What was the percentage yield?

# Organising organic reactions

There are several ways of organising the study of organic reactions. In this book the information is organised by functional group, so that subsequent chapters provide you with details of the typical reactions of the functional groups. Before you study these reactions, you need to know a little about the general types of reaction that occur.

You should be familiar with **acid–base** and reduction–oxidation (**redox**) reactions. Organic compounds frequently exhibit both these types of reaction. For example, ethanoic acid behaves as a typical acid, forming salts when reacted with alkalis such as aqueous sodium hydroxide:

$$CH_3COOH(aq) + NaOH(aq)$$
$$\rightarrow CH_3COONa(aq) + H_2O(l)$$

As with other acid–base reactions, a salt (sodium ethanoate) and water are formed.

Ethanol is readily oxidised in air to ethanoic acid (wine or beer soon become oxidised to vinegar if left exposed to the air):

$$CH_3CH_2OH(aq) + O_2(g)$$
$$\rightarrow CH_3COOH(aq) + H_2O(l)$$

In this redox reaction, oxygen is reduced to water.

There are several other types of reaction. These are substitution, addition, elimination and hydrolysis.

■ **Substitution** involves replacing an atom (or a group of atoms) by another atom (or group of atoms). For example, the bromine atom in bromoethane is substituted by the –OH group to form ethanol on warming with aqueous sodium hydroxide:

$$CH_3CH_2Br(l) + OH^-(aq)$$
$$\rightarrow CH_3CH_2OH(aq) + Br^-(aq)$$

■ **Addition** reactions involve two molecules joining together to form a single new molecule. If ethene and steam are passed over a hot phosphoric acid catalyst, ethanol is produced:

$$CH_2=CH_2(g) + H_2O(g) \rightarrow CH_3CH_2OH(g)$$

■ **Elimination** involves the removal of a molecule from a larger one. The addition of ethene to steam may be reversed by passing ethanol vapour over a hot catalyst such as pumice. A water molecule is eliminated:

$$CH_3CH_2OH(g) \rightarrow CH_2=CH_2(g) + H_2O(g)$$

■ **Hydrolysis** reactions involve breaking covalent bonds by reaction with water. The substitution of the bromine atom in bromoethane (above) by hydroxide is also a hydrolysis. The reaction proceeds much more slowly in water:

$$CH_3CH_2Br(l) + H_2O(l)$$
$$\rightarrow CH_3CH_2OH(aq) + HBr(aq)$$

# What is a reaction mechanism?

A balanced chemical equation shows the reactants and the products of a chemical change. It provides no information about the reaction pathway. The **reaction pathway** will include details of intermediate chemical species (molecules, radicals or ions) which have a transient existence between reactants and products. The **activation energy** for a reaction is the energy required to form these transient species (*figure 15.14a*). **Catalysts** are frequently used in reactions to increase the rate of reaction. They do this by providing an alternative reaction pathway with a lower activation energy (*figure 15.14b*).

If a reaction pathway with a lower activation energy is found, more molecules will have sufficient kinetic energy to react. Catalysts take part in the reaction mechanism, but they are recovered unchanged at the end of the reaction. Hence the catalyst does not appear in the balanced chemical equation for the reaction.

The mechanism is described using equations for the steps involved. You will meet the following organic mechanisms in this book:
■ free-radical substitution (page 296);
■ electrophilic addition (page 303);
■ nucleophilic substitution (page 329);
■ electrophilic substitution (page 322);
■ nucleophilic addition (page 353).
The terms free radical, electrophilic and nucleophilic refer to the nature of the attacking species (the reactant that starts a reaction by 'attacking' a bond on another reactant) in the reaction. These terms will be explained in the next section.

## Breaking bonds in different ways

A covalent bond consists of a pair of electrons lying between the nuclei of two atoms. The nega-

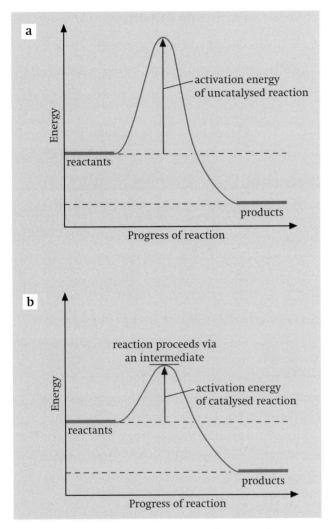

● **Figure 15.14** Activation energy diagrams for a reaction:
**a** without a catalyst;
**b** with a catalyst.

tively charged electrons attract both nuclei, binding them together. Such a bond may be broken in two different ways. We will consider these possibilities for hydrogen chloride. The dot-and-cross diagram for hydrogen chloride is:

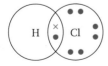

The bond may be broken so that each element takes one of the covalent bond electrons:

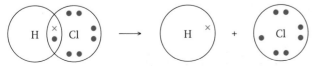

Each element now has a single unpaired electron. (In this example they have also become atoms.)

Atoms (or groups of atoms) with unpaired electrons are known as **free radicals**. When a covalent bond is broken to form two free radicals, the process is called **homolytic fission**. If a bond breaks homolytically, the energy is usually provided by ultraviolet light or high temperature.

Unpaired electrons are represented by a dot. Using dots for the unpaired electrons, the homolytic fission of bromomethane to form a methyl radical and a bromine radical may be represented as follows:

$$H_3C - Br \rightarrow CH_3{\cdot} + Br{\cdot}$$

Alternatively, a covalent bond may be broken so that one element takes both covalent bond electrons. Hydrogen chloride would form hydrogen ions and chloride ions:

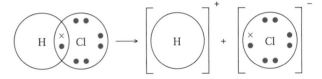

Notice that the more electronegative element takes both electrons. When a covalent bond is broken to form two oppositely charged ions, the process is called **heterolytic fission**. The bond in hydrogen chloride breaks heterolytically when the gas dissolves in water to form hydrochloric acid.

The movement of *two* electrons from the bond to the same atom is sometimes shown by a **curly arrow**. Using curly arrows, the heterolytic fission of bromomethane to form a positive methyl ion and a bromide ion may be represented as follows:

$$H_3C - Br \rightarrow CH_3{}^+ + Br^-$$

Positively charged ions that contain carbon, such as $CH_3{}^+$, are known as **carbocations**. (A negatively charged ion such as $CH_3{}^-$ is known as a **carbanion**.)

Free radicals, carbocations and carbanions are all highly reactive species. They react with molecules, causing covalent bonds to break and new covalent bonds to form.

Carbocations and carbanions are examples of reagents known as electrophiles and nucleophiles respectively. An **electrophile** (electron-lover) is an electron-pair acceptor which is attracted to an electron-rich molecule, leading to the formation of a new covalent bond between the electrophile and the molecule under attack. Electrophiles must be capable of accepting a pair of electrons. A **nucleophile** (nucleus-lover) is an electron-pair donor which is attracted to an atom with a partial positive charge, leading to the formation of a new covalent bond between the nucleophile and the atom under attack. Nucleophiles must possess a lone-pair of electrons for this new bond.

### SAQ 15.7

Draw dot-and-cross diagrams for the following species: $Br\cdot$, $Cl^-$, $CH_3^+$, $CH_3^-$, $CH_3\cdot$, $NH_3$, $BF_3$. Classify them as free radicals, electrophiles or nucleophiles. What do you notice about the outer electron shells of free radicals, electrophiles and nucleophiles?

# Isomerism

Most organic compounds have a molecular formula that is the same as one or more other compounds. This property is called isomerism. **Isomers** have the same molecular formula but the atoms are arranged in different ways. Isomerism arises for a number of reasons, including the ability of carbon to bond to itself and to most other elements in the Periodic Table. The atoms present in a given molecular formula may be treated rather like the children's construction toy Lego®, in that a given number of different pieces may be put together in a variety of ways.

## Structural isomerism

Structural isomerism describes the situation where chemicals of the same formula behave differently because the structures are different.

For example, the atoms of butane, $C_4H_{10}$, can be put together in two different ways. Try building models of these two isomers (or use a molecular modelling program on a computer). The two isomers behave in a very similar way chemically. The most noticeable difference in their properties is their boiling points. One isomer is more compact. This reduces the intermolecular forces as the molecules cannot approach each other so closely. This isomer has a boiling point of $-11.6\,°C$. The isomer which is less compact has a boiling point of $-0.4\,°C$. The displayed formulae and the names

of these two structural isomers are:

butane

methylpropane

### SAQ 15.8

Copy the displayed formulae of the structural isomers of butane. Label each isomer with its appropriate boiling point.

The molecular formula $C_2H_6O$ provides a very different example of structural isomerism. It has two isomers: ethanol, $C_2H_5OH$, and methoxymethane, $CH_3OCH_3$. Molecular models of these two isomers are shown in *figure 15.15*. Ethanol is an alcohol whilst methoxymethane is the simplest member of the homologous series of ethers, which are characterised by a $-COC-$ group. As they contain different functional groups, they have very different chemical and physical properties. Ethanol is able to form intermolecular hydrogen bonds; methoxymethane has weaker dipole–dipole intermolecular forces. Consequently the boiling point of ethanol ($78.5\,°C$) is considerably higher than that of methoxymethane ($-25\,°C$). Alcohols take part in many different reactions. Ethers, apart from being highly flammable, are relatively inert.

It is quite easy to mistake the flexibility of molecular structures for isomerism. For example, if you build a model of pentane, $C_5H_{10}$, you will find it is very flexible (*figure 15.16* shows three of the possibilities). The flexibility of a carbon chain arises because atoms can rotate freely about a carbon–carbon single bond. You should be careful

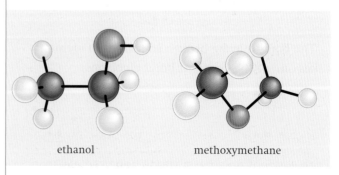

ethanol                    methoxymethane

● **Figure 15.15** Structural isomers of $C_2H_6O$.

when drawing displayed formulae of isomers. The following structures are not isomers. They are actually the same molecule:

$$\begin{array}{ccccc} & H & H & H & H & H \\ & | & | & | & | & | \\ H- & C- & C- & C- & C- & C-H \\ & | & | & | & | & | \\ & H & H & H & H & H \end{array}$$

These are all the same molecule; compare the displayed formula with the models in *figure 15.16*. Displayed formulae give a false impression of these structures. Remember that there is a tetrahedral arrangement of atoms round each carbon atom (with bond angles of 109.5°, not 90° as in displayed formulae).

## SAQ 15.9

Draw the displayed formulae for all the structural isomers of hexane.

## Stereoisomerism

In **stereoisomerism**, the same atoms are joined to each other in different spatial arrangements. Geometric and optical isomerism are two types of this stereoisomerism.

### Geometric (or *cis–trans*) isomerism

Whilst atoms on either side of a carbon–carbon single bond can rotate freely, those either side of a carbon–carbon double bond cannot. Try making models of but-2-ene, $CH_3CH=CHCH_3$. Two geometric (or *cis–trans*) isomers are possible. You should obtain models similar to those shown in *figure 15.17*. (In *cis*-but-2-ene, the methyl groups are on the *same* side of the double bond. In *trans*-but-2-ene, they lie *across* the double bond.)

## SAQ 15.10

**a** Draw the geometric isomers of 1,2-dichloroethene, CHCl=CHCl, and label them as *cis* or *trans*.

**b** Copy the following structures and indicate which can exhibit geometric isomerism by drawing the second isomer and labelling the two isomers as *cis* or *trans*.

$$\underset{H}{\overset{Br}{>}}C=C\underset{H}{\overset{Br}{<}} \qquad \underset{H}{\overset{Br}{>}}C=C\underset{H}{\overset{H}{<}} \qquad \underset{H}{\overset{Br}{>}}C=C\underset{H}{\overset{CH_3}{<}} \qquad \underset{H}{\overset{Br}{>}}C=C\underset{CH_3}{\overset{CH_3}{<}}$$

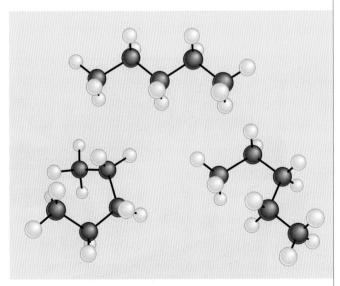

● **Figure 15.16** Models showing the flexibility of pentane. These forms are the same molecule, they are not isomers. The flexibility is due to the free rotation about the C–C single bond.

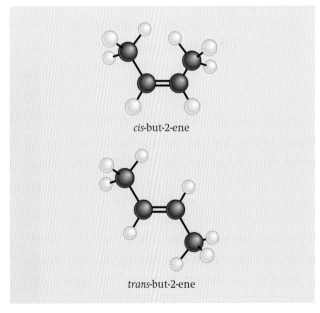

*cis*-but-2-ene

*trans*-but-2-ene

● **Figure 15.17** Geometric or *cis–trans* isomers of but-2-ene.

## Optical isomerism

The simplest form of optical isomerism occurs when a carbon atom is joined to four different groups. The groups can be arranged in two different ways and the two isomers so formed are mirror images of each other, which cannot be superimposed. Try making models of the amino acid alanine.

$$H - \underset{\underset{NH_2}{|}}{\overset{\overset{CH_3}{|}}{C}} - CO_2H$$

If you have made two models that are mirror images of each other, you will find that you are unable to superimpose them so that they match. Molecular models of the two **optical isomers** (enantiomers) of alanine are shown in *figure 15.18*.

Molecules that are mirror images, and so cannot be superimposed, are known as **chiral molecules**. The name comes from the Greek for hand. Place your hands together with the palms in contact. Hands are mirror images of each other. Place one hand on top of the other with both palms uppermost. Your thumbs are now on opposite sides. Like chiral molecules, hands cannot be superimposed. Optical isomerism is often referred to as chirality. The carbon atom which carries four different groups is a **chiral centre**.

Many of the molecules found in living organisms contain chiral centres. Usually only one of the isomers is biochemically active. This is not surprising when you consider the shape selectivity of, for example, enzymes. Medicines that have chiral molecules may need to be administered as a pure isomer. Synthetic organic reactions usually result in a mixture containing equal amounts of both isomers (a racemic mixture). Purification of such mixtures can be done by crystallisation with a chiral acid or base. However, new separation techniques such as chiral high-performance liquid chromatography are enabling much better separations (*figure 15.19*). To avoid expensive separation

techniques, a few 'leading technology companies' are now using synthetic routes which produce only the required isomer.

### SAQ 15.11

a Draw the optical isomers of bromochlorofluoromethane.

b Copy the following formulae and mark the chiral centres with an asterisk:

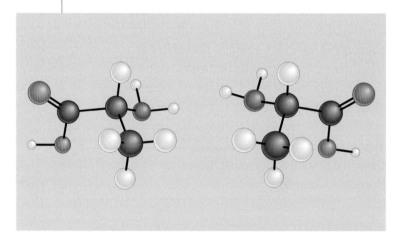

Optical isomers, like other isomers, have the same molecular formulae. As stereoisomers, they have the same atoms and the same bonds between

● **Figure 15.18** Ball-and-stick models of alanine enantiomers.

● **Figure 15.19** High-performance liquid chromatography equipment.

atoms. However, the bonds are arranged differently in space. The molecule CHBrClF provides a simple example of optical isomerism. The displayed formula of CHBrClF is shown below.

Displayed formulae give no indication of the spatial arrangement of the atoms in this molecule.

To display the optical isomers, we need to use three-dimensional formulae:

In these diagrams the solid wedge is coming towards you, the dashed wedge is away from you.

Rotation of the right-hand structure about the C–H bond produces

Notice that in the two structures the F, C and H atoms are in the same spatial position but the Br and Cl are interchanged. If the two isomers are placed on top of each other, as follows, they do not match. We say they are non-superimposable.

A key feature of a chiral centre in an organic molecule is the presence of four different groups

on a carbon atom. The chiral centre in CHBrClF is labelled with an asterisk in the following diagram:

When drawing three-dimensional formulae by hand, it saves time to use a dotted line instead of the dashed wedge.

In this book we use the dashed wedge to provide a more three-dimensional effect. You will find it helps to visualise these structures if you use a model kit (or modelling software on a computer) to make these two isomers. (Use the colours shown in *table 15.1* on page 269 for the different atoms.) Molecular models of these isomers are shown in *figure 15.20*.

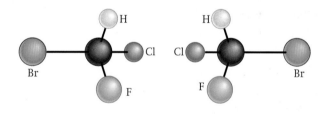

● **Figure 15.20** Ball-and-stick models of the optical isomers of CHBrClF.

With the exception of glycine, the α-amino acids all have a chiral centre at the α-carbon atom (the α-carbon atom is the one next to the carboxylic acid group). For example, alanine has the structure

$$H_2N—\overset{\overset{CH_3}{|}}{\underset{\underset{H}{|}}{C^*}}—COOH$$

## SAQ 15.12
Draw three-dimensional formulae to show the two optical isomers of alanine.

You will have already seen that many naturally occurring compounds are predominantly found as one of two isomeric forms. This type of isomerism is called optical isomerism.

It is not hard to find the reasons why only one of the two isomers predominates naturally. As life has evolved, the biochemical processes that take place in organisms have also evolved. Many of these processes require molecules of a specific shape for reactions to occur. For example, neuro-transmitters interact with sites on nerve cells that exactly accommodate both their shape and the intermolecular forces arising from the arrangement of atoms present. A different isomer of a specific neurotransmitter could not interact with these sites. Dopa is a neurotransmitter that exhibits optical isomerism. Only one form of dopa (L-dopa) is active in the brain. *Figure 15.21* shows a molecular model of L-dopa.

In this section, we shall look at examples of stereoisomerism. We shall also look at the stepwise synthesis of organic compounds. This provides an opportunity to bring together your knowledge and understanding of organic chemistry. We shall also look at the way chemists are trying to mimic nature by selecting synthetic routes to produce only the active isomer when manufacturing a medicine.

### SAQ 15.13

Draw the three-dimensional formula of L-dopa using the molecular model in *figure 15.21*. Alongside, mark a mirror plane and draw the three-dimensional formula of the isomer of L-dopa. Label this isomer D-dopa.

L-dopa is used in the treatment of Parkinson's disease. This disease causes much suffering and is characterised by tremors in the hands and loss of balance. The L-dopa must be free of D-dopa as the latter has many unpleasant side-effects. Increasingly, chemists are finding that, where a medicine has a chiral centre, one isomer is more beneficial than the other is. In some instances, as with D-dopa, one isomer has undesirable effects. Many chemical companies are seeking routes to produce chiral medicines containing only the beneficial isomer. A medicine containing only the beneficial isomer will require a smaller dose as only half the quantity of the medicine is needed. Pharmacological activity will be improved and side-effects reduced or even eliminated.

● **Figure 15.22** The leaves and bark of willow trees were used as a 'folk' medicine to reduce a fever and to relieve pain.

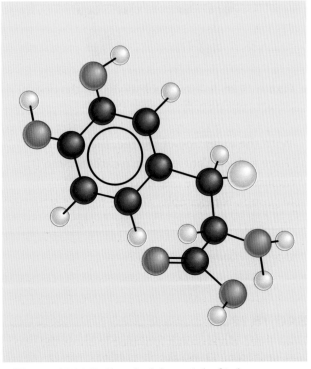

● **Figure 15.21** Ball-and-stick model of L-dopa.

Undesirable effects proved to be a particular problem with the drug thalidomide, which was prescribed to pregnant women as a sedative during the early 1960s. Indeed, thalidomide was for a time the preferred sedative during pregnancy as the alternatives, such as valium, were addictive. Unfortunately, one of the isomers of thalidomide proved to have disastrous side-effects, causing babies to be born with congenital deformities (teratogenicity). Not surprisingly, thalidomide was quickly withdrawn from use. It is now mandatory for tests to be carried out on possible new medicines for teratogenicity.

**Note**: In the examples used in the rest of this chapter, some compounds are used that are discussed in the A2 sections of this book. These are for illustration only and do *not* need to be studied for the AS course.

# How do we design molecules?

If we wish to design a molecule for a particular purpose, one approach is to identify the structural features that will achieve the desired result. The structural features of interest may be associated with the shape of the molecule or with the functional groups present. It is often possible to see a relationship between these structural features and the behaviour of the molecule in the body (pharmacological activity).

Some of the milder pain killers such as aspirin are derived from 2-hydroxybenzoic acid (salicylic acid). (These compounds are also used to reduce the effects of fevers.) Many modern medicines are related to naturally occurring compounds used in 'folk' medicine.

## SAQ 15.14

The structures of aspirin, 2-hydroxybenzoic acid and salicin are:

aspirin

2-hydroxybenzoic acid
(salicylic acid)

salicin

Copy these diagrams and circle the common structural feature.

For example, a derivative of salicylic acid, called salicin, is present in willow bark and willow leaves (*figure 15.22*). An infusion of willow leaves was recommended by Hippocrates (in 400 BC) for relieving pain whilst giving birth. A brew made from willow bark was used in the eighteenth century to reduce fever.

The part of the molecules that you have circled in *SAQ 15.14* is the part which gives rise to their similar pharmacological activity. Such a structural feature is known as a **pharmacophore**. Investigation of other potential pain killers might focus on making similar molecules with this common structural feature.

## SAQ 15.15

Which of these compounds might have potential as mild pain killers?

A    B    C

Medicines act by binding to **receptor molecules** present in the body. In order to bind to a receptor molecule and produce the desired pharmacological effect, the medicine molecule must have the following features.

- A shape which fits the receptor molecule.
- Groups which are capable of forming intermolecular bonds to complementary groups on the receptor molecules. These intermolecular bonds may involve hydrogen bonding, ionic attraction, dipole–dipole forces or instantaneous dipole–induced dipole forces.

Computers are now used to examine the relationship between a molecule and a receptor site. Such molecular modelling has greatly speeded up the process of designing new medicines; the interactions and fit of a potential medicine with a biological receptor molecule can be studied before the medicine is synthesised (*figure 15.23*). Before molecular modelling became available, the synthesis of a new medicine involved far more trial and error with many more compounds being

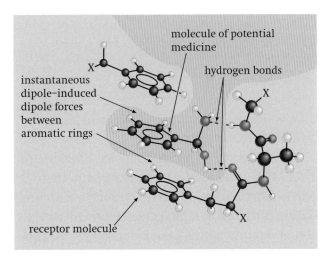

● **Figure 15.23** The interaction between a receptor molecule and a potential medicine.

prepared for testing. With molecular modelling, only those molecules that show potential after computer tests are made and tested. Molecular modelling on a computer thus provides a powerful tool for the design of medicines and many other compounds (such as pesticides or polymers).

### SAQ 15.16

Which of these compounds would you choose to investigate for pharmacological activity at the receptor site shown in *figure 15.23*?

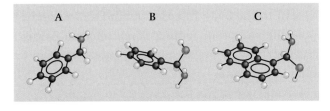

# Routes to new molecules

Even simple molecules such as aspirin may have several functional groups present. There may be a suitable, readily available molecule with a structure very close to the one desired. If such a starting material exists, it may be possible to achieve the desired product in a one-step synthesis. A one-step synthesis involves converting the starting material to the product by means of a single reaction. For example, a natural penicillin may be modified to produce a new penicillin with enhanced antibacterial activity. However, it is much more likely that several separate reactions

may be needed to convert a suitable starting compound to the desired product: a multi-step synthesis is required.

Planning a multi-step synthesis requires a sound knowledge of many different reactions. The reactions that you have met in your study of advanced chemistry provide you with the basis for planning the syntheses of a surprisingly wide range of organic compounds. We shall now review these reactions. This review should enable you to use reactions effectively in planning multi-step syntheses of your own, as well as helping you to learn the reactions more thoroughly. The reactions are best divided into two groups: aliphatic reactions and aromatic reactions.

## Aliphatic reactions

You may have already seen a connection between the reactions of a number of functional groups. These are summarised in *figure 15.24*, which shows the names of the functional groups, together with arrows to indicate the interconversions possible.

## Aromatic reactions

*Figure 15.25* provides you with the framework for reactions involving aromatic compounds.

Try copying and displaying the reaction summaries (from *figures 15.24* and *15.25*) where you will look at them regularly – this will help you to learn the reactions and their conditions. Note the central role of halogenoalkanes in these synthetic routes. The frameworks given in *figures 15.24* and *15.25* are also suitable for making annotated charts to provide summaries of reaction mechanisms or for summaries of tests for the different groups.

You can use the reaction summaries to plan multi-step syntheses. Suppose we wish to convert ethene to ethanoic acid. A possible route is to convert ethene to ethanol, which is then oxidised to ethanoic acid. Alternatively, ethene could be converted to bromoethane, which is then hydrolysed to ethanol, and this is oxidised to ethanoic acid. This alternative involves an extra reaction step; you should usually try to complete a synthesis in as few steps as possible (remember that material is lost at each stage when preparing organic compounds: reaction yields seldom approach 100%).

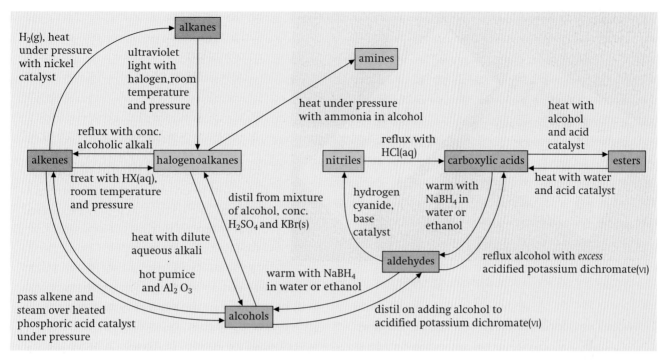

● **Figure 15.24** A summary of reactions of the functional groups.

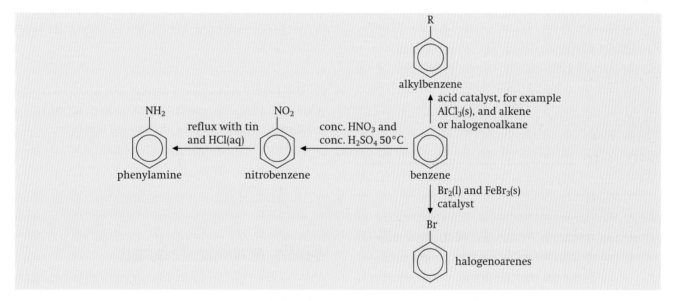

● **Figure 15.25** A summary of reactions involving aromatic compounds.

### *SAQ 15.17*

Outline how you might carry out the following conversions involving two- or three-step syntheses. Include the conditions required for the reactions. Start by drawing the structural formulae of the initial and final compounds.

**a** Ethene to ethylamine.

**b** Benzaldehyde to ethyl benzoate.

**c** 1-bromopropane to butanoic acid.

**d** Butan-2-one to 2-aminobutane.

# Carrying out a synthesis

The synthesis of a simple medicine, such as paracetamol or aspirin (*figure 15.26*), can provide an exciting basis for an investigation. The structures of paracetamol and aspirin are:

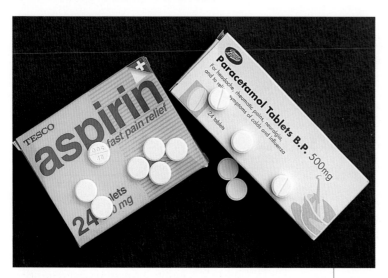

● **Figure 15.26** Aspirin and paracetamol are products of multi-step syntheses.

When considering such an investigation, there are a number of criteria to consider. A good investigation will have sufficient scope to allow you to demonstrate your skills in planning, implementing, analysing evidence and drawing conclusions, evaluating evidence and procedures. As these skills all carry similar weight in the assessment of your investigation, it is important that you design your investigation in such a way as to allow you to address each skill.

### SAQ 15.18 _____

Outline a possible route from phenol to paracetamol.

If you have answered *SAQ 15.18*, you should have a three-step synthesis. At the end of the first step you will have a mixture of isomers to separate. As they are solids, this may be possible using fractional crystallisation. Alternatively, chromatography may be used. The second step involves a steam distillation. All this takes time, and in the limited amount of practical time that you have for your investigation you may only manage to complete this synthesis two (possibly three) times. As this will produce very limited results, you will have insufficient opportunity to discuss the effects of variables or to produce a well-developed discussion of your results. You may have made a couple of samples of paracetamol with yields and melting points to comment on, but little else.

A better approach for the purpose of an investigation is to concentrate on investigating the best conditions to optimise the yield at a particular step. Studying the effect of different conditions on a single reaction step will give a range of results for discussion. For example, the first step to paracetamol involves the nitration of phenol. Different conditions could be tried – a range of temperatures; a range of concentrations of nitric acid; different lengths of reaction time; and so on. Analysis of the products obtained in this first step may be carried out at intervals during the reaction using thin-layer chromatography. Comparisons may be made of product yield and purity.

If you carry out an investigation in this way, you will be working in the same way as a process development chemist, repeating the reaction whilst making minor changes to achieve the optimum yield (you could even consider costs of energy and materials). You will have extensive results to discuss and you can still make a sample of paracetamol.

### SAQ 15.19 _____

Outline a possible conversion of ethanol to ethyl ethanoate via ethanoic acid. Suggest a possible sequence of experiments to investigate optimising the yield of the ester. Indicate which variables are being studied and which are being controlled.

## Deciding on masses of reactants

If you choose to carry out an organic synthesis for your project, you will need to calculate the appropriate reacting masses (for liquids you may choose to use volumes, for solutions you will need to know the concentrations to decide on the volumes required). These will need to be appropriate for the capacity of the reaction flask that you will use.

Calculate reacting quantities using the stoichiometric equation for the reaction. The approach is similar to that used earlier in this chapter when deciding which reactant is in excess for the calculation of percentage yield. You may wish to use exact amounts or to have one (possibly cheaper) reagent in excess.

## SAQ 15.20

Write a balanced equation for the conversion of ethanol to bromoethane using hydrogen bromide. Calculate the mass of ethanol required to react with 2.0 g of hydrogen bromide.

Earlier in this chapter, we discussed the calculation of the yield of product after a single reaction step. To calculate the overall yield for a multi-step synthesis, you multiply the percentage yield of the last step by the fractional yield for the preceding steps. For example, if a three-step synthesis has yields of 70% at each step, the overall yield is:

$$\frac{70}{100} \times \frac{70}{100} \times 70\% = 34\%$$

## Purifying and identifying the product

You will need to consider how to purify your product (called the target molecule in the pharmaceutical industry). Confirming that you have made the target molecule is called characterisation. This can be done in a variety of ways. Chromatography can be particularly useful for confirming purity as well as identity. Other methods of characterising a product include melting point and boiling point determinations, electrophoresis, mass spectrometry and the use of spectroscopic techniques. The spectroscopic techniques are described in chapter 23. You may have the opportunity to study them in more depth in the Spectroscopy option.

## Safety

Before you start any practical work, you must check your proposed experiments for hazards and establish the precautions that you need to take to work safely. This is called a risk assessment and your teacher will provide guidance on how to do this. Your teacher will also expect to check your risk assessment before allowing you to start practical work.

## A two-stage synthesis

2-Hydroxypropanoic acid (lactic acid) may be prepared by the addition of hydrogen cyanide to ethanal. However, due to the toxicity of hydrogen cyanide, you will not be performing this synthesis in school! The reaction is a good example of a nucleophilic addition reaction. Following the addition of hydrogen cyanide, the product is hydrolysed by refluxing with aqueous hydrochloric acid.

The two stages of this reaction are as follows:

Note that, over the two stages of this reaction, the carbon chain length has grown by one carbon atom from two in ethanal to three in the 2-hydroxypropanoic acid. Reactions such as this provide synthetic chemists with a route for lengthening a carbon chain.

## SAQ 15.21

a 2-Hydroxypropanoic acid exists as two isomers. Identify the type of isomerism present and draw appropriate diagrams to illustrate the two isomers.

b  (i) Describe, using structural formulae and curly arrows, the mechanism of the addition of HCN to ethanal.

   (ii) Explain why the nucleophilic addition of HCN to ethanal is catalysed by a base.

   (iii) Suggest, with reference to your answer to **b**(i), why an equimolar mixture of 2-hydroxy-propanoic acid is formed in this nucleophilic addition reaction.

## Designing molecules in industry

The use of molecular modelling in the design of a new medicine has already been mentioned, as have the many tools used by chemists in the characterisation of a compound. The use of all these tools has given us greatly increased capabilities in our search for new medicines. However, the search would not be possible without a wide range of other specialists including botanists, instrument designers and operators, computer scientists, biochemists, statisticians, geneticists and molecular biologists. All these specialists work with chemists in a team with a common goal. Any one of them might have the idea which provides the breakthrough to a new medicine. In terms of a career, working in such a team must be one of the most creative activities possible. Indeed, Lord Porter (winner of the 1967 Nobel Prize for Chemistry) has said: 'We chemists have not yet discovered how to make gold but, in contentment and satisfaction with our lot, we are the richest people on Earth.'

# SUMMARY (AS)

- All organic compounds contain carbon and hydrogen. Most organic compounds also contain other elements, such as oxygen, nitrogen and chlorine.

- Chemists use a wide variety of formulae to represent organic molecules. These include general, empirical, molecular, structural, skeletal, displayed and three-dimensional formulae.

- Functional groups, which have their own characteristic reactions, are attached to the hydrocarbon framework of an organic molecule. Alkenes, arenes, halogen atoms, alcohols, aldehydes and ketones, carboxylic acids, esters, amines, amides and nitriles are examples of functional groups.

- Chemists use a wide variety of formulae to represent organic molecules. These include general, empirical, molecular, structural, skeletal, displayed and three-dimensional formulae.

- Various types of molecular models (ball-and-stick, space-filling) are used to visualise organic molecules.

- Organic molecules are named in a systematic way, related to their structures.

- The empirical formula of an organic compound is found by combustion analysis.

- Practical techniques used in the preparation of organic compounds include reflux, distillation, vacuum filtration, separation of immiscible liquids in a separating funnel and recrystalisation.

- Most organic preparations involve equilibrium reactions and/or lead to losses of product during separation and purification. The percentage yield indicates the proportion of the maximum yield that has been obtained.

- The study of organic reactions is traditionally organised by functional group. Each functional group has its own characteristic reactions.

- Reactions may also be studied by type or by mechanism. Organic compounds may show the following types of reaction: acid–base, redox, substitution, addition, elimination or hydrolysis.

- Reaction mechanisms may involve electrophiles, nucleophiles or free radicals. Each of these reagents is capable of forming a new covalent bond to the atom attacked. Electrophiles are electron-pair acceptors. Nucleophiles are electron-pair donors. Free radicals are highly reactive, attacking any atom with which they are capable of forming a bond.

- Covalent bonds may be broken homolytically to form two free radicals, each with an unpaired electron. Polar bonds will frequently break heterolytically to form one cation and one anion.

- Curly arrows show the movement of two electrons in a reaction mechanism.

- The study of organic reactions is traditionally organised by functional group. Each functional group has its own characteristic reactions.

◆ Organic molecules with the same molecular formula but with different structures are called isomers. Three common types of isomerism are structural, *cis–trans* (or geometrical) and optical. Structural isomers have different structural formulae, *cis–trans* isomers have different displayed formulae and optical isomers have different three-dimensional formulae. Optical isomers are molecules that are mirror images of each other. They contain one or more chiral centres.

◆ Stereoisomers contain the same atoms with the same order of bonds but with different spatial arrangements of the atoms. *Cis–trans* and optical isomers are examples of stereoisomers.

◆ *Cis–trans* isomers are found in alkenes where the carbon–carbon double bond, C=C, prevents rotation. The presence of two identical atoms or groups on opposite sides of the double bond can then give rise to *cis–trans* isomers.

◆ Optical isomers are molecules that are non-superimposable mirror images of each other. Such molecules contain a carbon atom which is a chiral centre. This chiral centre has four different atoms or groups attached to it. With the exception of glycine, α-amino acids exhibit optical isomerism.

◆ Both natural biochemicals and modern medicines contain chiral molecules. Generally, only one of the isomers is beneficial to living organisms. The other isomer may have undesirable effects. The beneficial isomer has the appropriate shape and pattern of intermolecular forces to interact with a receptor molecule in a living organism.

◆ Chemists are now producing medicines containing single isomers rather than a mixture of isomers. This enables the dose to be halved, improves pharmacological activity (behaviour of molecule in an organism) and reduces side-effects.

◆ Molecular design of a new medicine is made possible with a sound understanding of the structural features that produce medical effects. The computerised study of the interactions between molecules and biological receptors has become a powerful tool in the search for new medicines.

◆ Many multi-step syntheses can be planned using the reactions of the functional groups discussed in this book.

◆ The preparation of a new compound will involve safety considerations, making decisions on quantities of reagents to use, establishing what conditions provide the best yield, and purification and characterisation of the product.

◆ In the design and production of a new medicine, chemists work as part of a team that includes a wide range of other specialists such as molecular biologists, chemical engineers and computer scientists.

# Questions (AS)

1 a Explain the following terms and give an example of each:
  (i) electrophile;
  (ii) nucleophile;
  (iii) free radical.

 b Write balanced equations to illustrate:
  (i) electrophilic addition;
  (ii) nucleophilic substitution;
  (iii) free-radical substitution.

2 a Explain, using examples, the following terms used in organic chemistry:
  (i) general formula;
  (ii) homologous series.

 b The Cl–Cl bond can be broken either by homolytic fission or by heterolytic fission. Explain, with the aid of suitable equations, what you understand by the terms **homolytic fission** and **heterolytic fission**.

3 a An organic compound of bromine, **X**, has a molecular mass of 137 and the following percentage composition by mass: C, 35.0%; H, 6.6%; Br, 58.4%.
  (i) Calculate the empirical formula of compound **X**.
  (ii) Show that the molecular formula of **X** is the same as the empirical formula.

 b (i) Draw displayed formulae for all the possible structural isomers of **X**.
  (ii) Name the structural isomers that you have drawn in (i).
  (iii) Draw the skeletal formulae for the isomers that you have drawn in (i).

4 But-2-ene and butan-2-ol both exhibit stereoisomerism.
 a Explain what is meant by the term **stereoisomerism**.
 b Name the **type** of stereoisomerism shown by but-2-ene and butan-2-ol.
 c Using appropriate types of formulae, illustrate your answers to **b** for but-2-ene and butan-2-ol. Draw **two** structures for each type of isomerism.

# Hydrocarbons: alkanes (AS)

## Physical properties of alkanes

The homologous series (see page 270) of alkanes has the general formula $C_nH_{2n+2}$. Alkanes are non-polar molecules containing only C–H and C–C covalent bonds. As all the C–C bonds are single bonds, alkanes are described as saturated **hydrocarbons**. Unsaturated hydrocarbons, such as the alkenes, contain one or more double bonds between carbon atoms.

The atoms in alkanes are held together by σ orbitals. A σ **orbital** lies predominantly along the axis between two nuclei. It may be regarded as being formed by the overlap of two atomic σ orbitals. The two electrons in the orbital attract both nuclei, binding them together in a σ bond. The geometry of alkane molecules is based on the tetrahedral arrangement of four covalent σ bonds round each carbon atom. The σ bonds lie between a carbon atom and either a hydrogen atom or another carbon atom. All bond angles are 109.5°. The molecules can rotate freely about each carbon–carbon single bond. This freedom to rotate allows a great degree of flexibility to alkane chains. The σ bonds in ethane are shown in *figure 16.1*.

The physical states of alkanes at room temperature and pressure change from gases to liquids to

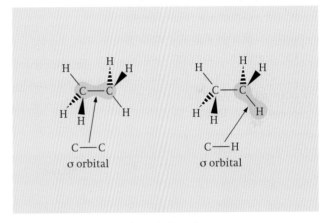

● **Figure 16.1** The σ bonds in ethane.

solids as the number of carbon atoms in the alkane molecule increases. We say that the **volatility** of the alkanes decreases with increasing number of carbon atoms in the alkane molecule. Volatility is the ease with which a liquid turns to vapour. We can examine this trend by plotting graphs of the melting or boiling points of alkanes against the number of carbon atoms present. *Figure 16.2* shows such a graph of the melting points for the straight-chain alkanes, butane to dodecane and eicosane. The term straight-chain indicates no branching is present in the molecule's carbon chain.

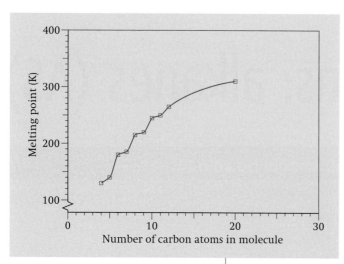

● **Figure 16.2** Melting points of straight-chain alkanes.

a *Table 16.1* contains the boiling points of the first twelve alkanes, and eicosane, $C_{20}H_{42}$. Plot these boiling points on the vertical axis of a graph against the number of carbon atoms present. Compare the shape of your graph with the melting point graph (*figure 16.2*).

| Alkane | Molecular formula | Boiling point (K) |
|---|---|---|
| methane | $CH_4$ | 109 |
| ethane | $C_2H_6$ | 185 |
| propane | $C_3H_8$ | 231 |
| butane | $C_4H_{10}$ | 273 |
| pentane | $C_5H_{12}$ | 309 |
| hexane | $C_6H_{14}$ | 342 |
| heptane | $C_7H_{16}$ | 372 |
| octane | $C_8H_{18}$ | 399 |
| nonane | $C_9H_{20}$ | 424 |
| decane | $C_{10}H_{22}$ | 447 |
| undecane | $C_{11}H_{24}$ | 469 |
| dodecane | $C_{12}H_{26}$ | 489 |
| eicosane | $C_{20}H_{42}$ | 617 |

● **Table 16.1** The boiling points of straight-chain alkanes.

Volatility is determined by the strength of the intermolecular forces between alkane molecules.

a Name the type of intermolecular forces found in alkanes. Give a reason for your answer, and

b explain the trends in the melting and boiling points of the alkanes in terms of these inter-molecular forces.

*Table 16.2* shows the boiling points for pentane and isomers of pentane. 2-methylbutane has one methyl group as a branch, 2,2-dimethyl-propane has two methyl group branches.

Again, a trend is apparent. As the number of branches in the chain increases, the boiling point decreases. The isomers all have the same number of carbon and hydrogen atoms, so we cannot explain the trend in terms of an increasing number of electrons. Look at the space filling models for these isomers, also shown in the table.

As the isomers become more branched, the overall shape of the molecule changes from that of a flexible long balloon (pentane) to one resembling a spherical balloon (2,2-dimethylpropane). The long balloon shape of pentane molecules allows them to pack more closely together than the spherical shape of 2,2-dimethylpropane. The intermolecular forces increase when the molecules approach more closely so the boiling point of pentane is higher than that of 2,2-dimethylpropane. The boiling point of 2-methylbutane, with only one branching point in the carbon chain, lies between the other two isomers.

| Alkane | Structural formula | Boiling point (K) | Space filling model |
|---|---|---|---|
| pentane | $CH_3CH_2CH_2CH_2CH_3$ | 309 | |
| 2-methylbutane | $CH_3CHCH_2CH_3$ with $CH_3$ above | 301 | |
| 2,2-dimethylpropane | $CH_3CCH_3$ with $CH_3$ above and $CH_3$ below | 283 | |

● **Table 16.2** The boiling points of pentane and its isomers.

# Chemical properties of alkanes

## Combustion in air

Alkanes make excellent fuels. Complete combustion in an excess of air produces carbon dioxide and water. For example, butane is used as a fuel in camping gas stoves. The equation for the combustion of butane is:

$$C_4H_{10}(g) + 6\tfrac{1}{2}O_2(g) \rightarrow 4CO_2(g) + 5H_2O(l)$$

Natural gas, used for cooking and heating in many homes (*figure 16.3*), is predominantly methane. Whether using natural gas or butane camping gas, it is important to ensure a good supply of air. If there is insufficient oxygen, incomplete combustion will occur, with the formation of carbon monoxide instead of carbon dioxide. For example, with methane the equation for complete combustion is:

$$CH_4(g) + 2O_2(g) \rightarrow CO_2(g) + 2H_2O(l)$$

The equation for incomplete combustion and formation of carbon monoxide is:

$$CH_4(g) + 1\tfrac{1}{2}O_2(g) \rightarrow CO(g) + 2H_2O(l)$$

Carbon monoxide is a poisonous gas which bonds to the iron of haemoglobin in the blood in preference to oxygen. Carbon monoxide is colour-less and odourless, so its presence is not noticed. Early symptoms of poisoning by carbon monoxide include the skin flushing red, headache and nausea. Many deaths result from the use of faulty

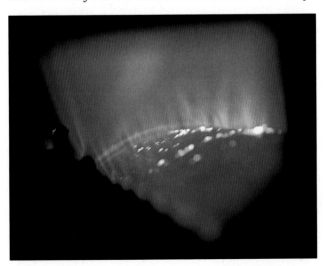

● **Figure 16.3** In a gas boiler the complete combustion of natural gas produces carbon dioxide and water.

gas fires in poorly ventilated rooms. It is impor-tant to have all gas equipment serviced annually and checked for carbon monoxide emissions. In the UK, legislation now requires adequate ventilation wherever there are gas installations. Property landlords are required by law to have their gas equipment checked annually.

### SAQ 16.3

A principal component of petrol is an isomer of octane ($C_8H_{18}$).

**a** Write balanced equations for the combustion of octane: (i) in a limited supply of air with the formation of carbon monoxide and water and (ii) in a supply of air which ensures complete combustion with the formation of carbon dioxide and water.

**b** Using your equations from part **a**, calculate: (i) the additional number of moles of oxygen required to prevent the formation of carbon monoxide on combustion of one mole of octane and (ii) the additional volume of air required (assume one mole of a gas occupies $24.0\,dm^3$ and that air contains 20% oxygen).

## The substitution reaction of alkanes

Alkanes are remarkably inert compounds. A reason for the inertness of alkanes arises from their lack of polarity. As carbon and hydrogen have very similar electronegativities, alkanes are non-polar molecules. Consequently, alkanes are not readily attacked by common chemical reagents. Most reagents that you have met are highly polar com-pounds. For example, water, acids, alkalis and many oxidising and reducing agents (see page 95) are polar, and they usually initiate reactions by their attraction to polar groups in other compounds. Such polar reagents do not react with alkanes.

Some non-polar reagents will react with alkanes. The most important of these are the halogens, which, in the presence of ultraviolet light, will *substitute* hydrogen atoms in the alkane with halogen atoms. For example, when chlorine is mixed with methane and exposed to sunlight, chloromethane is formed and hydrogen chloride gas is evolved:

$$CH_4(g) + Cl_2(g) \rightarrow CH_3Cl(g) + HCl(g)$$

Because the reaction requires ultraviolet light, it is called a photochemical reaction.

Further substitution is possible, in turn producing dichloromethane, trichloromethane and tetra-chloromethane. Other halogens, such as bromine, produce similar substitution products. With hexane, for example, bromine produces bromohexane (*figure 16.4*):

$$C_6H_{14}(l) + Br_2(l)$$
$$\rightarrow C_6H_{13}Br(l) + HBr(g)$$

● **Figure 16.4** The reaction of bromine with hexane in ultraviolet light.

## The substitution mechanism

The overall equation for a reaction gives no clue as to the stages involved between reactants and products. The sequence of stages is known as the **mechanism** of a reaction. For example, the energy of ultraviolet light is sufficient to break the Cl–Cl bond. Absorption of light energy causing a bond to break is known as photodissociation. Homolytic fission (page 279) occurs and two chlorine atoms are formed, each having seven electrons in their outer shell. The chlorine atoms each have one unpaired electron and are thus free radicals (page 279). Free radicals react very rapidly with other molecules or chemical species. As **homolytic fission** of a chlorine molecule must occur before any chloromethane can be formed, it is known as the **initiation step**.

$$Cl-Cl(g) \xrightarrow{\text{UV light}} Cl\cdot(g) + Cl\cdot(g)$$

The reaction of a chlorine free radical with a methane molecule produces hydrogen chloride and a $CH_3\cdot$ (methyl) free radical. The dot indicates the unpaired electron. The carbon atom in this $CH_3\cdot$ fragment also has seven electrons in its outer shell. A methyl free radical can react with a chlorine molecule to produce chloromethane and a new chlorine free radical:

$$Cl\cdot(g) + H-CH_3(g) \rightarrow Cl-H(g) + CH_3\cdot(g)$$

$$CH_3\cdot(g) + Cl-Cl(g) \rightarrow CH_3Cl(g) + Cl\cdot(g)$$

These two steps enable the reaction to continue. In the first step, a chlorine free radical is used up. The second step releases a new chlorine free radical, which allows repetition of the first step. The reaction will continue for as long as there is a supply of methane molecules and undissociated chlorine molecules. The two steps constitute a **chain reaction** and are known as the **propagation steps** of the reaction.

The reaction to form chloromethane and hydrogen chloride ceases when the supply of reagents is depleted. There is a variety of possible termination steps. These include recombination of chlorine free radicals to form chlorine molecules. Alternatively, two methyl free radicals can combine to form an ethane molecule:

$$Cl\cdot(g) + Cl\cdot(g) \rightarrow Cl_2(g)$$

$$CH_3\cdot(g) + CH_3\cdot(g) \rightarrow CH_3CH_3(g)$$

These, or any other, **termination step** will remove free radicals and disrupt the propagation steps, thus stopping the chain reaction.

The four steps (initiation, two propagation steps and one of two termination steps) involved in the formation of chloromethane and hydrogen chloride from methane and chlorine constitute the mechanism of this reaction. As the reaction is a substitution involving free radicals, it is known as a **free-radical substitution**.

## SAQ 16.4

**a** Which of the following reagents are likely to produce free radicals in ultraviolet light?

$HCl(aq)$, $Br_2(l)$, $NaOH(aq)$, $Cl_2(g)$, $KMnO_4(aq)$.

**b** Write balanced equations for the reactions of butane with those reagents that produce free radicals.

# SUMMARY (AS)

◆ Alkanes are saturated hydrocarbons with the general formula $C_nH_{2n+2}$. At room temperature the alkanes from methane to butane are gases; pentane to $C_{16}H_{34}$ are liquids; $C_{17}H_{36}$ and above are waxy solids.

◆ The melting and boiling points of alkanes increase with the length of the hydrocarbon chains. The increase may be explained in terms of increasing attraction between the non-polar alkanes with increasing chain length. The intermolecular forces are instantaneous dipole-induced dipole (or van der Waals') forces.

◆ For a given straight-chain alkane, the boiling points of its branched chain isomers are lower because the branched molecules cannot approach as closely.

◆ Alkanes are relatively unreactive as they are non-polar. Most reagents are polar and do not usually react with non-polar molecules.

◆ Alkanes burn completely to carbon dioxide and water and are widely used as fuels.

◆ Chlorine or bromine substitute for hydrogen atoms in alkanes in the presence of ultraviolet light producing halogenoalkanes.

◆ The Cl–Cl or Br–Br bond is broken in a photodissociation reaction producing reactive Cl· or Br· free radicals. This process is described as homolytic fission as each free radical retains one electron from the covalent bond. The initiation step of free-radical substitution is followed by propagation steps involving a chain reaction which regenerates the halogen free radicals. Termination of the reaction may occur, for example, when two free radicals combine.

# Questions (AS)

**1 a** Petrol is a mixture of alkanes containing 6 to 10 carbon atoms per molecule. Some of these alkanes are isomers of one another.

   (i) Explain the term **isomers**.

   (ii) State the molecular formula of an alkane present in petrol.

**b** The major hydrocarbon in camping gas is butane. Some camping gas was reacted with chlorine to form a mixture of isomers.

   (i) What conditions are required for this reaction to take place?

   (ii) Two isomers, **A** and **B**, were separated from this mixture. These isomers had a molar mass of $92.5\,\text{g}\,\text{mol}^{-1}$. Deduce the molecular formula of these two isomers.

   (iii) Draw the displayed formulae of **A** and **B** and name each compound.

**2** Alkanes burn readily and react rapidly with free radicals produced by the action of ultraviolet light on chlorine, $Cl_2$, or bromine, $Br_2$, molecules. However, they are remarkably unreactive with common laboratory acids or alkalis such as concentrated sulphuric acid, $H_2SO_4$, or aqueous sodium hydroxide, NaOH.

**a** Write a balanced equation for the complete combustion of heptane, $C_7H_{16}(l)$. Include state symbols in your equation.

**b** (i) Describe the formation of bromine free radicals, $Br\cdot$, from bromine molecules in ultraviolet light.

   (ii) Describe, using balanced equations, the reaction steps involved in the substitution reaction of bromine free radicals with hexane, $C_6H_{14}$, to form bromohexane, $C_6H_{13}Br$.

# Hydrocarbons: alkenes (AS)

## By the end of this section you should be able to:

6 state that alkenes are *unsaturated* hydrocarbons;

7 state and explain the bonding in alkenes in terms of the overlap of adjacent p orbitals to form a π bond;

8 state and explain the shape of ethene and other related molecules;

9 describe the chemistry of alkenes, for example by certain *addition reactions* of ethene and propene;

10 define an *electrophile* as an *electron pair acceptor*;

11 describe how *heterolytic fission* leads to the mechanism of *electrophilic addition* in alkenes, typified by bromine and ethene to form 1,2-dibromoethane;

12 describe the oxidation of alkenes by cold, dilute manganate(VII) ions to form the diol;

13 describe the oxidation of alkenes by hot, concentrated manganate(VII) ions leading to the rupture of the C=C bond;

14 describe the *addition polymerisation* of alkenes, for example ethene and propene;

15 deduce the repeat unit of a *polymer* obtained from a given *monomer*;

16 identify, in a given section of polymer, the monomer from which it was obtained;

17 outline the use of alkenes in the industrial production of organic compounds;

18 outline the difficulties in disposing of polymers, for example non-biodegradability or toxic combustion products;

19 outline, for polymers, the movement towards recycling, the combustion of waste for energy production and their use as a feedstock for cracking in the production of useful organic compounds;

20 outline the role of chemists in minimising damage to the environment.

A number of biologically important molecules are alkenes. Many of these are based on the simple diene, isoprene (2-methylbuta-1,3-diene):

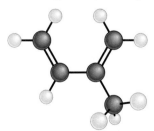

Some trees can be tapped for their latex or natural rubber (*figure 16.5*). Latex is a polymer of isoprene. The natural oil, limonene, present in the rind of oranges and lemons is derived from two isoprene units:

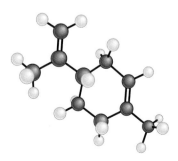

● **Figure 16.5** Scraping the bark off a rubber tree in this way causes the liquid rubber to accumulate at one point, where it can be collected.

Alkenes are used to make many chemicals that feature prominently in modern life. Some examples of these chemicals are shown in *figure 16.6*.

# Physical properties of alkenes

Simple alkenes are **hydrocarbons** that contain one carbon–carbon double bond. The simplest alkene is ethene, $CH_2=CH_2$. The general formula of the homologous series of alkenes is $C_nH_{2n}$.

● **Figure 16.6** A range of products produced from alkenes, including poly(chloroethene) window frames, ethane-1,2-diol (used in antifreeze) and industrial methylated spirits (mainly ethanol with methanol added to avoid alcohol tax – used as a solvent).

**SAQ 16.5** _____
Draw a dot-and-cross diagram for ethene. Predict the shape of the molecule and give estimates of the bond angles.

# Bonding in alkenes: σ and π bonds

Electrons in molecules occupy σ and π molecular orbitals. A π bond lies predominantly in two lobes, one on each side of a σ bond. Overlap of two atomic p orbitals produces a π molecular orbital or π **bond**. To ensure maximum overlap, ethene must be a planar molecule. A single covalent bond, such as C–C or C–H, consists of a σ bond. Double bonds such as C=C consist of one σ bond and one π bond.

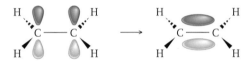

overlap of p orbitals produces
π molecular orbitals

Compounds which contain π bonds, such as ethene, are called unsaturated compounds. The term **unsaturated** indicates that the compound will combine by *addition* reactions with hydrogen or other chemicals, losing its multiple bonds.

**Saturated** compounds contain only *single* carbon–carbon bonds. The terms 'saturated' and 'unsaturated' are often used in connection with oils and fats. The molecules in vegetable oils contain several double bonds – they are described as polyunsaturated. In hard margarine, hydrogen has been added to these double bonds so the margarine is now saturated. However, several of the fatty acids which are essential to our diet are polyunsaturated and so, to ensure that these fatty acids are retained, much modern margarine is only partially saturated.

# Cis–trans isomerism

Many alkenes exhibit *cis–trans* **isomerism**; we shall consider an example. Natural rubber is a polymer of 2-methylbuta-1,3-diene (or isoprene, page 299). The repeating unit contains a carbon–carbon double bond. All the links between the isoprene units are on the same side of this double bond.

This arrangement is described as the *cis* isomer:

$$-\overset{H_2}{\underset{}{C}}\diagdown\underset{H_3C}{\overset{}{C}}=\underset{H}{\overset{}{C}}\diagup\overset{H_2}{\underset{}{C}}-\overset{H_2}{\underset{}{C}}\diagdown\underset{H_3C}{\overset{}{C}}=\underset{H}{\overset{}{C}}\diagup\overset{H_2}{\underset{}{C}}-\overset{H_2}{\underset{}{C}}\diagdown\underset{H_3C}{\overset{}{C}}=\underset{H}{\overset{}{C}}\diagup\overset{H_2}{\underset{}{C}}-$$

*cis*-poly(2-methylbuta-1,3-diene): natural rubber

Natural rubber is the familiar material used for balloons, rubber gloves and condoms.

Another possible arrangement has the links between each 2-methylbuta-1,3-diene unit on alternate sides of the double bond. As they lie across the double bond, this is the *trans* isomer. It is found naturally as gutta-percha, which is a grey, inelastic, horny material obtained from the percha tree in Malaysia. It is used in the manufacture of golf balls.

*trans*-poly(2-methylbuta-1,3-diene): gutta-percha

Both *cis*- and *trans*-2-methylbuta-1,3-diene can be manufactured from 2-methylbuta-1,3-diene using appropriate Ziegler–Natta catalysts. Such catalysts were developed by the German chemist Karl Ziegler and the Italian chemist Giulio Natta, and are based on triethylaluminium and titanium(IV) chloride. Ziegler and Natta made a substantial contribution to the development of polymers and were jointly awarded the Nobel prize for chemistry in 1963.

*Cis–trans* isomerism is frequently encountered in alkenes, and arises because rotation about a double bond cannot occur unless the π bond is broken. In addition to a double bond, the molecule must have two identical groups, one on each of the two carbon atoms involved in the double bond. The other two groups must be different to this identical pair. But-2-ene is the simplest alkene to show *cis–trans* isomerism:

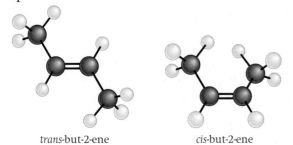

*trans*-but-2-ene          *cis*-but-2-ene

In the *cis* isomer, two methyl groups are on the same side of the double bond; in the *trans* isomer they are on opposite sides.

## SAQ 16.6

Consider the following:

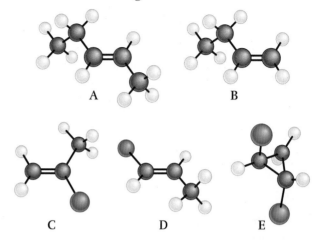

A          B

C          D          E

**a** Which, apart from **A**, can exist as *cis–trans* isomers?

**b** Draw and name the structural formulae for the pair of *cis–trans* isomers for **A**.

# Characteristic reactions of alkenes

Most alkene reactions involve breaking the π bond. This is weaker than the C–C σ bond and reacts with a variety of reagents.

## Addition reactions to the double bond

The characteristic reaction of an alkene involves a simple molecule (such as hydrogen, water or bromine) joining across the double bond to form a single product. Such reactions are called **addition reactions**. Addition reactions are the second important type of organic reactions that you will meet.

### Addition of hydrogen

This converts the unsaturated alkene to a saturated alkane. Hydrogen gas and a gaseous alkene are passed over a finely divided nickel catalyst supported on an inert material. The equation for the addition of hydrogen to cyclohexene is:

$$\bighexagon + H_2 \longrightarrow \bighexagon$$

## The molecules of sight

The molecule that is responsible for initiating the signal to our brain, which allows us to see, is called retinal. This molecule is present in the rod and cone cells of the eye. One of its isomers is responsible for the absorption of light. Each double bond is locked into position, preventing rotation. When this isomer absorbs light, one of the two electron-pairs in a double bond is split apart. This allows the retinal molecule to change its shape by rotating around the single bond left behind. After bond rotation, the two electrons that were split apart by the absorption of light come together, fixing the molecule in its new shape and preventing further rotation. This is shown in the reaction sequence in *figure 16.7*. The dramatic change of shape affects the shape of the protein to which the retinal is attached. This causes a signal to be sent via the optic nerve to the brain. The new *trans*-retinal isomer breaks away from the protein and is converted back to *cis*-retinal, ready for further light absorption.

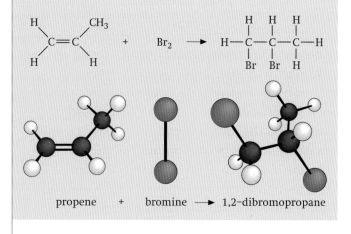

only one of the double bonds (labelled A here) is broken by the absorption of light energy, *hf*

● **Figure 16.7** The change of shape of a retinal molecule by rotation about the single bond that results from absorption of light.

In the *cis* isomer, two methyl groups are on the same side of the double bond; in the *trans* isomer, they are on opposite sides. The breaking of one of the bonds in a double bond by light absorption is not a usual reaction for alkenes.

Another example is the manufacture of margarine from vegetable oil over a nickel catalyst at a temperature of about 450 K and a hydrogen pressure of up to 1000 kPa (*figure 16.8*).

### Addition of halogens

When an alkene such as propene is bubbled through a solution of bromine at room temperature, the bromine solution is rapidly decolorised from its characteristic orange colour (*figure 16.9*). Unlike free-radical substitution on an alkane, this reaction does not require ultraviolet light and will occur in total darkness. The bromine joins to the propene to form 1,2-dibromopropane:

$$CH_3CH=CH_2 + Br_2 \longrightarrow CH_3CHBrCH_2Br$$

propene + bromine ⟶ 1,2–dibromopropane

Chlorine and iodine produce similar addition products. Fluorine is too powerful an oxidant and tends to ignite hydrocarbons!

● **Figure 16.8** A hydrogenation vessel for making margarine.

● **Figure 16.9** The reaction of ethene with a solution of bromine. This characteristic reaction provides a test for an alkene (*table 16.3*).

| Test | Observation if an alkene is present |
|------|-------------------------------------|
| shake alkene with bromine water | orange bromine water is decolorised |

● **Table 16.3** Simple test for an alkene.

### Addition of hydrogen halides

Hydrogen halides also add readily to alkenes. Ethene produces chloroethane on bubbling through concentrated aqueous hydrochloric acid at room temperature:

$$CH_2{=}CH_2(g) + HCl(aq) \rightarrow CH_3CH_2Cl(l)$$

The reactivity of the hydrogen halides increases from HF to HI, following the order of decreasing bond energy. Hydrogen fluoride will react with an alkene only under pressure. Alkenes such as propene can give rise to two different products:

$$CH_3CH{=}CH_2 + HBr \rightarrow CH_3CHBrCH_3 \text{ or}$$
$$CH_3CH_2CH_2Br$$

The normal product is 2-bromopropane, $CH_3CHBrCH_3$.

### Addition of steam

This is a route to making alcohols. Industrially, steam and a gaseous alkene are passed over a solid catalyst. A temperature of 600 K and a pressure of 6 MPa are used in the presence of a phosphoric acid $H_3PO_4$ catalyst. The addition of steam to ethene produces ethanol:

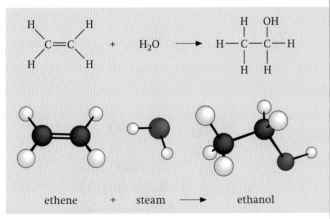

ethene  +  steam  ⟶  ethanol

## The mechanism of addition

Although bromine and ethene are non-polar reagents, the bromine molecule becomes polarised when close to a region of negative charge such as

the ethene π bond. The π bond then breaks, with its electron-pair forming a new covalent bond to the bromine atom, which carries a partial, positive charge. At the same time, the bromine molecule undergoes heterolytic fission (page 279). Heterolytic fission involves both electrons in the bond moving to the same atom. These changes produce a bromide ion and a positively charged carbon atom (a **carbocation**) in the ethene molecule (*figure 16.10*).

Carbocations are highly reactive and the bromide ion rapidly forms a second carbon–bromine covalent bond to give 1,2-dibromoethane.

In this mechanism, the polarised bromine molecule has behaved as an electrophile. An **electrophile** is a reactant which is attracted to an electron-rich centre or atom, where it accepts a pair of electrons to form a new covalent bond. The reaction is an example of one which proceeds by an **electrophilic addition** mechanism.

● **Figure 16.10** The formation of a carbocation in the bromination of ethene.

### SAQ 16.7

a Draw a dot-and-cross diagram of the carbocation formed in an electrophilic addition to ethene. How many electrons are there on the positively charged carbon atom? Explain how this atom completes its outer electron shell when it combines with a bromide ion.

b Suggest a mechanism for the addition of hydrogen chloride to ethene.

c If the reaction of bromine with ethene is carried out in ethanol containing some lithium chloride, a second, chlorine-containing, product is formed, as well as 1,2-dibromoethane. Suggest a structure for this second product.

d Which of the following are likely to behave as electrophiles:
$Cl_2(g)$, $Na^+(aq)$, $F^-(aq)$, $H_2(g)$, $SO_3(g)$, $ICl(g)$?
Give an explanation in each case.

## Reactions of alkenes with manganate(VII) ions, $MnO_4^-$

Alkenes undergo a different type of reaction with manganate(VII) ions, depending on the conditions. When shaken with dilute acidified or dilute alkaline potassium manganate(VII), alkenes react readily at room temperature. The purple colour disappears and a diol is formed.

$$CH_2=CH_2 + H_2O + [O] \rightarrow HOCH_2CH_2OH$$
ethan-1,2–diol

When alkenes are heated with an acidified solution of potassium manganate(VII), any diol formed is split into two fragments which are oxidised further to ketones or carboxylic acids. For example:

- ethene will give carbon dioxide

$$CH_2 = CH_2 \longrightarrow HOCH_2CH_2OH \longrightarrow \underset{H}{\overset{O}{\underset{|}{\overset{\|}{C}}}} + \underset{H}{\overset{O}{\underset{|}{\overset{\|}{C}}}} \longrightarrow O_2C + CO_2$$

- propene will give ethanoic acid and carbon dioxide

$$CH_3 - \underset{H}{\overset{H}{\underset{|}{\overset{|}{C}}}} = CH_2 \longrightarrow CH_3 - \underset{OH}{\overset{H}{\underset{|}{\overset{|}{C}}}} + CH_2OH \longrightarrow CH_3 - \overset{O}{\underset{OH}{\overset{\|}{C}}} + CO_2$$

- 2-methyl prop-1-ene will give propanone and carbon dioxide

$$CH_3 - \underset{CH_3}{\overset{|}{\underset{|}{C}}} = CH_2 \longrightarrow CH_3 - \underset{CH_3}{\overset{OH}{\underset{|}{\overset{|}{C}}}} + CH_2OH \longrightarrow \underset{CH_3}{\overset{CH_3}{C}} = O + CO_2$$

Identification of the compounds produced indicates where the carbon–carbon double bond was in the alkene.

# Polymerisation of alkenes

During polymerisation, an alkene undergoes an addition reaction to itself. As one molecule joins to a second, a long molecular chain is built up. The reactions are initiated in various ways and the initiator may become incorporated at the start of the polymer chain. Ignoring the initiator, the empirical formula of an addition polymer is the same as the alkene it comes from. This type of reaction is called **addition polymerisation**. Many useful polymers are obtained via addition polymerisation of different alkenes.

Poly(ethene) was first produced accidentally by two scientists (Eric Fawcett and Reginald Gibson) in 1933. The reaction involves ethene adding to itself in a chain reaction. It is a very rapid reaction, chains of up to 10 000 ethene units being formed in one second. The product is a high-molecular-mass straight-chain alkane. It is a polymer and is a member of a large group of materials generally known as plastics. The alkene from which it is made is called the **monomer** and the section of polymer that the monomer forms is called the **repeat unit** (often shown within brackets in structural formulae):

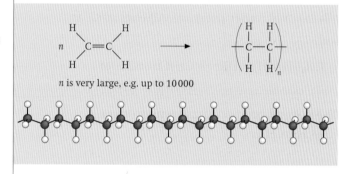

$n$ is very large, e.g. up to 10 000

Other important poly(alkene)s include poly(chloroethene) and poly(phenylethene).

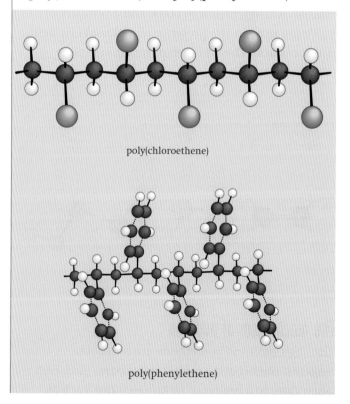

poly(chloroethene)

poly(phenylethene)

They are more commonly known as PVC and poly-styrene respectively. Note how the systematic name is derived by putting the systematic name of the alkene in brackets, and prefixing this with 'poly'.

The skeletal formulae of the monomers, chloroethene (traditionally vinyl chloride) and phenylethene (styrene), are as follows:

chloroethene          phenylethene

Note that when a benzene ring becomes a group attached to an alkene its name changes to phenyl (from 'phene', an old name for benzene). The phenyl group may also be written as $C_6H_5-$.

## SAQ 16.8

**a** Write balanced equations for the formation of poly(chloroethene) and poly(phenylethene) using displayed formulae. Show the repeat unit in brackets.

**b** A polymer which is often used to make plastic boxes for food storage has the structure:

$$\text{CH}_3 \quad \text{CH}_3 \quad \text{CH}_3 \quad \text{CH}_3$$

Draw displayed formulae to show (i) the repeat unit of this polymer and (ii) the monomer from which it is made. Label your diagrams with the appropriate systematic names.

We now have several methods for the addition polymerisation of alkenes. These methods provide

● **Figure 16.11** Some products made from poly(alkene)s.

● **Figure 16.12** A beach littered with poly(alkene) waste products, on Holy Island, near the coast of Anglesey in Wales.

the wide variety of poly(alkene)s for the many applications of these versatile materials. *Figure 16.11* shows some examples of these uses. The use of poly(alkene)s has created a major problem when we wish to dispose of them. *Figure 16.12* is a sight familiar to us all. As they are alkanes, they break down very slowly in the environment. They are resistant to most chemicals and to bacteria (they are non-biodegradable). It might seem desirable to collect waste poly(ethene), sort it and recycle it into new products (as in *figure 16.13*).

Some praiseworthy attempts at recycling are being made, mostly of manufacturing waste. However, the current costs of recycling in terms of the energy used in collecting and reprocessing domestic waste plastic is often greater than that used in making new material. A second option is

● **Figure 16.13** Recycling poly(alkene)s into a new product. Different types of polymers must be separated if the plastics are to be recycled. A mixture of polymers will produce a very inferior plastic.

to burn the poly(ethene) to provide energy. The energy released on its combustion is about the same as the energy used in its production. It is potentially a good fuel as it is a hydrocarbon and would reduce the amount of oil or other fossil fuels burned. It could be burnt with other combustible household waste. This would save considerable landfill costs and provide a substantial alternative energy source. Modern technology is such that the waste could be burnt cleanly and with less pollution than from traditional fossil-fuel power stations. The carbon dioxide produced would not add to the total emissions of this greenhouse gas but replace emissions from burning other fossil fuels. Other pollutant gases, such as hydrogen chloride from PVC, can be removed by the use of gas scrubbers. In a gas scrubber, acidic gases are dissolved and neutralised in a spray of alkali. European Union legislation requires household waste incinerators to use gas scrubbers. *Figure 16.14* shows a modern waste incinerator in Vienna.

A third option is feedstock recycling. In view of the limitations of mechanical recycling, BP (British Petroleum) developed a method for processing mixed and contaminated plastics. They have now built a pilot plant at their refinery site in Grangemouth, Scotland. In the plant the polymers are cracked (see page 311) to produce a mixture of hydrocarbons. The mixture contains alkanes, alkenes and arenes which provide additional feedstock for the main refinery. Alkenes, once separated, may once again be made into polymers such as poly(ethene) or poly(propene).

● **Figure 16.14** The incinerator in Vienna is not only clean, it is also a tourist attraction!

## SUMMARY (AS)

◆ The homologous series of alkenes has the general formula $C_nH_{2n}$. Alkenes are unsaturated hydrocarbons with one carbon–carbon double bond consisting of a $\sigma$ bond and a $\pi$ bond.

◆ Ethene is a planar molecule, other alkenes are planar of the double bond and the four adjacent atoms. Many alkenes have *cis–trans* isomers which arise because rotation about the double bond is prevented.

◆ Alkenes are more reactive than alkanes because they contain a $\pi$ bond. The characteristic reaction of the alkene functional group is addition, which occurs across the $\pi$ bond. For example ethene produces: ethane with hydrogen over a nickel catalyst; 1,2-dibromoethane with bromine at room temperature; chloroethane with hydrogen chloride at room temperature; ethanol with steam in the prescence of $H_3PO_4$.

◆ The mechanism of the reaction of bromine with ethene is electrophilic addition. Electrophiles accept a pair of electrons from an electron-rich atom or centre, in this case the $\pi$ bond. A carbocation intermediate is formed after the addition of the first bromine atom. This rapidly reacts with a bromide ion to form 1,2-dibromoethane.

◆ Alkenes produce many useful polymers by addition polymerisation. For example, poly(ethene) from $CH_2=CH_2$, poly(propene) from $CH_3CH=CH_2$, poly(chloroethene) from $CH_2=CHCl$ and poly(tetrafluoroethene) from $CF_2=CF_2$ (see chapter 17, page 331).

◆ The disposal of polymers is difficult as they are chemically inert and non-biodegradable. When burnt, they may produce toxic products such as hydrogen chloride from PVC (poly(chloroethene)). Whilst much manufacturing waste plastic is recycled, the costs of collecting and sorting most domestic waste plastic are too high to make recycling worthwhile. Use of the energy released on combustion (for heating buildings) is a better option for domestic waste, but treatment of flue gases is required to remove toxic pollutants. A third option is feedstock recycling where the polymers are cracked to form alkenes. The alkenes are separated and used as feedstock to make new polymers.

# Questions (AS)

3 The following diagrams show the structures of four isomers of molecular formula $C_4H_8$.

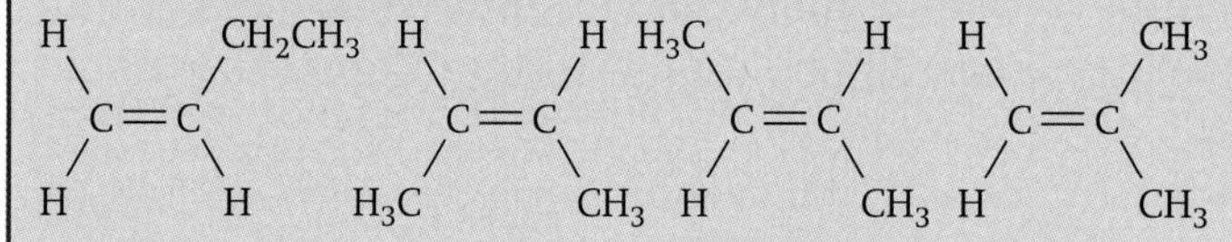

A      B      C      D

a (i) To which class of compounds do the four isomers belong?
  (ii) Which two diagrams show compounds that are *cis–trans* isomers?
b Compound A reacts with hydrogen bromide.
  (i) Draw the displayed formulae of the two possible products and give their systematic names.
  (ii) What type of reaction has taken place?
  (iii) What type of mechanism is involved?
c Compound C produces one product with steam in the presence of phosphoric acid.
  (i) What type of reaction has occurred?
  (ii) Draw the structural formula for this product and label it with its systematic name.

4 Chlorine can react with ethene and with methane. It reacts readily with ethene in the dark but does not react with methane unless sunlight or another source of UV light is present. For each reaction, write a balanced equation, describe the mechanism and state clearly whether or not the chlorine undergoes homolytic fission or heterolytic fission.

5 Cracking of the unbranched compound E, $C_6H_{14}$, produced the saturated compound F and an unsaturated hydrocarbon G ($M_r$, 42). Compound F reacted with bromine in UV light to form a monobrominated compound H and an acidic gas I. Compound G reacted with hydrogen bromide to form a mixture of two compounds J and K.
a Use this evidence to suggest the identity of each of compounds E to K. Include equations for the reactions in your answer.
b Oil companies often 'reform' compounds such as E. Explain why this is done and suggest two organic products of the reforming of E.
c Predict the structure of the polymer that could be formed from compound G.

# Hydrocarbons: fuels (AS)

## By the end of this section you should be able to:

21 explain the use of crude oil as a source of hydrocarbons (separated by fractional distillation) which can be used directly as fuels or for processing into petrochemicals;

22 state that branched alkanes, cycloalkanes and arenes are used in petrol to promote efficient combustion;

23 describe the use of *cracking* to obtain more useful alkanes and alkenes;

24 describe the use of *reforming* to obtain cycloalkanes and arenes;

25 describe the use of *isomerisation* to obtain branched alkanes;

26 describe and explain how the combustion reactions of alkanes lead to their use as fuels in industry, in the home and in transport;

27 outline the value to society of fossil fuels in relation to needs for energy and raw materials, the non-renewable nature of fossil fuel reserves and the need to develop renewable fuels, for example biofuels, which do not further deplete finite energy resources.

## Sources of hydrocarbons

The fossil deposits of crude oil and natural gas have been the primary sources of alkanes throughout the twentieth century. Much of the wealth of the industrialised world can be ascribed to this exploitation of a natural resource. The vast majority of these deposits have been used to provide fuel for heating, electricity generation and transport. Smaller, but significant, proportions have been used to produce lubricants and to provide a source of hydrocarbons for the chemical process industry. In the UK, the chemical and petrochemical industries are by far the biggest contributors towards a positive balance in the value of manufacturing trade with the rest of the world. The UK chemical industry employs approximately 250 000 people and, in 1996 produced about 11% of total industrial output. *Figure 16.15* shows just how

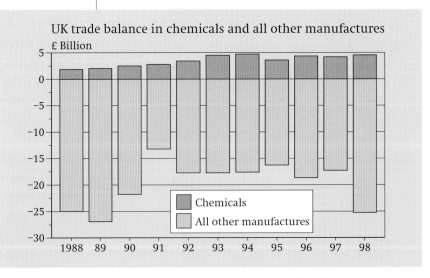

● **Figure 16.15** UK trade balance in chemicals and all other manufactures. The chemical industry is UK manufacturing's number one exporter. With exports of £22.5bn and imports of £18.1bn it earned a trade surplus of £4.4bn in 1998.

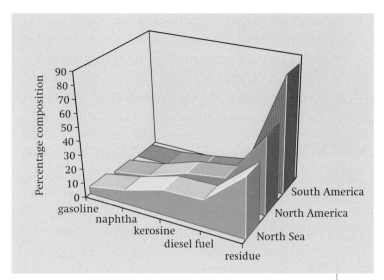

● **Figure 16.16** Breakdown of compositions of oils by oil fractions. North Sea oil contains a higher proportion of the gasoline and naphtha fractions than oils from North or South America.

dependent the UK is on its chemical industry for the size of manufacturing exports.

Crude oil is a complex mixture of hydrocarbons. The composition of oil from different places varies considerably (*figures 16.16* and *16.17*). Three main series of hydrocarbons are present: arenes, cycloalkanes and alkanes. Arenes are hydrocarbons containing one or more benzene rings (see page 272). At a given boiling point, the densities of these decrease in the order arenes > cycloalkanes > alkanes. This provides a method for comparing the compositions of different oils.

## Separating the hydrocarbons in crude oil

Crude oil must be refined so that use can be made of the wide variety of hydrocarbons present. In

● **Figure 16.17** Californian crude is rich in cycloalkanes!

general, chemists separate mixtures of similar liquids by **fractional distillation**. This technique relies on differences in boiling points of the different molecules in the liquid. Fractional distillation can be successful even where differences in boiling point are small. As crude oil is such a complex mixture, it is first broken down into fractions. Each fraction consists of a mixture of hydrocarbons with a much narrower range of boiling points than the full range of hydrocarbons in crude oil. This separation into fractions is known as fractional distillation. Further distillation processes in an oil refinery enable separation of the hydrocarbons in a fraction where this is desired. We shall consider fractional distillation in more detail by looking at one type of column for such a distillation.

Prior to entering a fractional distillation column (*figure 16.18*), the crude oil must be

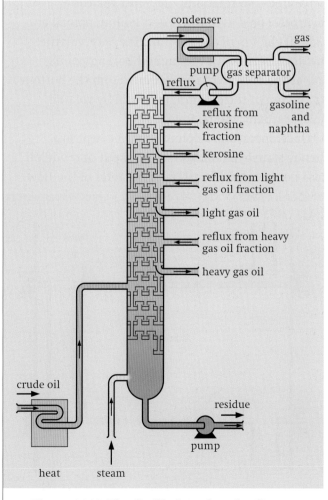

● **Figure 16.18** The distillation of crude oil.

vaporised. This is achieved by passing the crude oil through pipes in a furnace where the oil is heated to 650 K. The resulting mixture of liquid and vapour is fed into the distillation column at a point above the bottom. The column (which may be up to 100 m in height) is divided by a number of steel 'trays' (40 to 50 in a 100 m column). Vapour passes up the column through the trays via holes (figure 16.19). Each tray is like a sieve. Liquid flows down the column from tray to tray over a 'weir'.

There is a temperature gradient between the (hot) bottom of the column and the (cool) top of the column. When vapour passes through a tray, the hot vapour comes into contact with a slightly cooler liquid. Some of the hydrocarbon molecules in the vapour will condense, causing more volatile hydrocarbons in the liquid to evaporate. An individual tray will contain a liquid mixture of hydrocarbons with a narrow range of boiling points.

By the time 40 to 50 such condensations and evaporations have taken place, the crude oil has separated into fractions. The most volatile hydrocarbons (with the lowest boiling points) are now at the top of the column. The least volatile hydrocarbons (with the highest boiling points) are at the bottom of the column. From the bottom to the top of the column, increasingly volatile hydrocarbons will be found.

Once operating, a column may be kept in a steady state by maintaining the input of crude oil at a flow rate which balances the total of the flow rates at which the fractions are removed. You can create a similar steady state when you are taking a bath! If you continue to run hot water when the bath is full, the bath water will not overflow the sides providing you adjust the flow of hot water to be the same as the flow down the overflow pipe. When a steady state exists, the compositions of the liquid and vapour at any one tray do not vary. This enables the various fractions to be drawn from the column at appropriate points. An individual tray will contain a mixture of hydrocarbons with quite a narrow range of boiling points.

A fractional distillation column is designed to separate crude oil into the following fractions: refinery gases, gasoline and naphtha, kerosine, gas (diesel), oil, and residue. The refinery gases consist of simple alkanes containing up to four carbon atoms. They are used as fuels or as a source (or feedstock) for building other molecules. Gasoline contains alkanes with five to ten carbon atoms and is used as petrol. Naphtha is the fraction of crude oil which is the most important source of chemicals (or feedstock) for the chemical process industry. Other fractions and natural gas are of lesser importance. Kerosine is used for jet fuels and for domestic heating. Gas oil is used as diesel fuel and as a feedstock for catalytic cracking. The residue is used as a source of lubricating oils and waxes and bitumen. Bitumen mixed with crushed stone is the tarmac used to surface roads. Figure 16.20 shows a distillation column in a modern oil refinery.

## Further treatment

After distillation, the different hydrocarbon fractions are treated in a variety of different ways. These include processes such as vacuum distillation

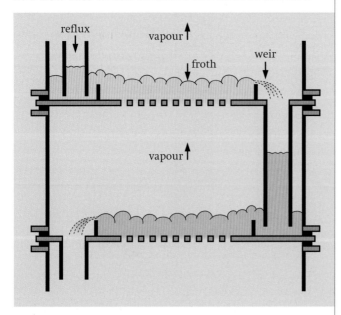

● **Figure 16.19** Trays in a fractionating column.

● **Figure 16.20** The skyline of an oil refinery is dominated by fractional distillation columns.

(to separate out less volatile components such as lubricating oils and waxes from the residue), desulphurisation (to remove sulphur) and cracking (to produce more gasoline and alkenes). There is insufficient gasoline and naphtha fractions from the primary distillation to satisfy the demand for petrol, so higher boiling fractions are cracked to produce more gasoline and naphtha. Modern petrol engines require higher proportions of branched-chain alkanes, cycloalkanes and arenes to promote efficient combustion. These are produced by reforming and isomerisation.

**Cracking** involves heating the oil fraction with a catalyst. Under these conditions, high-molecular-mass alkanes are broken down into low-molecular-mass alkanes as well as alkenes. Both C–C and C–H bonds are broken in the process. As the bond-breaking is a random process, a variety of products, including hydrogen, are possible and some of the intermediates can react to produce branched-chain alkane isomers. For example, a possible reaction equation for decane is:

$CH_3CH_2CH_2CH_2CH_2CH_2CH_2CH_2CH_2CH_3$
decane

$\longrightarrow CH_3CH_2CH = CH_2$ + $\begin{array}{c} H \\ | \\ H_3C - C - CH_2CH_2CH_3 \\ | \\ CH_3 \end{array}$
but-1-ene

2-methylpentane

The chemical industry uses alkenes such as ethene for a variety of products (for example, poly(ethene) from ethene). 2,2,4-Trimethylpentane is an important component of petrol.

### SAQ 16.9

Write balanced equations showing the structural formulae for all the possible products formed on cracking pentane.

In the catalytic cracker (*figure 16.21*) the hot, vaporised oil fraction and the catalyst behave as a fluid. The seething mixture is called a fluidised bed. Some of the hydrocarbon mixture is broken down to carbon, which blocks the pores of the catalyst. The fluidised bed of the catalyst is pumped into a regeneration chamber, where the carbon coke is burnt off in air at a high temperature, allowing the catalyst to be recycled.

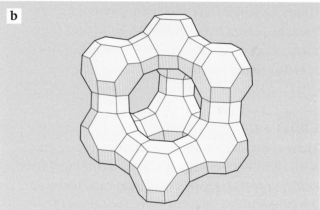

● **Figure 16.21**
**a** A catalytic cracker occupies the bulk of the central part of this photograph.
**b** A computer graphic showing the framework of zeolite Y, a modern catalyst used to crack hydrocarbons.

**Reforming** involves the conversion of alkanes to cycloalkanes, or of cycloalkanes to arenes. Reforming reactions are catalysed by bimetallic catalysts. For example, a cluster of platinum and rhenium atoms is very effective at removing hydrogen from methylcyclohexane to form methylbenzene:

⬡–$CH_3$ $\longrightarrow$ ⬡–$CH_3$ + $3H_2$

A catalyst containing clusters of platinum and iridium atoms enables conversion of straight-chain alkanes to arenes:

$CH_3CH_2CH_2CH_2CH_2CH_3$ $\longrightarrow$ ⬡ + $4H_2$

These metal clusters are between 1 and 5nm in diameter and are deposited on an inert support such as aluminium oxide. The rhenium and iridium help prevent the build-up of carbon deposits, which reduce the activity of the catalysts.

**Isomerisation** involves heating the straight-chain isomers in the presence of a platinum catalyst:

$$CH_3CH_2CH_2CH_2CH_2CH_3 \longrightarrow H_3C - \overset{\overset{\displaystyle CH_3}{|}}{\underset{\underset{\displaystyle CH_3}{|}}{C}} - CH_2CH_3$$

The resulting mixture of straight- and branched-chain isomers then has to be separated. This is done by using a molecular sieve, which is another type of zeolite that has pores through which the straight-chain isomers can pass (figure 16.22). The branched-chain isomers are too bulky and thus are separated off; the straight-chain molecules are recycled to the reactor.

# Fuels

Many substances burn in reactions with oxygen, with transfer of energy to the surroundings (figure 16.23). Only those used on a large scale, however, are properly described as fuels. Oxidation of chemicals in the fuels coal, petroleum and gas provides over 90% of the energy used in most industrialised countries; hydroelectricity and nuclear power together supply about 9%.

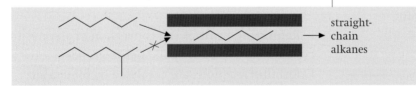

● **Figure 16.22** Shape selectivity by a zeolite catalyst – separation of isomers by a molecular sieve.

| Fuel | Formula | Relative molecular mass | Energy released per mole ($kJ\,mol^{-1}$) | Energy released per kilogram ($kJ\,kg^{-1}$) |
|------|---------|-------------------------|-------------------------------------------|---------------------------------------------|
| Carbon (coal) | $C(s)$ | 12 | −393 | −32 750 |
| Methane | $CH_4(g)$ | 16 | −890 | −55 625 |
| Octane | $C_8H_{18}(l)$ | 114 | −5512 | −48 350 |
| Methanol | $CH_3OH(l)$ | 32 | −715 | −22 343 |
| Hydrogen | $H_2(g)$ | 2 | −286 | −143 000 |

● **Table 16.4** Comparison of fuels in terms of energy released.

## What makes a good fuel?

The essential reaction for any chemical fuel is:

fuel + oxygen (or other oxidiser)
→ oxidation products + energy transfer

### SAQ 16.10

Write balanced equations for the complete combustion of the fuels shown in table 16.4.

Though different fuels are needed for different purposes the ideal characteristics include the following.

■ *A fuel should react with an oxidiser to release large amounts of energy*
It is interesting to compare fuels on the basis of energy per unit amount of material (mole) and energy per unit mass (kilogram) (table 16.4). Remember that fuels are usually purchased in litres, kilograms or tonnes, not in moles.

### SAQ 16.11

From the data in table 16.4, compare hydrogen with methane. Why are the values for the energy released per kilogram so different when compared with the energy released per mole?

● **Figure 16.23** Gases from oilfields are often disposed of by being burnt as controllable 'flares'. This is a waste of gas but the costs of collection, storage and transportation are higher than the income available from selling the gas for other uses.

■ *A fuel must be oxidised fairly easily, ignite quickly and sustain burning without further intervention*
Gaseous or easily vaporised fuels usually perform well, as they mix easily and continuously with air/oxygen, which helps the reaction. Solid fuels (coal) are sometimes powdered for use in large industrial furnaces.

■ *A fuel should be readily available, in large quantities and at a reasonable price*
The availability and price of oil, for example, affect national economies so much that governments can fall and countries go to war when these change. The price of any fuel includes many factors: the costs of finding it; extraction, refining and transportation; all the company overheads, such as buildings, salaries and advertising; fuel taxes levied by governments; and the capital costs of the equipment needed to burn it. During the 1960s Britain changed the main gas supply from 'coal gas' (mainly hydrogen and carbon monoxide) to 'natural gas' (methane). This required a large-scale and expensive programme of adapting gas burners in industries and homes to suit the slower burning rate of methane. The advantages were that large supplies of methane were becoming available from gas-fields near to the British coast and that methane was thought to be a much 'cleaner' and safer fuel than the coal gas produced in dirty gas-works in most towns (*figure 16.24*).

■ *A fuel should not burn to give products that are difficult to dispose of, or are unpleasant or harmful*
This is a considerable problem for most fuels (see below), as hydrogen is the only fuel with a safe, non-polluting product from its oxidation reaction to water.

■ *A fuel should be convenient to store and transport safely and without loss*
Over the ages, people have tackled many problems of fuel storage, from how to keep wood dry to how to keep liquid oxygen extremely cold and safe for space flight (*figure 16.25*). If gases such as methane and hydrogen are to be used as alternatives to petrol in vehicles, the problems of storage of large amounts of gas must be solved. People are worried about storing these gases under high pressure in cylinders.

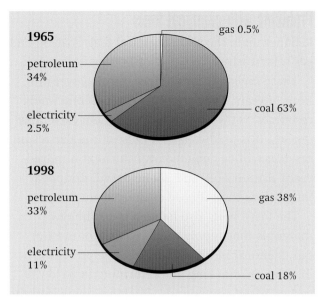

● **Figure 16.24** Changing use of fuel in Britain, 1965–98. Use of coal has greatly declined as methane gas is used for domestic and industrial energy supply, and many more gas-fuelled power stations for generating electricity are built.

Scientists are developing some interesting ways, however, of storing hydrogen as its solid compounds, such as the hydrides of metals: $FeTiH_2$ or $LaNi_5H_7$ or $MgNiH_4$. These hydrides release hydrogen when warmed gently and they may enable safe hydrogen-fuelled motor transport.

### SAQ 16.12

**a** Why is oxygen transported into space in liquid form instead of as gas?

**b** Why are large quantities of liquid or gaseous fuels often stored in spherical tanks?

● **Figure 16.25** A space shuttle is propelled by fuels including liquid oxygen. Note the spherical storage tank for fuel on the right-hand side of the picture.

# Problems with chemical fuels

Reliance upon the main chemical fuels coal, oil and gas is increasingly a matter of worldwide concern.

These fuels are 'fossil fuels', formed over millions of years. They are, in effect, non-renewable resources, yet we are consuming them extremely quickly. It is predicted that most of the Earth's oil reserves will be depleted over the next hundred years. Britain's oil- and gas-fields will disappear long before that, if used at the present rate.

The fossil fuels also happen to be the raw materials that supply the feedstock for most of our chemical industry. They may be processed by distillation, cracking and reforming to yield the carbon-based compounds which are made into the polymers, medicines, solvents, adhesives, etc., that modern society would find difficult to replace (see chapter 12). For how long can we afford to carry on burning the feedstock?

Oxidation of the carbon-based compounds in fuels produces vast amounts of carbon dioxide ($CO_2$). At one time carbon dioxide was considered to be a relatively harmless gas. Now it is known to be a major contributor to the 'greenhouse effect', which causes an increase in atmospheric temperatures. Some governments are so concerned about this effect, which could bring about disastrous climatic change, that many means of reducing carbon dioxide levels in the atmosphere are being considered. Britain has set a target of reducing $CO_2$ emissions by 35% of the 1992 levels by the year 2000. The simplest solution would be an outright ban on the use of coal, oil and methane. Governments are understandably reluctant to take such drastic action, as national economies have become so dependent on these fuels. However, we may see increasing 'carbon taxes' (extra taxes levied upon use of carbon-compound fuels) and other means of restricting their use.

Spillage of fuel often causes great damage to local environments (*figure 16.26*). This damage ranges from streams and ponds polluted by leaky fuel tanks to major disasters when oil tankers break open. There can be immense loss of animal and plant life and enormous costs of cleaning up.

Inefficient burning of carbon-based fuels in defective furnaces and domestic gas fires and in poorly tuned engines produces the very poisonous gas, carbon monoxide. Instead of:

$$C(s) + O_2(g) \rightarrow CO_2(g)$$

partial oxidation gives:

$$2C(s) + O_2(g) \rightarrow 2CO(g)$$

Inhalation of carbon monoxide may cause death, as it interferes with the transport of oxygen in the bloodstream. Other dangerous gases produced by the burning of fuels include nitrogen oxides and sulphur oxides, which form strongly acidic solutions in water (hence 'acid rain') (*figure 16.27*). A large variety of compounds, including carcinogens, appear in the smoke from burning coal and wood (*figure 16.28*).

## SAQ 16.13

What are the reactions of nitrogen(IV) oxide ($NO_2$) and the sulphur oxides ($SO_2$ and $SO_3$) with water? Write equations for these reactions.

● **Figure 16.26** The oil tanker *Braer* broke open and spilled large amounts of oil around the Shetland Islands in 1993.

● **Figure 16.27** These trees in Germany were killed by the effects of acid rain, caused mainly by the sulphur oxides produced from burning coal.

● **Figure 16.28** Acidic gases, such as sulphur dioxide are removed by reaction with calcium oxide. The calcium sulphate produced is used to make plasterboard. The 'smoke' is actually water vapour.

# Alternatives to fossil fuels

## Biofuels

*Plants* can be grown to be used *directly* as fuels, e.g. wood. Plants can also be grown for *conversion* into fuels, e.g. sugar from sugar cane is easily fermented into ethanol. This can be used directly as an alternative to petrol or mixed with petrol. There is increasing use of natural oils, such as rapeseed or sunflower oil, as part of diesel fuels.

Plants convert atmospheric carbon dioxide by photosynthesis to cellulose and other plant material. If crops are used either directly as, or for conversion into, a fuel, the carbon dioxide released to the atmosphere simply replaces that removed during plant growth. Scientists working for Shell are exploring the potential for growing forests of fast cropping trees and using the biomass (plant material) as a renewable energy source. The biomass is dried and chipped before being converted to gas and bio-oil by heating in the absence of air. The gas or bio-oil is then used to fuel a gas turbine to generate electricity. Greater overall efficiency results when the biomass is first converted to gas and bio-oil.

*Waste products:* Large municipal landfill sites produce significant quantities of biogas by anaerobic decay of biological materials. In the past, this gas often seeped into the atmosphere where it can form an explosive mixture with air. Now, it is collected in pipes and often flared for safe disposal. Biogas is mainly composed of methane which has a much greater greenhouse effect than its combustion product carbon dioxide. In a few cases, the collection and combustion of biogas from landfill sites is being used to generate electricity.

■ *Advantages:* renewable; helps to reduce waste; used with simple technology.
■ *Disadvantages:* not large enough supply to replace fossil fuels at present rates of use.

## Methanol ($CH_3OH$)

This simple alcohol can be made quite cheaply from methane. It is often used in racing cars (figure 16.29).

■ *Advantages:* methanol burns cleanly and completely; little carbon monoxide is produced.
■ *Disadvantages:* methanol is more toxic than ethanol; it provides much less energy per litre than petrol; mixtures of methanol and petrol absorb water and car engines may corrode; methanol and petrol tend to separate into layers; combustion of methanol produces the carcinogenic aldehyde methanal when there is insufficient air.

## Nuclear fuels

*Fission:* Energy is released when the nuclei of atoms of isotopes of uranium U-235 undergoes fission (splitting) in a chain reaction (figure 16.30). Very large amounts of energy are available from this process. The energy is normally used in power stations to heat water to drive electricity-generating steam turbines.

● **Figure 16.29** This 'ChampCar', driven by Juan Montoya, is fuelled by methanol.

- *Advantages*: no carbon, nitrogen or sulphur oxides as polluting by-products.
- *Disadvantages*: radioactive waste products are difficult to store and treat; safety systems to contain radioactivity are very costly.

*Fusion*: Energy is released when deuterium and tritium 'fuse' to form helium:

$${}^{2}_{1}H + {}^{3}_{1}H \longrightarrow {}^{4}_{2}He + {}^{1}_{0}n$$

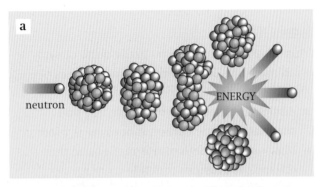

- **Figure 16.30** Nuclear energy.
- **a** Nuclear fission: a neutron colliding with a uranium nucleus causes fission and the release of energy and more neutrons.
- **b** Fuel rods containing uranium-235 being loaded into a nuclear reactor. The top of the reactor core is kept under 11 metres of water to protect the workers from the intense radiation.

- *Advantages*: potentially almost limitless as an energy supply as the 'fuels' come from water.
- *Disadvantages*: no fusion reactors are yet producing energy at economic rates; they are extremely costly.

### Moving air: wind

The energy of moving air is transferred into the motion of windmills and wind turbines (*figure 16.31*). Much science and technology is being devoted to improving the efficiency of the wind machines, and they soon may provide over 10% of the UK energy needs.

- *Advantages*: renewable; pollution- and waste-free; can be used in locality where energy is needed.
- *Disadvantages*: high initial expense for large-scale generation of electricity; not a reliable source in calm weather; large 'wind-farms' have environmental impact: both noise and visual.

### Moving water

*Hydroelectricity*: Water stored behind dams or from waterfalls can be released through turbines and generate electricity (*figure 16.32a*) or be used directly to turn wheels in mills. Hydroelectricity is a major source of power in many countries.

*Waves*: The motion of waves is used to cause oscillating motion in various devices and to generate electricity (*figure 16.32b*).

*Tides*: Incoming tides in river estuaries fill up large water stores behind barrages across the river. The water can be released through turbines to generate electricity.

- **Figure 16.31** This wind-farm in Spain includes many wind turbines for generating electricity.

● **Figure 16.32**
a A hydroelectric power station is sited below the storage lake and dam.
b This device, on a sea inlet in Islay, Scotland, uses the motion of waves to generate electricity. Other wave motion devices are used out at sea.

■ *Advantages*: renewable; quite predictable; pollution- and waste-free; can be used on large scale.
■ *Disadvantages*: costly to install; environmental impact of dams and barrages.

### Sunlight: solar heating and photovoltaics

*Solar panels*, which are panels of solar heat collectors, are used to heat water in parts of the world where sunshine is plentiful (*figure 16.33a*).

*Photovoltaic cells* convert light into electricity (*figure 16.33b*). In future, large satellites may generate electricity and beam energy by microwave to Earth:
■ *Advantages*: renewable; pollution-free with no waste products.
■ *Disadvantages*: low sunlight levels in UK; none at night; photovoltaics have high initial costs; very large arrays needed for large-scale production of electricity.

### Geothermal: hot rocks

Some distance below the surface of the Earth, the temperature is high (about 85 °C at 2 km below). Water pumped into wells in the hot rock zone is

● **Figure 16.33**
a Solar water heaters on a roof top in Kathmandu, Nepal.
b A lighthouse in Shetland that uses photovoltaic cells to charge storage batteries.

heated; the extracted hot water can be used to heat buildings (*figure 16.34*).
■ *Advantages*: almost unlimited source.
■ *Disadvantages*: not widely available; expensive initially; technological problems.

● **Figure 16.34** Geothermal power stations are widely used in Iceland where hot rocks are near the surface. The four wells in this station provide enough steam to drive a power plant producing 100 megawatts of thermal energy and 2.7 megawatts of electricity. The steam is also used to heat cold water, which is then piped to the capital, Reykjavik, for heating and washing.

## Hydrogen

Many scientists believe that we should run a 'hydrogen economy'. Hydrogen can be extracted quite cheaply from water by electrolysis. Much scientific and technological effort is being spent on effective storage and transport systems.

■ *Advantages*: no pollution, as water is the only waste product from burning hydrogen in air (*figure 16.35*); available in large quantities.

■ *Disadvantages*: regarded as too dangerously explosive by many people (*figure 16.36*); difficult to store and use for transport or in domestic situations.

● **Figure 16.35** A prototype hydrogen-powered car.

● **Figure 16.36** The fate of the airship *Hindenburg* in 1937. Hydrogen was not used as fuel but to keep the airship buoyant. This and similar tragedies have made people very cautious about the use of hydrogen as a fuel for transport, but with careful planning it can be used at least as safely as petrol.

## Electricity from chemical cells

Cells work by using oxidation and reduction reactions (redox systems) in which electrons are transferred. Cells act as convenient stores of electricity (*figure 16.37a*). There is much research into batteries (collections of cells) that will provide energy in sufficient quantities to power cars and lorries. The familiar lead–acid batteries, used in many delivery vans in towns, may be replaced in the future by other batteries using, for example, sodium and sulphur.

Fuel cells are of great interest (*figure 16.37b*). In these, redox reactions between hydrogen and oxygen, or alcohols and oxygen, take place over catalysts. Fuel cells are very clean and efficient, and are used in small spacecraft. They have not yet been developed for very large-scale generation of electricity.

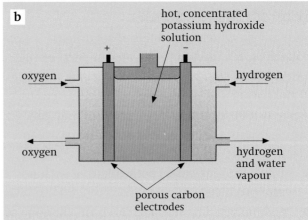

● **Figure 16.37**
**a** This vehicle is powered by a number of rechargeable lead–acid batteries, seen underneath.
**b** A simple fuel cell using the hydrogen–oxygen reaction. The gases must be supplied continuously to the electrodes, so a fuel cell is not a 'store' of electricity. This cell provides a voltage of 1.23 V and can be designed to give 70% efficiency in converting the energy of the reaction to electricity.

## SUMMARY (AS)

◆ Currently, natural gas and crude oil are our major sources of hydrocarbons. The majority of hydrocarbons release large amounts of energy on combustion and are used as fuels for electricity generation, industry, homes or transport.

◆ A significant proportion of these hydrocarbons are converted into a wide range of chemical products.

◆ Cracking of the less useful fractions from crude oil produces a range of more useful alkanes and alkenes. The branched-chain alkanes are suitable for petrol and the alkenes are used to make polymers and other chemical products such as anti-freeze.

◆ Isomerisation converts straight chain alkanes into more of the branched-chain alkanes. Reforming converts alkanes to cycloalkanes or arenes. Branched-chain alkanes, cycloalkanes and arenes all improve the efficiency of combustion in modern petrol engines.

◆ Our reserves of fossil fuels such as gas and oil are limited; once these reserves are exhausted, alternative sources of energy will be needed by society. In the search for alternatives, chemists and other scientists are now working to develop renewable fuel sources such as biofuels.

## Questions (AS)

6 Give an account of what is meant by the term **cracking**. Illustrate your answer by reference to the cracking of decane and the variety of products obtained. Comment on the importance of the cracking process.

7 Various processes are carried out in an oil refinery to provide sufficient petrol of the appropriate quality for modern car engines. Three of these reactions are illustrated below:

Cracking, for example:
Reaction 1

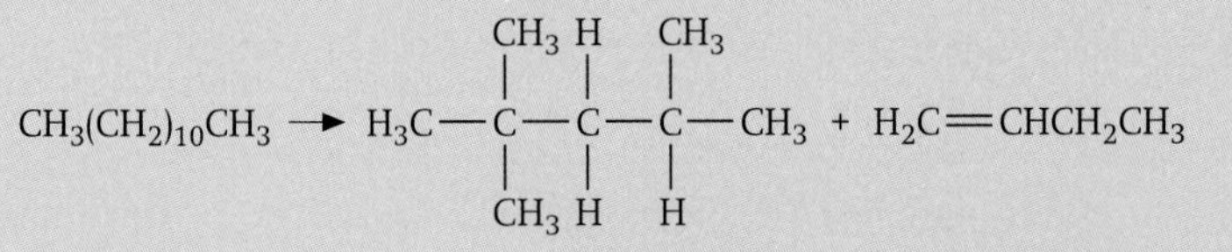

$$CH_3(CH_2)_{10}CH_3 \rightarrow H_3C-\underset{\underset{CH_3}{|}}{\overset{\overset{CH_3}{|}}{C}}-\underset{\underset{H}{|}}{\overset{\overset{H}{|}}{C}}-\underset{\underset{H}{|}}{\overset{\overset{CH_3}{|}}{C}}-CH_3 + H_2C{=}CHCH_2CH_3$$

   A                              B                        C

Isomerisation, for example
Reaction 2
$$CH_3CH_2CH_2CH_2CH_3 \rightarrow D$$

Reforming, for example
Reaction 3
$$\underset{E}{C_6H_{12}} \rightarrow \underset{F}{C_6H_6} + G$$

a Name the compounds **A**, **B** and **C** in reaction 1.

b Suggest a structure for compound **D** in reaction 2.

c (i) Draw skeletal formulae for compounds **E** and **F** in reaction 3.

  (ii) Name the product **G** in reaction 3. Write a balanced equation for this reaction.

# Hydrocarbons: arenes (A2)

## By the end of this section you should be able to:

28  show understanding of the concept of *delocalisation* of electrons as used in a model of benzene;

29  describe the *electrophilic substitution* of arenes with concentrated nitric acid in the presence of concentrated sulphuric acid, a halogen in the presence of a halogen carrier, and a halogenoalkane such as chloromethane in the presence of a halogen carrier (Friedel–Crafts reaction);

30  describe the mechanism of *electrophilic substitution* in arenes, using the mononitration of benzene as an example;

31  describe the electrophilic substitution (with halogen carrier) and nucleophilic substitution (free radical) of methylbenzene by chlorine;

32  understand whether halogenation will occur in the side-chain or aromatic nucleus depending on reaction conditions;

33  describe the oxidation of the side-chain (e.g. in methylbenzene) to give a carboxylic acid;

34  understand that reactions of arenes, such as those in point 29 above, are used by industry during the synthesis of commercially important materials, for example explosives, pharmaceuticals and dyes (from nitration), and polymers such as polystyrene (from alkylation);

35  explain the relative resistance to bromination of benzene, compared with cyclohexene, in terms of *delocalisation* of the benzene ring.

## Introduction

The simplest arene is benzene. Benzene is added to unleaded petrol and is used to make many other chemicals, as shown in the pie chart (*figure 16.38*): 65% of benzene is used to make alkylbenzenes. These include ethylbenzene (used to make phenylethene, the monomer for poly(phenylethene), more commonly known as polystyrene); dodecylbenzene (which is used to make detergents) and 1-methylethylbenzene (cumene), used to make phenol and propanone. Benzene is the feedstock for the manufacture of compounds as varied as medicines, dyes and explosives (*figure 16.39*). Cyclohexane, which is a starting material for making nylon, is also made from benzene. You will not use benzene in a school laboratory as it is believed to cause leukaemia. Benzene is a planar hexagonal molecule. This

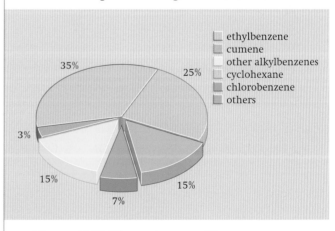

- **Figure 16.38** The main uses of benzene.

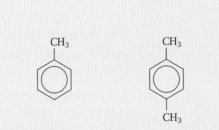

methylbenzene (toluene) and 1,4-dimethylbenzene (xylene) – additives which improve the performance of petrol

vanillin – present in oil of vanilla extracted from the pod of the vanilla orchid, and familiar as vanilla flavouring

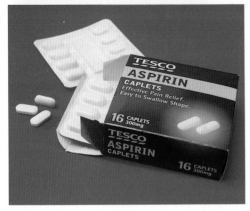

aspirin – used as an analgesic (pain killer)

a diazo dye – used as colouring in paints and on fabrics

● **Figure 16.39** Some compounds manufactured from benzene.

structure has considerable chemical stability. Kekulé was first to suggest that benzene was a cyclic molecule but he also thought benzene had alternating single and double carbon–carbon bonds. Such a structure would have two different lengths for the carbon–carbon bonds. The single and double bonds may be placed in two alternative positions:

(It may help you to see these as alternative positions if you imagine that you are standing on the carbon atom at 12 o'clock: one structure will have the double bond on your left, the other has the double bond on the right.)

The Kekulé structure for benzene would be expected to show the typical addition reactions of an alkene. However, benzene undergoes addition reactions far less easily than a typical alkene. For example, an alkene such as cyclohexene will rapidly decolourise aqueous bromine in the dark. Bromine must be dissolved in boiling benzene and exposed to ultraviolet light before addition occurs (see page 325).

Also, the carbon–carbon bond lengths in benzene molecules are all identical, with lengths intermediate between those of single and double bonds (*table 16.5*).

The current model of the bonding in benzene accounts for these observations. Each carbon atom contributes one electron to a π bond. However, the π bonds formed do not lie between pairs

| Bond | Bond length (nm) |
|------|------------------|
| C–C | 0.154 |
| C=C | 0.134 |
| benzene C–C | 0.139 |

● **Table 16.5** Carbon–carbon bond lengths.

of carbon atoms as in an alkene: the π bonds spread over all six carbon atoms. The electrons occupy three delocalised π orbitals. They are said to be **delocalised** as they are not localised between adjacent pairs of carbon atoms but are spread over all six. (An alkene π bond *is* localised between a pair of carbon atoms.) The π molecular orbitals are formed by overlap of carbon p atomic orbitals. To achieve maximum overlap, the benzene molecule must be planar. One of the delocalised π molecular orbitals is shown below:

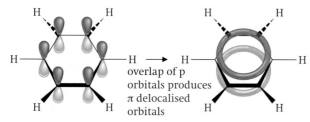

This model produces six C–C bonds of the same length, as observed. The planar shape is clearly seen in a space-filling molecular model of benzene:

The reluctance of benzene to undergo addition reactions is due to the increased energetic stability that the delocalised system gives it (see page 326).

# Substitution reactions

Breaking the delocalised π electron system on benzene requires a considerable input of energy. Arenes such as benzene exhibit many reactions in which the delocalised system is retained. The majority of these are substitution reactions. Groups which may directly replace a hydrogen atom on a benzene ring include halogen atoms, nitro (–$NO_2$) groups and alkyl groups.

# The formation of nitroarenes

The explosive trinitrotoluene (TNT) is made by substituting **nitro groups**, –$NO_2$, for hydrogen atoms on the benzene ring of methylbenzene (toluene). It is explosive because the nitro groups bring six oxygen atoms into close proximity to the carbon atoms of the benzene ring. When detonated (*figure 16.40*), the compression pushes these atoms closer together, causing rapid formation of carbon dioxide and water vapour, and leaving the nitrogen atoms to join together as nitrogen molecules. The explosion is caused by the very large and rapid increase in volume as the solid TNT is converted to gases. (There is not sufficient oxygen to convert all the carbon to carbon dioxide, so carbon is also formed and is seen as black smoke.)

In addition to its use in explosives, the nitro group is a versatile and useful group in the preparation of drugs and dyestuffs.

Until the hazardous nature of benzene was fully appreciated and its use in schools and colleges was banned, the preparation of nitrobenzene was a routine practical in A level chemistry. You may have the chance to nitrate a substituted benzene such as the much less harmful methyl benzoate. Both benzene and methyl benzoate require the use of **nitrating mixture**. This is a mixture of concentrated nitric acid and concentrated sulphuric acid. For benzene, the reaction mixture is heated gently under reflux at a temperature of about 50–55 °C. Careful temperature control is needed to minimise the formation of dinitrobenzene. The reaction equation is:

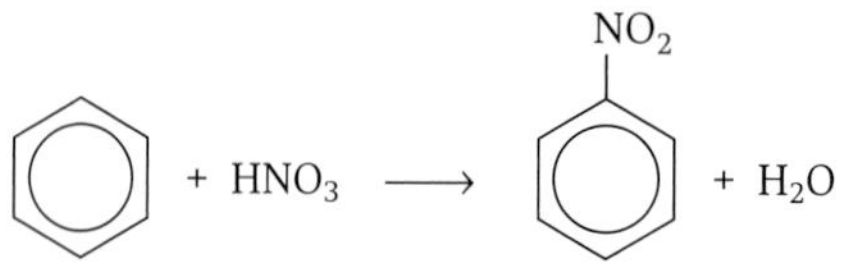

$$\text{benzene} + HNO_3 \longrightarrow \text{nitrobenzene} + H_2O$$

This is a substitution in which a hydrogen atom has been replaced by the nitro group, –$NO_2$.

The mechanism of nitration involves an electrophilic substitution. The function of the sulphuric acid in the nitrating mixture is to generate the attacking species from the nitric acid. (An attacking species may be a reactive molecule, a free radical or an ion.) The benzene ring has a high electron charge density associated with the delocalised π electrons. Hence an attacking

● **Figure 16.40** The use of trinitrotoluene (TNT) as an explosive in quarrying.

reagent that is attracted by this negative charge is needed – an electrophile. An electrophile must be capable of forming a new covalent bond to carbon if it is to react successfully.

The electrophile produced in the nitrating mixture is the nitryl cation, $NO_2^+$:

$$HNO_3 + H_2SO_4 \rightarrow H_2NO_3^+ + HSO_4^-$$
$$H_2NO_3^+ \rightarrow NO_2^+ + H_2O$$

There are two stages in the mechanism of electrophilic substitution by the $NO_2^+$ ion. Figure 16.41 shows this mechanism using curly arrows.

1 Electrophilic attack by the nitronium ion takes place as the positively charged ion is attracted by the delocalised π electrons on benzene. A

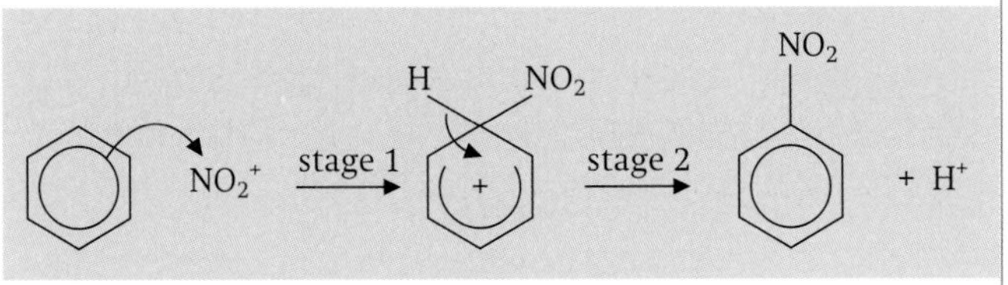

● **Figure 16.41** Electrophilic substitution on benzene.
*Stage 1.* Notice that the curly arrow starts at the delocalised π electrons and finishes on the nitrogen atom in $NO_2^+$. Two electrons are lost from the delocalised π electrons to produce a new covalent bond to the nitrogen atom in $NO_2^+$.
The intermediate is a cation with a single positive charge and a 'horseshoe' representing delocalisation of four electrons over five carbon atoms.
*Stage 2.* The second curly arrow moves two electrons from the C–H bond to restore the full delocalised system of six π electrons. Nitrobenzene and $H^+$ are formed. The circle in the benzene ring of the product shows that the full delocalised π electron system has been restored.

new covalent bond forms to one of the carbon atoms in the benzene ring. This carbon atom is now saturated, so the delocalised π electrons, together with the positive charge from the $NO_2^+$, are shared by the remaining five carbon atoms.

2 Loss of a proton ($H^+$) produces nitrobenzene and restores the full delocalised π electron system.

Thus in electrophilic substitution, the chemical stability of the benzene ring is retained.

### SAQ 16.14

**a** Draw and name three isomers which might be produced following electrophilic substitution of $NO_2^+$ for one hydrogen atom in methylbenzene.

**b** TNT has the systematic name 1-methyl-2,4,6-trinitrobenzene. Draw the structural formula of TNT.

## The formation of halogenoarenes

Benzene also undergoes an electrophilic substitution reaction with chlorine or bromine. For example, if chlorine is bubbled through benzene in the presence of a halogen carrier, chlorobenzene is formed at room temperature:

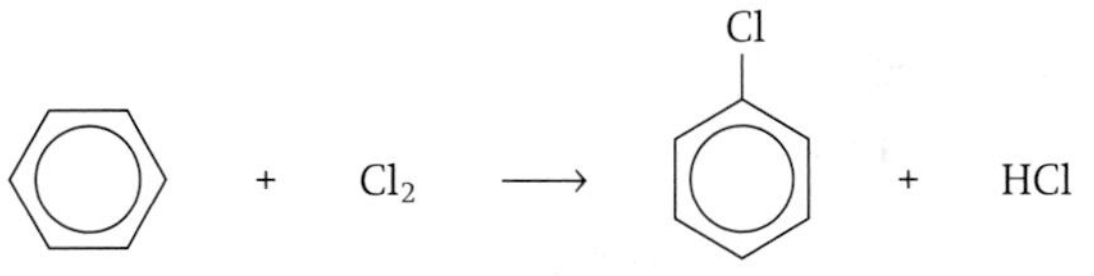

The halogen carrier is usually introduced as metallic iron. This reacts with the chlorine to produce anhydrous iron(III) chloride. Iron(III) chloride is a covalent chloride and is soluble in the benzene.

The effect of the iron(III) chloride is to polarise the chlorine molecule so that it behaves as an electrophile:

$$\overset{\delta+}{Cl} \text{---} \overset{\delta-}{Cl} \text{---} FeCl_3$$

The dotted lines show bonds breaking between chlorine atoms and forming between a chlorine atom and the iron(III) chloride. Anhydrous aluminium chloride may also be used as a halogen carrier.

### SAQ 16.15

Suggest the stages involved in the mechanism for substitution by chlorine on benzene.

Halogenation of methylbenzene, $C_6H_5CH_3$, could involve substitution of a halogen atom in either the aromatic ring or in the side-chain. As we have just seen with benzene, substitution in the aromatic ring would be an example of electrophilic substitution and a halogen carrier would be necessary.

When methylbenzene is reacted with chlorine in the presence of anhydrous aluminium chloride, two products are formed.

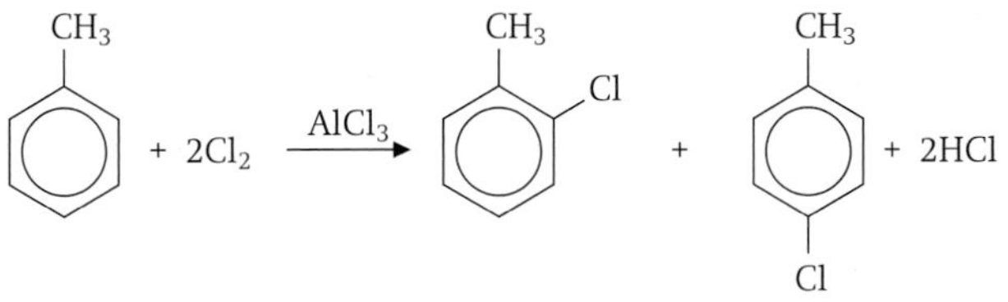

2-chloromethyl-benzene    4-chloromethyl-benzene

The methyl group is unaffected in this reaction because it undergoes nucleophilic substitution. If the conditions for the chlorination are to pass chlorine into boiling methylbenzene in the presence of ultraviolet light, substitution occurs only in the side-chain.

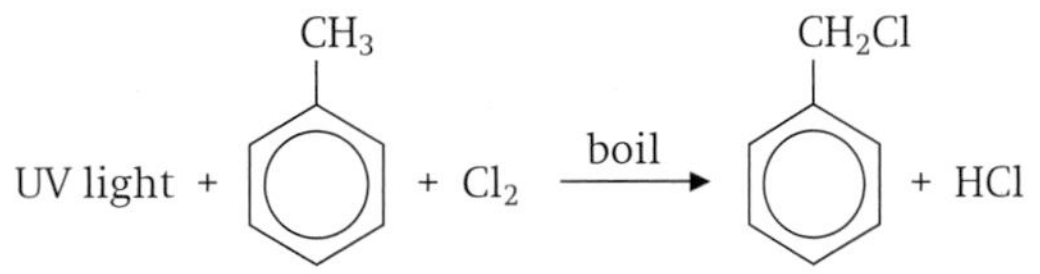

chloromethyl-benzene

This is an example of a free-radical reaction.

# Electrophilic substitution in substituted arenes

Any aromatic compound that has a side-chain can undergo reactions in both the side-chain and the aromatic ring. Electrophilic substitution can always occur in the ring but *where* this substitution occurs depends on the side-chain present.

As we have just seen, the chlorination of methylbenzene produces substitution in positions 2 and 4. However, if nitrobenzene is chlorinated, substitution occurs in position 3.

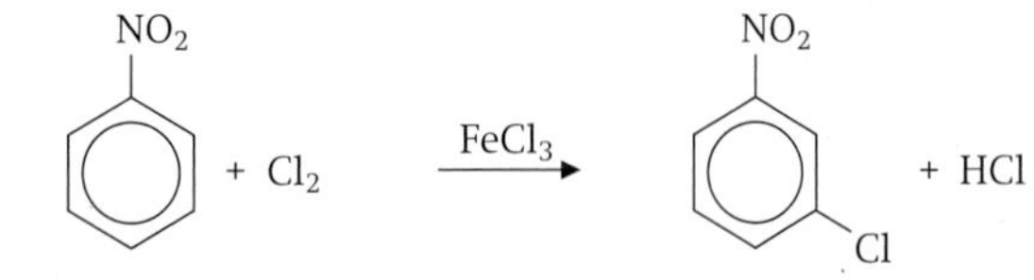

nitrobenzene    3-chloronitrobenzene

Study of many such reactions shows that certain side-chains attached to an aromatic ring are 2,4-directing while others are 3-directing. Note that positions 2 and 6 are equivalent, as are positions 3 and 5.

Groups which direct substitution to positions 2 and 4 (and 6) include $-CH_3$, $-OH$ and $-NH_2$. The methyl group donates electrons to the benzene ring inductively, thus increasing its electron charge density. Both $-OH$ groups and $-NH_2$ groups contain lone pairs of electrons and these can overlap with the delocalised $\pi$ electrons, again increasing electron charge density – particularly at positions 2, 4 and 6.

Groups which direct substitution to position 3 (and 5) include $-NO_2$ and $-COOH$. Each of these groups has an oxygen atom next to the atom (N or C) that is attached to the benzene ring. The electronegative oxygen atom withdraws electrons from the N or C atom, leaving it $\delta+$. This in turn reduces the electron charge density of the benzene ring in positions 2, 4 and 6, so substitution occurs in position 3 (and sometimes 5) because of the relatively higher charge density here.

# The formation of alkylarenes

Alkylarenes are made using the Friedel–Crafts-type reaction. This makes use of a halogen carrier and a halogenoalkane. With chloromethane, for example, benzene forms methylbenzene:

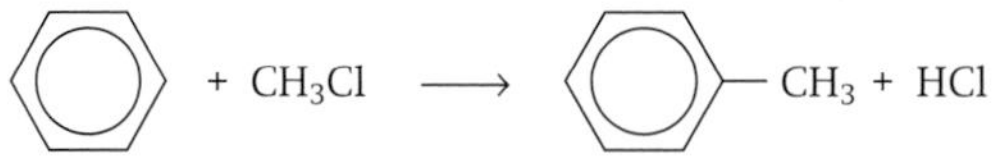

## SAQ 16.16

a Suggest a suitable halogen carrier to use in the reaction of benzene with chloromethane.

b Suggest suitable reactants which might lead to the formation of the following compound in the presence of a halogen carrier.

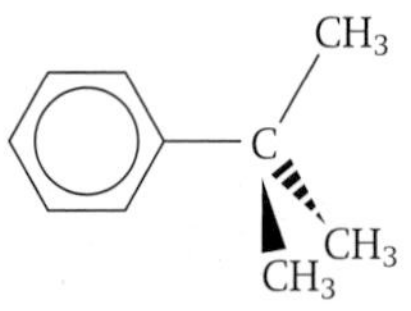

c Write a balanced equation using your suggested reactants.

Ethylbenzene is an important alkylbenzene that is used to make phenylethene (styrene). Ethylbenzene can be made from benzene and chloroethane using a Friedel–Crafts catalyst. However, industrially ethylbenzene is made more cheaply from benzene and ethene, as follows.

$$\text{benzene} + CH_2{=}CH_2 \xrightarrow[\substack{600\text{ K} \\ 40\text{ atm}}]{\substack{AlCl_3 \\ \text{catalyst}}} \text{ethylbenzene}$$

$$\text{ethylbenzene} \xrightarrow[900\text{ K}]{\substack{Fe_2O_3 \\ \text{catalyst}}} \text{phenylethene}$$

Phenylethene is the monomer for the production of the poly(phenylethene). This polymer is the familiar plastic (polystyrene) foam that is widely used in an expanded form for packaging and insulation. Polystyrene is also used for industrial mouldings, telephones, the casing of portable stereos and CD players and toys (*figure 16.42*).

# Addition of halogens to benzene

The Kekulé structure of benzene with three alternating carbon–carbon double bonds would suggest that benzene might readily undergo an addition reaction with a halogen such as chlorine or bromine. We have already seen that chlorine and bromine, in the presence of a **halogen carrier**, produce substituted products. For example, bromine in the presence of anhydrous iron(III) bromide produces bromobenzene.

$$\text{benzene} + Br_2 \xrightarrow[\text{FeBr}_3]{\text{anhydrous}} \text{bromobenzene} + HBr$$

Addition of bromine to benzene is much more difficult to achieve. This is somewhat surprising if we represent benzene by the Kekulé structure.

$$\text{benzene} + 3Br_2 \longrightarrow \text{product}$$

Our knowledge of the addition of bromine to an alkene such as cyclohexene would suggest that this reaction would require mild reaction conditions. Cyclohexene produces 1,2-dibromo-cyclohexane on shaking cyclohexene with bromine water. Indeed, this reaction is used as a quick test to show the presence of an alkene.

$$\text{cyclohexene} + Br_2 \longrightarrow \text{1,2-dibromocyclohexane}$$

The relative resistance of benzene to bromination as compared to cyclohexene may be explained in terms of delocalisation of the $\pi$ electrons in the benzene ring.

Benzene requires more vigorous reaction conditions for the addition of a halogen such as chlorine or bromine because of the chemical stability of the delocalised $\pi$ electron system. Extra energy is required to overcome this stability. We shall examine this in more detail for the chlorination of benzene.

Benzene has been used to manufacture the chlorinated insecticide Lindane.

Use of chlorinated hydrocarbon insecticides has now virtually ceased. This follows the discovery of a link between their use and a decline in the population of peregrine falcons (*figure 16.43*).

● **Figure 16.42**
Some uses of polystyrene.

● **Figure 16.43** Peregrine falcon populations have increased significantly since chlorinated hydrocarbon insecticides have been replaced by new, safer alternatives.

## SAQ 16.17

**a** What does the use of ultraviolet light suggest about the nature of the attacking species in the addition of chlorine to benzene?

**b** How does your suggestion compare to the attacking species in the addition of chlorine to an alkene?

A comparison of the enthalpy changes for the reactions of chlorine with benzene or cyclohexene provides a measure of the extra energetic stability of benzene. The equations and enthalpy changes are as follows:

$$\text{(l)} + Cl_2(g) \longrightarrow \text{(l)}; \Delta H = -183.7\,\text{kJ mol}^{-1}$$

$$\text{(l)} + 3Cl_2(g) \longrightarrow \text{(l)}; \Delta H = -399.1\,\text{kJ mol}^{-1}$$

If benzene had the Kekulé (or cyclohexatriene) structure with alternating single and double bonds, it would be reasonable to suppose that the enthalpy change on reacting benzene with three moles of chlorine would be three times that of the addition of one mole of chlorine to a mole of cyclohexene:

$$\text{(l)} + 3Cl_2(g) \longrightarrow C_6H_6Cl_6(l); \Delta H = -551.1\,\text{kJ mol}^{-1}$$

However, this is $152\,\text{kJ mol}^{-1}$ more exothermic than the experimentally derived value. The extra energy is needed to overcome the delocalisation of the $\pi$ electron bonds. This energy is sometimes referred to as the **stabilisation** (or delocalisation) energy of benzene.

# SUMMARY (A2)

◆ Arenes have considerable energetic stability because of the delocalised π electrons. Arenes require much more vigorous reaction conditions to undergo addition reactions because of this extra stability.

◆ Arene chemistry is dominated by substitution reactions that enable arenes to retain the delocalised π electrons. Hydrogen atoms on the benzene ring may be replaced by a variety of other atoms or groups including halogen atoms, nitro ($-NO_2$) groups and alkyl groups.

◆ Halogenation in the ring using a halogen carrier is electrophilic substitution; halogenation in the side-chain in the presence of ultraviolet light is free-radical substitution.

◆ Side-chains affect the position of second substitution in the ring. $-CH_3$, $-OH$ and $-NH_2$ groups are 2,4-directing. $-NO_2$ and $-COOH$ groups are 3-directing.

◆ The variety of substitution reactions on benzene provides access to many useful compounds including medicines, dyes, explosives and polymers.

# Questions (A2)

**8**  **a** Using a suitable diagram, describe and explain the bonding in methylbenzene.

 **b** Aerosols to ease the pain of wasp stings may contain the local anaesthetic, benzocaine. The structure of benzocaine is shown below.

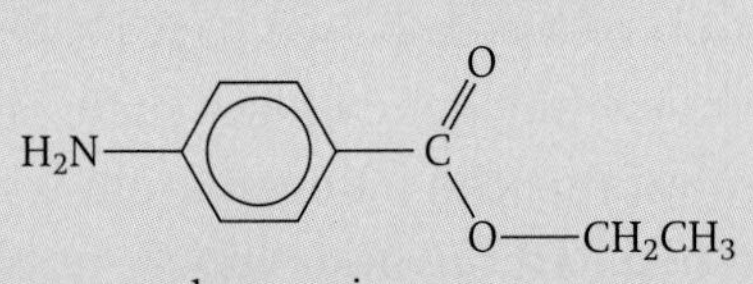

benzocaine

In the production of benzocaine, ethyl 4-nitrobenzoate is converted to benzocaine. Ethyl 4-nitrobenzoate is itself made from 4-nitrobenzoic acid. The structure of 4-nitrobenzoic acid is shown below.

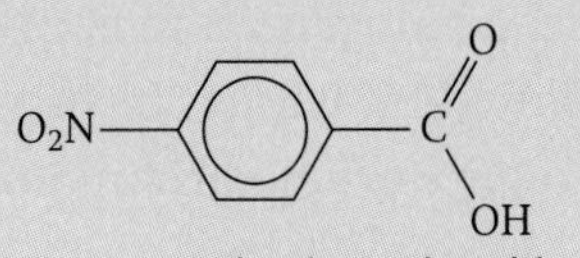

4-nitrobenzoic acid

 (i) State the reagents and conditions for the introduction of a nitro group, $NO_2^-$, into the benzene ring.

 (ii) Write a balanced equation for the formation of 4-nitrobenzoic acid from benzoic acid.

 (iii) Describe the mechanism of this reaction, using 4-nitrobenzoic acid to illustrate this mechanism.

# CHAPTER 17

# Halogenoalkanes (AS)

**By the end of this chapter you should be able to:**

1 describe substitution reactions of halogenoalkanes, typified by reactions of bromoethane;

2 define the term *nucleophile* as an electron pair donor;

3 describe the mechanism of *nucleophilic substitution* in the hydrolysis of primary halogenoalkanes;

4 explain the rates of hydrolysis of primary halogenoalkanes in terms of the *relative bond enthalpies* of the C–Hal bond (C–F, C–Cl, C–Br and C–I). Aqueous silver nitrate in ethanol can be used to compare these rates;

5 describe the *elimination* of hydrogen bromide from halogenoalkanes, typified by bromoethane, with hot ethanolic sodium hydroxide;

6 outline the uses of fluoroalkanes and fluorohalogenoalkanes, chloroethene and tetrafluroethene, and halogenoalkanes;

7 outline the role of chemists in minimising damage to the environment by, for example, developing alternatives to CFCs in an effort to halt the depletion of the ozone layer.

This chapter deals with the properties and reactions of the simple halogenoalkanes. These have the general formula $C_nH_{2n+1}X$, where X is a halogen atom: one of F, Cl, Br or I. They are named by prefixing the name of the alkane with fluoro, chloro, bromo or iodo and a number to indicate the position of the halogen on the hydrocarbon chain. For example, $CH_3CH_2CHClCH_3$ is 2-chlorobutane.

### SAQ 17.1

Name the following compounds: $CH_3CH_2CH_2I$, $CH_3CHBrCH_3$ and $CBrF_2CBrF_2$.

## The classification of halogenoalkanes

Halogenoalkanes are classified according to their structures (*figure 17.1*) in a similar way to the classification of alcohols (see pages 338–9).

- In a primary halogenoalkane such as 1-chlorobutane, the halogen atom is covalently bonded to a carbon atom which, in turn, has a covalent bond to just *one* other carbon atom.

- In a secondary halogenoalkane such as 2-chlorobutane, the halogen atom is covalently bonded to a carbon atom which, in turn, has covalent bonds to *two* other carbon atoms.

- In a tertiary halogenoalkane such as 2-chloro-2-methylpropane, the halogen atom is covalently bonded to a carbon atom which, in turn, has covalent bonds to *three* other carbon atoms.

### SAQ 17.2

What type of isomerism is shown by the compounds in *figure 17.1*?

Draw the structural formula of one further isomer of $C_4H_9Cl$. Is this a primary, a secondary or a tertiary chloroalkane?

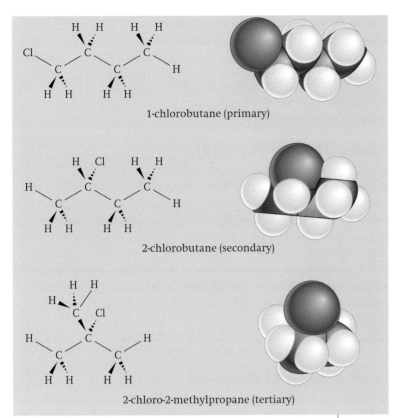

● **Figure 17.1** The classification of halogenoalkanes as primary, secondary or tertiary.

# Physical properties

Typically, halogenoalkanes and halogenoarenes are volatile liquids that do not mix with water.

## SAQ 17.3

**a** Explain why 1-chloropropane, $C_3H_7Cl$, is a liquid at room temperature (boiling point = 46.7°C) whereas butane, $C_4H_{10}$, is a gas (boiling point = 0°C).

**b** Why is it that halogen compounds such as 1-chloropropane do not mix with water?

# Nucleophilic substitution

The predominant type of chemical reaction shown by halogenoalkanes involves substitution of the halogen by a variety of other groups. As the halogen atom is more electronegative than carbon, the carbon–halogen bond is polar:

In a substitution reaction, the halogen atom will leave as a halide ion. This means that the atom or group of atoms replacing the halogen atom must possess a lone-pair of electrons. This lone-pair is donated to the slightly positive, δ+, carbon atom, and a new covalent bond forms. A chemical that can donate a pair of electrons, with the subsequent formation of a covalent bond, is called a nucleophile.

The mechanism for the nucleophilic substitution of bromine in bromomethane by a hydroxide ion is:

Nucleophilic attack is followed by loss of the bromine atom as a bromide ion. A new covalent bond between the nucleophile and carbon is formed. Overall a substitution reaction has occurred.

Some nucleophiles possess a net negative charge but this is not necessary for nucleophilic behaviour. Nucleophiles which will substitute for the halogen atom in halogenoalkanes include the hydroxide ion, water and ammonia. The conditions and equations for these reactions follow.

## Nucleophilic substitution in a tertiary halogenoalkane

The mechanism of nucleophilic substitution in a tertiary halogenoalkane is different from that discussed above for a primary halogenoalkane.

The hydrolysis of 2-bromo-2-methylpropane involves the breaking of the C–Br bond followed by attack by OH⁻ ions on the resulting carbocation.

The electron-releasing methyl groups enhance the stability of the carbocation, thus changing the mechanism of the hydrolysis.

Primary halogenoalkanes react by collision between the halide and the nucleophile. The reaction is first order with respect to each compound (see chapter 8). Tertiary halogenoalkanes react in a two-stage process with a slow (rate-determining) first stage. Secondary halogenoalkanes undergo nucleophilic substitution by a mixture of the two mechanisms.

## Hydrolysis

As the halogenoalkanes do not mix with water, they are mixed with ethanol before being treated with dilute aqueous sodium hydroxide. Warming the mixture causes a nucleophilic substitution to occur, producing an alcohol. The same hydrolysis reaction will occur more slowly without alkali, if the halogenoalkane is mixed with ethanol and water. The equation for the hydrolysis of bromoethane with alkali is:

$$CH_3CH_2Br + OH^- \rightarrow CH_3CH_2OH + Br^-$$

The equation for the hydrolysis of bromoethane with water is:

$$CH_3CH_2Br + H_2O \rightarrow CH_3CH_2OH + HBr$$

### SAQ 17.4

Write a balanced equation for the alkaline hydrolysis of 2-bromo-2-methylpropane, using structural formulae for the organic compounds. Name the organic product.

### The relative rates of hydrolysis of 1-halogenobutanes

Hydrolysis gets easier as you change the halogen from chlorine to bromine to iodine. At first sight this may seem strange, since the polarity of the carbon–halogen bond decreases from chlorine to iodine. You might expect that a less positively charged carbon atom would react less readily with the nucleophilic hydroxide ion.

However, examination of the carbon–halogen bond enthalpies (*table 17.1*) shows that the strength of the bond decreases significantly from C–Cl to C–I. This suggests that the ease of breaking the carbon–halogen bond is more important than the size of the positive charge on the carbon atom. A nucleophile may be attracted more strongly to the carbon atom but, unless it forms a stronger bond to carbon, it will not displace the halogen.

The carbon–fluorine bond does not undergo nucleophilic substitution because it is the strongest carbon–halogen bond. Despite its high polarity, no nucleophile will displace it. This accounts for the very high stability of the fluoroalkanes.

You can observe the relative rates of hydrolysis of halogenoalkanes by adding aqueous ethanolic silver nitrate to the reaction mixture and timing the first appearance of a silver halide precipitate (*figure 17.2*). This will form as soon as sufficient halide ions have been formed by the hydrolysis of the halogenoalkane. For example:

$$Ag^+(aq) + Cl^-(aq) \rightarrow AgCl(s)$$

- 1-chlorobutane slowly produces a faint white precipitate of silver chloride.
- 1-bromobutane produces a white precipitate of silver bromide rather more rapidly.
- 1-iodobutane produces a yellow precipitate of silver iodide most rapidly.

| Bond | Bond enthalpy (kJ mol$^{-1}$) |
|------|------------------------------|
| C–F | 467 |
| C–Cl | 340 |
| C–Br | 280 |
| C–I | 240 |

- **Table 17.1** Bond enthalpies of carbon–halogen bonds.

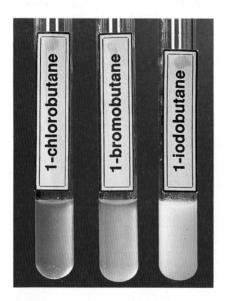

- **Figure 17.2** The hydrolysis of halogenoalkanes by aqueous ethanolic silver nitrate after 15 minutes. The silver nitrate produces an insoluble precipitate of a silver halide.

## Reaction with ammonia

If halogenoalkanes are mixed with an excess of ethanolic ammonia and heated under pressure, amines are formed. For example, bromoethane will form ethylamine:

$$CH_3CH_2Br + NH_3 \rightarrow CH_3CH_2NH_2 + HBr$$

Ethylamine is a primary amine.

### SAQ 17.5

Explain why ammonia behaves as a nucleophile in the formation of ethylamine, and suggest a mechanism for this reaction. What will happen to the hydrogen bromide formed?

## Reaction with cyanide ions

When halogenoalkanes are heated under reflux with ethanolic sodium cyanide or potassium cyanide, nitriles are formed, for example:

$$CH_3CH_2Br + KCN \rightarrow CH_3CH_2CN + KBr$$
$$\text{in ethanol} \quad \text{propanenitrile}$$

The product contains one more carbon atom than the original halogenoalkane. This reaction can, therefore, be useful in organic synthesis (see chapter 15, page 289).

## Elimination reactions

Halogenoalkanes undergo nucleophilic substitution reactions with aqueous alcoholic sodium hydroxide to produce alcohols. However, if halogenoalkanes are refluxed with a purely alcoholic solution of sodium hydroxide, a different reaction occurs. For example, bromoethane will produce ethene:

$$CH_3CH_2Br + NaOH \rightarrow CH_2{=}CH_2 + NaBr + H_2O$$

This involves the elimination of hydrogen bromide, leaving an alkene. The hydrogen bromide is neutralised by the alkali. Under these conditions, the rate of the elimination reaction is faster than the rate of the nucleophilic substitution reaction. At lower temperatures, the substitution reaction proceeds at a faster rate.

# The uses of halogen compounds

As a functional group, the halogen atom provides chemists with useful routes to the synthesis of other compounds. This is a more important use of organic halogen compounds than their usefulness as products in themselves. For example, the synthesis of a medicine such as ibuprofen requires alkyl groups to be joined to benzene. This is achieved by reactions between halogenoalkanes and benzene. Ibuprofen is an anti-inflammatory medicine that brings relief to many people suffering from rheumatoid arthritis (which causes painful inflammation of the joints).

Halogenoalkanes which do have direct applications include the polymers poly(chloroethene), better known as PVC, and poly(tetrafluoroethene) (*figure 17.3*); several CFCs, for example dichlorodifluoromethane or trichlorofluoromethane, which have been used as refrigerants, aerosol propellants or blowing agents (for producing foamed polymers); $CCl_2FCClF_2$ as a dry cleaning solvent or degreasing agent for printed circuit boards, and firefighting compounds such as bromochlorodifluoromethane (*figure 17.4*). When combustible materials are ignited, free radicals are generated. These free radicals propagate a seemingly unlimited variety of combustion reaction steps which produce more free

● **Figure 17.3** Poly(tetrafluoroethene), PTFE, is used in the non-stick coating on saucepans and in waterproof clothing.

● **Figure 17.4** Bromochlorodifluoromethane, BCF, is very effective at extinguishing fires. However, it is not now in general use because the breakdown products are poisonous.

radicals. By diverting or terminating these free radical steps we can extinguish the combustion. Bromochlorodifluoromethane (or BCF) is used in some fire extinguishers. The presence of a bromine atom confers flame-retarding qualities on the product. The high temperatures in fires break this compound down, producing free radicals such as Br·(g). These react rapidly with other free radicals produced during combustion, quenching the flames.

# Chemists and the environment

## Trouble in the ozone layer

Chlorofluorocarbons (CFCs) are regularly blamed for causing damage to our environment. Although they absorb much more infrared radiation per molecule than carbon dioxide, their contribution to the 'greenhouse effect' is very low due to their very low abundance in the atmosphere (carbon dioxide is the main cause of the 'greenhouse effect'). More importantly, CFCs are responsible for a thinning of the protective ozone layer (*figure 17.5*) in the stratosphere. (Ozone absorbs significant quantities of harmful ultraviolet radiation and thus protects us from skin cancer.) CFCs are still

used in air conditioners and were formerly used as refrigerants and aerosol propellants. They were chosen for these purposes as they are gases that liquefy easily when compressed. They are also very unreactive, non-flammable and non-toxic. (Before CFCs were used as refrigerants, highly toxic compounds such as ammonia or sulphur dioxide were used in domestic refrigerators. Leakage of ammonia or sulphur dioxide caused a number of deaths in the 1920s. As a result, some parts of the USA took the drastic measure of banning these early domestic refrigerators.)

The high stability of CFCs has been part of the cause of the problems in the ozone layer. This has enabled concentrations of CFCs to build up in the atmosphere. When they reach the stratosphere, CFCs absorb ultraviolet radiation, which causes photodissociation of carbon–chlorine bonds. For example:

$$CF_2Cl_2(g) \xrightarrow{\text{UV light}} CF_2Cl\cdot(g) + Cl\cdot(g)$$

Very reactive chlorine free radicals, Cl·(g), are formed.

These radicals catalyse the decomposition of ozone to oxygen. The overall reaction equation is:

$$2O_3(g) \rightarrow 3O_2(g)$$

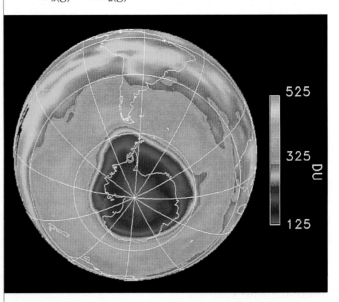

● **Figure 17.5** Representation of satellite measurements of the ozone 'hole' over Antarctica. Ozone concentration is measured in Dobson units (DU). The depletion of ozone reaches a maximum in October, the Antarctic spring, and is probably due mainly to the effects of chlorofluorocarbons (CFCs).

The developments of compounds such as CFCs and BCF illustrate aspects of the work of chemists which benefit society and the environment. Unwanted fires cause considerable economic and environmental damage.

Often, chemists respond to the needs of society by developing new, safer products. This happened in 1928 when Thomas Midgeley (an American engineer) was asked to find a safer alternative to the early refrigerants sulphur dioxide and ammonia. He suggested the use of $CF_2Cl_2$ and demonstrated its lack of toxicity by inhaling the gas and blowing out a candle!

In recent years, we have learnt that the introduction of CFCs like $CF_2Cl_2$ were not without environmental consequences. These consequences have been identified by chemists and other scientists. An understanding of the processes involved has also helped in the search for safer replacements, as you will see in chapter 8. Nowadays, chemists are designing new 'ozone-friendly' chemicals to replace the destructive CFCs. The compound 1,1,1,2-tetrafluoroethane, $CF_3CH_2F$, is now being manufactured as an appropriate alternative. The presence of the hydrogen atoms increases the reactivity of this compound relative to CFCs, so that it is broken down in the lower atmosphere much more rapidly. If it does reach the stratosphere, it does not produce the damaging chlorine free radicals. The use of such alternatives should allow the ozone layer to recover, although the process may well be slow.

## Reactions of chlorobenzene, $C_6H_5Cl$ (A2 only)

Unlike halogenoalkanes, chlorobenzene cannot be hydrolysed, even by boiling it with aqueous sodium hydroxide. Attack by a nucleophile on the carbon atom to which the chlorine atom is attached is difficult because the carbon atom is shielded by the delocalised $\pi$ electrons on either side of the ring. In addition, the C–Cl bond is strengthened by overlap of p electrons from the chlorine atom with the $\pi$ electron cloud of the ring.

## SUMMARY (AS)

◆ Halogenoalkanes have the general formula $C_nH_{2n+1}X$, where X is F, Cl, Br or I. They are named by prefixing the name of the alkene with fluoro, chloro, bromo or iodo and a number to indicate the position of the halogen on the hydrocarbon chain.

◆ Halogenoalkanes react with a wide range of nucleophiles. Nucleophiles possess a pair of electrons, which is donated to the positively charged carbon atom in a C–X bond. The halogen is substituted by the nucleophile, which forms a new covalent bond to the carbon atom attacked.

◆ Bromoethane produces the following products on reaction with the following nucleophiles:
  ● ethanol on warming with water or aqueous alkali;
  ● ethylamine on heating under pressure with alcoholic ammonia.

◆ The reactivities of different halogenoalkanes depends on the relative strengths of the C–X bonds. The C–F bond is very unreactive due to its high bond energy. The rate of hydrolysis of the C–X bond increases from chlorine to iodine as the bond energy decreases.

◆ On heating bromoethane with a strong base dissolved in ethanol, elimination of hydrogen bromide takes place and ethene is formed.

◆ Poly(tetrafluoroethene) (a fluoroalkane) is an important polymer valued for its inertness, high melting point and smooth, slippery nature. It is used for non-stick saucepans and electrical insulation. PVC, poly(chloroethene) is a very widely used material.

◆ Chlorofluoroalkanes have been used extensively as they are inert, non-toxic, non-flammable compounds that have appropriate physical properties for use as propellants, refrigerants, blowing agents or cleaning solvents.

◆ Chemists play an important role, for example in the development of alternatives to CFCs to provide for the perceived needs of society and to minimise damage to the environment.

◆ CFCs, which were used extensively in refrigerators and aerosol cans, are very unreactive. Their low reactivity means that they stay in the atmosphere for a long time. They are broken down by ultraviolet radiation to release chlorine free radicals, which have reduced the concentration of ozone in the stratosphere.

◆ $CF_3CH_2F$ is being introduced as a replacement for various CFCs in refrigerants and aerosols.

◆ Bromochlorodifluoromethane (BCF), $CF_2ClBr$, has been used in some fire extinguishers. It is not now in general use because it produces poisonous breakdown products.

◆ Chlorobenzene cannot be hydrolysed like halogenoalkanes, even by boiling with NaOH(aq).

# Questions (AS)

1 There are four isomers of $C_4H_9Br$. The isomer 2-bromo-2-methylpropane is shown below:

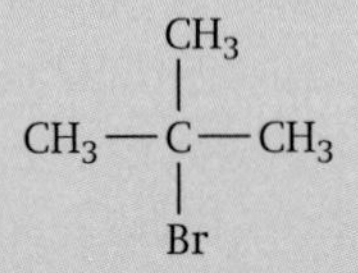

$$CH_3 - \underset{\underset{Br}{|}}{\overset{\overset{CH_3}{|}}{C}} - CH_3$$

  **a** Draw the other **three** isomers of $C_4H_9Br$ and classify each as either primary, secondary or tertiary.

  **b** Describe the mechanism of the nucleophilic substitution of 2-bromo-2-methylpropane using aqueous sodium hydroxide.

2 On heating, the compound 1-bromobutane, $CH_3CH_2CH_2CH_2Br$, undergoes reactions, as shown in the scheme below:

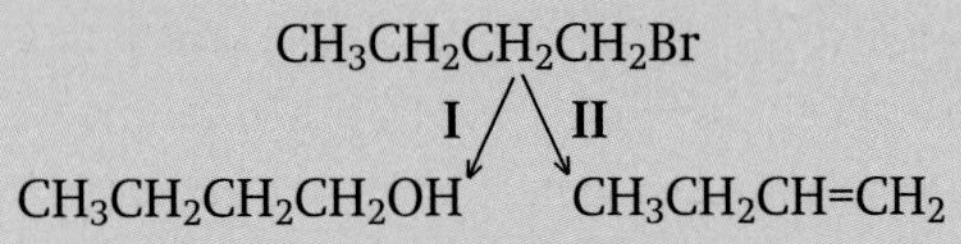

$$CH_3CH_2CH_2CH_2Br$$
$$\overset{I}{\swarrow} \overset{II}{\searrow}$$
$$CH_3CH_2CH_2CH_2OH \qquad CH_3CH_2CH=CH_2$$

  **a** For each of the two reactions shown, name the reagents and the solvents used.

  **b** If 1-chlorobutane was used in reaction **I** in place of 1-bromobutane, what difference (if any) would you expect in the rate of reaction? Explain your answer.

  **c** If 2-bromo-2-methylpropane was used in reaction **I** in place of 1-bromobutane, what difference (if any) would you expect in the rate of reaction? Explain your answer.

3 Many halogenated carbon compounds are important in industry, but their disposal can cause major environmental problems. Using halogenated solvents and polymers as examples, discuss the problems associated with their disposal and indicate which part of the environment is likely to be affected in each case.

# Hydroxy compounds: alcohols (AS)

## By the end of this section you should be able to:

1 explain, in terms of hydrogen bonding, the water solubility and relatively low *volatility* of alcohols;

2 describe and explain the industrial production of ethanol by the reaction of steam with ethene in the presence of $H_3PO_4$;

3 describe the chemistry of alcohols, typified by the reactions of ethanol;

4 describe the classification of alcohols into primary, secondary and tertiary alcohols;

5 describe the oxidation of primary alcohols to form aldehydes and carboxylic acids, the oxidation of secondary alcohols to form ketones, and the resistance to oxidation of tertiary alcohols;

6 outline the use of ethanol as a fuel and methanol as a petrol additive;

7 identify, from *an infrared spectrum*, an alcohol, *a carbonyl compound* and a carboxylic acid;

8 deduce the presence of a $CH_3CH(OH)-$ group in an alcohol from its reaction with alkaline aqueous iodine to form tri-iodomethane (A2 only).

The homologous series of aliphatic alcohols has the general formula $C_nH_{2n+1}OH$. They are named by replacing the final '-e' in the name of the alkane with '-ol'. The position of the alcohol group is indicated by a number. For example, $CH_3CH_2CH(OH)CH_3$ is butan-2-ol.

## Physical properties of alcohols

### Miscibility with water

Miscibility is a measure of how easily a liquid mixes; it is the equivalent of solubility for solids. The miscibility of alcohols may be understood in terms of their ability to form hydrogen bonds to water. Methanol and ethanol are freely miscible in water in all proportions. When water and ethanol mix, some of the hydrogen bonds between the molecules in the separate liquids are broken. These are replaced by hydrogen bonds between water and ethanol. There is no significant gain or loss in energy. *Figure 18.1* shows a molecular model of hydrogen bonds between water and ethanol.

The miscibility of alcohols in water decreases with increasing length of the hydrocarbon chain. Although the hydroxyl group can still form hydrogen bonds to water, the long hydrocarbon chain disrupts hydrogen bonding between other water molecules. The hydrocarbon chains do not form strong intermolecular bonds with water molecules, because the hydrocarbon chains are essentially non-polar and only exert weak van der Waals' forces.

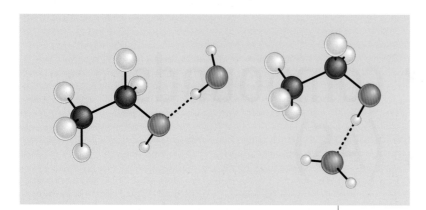

● **Figure 18.1** Hydrogen bonding between ethanol and water (the hydrogen bonds are represented by dotted lines). The bonds form between an oxygen lone-pair and a hydrogen atom.

## Volatility of alcohols

Hydrogen bonding between alcohol molecules reduces their **volatility** considerably. Volatility is the ease with which a liquid turns to vapour. The intermolecular forces are significantly stronger in alcohols than in alkanes of comparable size and shape. *Table 18.1* shows the boiling points of some alcohols together with the boiling points of comparable alkanes. To allow for the atoms in the –OH group, each alcohol is compared to the alkane with one more carbon atom. The higher the boiling point, the less volatile the liquid.

All the alcohols in *table 18.1* have boiling points significantly above those of the comparable alkanes.

## Industrial production of ethanol

Most industrial ethanol is made by the addition reaction of steam with ethene in the presence of a phosphoric acid catalyst.

$$CH_2=CH_2(g) + H_2O(g) \rightarrow CH_3CH_2OH(g)$$

Ethanol is widely used as a solvent. It is often sold as methylated spirit which is ethanol to which a quantity of other compounds such as methanol, methylbenzene or pyridine has been added. These compounds are either toxic or foul-tasting and are added to deter members of the public from drinking the methylated spirit.

# The reactions of alcohols

Alcohol reactions may be divided into groups, according to which bonds are broken. The bonds present in a typical alcohol such as ethanol are shown in *table 18.2*, together with their average bond enthalpies (see page 76).

### SAQ 18.1

When a bond is broken, is the energy absorbed or released? Place the bonds in *table 18.2* in order of increasing strength.

Although the O–H bond is the strongest, it is also the most polar. The atoms involved in polar bonds are more susceptible to attack by polar reagents, so the O–H bond is not necessarily the most difficult bond to break in ethanol.

### SAQ 18.2

**a** Apart from the O–H bond, which other bond in an alcohol is very polar?
**b** Why are this bond and the O–H bond so polar?
**c** Polar reagents include electrophiles and nucleophiles. Explain what is meant by each of these terms.

| Bond | Bond enthalpy (kJ mol⁻¹) |
|------|------|
| C–C | 350 |
| C–H | 410 |
| C–O | 360 |
| O–H | 460 |

● **Table 18.2** Bonds and bond enthalpies in ethanol.

| Alcohol | Boiling point (K) | Intermolecular forces | Alkane | Boiling point (K) | Intermolecular forces |
|---------|-------------------|-----------------------|--------|-------------------|-----------------------|
| ethanol | 352 | hydrogen bonds | propane | 231 | van der Waals' |
| propan-1-ol | 371 | hydrogen bonds | butane | 273 | van der Waals' |
| butan-1-ol | 390 | hydrogen bonds | pentane | 309 | van der Waals' |

● **Table 18.1** Boiling points of alcohols and alkanes of comparable size and shape.

We shall now look at the reactions of alcohols in order, according to which bonds are broken.

# Reactions in which the O-H bond is broken

### Reaction with sodium

Metallic sodium reacts more gently with ethanol than with water, producing a steady stream of hydrogen. As ethanol is less dense than sodium, the metal sinks in ethanol, rather than floating as it does on water. The resulting solution turns phenolphthalein indicator pink (*figure 18.2*) and produces a white solid on evaporation. The white solid is the ionic organic compound called sodium ethoxide, $CH_3CH_2O^-Na^+$. The equation for the reaction is:

$$2CH_3CH_2OH(l) + 2Na(s)$$
$$\rightarrow 2CH_3CH_2O^-Na^+(\text{alcoholic}) + H_2(g)$$

The $CH_3CH_2O^-$ ion is an ethoxide ion. In general, aliphatic alcohols produce alkoxide ions with sodium. This reaction may be compared to the reaction of sodium with water, in which one of the O–H bonds in a water molecule is broken, leaving a hydroxide ion:

$$2H_2O(l) + 2Na(s) \rightarrow 2Na^+OH^-(aq) + H_2(g)$$

As sodium reacts more gently with ethanol than with water, industrial methylated spirit is used to safely destroy small quantities of sodium. You will find that industrial methylated spirit is used in school and college laboratories rather than pure ethanol. Pure ethanol is much more expensive.

● **Figure 18.2** Sodium reacting with ethanol. Phenolphthalein indicator has also been added. The pink colour shows that the alkaline ethoxide ion, $CH_3CH_2O^-$, has been formed.

The reactivity of other aliphatic alcohols with sodium decreases with increasing length of the hydrocarbon chain. All reactions between aliphatic alcohols and sodium produce hydrogen and an ionic product. The organic anions formed have the general name alkoxide ions.

### The formation of esters

When ethanol is warmed with ethanoic acid in the presence of a strong acid catalyst, an ester, ethyl ethanoate, is formed. During this reaction the O–H bond in ethanol is broken. Ethyl ethanoate smells strongly of pears. Other esters of aliphatic alcohols and carboxylic acids also have characteristic fruity odours. Many of these esters are found naturally in fruits. The equation for the formation of ethyl ethanoate is:

$$CH_3CH_2OH + H_3C - \overset{\overset{\displaystyle O}{\|}}{C} - OH \rightleftharpoons H_3C - \overset{\overset{\displaystyle O}{\|}}{C} - OCH_2CH_3 + H_2O$$

Concentrated sulphuric acid is usually used as the acid catalyst and the mixture is refluxed (pages 274–5). The impure ester is obtained from the reaction mixture by distillation. The reaction mixture contains an equilibrium mixture of reactants and products.

Esters may also be prepared by reaction of an alcohol with an acyl chloride (acylation). Acyl chlorides react very vigorously and exothermically with alcohols, releasing hydrogen chloride gas. No catalyst is required and the reaction mixture may require cooling to slow down the reaction. The equation for the reaction of ethanol with ethanoyl chloride is:

$$CH_3CH_2OH + H_3C - \overset{\overset{\displaystyle O}{\|}}{C} - Cl \rightleftharpoons H_3C - \overset{\overset{\displaystyle O}{\|}}{C} - OCH_2CH_3 + HCl$$

# Reactions in which the C-O bond is broken

### Substitution to form halogenoalkanes

When ethanol is heated with concentrated sulphuric acid and solid sodium (or potassium) bromide, bromoethane is formed. This method provides a standard route to other halogenoalkanes from the corresponding alcohols. You should bear in mind that halogenoalkanes are important intermediates in the formation of many other compounds. You can learn more about halogenalkanes in chapter 17.

Concentrated sulphuric acid and sodium bromide react to produce hydrogen bromide and sodium hydrogen sulphate. In the absence of an alcohol, the hydrogen bromide would escape as a gas:

$$NaBr(s) + H_2SO_4(l) \rightarrow NaHSO_4(s) + HBr(g)$$

When ethanol is present, the hydrogen bromide acts as a nucleophile, substituting a bromine atom for the hydroxyl, –OH, group on the alcohol:

$$C_2H_5OH(l) + HBr(g) \rightarrow C_2H_5Br(l) + H_2O(l)$$

Note that this reaction is the reverse of the hydrolysis of a halogenoalkane (page 330). Bromoethane distils from the hot liquid. The product is usually collected under water. Excess hydrogen bromide dissolves in the water. *Figure 18.3* shows the apparatus used to produce a small sample of bromoethane in the laboratory.

● **Figure 18.3** Bromoethane forms when a mixture of ethanol, concentrated sulphuric acid and sodium bromide crystals is heated. The product distils from the reaction mixture and collects as oily droplets under water.

**SAQ 18.3**
**a** Draw a dot-and-cross diagram of hydrogen bromide.
**b** Indicate the polarity of the hydrogen bromide on your diagram.
**c** Draw the displayed formula for ethanol and indicate the polarity of the carbon–oxygen bond.
**d** Using curly arrows, draw diagrams to show the replacement of the hydroxyl group by a bromine atom.
**e** Complete your reaction scheme by showing the formation of water.

Halogenoalkanes containing chlorine or iodine can also be made from alcohols.

Chloroalkanes can be made by reacting alcohols with phosphorus(III) chloride, $PCl_3$, phosphorus(V) chloride, $PCl_5$, or sulphur dichloride oxide, $SOCl_2$. For example:

$$CH_3CH_2OH + PCl_5 \rightarrow CH_3CH_2Cl + HCl + POCl_3$$
$$CH_3CH_2OH + SOCl_2 \rightarrow CH_3CH_2Cl + HCl + SO_2$$

Iodoalkanes can be made by warming an alcohol with a mixture of red phosphorus and iodine. Posphorus(III) iodide is first formed which then reacts with the alcohol.

$$2P + 3I_2 \rightarrow 2PI_3$$
$$3CH_3OH + PI_3 \rightarrow 2CH_3I + P(OH)_3$$

**SAQ 18.4**
Compare the conditions for the hydrolysis of bromoethane with those for the reverse reaction. Explain how the different conditions enable the reaction to be reversed.

## Reactions that may also involve breaking C–C or C–H bonds

### Mild oxidation

Like halogenoalkanes (page 328), aliphatic alcohols may be classed as primary, secondary or tertiary.

■ In a primary alcohol, the –OH group is on a carbon atom which is bonded to only *one* other carbon atom. Ethanol is a primary alcohol.
■ In a secondary alcohol, the –OH group is on a carbon atom which is bonded to *two* other carbon atoms.

- In a tertiary alcohol, the −OH group is on a carbon atom which is bonded to *three* other carbon atoms.

Examples of primary, secondary and tertiary alcohols are:

$$H_3C-CH_2-CH_2-OH \qquad H_3C-\underset{H}{\overset{CH_3}{C}}-OH \qquad H_3C-\underset{CH_3}{\overset{CH_3}{C}}-OH$$

propan-1-ol
primary alcohol

propan-2-ol
secondary alcohol

2-methylpropan-2-ol
tertiary alcohol

## SAQ 18.5

Molecular models for six isomers of pentanol, $C_5H_{11}OH$, are shown in *table 18.3*. The oxygen atoms are coloured red. Draw and label the structural formulae for these isomers. Name those without names and classify each of the alcohols as primary, secondary or tertiary.

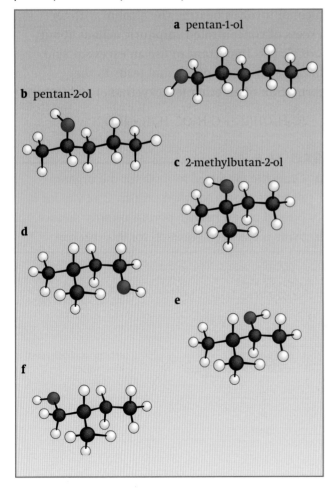

**a** pentan-1-ol
**b** pentan-2-ol
**c** 2-methylbutan-2-ol
**d**
**e**
**f**

- **Table 18.3** Isomers of pentanol.

Primary and secondary aliphatic alcohols are oxidised on heating with acidified aqueous potassium dichromate(VI); tertiary alcohols remain unchanged with this reagent (*figure 18.4*). As primary and secondary alcohols produce different, easily distinguished products, this reaction provides a useful means of identifying an unknown alcohol as primary, secondary or tertiary:

- Primary alcohols produce aldehydes on gentle heating with acidified dichromate(VI). As aldehydes are more volatile than their corresponding alcohols, they are usually separated by distillation as they are formed. On stronger heating under reflux with an excess of acidified dichromate(VI), the aldehydes are oxidised to carboxylic acids.
- Secondary alcohols produce ketones on gentle heating with acidified dichromate(VI).
- Tertiary alcohols do not react with acidified dichromate(VI).

During the oxidation reactions that occur with primary and secondary alcohols, the orange colour of the dichromate(VI) ion, $Cr_2O_7^{2-}(aq)$, changes to the green colour of the chromium(III) ion, $Cr^{3+}(aq)$.

Ethanol, a primary alcohol, produces the aldehyde ethanal on gentle heating with acidified dichromate(VI). You may prepare a sample of aqueous ethanal by distilling the aldehyde as it is formed when acidified dichromate(VI) is added dropwise to hot ethanol. Simplified equations are frequently used for the oxidation of organic

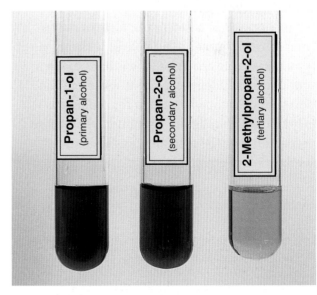

- **Figure 18.4** The colour changes that occur when primary, secondary and tertiary alcohols are treated with hot, acidified potassium dichromate(VI).

compounds, with the oxygen from the oxidising agent being shown as [O]:

$$CH_3CH_2OH + [O] \longrightarrow H_3C - \underset{\underset{\text{ethanal}}{}}{\overset{\overset{O}{\|}}{C}} - H + H_2O$$

Ethanal has a smell reminiscent of rotting apples. Further oxidation, by refluxing ethanol with an excess of acidified dichromate(VI), produces ethanoic acid:

$$H_3C - \overset{\overset{O}{\|}}{C} - H + [O] \longrightarrow H_3C - \underset{\underset{\text{ethanoic acid}}{}}{\overset{\overset{O}{\|}}{C}} - OH$$

You can separate aqueous ethanoic acid from the reaction mixture by distillation after it has been refluxing for 15 minutes. You can detect the ethanoic acid by its characteristic odour of vinegar and by its effect on litmus paper, which turns red.

The secondary alcohol propan-2-ol, on gentle heating with acidified dichromate(VI), produces the ketone propanone. No other products can be obtained even with prolonged refluxing of an excess of the reactants.

$$H_3C - \underset{\underset{H}{|}}{\overset{\overset{CH_3}{|}}{C}} - OH + [O] \longrightarrow H_3C - \underset{\underset{\text{propanone}}{}}{\overset{\overset{O}{\|}}{C}} - CH_3 + H_2O$$

Typically, ketones have pleasant odours resembling wood and fruit. Heptan-2-one is present in oil of cloves as well as in some fruits.

## Complete oxidation: combustion

Ethanol is used as a fuel in the form of methylated spirit; it burns with a pale blue flame, but it is rather volatile and the flame is hard to see in sunlight, so accidents can occur when refilling stoves. Many campers favour it for cooking as it may be carried in lighter containers than those needed for gas. The equation for the complete combustion of ethanol is:

$$C_2H_5OH(l) + 3O_2(g) \rightarrow 2CO_2(g) + 3H_2O(l);$$
$$\Delta H = -1367.3 \text{ kJ mol}^{-1}$$

C–C and C–H bonds are broken in this reaction, as ethanol is completely oxidised to carbon dioxide and water.

In some countries ethanol is blended with petrol to make a cheaper motor fuel. Methanol is used as a fuel for US ChampCar racing.

## Dehydration to alkenes

You can produce alkenes by eliminating hydrogen halide from halogenoalkanes or water from alcohols. For example, if ethanol vapour is passed over a hot, porous ceramic surface, both C–O and C–H bonds are broken producing ethene and water:

$$C_2H_5OH(g) \rightarrow CH_2{=}CH_2(g) + H_2O(g)$$

The ceramic surface acts as a catalyst; the pores of the ceramic provide a large surface area. The high temperature, catalyst and large surface area all increase the rate of this reaction. The reaction is often referred to as **dehydration**, because a water molecule is removed. *Figure 18.5* shows how you can prepare a small sample of ethene by this method. (Note the similarity to the cracking of an alkane – see page 311.)

An alternative method of dehydrating an alcohol involves heating the alcohol with an excess of concentrated sulphuric acid at about 170 °C. It is important to use an excess of acid, because an excess of ethanol leads to the formation of an ether (ethoxyethane) and water:

$$2C_2H_5OH(l) \rightarrow C_2H_5OC_2H_5(l) + H_2O(l)$$

## SAQ 18.6

**a** Draw the displayed formula for the organic product produced when propan-2-ol vapour is passed over a heated, porous ceramic surface.

**b** Write a balanced equation for this reaction.

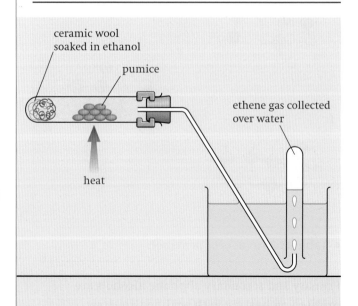

ceramic wool soaked in ethanol

pumice

ethene gas collected over water

heat

● **Figure 18.5** The dehydration of ethanol.

# The uses of alcohols

## ■ Fuels

Alcohols have high enthalpies of combustion. The uses of ethanol and methanol as fuels have already been mentioned (see also page 77). Unleaded petrol contains about 5% of methanol and 15% of an ether known as MTBE (which is made from methanol). The rapid increase in the number of vehicles which can use unleaded fuel caused MTBE production to grow faster than that of any other chemical.

## ■ Solvents

As alcohols contain the polar hydroxyl group and a non-polar hydrocarbon chain, they make particularly useful solvents. They will mix with many other non-polar compounds and with polar compounds. Methanol and ethanol will also dissolve some ionic compounds.

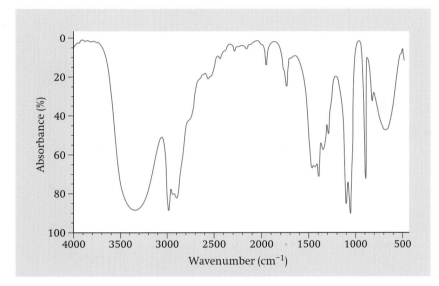

● **Figure 18.6** The infrared spectrum of ethanol.

| Functional Group | Location | Wavenumber (cm$^{-1}$) | Absorbance |
|---|---|---|---|
| O–H | alcohols | 3200–3600 | strong, broad |
| O–H | carboxylic acids | 2500–3500 | medium, very broad |
| C=O | aldehydes, ketones, acids and esters | 1680–1750 | strong, sharp |

● **Table 18.4** Infrared absorption frequencies of some functional groups.

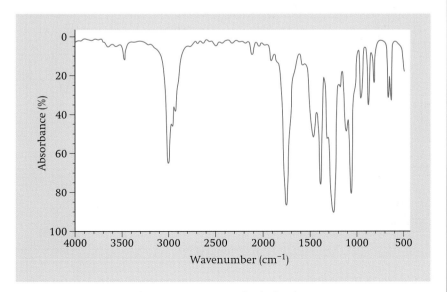

● **Figure 18.7** The infrared spectrum of ethyl ethanoate.

# Structural identification using infrared spectroscopy

In a modern infrared spectrometer, a beam of infrared radiation is passed through a sample of the chemical to be identified. Computer analysis enables the absorbance of radiation to be measured at different frequencies. Study of the resulting spectrum enables the presence (or absence) of particular functional groups to be established. *Figure 18.6* shows the infrared spectrum of ethanol. Notice that absorbance increases in a downward direction. An unusual unit is used to measure frequency, the wavenumber or cm$^{-1}$. *Table 18.4* shows the absorption frequencies which we shall use in this unit.

Look again at the infrared spectrum of ethanol in *figure 18.6*. Most of the absorptions are sharp and some overlap. The absorption of interest is the strong, broad absorption at about 3420 cm$^{-1}$, which shows the presence of the O–H group.

(The O–H absorptions are usually broadened by the effect of hydrogen bonding between molecules.)

If ethanol is warmed with ethanoic acid in the presence of a few drops of concentrated sulphuric acid, ethyl ethanoate (see page 337) is formed:

$$CH_3 - C \overset{\displaystyle O}{\underset{\displaystyle O - CH_2CH_3}{\Big\langle}}$$

How do we know that the ester is present? The infrared spectrum of a pure sample of ethyl ethanoate is shown in *figure 18.7*.

Note the absence of the strong, broad absorption from the O–H group in ethanol. Instead, there is a strong, sharp absorption at 1720 cm$^{-1}$ which arises from the C=O group.

When ethanol is refluxed with an excess of potassium dichromate and dilute sulphuric acid, ethanoic acid is formed (see page 340). Infrared spectroscopy again helps us to distinguish the product from ethanol. The infrared spectrum of a pure sample of ethanoic acid is shown in *figure 18.8*.

The strong, very broad absorption between 2500 and 3500 cm$^{-1}$ is partly due to the O–H group in the acid. (Although groups containing C–H bonds also absorb in this region, they are of little help in identification as such bonds are present in all organic compounds.) Compare the spectrum of ethanoic acid with that of ethanol. There are clear differences between the two spectra.

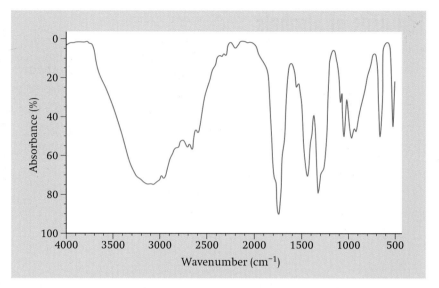

● **Figure 18.8** The infrared spectrum of ethanoic acid.

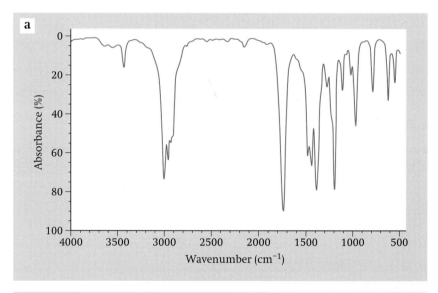

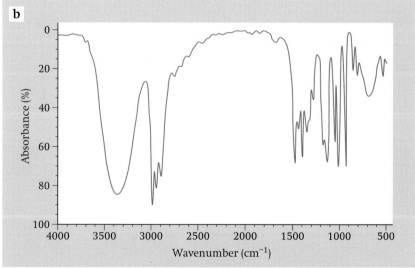

● **Figure 18.9** The infrared spectra of butanone and butan-2-ol, for use with SAQ 18.8.

a  Draw the structural formula of ethanoic acid.
b  Apart from the O–H group, which other group
   can be identified in the spectrum for ethanoic
   acid?  Use *figure 18.8* to record the absorbance
   and frequency of this bond.

Oxidation of a primary alcohol under milder conditions produces an aldehyde, for example ethanal
from ethanol. Oxidation of secondary alcohols
produces ketones, for example propanone from
propan-2-ol (see page 340).

The infrared spectra of butan-2-ol and butanone are
shown in *figure 18.9*.

Identify which of **a** or **b** is butanone. Explain your
reasoning.

# The tri-iodomethane reaction (A2 only)

Alcohols containing the $CH_3CH(OH)-$ group, for
example $CH_3CH(OH)CH_3$ and $CH_3CH_2OH$, give a
yellow precipitate of tri-iodomethane (also known
as iodoform), $CHI_3$, when warmed with alkaline
aqueous iodine (see *figure 18.10*).

In the first stage of the reaction, the alcohol is
oxidised to the corresponding carbonyl compound. For example:

$$CH_3CH(OH)CH_3 \xrightarrow[\text{NaOH(aq)}]{I_2} CH_3COCH_3$$

● **Figure 18.10**  Tri-iodomethane crystals form when
ethanol reacts with aqueous alkaline iodine.

This carbonyl compound is then halogenated and
hydrolysed. For example:

$$CH_3COCH_3 \xrightarrow[\text{NaOH(aq)}]{I_2} CH_3COCI_3 \xrightarrow[\text{NaOH(aq)}]{H_2O} CH_3CO_2^- + CHI_3$$

The formation of the yellow precipitate confirms
the presence of the $CH_3CH(OH)-$ group in the
original alcohol. (See also the reactions of
carbonyl compounds in chapter 19.)

What are the organic products formed when ethanol
is warmed with alkaline aqueous iodine?

# SUMMARY (AS)

◆ Alcohols are soluble or partly miscible in water because hydrogen bonds can form between water molecules and the –OH group. Hydrogen bonding reduces the volatility of alcohols when compared to hydrocarbon molecules of similar size.

◆ Industrially, ethanol is produced by the addition reaction of steam to ethene using $H_3PO_4$ as a catalyst.

◆ Hydrogen bonding reduces the volatility of alcohols when compared to molecules of similar size.

◆ Alcohol reactions may be grouped together by the bond(s) broken: the O–H bond, the C–O bond or the C–C and C–H bonds.

◆ The O–H bond is broken either by sodium to form an alkoxide and hydrogen or by carboxylic acids to form an ester and water.

◆ The C–O bond is broken by nucleophilic halides in, for example, hydrogen bromide.

◆ C–C and C–H bonds are broken by oxidation or elimination reactions.

◆ Oxidation of a primary alcohol occurs in two steps: an aldehyde is formed first and this is oxidised further to a carboxylic acid. Secondary alcohols are oxidised to ketones. Tertiary alcohols are not oxidised under mild conditions. Mild oxidation is usually achieved by heating the alcohol with acidified dichromate(VI).

◆ Complete oxidation of alcohols occurs on combustion to form carbon dioxide and water.

◆ Elimination of water from an alcohol produces an alkene; the reaction is a dehydration. Dehydration may be carried out by passing ethanol vapour over a heated porous surface.

◆ Both methanol and ethanol are useful fuels. Alcohols are also used as solvents.

◆ Infrared spectroscopy enables identification of alcohols, aldehydes and ketones, carboxylic acids and esters by the presence of O–H and C=O absorption frequencies in the spectra.

◆ Alcohols containing the $CH_3CH(OH)-$ group give a yellow precipitate of $CHI_3$ with alkaline aqueous iodine (A2 only).

# Questions (AS)

**1** **a** **(i)** Explain what is meant by the term **structural isomerism**.

   **(ii)** Draw the displayed formulae for all of the alcohols with the molecular formula $C_4H_{10}O$, classifying each as primary, secondary or tertiary.

   **b** For one primary, one secondary and one tertiary alcohol you identified in **a**, describe its reaction, if any, with acidified aqueous potassium dichromate(VI), naming the organic products of the reaction.

**2** Esters are often described as having 'fruity smells'. An ester can be prepared in the laboratory by the reaction of an alcohol and a carboxylic acid in the presence of an acid catalyst.

   **a** Ethanol reacts with 2-methylbutanoic acid to produce an ester which is found in ripe apples.

   **(i)** Draw the displayed formula of 2-methylbutanoic acid.

   **(ii)** When ethanol reacts with 2-methylbutanoic acid, the ester produced has the formula $CH_3CH_2CH(CH_3)CO_2CH_2CH_3$. Write a balanced equation for the formation of this ester.

   **b** The following experiment was carried out by a student:

   A 9.2 g sample of ethanol and 20.4 g of 2-methylbutanoic acid were mixed in a flask and 2.0 g of concentrated sulphuric acid was added. The mixture was refluxed for four hours and then fractionally distilled to give 17.4 g of the crude ester. The ester was washed repeatedly with aqueous sodium carbonate until there was no more effervescence. After further washing with distilled water and drying, 15.6 g of pure ester were obtained.

By referring to the experimental procedure above,

   **(i)** explain the meaning of **refluxed**;

   **(ii)** explain why the crude ester was washed repeatedly with aqueous sodium carbonate;

   **(iii)** state which gas was responsible for the **effervescence**.

   **(iv)** Calculate how many moles of each reactant were used. [Ethanol, $M_r$ : 46; 2-methylbutanoic acid, $M_r$ : 102.]

   **(v)** Use your answers to **a(ii)** and to **b(iv)** to calculate the percentage yield of pure ester obtained in the above experiment.

**3** An alcohol **A**, $C_4H_9OH$, is warmed with acidified potassium dichromate(VI). The colour of the reaction mixture changes from orange to green. Distillation of the green mixture produces a colourless liquid containing product **B**. The infrared spectrum of **B** is shown below:

   **a** Use the spectrum above to identify two functional groups present in the product **B**.

   **b** **(i)** Suggest a structure for the alcohol **A**. Draw a displayed formula of your suggested structure.

   **(ii)** Name the alcohol that you have drawn.

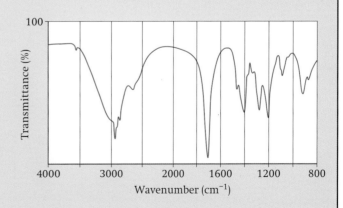

# Hydroxy compounds: phenols (A2)

## By the end of this section you should be able to:

7  describe the reactions of phenol with bases and with sodium to form salts;

8  describe the nitration and bromination of phenol;

9  explain the relative ease of bromination of phenol, compared with benzene, in terms of activation of the benzene ring;

10  explain the relative acidities of water, phenol and ethanol;

11  state the uses of phenols in antiseptics and disinfectants.

## Phenols and their properties

**Phenols**, like alcohols, occur widely in nature. In phenols, the –OH group is joined to a benzene ring. Two very different examples are vanillin and estradiol.

■ Vanillin is found in the seed pods of the vanilla orchid. It is widely used as a flavouring in foods like chocolate or ice cream. The structure of vanillin is:

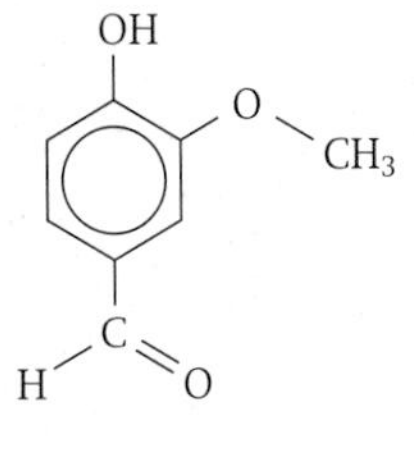

■ Estradiol is an important female sex hormone. It maintains female sexual characteristics and stimulates RNA synthesis (and hence promotes growth). Estradiol contains a secondary alcohol as well as a phenol. The structure of estradiol is:

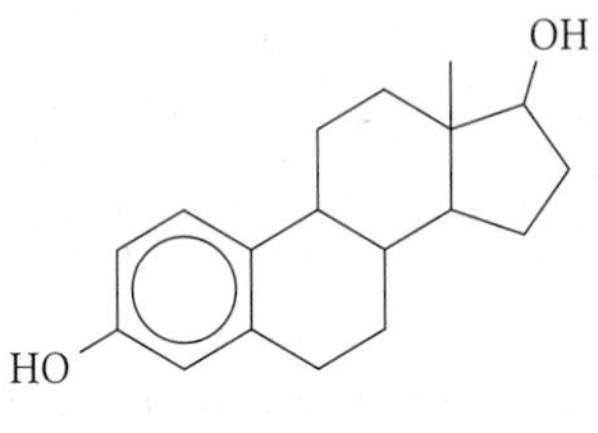

### SAQ 18.10

a  Copy the structures of vanillin and estradiol.

b  Label the phenolic –OH group on each.

c  Identify and label any other functional groups present.

## Solubility in water

Phenol is sparingly soluble in water. The –OH group forms hydrogen bonds to water, whilst the benzene ring reduces the solubility because it forms only weak van der Waals' bonds to other molecules. Two liquid layers are formed if a sufficient amount of phenol crystals is added to water (*figure 18.11*). The excess phenol absorbs water (again, by forming hydrogen bonds) and produces a lower liquid layer. This lower layer is a solution of water in phenol, the upper layer being a solution of phenol in water.

## Reactions in which the O–H bond is broken

### The reaction with bases

As phenol is a weak acid, it neutralises strong bases. For example, with sodium hydroxide the products are sodium phenoxide and water:

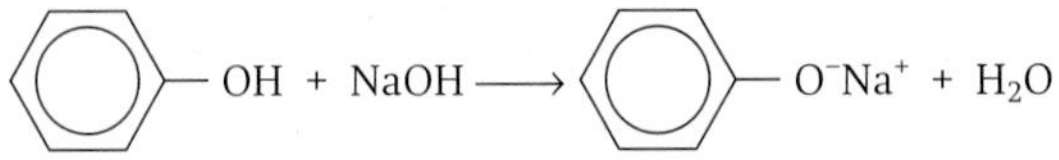

Sodium phenoxide is an ionic compound. Phenol dissolves completely in aqueous sodium hydroxide, but it is only sparingly soluble in water.

Addition of a strong acid to a solution of sodium phenoxide produces the reverse of the reaction with sodium hydroxide. Initially, a milky emulsion of phenol in water forms. This is followed by phenol separating out as a dense, oily liquid layer. We can represent the equation as:

$$\text{C}_6\text{H}_5\!-\!\text{O}^-\text{Na}^+ + \text{H}^+ \longrightarrow \text{C}_6\text{H}_5\!-\!\text{OH} + \text{Na}^+$$

## Reaction with sodium

Phenol reacts vigorously with sodium:

$$2\,\text{C}_6\text{H}_5\!-\!\text{OH} + 2\text{Na} \longrightarrow 2\,\text{C}_6\text{H}_5\!-\!\text{O}^-\text{Na}^+ + \text{H}_2$$

Sodium phenoxide is formed and hydrogen is liberated. The greater reactivity (in comparison with ethanol) is again due to the weak acidity of phenol.

# Reactions involving the benzene ring

Phenol undergoes electrophilic substitution reactions far more readily than benzene. The hydroxyl group, −OH, raises the electron charge density of the benzene π orbitals, considerably enhancing the reactivity of phenol towards electrophiles. The carbon−oxygen bond in phenol has about 16% double-bond character. This is caused by a partial delocalisation into the benzene ring of lone-pair electrons on the oxygen. The increased electron charge density is greatest at the 2, 4 and 6 positions on the ring.

## Substitution with bromine

Aqueous phenol decolorises bromine water to form a white precipitate of 2,4,6-tribromophenol (*figure 18.12*):

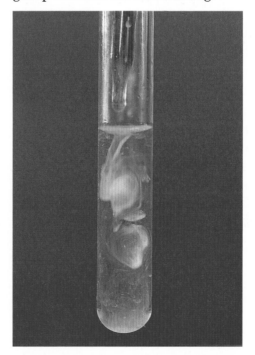

$$\text{C}_6\text{H}_5\text{OH} + 3\text{Br}_2 \longrightarrow \text{C}_6\text{H}_2\text{Br}_3\text{OH} + 3\text{HBr}$$

Similar reactions occur with chlorine and iodine. Contrast these very mild conditions with the need to use pure bromine and pure benzene, together with an iron(III) bromide catalyst, to produce the mono-substituted bromobenzene.

The presence in phenol of the −OH group increases the susceptibility of the benzene ring to electrophilic attack. The oxygen in the −OH group has two lone pairs of electrons. These can overlap with the delocalised π electrons, partially extending delocalisation to the oxygen atom. Overall, the π electron charge density is increased (especially at the 2, 4 and 6 positions). Chemists say the −OH group activates the benzene ring.

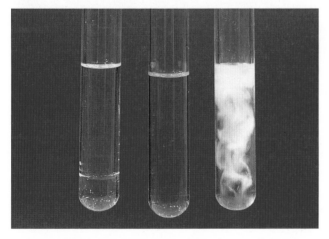

● **Figure 18.11** The left-hand tube shows phenol in water: the phenol does not mix, and settles out at the bottom of the tube. The central tube contains phenol dissolved in alkali. The right-hand tube shows the formation of a milky emulsion when the alkaline phenol is acidified.

● **Figure 18.12** The reaction that occurs when bromine water is added to aqueous phenol.

## SAQ 18.11

How does bromine in aqueous solution become sufficiently polar to achieve electrophilic substitution on phenol?

### Nitration

The activated benzene ring in phenol results in it being nitrated by dilute nitric acid at room temperature.

OH     dil HNO₃ →    OH, NO₂    +    OH ... NO₂

With dilute nitric acid a mixture of 2-nitrophenol and 4-nitrophenol is formed. When concentrated nitric acid is used, 2,4,6-trinitrophenol is formed.

This is commonly known as picric acid and is an explosive.

# The uses of phenol

Phenol is used to manufacture a wide range of useful chemical products (*figure 18.13*). A dilute aqueous solution of phenol was first used in 1865 as an antiseptic by Lister. Phenol was soon widely used in hospitals and greatly reduced the number of infections, particularly during surgery. Phenol as the solid or in concentrated form is harmful by skin absorption and can cause burns. Safer compounds such chlorophenols have now largely replaced phenol in antiseptics and disinfectants.

## The acidity of alcohols

Phenol ionises slightly in water. The O–H bond in phenol breaks to form a hydrogen ion and a negative phenoxide ion. This bond breaking occurs more readily in a phenol molecule than in a water molecule, because the phenoxide ion is stabilised by a partial delocalisation over the benzene ring of the negative charge on the oxygen atom. Phenol is therefore more acidic than water.

$$\text{\footnotesize (ring)}-OH \rightleftharpoons \text{\footnotesize (ring)}-O^- + H^+$$

Ethanol ionises even less than water. The positive inductive effect in ethanol increases the electron charge density on the oxygen atom. This increases the ability of the ethoxide ion to attract hydrogen ions, so ethanol is less acidic than water.

The order of acid strength decreases as:

phenol (most acidic) > water > ethanol

All three are very weak acids in comparison to other weak acids that you may meet. Acids (or bases) which are fully ionised in solution are known as strong acids (or strong bases). Chapter 7 has more on acids and bases.

● **Figure 18.13** Compact discs, the adhesive Araldite and TCP are all manufactured using phenol as a raw material.

# SUMMARY (A2)

◆ Phenols are acidic (relative to aliphatic alcohols) and form phenoxides on reaction with sodium hydroxide. The acidity of phenol is due to stabilisation of the negative charge in the phenoxide ion into the π electron system on the benzene ring.

◆ The reaction of sodium with phenol produces sodium phenoxide and hydrogen.

◆ The –OH group enhances the reactivity of the benzene ring towards electrophiles. Bromine water is decolourised by phenol, producing a white precipitate of 2,4,6-tribromophenol.

# Questions (A2)

5 Wood contains an arene-based polymer known as lignin. Approximately a quarter of the dry weight of wood is lignin. The lignin polymer is built from more than one monomer molecule, with 4-hydroxycinnamyl alcohol being the most frequent. The structure of 4-hydroxycinnamyl alcohol is shown below.

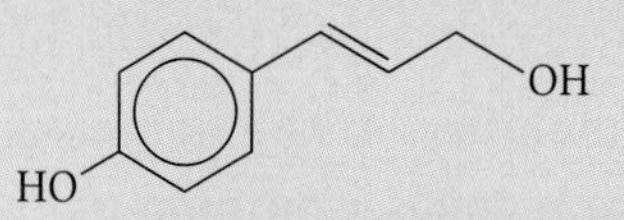

4-hydroxycinnamyl alcohol

a Describe what you might observe when 4-hydroxycinnamyl alcohol is treated with the following reagents. In each case, suggest a structure for the organic product(s).
   (i) Aqueous sodium hydroxide, NaOH(aq).
   (ii) Hot, acidified aqueous potassium dichromate(VI).
   (iii) Aqueous bromine, $Br_2$(aq).

Recent research has shown that, in the kitchen, use of a wooden chopping board may be more hygienic than one made from poly(propene).

b With reference to the structure of 4-hydroxycinnamyl alcohol, comment on this research finding.

# CHAPTER 19

# Carbonyl compounds (AS)

## By the end of this chapter you should be able to:

1 describe the reduction of *carbonyl compounds* using $NaBH_4$ to form alcohols;

2 describe the mechanism for *nucleophilic addition* reactions of hydrogen cyanide (in the presence of potassium cyanide) with aldehydes and ketones;

3 describe the use of 2,4-dinitrophenylhydrazine to detect the presence of a carbonyl group in an organic compound and to identify a carbonyl compound from the melting point of the derivative;

4 describe the use of Fehling's solution and Tollens' reagent to detect the presence of an aldehyde group and to distinguish between aldehydes and ketones, as explained in terms of the oxidation of aldehydes to carboxylic acids with reduction of $Cu^{2+}$ ions to $Cu_2O$ and reduction of silver ions to silver;

5 describe the reaction of compounds containing the $CH_3CO-$ group with alkaline aqueous iodine (A2 only).

You first encountered carbonyl compounds in chapter 18a, in the form of aldehydes and ketones. Aldehydes are formed in the first stage of oxidation of primary alcohols whilst ketones are the only product formed on oxidation of secondary alcohols.

Both aldehydes and ketones contain the carbonyl group, C=O. In aldehydes, the carbon atom of this group is joined to at least one hydrogen atom. The aldehyde group is often written as –CHO. (This must not be confused with the hydroxyl functional group in alcohols, which is written as $\geqslant$COH.) In ketones, the carbonyl group is joined to two other carbon atoms, so the simplest ketone, propanone, must contain three carbon atoms. *Table 19.1* shows the first few members of the homologous series of aldehydes and ketones. Common names of these compounds are shown in brackets. Note that aldehydes are named by taking the alkane stem and replacing the '-e' with '-al'; with ketones the '-e' is replaced by '-one'.

Aliphatic aldehydes and ketones occur widely. The simple sugars, such as glucose and fructose, are present in aqueous solutions as equilibrium mixtures of chain and ring forms (*figure 19.1*). The chain form of glucose has an aldehyde group at one end, whilst the chain form of fructose contains a ketone group. Aldehydes and ketones frequently contribute to the distinctive odours of foods and plants, though odour depends more on the overall shape of a molecule rather than on the functional groups present. Heptan-2-one is responsible for the odour of blue cheese (*figure 19.2*).

| Aldehydes | | Ketones | |
|---|---|---|---|
| **Name** | **Structural formula** | **Name** | **Structural formula** |
| methanal (formaldehyde) | HCHO | | |
| ethanal (acetaldehyde) | $CH_3CHO$ | | |
| propanal | $CH_3CH_2CHO$ | propanone (acetone) | $(CH_3)_2CO$ |
| butanal | $CH_3CH_2CH_2CHO$ | butanone | $CH_3COCH_2CH_3$ |

● **Table 19.1** The homologous series of aldehydes and ketones.

glucose (chain form)    -glucose (ring form)    fructose (chain form)    fructose (ring form)

● **Figure 19.1** Chain and ring forms of sugars.

Another example of a naturally occurring ketone is carvone. This is a chiral molecule and exists as two optical isomers (page 282) with very different odours. One optical isomer is responsible for the odour of spearmint, whilst the other is the principal odour in caraway seed (*figure 19.3*).

### SAQ 19.1

Copy the structures for carvone and the chain forms of glucose and fructose. Label the aldehyde and ketone groups present. Mark the chiral carbon atom in carvone with an asterisk.

● **Figure 19.2** The ketone, heptan-2-one, is responsible for the odour of blue cheese.

The simplest aromatic aldehyde is benzaldehyde, $C_6H_5CHO$, and the simplest aromatic ketone is phenylethanone, $C_6H_5COCH_3$:

benzaldehyde    phenylethanone

The aromatic carbonyl compounds have very distinctive, almond-like odours. Benzaldehyde is used to make almond essence, the flavouring used in Bakewell tarts and puddings. Benzaldehyde also contributes to the flavours of many fruits such as almonds, cherries, apricots, plums and peaches (*figure 19.4*). Such fruits contain amygdalin, $C_{20}H_{27}O_{11}N$. This molecule is hydrolysed by enzymes, forming benzaldehyde, glucose and hydrogen cyanide, HCN:

$$C_{20}H_{27}O_{11}N + 2H_2O \rightarrow C_6H_5CHO + 2C_6H_{12}O_6 + HCN$$

Hydrogen cyanide is a toxic, colourless gas which also has an aroma of almonds. It contributes to the flavour of the fruits. Fortunately it is not a danger as it is only present at a very low concentration!

carvone

● **Figure 19.3** The very different flavours of spearmint, **a**, and caraway, **b**, are produced by the enantiomers of the ketone, carvone, **c**.

● **Figure 19.4** Benzaldehyde contributes to the flavours of many fruits.

*SAQ 19.2* _____

Amygdalin is an example of a glycoside. Many different glycosides occur naturally in plants. They are built up from glucose and either an alcohol or phenol. The structure of amygdalin is shown in *figure 19.5*.

**a** Identify the parts of the amygdalin molecule which give rise to
   (i) hydrogen cyanide
   (ii) benzaldehyde
   (iii) glucose.

**b** Explain what is meant by the term **hydrolysis**.

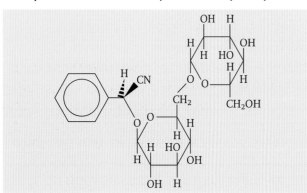

● **Figure 19.5** The structure of amygdalin.

# Physical properties

The carbonyl group is significantly polar:

$$\overset{\delta+}{\underset{/}{\diagdown}}C = \overset{\delta-}{O}$$

The polarity is sufficient to enable the lower members of the homologous series of aldehydes and ketones to be completely miscible with water.

Water will form hydrogen bonds to the carbonyl group:

$$\overset{\delta+}{\underset{/}{\diagdown}}C = \overset{\delta-}{O} \cdots \overset{H}{\diagdown} O - H$$

*SAQ 19.3* _____

Explain the following in terms of intermolecular forces:

'Aldehydes and ketones containing more than four carbon atoms become increasingly immiscible with water.'

# Redox reactions

## Reduction

Aldehydes are obtained by mild oxidation of primary alcohols, and ketones are formed when secondary alcohols are oxidised (see page 339). Aldehydes or ketones may be reduced to their respective alcohols. Sodium tetrahydridoborate, $NaBH_4$, is a suitable reducing agent. The aldehyde or ketone is warmed with the reducing agent using water or ethanol as a solvent. It is usual to represent $NaBH_4$ by [H] in the equation for the reduction. (Compare this to the use of [O] in the equations for the oxidation of alcohols with acidified dichromate(VI).) Here are two examples.

Ethanal is reduced to ethanol:

$$CH_3CHO + 2[H] \rightarrow CH_3CH_2OH$$

Propanone is reduced to propan-2-ol:

$$CH_3COCH_3 + 2[H] \rightarrow CH_3CH(OH)CH_3$$

The reactions may also be regarded as addition of hydrogen to the carbonyl double bond. Remember that, under different conditions, hydrogen may also add to the carbon–carbon double bond in alkenes.

*SAQ 19.4* _____

Draw the structural formulae for the products obtained when the following are treated with $NaBH_4$:
**a** butanone
**b** butanal.

## Oxidation

Under mild conditions, aldehydes are oxidised further to carboxylic acids. The aldehyde is usually refluxed with acidified potassium dichromate(VI). Ketones are not oxidised under these conditions. We have already studied the oxidation of primary alcohols to aldehydes and aldehydes to carboxylic acids in chapter 18a, and you may find it helpful to revise that section now.

### SAQ 19.5

Draw the skeletal formula for the product formed when butanal is refluxed with acidified potassium dichromate(VI).

## Addition of hydrogen cyanide

Both aldehydes and ketones will react with hydrogen cyanide. The product is a hydroxynitrile. For example, propanal will form 2-hydroxybutanenitrile:

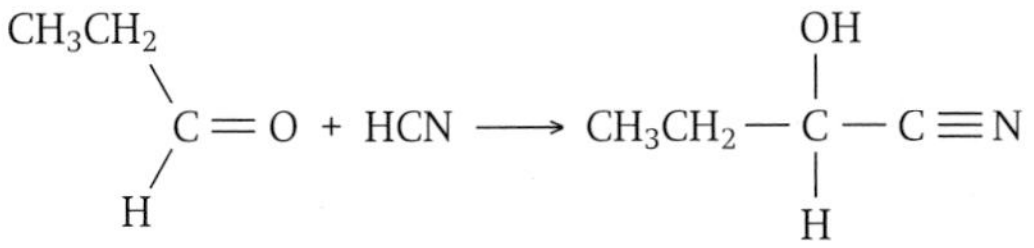

$$CH_3CH_2\ \backslash C=O + HCN \longrightarrow CH_3CH_2-C-C\equiv N$$

Notice that this reaction introduces an extra carbon atom into the molecule. Hence the stem name changes from propane to butane.

Unlike addition to alkenes, which involves an electrophilic mechanism (chapter 16b), the polarity of the carbonyl compounds allows **nucleophilic addition** to occur. The reaction is catalysed by the presence of a base. Hydrogen cyanide is a very weak acid and the presence of a base increases the concentration of cyanide ions. The cyanide ion is a stronger nucleophile than hydrogen cyanide. The lone-pair of electrons on the carbon atom in the cyanide ion attacks the positively charged carbon atom of the carbonyl group:

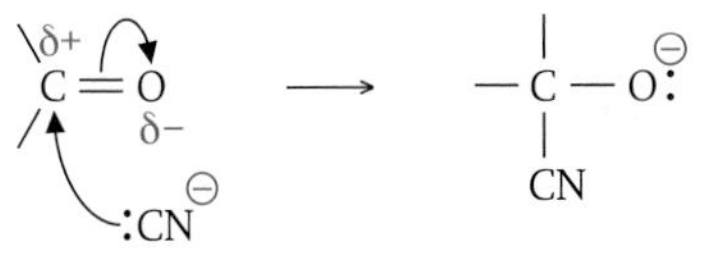

The intermediate ion rapidly reacts with a proton (either from an HCN molecule or from a water

molecule in the solvent) to form the hydroxynitrile:

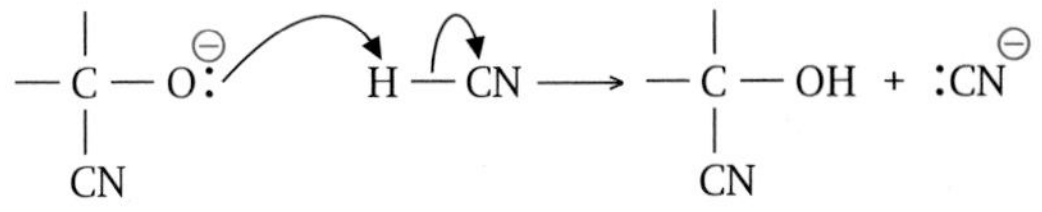

The reaction has considerable synthetic importance due to the formation of a new carbon–carbon bond. The nitrile group is readily converted to a carboxylic acid by hydrolysis:

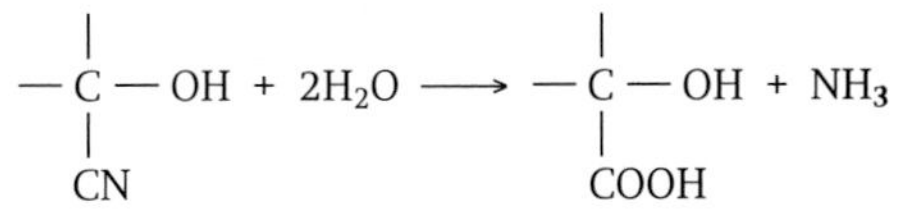

Hydrolysis is achieved by refluxing with aqueous acid or aqueous alkali.

Alternatively, reduction of the nitrile group produces an amine:

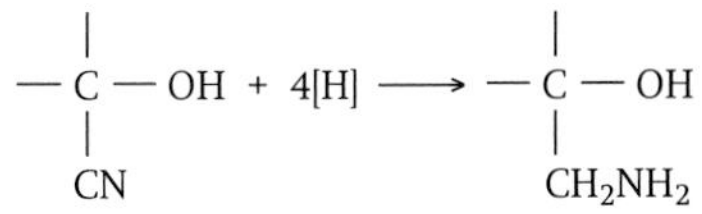

Reduction is carried out using sodium and ethanol.

# Characteristic tests

## A test for the presence of the carbonyl group, C=O

When a solution of 2,4-dinitrophenylhydrazine is added to an aldehyde or a ketone, a deep yellow or orange precipitate is formed (figure 19.6). The test is quite specific for an aldehyde or ketone carbonyl bond. No precipitate is produced with carboxylic acids or with esters, although each of these classes of compounds contain carbonyl groups. The reaction involves an addition across the double bond followed by elimination of a water molecule. The yellow precipitate is a 2,4-dinitrophenylhydrazone.

We use 2,4-dinitrophenylhydrazine rather than phenylhydrazine because it gives better precipitates. These precipitates are easily recrystallised. Recrystallisation, followed by the determination of the melting point of the 2,4-dinitrophenylhydrazone product and determination of the boiling point of the aldehyde or ketone, can help to identify an unknown carbonyl compound.

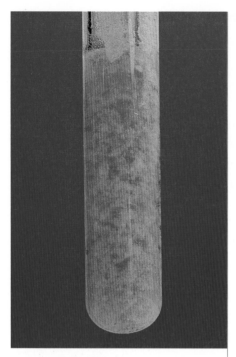

● **Figure 19.6** Propanone reacts with 2,4-dinitrophenylhydrazine to form a 2,4-dinitrophenyl-hydrazone.

The equation for the reaction of ethanal with 2,4-dinitrophenylhydrazine is:

atoms lost in condensation reaction to form water

2,4-dinitrophenylhydrazine          2,4-dinitrophenylhydrazone

As water is eliminated in the formation of the carbon–nitrogen double bond in the hydrazone, the reaction is a **condensation reaction**. In general, a condensation reaction is one in which two molecules join together to form a larger molecule, with elimination of a small molecule (which is often water, but may be methanol, hydrogen chloride, ammonia, etc.).

## Distinguishing between aldehydes and ketones

Aldehydes produce carboxylic acids when treated with mild oxidising agents. Ketones are not oxidised by these reagents. Suitable mild oxidising agents, together with the observations seen when they are used to oxidise an aldehyde, are shown in *table 19.2*. The observations are illustrated in *figure 19.7*.

● **Figure 19.7** 'Before' and 'after' situations for the oxidation of ethanal by **a** acidified potassium dichromate(VI) and **b** Tollens' reagent.

| Oxidising agent | Conditions | Observation on oxidation of an aldehyde | Explanation of observation |
|---|---|---|---|
| acidified potassium dichromate(VI) | boil gently (reflux) | the orange solution turns green | the orange dichromate(VI) ion, $Cr_2O_7^{2-}$, is reduced to green chromium(III) ion, $Cr^{3+}$ |
| Fehling's solution (an alkaline solution of $Cu^{2+}$ complex ions) | warm | red precipitate | the $Cu^{2+}$ ion is reduced to red $Cu_2O$ |
| Tollens' reagent (an aqueous solution of silver nitrate in excess ammonia) | warm | a silver mirror forms on the sides of the test tube from the colourless solution | the silver(I) ion is reduced to silver metal |

● **Table 19.2** The effects of oxidising agents on aldehydes.

## A test for the presence of the CH₃CO– group (A2 only)

Methyl ketones, which contain the CH₃CO– group, give a yellow precipitate of tri-iodomethane (iodoform), $CHI_3$, when warmed with alkaline aqueous iodine (see also chapter 18a, page 343 and *figure 18.10*). For example:

$$C_2H_5COCH_3 \xrightarrow[NaOH(aq)]{I_2} C_2H_5COCI_3 \xrightarrow[NaOH(aq)]{H_2O} C_2H_5CO_2^- + CHI_3$$

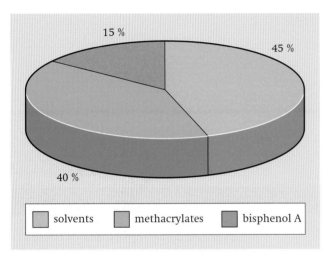

15 %

45 %

40 %

solvents    methacrylates    bisphenol A

● **Figure 19.8** The major uses of propanone.

The formation of the yellow precipitate confirms the presence of the CH₃CO– group in the original ketone.

Some uses of propanone are shown in *figures 19.8* and *19.9*.

● **Figure 19.9** Methacrylate polymerises to a bright, transparent product that is used extensively in vehicle light clusters.

## SUMMARY (AS)

◆ Aldehydes and ketones contain the carbonyl group, C=O. In aldehydes the carbonyl group is joined to just one other carbon atom; in ketones the carbonyl group is joined to two other carbon atoms.

◆ The systematic names of aldehydes are derived from the name of the alkane with the '-e' repaced by '-al'. Similarly ketones are named with the '-e' replaced by '-one'.

◆ As the carbonyl group is very polar, aldehydes and ketones are water soluble.

◆ Carbonyl compounds are readily reduced by $NaBH_4$. Reduction of an aldehyde produces a primary alcohol; reduction of a ketone produces a secondary alcohol.

◆ Aldehydes are readily oxidised under mild conditions to carboxylic acids. Ketones are not oxidised under mild conditions.

◆ The polar nature of the carbonyl group in aldehydes and ketones enables them to undergo nucleophilic addition of hydrogen cyanide to form hydroxynitriles.

◆ The mechanism of nucleophilic addition involves attack on the carbon atom of a cyanide ion by a lone-pair of electrons. A covalent bond forms to the positively charged carbon atom of the C=O bond. The π bond breaks and produces a negative charge on the oxygen of the C=O, which removes a hydrogen ion from a hydrogen cyanide molecule, forming the hydroxynitrile and another cyanide ion. The reaction is catalysed by sodium cyanide.

◆ The reagent 2,4-dinitrophenylhydrazine produces a yellow precipitate with aldehydes and ketones. A condensation reaction is involved (water is eliminated).

◆ As aldehydes are readily oxidised, they may be distinguished from ketones on warming with suitable oxidising reagents: acidified potassium dichromate(VI) turns from orange to green; Tollens' reagent produces a silver mirror.

◆ Propanone is an important solvent.

◆ Ketones containing the $CH_3CO-$ group give a yellow precipitate of $CHI_3$ with alkaline aqueous iodine (A2 only).

# Questions (AS)

1 Cinnamaldehyde is present in the spice cinnamon. It is used as a flavouring in biscuits, cakes and mulled wine. Cinnamon is also known for its ability to release gases produced by bacteria from the intestine or the stomach, either as a burp or flatulence. The structure of cinnamaldehyde is shown below.

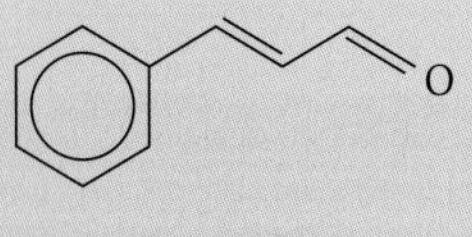

cinnamaldehye

   a   (i) A sample of cinnamaldehyde was refluxed with dilute sulphuric acid and potassium dichromate(VI). Draw a skeletal formula to show the structure of the product.

      (ii) Give the name or formula of the reagent which will reduce cinnamaldehyde to cinnamyl alcohol.

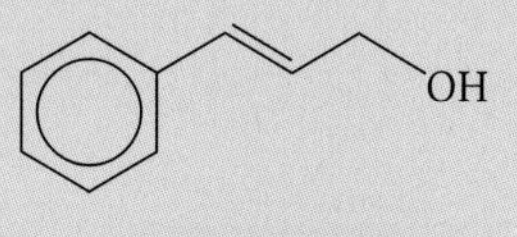

cinnamyl alcohol

      (iii) Give the systematic name of cinnamyl alcohol.

   b   (i) Describe a chemical test to show the presence of the carbonyl, >C=O, bond in cinnamaldehyde. Give the observations expected.

      (ii) Describe a chemical test to show that cinnamaldehyde is an aldehyde and not a ketone. Give the observations expected.

2 Describe the mechanism of the nucleophilic addition of hydrogen cyanide, HCN, to propanone, $CH_3COCH_3$. Explain in your answer why the reaction is catalysed by cyanide ions, $CN^-$.

# Carboxylic acids and derivatives (AS)

**By the end of this section you should be able to:**

1  describe the formation of carboxylic acids from alcohols, aldehydes and nitriles;

2  describe the reactions of carboxylic acids, typified by ethanoic acid, with aqueous alkalis to form carboxylates (salts) and with alcohols, in the presence of an acid catalyst, to form *esters*;

3  describe the *acid and base hydrolysis of esters* to form carboxylic acids and carboxylates, respectively;

4  state the uses of esters in perfumes and flavourings.

● **Figure 20.1** Lemonade often contains benzoic acid as a preservative. Citric acid is present naturally in lemons.

The carboxylic acid functional group is –COOH. This consists of a hydroxyl group joined to a carbonyl group. Simple carboxylic acids are present in many foods. The sharp acidic taste of vinegar is caused by the ethanoic acid (acetic acid) present. Ethanoic acid has the formula $CH_3COOH$. The simplest aromatic carboxylic acid, benzoic acid, is used as a flavouring and a preservative in sparkling drinks such as lemonade. The acidity of lemons is caused by citric acid (*figure 20.1*). The structures of benzoic acid and citric acid are:

benzoic acid

citric acid

Esters are derivatives of carboxylic acids and are present in many foods. In esters, the hydrogen in the carboxylic acid group is replaced by an alkyl or an aryl group. Aliphatic esters have distinctive, fruity flavours. They are one of the principal flavouring components in most fruits (*figure 20.2*): ethyl 2-methylbutanoate is one component of the flavour of ripe apples; 3-methylbutyl ethanoate contributes to the flavour of ripe pears.

ethyl 2-methylbutanoate

3-methylbutyl ethanoate

## SAQ 20.1

Classify the following compounds as carboxylic acids or esters:

a  $CH_3CH_2CH_2COOCH_3$

b  $CH_2ClCOOH$

c  $HCOOCH_2CH_2CH_3$.

● **Figure 20.2** Esters are principal flavour components in ripe fruits.

# Carboxylic acids

The structure of the carboxylic acid group is:

Carboxylic acids are named by taking the name of the alkane and replacing the final '-e' with '-oic acid'. The first four members of the homologous series of

● **Figure 20.3** Oleic acid can be obtained from olive oil, which contains an ester of oleic acid.

| Structural formula | Systematic name | Common name |
|---|---|---|
| HCOOH | methanoic acid | formic acid |
| $CH_3COOH$ | ethanoic acid | acetic acid |
| $CH_3CH_2COOH$ | propanoic acid | propionic acid |
| $CH_3CH_2CH_2COOH$ | butanoic acid | butyric acid |

● **Table 20.1** The first four members of the homologous series of carboxylic acids.

aliphatic carboxylic acids are shown in *table 20.1*. Note that the carbon atom of the carboxylic acid is counted as a carbon atom from the parent alkane. The general formula for the aliphatic carboxylic acids is $C_nH_{2n+1}COOH$.

## Sources of carboxylic acids

### Natural sources

Both petroleum fractions and natural oils provide sources of carboxylic acids. The naphtha crude oil fraction is an important starting material for making other chemicals; it is called a **feedstock**. Large quantities of ethanoic acid are made by the catalytic oxidation of naphtha.

The irritation caused by a stinging nettle is caused by methanoic acid. Butanoic acid gives a very unpleasant odour to rancid butter.

Vegetable oils (*figure 20.3*) and animal fats are esters of carboxylic acids and the alcohol propane-1,2,3-triol (also known as glycerol). Hydrolysis of these oils or fats provides an important source of carboxylic acids with longer chains of carbon atoms. Some examples are shown in *table 20.2*.

In general, carboxylic acids that are obtained from oils or fats are called **fatty acids**. They usually contain an even number of carbon atoms and form unbranched chains. Fatty acids with one carbon–carbon double bond are said to be mono-unsaturated. They are polyunsaturated if they contain more than one carbon–carbon double bond. Each double bond will give rise to geometric isomers.

### Synthetic sources

In the laboratory, there are a variety of synthetic routes to carboxylic acids. These methods include the oxidation of primary alcohols or aldehydes (chapter 18a) and the hydrolysis of nitriles (chapter 19).

| Common name | Systematic name | Skeletal formula | Principal source |
|---|---|---|---|
| lauric acid | dodecanoic acid | ∿∿∿∿COOH | coconut oil |
| myristic acid | tetradecanoic acid | ∿∿∿∿∿COOH | nutmeg seed oil |
| stearic acid | octadecanoic acid | ∿∿∿∿∿∿COOH | animal fats |
| oleic acid | octadeca-*cis*-9-enoic acid | ∿∿∿=∿∿COOH | olive oil |

● **Table 20.2** Some natural carboxylic acids.

Primary alcohols and aldehydes can be oxidised to carboxylic acids by heating with an acidified solution of potassium dichromate(VI). In order to prepare a carboxylic acid from the corresponding primary alcohol, it is necessary to heat the reagents under reflux in order to oxidise the more volatile aldehyde which is formed as an intermediate.

$$CH_3CH_2OH + 2[O] \xrightarrow[\text{heat}]{K_2Cr_2O_7(aq)/H^+(aq)} CH_3COOH + H_2O$$

ethanol $\qquad\qquad$ ethanoic acid

$$CH_3CH_2CHO + [O] \xrightarrow[\text{heat}]{K_2Cr_2O_7(aq)/H^+(aq)} CH_3CH_2COOH$$

propanal $\qquad\qquad$ propanoic acid

Nitriles are hydrolysed to the corresponding carboxylic acid by heating with a mineral acid such as aqueous sulphuric acid.

$$CH_3CN + 2H_2O \xrightarrow[\text{heat}]{H_2SO_4(aq)} CH_3COOH + NH_3$$

ethanenitrile $\qquad$ ethanoic acid

In the acid solution, the ammonia will form ammonium sulphate.

If aqueous sodium hydroxide is used for the hydrolysis, the sodium salt of the carboxylic acid will be formed. The carboxylic acid may be obtained by heating this salt with a mineral acid.

## SAQ 20.2

**a** Draw the skeletal formula of hexadecanoic acid (palmitic acid).

**b** Draw the skeletal formula of the *trans* isomer of oleic acid.

**c** Name the following fatty acid:

**d** Draw the displayed formula of and name the carboxylic acid formed on oxidation of 2-methylpropan-1-ol.

**e** Draw the displayed formula of and name the carboxylic acid formed on hydrolysis of propanenitrile.

# The reactions of carboxylic acids

You first met the hydroxyl group in chapter 18a, and the carbonyl group in chapter 19. In carboxylic acids these two groups combine to form the carboxylic acid functional group, $-COOH$. The combination of these two groups modifies the properties of each of them.

### Behaviour as acids

The proximity of the polar carbonyl group enables the hydroxyl group to ionise partly in water. Hence carboxylic acids are weak acids – unlike alcohols, which do not ionise to any significant degree in water.

The ionisation of the carboxyl group is due to delocalisation of the negative charge over the carbon and oxygen atoms. This delocalisation increases the energetic stability of the anion, producing an equilibrium in aqueous solution:

Carboxylic acids form salts when reacted with metals (such as magnesium or zinc), alkalis, carbonates and basic metal oxides. In addition to producing a salt in the reaction with a carboxylic acid:

- metals produce hydrogen;
- alkalis and basic metal oxides produce water;
- carbonates produce carbon dioxide and water.

For example, if you neutralise ethanoic acid with sodium hydroxide, sodium ethanoate and water are formed:

$$CH_3COOH(aq) + NaOH(aq) \rightarrow CH_3COONa(aq) + H_2O(l)$$

## SAQ 20.3

Write balanced equations for the reactions of:

**a** zinc with propanoic acid;

**b** sodium carbonate with methanoic acid;

**c** magnesium oxide with ethanoic acid;

**d** benzoic acid with sodium hydroxide.

You can titrate ethanoic acid, or wine that has been oxidised to vinegar, against sodium hydroxide to determine the concentration of acid present (*figure 20.4*). Vinegar is between 6% and 10% ethanoic acid. As ethanoic acid is a weak acid, an indicator for the titration of a strong base against a weak acid is required (such as phenolphthalein).

● **Figure 20.4** The concentration of ethanoic acid in vinegar may be found by titration.

# Esters

The ester functional group is:

Esters are formed by the reaction of an alcohol with a carboxylic acid.

The name of an ester comes partly from the parent alcohol and partly from the parent acid. The alcohol part of the name is placed first and is separated by a space before the acid part of the name. An example is ethyl propanoate:

$$\underbrace{CH_3CH_2-O}_{\text{ethyl}}\underbrace{\overset{\overset{\displaystyle O}{\|}}{C}-CH_2CH_3}_{\text{propanoate}}$$

A range of isomers may be formulated by moving carbon atoms from one side of the ester group to the other. Ethyl propanoate has methyl butanoate, propyl ethanoate and butyl methanoate as isomers (all of which are esters).

## SAQ 20.4

**a** Draw skeletal formulae for isomers of ethyl propanoate that are esters and don't have branched carbon chains, and name them.

**b** Further isomers with the same molecular formula as ethyl propanoate are possible. Draw the skeletal formulae of as many of these as you can and name them.

# Formation of esters

The formation of an ester from a carboxylic acid is known as **esterification**. You can prepare ethyl ethanoate by warming a mixture of ethanol and glacial ethanoic acid in the presence of concentrated sulphuric acid as a catalyst. (Glacial ethanoic acid is pure ethanoic acid, free of water. It is called glacial because it freezes in the bottle at 16.7 °C (*figure 20.5*).) The equation for the formation of ethyl ethanoate is:

$$H_3C-\overset{\overset{\displaystyle O}{\|}}{\underset{\displaystyle O-H}{C}} + CH_3CH_2OH \rightleftharpoons H_3C-\overset{\overset{\displaystyle O}{\|}}{\underset{\displaystyle O-CH_2CH_3}{C}} + H_2O$$

ethyl ethanoate

You can make esters of aliphatic alcohols in this way.

## SAQ 20.5

**a** (i) Draw the structural formula of 1-methylethyl propanoate.
   (ii) Name the carboxylic acid and the alcohol which would form 1-methylethyl propanoate.
   (iii) Write a balanced equation for the formation of 1-methylethyl propanoate using structural formulae.

**b** (i) Name the ester formed on reaction of methanoic acid with butan-1-ol.
   (ii) Write a balanced equation for the reaction of methanoic acid with butan-1-ol using structural formulae.

● **Figure 20.5** Glacial ethanoic acid freezes at 16.7 °C.

# The hydrolysis of esters

Esters may be hydrolysed by refluxing with either an acid or an alkali. Refluxing with an acid simply reverses the preparation of the ester from an alcohol and a carboxylic acid. The acid catalyses the reaction. The reaction is an equilibrium; hence there are always molecules of both reactants and products present after the reaction. The equation for the acid hydrolysis of ethyl ethanoate is:

$$H_3C-C\!\!\begin{array}{c}O\\\\O-CH_2CH_3\end{array} + H_2O \underset{}{\overset{H^+(aq)}{\rightleftharpoons}} H_3C-C\!\!\begin{array}{c}O\\\\O-H\end{array} + CH_3CH_2OH$$

When an ester is refluxed with an alkali such as aqueous sodium hydroxide, it is fully hydrolysed to the alcohol and the sodium salt of the acid. The equation for the base hydrolysis of ethyl ethanoate is:

$$H_3C-C\!\!\begin{array}{c}O\\\\O-CH_2CH_3\end{array} + OH^- \longrightarrow H_3C-C\!\!\begin{array}{c}O\\\\O^-\end{array} + CH_3CH_2OH$$

When the ester is a benzoate, base hydrolysis with aqueous sodium hydroxide produces an aqueous solution of sodium benzoate. Subsequent acidification produces a white precipitate of benzoic acid, as benzoic acid is only sparingly soluble in water (*figure 20.6*).

## SAQ 20.6

a Write a balanced equation for the base hydrolysis of methyl benzoate. Name the products.

b Write a balanced equation for the acid hydrolysis of methyl propanoate. Name the products.

● **Figure 20.6** Benzoic acid precipitates when sodium benzoate is acidified.

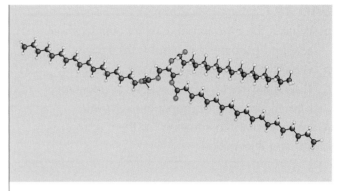

● **Figure 20.7** A triglyceride.

# Fats as natural esters

Vegetable oils and animal fats provide an important store of energy for plants and animals. Oils and fats are esters of propane-1,2,3-triol. This alcohol has three hydroxyl groups, each of which can form an ester when reacted with a carboxylic acid. When only *one* of the alcohol groups has been esterified, the product is called a monoglyceride. In diglycerides, any *two* of the alcohol groups have been esterified. Triglycerides have had all *three* alcohol groups esterified. You can use different carboxylic acids to esterify each of the hydroxyl groups. *Table 20.2* (page 358) shows a few of the carboxylic acids which form these esters. *Figure 20.7* shows a molecular model of a triglyceride.

We shall look more closely at the structure of one triglyceride containing the fatty acid octadecanoic acid (stearic acid). The structures of propane-1,2,3-triol and octadecanoic acid are:

$$\begin{array}{c}CH_2OH\\|\\CHOH\\|\\CH_2OH\end{array} \qquad \begin{array}{c}O\\\|\\C-(CH_2)_{16}CH_3\\/\\HO\end{array}$$

propane-1,2,3-triol (glycerol)　　　octadecanoic acid (stearic acid)

The triglyceride formed from three moles of octadecanoic acid and one mole of propane-1,2,3-triol is:

$$H_3C(H_2C)_{16}-\overset{\overset{\displaystyle O}{\|}}{C}-O-\!\!\begin{array}{c}H_2C-O-\overset{\overset{\displaystyle O}{\|}}{C}-(CH_2)_{16}CH_3\\|\\CH\\|\\H_2C-O-\overset{\overset{\displaystyle O}{\|}}{C}-(CH_2)_{16}CH_3\end{array}$$

## SAQ 20.7

a What is the other product when octadecanoic acid and propane-1,2,3-triol form a triglyceride?

b What type of reaction has taken place?

c How many moles of this second product are formed per mole of propane-1,2,3-triol?

d Write a balanced equation for the reaction using structural formulae.

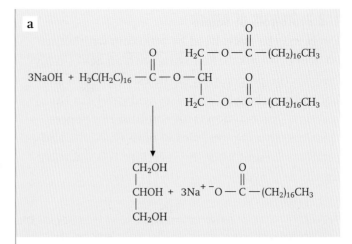

Fats and oils can be hydrolysed (like other esters) by heating with an acid or a base. When they are refluxed with sodium hydroxide, they are converted into propane-1,2,3-triol and the sodium salts of the fatty acids present. These sodium salts of fatty acids are soaps, so this hydrolysis is known as a **saponification**, meaning 'the forming of soap' (from *sapo*, the Latin word for soap). The reaction forms the basis of our modern soap-making industry. Soap making has been known to humans for many thousands of years. Soap is described in the Bible (Jeremiah 2:22). In the first century AD, the Roman historian Pliny described a method of soap manufacture that used goats' fat and beech-wood ashes.

The equation for the saponification of the triglyceride prepared from propane-1,2,3-triol and octadecanoic acid is given in *figure 20.8a*. After the saponification process, the soap is present in solution. It is precipitated as a solid by adding an excess of sodium chloride to the reaction mixture – a process known as salting out. Modern soaps (*figure 20.8b*) are made from blends of oils to produce particular combinations of properties.

## The uses of esters

Significant quantities of esters are used as solvents in the chemical industry and as adhesives. Nail varnish (or its remover) and whiteboard marker pens may contain ethyl ethanoate as a solvent.

The flavours and fragrances of different esters are widely used to produce food flavourings and perfumes. The natural flavours of fruits are the result of subtle blends of hundreds of organic compounds. Many of these compounds are esters of aliphatic alcohols and simple carboxylic acids. In this context, we have already mentioned ethyl 2-methylbutanoate and 3-methylbutyl ethanoate. *Table 20.3* shows a number of esters with their

● **Figure 20.8**

a The saponification reaction produces soap.

b A noodling machine, part of the soap-making process.

approximate associated flavours and their molecular models.

The fragrance of a flower or plant is produced by volatile organic compounds. These may be extracted as the 'essential oil' of the flower or plant. These essential oils are the basis of the perfume industry; they contain a variety of compounds such as esters, aldehydes, terpenes and phenols. (The distinguishing feature of terpenes is that they are built up from a common five-carbon-atom unit based on 2-methylbuta-1,3-diene (isoprene).)

| Flavour | Esters | Molecular model |
|---|---|---|
| apple | ethyl 2-methylbutanoate | |
| pear | 3-methylbutyl ethanoate | |
| banana | 1-methylbutyl ethanoate | |
| pineapple | butyl butanoate | |

● **Table 20.3** Some esters and their associated flavours.

● **Figure 20.9** Oil of jasmine is a natural oil used in perfumes. It used to be obtained from the jasmine plant, but now it is manufactured using phenylmethanol and ethanoic acid.

oil of jasmine

Oil of jasmine (*figure 20.9*), traditionally obtained from the plant jasmine, is now produced by chemical synthesis and is thus cheaply and readily available. Oil of jasmine is phenylmethyl ethanoate.

The perfume industry now relies heavily on chemical synthesis to provide the basic fragrances for many expensive perfumes.

# SUMMARY (AS)

◆ The carboxylic acid functional group is –COOH. Carboxylic acids are found naturally in many foods. The systematic name for a carboxylic acid derives from the name of the alkane, with the '-e' replaced by '-oic acid'.

◆ Carboxylic acids may be made by oxidation of primary alcohols or by hydrolysing a nitrile. Industrially, they are obtained from fats or by the oxidation of a petroleum feedstock. Carboxylic acids may be reduced to primary alcohols (via aldehydes) using $NaBH_4$.

◆ The close proximity of the carbonyl group to the hydroxyl group is responsible for the acidic behaviour of carboxylic acids. They readily form salts with alkalis, bases or carbonates.

◆ Esters are formed when carboxylic acids react with alcohols. A water molecule is released in the reaction. The ester functional group is

$$-\overset{\overset{\text{O}}{\|}}{\text{C}}-\text{O}-\text{C}$$

◆ Esters of aliphatic alcohols have fruity odours and are principal components of the flavours of many fruits. Fats and oils are esters of propane-1,2,3-triol (glycerol) and long-chain carboxylic acids.

◆ Esters are hydrolysed to form alcohols and carboxylic acids by warming the ester with an acid catalyst. Warming an ester with an alkali produces an alcohol and a carboxylic acid salt. Alkaline hydrolysis of a fat or oil produces propane-1,2,3-triol and the salt of a fatty acid. These salts are soaps, so the hydrolysis of a fat or oil is often called saponification.

◆ Esters are used as flavours and fragrances. Apart from its use in vinegar, ethanoic acid is an important feedstock for the chemical industry.

# Questions (AS)

1 An ester found in ripe apples which contributes to the flavour of the apples is ethyl 2-methylbutanoate.

a Draw the structural formula of ethyl 2-methylbutanoate.

b (i) Draw the structural formulae of the alcohol and carboxylic acid that you would use to make ethyl 2-methylbutanoate.

(ii) Write a balanced equation for the formation of ethyl 2-methyl-butanoate.

c A student carried out the following experiment using samples of the alcohol and acid identified in b (i).

● A 9.2 g sample of alcohol ($M_r$: 46) and 20.4 g of carboxylic acid ($M_r$: 102) were mixed in a flask.

● 2.0 g of concentrated sulphuric acid was added.

● The mixture was refluxed for several hours and then fractionally distilled.

● 17.4 g of crude ester were obtained.

● The ester was washed using aqueous sodium carbonate. The washing was repeated with fresh aqueous sodium carbonate until no more gas was produced.

● The ester was then washed with distilled water and dried over anhydrous calcium chloride.

● 15.6 g of pure ester were obtained.

(i) What is meant by the term **refluxed**?

(ii) Write a balanced equation for the reaction of the carboxylic acid with aqueous sodium carbonate.

(iii) How many moles of each reactant were used by the student to make the ester?

(iv) Calculate the percentage yield of the pure ester that the student obtained in this experiment.

# Carboxylic acids and derivatives (A2)

**By the end of this section you should be able to:**

5 explain the acidity of carboxylic acids and of chlorine-substituted ethanoic acids in terms of their structure;

6 describe the formation of acyl chlorides from carboxylic acids;

7 describe the hydrolysis of acyl chlorides;

8 describe the reactions of acyl chlorides with alcohols, phenols and primary amines;

9 describe the formation of phenyl benzoate;

10 explain the relative ease of hydrolysis of acyl chlorides, alkyl chlorides and aryl chlorides.

## The acidity of carboxylic acids

As has been discussed earlier in this chapter (see page 359), carboxylic acids are weak acids.

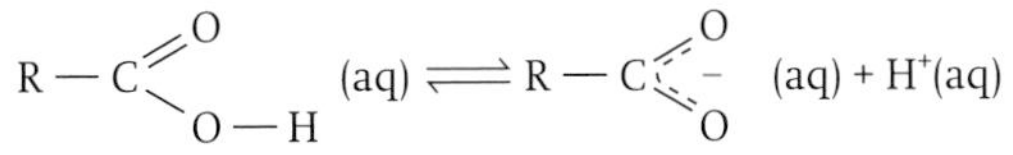

$$R-C\overset{O}{\underset{O-H}{\lessgtr}} (aq) \rightleftharpoons R-C\overset{O}{\underset{O}{\lessgtr}}^{-} (aq) + H^{+}(aq)$$

The anion is stabilised by the delocalisation of the negative charge over the carbon and oxygen atoms. The presence of electron-withdrawing or electron-donating groups or atoms adjacent to the −COOH group affects the energetic stability of the anion.

| Acid | $K_a$ (mol dm$^{-3}$) | $pK_a$ |
|------|------------------------|--------|
| Cl$_3$CCOOH | $2.3 \times 10^{-1}$ | 0.7 |
| Cl$_2$CHCOOH | $5.0 \times 10^{-2}$ | 1.3 |
| ClCH$_2$COOH | $1.3 \times 10^{-3}$ | 2.9 |
| HCOOH | $1.6 \times 10^{-4}$ | 3.8 |
| CH$_3$COOH | $1.7 \times 10^{-5}$ | 4.8 |
| CH$_3$CH$_2$COOH | $1.3 \times 10^{-5}$ | 4.9 |

● **Table 20.4** Acid dissociation constants for some carboxylic acids.

*Table 20.4* shows that as chlorine atoms progressively replace the hydrogen atoms in ethanoic acid to form mono-, di- and tri-chloroethanoic acids the extent of ionisation increases. Thus trichloroethanoic acid is a significantly stronger acid than ethanoic acid, because of the increased stabilisation of the anion by the three electron-withdrawing chlorine atoms.

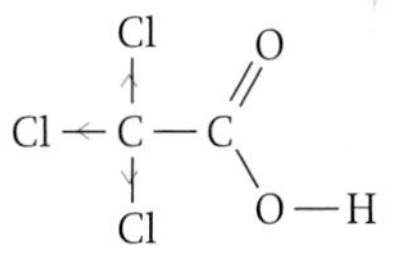

$$Cl\leftarrow\overset{\overset{\textstyle Cl}{|}}{\underset{\underset{\textstyle Cl}{|}}{C}}-C\overset{O}{\underset{O-H}{\lessgtr}}$$

When the group next to the −COOH group is electron releasing, the opposite effect is observed. From methanoic acid to propanoic acid, the anion becomes progressively less stable due to the increasing size of the electron-releasing alkyl group and $K_a$ decreases in value.

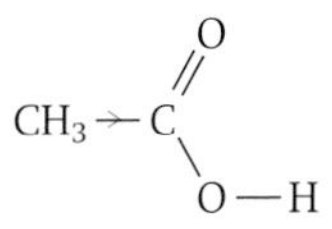

$$CH_3\rightarrow C\overset{\textstyle O}{\underset{\textstyle O-H}{\lVert}}$$

# Acyl chlorides

Acyl chlorides are derivative of carboxylic acids in which the –OH group has been replaced by a Cl atom. The acyl chloride group is –COCl. A typical acyl chloride is ethanoyl chloride, $CH_3COCl$.

Acyl chlorides may be prepared by heating the corresponding carboxylic acid with phosphorus(III) chloride, $PCl_3$, or with sulphur dichloride oxide, $SOCl_2$.

$$3RCOOH + PCl_3 \rightarrow 3RCOCl + H_3PO_3$$
$$RCOOH + SOCl_2 \rightarrow RCOCl + SO_2 + HCl$$

The resulting acyl chlorides are usually liquids which fume in moist air and have an irritating smell. The structure of the acyl chloride group is

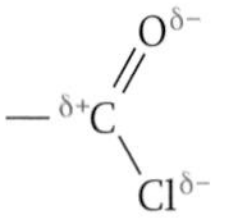

The electronegative chlorine and oxygen atoms withdraw electrons from the carbon atom, making it reactive to nucleophilic attack.

## Reactions of acyl chlorides

### Reactions with water

Acyl chlorides react vigorously with water at room temperature, being hydrolysed to the corresponding carboxylic acid and HCl. For example:

propanoyl chloride — propanoic acid

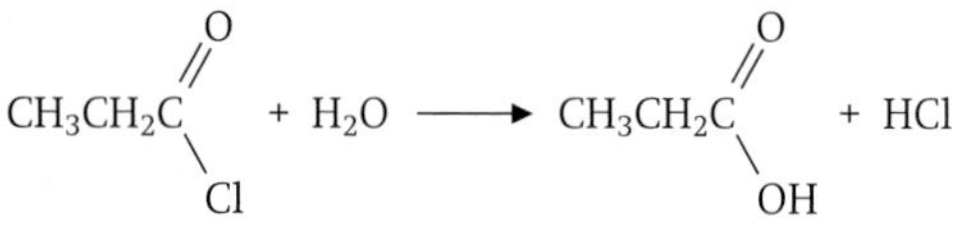

### Reactions with alcohols

Alcohols react vigorously with acyl chlorides to form esters. For example:

ethanoyl chloride — ethanol — ethyl ethanoate

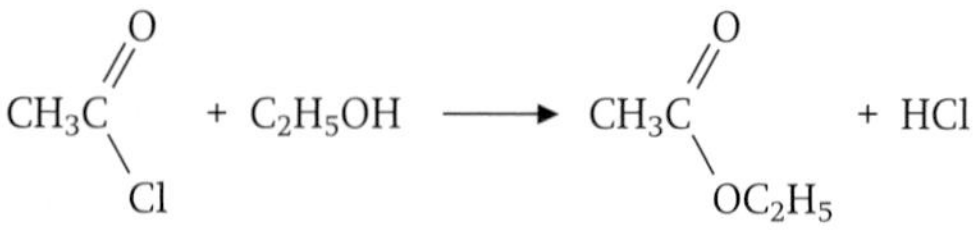

### Reactions with phenols

Acyl chlorides react readily on warming with phenols. In such reactions, the phenol is dissolved in aqueous sodium hydroxide. The corresponding phenyl ester is formed; this is an important method of making phenyl esters because phenol does not react with carboxylic acids.

The formation of phenyl benzoate, using benzoyl chloride, $C_6H_5COCl$, is an example of such a reaction.

benzoyl chloride — sodium phenoxide — phenyl benzoate

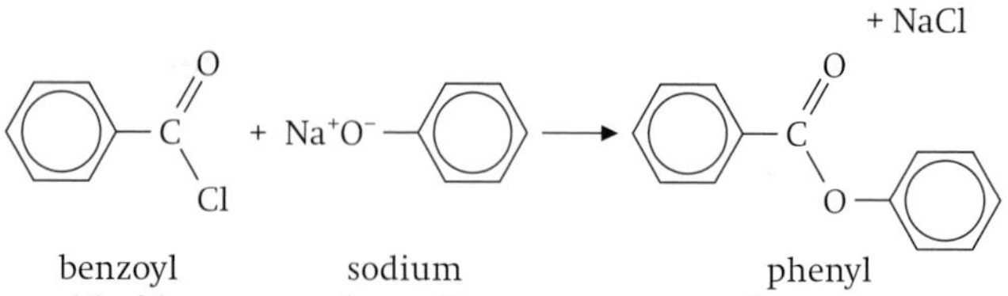

**SAQ 20.8**

Eugenol is an important compound in many spices, such as cinnamon.

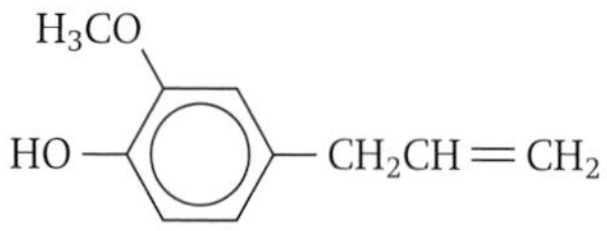

(The $CH_3O$– group is inert and can be ignored.) Draw the structure of the organic product formed when eugenol, dissolved in NaOH(aq), reacts with ethanoyl chloride.

### Reactions with amines

Amines react vigorously with acyl chlorides, forming substituted amides. For example:

*N*-methylethanamide

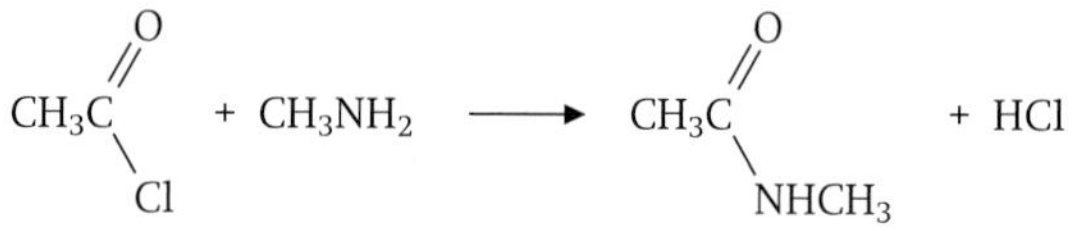

## The relative ease of hydrolysis of acyl chlorides, alkyl chlorides and aryl chlorides

The hydrolysis of compounds such as alkyl chlorides is an example of nucleophilic substitution (see chapter 17, page 329). The lone-pair of electrons on the water molecule is donated to the slightly positive δ+ carbon atom that is bonded to the chlorine atom.

For alkyl chlorides, the hydrolysis of chloroalkanes with water will take place following heating at 100 °C for several days. The reaction takes place more readily with aqueous sodium hydroxide.

For acyl chlorides, the reaction with water occurs very readily at room temperature. This is because the δ+ charge on the carbon atom of the –COCl group is significantly greater than in alkyl chlorides.

In aryl chlorides such as chlorobenzene, $C_6H_5Cl$, the chlorine atom is attached directly to the benzene ring. The carbon atom which would be attacked by a water molecule is shielded by the $\pi$ electron cloud above and below the benzene ring. This means that nucleophiles are repelled. Aryl chlorides, therefore, are not hydrolysed under these conditions.

The relative ease of hydrolysis is

acyl chlorides >> alkyl chlorides >> aryl chlorides

# SUMMARY (A2)

◆ Carboxylic acids are weak acids. When electron-withdrawing atoms, such as chlorine, are on the carbon atom adjacent to the −COOH group, acid strength is increased. When electron-releasing groups are present, acid strength is decreased.

◆ Acyl chlorides are made by reacting carboxylic acids with chlorinating compounds such as phosphorus(III) chloride.

◆ Acyl chlorides are more reactive than carboxylic acids and are good intermediates. They react with alcohols and phenols to form esters, and with amines to form amides.

◆ The ease of hydrolysis of chlorine-containing compounds is acyl chlorides >> alkyl chlorides >> aryl chlorides.

# Questions (A2)

2 Esters can be prepared from carboxylic acids or from acyl chlorides.

  a State the reagents and essential conditions necessary to make methyl propanoate directly from a carboxylic acid.

  b State the reagents and essential conditions necessary to make phenyl benzoate from an acyl chloride.

    In each case, write an equation for the reaction.

3 Using benzoic acid as starting material, copy and complete the synthetic pathways shown below.

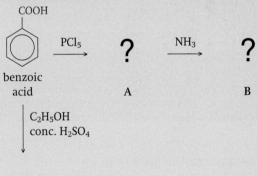

# CHAPTER 21

# Nitrogen compounds (A2)

## By the end of this chapter you should be able to:

1 describe the formation of ethylamine by nitrile reduction and of phenylamine by reduction of nitrobenzene;

2 explain the basicity of primary amines and the relative basicities of ethylamine and phenylamine in terms of the *inductive effect* and the influence of the delocalised electrons in the benzene ring;

3 describe the reactions of *primary amines* with acids to form salts;

4 describe the reaction of phenylamine with aqueous bromine;

5 describe the synthesis of an *azo dye* by reaction of phenylamine with nitrous acid with the formation of a *diazonium salt*, followed by coupling with phenols under alkaline conditions;

6 describe the use of reactions that produce diazonium salts in the formation of dyestuffs;

7 describe the formation of amides from primary amines and acyl clorides;

8 describe amide hydrolysis on treatment with aqueous alkali or acid;

9 state the general formula for an $\alpha$-amino acid as $RCH(NH_2)COOH$;

10 describe the acid–base properties of $\alpha$-amino acids and the formation of *zwitterions*;

11 explain the formation of a *peptide linkage* between $\alpha$-amino acids leading to the idea that polypeptides and proteins are *condensation polymers*;

12 describe the acid hydrolysis of proteins and peptides to form $\alpha$-amino acids;

13 describe the formation of polyamides.

N itrogen may be present in an organic molecule in a number of functional groups.

The **amine functional group**, $-NH_2$, occurs in a wide variety of compounds. These range from simple amines to medicines, dyes and giant biological macromolecules. The smell given off by rotting animal flesh is largely caused by amines such as putrescine, $NH_2(CH_2)_4NH_2$, and cadaverine, $NH_2(CH_2)_5NH_2$. Urea, present in urine, has the structure:

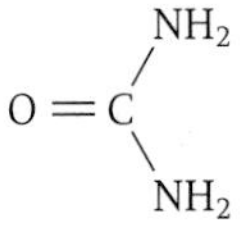

Amphetamine is a medicine used as a stimulant that mimics the effect of noradrenaline. Noradrenaline is a neurotransmitter that prepares animals for a rapid response when, for example, they are suddenly frightened (*figure 21.1*). Noradrenaline and amphetamine increase the heart rate, dilate the air passages in the lungs and increase sweating. They have similar structures:

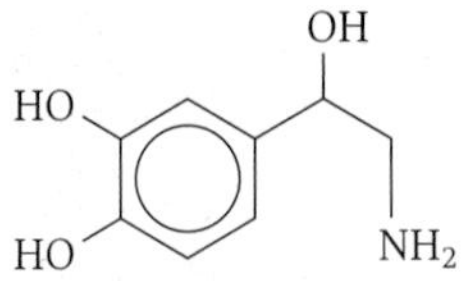

noradrenaline

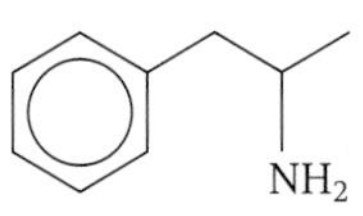

amphetamine

● **Figure 21.1** When springbok are frightened they will take flight, frequently leaping high into the air (an activity known as 'pronking'). The rapid response is triggered by a release of noradrenaline.

The double helix present in DNA is held together by hydrogen bonds between pairs of bases (*figure 21.2*). Amine functional groups are involved in some of these hydrogen bonds. The hydrogen bonds between the cytosine and guanine bases are shown in *figure 21.2b*.

Amino acids also contain the amine group. For example:

$$HOOC \cdots \underset{H}{\overset{CH_3}{\underset{|}{C}}} NH_2$$

**SAQ 21.1**

Copy the diagram of hydrogen bonds between the cytosine and guanine bases (*figure 21.2b*). Draw circles round the amine functional groups and label them.

■ The **amide** functional group, –CONH–, is present in proteins and polyamides. Some synthetic polymers, such as nylon, are polyamides. The repeat units of a protein and a polyamide are:

repeat unit of a protein

repeat unit of a polyamide

**SAQ 21.2**

Copy the repeat units of a protein and a polyamide. Draw circles round the amide functional groups and label them.

■ The **nitrile** functional group, –CN, is used to introduce an additional carbon atom during organic synthesis (see page 289). However, it is also present in the synthetic polymer used to make acrylic fibre. Poly(ethenenitrile) (also called polyacrylonitrile) is made by polymerising ethenenitrile:

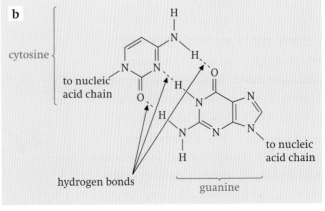

● **Figure 21.2 a** Watson and Crick with their first model of DNA.  **b** Hydrogen bonds between a base pair in DNA.

● **Figure 21.3** Acrylics are used in clothing and furnishing materials.

Poly(ethenenitrile) is used to make acrylic fibre, which is widely used for clothing and furnishing fabrics. It is an interesting thought that when we wear acrylic garments (*figure 21.3*), we cover ourselves in cyanide (nitrile) groups. Sodium cyanide and hydrogen cyanide are highly toxic but, fortunately, the cyanide groups in acrylic fabric are firmly bonded in the polymer, and represent no danger. However, a hazard can arise if the material is burned and the fumes are inhaled. As a result, modern acrylic fibre is modified by the inclusion of some chloroethene. The chlorine atoms provide a substantially increased resistance to combustion.

# Primary amines

The primary amines which we shall study in detail are ethylamine and phenylamine. Models of their structures are shown in *figure 21.4*. Primary aliphatic amines are generally water-soluble. The hydrogen atoms in the amine group, $-NH_2$, form hydrogen bonds to the oxygen atoms in the water molecules. A hydrogen atom in water may also hydrogen-bond to the nitrogen of the amino group (*figure 21.5*). The solubility in water of the primary aliphatic amines reduces as the

number of carbon atoms in the alkyl group increases. Alkyl groups are non-polar and can only form weak, instantaneous dipole–induced bonds to other molecules. The breaking of these bonds provides insufficient energy to disrupt the much stronger hydrogen bonding between water molecules. (Phenylamine also has a low solubility in water, for the same reason.)

## The preparation of amines

Here are two methods for preparing ethylamine.

■ Heating bromoethane with an excess of a hot, ethanolic solution of ammonia produces ethylamine:

$$CH_3CH_2Br + NH_3 \rightarrow CH_3CH_2NH_2 + HBr$$

You first met this reaction in chapter 17. The excess ammonia reacts with the HBr forming ammonium bromide, $NH_4Br$:

$$NH_3 + HBr \rightarrow NH_4Br$$

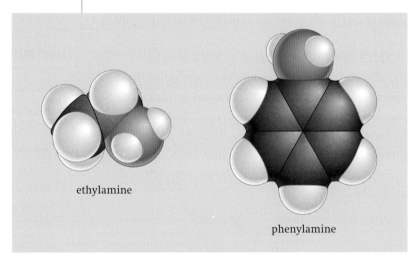

ethylamine

phenylamine

● **Figure 21.4** Amines.

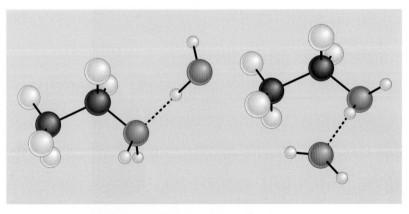

● **Figure 21.5** The formation of hydrogen bonds between water and ethylamine.

- Reducing ethanenitrile with hydrogen produces ethylamine:

$$CH_3CN + 4[H] \rightarrow CH_3CH_2NH_2$$

Sodium and ethanol may be used for this reduction. We also discussed the reduction of a nitrile to an amine in chapter 19 (page 353). Phenylamine is prepared by reducing nitrobenzene:

The reduction is carried out using tin and concentrated hydrochloric acid. The product is separated from the reaction mixture by steam distillation, which involves distilling the mixture whilst passing steam through the mixture (*figure 21.6*). Arenes are readily nitrated, so the reduction of nitroarenes provides a standard route to aromatic amines.

### SAQ 21.3

Give the name and structural formula of the organic product from the reactions of:
**a** propanenitrile with hydrogen (from sodium and ethanol)
**b** 4-nitrophenol with tin and hydrochloric acid.

● **Figure 21.6** This student is carrying out a steam distillation.

## Amines as bases

Amines are related to ammonia, which is a weak base. Weak bases will accept a proton from water to form an alkaline solution. The equation for the reaction of ammonia with water is:

Ammonia has a lone-pair of electrons on the nitrogen atom. This lone-pair accepts a proton from a water molecule to form the ammonium ion. A mixture of ammonia and ammonium ions is present in an aqueous solution of ammonia. If we represent a general amine by the formula $RNH_2$, the general equation for the reaction with water is:

$$RNH_2(aq) + H_2O(l) \rightleftharpoons RNH_3^+(aq) + OH^-(aq)$$

For example, ethylamine accepts a proton to form the ethylammonium ion:

The base strengths of ethylamine and phenylamine relative to ammonia are shown in *table 21.1*. The order of base strength is due to the **inductive effects** of the ethyl and phenyl groups.

- Alkyl groups have a positive inductive effect. This means that they have a tendency to push electrons towards a neighbouring atom. In ethylamine, the effect of this is to increase slightly the electron charge density on the nitrogen atom. This increased charge density on the nitrogen atom enhances its ability to donate its lone-pair of electrons to a proton, so ethylamine is a stronger base than ammonia.
- The phenyl group has a negative inductive effect. The electron charge density on the nitrogen atom in phenylamine is decreased.

| Amine | Order of base strength |
|---|---|
| phenylamine | |
| ammonia | increasing strength |
| ethylamine | |

● **Table 21.1** Relative base strengths of amines and ammonia.

Consequently, the ability of phenylamine to accept a proton is decreased, so it is a weaker base than ammonia. This effect is further enhanced in phenylamine because the lone-pair of electrons on the nitrogen atom becomes partially delocalised over the benzene ring.

## Making salts with amines

Bases are neutralised by acids to form salts. For example, ammonia with hydrochloric acid produces ammonium chloride:

$$NH_3(aq) + HCl(aq) \rightarrow NH_4^+(aq) + Cl^-(aq)$$

Amines also produce salts. Ethylamine with hydrochloric acid forms ethylammonium chloride:

$$C_2H_5NH_2(aq) + HCl(aq) \rightarrow C_2H_5NH_3^+(aq) + Cl^-(aq)$$

Phenylamine forms phenylammonium chloride:

Phenylamine is only sparingly soluble in water, but it dissolves readily in hydrochloric acid because a salt is formed. Addition of alkali to this salt solution causes phenylamine to be released. Initially, a milky emulsion forms, which usually breaks down into oily drops (*figure 21.7*). (Compare this to the behaviour of a solution of phenol in aqueous alkali on treatment with hydrochloric acid (page 346).)

### SAQ 21.4

Write balanced equations for the reactions of:
**a** nitric acid with butylamine;
**b** hydrochloric acid with 4-aminophenol;
**c** sodium hydroxide with 4-aminophenol.

## Reactions specific to phenylamine

### Reaction with aqueous bromine

When phenylamine is mixed with aqueous bromine, a white precipitate of 2,4,6–tribromophenylamine is formed and the bromine is decolorised.

● **Figure 21.7** The left-hand tube contains brown phenylamine, which does not mix with water. The central tube contains a solution of phenylamine in acid. A white emulsion forms when alkali is added to this solution.

As with phenol (see chapter 18b, page 347) the presence of the $-NH_2$ group increases the susceptibility of the benzene ring to electrophilic attack. The $-NH_2$ group, like the $-OH$ group, has one lone pair of electrons that overlap with the delocalised $\pi$ electrons of the benzene ring and activate it.

### Diazonium salt formation and coupling reactions

When a reaction mixture of phenylamine and nitrous acid is kept below 10°C, a diazonium salt is formed (the diazonium ion is $-N_2^+$). This reaction is known as a **diazotisation** reaction:

(The nitrous acid needed for these reactions is unstable and is produced by reacting sodium nitrite with dilute hydrochloric acid.)

The diazonium ion, $-N_2^+$, is rather unstable and decomposes readily to nitrogen. However, delocalisation of the diazonium ion $\pi$-bond electrons over a benzene ring stabilises phenyldiazonium sufficiently for it to form at low temperatures.

The phenyldiazonium ion behaves as an electrophile, and will attack another arene molecule such as phenol. Electrophilic substitution takes place at the 4 position, producing 4-hydroxyphenylazobenzene (*figure 21.8*). The reaction is known as a **coupling reaction**:

The compound formed is an energetically stable, yellow azo dye (the **azo group** is $-N=N-$). The stability is due to extensive delocalisation of the electrons via the nitrogen–nitrogen double bond.

The dye 4-hydroxyphenylazobenzene is just one of the wide range of dyes that can be made from aromatic amines and other arenes. These are known as diazonium dyes. They are very stable, so they do not fade. Another example is the indicator methyl orange (*figure 21.9*) which has the structure:

● **Figure 21.8** A diazonium dye is formed when phenyldiazonium chloride is added to an alkaline solution of phenol.

● **Figure 21.9** Methyl orange is used as an indicator.

## SAQ 21.5

Draw the displayed formula for the azo dye produced on reacting 4-aminophenol with nitrous acid (in dilute hydrochloric acid) below 10 °C and coupling the resulting diazonium salt with phenol. Write balanced equations for the reactions involved.

# Amides

As discussed in chapter 20b (page 366), acyl chlorides react with primary **amines** to form substituted amides which contain the group $-CONH-$.

$$CH_3C\begin{smallmatrix}O\\||\\Cl\end{smallmatrix} + CH_3NH_2 \longrightarrow CH_3C\begin{smallmatrix}O\\||\\NHCH_3\end{smallmatrix} + HCl$$

N-methylethanamide

If an excess of amine is used, it will react with the hydrogen chloride produced.

$$CH_3NH_2 + HCl \rightarrow CH_3\overset{+}{N}H_3\ Cl^-$$

## The hydrolysis of amides

Amides may be hydrolysed by heating under reflux with either an acid or an alkali.

Refluxing with an acid will produce the corresponding carboxylic acid and primary amine:

$$CH_3C\begin{smallmatrix}O\\||\\NHCH_3\end{smallmatrix} + H_2O \xrightarrow{H^+(aq)} CH_3C\begin{smallmatrix}O\\||\\OH\end{smallmatrix} + CH_3NH_2$$

The amine will react with any excess acid.

If aqueous alkali is used for the hydrolysis, the corresponding salt of the acid will be formed, together with the amine.

$$CH_3C\overset{O}{\underset{NHCH_3}{\big<}} + NaOH(aq) \longrightarrow CH_3C\overset{O}{\underset{O^-Na^+}{\big<}} + CH_3NH_2$$

# Amino acids

There are about twenty naturally occurring amino acids. Their general structure is:

$$R\overset{NH_2}{\underset{COOH}{\overset{|}{\underset{|}{C}}}}H$$

They are all α-**amino acids**, which have the amino group and the carboxylic acid group attached to the same carbon atom. In the simplest amino acid, glycine, the 'R' is a hydrogen atom. In the next simplest amino acid, alanine, the 'R' is a methyl group, $CH_3$.

Amino acids are bifunctional, that is they have two functional groups present in the molecule: the carboxylic acid group, $-COOH$, and the amino group, $-NH_2$. As one of these groups is acidic and the other group is basic, they can interact with one another. The $-COOH$ group donates a proton to the $-NH_2$ group. This forms an 'internal' salt known as a **zwitterion**:

$$R\overset{NH_2}{\underset{COOH}{\overset{|}{\underset{|}{C}}}}H \longrightarrow R\overset{\overset{+}{N}H_3}{\underset{COO^-}{\overset{|}{\underset{|}{C}}}}H$$

a zwitterion

The zwitterion has a significant effect on the properties of amino acids. It is the predominant form of the amino acid in the solid phase or in aqueous solution. The ionic charges increase the attractive forces between the amino acids in the solid, and so raise the melting point significantly above that of related compounds with similar numbers of atoms and electrons. The amino acid glycine, $NH_2CH_2COOH$, decomposes at 262°C without melting, whereas propanoic acid, $CH_3CH_2COOH$, melts at −21°C.

Amino acids form salts when reacted with acids or bases. On addition of a dilute solution of a strong acid (for example, aqueous hydrochloric acid), the zwitterion will accept a proton. The product now carries a net positive charge and may be crystallised as the chloride salt:

$$R\overset{\overset{+}{N}H_3}{\underset{COO^-}{\overset{|}{\underset{|}{C}}}}H + H^+ \longrightarrow R\overset{\overset{+}{N}H_3}{\underset{COOH}{\overset{|}{\underset{|}{C}}}}H$$

Addition of dilute aqueous sodium hydroxide removes the proton from the $-NH_3^+$ group in the zwitterion. This leaves a negatively charged ion:

$$R\overset{\overset{+}{N}H_3}{\underset{COO^-}{\overset{|}{\underset{|}{C}}}}H + OH^- \longrightarrow R\overset{NH_2}{\underset{COO^-}{\overset{|}{\underset{|}{C}}}}H + H_2O$$

Hence at high pH, amino acids are negatively charged in aqueous solution. At low pH, they are positively charged.

## SAQ 21.6

a Draw the structural formulae for the ions present when glycine, $NH_2CH_2COOH$, is dissolved in:
  (i) aqueous hydrochloric acid;
  (ii) aqueous sodium hydroxide.
b Write balanced equations for the reaction of aqueous glycine with:
  (i) aqueous hydrochloric acid;
  (ii) aqueous sodium hydroxide.

# Optical isomerism in amino acids

With the exception of glycine, amino acids have four different groups round the α carbon atom, and optical isomers are possible (see chapter 15a for more on this subject). The mirror images of the optical isomers of alanine may be drawn using three-dimensional formulae:

mirror plane

When you need to represent a pair of optical isomers, draw one isomer using the three-dimensional representation. Next, imagine reflecting this isomer in a mirror plane, and draw the other isomer.

## SAQ 21.7

**a** Leucine has the structure:

$$H_2N - \overset{\overset{\displaystyle H}{|}}{\underset{\underset{\displaystyle CH_2}{|}}{C}} - COOH$$

$$CH(CH_3)_2$$

Draw three-dimensional formulae to show the optical isomers of leucine.

**b** Isoleucine has more than one chiral centre. It has the structure:

$$H_2N - \overset{\overset{\displaystyle H}{|}}{\underset{\underset{\displaystyle CHCH_2CH_3}{|}}{C}} - COOH$$

$$CH_3$$

Copy this structure and mark the chiral centres with asterisks.

# Proteins and polypeptides

Proteins and **polypeptides** are important molecules in living organisms. Muscle and hair are composed of fibres containing long protein molecules. Enzymes are soluble proteins that catalyse many biochemical reactions. Proteins, like nylon, are also examples of polyamides.

Polypeptides are formed when amino acids undergo condensation polymerisation. Two amino acids join together via a **peptide link** to form a dipeptide and a water molecule – the peptide link is simply the name we use for the amide link in polypeptides and proteins:

Three amino acids produce a tripeptide and two water molecules. Polypeptides and proteins contain a large number of amino acid units. (Proteins generally have much larger relative molecular masses then polypeptides.) In nature, proteins often consist of two or more polypeptides held together by intermolecular forces (such as hydrogen bonds). The sequence of amino acids in a protein is known as the primary structure of that protein.

Hydrolysis of a protein involves breaking the peptide links by reaction with water. So hydrolysis is the reverse of the condensation polymerisation of amino acids to form a protein. In living organisms, condensation polymerisation of amino acids and hydrolysis of proteins are both catalysed by enzymes. In the laboratory, acids or alkalis are used to catalyse the hydrolysis of proteins. Since each peptide link is broken, this is simply an extended example of the hydrolysis of an amide. Polyamides and polyesters are also hydrolysed to their monomers by refluxing with an acid catalyst.

## SAQ 21.8

Aspartame is the methyl ester of the dipeptide formed between aspartic acid and phenylalanine (*figure 21.10*). Its skeletal formula is:

It is used as a sweetener in many 'diet' soft drinks. Aspartame has two links that may be hydrolysed.

**a** Copy the skeletal formula of aspartame. Mark the bonds that may be broken by hydrolysis, and label them with the names of the types of linkages present.

**b** Write a balanced equation for the acid hydrolysis of aspartame and name all the products.

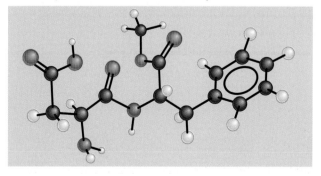

● **Figure 21.10** Aspartame.

# Polyamides

Synthetic **polyamides** (nylons) are polymers which also contain the $-CONH-$ group. They are formed by reaction between diamines (e.g. $H_2N(CH_2)_6NH_2$) and diacids (e.g. $HOOC(CH_2)_4COOH$). For a fuller treatment of polyamides see chapter 22b, page 386.

# SUMMARY (A2)

- Nitrogen appears in organic compounds in the following functional groups:

$-NH_2$     $\overset{O}{\underset{}{\overset{\|}{-C}}}-NH-$     $-CN$     $-N=N-$

amine     amide     nitrile     azo

  Such groups are common amongst the bio-chemical molecules found in living things.

- Ethylamine is prepared either by treating bromoethane with an excess of hot, ethanolic ammonia or by reducing ethanenitrile. Phenylamine is prepared by reducing nitrobenzene using tin and hydrochloric acid.

- Like ammonia, amines behave as bases, readily accepting protons to form salts. Ethylamine is a stronger base than ammonia because the alkyl group has a positive inductive effect; phenylamine is a weaker base than ammonia because the phenyl group has a negative inductive effect. Phenylamine is also a weaker base due to the partial delocalisation of a pair of electrons from nitrogen over the benzene ring.

- Phenylamine reacts with nitrous acid on warming to give nitrogen and phenol. Below 10°C, the products are phenyldiazonium chloride and water; this reaction is called diazotisation.

- Diazonium salts react with other aromatic compounds (such as phenol) to form dyes; this is known as a coupling reaction. Diazonium dyes are commercially useful. Some indicators are diazonium dyes. The colour of diazonium dyes arises from the extensively delocalised π-electron system.

- There are about twenty naturally occurring amino acids with the general formula $RCH(NH_2)COOH$. 'R' may be H, $CH_3$ or another organic group. The amino group interacts with the acid group to form an internal salt or zwitterion. Amino acids react with both acids and bases to form salts.

- With the exception of glycine, amino acids possess a chiral carbon atom (a chiral atom has four different groups attached) and so optical isomers are possible.

- Polypeptides form when amino acids undergo condensation polymerisation. Two amino acids join together by a peptide (or amide) link to form a dipeptide and water. Repetition of this process leads to polypeptides and proteins.

- Proteins or polypeptides are hydrolysed by refluxing in a strong acid, such as HCl(aq), to form α-amino acids.

# Questions (A2)

**1** The last step in the synthesis of benzocaine involves the following conversion.

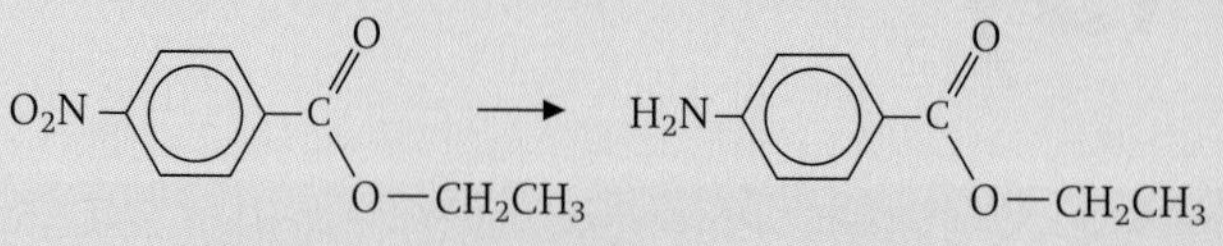

**a** (i) State the reactants and conditions required to carry out this conversion.

(ii) Give the systematic name of benzocaine.

**b** A student treated a sample of benzocaine with dilute hydrochloric acid at a temperature of 5°C. She then added aqueous sodium nitrite whilst maintaining a temperature of 5°C. After the mixture had stood for 10 minutes, she added the mixture dropwise to a solution of phenol in aqueous sodium hydroxide. A deep yellow-orange precipitate was formed.

Explain the chemical changes, with the aid of equations, which take place during the following steps.

(i) When benzocaine is treated with dilute hydrochloric acid at a temperature of 5°C.

(ii) When the mixture is added to aqueous sodium nitrite whilst maintaining the temperature at 5°C.

(iii) When the mixture from **b** (ii) was added to a solution of phenol in aqueous sodium hydroxide.

**2** The structures of the α-amino acids glycine and alanine are shown below.

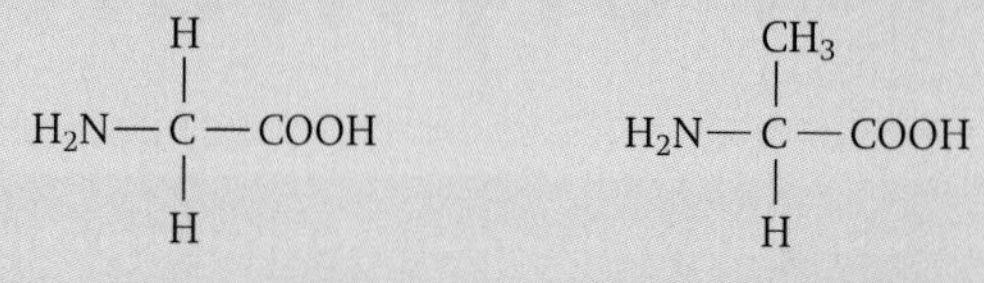

**a** Give the systematic names of glycine and alanine.

**b** Describe and explain, with the aid of equations, the effect of adding the following to an aqueous solution of glycine.

(i) dilute hydrochloric acid

(ii) dilute sodium hydroxide.

**c** Draw a structural formula for alanine to show what is meant by the word **zwitterion**.

**d** α-amino acids, such as glycine and alanine, polymerise to form peptides and proteins.

(i) Illustrate this polymerisation by writing a balanced equation to show the dipeptide formed between two molecules of alanine.

(ii) In your answer to **d** (i), draw a circle round the peptide link.

(iii) State the type of polymerisation taking place when peptides and proteins are formed from α-amino acids.

# Polymers (AS)

**By the end of this section you should be able to:**

1 describe the characteristics of *addition polymerisation*, typified by poly(phenylethene);

2 identify that some alkenes, typified by propene, can produce addition polymers that are *atactic*, *isotactic* and/or *syndiotactic*;

3 recognise the difficulty of the disposal of poly(alkenes), i.e. non-biodegradability and harmful combustion products.

**P**olymers are macromolecules that are built up from very large numbers of small molecules known as monomers. Many natural polymers are known. For example, proteins are polymers of amino acids, natural rubber is a polymer of isoprene (see chapter 16b) and DNA is a polymer of nucleotides. Nucleotides consist of an organic base, such as adenine in adenosine triphosphate (ATP, the chemical that carries energy within cells), bonded to a sugar, such as ribose, which is in turn joined to one or more phosphate ions:

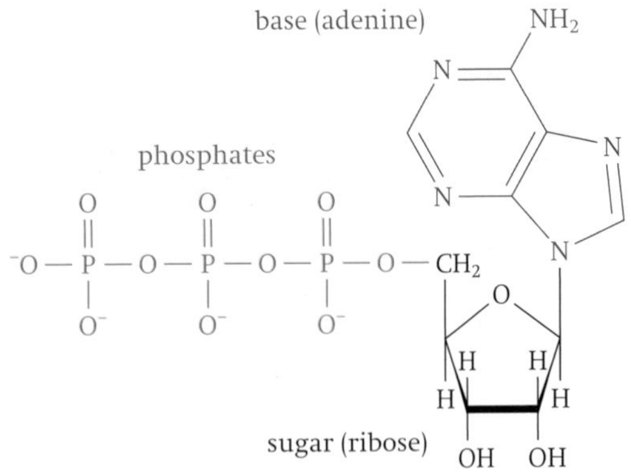

The polymer chain in DNA consists of a sugar–phosphate backbone. Two such backbones are linked by hydrogen bonds between pairs of bases to form a double helix.

Many polymers were discovered by chemists in the twentieth century. Some of these polymers were made by modifying naturally occurring materials. For example, cellulose is converted into cellulose ethanoate (acetate) by an esterification reaction:

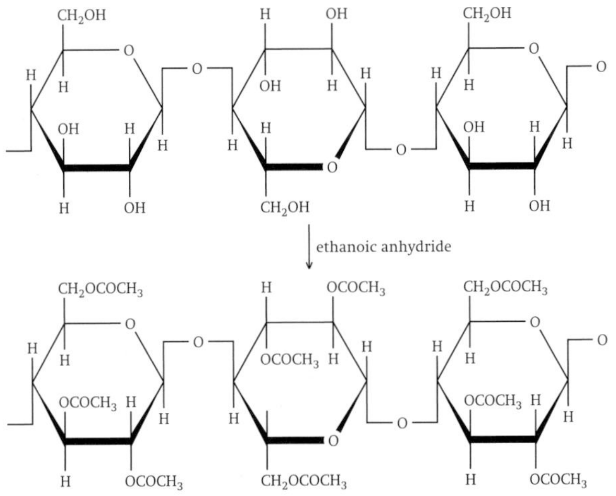

Other polymers were discovered by accident when the chemists concerned were pursuing a very different goal: examples include Bakelite® (*box 22A*), poly(tetrafluoroethene) and poly(ethene).

Nowadays, our understanding of the reactions and structures of polymers is much greater. Computer molecular modelling (page 285) is being used to design polymers with specific properties before the compounds are synthesised by chemists.

Polymer properties are dependent on a variety of factors such as chain length, crystallinity (crystallinity is greater when the molecules pack more closely), the degree of chain-branching or cross-linking and the strength of the intermolecular forces. The properties can be modified by the way

**Box 22A Bakelite®**

In 1872, Adolf von Baeyer made a resin by heating phenol with an aldehyde. He threw this resin away because he could not see a use for the material. The resin was re-investigated by Leo Hendrik Baekeland who, in 1910, set up a company to manufacture the material (which he called Bakelite®) for use in making electrical sockets and plugs. Since Baekeland's day, the material used in these components has changed several times. In the 1990s, polyester, polycarbonate and acrylonitrilebutadiene styrene copolymer (ABS) are used for these components (*figure 22.1*). Once Bakelite® has been formed it cannot be melted, so it is a *thermosetting* polymer; the new materials can be melted and moulded many times (they are *thermoplastic* polymers), making fabrication much easier.

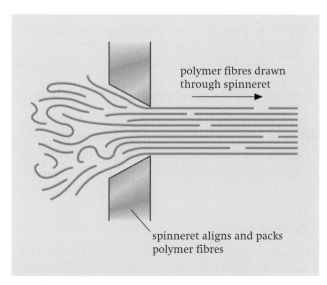

● **Figure 22.1** Electrical sockets and plugs are made from thermoplastic polymers.

● **Figure 22.2** The packing of polymer chains increases the tensile strength of a fibre.

the polymer is treated. For example, if the polymer is drawn (pulled through a small hole) whilst being formed into a fibre, the molecules tend to become more ordered. The intermolecular forces are increased because the polymer chains are more closely packed; the tensile strength of the fibre is therefore greater (*figure 22.2*). Properties are also modified by mixing the polymer with other materials. Glass fibre will produce a much stronger and more rigid material; plasticisers will produce a more flexible material. Canoes are made of glass-fibre-reinforced poly(phenylethene) (*figure 22.3a*). The bags and tubing for blood transfusions are made from a poly(chloroethene) composite containing a plasticiser (*figure 22.3b*).

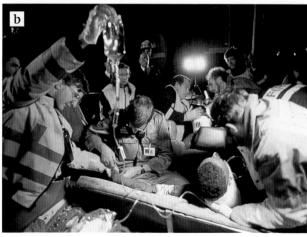

● **Figure 22.3**
**a** Canoes are often made from glass-reinforced poly(phenylethene).
**b** Blood bags are made from poly(chloroethene).

# The formation of polymers

## Addition polymerisation

Alkenes polymerise by addition reactions. The alkene undergoes an addition to itself. As further molecules are added, a long molecular chain is built up. The reactions are initiated in various ways and an initiating chemical (**initiator**) may become incorporated at the start of the polymer chain. Ignoring the initiator, the empirical formula of an addition polymer is the same as the alkene it comes from. This type of reaction is called **addition polymerisation**. Many useful polymers are obtained via addition polymerisation of different alkenes.

Poly(ethene) was first produced accidentally by Eric Fawcett and Reginald Gibson in 1933. The reaction involves ethene adding to itself in a chain reaction. It is a very rapid reaction, with chains of up to 10 000 ethene units being formed in one second. The product is a high molecular mass, straight-chain alkane. It is a polymer and is a member of a large group of materials generally known as plastics. The alkene from which it is made is called the **monomer**, and the section of polymer that the monomer forms is called the **repeat unit** (often shown within brackets in structural formulae):

$$n \quad \begin{array}{c} H \\ \diagdown \\ C = C \\ \diagup \\ H \end{array} \begin{array}{c} H \\ \diagup \\ \diagdown \\ H \end{array} \qquad \left[ \begin{array}{cc} H & H \\ | & | \\ C - C \\ | & | \\ H & H \end{array} \right]_n$$

Skeletal formulae for two other important poly(alkene)s, poly(chloroethene) and poly(phenylethene), are:

poly(chloroethene)

poly(phenylethene)

Poly(chloroethene) and poly(phenylethene) are more commonly known as PVC and polystyrene, respectively. Note how the systematic name is derived by putting the systematic name of the monomer in brackets and prefixing this with 'poly'. The skeletal formulae of the monomers, chloroethene (old name vinyl chloride) and phenylethene (old name styrene), are as follows:

chloroethene      phenylethene

The synthesis of phenylethene from benzene is described in chapter 16d (page 325).

### SAQ 22.1

a Acrylic fibre is often used in furnishing fabric or as a wool substitute in sweaters. It is an addition polymer of propenenitrile, $CH_2$=CHCN (also called acrylonitrile). Write a balanced equation for the polymerisation of propenenitrile. Use a displayed formula in your equation to indicate the repeat unit of this polymer.

b A polymer which is often used to make plastic boxes for food storage has the structure:

$$CH_3 \quad CH_3 \quad CH_3 \quad CH_3$$

Draw displayed formulae to show (i) the repeat unit of this polymer and (ii) the monomer from which it is made. Label your diagrams with the appropriate systematic names.

There are several ways of bringing about the addition polymerisation of alkenes. These different methods produce polymers with different properties, which provide the wide variety of poly(alkene)s for the many applications of these versatile materials.

### Stereoregular polymers

In 1953, a German chemist Karl Ziegler discovered a new catalyst which produced very long molecules of poly(ethene) with very little chain-branching. Before 1953, the poly(ethene) produced contained shorter polymer chains with many chain-branches present. Chain-branching in a polymer prevents close-packing of the polymer molecules. The molecules in Ziegler's polymer, with little chain-branching present, could pack more closely. The new polymer thus had a higher density and a higher melting point and was suitable for many new applications. It became known as high-density poly(ethene) or hdpe. The earlier polymer became known as ldpe (low-density poly(ethene)). Ziegler was able to patent his discovery and became a millionaire.

An Italian chemist Giulio Natta believed that Ziegler's catalyst would make it possible to synthesise polymers with a regular structure. In 1954, Natta developed Ziegler's catalyst to prepare poly(propene). Using different Ziegler-type catalysts he prepared three different forms of poly(propene).

All contained long molecular chains. One form was highly crystalline with all the methyl groups ordered on one side of the polymer chain. Natta called this form **isotactic** poly(propene) (*figure 22.4a*). Natta's second form of poly(propene) was amorphous with the methyl groups randomly arranged along the polymer chain. He called this form atactic poly(propene) (*figure 22.4b*). A third form has the methyl groups alternating between one side of the polymer chain and the other. This is known as syndiotactic poly(propene) (*figure 22.4c*). Only the isotactic and syndiotactic forms are stereoregular.

In *figure 22.4* molecular models of short sections of poly(propene) show the different structures of the three types. Ziegler and Natta shared the 1963 Nobel Prize for Chemistry for their work on these new polymerisation catalysts.

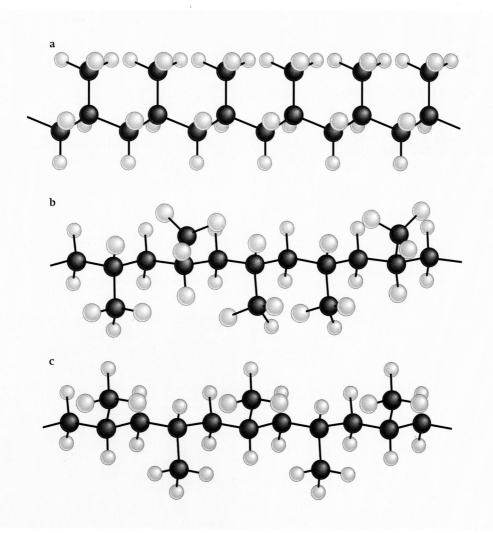

● **Figure 22.4** Molecular models of the three forms of poly(propene):
**a** isotactic poly(propene), **b** atactic poly(propene), **c** syndiotactic poly(propene).

| Properties | Structure | Uses |
|---|---|---|
| Isotactic poly(propene): regular structure, a rigid, tough, crystalline polymer which can withstand heat | 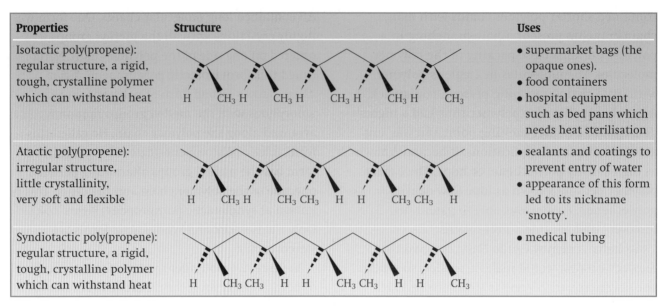 | • supermarket bags (the opaque ones). • food containers • hospital equipment such as bed pans which needs heat sterilisation |
| Atactic poly(propene): irregular structure, little crystallinity, very soft and flexible | | • sealants and coatings to prevent entry of water • appearance of this form led to its nickname 'snotty'. |
| Syndiotactic poly(propene): regular structure, a rigid, tough, crystalline polymer which can withstand heat | | • medical tubing |

• **Table 22.1** Structures, properties and uses of poly(propene).

*Table 22.1* shows the molecular structures, properties and uses of these three polymers.

## SAQ 22.2

Atactic and isotactic forms of pvc are shown in the following molecular models.

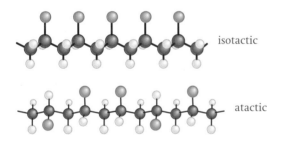

a Draw three-dimensional formulae to show isotactic and atactic forms of pvc.
b How will isotactic and atactic forms of pvc differ in their:
  (i) hardness and rigidity
  (ii) resistance to heat?
c Explain your answers to part **b** in terms of inter-molecular forces.

## Processing of poly(alkene)s

Poly(alkene)s are thermoplastic, so they are easily made into different products by a variety of techniques. The molten polymer may be forced under pressure into a mould (injection moulding) or forced through a die to form pipes or other continuously moulded shapes (extrusion moulding). Fibres are produced by forcing the molten polymer through a die with fine holes (a spinneret). The emerging polymer is cooled in an air current to produce a continuous filament which may be spun into a yarn (the process is called melt spinning). Alternatively, a softened polymer sheet can be moulded into a shape under reduced pressure (vacuum forming) or under increased air pressure (blow moulding). An example of one of these techniques is shown in *figure 22.5*.

• **Figure 22.5** A stage in the production of poly(ethene) film.

## Disposing of poly(alkenes)

The large-scale use of poly(alkenes) has led to a large problem when their disposal is attempted. Pollution like that shown in *figure 22.6* is very common. Poly(alkenes) are alkanes and so show the lack of reactivity of alkanes (see chapter 16a, page 295). Poly(alkenes) decompose very slowly in the environment, so if they are disposed of in landfill sites they do not break down. They are resistant to bacteria (they are non-biodegradable) and they are resistant to most chemicals. However, you do need to bear in mind that it is these properties that make them so useful in the first place.

Other methods of dealing with waste poly(alkenes) have been considered.

■ One option is to collect waste poly(alkenes), sort them and then recycle them into new products (*figure 22.7*). The problem with this approach is that the cost of recycling, in terms of the amount of energy used to collect and reprocess the material, can be greater than the amount of

● **Figure 22.7** Recycling polymers is one way of combating the problem of polymer waste.

energy used to make the new products from new material.

■ Another option is to burn the poly(alkenes). As they are hydrocarbons they are good fuels (see page 295). Burning waste poly(alkenes) would both deal with the problem of disposing of them and also reduce the amount of oil or other fossil fuels burned as fuels. In the past, there have been problems with pollution from burning waste poly(alkenes), but modern incinerators produce less pollution than traditional fossil-fuel power stations (see chapter 16b and *figure 16.14*, page 306).

■ A third option is to subject the poly(alkenes) to high-temperature pyrolysis. This process enables the polymers to be broken down into smaller, useful molecules. High-temperature pyrolysis is similar to the cracking of alkanes (see chapter 16c, page 311). A mixture of hydrocarbons is produced, containing alkanes, alkenes and arenes. The alkenes could then be used to make more poly(alkenes) once they have been through a separation process.

## SAQ 22.3

Suggest some small molecules that might be produced by pyrolysis of poly(ethene). Explain how your suggestions would be useful.

● **Figure 22.6** Polymer waste is not easy to dispose of – it is usually not biodegradable.

# SUMMARY (AS)

◆ Polymers are macromolecules that are built up from a very large number of small molecules known as monomers.

◆ Natural polymers include proteins, DNA and rubber. Many synthetic polymers have been discovered by accident (for example, poly(ethene) and Bakelite®). Polymers are now being designed to fulfil specific functions.

◆ The properties of polymers depend on chain length, intermolecular forces, degree of chain branching, crystallinity and additives.

◆ Addition polymerisation occurs when a monomer joins to itself by an addition reaction. Alkenes polymerise in this way. Poly(ethene), poly(chloroethene) and poly(phenylethene) are important alkene polymers.

◆ Poly(alkene)s are non-biodegradable and are also very resistant to chemical decomposition. Disposal of poly(alkene) waste has become a problem. The waste may be buried or recycled and reprocessed. Alternatively, poly(alkene) waste may be incinerated as a 'clean' fuel. Gas scrubbers are required to remove polluting gases such as hydrogen chloride from poly(chloroethene) incineration.

# Questions (AS)

1 Explain, with suitable examples, the meaning of each of the following terms:
   a monomer;
   b polymer;
   c addition polymerisation;
   d repeat unit.

# Polymers (A2)

**By the end of this section you should be able to:**

4  describe the characteristics of *condensation polymerisation* in polyesters typified by Terylene, in polyamides, typified by nylon-6,6 and Kevlar and in polypeptides and proteins;

5  suggest the type of polymerisation reaction from a given monomer or pair of monomers or from a given section of a polymer molecule;

6  deduce the *repeat unit* of a polymer obtained from a given monomer or pair of monomers;

7  identify, in a given section of polymer, the monomer(s) from which it was obtained.

## Condensation polymerisation

### Polyester formation

A significant proportion of clothing is made using polyester fibre. Polyester is also used to make plastic bottles for drinks (*figure 22.8*). Polyester is made by polymerising ethane-1,2-diol with benzene-1,4-dicarboxylic acid (terephthalic acid). As each ester link is made, a water molecule is lost – a condensation reaction occurs. So the formation of a polyester is an example of **condensation** **polymerisation**. The reaction requires a catalyst such as antimony(III) oxide at about 280°C. An equation for the reaction is:

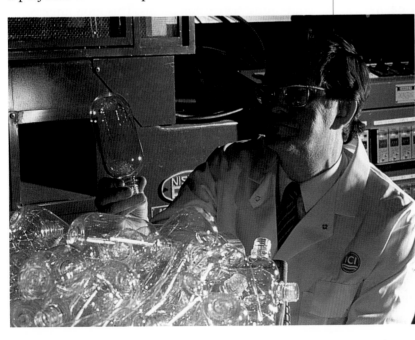

● **Figure 22.8** Poly(ethylene terephthalate), a polyester, is widely used for drinks bottles as a replacement for glass.

The resulting polymer is fairly rigid because of the 1,4 links across the benzene ring. The 1,4 links produce a more linear polymer, which enables the polymer chains to pack more closely. Close-packing produces strong intermolecular forces, which enable the polymer to be spun into strong threads for the clothing industry.

### SAQ 22.4

The external mirror housings of some vehicles have been made from PBT, or poly(butylene terephthalate). This material provides excellent protection to the mirror glass whilst driving off-road. The structure of PBT is:

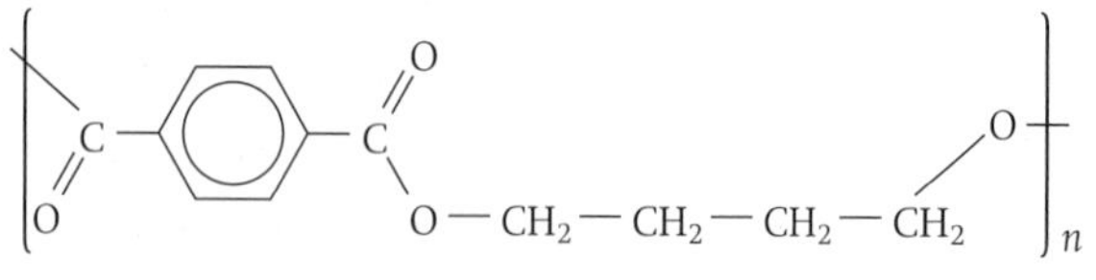

Draw displayed formulae to show the two monomers used to make PBT. Write an equation for the reaction.

# Polyamide formation

Wallace Carothers carried out research for Du Pont in 1928 in order to find new polymers that might be used for making fabric. At that time, it was known that wool and silk were proteins and that they contained the **peptide linkage**, −NHCO−. Because of this, Carothers set out to make polymers systematically, using condensation reactions involving amines and carboxylic acids.

In order to make a polymer, he realised that he needed monomers which had two functional groups present. The monomer could have an amino group at one end and a carboxylic acid group at the other. Alternatively, two monomer units could be used, one with an amino group at both ends, the other with a carboxylic acid group at both ends. Both approaches led to the discovery of new polymers, which are now widely used to make fibres.

Use of the diamine, 1,6-diaminohexane, together with the dicarboxylic acid, hexanedioic acid (commonly called adipic acid) produces a nylon called nylon-6,6. An amino group undergoes a condensation reaction with a carboxylic acid group. A water molecule is released and a C–N bond is formed. This can occur at each end of the two monomer molecules, so a condensation polymerisation is possible:

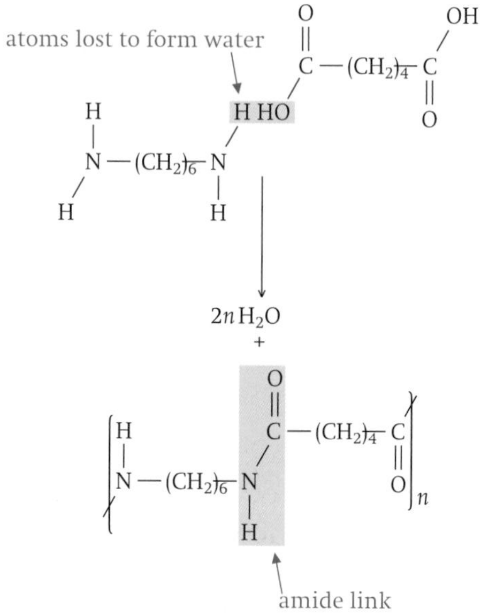

The product is a long chain of alternating monomer residues linked by amide groups, −NHCO−. Such polymers are called **polyamides**. Notice that each of the two monomer units contains six carbon atoms. This is why it is called nylon-6,6. Nylons are given names that indicate the number of carbon atoms in each monomer unit.

Nylon-6 is made from a single monomer containing six carbon atoms. This monomer is caprolactam, a cyclic amide. The caprolactam ring is polymerised to nylon-6 by heating:

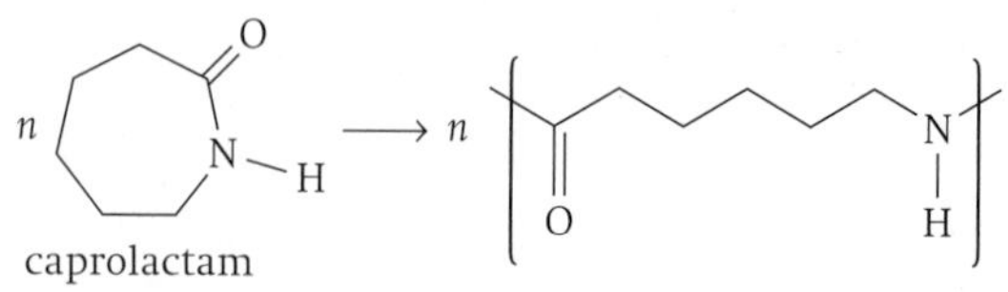

Caprolactam is formed from 6-aminohexanoic acid by a condensation reaction:

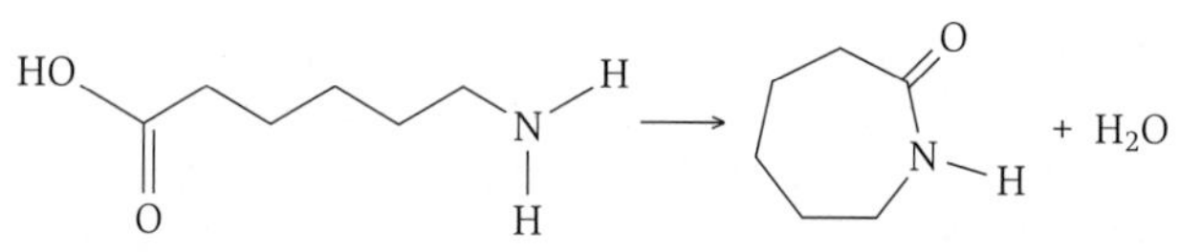

## SAQ 22.5

Kevlar is a polyamide made by Du Pont. It has some remarkable properties, including fire resistance and a much higher tensile strength than steel. Kevlar is being used to make protective clothing for fire-fighters, bullet-proof vests, crash helmets for motor cyclists and tail fins for jumbo jets, and it is used instead of steel in radial tyres. The structure of this remarkable polymer is:

Draw a displayed formula to show the repeat unit in Kevlar and label the amide link clearly. Draw displayed formulae of the two monomer units required to make Kevlar. Write a balanced equation for the reaction.

Nylon forms a very strong fibre by melt spinning, during which the molecules become oriented along the axis of the fibre. This increases the opportunities for hydrogen bonds to form between the molecules. The hydrogen bonds also provide nylon with greater elasticity than is present in fibres without hydrogen bonds (such as poly(propene)). The hydrogen bonds tend to pull the molecules back to their original positions after the fibre has been stretched. This is why nylon is the most popular fibre for making tights. Tights made from many other fibres would tend to sag and lose their shape. The combination of strength and elasticity are also important properties in a climbing rope (*figure 22.9*).

# Proteins and polypeptides

Twenty α-amino acids occur naturally in the human body. These make up a wide variety of natural polymers known as peptides and proteins. Peptides are smaller molecules than proteins. *Figure 22.10* shows the structure of a protein.

Peptides and proteins are formed by condensation polymerisation. A peptide link is formed between two amino acids with the loss of a water molecule. A peptide link may also be called an amide link. Hence both polyamides and proteins contain monomer units joined by the same link. You can find more about peptides and proteins in chapter 21.

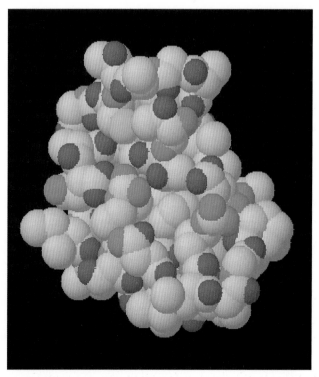

● **Figure 22.10** Structure of a relatively small protein. You can explore protein structures by visiting http://www.rcsb.org/pdb/

● **Figure 22.9** The climber is using nylon rope and slings for protection. Nylon has a very high tensile strength, coupled with considerable elasticity. Climbers rely on these properties to minimise the effects of a fall.

# The relation between the structure of the monomer and the polymer

**Addition polymers** are formed from unsaturated hydrocarbons without the formation of any other product. Saturated polymers, which may have substitutents at regular intervals along the hydrocarbon chain, are usually formed.

**Condensation polymers** are formed when two different types of monomer co-polymerise with the elimination of small molecules. The resulting polymer contains ester or peptide linkages at regular intervals along the polymer chain.

Inspection of the structure of the polymer can reveal the original monomers.

Consider the following polymers:

1
$$-\overset{\displaystyle F}{\underset{\displaystyle F}{\overset{|}{\underset{|}{C}}}}-\overset{\displaystyle F}{\underset{\displaystyle F}{\overset{|}{\underset{|}{C}}}}-\overset{\displaystyle F}{\underset{\displaystyle F}{\overset{|}{\underset{|}{C}}}}-\overset{\displaystyle F}{\underset{\displaystyle F}{\overset{|}{\underset{|}{C}}}}-\overset{\displaystyle F}{\underset{\displaystyle F}{\overset{|}{\underset{|}{C}}}}-\overset{\displaystyle F}{\underset{\displaystyle F}{\overset{|}{\underset{|}{C}}}}-$$

This is a 'hydrocarbon chain' which has been fully substituted by fluorine. There are no ester or peptide linkages. The polymer must, therefore, be an *addition polymer*, for which the repeat unit is

$$-\overset{\displaystyle F}{\underset{\displaystyle F}{\overset{|}{\underset{|}{C}}}}-\overset{\displaystyle F}{\underset{\displaystyle F}{\overset{|}{\underset{|}{C}}}}-$$

The polymer is actually poly(tetrafluoroethene), also known as PTFE or Teflon. It is used in non-stick coatings.

2  $-NH-(CH_2)_6-NH-CO-(CH_2)_8-CO-NH-(CH_2)_6-NH-CO-(CH_2)_8-CO-$

This is clearly a polyamide which has been formed by *condensation*. The repeat unit is $-(NH-(CH_2)_6-NH-CO-(CH_2)_8-CO)_n-$ and the monomers are $H_2N-(CH_2)_6-NH_2$ and $HOOC-(CH_2)_8-COOH$.

The polymer is actually nylon-6,10 because the diamine has six carbon atoms and the dicarboxylic acid has ten carbon atoms.

# SUMMARY (A2)

◆ Condensation polymerisation involves the loss of a small molecule (usually water) in the reaction between two monomer molecules. Both polyesters and polyamides are formed by condensation polymerisation.

◆ Polyester is formed by condensation polymerisation of benzene-1,4-dicarboxylic acid with ethane-1,2-diol.

◆ Polyamides are formed by condensation polymerisation between an amine group and a carboxylic acid group. These groups may be at either end of the same monomer or on different monomers. Nylon-6,6 is formed in a condensation polymerisation between 1,6-diaminohexane and hexanedioic acid. Nylon-6 is formed by heating caprolactam, which is produced from 6-aminohexanoic acid in a condensation reaction. The numbers in the names for nylons refer to the number of carbon atoms present in the monomers.

◆ Condensation polymerisation between the amino and carboxylic acid groups in amino acids produces a polypeptide or protein. The amide links in these polymers are known as peptide links.

# Questions (A2)

**2** Perspex is an acrylic polymer produced from the monomer methyl 2-methylpropenoate, shown below.

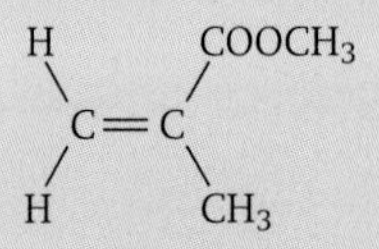

methyl 2-methylpropenoate

**a** **(i)** Suggest the type of polymerisation undergone by methyl 2-methylpropenoate.

**(ii)** Draw a section of the Perspex polymer chain produced by the polymerisation of methyl 2-methylpropenoate. On your diagram, circle the repeating unit in the polymer.

**b** Identify the **types** of intermolecular forces in Perspex and in poly(propene).

**c** Atactic poly(propene) has randomly arranged polymer chains. It is a soft, flexible material which melts at a low temperature. Isotactic poly(propene) is a rigid, tough, heat-resistant polymer.

**(i)** Explain, with the aid of structural formulae, the meaning of the terms **atactic** and **isotactic**.

**(ii)** Suggest why a close-packed polymer is tougher and has greater resistance to heat than a randomly arranged polymer.

**3** Kevlar is formed by a condensation polymerisation reaction.

**a** Explain the term **condensation polymerisation**.

**b** A section of Kevlar is shown below.

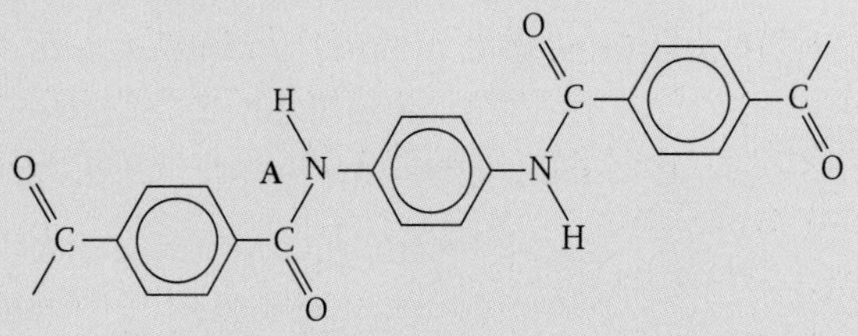

**(i)** Identify the functional group at **A**.

**(ii)** Use brackets to show the smallest repeating unit in the polymer chain.

**(iii)** Draw the structural formulae of the two monomers used to form Kevlar.

# CHAPTER 23

# Spectroscopy

## By the end of this chapter you should be able to:

1 use a simple *infrared spectrum* to identify the presence of functional groups in a molecule (limited to alcohols, OH, carbonyl compounds, C=O, carboxylic acids, COOH, and esters, COOR);

2 use the *molecular ion peak* in a *mass spectrum* to determine the relative molecular mass of an organic molecule;

3 predict, from the *high-resolution n.m.r. spectrum* of a simple molecule containing carbon, hydrogen and/or oxygen, the different types of proton present from *chemical shift* values, the relative numbers of each type of proton present from the relative peak area, the number of protons adjacent to a given proton from the *spin–spin splitting pattern*, limited to splitting patterns up to a quadruplet only, and possible structures for the molecule;

4 predict the chemical shifts and splitting patterns of the protons in a given molecule;

5 describe the use of D$_2$O to identify the n.m.r. signal from −OH groups.

Before the last century, the determination of organic structures was a difficult and time-consuming process. One trial-and-error approach was to build the suggested structure of a compound by synthesising it from simpler compounds of known structure. The synthetic product was then compared to the compound for which a structure was required. If both compounds had the same physical and chemical properties, they were likely to have the same structure.

Chemists now have a wide range of physical methods available for identifying the structure of a compound. In chapter 2, you met two of these methods, mass spectrometry and infrared spectroscopy. In particular, in chapter 2, you saw how mass spectrometry could be used to determine the mass number and percentage of each isotope present in a sample of an element. From such data, we can determine the relative atomic mass of the element. In chapter 18a, infrared spectroscopy was used to identify the functional groups >C=O and −OH in simple organic compounds such as alcohols or carboxylic acids.

## Infrared spectroscopy

The technique of **infrared spectroscopy** declined as n.m.r. spectrometers (see page 394) became more sophisticated. However, the introduction of modern infrared spectrometers has led to a resurgence of use of this once popular analytical technique. Modern infrared spectrometers (*figure 23.1*) are able to make use of sophisticated mathematical processing that enables spectra to be obtained from a much wider range of specimens. No special preparation is required with the most recent spectrometers and an **infrared spectrum** can, for example, be obtained from the surface of a solid sample. Earlier infrared spectrometers required time-consuming preparation of the sample before a spectrum could be recorded. In particular, modern infrared spectrometers are finding use in many areas:

■ in forensic science, for example, to identify paint samples following hit-and-run accidents – a knowledge of the composition of a paint sample can narrow the search for the driver of a car which failed to stop;

● **Figure 23.1** This infrared spectrometer is used to monitor levels of $NO_2$ in the atmosphere.

■ to rapidly identify different samples of polymers – this could help recycling, enabling separation of different polymers;

■ to identify compounds absorbed by a surface – this might be used to monitor health and safety in a laboratory where, for example, potential new medicines or pesticides were being synthesised, as both the flooring material and the surface of the bench can be checked for contamination.

In a modern infrared spectrometer, a beam of infrared radiation is passed through a sample. Computer analysis enables the absorbance of radiation to be measured at different frequencies. Study of the resulting spectrum enables the presence (or absence) of particular functional groups to be established. *Figure 23.2* shows the infrared spectrum of 2-hydroxybenzoic acid, which has the following structure:

COOH
OH

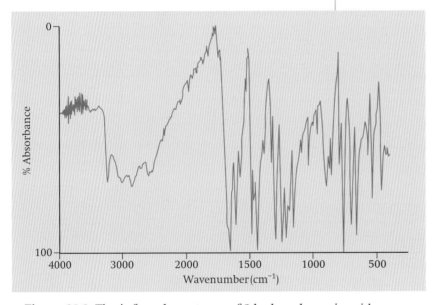

● **Figure 23.2** The infrared spectrum of 2-hydroxybenzoic acid.

Notice in *figure 23.2* that absorbance is shown increasing in a downward direction. An unusual unit is used to measure frequency, the wavenumber or $cm^{-1}$ (in other words, the number of waves in 1 cm).

*Table 23.1* shows the absorptions which we shall use in this chapter.

Look again at the infrared spectrum of 2-hydroxybenzoic acid in *figure 23.2*. Most of the absorptions are sharp, some overlap. The absorptions of interest are

1 the medium very broad absorption between 2500 and $3200\,cm^{-1}$, which is due in part to the presence of the carboxylic acid O–H group;

2 the sharper absorption at about $3250\,cm^{-1}$, which is likely to be due to the phenolic O–H group, free of hydrogen bonding;

| Bond | Location | Wavenumber $(cm^{-1})$ | Absorbance |
|---|---|---|---|
| O–H | hydrogen-bonded alcohols and phenols | 3200–3600 | strong, broad |
| O–H | free of hydrogen bonds in alcohols | 3580–3670 | medium–strong |
| O–H | hydrogen-bonded carboxylic acids | 2500–3300 | medium, very broad |
| C–O | alcohols, esters | 1000–1300 | strong |
| C=O | aldehydes, ketones, carboxylic acids and esters | 1680–1750 | strong, sharp |

● **Table 23.1** Infrared absorption frequencies.

3 the sharp absorption at about 1660 cm$^{-1}$, due to the carboxylic acid >C=O group;

4 the strong absorptions between 1000 and 1300 cm$^{-1}$ – as there are several of these we cannot be certain which is due to the carboxylic acid C–O group.

If 2-hydroxybenzoic acid is refluxed with ethanoic anhydride, $(CH_3CO)_2O$, in the presence of concentrated sulphuric acid as a catalyst, aspirin is formed:

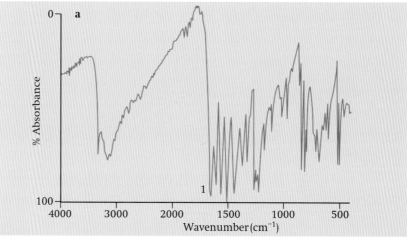

How do we know that aspirin is present? The infrared spectrum of a sample of aspirin is shown in *figure 23.3*. Note the presence of the following absorptions:

1 the strong broad absorption between 2500 and 3100 cm$^{-1}$, as in 2-hydroxybenzoic acid – again this is due in part to the presence of the carboxylic acid O–H group.

2 the two absorptions at 1690 and 1760 cm$^{-1}$ due to the presence of two carboxyl >C=O groups, each in a different environment.

Note the absence of the sharp absorption at 3250 cm$^{-1}$ from the O–H group in 2-hydroxybenzoic acid – this group is no longer present in aspirin.

### SAQ 23.1

Explain how the two carboxyl groups in aspirin lead to a different environment for the two >C=O groups.

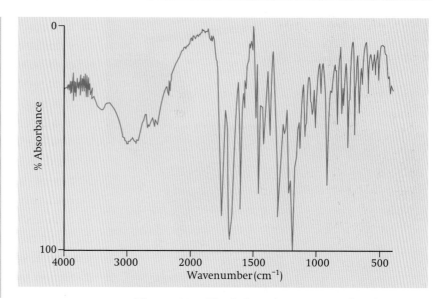

● **Figure 23.3** The infrared spectrum of aspirin.

### SAQ 23.2

*Figure 23.4* shows the infrared spectrum and a molecular model for paracetamol. Like aspirin, paracetamol is a widely used analgesic (pain killer).

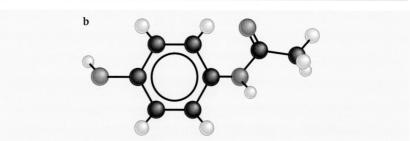

● **Figure 23.4a** The infrared spectrum of paracetamol. **b** Molecular model of paracetamol.

a Using the molecular model of paracetamol in *figure 23.4b*, draw the structural formula of paracetamol.

b Use the infrared spectrum in *figure 23.4a* to record the frequency of the absorption labelled **1**. Identify the bond that you would give rise to this absorption by labelling it '**1**' on your structure.

# Mass spectrometry

In chapter 2, you were introduced to the use of a mass spectrometer for the determination of relative atomic masses from relative isotopic masses and percentage abundance. A mass spectrometer may also be used to determine relative molecular masses. When a molecular compound is placed in a mass spectrometer, it is also ionised. The molecule will lose one electron, a positive ion will be formed and this can be detected. This ion, which will have a mass equal to the $M_r$ of the compound is called the **molecular ion**.

*Figure 23.5* shows the mass spectrum of dodecane. The molecular ion is shown by the peak with the highest mass/charge ratio. Hence the relative molecular mass of dodecane is shown by peak $M$, which has a mass/charge ratio of 170. The molecular formula of dodecane is $C_{12}H_{26}$ and the formula of the ion at peak $M$ is $C_{12}H_{26}^{+}$. When writing the formula of an ion, remember to include the positive charge. You will see that the mass spectrum of dodecane shows the presence of many other ions of lower mass/charge ratios. These correspond to fragment ions with the formulae shown on the spectrum. You will learn more about the use of such ions in determining the structure of an organic compound if you study Spectroscopy Option.

In some larger molecules, care is needed in selecting the molecular ion. This may occur when the relative abundance of the molecular ion is high compared to the fragment ions. The presence of about 1% of naturally occurring carbon-13 often means a smaller peak is visible at one mass unit above the molecular ion peak. An example is shown in the mass spectrum of another hydrocarbon shown in *figure 23.6*. The small peak is labelled the $M + 1$ peak to help distinguish it from the main molecular ion peak. The $M + 1$ peak shows the percentage abundance of molecules with one carbon-13 atom present in place of a carbon-12 atom.

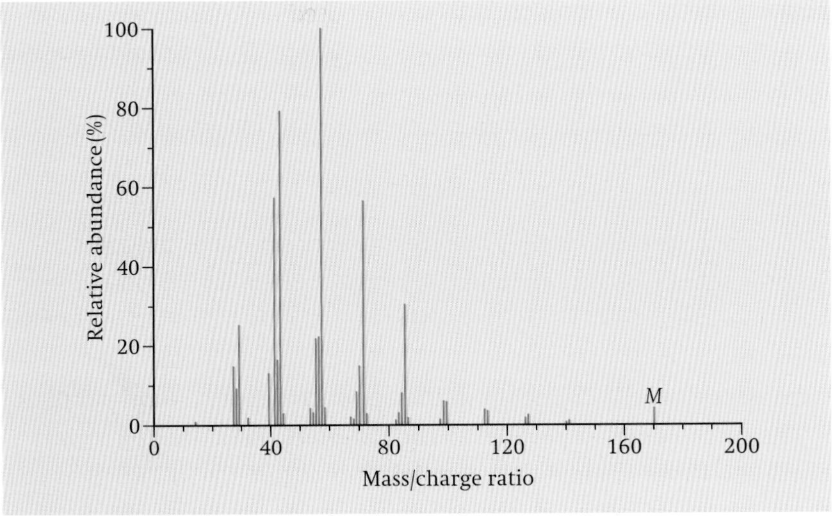

## SAQ 23.3

Using the mass spectrum in *figure 23.6*, determine the relative molecular mass of the hydrocarbon present. Be careful to use the larger peak, labelled $M$.

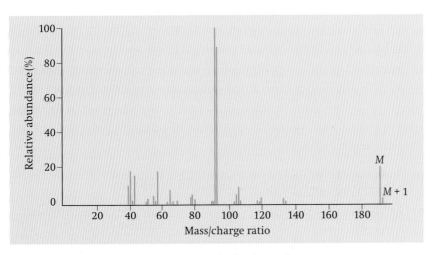

● **Figure 23.5** The mass spectrum of dodecane.

● **Figure 23.6** The mass spectrum of a hydrocarbon.

● **Figure 23.7** A mobile mass spectrometer used for environmental chemical analysis.

# Analytical applications of the mass spectrometer

## Water analysis

The very tiny amounts of industrial and agricultural organic chemicals that find their way into our water supplies can be monitored by means of a mass spectrometer. *Figure 23.7* shows a modern portable mass spectrometer that has been developed for this purpose. It is comforting to know that these instruments are capable of detecting such pollutants at levels well below the point where the pollutants might harm us. An example comes from SAC Scientific who have developed analytical methods for determining the concentration of triazine herbicides, which have been found in ground-water. These herbicides have been used to control weeds on railway lines,

but less persistent herbicides such as glyphosphate (Tumbleweed), which rapidly breaks down in soil into harmless products, are now being used.

## Drug analysis

In most sports competitions, a careful watch is kept for athletes who may have taken drugs to enhance their performance (*figure 23.8*). Mass spectrometry is linked with gas–liquid chromatography to provide a rapid method of detecting tiny quantities of a drug in a sample of blood or urine.

# Nuclear magnetic resonance spectroscopy

Nuclear magnetic resonance spectroscopy (n.m.r. spectroscopy) is a particularly powerful tool for the determination of the structure of a compound. In only a few minutes, it is possible for a chemist to have established the absolute structure for a simple organic compound. The technique can even be used to determine the structures of quite complex organic compounds. For this reason, it is a very popular method among chemists.

N.m.r. spectroscopy was developed from work by both chemists and nuclear physicists. The technique relies on the interaction between magnetic properties of certain nuclei and their chemical environment. Some nuclei (with odd mass numbers such as $^1H$ or $^{13}C$) have a property called 'spin' (like electrons). This spin gives the nuclei magnetic properties so that they behave like very small bar magnets. When a sample of a compound containing such nuclei is placed in a large magnetic field, a small majority of nuclei will line up in the same direction as the magnetic field (parallel to the field). The remaining nuclei will line up in the opposite direction (anti-parallel).

The nuclei aligned parallel to the magnetic field are at a lower energy to those aligned anti-parallel. The difference in energy is of the same frequency as electromagnetic radiation in the radio-frequency range. By subjecting the sample to a pulse of radio-frequency radiation, some of the nuclei will flip from the parallel to the anti-parallel alignment (*figure 23.9*).

Because electrons surround the nuclei, the energy needed for resonance varies slightly, depending on the local chemical environment. This slight variation is the key to structure determination. In the following section we shall focus on the use of proton n.m.r spectroscopy. This will enable the positions of protons (hydrogen atoms) in a compound to be determined.

## Use of n.m.r. to determine the structure of ethanol

A low-resolution **n.m.r spectrum** of ethanol consists of three lines, as shown in *figure 23.10*. You will notice several features in this spectrum:
- Unusually, the horizontal scale increases from right to left.
- The scale is labelled in terms of **chemical shift**, $\delta$ (ppm). The

● **Figure 23.8** Drug analysis is needed to detect the use of performance-enhancing drugs by athletes.

small peak at 0 ppm is due to a compound, tetramethylsilane, (TMS, $(CH_3)_4Si$), which is used as a reference standard.

■ The spectrum consists of three sharp peaks. The numbers at the top of each peak show the relative areas of each peak. The relative numbers of each type of proton are shown by relative peak areas.

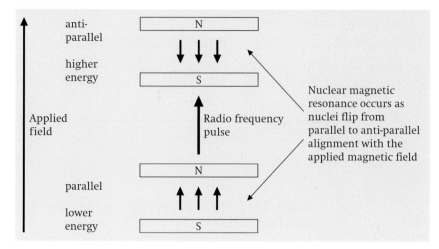

Nuclear magnetic resonance occurs as nuclei flip from parallel to anti-parallel alignment with the applied magnetic field

● **Figure 23.9** A nucleus may flip from parallel to anti-parallel alignment on absorption of energy from radio frequency radiation.

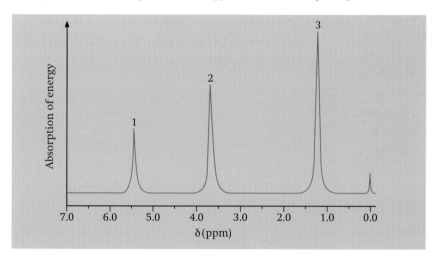

● **Figure 23.10** Low-resolution n.m.r. spectrum of ethanol.

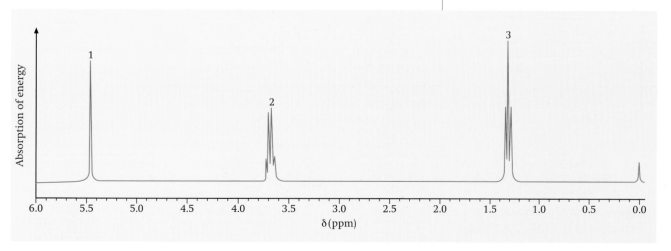

● **Figure 23.11** High-resolution n.m.r. spectrum of ethanol.

Ethanol has protons in three different chemical environments. Look at the structure of ethanol: $CH_3CH_2OH$. There are three protons on the first carbon, two on the second carbon and one on the oxygen atom. Each atom has different neighbours and so has a different chemical environment. Notice that these numbers correspond to the relative peak areas in the n.m.r. spectrum of ethanol. The peak at about 1.2 ppm is due to the $CH_3-$ protons; that at about 3.7 ppm is due to the $-CH_2-$ protons and that at about 5.4 ppm to the $-OH$ proton. For ethanol, a low-resolution spectrum confirms the structure.

It is not always so easy to establish a structure from a low-resolution spectrum. Indeed such spectra are not usually recorded. More information can be obtained from a high-resolution spectrum, as we shall see.

The high-resolution spectrum of ethanol is shown in *Figure 23.11*. Notice that there are still three main groups of peaks, with areas in the same ratio. However, two of the peaks are split. The CH₃– peak is split into a triplet, whilst the –CH₂– peak is split into a quartet. This splitting is caused by spins of protons on adjacent carbon atoms coupling with each other. A proton on an adjacent carbon will produce a small difference in the magnetic field experienced by a proton. The difference depends on whether the spin of the adjacent proton is parallel or anti-parallel to the applied magnetic field. Protons on the same carbon atom are equivalent and do not affect each other.

Consider a single proton, for example the –CH– proton in $CH_3CH(OH)COOH$. In this compound (lactic acid) there are three equivalent methyl (CH₃–) protons. The signal for these will be split into two signals (a doublet) of almost equal intensity as slightly more than half of the –CH– protons will have parallel spins, the rest being anti-parallel.

However, if we consider the arrangements of spin for the –CH₂– protons in ethanol, $CH_3CH_2OH$, we find more possibilities arise. We find that the methyl protons (CH₃–) are now split into a triplet of ratio 1:2:1. This ratio reflects the possible arrangements, shown in *figure 23.12*.

There is a general rule for predicting the number of signals in the **splitting pattern** of protons on a carbon atom by protons on an

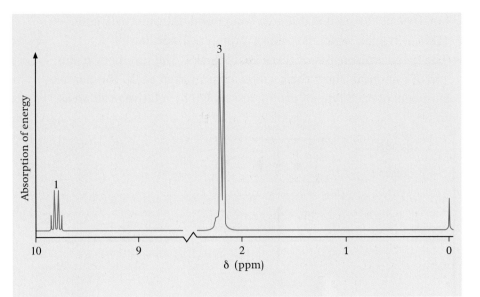

● **Figure 23.13** The n.m.r spectrum of an unknown molecule, $C_2H_4O$.

adjacent carbon. It is known as the *n* + 1 rule, where *n* = number of protons on the adjacent carbon. Hence for a –CH– proton, *n* = 1 so *n* + 1 = 2, and a doublet is produced. For –CH₂–, a triplet results and for CH₃–, a quartet.

| Type of proton | Chemical shift, δ (ppm) |
|---|---|
| R–CH₃ | 0.7–1.6 |
| R–CH₂–R | 1.2–1.4 |
| R₃CH | 1.6–2.0 |
| $-\overset{O}{\overset{\|\|}{C}}-CH_3 \quad -\overset{O}{\overset{\|\|}{C}}-CH_2-R$ | 2.0–2.9 |
| ⬡–CH₃  ⬡–CH₂–R | 2.3–2.7 |
| –O–CH₃  –O–CH₂–R | 3.3–4.3 |
| R–OH | 3.5–5.5 |
| ⬡–OH | 6.5–7.0 |
| ⬡–H | 7.1–7.7 |
| $R-\overset{O}{\overset{\|\|}{C}}-H \qquad ⬡-\overset{O}{\overset{\|\|}{C}}-H$ | 9.5–10 |
| $-\overset{O}{\overset{\|\|}{C}}-OH$ | 11.0–11.7 |

● **Table 23.2** Chemical shifts for some types of proton in n.m.r. spectra. All chemical shifts are relative to tetramethylsilane (TMS), δ = 0 ppm. The symbol 'R' represents an alkyl group.

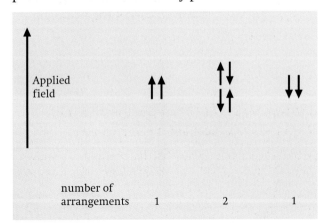

Applied field

number of arrangements    1      2      1

● **Figure 23.12** The arrangements possible for the two protons in –CH₂–. In ethanol, the –CH₂– protons cause the CH₃– peak to be split into a triplet with a 1:2:1 ratio.

## SAQ 23.4

By considering the possible arrangements of spin for the protons in a $CH_3-$ group, show that the splitting of the $-CH_2-$ protons in ethanol is a 1:3:3:1 quartet.

We will now look at the interpretation of the n.m.r. spectrum of an unknown molecule of molecular formula, $C_2H_4O$. The spectrum is shown in *figure 23.13*. *Table 23.2* provides information on the chemical shifts of different types of proton.

The information contained in *figure 23.13* may be summarised in *table 23.3*.

| Chemical shift, $\delta$ (ppm) | Relative number of protons | Splitting pattern |
|---|---|---|
| 2.2 | 3 | doublet |
| 9.8 | 1 | quartet |

● Table 23.3

From the splitting patterns given, the following can be deduced:

■ to produce a quartet the single proton at chemical shift 9.8 must be adjacent to a $-CH_3$ group.
■ to produce a doublet the three protons at chemical shift 2.2 must be adjacent to a $-CH-$ proton.

The types of proton are shown in *table 23.4*.

| Chemical shift, $\delta$ (ppm) | Type of proton |
|---|---|
| 2.2 | $CH_3-\overset{\displaystyle O}{\overset{\displaystyle \|}{C}}-R$ |
| 9.8 | $R-\overset{\displaystyle O}{\overset{\displaystyle \|}{C}}-H$ |

● Table 23.4

The structure of the compound is thus $CH_3CHO$ (ethanal), which agrees with the molecular formula of $C_2H_4O$.

## SAQ 23.5

A compound has the molecular formula $C_4H_8O_2$. The n.m.r. spectrum of this compound is shown in *figure 23.14*. The compound shows a strong sharp absorption in its infrared spectrum at 1750 cm$^{-1}$.

a Summarise the information from the n.m.r. spectrum in a table similar to *table 23.3*.
b From the splitting patterns, deduce which protons are on adjacent carbon atoms.

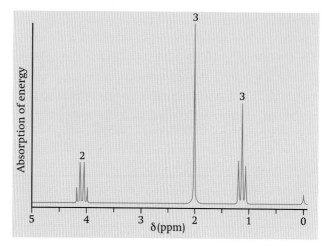

● **Figure 23.14** The n.m.r. spectrum of the compound with molecular formula $C_4H_8O_2$.

c Use *table 23.2*, together with the infrared data given above, to identify the types of proton present.
d Deduce the structural formula for this compound.

## Predicting an n.m.r. spectrum

When chemists set out to synthesise a compound, they may predict the n.m.r. spectrum of the desired compound. They can then compare the spectrum of the product with that of their desired compound. Computer programs are now available to make predictions of n.m.r. spectra from chemical structures. However, you will not be able to use such a program in an examination when you are asked to predict the spectrum of a simple compound. Fortunately, the process is quite straightforward for simple compounds, as the following example shows.

Suggest the chemical shifts and splitting patterns that you might observe for butanone. Butanone has the structure

$$CH_3 \underset{CH_2}{\diagdown} \overset{\displaystyle O}{\overset{\displaystyle \|}{C}} \diagup CH_3$$

First we check *table 23.2* for the chemical shifts. We can create a table for our predictions.

| Type of proton | Chemical shift, $\delta$ (ppm) | Relative number of protons | Splitting pattern |
|---|---|---|---|
| $CH_3-R$ | 1.2 | 3 | triplet |
| $-\overset{\displaystyle O}{\overset{\displaystyle \|}{C}}-CH_3$ | 2.0-2.9 | 3 | singlet |
| $-\overset{\displaystyle O}{\overset{\displaystyle \|}{C}}-CH_2-R$ | 2.0-2.9 | 2 | quartet |

The n.m.r. spectrum for butanone is shown in *figure 23.15*. Note that both $-CH_3$ protons are outside the range given in *table 23.2*. The ranges given in *table 23.2* may not always be appropriate. The chemical shift for a particular group of protons can be affected by factors outside the molecule such as the solvent used to run the spectrum.

### SAQ 23.6

Suggest the chemical shifts and splitting patterns that you might observe for methyl propanoate.

## Identifying the –OH signal

The –OH signal in the high-resolution n.m.r. spectrum of ethanol appears as a single peak. You may have wondered why the signal is not split by the protons on the neighbouring $-CH_2-$ group. The reason for this is that the –OH proton exchanges very rapidly with protons in traces of water (or acid) present as follows. The hydrogen atoms involved in this reversible exchange have been coloured red and blue to help you to see what takes place.

$$CH_3CH_2OH + H_2O \rightleftharpoons CH_3CH_2OH + HOH$$

This exchange is so rapid that the signal for the –OH protons becomes a single peak.

*Table 23.2* shows that –OH signals range from a chemical shift of 3.5–5.5 (for R–**OH** protons) through 6.5–7.0 (for phenol protons) to 11.0–11.7 (for carboxylic acid protons). Some of these ranges overlap with the signals for other protons and can make an n.m.r. spectrum less clear.

Fortunately, there is a simple remedy to this lack of clarity. The signal for the –OH group can be easily removed from the spectrum by adding a small amount of deuterium oxide, $D_2O$, to the n.m.r. sample. The deuterium atoms in $D_2O$ exchange reversibly with the protons in the –OH groups:

$$-OH + D_2O \rightleftharpoons -OD + HOD$$

Deuterium atoms ($^2H$) do not absorb in the same region of the spectrum as protons ($^1H$). The –OH signal disappears from the n.m.r. spectrum. This enables the –OH signal in the n.m.r. spectrum from the $D_2O$-free sample to be identified and any overlapping signals clarified.

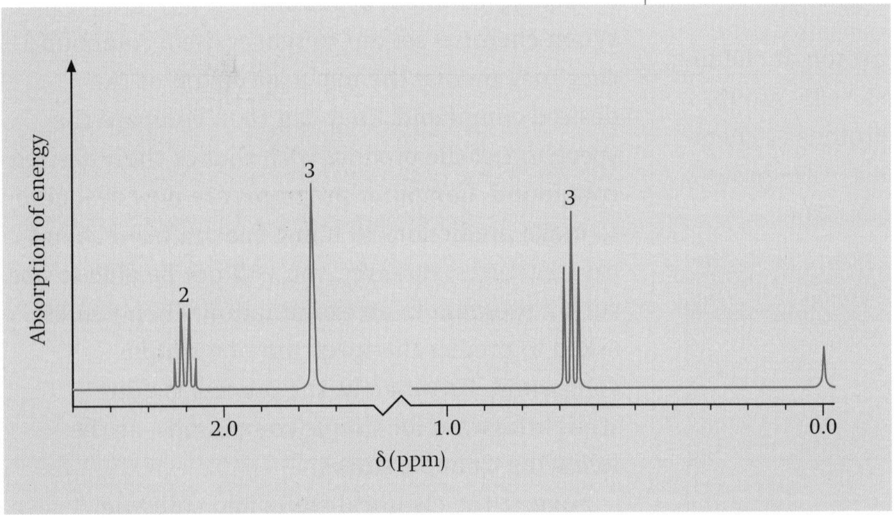

● **Figure 23.15** The n.m.r spectrum of butanone. Note that the chemical shift values differ from the predicted values. Such variation is not uncommon.

## SUMMARY

◆ The infrared spectrum of a compound enables the presence of different functional groups to be established. Groups such as $>C=O$ or $-O-H$ absorb radiation at different frequencies in the infrared. In infrared spectroscopy frequency is measured in units of $cm^{-1}$ (called wavenumbers).

◆ The mass spectrum of a compound enables the molecular mass of the compound to be determined using the molecular ion peak. The molecular ion peak, *M*, is the peak produced by the loss of one electron from a molecule of the compound.

◆ The n.m.r. spectrum of a compound provides detailed information about the structure of the compound. In particular, the spectrum for the protons, $^1H$, in a compound can provide a complete determination of the compound's structure.

◆ Protons in different chemical environments produce signals at different chemical shifts. The chemical shift provides information about the type of proton present.

◆ The area ratios of the signals correspond to the numbers of protons in the different chemical environments.

◆ Protons on neighbouring carbon atoms cause signals to be split. The splitting pattern establishes which groups of protons are on adjacent carbon atoms. The $n + 1$ rule predicts the splitting pattern.

◆ Protons on $-OH$ can be identified by the addition of $D_2O$ to the n.m.r. sample, which collapses the signal due to an $-OH$ proton.

# Questions

1  The empirical formula of compound A is $C_3H_6O_2$. The mass spectrum of compound A is shown below.

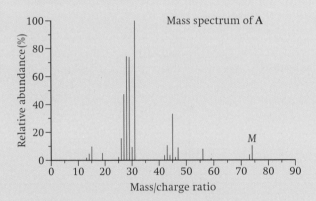

Mass spectrum of A

Relative abundance (%)

Mass/charge ratio

a  Use the molecular ion peak, M, to show that the molecular formula of A is the same as its empirical formula.

The infrared spectrum of A is shown below.

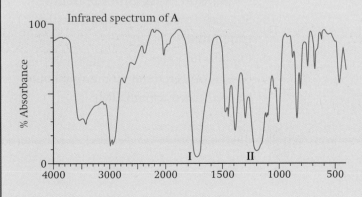

Infrared spectrum of A

% Absorbance

b  (i) Identify the types of bond which give rise to the absorptions labelled I and II in this infrared spectrum.
   (ii) Draw three structural isomers of A which contain the bonds identified in part b.

The n.m.r. spectrum of A is shown below.

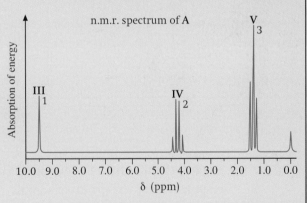

n.m.r. spectrum of A

Absorption of energy

δ (ppm)

c  Suggest the identity of the protons responsible for the groups of signals labelled III, IV and V in this n.m.r. spectrum. Use the number of protons present in each group, the splitting pattern and the chemical shift to explain your reasoning.

d  Suggest a possible structure for this compound, using information that you have obtained in parts a, b and c.

**2** Compound **B** is an aromatic hydrocarbon
with the molecular formula $C_8H_{10}O$.
The infrared spectrum of **B** is given below.

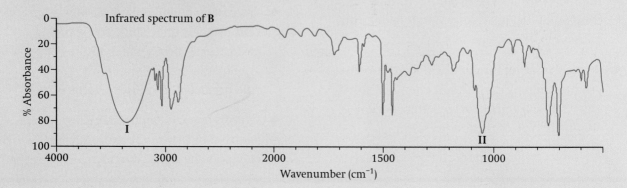

**a** Identify the types of bond which give
rise to the absorptions labelled **I** and **II**
in this infrared spectrum.

The n.m.r. spectrum of **B** is shown below.
Part of the spectrum has been expanded
to show three groups of signals more
clearly.

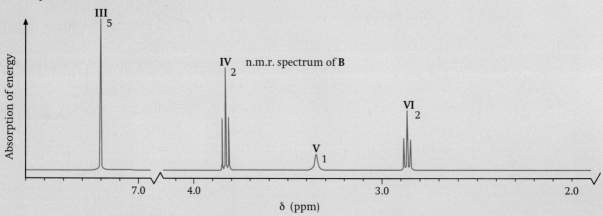

**b** (i) Suggest the identity of the protons
responsible for the group of signals
labelled **III**, using the chemical
shift and number of protons.

(ii) Suggest the identity of the protons
responsible for the groups of signals labelled **IV**, **V** and **VI** in this
n.m.r. spectrum. Use the number of
protons present in each group, the
splitting pattern and the chemical
shift to explain your reasoning.

**c** Suggest a possible structure for this
compound.

**d** Explain how the n.m.r. signal arising
from a proton in an −OH group could
be confirmed using $D_2O(l)$.

# Appendix: Periodic Table of the elements

Key:

| a |
|---|
| X |
| Name |
| b |

a = relative atomic mass
X = symbol
b = proton number

**s-Block**

| Period | I | II |
|--------|---|----|
| 1 | 1.0 H Hydrogen 1 | |
| 2 | 6.9 Li Lithium 3 | 9.0 Be Beryllium 4 |
| 3 | 23.0 Na Sodium 11 | 24.3 Mg Magnesium 12 |
| 4 | 39.1 K Potassium 19 | 40.1 Ca Calcium 20 |
| 5 | 85.5 Rb Rubidium 37 | 87.6 Sr Strontium 38 |
| 6 | 133 Cs Caesium 55 | 137 Ba Barium 56 |
| 7 | – Fr Francium 87 | – Ra Radium 88 |

**d-Block**

| | | | | | | | | | |
|---|---|---|---|---|---|---|---|---|---|
| 45.0 Sc Scandium 21 | 47.9 Ti Titanium 22 | 50.9 V Vanadium 23 | 52.0 Cr Chromium 24 | 54.9 Mn Manganese 25 | 55.9 Fe Iron 26 | 58.9 Co Cobalt 27 | 58.7 Ni Nickel 28 | 63.5 Cu Copper 29 | 65.4 Zn Zinc 30 |
| 88.9 Y Yttrium 39 | 91.2 Zr Zirconium 40 | 92.9 Nb Niobium 41 | 95.9 Mo Molybdenum 42 | – Tc Technetium 43 | 101 Ru Ruthenium 44 | 103 Rh Rhodium 45 | 106 Pd Palladium 46 | 108 Ag Silver 47 | 112 Cd Cadmium 48 |
| La to Lu 57 | 178 Hf Hafnium 72 | 181 Ta Tantalum 73 | 184 W Tungsten 74 | 186 Re Rhenium 75 | 190 Os Osmium 76 | 192 Ir Iridium 77 | 195 Pt Platinum 78 | 197 Au Gold 79 | 201 Hg Mercury 80 |
| Ac to Lr 89 | Rf Rutherfordium 104 | Db Dubnium 105 | Sg Seaborgium 106 | Bh Bohrium 107 | Hs Hassium 108 | Mt Meitnerium 109 | Unn Ununnillium 110 | Uuu Unununium 111 | Uub Ununbium 112 |

**p-Block**

| III | IV | V | VI | VII | 0 |
|-----|----|----|----|-----|---|
| | | | | | 4.0 He Helium 2 |
| 10.8 B Boron 5 | 12.0 C Carbon 6 | 14.0 N Nitrogen 7 | 16.0 O Oxygen 8 | 19.0 F Fluorine 9 | 20.2 Ne Neon 10 |
| 27.0 Al Aluminium 13 | 28.1 Si Silicon 14 | 31.0 P Phosphorus 15 | 32.1 S Sulphur 16 | 35.5 Cl Chlorine 17 | 39.9 Ar Argon 18 |
| 69.7 Ga Gallium 31 | 72.6 Ge Germanium 32 | 74.9 As Arsenic 33 | 79.0 Se Selenium 34 | 79.9 Br Bromine 35 | 83.8 Kr Krypton 36 |
| 115 In Indium 49 | 119 Sn Tin 50 | 122 Sb Antimony 51 | 128 Te Tellurium 52 | 127 I Iodine 53 | 131 Xe Xenon 54 |
| 204 Tl Thallium 81 | 207 Pb Lead 82 | 209 Bi Bismuth 83 | Po Polonium 84 | At Astatine 85 | Rn Radon 86 |
| | Uuq Ununquadium 114 | | Uuh Ununhexium 116 | | |

**f-Block**

| 139 La Lanthanum 57 | 140 Ce Cerium 58 | 141 Pr Praseodymium 59 | 144 Nd Neodymium 60 | – Pm Promethium 61 | 150 Sm Samarium 62 | 152 Eu Europium 63 | 157 Gd Gadolinium 64 | 159 Tb Terbium 65 | 163 Dy Dysprosium 66 | 165 Ho Holmium 67 | 167 Er Erbium 68 | 169 Tm Thulium 69 | 173 Yb Ytterbium 70 | 175 Lu Lutetium 71 |
|---|---|---|---|---|---|---|---|---|---|---|---|---|---|---|
| Ac Actinium 89 | Th Thorium 90 | Pa Protactinium 91 | U Uranium 92 | Np Neptunium 93 | Pu Plutonium 94 | Am Americium 95 | Cm Curium 96 | Bk Berkelium 97 | Cf Californium 98 | Es Einsteinium 99 | Fm Fermium 100 | Md Mendelevium 101 | No Nobelium 102 | Lr Lawrencium 103 |

# Answers to self-assessment questions

## Chapter 1

**1.1** **a** U-235 has 92 protons, 92 electrons and 143 neutrons.

U-238 has 92 protons, 92 electrons and 146 neutrons.

**b** $K^+$-40 has 19 protons, 18 electrons and 21 neutrons.

$Cl^-$-37 has 17 protons, 18 electrons and 20 neutrons.

**1.2** All the isotopes have the same number and arrangement of electrons and this controls their chemical properties.

**1.3** **a** Sodium has 11 electrons in all. There is one electron in its outer shell ($n = 3$) and this is the easiest to remove. The second ionisation energy shows the energy required to remove an electron from the next inner (filled) shell ($n = 2$).

The ninth electron to be removed is in shell $n = 2$ and the tenth is in shell $n = 1$, which is closest to the nucleus.

**b** The first electron is in the outer shell $n = 3$.

The relatively low increases from the second to the ninth ionisation energies show that eight electrons are in the same shell $n = 2$. The tenth and eleventh electrons are in the shell $n = 1$.

**1.4** Group II. The first and second ionisation energies are fairly close in value. There is a large increase between the second and third ionisation energies, which shows that the second and third electrons are in a different shell. This indicates that there are two electrons in the outer shell.

**1.5** See *figure*.

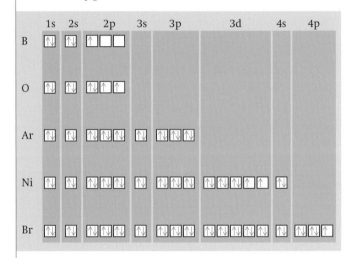

## Chapter 2

**2.1** Relative atomic mass of neon

$$= \frac{90.9 \times 20 + 0.3 \times 21 + 8.8 \times 22}{100} = 20.18$$

**2.2** **a** $24.3 + 2 \times 35.5 = 95.3$

**b** $63.5 + 32.1 + 4 \times 16.0 = 159.6$

**c** $2 \times 23.0 + 12.0 + 3 \times 16.0 + 10(2 \times 1.0 + 16.0) = 286.0$

**2.3** **a** $^{90}Zr$, $^{91}Zr$, $^{92}Zr$, $^{94}Zr$, $^{96}Zr$

**b** $A_r(Zr)$

$$= \frac{51.5 \times 90 + 11.2 \times 91 + 17.1 \times 92 + 17.4 \times 94 + 2.8 \times 96}{100}$$

$$= 91.3$$

**2.4** **a** $\dfrac{35.5}{35.5} = 1$ mol Cl atoms

**b** $\dfrac{71}{2 \times 35.5} = 1$ mol $Cl_2$ molecules

**2.5** **a** $6 \times 10^{23}$ Cl atoms

**b** 1 mol $Cl_2$ molecules = 2 mol Cl atoms
$= 2 \times 6 \times 10^{23} = 1.2 \times 10^{24}$

**2.6** **a** $CO_2 = 12.0 + 2 \times 16.0 = 44.0\,g$

∴ mass 0.1 mol $CO_2 = 0.1 \times 44.0$

$= 4.40\,g$

**b** $CaCO_3 = 40.1 + 12.0 + 3 \times 16.0$

$= 100.1\,g$

∴ mass 10 mol $CaCO_3 = 10 \times 100.1$

$= 1001\,g$

**2.7** **a** From equation, mole ratio $H_2 : Cl_2 = 1 : 1$

∴ mass ratio = 2.0 : 71.0 or 1 : 35.5

**b** $HCl = 1.0 + 35.5 = 36.5 = 1$ mol HCl

∴ as 1 mol $H_2$ produces 2 mol HCl,

0.5 mol $H_2$ produces 1 mol HCl.

∴ $2.0 \times 0.5$

$= 1.0\,g$ $H_2$ produces $36.5\,g$ HCl.

**2.8** 1000 tonne $Fe_2O_3$ produce

$112 \times \dfrac{1000}{160}$ tonne = 700 tonne Fe

∴ 1 tonne Fe requires $\dfrac{1000}{700}$ tonne $Fe_2O_3$

$= 1.43$ tonne

∴ mass ore $= 1.43 \times \dfrac{100}{12} = 11.9$ tonne

**2.9** **a** $C_3H_7$  **b** HO

**2.10**

| | **Cu** | **O** |
|---|---|---|
| Amount (mol) | $\dfrac{0.635}{63.5} = 0.0100$ | $\dfrac{0.080}{16.0} = 0.00500$ |
| Ratio (mol) | 2 | 1 |

∴ Empirical formula is $Cu_2O$.

**2.11** **a** Mass C in $1.257\,g$ $CO_2$

$= \dfrac{12.0}{44.0} \times 1.257 \quad = 0.343\,g$

Mass H in $0.514\,g$ $H_2O$

$= \dfrac{2 \times 1.0}{18.0} \times 0.514 \quad = 0.057\,g$

(Check: $0.343 + 0.057 = 0.400\,g$ = mass of hydrocarbon sample.)

| | **C** | **H** |
|---|---|---|
| Amount (mol) | $\dfrac{0.343}{12.0} = 0.0286$ | $\dfrac{0.057}{1.0} = 0.057$ |
| Ratio (mol) | 1 | 1.99 |

∴ Empirical formula is $CH_2$; $M_r(CH_2) = 14$.

**b** As $84 = 6 \times 14$, molecular formula is $C_6H_{12}$.

**2.12** **a** $MgBr_2$     **d** $Na_2SO_4$

**b** HI           **e** $KNO_3$

**c** CaS          **f** $NO_2$

**2.13** **a** Potassium carbonate

**b** Aluminium sulphide

**c** Lithium nitrate

**d** Calcium phosphate

**e** Silicon dioxide

**2.14** **a** $2Al + Fe_2O_3 \rightarrow Al_2O_3 + 2Fe$

**b** $2C_8H_{18} + 25O_2 \rightarrow 16CO_2 + 18H_2O$

or $C_8H_{18} + \frac{25}{2}O_2 \rightarrow 8CO_2 + 9H_2O$

**c** $2Pb(NO_3)_2 \rightarrow 2PbO + 4NO_2 + O_2$

**2.15** **a** $Cl_2(aq) + 2Br^-(aq) \rightarrow 2Cl^-(aq) + Br_2(aq)$

**b** $Fe^{3+}(aq) + 3OH^-(aq) \rightarrow Fe(OH)_3(s)$

**2.16** **a** Amount nitric acid

$= \dfrac{25}{1000} \times 0.1 = 2.5 \times 10^{-3}\,mol$

**b** Volume $= \dfrac{50}{1000} = 5 \times 10^{-2}\,dm^3$

∴ concentration $= \dfrac{0.125}{5 \times 10^{-2}}$

$= 2.5\,mol\,dm^{-3}$

**2.17** **a** $CH_3COOH = 12.0 + 3 \times 1.0 + 12.0$

$+ 2 \times 16.0 + 1.0 = 60.0$

∴ concentration $= 0.50 \times 60 = 30.0\,g\,dm^{-3}$

**b** $NaOH = 23.0 + 16.0 + 1.0 = 40.0$

∴ concentration $= \dfrac{4.00}{40.0} = 0.100\,mol\,dm^{-3}$

(N.B. Three significant figures in these answers.)

**2.18** **a** Amount KOH

$= \dfrac{20}{1000} \times 0.100 = 2 \times 10^{-3}\,mol$

$KOH + HCl \rightarrow KCl + H_2O$

∴ amount KOH = amount HCl

$= 2 \times 10^{-3}\,mol$

Volume HCl $= \dfrac{25.0}{1000} = 2.5 \times 10^{-2}\,dm^3$

∴ concentration HCl

$= \dfrac{2 \times 10^{-3}}{2.5 \times 10^{-2}} = 0.08\,mol\,dm^{-3}$

**b** $36.5 \times 0.08 = 2.92\,g\,dm^{-3}$

**2.19** Amount $HNO_3$

$= \dfrac{24}{1000} \times 0.050 = 1.20 \times 10^{-3}\,\text{mol}$

∴ stoichiometric mole ratio nitric acid: iron hydroxide is

$1.20 \times 10^{-3} : 4.00 \times 10^{-4}$    i.e. 3:1

Iron hydroxide contains three hydroxide ions to exactly neutralise three $HNO_3$ molecules. So equation is

$3HNO_3(aq) + Fe(OH)_3(s) \rightarrow Fe(NO_3)_3(aq) + 3H_2O(l)$

**2.20 a** Amount He $= \dfrac{2.4}{24} = 0.10\,\text{mol}$

**b** 0.5 mol propane $= 0.5 \times 24 = 12\,\text{dm}^3$

1.5 mol butane $= 1.5 \times 24 = 36\,\text{dm}^3$

∴ total volume $= 48\,\text{dm}^3$

**2.21**

| hydrocarbon Y(g) + $O_2$(g) $\rightarrow$ $CO_2$(g) + $H_2O$(l) | | | |
|---|---|---|---|
| gas volumes ($cm^3$) | 20 | 60 | 40 |
| gas volume ratio | 1 | 3 | 2 |
| gas mole ratio | 1 | 3 | 2 |

As 2 mol of carbon dioxide are obtained from 1 mol of the hydrocarbon, each hydrocarbon molecule contains 2 carbon atoms.

2 mol of carbon dioxide requires 2 out of the original 3 mol of oxygen.

Hence 1 mole of oxygen molecules, $O_2$(g), are left to combine with hydrogen atoms from the hydrocarbon to form water.

1 mole of $O_2$(g) produce 2 mol of water. Hence there must be $2 \times 2 = 4$ hydrogen atoms present in the hydrocarbon.

**a** The formula of the hydrocarbon is $C_2H_4$. Strictly speaking, as this formula has been obtained from ratios, hydrocarbon Y could be any hydrocarbon with the empirical formula $CH_2$. The relative molecular mass of hydrocarbon Y is needed for a full identification. (In the worked example above SAQ 2.21, the formula of hydrocarbon X happens to be unique.)

**b** $C_2H_4(g) + 3O_2(g) \rightarrow 2CO_2(g) + 2H_2O(l)$

# Chapter 3

**3.1** At negative electrode:    $Cu^{2+} + 2e^- \rightarrow Cu$

At positive electrode:    $2Br^- \rightarrow Br_2 + 2e^-$

**3.2 a–d** See *figure*.

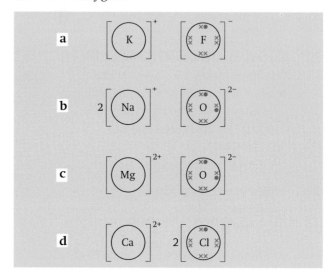

**3.3 a** See *figure*.

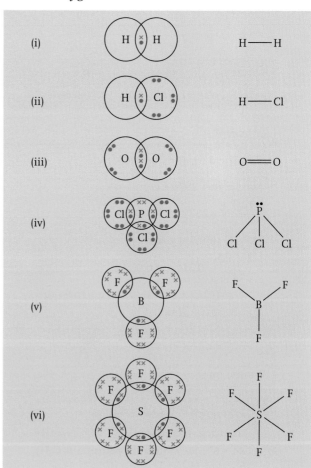

**b** BF₃: Outer shell of boron contains six electrons.
SF₆: Outer shell of sulphur contains 12 electrons.

**3.4** **a–c** See *figure*.

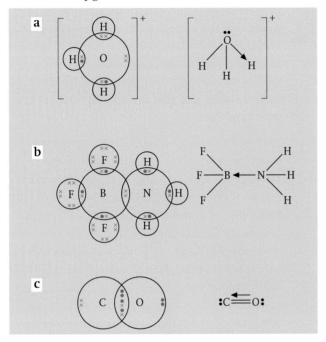

**3.5** **a–d** See *figure*.
Thus, **a** is non-polar; and **b**, **c** and **d** are polar.

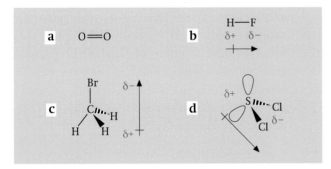

**3.6** **a** See *figure*.

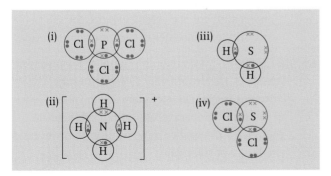

**b** (i) triangular pyramid
(ii) tetrahedral
(iii) non-linear
(iv) non-linear

**3.7** **a** Copper provides better heat transfer as it has a thermal conductivity that is five times higher than that of iron (stainless steel has a lower thermal conductivity than iron).

**b** Copper has more than three times the density of aluminium. The electrical conductivity of copper is 1.5 times that of aluminium. Aluminium cables will be lighter than copper whilst still being good conductors of electricity. The lighter cables enable less massive (and less unsightly) pylons to be used. As the tensile strength of aluminium is low, aluminium cables are reinforced with a steel core to increase their strength.

**c** Copper has the highest electrical and thermal conductivities. Its high thermal conductivity helps to keep equipment such as transformers cool.

**3.8** As water molecules are free to rotate, the positive charge on the rod repels the positive end of a water molecule whilst attracting the negative end. The overall effect is thus an attraction. The effect will be the same if the charge on the rod is negative rather than positive.

**3.9** See *figure*.

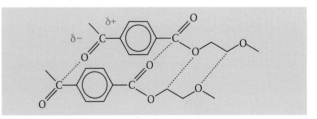

Dotted lines show the dipole–dipole forces. (Note: Extrusion through spinnerets causes more molecules to line up closely, increasing the intermolecular forces (and hence the strength of the fibre) by the closer contact.)

**3.10** Underlying increase is due to increasing instantaneous dipole–induced dipole forces as the number of electrons and protons present in the molecules rise. The value for water based on this underlying trend would be about 18 kJ mol⁻¹.

The much higher value observed for water is due to the presence of much stronger intermolecular forces.

**3.11** The O–H····O distance in ice is 0.159 + 0.096 nm = 0.255 nm. The effect of this is to produce a structure that occupies more space than that required when ice melts and many hydrogen bonds break. For a given mass, ice occupies a greater volume than water, so its density is less.

**3.12** Washing-up liquid lowers the surface tension of water. This reduces the hydrogen bonding at the surface to the point where it is no longer sufficient to keep the needle afloat.

**3.13** **a** Underlying increase is due to increasing instantaneous dipole–induced dipole forces as the number of electrons and protons present in the molecules rise.
**b** The much higher value observed for ammonia is due to the presence of hydrogen bonds, N–H····N.

**3.14** **a**

**b** See *figure*.

# Chapter 4

**4.1** There is no hydrogen bonding in methane.

**4.2** **a** Temperature increasing is another way of saying that the average energy of the particles is increasing. Thus, the number of particles with high energies increases, and their kinetic energy can overcome the intermolecular forces that hold the particles together. When this happens, the particles with higher-than-average energy can escape from the liquid into the gas.
**b** With very few exceptions, every substance has its own particular boiling point because it is made of a unique set of molecules that have their own unique set of intermolecular forces,

and therefore a unique temperature at which these forces can be overcome.

**4.3** The molecules most likely to leave the surface at first are the most energetic. Thus, if ethanol or propanone loses some of its most energetic molecules, the average energy of the remainder goes down. Therefore, the temperature of the liquid goes down. As the temperature of the liquid goes down, the heat from your hand gives energy to those molecules that are left. This results in your hand cooling.

**4.4** Water vapour escapes from the Earth's surface (damp ground, lakes, seas, etc.), rises in the atmosphere, and as it does so it cools. When a region of the atmosphere becomes saturated with water vapour, tiny water droplets start to form. Clouds are large collections of these tiny droplets. A number of things can happen to a cloud. If the surrounding atmosphere is not saturated with water vapour, the droplets will lose more molecules to the surroundings by evaporation than they gain; in this situation the cloud disperses. If a state of equilibrium is reached with the surroundings, then the cloud will just go on existing. If there is slight imbalance with the surroundings, the cloud may (i) gradually get smaller as the water droplets slowly evaporate, or (ii) get bigger as more water droplets form because the surrounding atmosphere becomes saturated with water vapour. In the latter case, eventually the droplets themselves will coalesce and be too heavy to be supported in the atmosphere: the result is rain.

**4.5** **a** The average energy increases.
**b** Note that not every molecule is bound to suffer an increase; some may travel more slowly than before owing to the way they collide with other molecules; but the overall effect is for the majority of molecules to increase their energies.

**4.6** Because the pressure is the same (atmospheric pressure), the reason why the volumes are different is that the cylinders are in rooms kept at different temperatures. Cylinder B is in the room with the higher temperature (the volume is the larger of the two).

**4.7** We have $P = 100 \, \text{kPa} = 100 \times 10^3 \, \text{Pa}$, $V = 1 \, \text{dm}^3$ $= 1 \times 10^{-3} \, \text{m}^3$ and $T = 20\,°\text{C} = (20 + 273)\,\text{K} = 293\,\text{K}$, so that $n = \dfrac{PV}{RT} = \dfrac{100 \times 10^3 \, \text{Pa} \times 10^{-3} \, \text{m}^3}{8.314 \, \text{J K}^{-1}\text{mol}^{-1} \times 293 \, \text{K}} = 0.041 \, \text{mol}$.

**4.8** As the balloon rises, the pressure of the atmosphere decreases, thus the gas inside will expand and the envelope expands. If the envelope were full at the start, it would be likely to burst at high altitude. High-altitude balloons are often coated with a bright silver-coloured coating. This helps to reflect the Sun's rays and keep the balloon cool, thus preventing even more expansion taking place. (The silver layer can also help the balloon to show up on radar.)

**4.9** a Volume occupied = $64 \times 10^{-30}\,\text{m}^3 \times 6.02 \times 10^{23}\,\text{mol}^{-1} = 3.85 \times 10^{-5}\,\text{m}^3 = 38.5\,\text{cm}^3$
   b This is about 0.2% of the total volume.

**4.10** At low pressure the particles are very far apart, so the influence of intermolecular forces is very slight. Also, the proportion of the total volume that the molecules occupy becomes extremely small; i.e. the molecules can be assumed to be like points. These are the assumptions made about ideal gases.

**4.11** At room temperature and pressure, 1 mol occupies about $24\,\text{dm}^3$. Thus the answers are:
   a $48\,\text{dm}^3$
   b $6\,\text{dm}^3$

**4.12** a The liquid can evaporate from the tip of the small syringe. Therefore less liquid is injected than was weighed out.
   b It increases the value of the relative molecular mass. To see why, let us take an impossible example, but one that illustrates the working. Suppose the syringe and liquid start out with a mass of 3 g, and that after injection their mass is 1 g. We believe that 2 g of liquid has been injected. However, let us assume that 1 g of liquid actually evaporated before the injection took place. Therefore the actual mass injected was only 1 g. If the gas occupied $100\,\text{cm}^3$ at room temperature and pressure, we would calculate the relative molecular mass to be $2\,\text{g mol}^{-1} \times 24\,000\,\text{cm}^3/100\,\text{cm}^3 = 480\,\text{g mol}^{-1}$ (We have already said that the numbers are not very likely!) Its true value should be $1\,\text{g mol}^{-1} \times 24\,000\,\text{cm}^3/100\,\text{cm}^3 = 240\,\text{g mol}^{-1}$ i.e. half the experimental result.

**4.13** You should find that $M(\text{propanone}) = 58.6\,\text{g mol}^{-1}$. Propanone has the formula $(CH_3)_2CO$, and a relative molecular mass of about $58\,\text{g mol}^{-1}$, so the result is reasonable.

# Chapter 5

**5.1** Exothermic: crystallisation; magnesium oxide formation.
   Endothermic: evaporation; copper oxide from copper carbonate.

**5.2** a (i) $2C(s) + 3H_2(g) \rightarrow C_2H_6(g)$;
   $$\Delta H_f^\ominus = -84.7\,\text{kJ mol}^{-1}$$
   (ii) $2Al(s) + \frac{3}{2}O_2(g) \rightarrow Al_2O_3(s)$;
   $$\Delta H_f^\ominus = -1669\,\text{kJ mol}^{-1}$$

   b See *figure*.

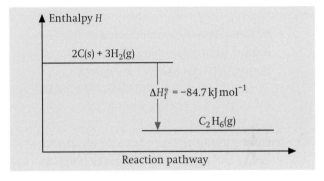

**5.3** a *Figure 5.6a*: either $\Delta H_r^\ominus$ or $\Delta H_c^\ominus$
   *Figure 5.6b*: $\Delta H_r^\ominus$
   b (i) $C_8H_{18}(l) + 12\frac{1}{2}O_2(g) \rightarrow 8CO_2(g) + 9H_2O(l)$;
   $$\Delta H_c^\ominus = -5512\,\text{kJ mol}^{-1}$$
   (ii) $C_2H_5OH(l) + 3O_2(g) \rightarrow 2CO_2(g) + 3H_2O(l)$;
   $$\Delta H_c^\ominus = -1371\,\text{kJ mol}^{-1}$$
   c One mole of water is formed by burning one mole of hydrogen.

**5.4** $\Delta H_c^\ominus(H_2)$ is calculated directly from experimental measurements. $\Delta H_f^\ominus(H_2O)$ is found from bond energies, which are average values calculated from measurements in a number of different experiments.

**5.5** The value in the data book was calculated from much more accurate experimental data. Some of the energy transferred from the burning propanol would not change the temperature but would be 'lost' in heating the apparatus and surroundings.

**5.6** The reaction that produces the enthalpy change is the same in each case of reaction between these acids and alkalis. Only $H^+(aq)$ and $OH^-(aq)$ are involved:
$$H^+(aq) + OH^-(aq) \rightarrow H_2O(l)$$

**5.7 a & b**

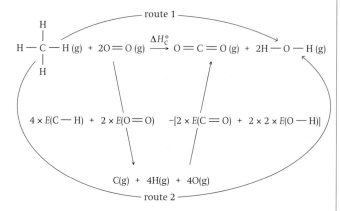

**c** By Hess's law the enthalpy change for route 1 = enthalpy change for route 2.
Hence $\Delta H_c^\ominus = 4 \times E(C\text{–}H) + 2 \times E(O{=}O)$
$\qquad\qquad - [2 \times E(C{=}O) + 2 \times 2 \times E(O\text{–}H)]$
$\quad = 4 \times 413 + 2 \times 498 - (2 \times 805 + 2 \times 2 \times 464)$
$\quad = -818\,\text{kJ mol}^{-1}$

**d** Bond enthalpies used are based on average values and are based on breaking bonds in gaseous molecules. Water molecules are present in the gaseous state in the bond enthalpy calculation. $\Delta H_c^\ominus$ should refer to the liquid state for water, so the experimental value will be more accurate.

**5.8 a**

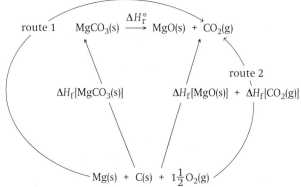

**b** The enthalpy change for route 1
$= \Delta H_f^\ominus[\text{MgCO}_3(\text{s})] + \Delta H_r^\ominus$
The enthalpy change for route 2
$= \Delta H_f^\ominus[\text{MgO}(\text{s})] + \Delta H_f^\ominus[\text{CO}_2(\text{g})]$
Applying Hess's law
$\Delta H_f^\ominus[\text{MgCO}_3(\text{s})] + \Delta H_r^\ominus = \Delta H_f^\ominus[\text{MgO}(\text{s})] + \Delta H_f^\ominus[\text{CO}_2(\text{g})]$
or
$(-1096) + \Delta H_r^\ominus = (-602) + (-394);$
$\qquad\qquad\qquad \Delta H_r^\ominus = +100\,\text{kJ mol}^{-1}$

**5.9 a & b**

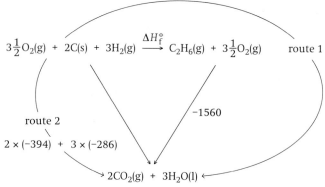

**c** Applying Hess's law
$\Delta H_f^\ominus + (-1560) = 2 \times (-394) + 3 \times (-286)$
$\Delta H_f^\ominus = 2 \times (-394) + 3 \times (-286) - (-1560)$
$\qquad = -86\,\text{kJ mol}^{-1}$

**5.10 a** The energy change associated with a chemical reaction.

**b** A chemical change in which energy is released to the surroundings; $\Delta H^\ominus$ is negative.

**c** A chemical change in which energy is taken in from the surroundings; $\Delta H^\ominus$ is positive.

**5.11** The total enthalpy change for a chemical reaction is independent of the route by which the reaction takes place, provided initial and final conditions are the same.

**5.12 a** $\frac{1}{2}O_2(\text{g}) \rightarrow O(\text{g})$

**b** $Cs(\text{g}) \rightarrow Cs^+(\text{g}) + e^-$

**c** $K(\text{s}) + \frac{1}{2}Cl_2(\text{g}) \rightarrow KCl(\text{s})$

**d** $I(\text{g}) + e^- \rightarrow I^-(\text{g})$

**e** $Ba(\text{s}) \rightarrow Ba(\text{g})$

**5.13 a** See *figure*.

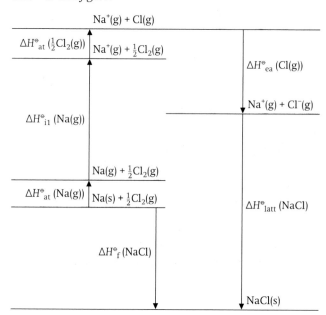

**b** $-787\,\text{kJ}\,\text{mol}^{-1}$

**5.14 a** See *figure*.

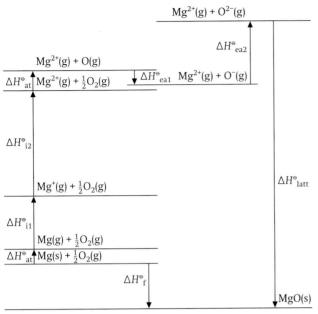

**b** See *figure*.

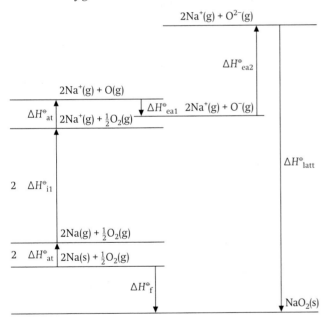

**5.15 a** CaO      **b** $K_2O$      **c** $SrI_2$

**5.16** LiF, $Li_2O$, MgO.

LiF is composed of singly charged ions so has the least attraction between ions, $Li_2O$ has one doubly charged ion and MgO has two doubly charged ions so has the most attraction between ions.

**5.17** $Mg^{2+}$ has a greater charge density than $Ca^{2+}$ because it is smaller, therefore it polarises the anion to a greater extent which aids decomposition.

# Chapter 6

**6.1** C in $CO_3^{2-}$ has an oxidation state of +4.
Al in $Al_2Cl_6$ has an oxidation state of +3.

**6.2 a** at the anode
$$4OH^-(aq) \rightarrow 2H_2O(l) + O_2(g) + 4e^-$$
**b** at the cathode
$$Ag^+(aq) + e^- \rightarrow Ag(s)$$

**6.3** For the $Fe^{2+}/Fe$ half-cell:
**a** $Fe^{2+} + 2e^- \rightarrow Fe$
**b** $-0.44\,\text{V}$
**c** $Fe^{2+}$: $1.00\,\text{mol}\,\text{dm}^{-3}$

For the $Cr^{2+}/Cr$ half-cell:
**a** $Cr^{2+} + 2e^- \rightarrow Cr$
**b** $-0.91\,\text{V}$
**c** $Cr^{2+}$: $1.00\,\text{mol}\,\text{dm}^{-3}$

For the $Ag^+/Ag$ half-cell:
**a** $Ag^+ + e^- \rightarrow Ag$
**b** $+0.80\,\text{V}$
**c** $Ag^+$: $1.00\,\text{mol}\,\text{dm}^{-3}$

In all three cells the temperature must be 298 K and in the standard hydrogen electrodes the $H^+(aq)$ concentration must be $1.00\,\text{mol}\,\text{dm}^{-3}$, the $H_2$ pressure must be 1 atmosphere and electrical contact must be made by platinum.

**6.4** $+1.52\,\text{V}$

**6.5** 298 K, all gases at pressure of 1 atmosphere, all relevant concentrations at $1.00\,\text{mol}\,\text{dm}^{-3}$.

**6.6** Platinum does not take part in reactions.

**6.7** See *figure*.

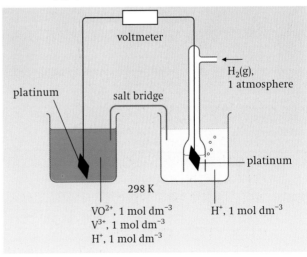

voltmeter

$H_2(g)$, 1 atmosphere

platinum

salt bridge

platinum

298 K

$VO^{2+}$, 1 mol dm$^{-3}$
$V^{3+}$, 1 mol dm$^{-3}$
$H^+$, 1 mol dm$^{-3}$

$H^+$, 1 mol dm$^{-3}$

**6.8** $S + 2e^- \rightleftharpoons S^{2-}$; $E^\ominus = -0.51\,\text{V}$

**6.9** See *figure*.

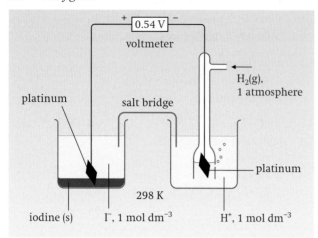

**6.10** **a** $Cr^{3+}$

**b** Ag

**6.11** **a** See *figure*.

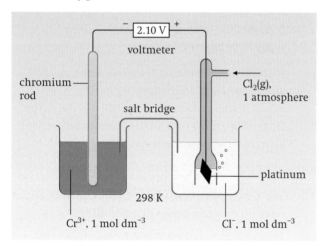

**b** 2.10 V

**c** chlorine half-cell

**6.12** **a** See *figure*.

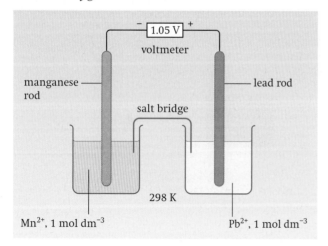

**b** 1.05 V

**c** lead half-cell

**6.13** **a** $Zn + 2Ag^+ \rightarrow Zn^{2+} + 2Ag$

**b** $Cu + 2Fe^{3+} \rightarrow Cu^{2+} + 2Fe^{2+}$

**c** $Cr + \frac{3}{2}Cl_2 \rightarrow Cr^{3+} + 3Cl^-$

**d** $Pb^{2+} + Mn \rightarrow Mn^{2+} + Pb$

**e** On your diagrams you should have shown the following electron flow in each external circuit.

part **a**: from the $Zn^{2+}/Zn$ half-cell to the $Ag^+/Ag$ half-cell

part **b**: from the $Cu^{2+}/Cu$ half-cell to the $Fe^{3+}/Fe^{2+}$ half-cell

part **c**: from the $Cr^{3+}/Cr$ half-cell to the $Cl_2/Cl^-$ half-cell

part **d**: from the $Mn^{2+}/Mn$ half-cell to the $Pb^{2+}/Pb$ half-cell.

**6.14** $Fe^{3+} + I^- \rightarrow Fe^{2+} + \frac{1}{2}I_2$

**6.15** **a** yes

$MnO_4^- + 5Cl^- + 8H^+ \rightarrow Mn^{2+} + \frac{5}{2}Cl_2 + 4H_2O$

$MnO_4^- + 8H^+ + 5e^- \rightleftharpoons Mn^{2+} + 4H_2O$, with its *more* positive $E^\ominus$ value, will proceed in a forward direction while $Cl_2 + 2e^- \rightleftharpoons 2Cl^-$ proceeds in a backward direction.

**b** no

$MnO_4^- + 8H^+ + 5e^- \rightleftharpoons Mn^{2+} + 4H_2O$, with its *less* positive $E^\ominus$ value, cannot proceed in a forward direction while $F_2 + 2e^- \rightleftharpoons 2F^-$ proceeds in a backward direction.

**c** yes

$V^{2+} + H^+ \rightarrow \frac{1}{2}H_2 + V^{3+}$

$2H^+ + 2e^- \rightleftharpoons H_2$, with its *more* positive $E^\ominus$ value, will proceed in a forward direction while $V^{3+} + e^- \rightleftharpoons V^{2+}$ proceeds in a backward direction.

**d** no

$2H^+ + 2e^- \rightleftharpoons H_2$, with its *less* positive $E^\ominus$ value, cannot proceed in a forward direction while $Fe^{3+} + e^- \rightleftharpoons Fe^{2+}$ proceeds in a backward direction.

**6.16** **a** (i) $E$ = more than 1.33 V

(ii) $E$ = less than 1.33 V

(iii) $E$ = less than 1.33 V

**b** (i) stronger oxidising agent

(ii) weaker oxidising agent

(iii) weaker oxidising agent

**c** high concentration $Cr_2O_7^{2-}$, high concentration $H^+$, low concentration $Cr^{3+}$

**d** Increasing the concentrations of reactants forces equilibrium to shift to the right in order to reduce these concentrations. Therefore, $E$ goes up and the $Cr_2O_7^{2-}/H^+$ solution becomes a stronger oxidising agent.

**6.17** $E^\ominus$-based predictions refer to standard conditions, but lab conditions are not usually standard. (However, if the $E^\ominus$ values for the two half-equations differ by more than 0.30 volts, $E^\ominus$-based predictions are usually correct.)

$E^\ominus$ values may predict that a reaction will occur, even though in reality the reaction may have such a slow rate that it is not observed.

**6.18** Add a catalyst; increase temperature; increase concentration of dissolved reactants; increase pressure of gaseous reactants; increase surface area of solid reactants.

**6.19** The two half-equations are:

$2H_2O + 2e^- \rightleftharpoons H_2 + 2OH^-; E^\ominus = -0.83\,V$

$O_2 + 2H_2O + 4e^- \rightleftharpoons 4OH^-; E^\ominus = +0.40\,V$

In the cell, the bottom half-equation, which has the more positive value of $E^\ominus$, gains electrons and will proceed in the forward direction. The top half-equation, with its more negative $E^\ominus$ value, will proceed in the backward direction.

The cell voltage is given by

$E^\ominus_{cell} = +0.40 - (-0.83)$
$\qquad = 1.23\,V$

**6.20** **a** anode: $4OH^-(aq) \rightarrow 2H_2O(l) + O_2 + 4e^-$
cathode: $Cu^{2+}(aq) + 2e^- \rightarrow Cu(s)$

The removal of copper ions from the solution causes it to become colourless.

**b** cathode: $2H^+(aq) + 2e^- \rightarrow H_2(g)$

# Chapter 7

**7.1** The system is not closed, water will evaporate.

**7.2** **a** The position of equilibrium would move towards the reactants. A new position of equilibrium will be established with a lower concentration of the ester (and water).

**b** Use a large excess of ethanol or ethanoic acid. (Preferably whichever is cheaper!). Remove the ethyl ethanoate as it is formed (the ester may be distilled from the mixture).

**7.3** **a** No change occurs as there are equal numbers of gaseous molecules on either side of the equation.

**b** There are fewer gaseous molecules on the right hand side of the equation. There is a reduction in volume moving from reactants to products so more $NH_3(g)$ is formed.

**7.4** **a** As the $[CO_2]$ builds up in the crocodile's blood, the position of equilibrium moves to the right and $[HCO_3^-]$ increases.

**b** (i) As the $[CO_2]$ builds up, more $O_2$ is released, so $[Hb]$ increases and $[HbO_2]$ decreases. $[O_2]$ continues to fall as it is used for tissue respiration.

(ii) The position of equilibrium moves to the left.

**7.5** experiment 1, $K_c = 0.231$;
experiment 4, $K_c = 0.272$.

**7.6** The ten moles of hydrogen iodide begin to dissociate, forming hydrogen and iodine:
$2HI(g) \rightleftharpoons H_2(g) + I_2(g)$
For every molecule of iodine formed, two molecules of hydrogen iodide have to split up. To form 0.68 moles of iodine molecules, $2 \times 0.68$ moles of hydrogen iodide must dissociate. This means a total loss of 1.36 moles of hydrogen iodide, from 10 down to 8.64 moles.

**7.7** **a** $K_c = \dfrac{[N_2O_4(g)]}{[NO_2(g)]^2}\,dm^3\,mol^{-1}$

**b** $K_c = \dfrac{[NO_2(g)]^2}{[NO(g)]^2[O_2(g)]}\,dm^3\,mol^{-1}$

**c** $K_c = \dfrac{[NH_3(g)]^2}{[N_2(g)]\,[H_2(g)]^3}$

The units for $K_c$ are given by:

$\text{units }(K_c) = \dfrac{(mol\,dm^{-3})^2}{(mol\,dm^{-3})\,(mol\,dm^{-3})^3}$

$= \dfrac{mol^2\,dm^{-6}}{mol\,dm^{-3}\,mol^3\,dm^{-9}} = \dfrac{1}{mol^2\,dm^{-6}}$

$= dm^6\,mol^{-2}$

**7.8**

| | $H_2(g)$ | $+$ | $CO_2(g)$ | $\rightleftharpoons$ | $CO(g)$ | $+$ | $H_2O(g)$ |
|---|---|---|---|---|---|---|---|
| initial concentrations $(mol\,dm^{-3})$ | 10.00 | | 90.00 | | 0 | | 0 |
| equilibrium concentrations $(mol\,dm^{-3})$ | 10.00 − 9.47 = 0.53 | | 90.00 − 9.47 = 80.53 | | 9.47 | | 9.47 |

$K_c = \dfrac{[CO][H_2O]}{[H_2][CO_2]}$

$= \dfrac{9.47 \times 9.47}{0.53 \times 80.53}$

$= 2.10$

(No units as in this homogeneous reaction total moles reactants = total moles products, so units cancel out.)

**7.9** $K_c$ decreases.

**7.10** **a** $K_p = \dfrac{p(NO)^2}{p(N_2)\,p(O_2)}$ no units

**b** $K_p = \dfrac{p(C_2H_5OH)}{p(C_2H_4)\,p(H_2O)}$ $Pa^{-1}$

**7.11** **a**

(i) Total moles gas = 0.925 + 2.775 + 0.150 = 3.850 mol

|  | $N_2(g)$ | + | $3H_2(g)$ | $\rightleftharpoons$ | $2NH_3(g)$ |
|---|---|---|---|---|---|
| mole fraction | $\dfrac{0.925}{3.850}$ | | $\dfrac{2.775}{3.850}$ | | $\dfrac{0.150}{3.850}$ |
| | = 0.240 | | = 0.721 | | = 0.039 |

(ii) partial pressure (kPa)

$0.240 \times 5000$ $\quad$ $0.721 \times 5000$ $\quad$ $0.039 \times 5000$

$\quad = 1200$ $\qquad\qquad = 3605$ $\qquad\qquad = 195$

**b** (i) $K_p = \dfrac{(195)^2}{(1200) \times (3605)^3} = 6.76 \times 10^{-10}$

(ii) $K_p$ units $= \dfrac{kPa^2}{kPa \times kPa^3} = kPa^{-2}$

**7.12** **a** (i) $Ca(s) + 2H^+(aq) \rightarrow Ca^{2+}(aq) + H_2(g)$

(ii) $2H^+(aq) + SrO(s) \rightarrow Sr^{2+}(aq) + H_2O(l)$

(iii) $2H^+(aq) + BaCO_3(s)$
$\quad\quad \rightarrow Ba^{2+}(aq) + CO_2(g) + H_2O(l)$

**b** (i) calcium chloride, $CaCl_2$;

(ii) strontium chloride, $SrCl_2$;

(iii) barium chloride, $BaCl_2$.

**7.13** **a** $H_2SO_4(aq) + H_2O(l) \rightleftharpoons H_3O^+(aq) + HSO_4^-(aq)$

B–L acid $\qquad$ B–L base $\quad$ B–L acid $\qquad$ B–L base

**b** $CH_3COOH(aq) + H_2O(l) \rightleftharpoons CH_3COO^-(aq) + H_3O^+(aq)$

B–L acid $\qquad\qquad$ B–L base $\quad$ B–L base $\qquad\qquad$ B–L acid

**c** $CH_3NH_2(aq) + H_2O(l) \rightarrow CH_3NH_3^+(aq) + OH^-(aq)$

B–L base $\qquad\qquad$ B–L acid $\quad$ B–L acid $\qquad\qquad$ B–L base

**d** $NH_3(g) + HCl(g) \rightarrow NH_4^+(s) + Cl^-(s)$

B–L base $\quad$ B–L acid $\qquad$ B–L acid $\quad$ B–L base

**7.14** Pure water is a poor conductor of electricity, which shows that it contains very few ions that can carry a direct current.

**7.15** $K_c = \dfrac{[H^+][OH^-]}{[H_2O]}$

$K_c$ is very small, so the concentrations of the products must be very much smaller then the concentration of water itself. This indicates that only a tiny proportion of pure water exists at any one time as protons and hydroxide ions, a deduction backed by the evidence that water is a poor conductor of electricity.

**7.16** **a** 3.52

**b** 2.00

**c** 7.40

**7.17** **a** 0.0

**b** 0.3

**c** The aqueous solution contains 3 g of hydrogen chloride, HCl, per $dm^3$. To find the pH we need the hydrogen ion concentration in $mol\,dm^{-3}$. The relative molecular mass of HCl
= (1 + 35.5) = 36.5.
Thus the concentration of hydrogen chloride
$= 3/36.5\,mol\,dm^{-3}$
$= 0.082\,mol\,dm^{-3}$
Because the hydrogen chloride dissociates completely to form hydrogen ions and chlorine ions, the concentration of hydrogen ions is $0.082\,mol\,dm^{-3}$. The pH of this acid $= -\log_{10}[H^+]$
$= -\log_{10}[0.082] = 1.1$.

**d** Potassium hydroxide dissociates completely in solution:

$$KOH(s) \xrightarrow{\;H_2O\;} K^+(aq) + OH^-(aq)$$

0.001 mol $\qquad$ 0.001 mol 0.001 mol

The concentration of hydroxide ions is the same as the concentration of the potassium hydroxide.
$K_w = [H^+][OH^-] = 1 \times 10^{-14}\,mol^2\,dm^{-6}$
so
$[H^+] = 1 \times 10^{-14}\,mol^2\,dm^{-6}/[OH^-]$
$\quad = 1 \times 10^{-14}\,mol^2\,dm^{-6}/0.001\,mol\,dm^{-3}$
$\quad = 1 \times 10^{-11}\,mol\,dm^{-3}$
The pH of this acid
$\quad = -\log_{10}[H^+] = -\log_{10}[10^{-11}] = 11.0$

**e** Sodium hydroxide ionises completely in aqueous solution:

$$NaOH(s) \xrightarrow{\;H_2O\;} Na^+(aq) + OH^-(aq)$$

The relative molecular mass of NaOH
= (23 + 16 + 1) = 40.
An aqueous solution containing 0.2 g of NaOH per $dm^3$ contains (0.2/40)mol NaOH,
i.e. $5 \times 10^{-3}\,mol\,dm^{-3}$. The concentration of hydroxide ions is therefore $5 \times 10^{-3}\,mol\,dm^{-3}$.
$k_w = [H^+][OH^-] = 1 \times 10^{-14}\,mol^2\,dm^{-6}$
$\therefore [H^+] \times 5 \times 10^{-3} = 1 \times 10^{-14}$

$[H^+] = \dfrac{1 \times 10^{-14}}{5 \times 10^{-3}} = 2 \times 10^{-12}\,mol\,dm^{-3}$

$\therefore pH = -\log_{10}[H^+] = -\log_{10}(2 \times 10^{-12})$
$\qquad\qquad = 11.7$

**7.18** See *table*.

| Acid | Base |
|------|------|
| $HNO_3$ | $NO_3^-$ |
| $H_2SO_3$ | $HSO_3^-$ |
| $[Fe(H_2O)_6]^{3+}$ | $[Fe(H_2O)_5(OH)]^{2+}$ |
| $HF$ | $F^-$ |
| $HNO_2$ | $NO_2^-$ |
| $HCOOH$ | $HCOO^-$ |
| $C_6H_5COOH$ | $C_6H_5COO^-$ |
| $CH_3COOH$ | $CH_3COO^-$ |
| $C_2H_5COOH$ | $C_2H_5COO^-$ |
| $[Al(H_2O)_6]^{3+}$ | $[Al(H_2O)_5(OH)]^{2+}$ |
| $CO_2 + H_2O$ | $HCO_3^-$ |
| $SiO_2 + H_2O$ | $HSiO_3^-$ |
| $HCO_3^-$ | $CO_3^{2-}$ |
| $HSiO_3^-$ | $SiO_3^{2-}$ |
| $H_2O$ | $OH^-$ |

**7.19**   **a** pH = 2.95

      **b** pH = 3.5. Aqueous solutions of aluminium salts are surprisingly acidic. An accidental tipping of aluminium salts into a reservoir in Cornwall created tap-water acidic enough to dissolve copper from pipes and to worry large numbers of people about the possibility of being poisoned.

      **c** pH = 2.4

**7.20** Strong acid–strong base: the slope of the graph is steep over the range pH = 3.5 to pH = 10. Any indicator with a colour-change range within these limits is suitable: bromocresol green, methyl red, bromothymol blue or phenolphthalein. The others in the table are not suitable.

**7.21** Strong acid–weak base: the slope is steep over the range 7.0–2.0. The indicators we could use are methyl yellow, methyl orange, bromophenol blue, bromocresol green or methyl red. We might get away with using bromothymol blue, but all the others in the table are unsuitable.

**7.22** Weak acid–strong base: methyl orange starts changing colour when the pH is 3.2 and stops at pH 4.4. A large amount of strong base would have to be added to cover this range, so there would be no degree of accuracy.

**7.23**   **a** Strong acid–weak base: methyl orange or bromophenol blue.

      **b** Strong acid–strong base: bromocresol green, methyl red, bromothymol blue or phenolphthalein.

      **c** The equilibrium constant for aspirin is similar to that of methanoic acid, so aspirin is a weak acid. Potassium hydroxide is a strong base, so the sensitive region for the indicator would be in the range pH 7–11. Phenolphthalein would be the best choice of indicator.

**7.24**   **a** The conjugate acid is $NH_4^+$ and the conjugate base is $NH_3$.

      **b** (i) When dilute hydrochloric acid is added, the additional hydrogen ions are accepted by the ammonia molecules.

          (ii) When dilute sodium hydroxide is added, the equilibrium shifts to the left, trapping the $OH^-(aq)$ ions.

**7.25**   **a** The equation for the equilibrium reaction is
$HCOOH(aq) \rightleftharpoons H^+(aq) + HCOO^-(aq)$
from which we can write the equilibrium constant expression
$$K_a = \frac{[H^+][HCOO^-]}{[HCOOH]}$$
Rearranging this equation
$$[H^+] = K_a \times \frac{[HCOOH]}{[HCOO^-]} \, mol\,dm^{-3}$$
Substituting the data given produces
$$[H^+] = 1.6 \times 10^{-4} \times \frac{0.0500}{0.100} \, mol\,dm^{-3}$$
$$= 8.00 \times 10^{-5} \, mol\,dm^{-3}$$
so
$$pH = -\log_{10}(8.00 \times 10^{-5})$$
$$= -(-4.096) = 4.10$$

      **b** Using the method in part **a**, pH = 4.8

**7.26**   **a** $K_a = 4.5 \times 10^{-7} \, mol\,dm^{-3}$

      **b** Carbonic acid, $H_2CO_3$

      **c** $HCO_3^-(aq)$

**7.27** Solubility of $PbCl_2$ = 0.70 g per 100 cm$^3$
$$= 7.00 \, g\,dm^{-3}$$
$$= \frac{7.00}{278} = 2.52 \times 10^{-2} \, mol\,dm^{-3}$$
$[Pb^{2+}] = 2.52 \times 10^{-2} \, mol\,dm^{-3}$
$[Cl^-] = 2 \times 2.52 \times 10^{-2} \, mol\,dm^{-3}$
$K_{sp} = [Pb^{2+}][Cl^-]^2 = 2.52 \times 10^{-2} \times (2 \times 2.52 \times 10^{-2})^2$
$$= 6.40 \times 10^{-5}$$

**7.28** Let $x$ be the solubility of $Ag_2CrO_4$ in $mol\,dm^{-3}$

$[CrO_4^{2-}] = x\,mol\,dm^{-3}$

$[Ag^+] = 2x\,mol\,dm^{-3}$

$K_{sp} = [Ag^+]^2[CrO_4^{2-}] = 4x^3 = 1.00 \times 10^{-12}$

$$x = \sqrt[3]{\frac{1.00 \times 10^{-12}}{4}}$$

$$= 6.30 \times 10^{-5}\,mol\,dm^{-3}$$

# Chapter 8

**8.1** **a** $CaCO_3 = 40 + 12 + (3 \times 16) = 100$

Amount of $CaCO_3 = \dfrac{2.00}{100} = 0.0200\,mol$

$150\,cm^3$ of $2\,mol\,dm^{-3}$ HCl contains $\dfrac{150}{1000} \times 2\,mol$ HCl

$= 0.300\,mol$ HCl

**b** From the equation, 2 mol HCl react with 1 mol $CaCO_3$. Therefore 0.0200 mol $CaCO_3$ require 0.0400 mol HCl. As 0.300 mol HCl is present, acid is in excess.

**c** The excess is 0.300 − 0.0400 = 0.260 mol.

**d** When the acid is in excess, the acid concentration is reasonably constant, so the concentration variable is controlled.

**8.2** **a** 1.0 M HCl   −0.18 g

2.0 M HCl   −0.37 g

**b** Mass loss is approximately doubled, so rate is also doubled.

**c** Reaction rate is directly proportional to the concentration of HCl.

**8.3** $2C_2H_2(g) + 5O_2(g) \rightarrow 4CO_2(g) + 2H_2O(g)$

**8.4** A spark or match might provide the activation energy.

**8.5** *Figure 8.19a* has lower entropy than *figure 8.19b*, so *figure 8.19b* represents the more stable state.

**8.6** **a** Infrared

**b** $2.00 \times 10^{-13}\,s$

**8.7** Experimental evidence shows that the rate of reaction is directly proportional to the concentration of cyclopropane. If the concentration of cyclopropane is halved, the rate of reaction is halved.

**8.8** Students' own answers.

**8.9** The reaction is first order with respect to cyclopropane and first order overall.

**8.10** By titrating small samples of the reaction mixture with standardised base, for example $1.0\,mol\,dm^{-3}$ aqueous sodium hydroxide, you could find the concentration of hydrochloric acid as the reaction progressed. You could also monitor this concentration using either a pH meter or a conductivity meter. Both devices respond to changes in hydrogen ion concentration, which is itself an indication of the concentration of hydrochloric acid.

**8.11** (Remember that the temperature of the reaction mixture must be constant throughout).

**a** (i) Both reactants are affecting the rate.

(ii) Several approaches are possible. To provide a fair test, the experiment should be designed to study the effect of changing the concentration of only one reagent. One approach is to ensure a large excess of methanol. Relative to the concentration of HCl, the methanol concentration could then be assumed to be constant. This would allow the concentration of the acid to be monitored. The data obtained would enable the order with respect to the HCl to be deduced.

**b** Separate experiments need to be conducted. In each experiment, the concentration of just one reactant is allowed to change, with other reactants present in excess. The effect of changing the concentration of $H^+(aq)$ can be investigated by the addition of a strong acid (such as sulphuric acid). Similarly, the effect of changing the concentration of $Cl^-(aq)$ can be investigated by the addition of sodium chloride.

**8.12** **a** The reaction rate = $k[N_2O_5]$, so the order of the reaction is 1.

**b** $k = 1.05 \times 10^{-5}\,s^{-1}$

**8.13** **a** Reaction rate = $k[H^+][CH_3COCH_3][I_2(aq)]^0$

**b & c** Substituting data from experiment 1 in the rate equation:

$10.9 \times 10^{-6}\,mol\,dm^{-3}\,s^{-1}$

$= k \times 1.25\,mol\,dm^{-3} \times 0.5\,mol\,dm^{-3}$

$k = \dfrac{10.9 \times 10^{-6}\,\cancel{mol\,dm^{-3}}\,s^{-1}}{1.25\,\cancel{mol\,dm^{-3}} \times 0.5\,mol\,dm^{-3}}$

$= 1.74 \times 10^{-5}\,mol^{-1}\,dm^3\,s^{-1}$

**8.14**

**8.15** To provide a very large surface area for reaction.

**8.16** Air.

# Chapter 9

**9.1** The properties predicted for eka-silicon are close to those now known for germanium.

**9.2** **a** Elements may have several isotopes – atoms with the same number of protons but different numbers of neutrons and hence different masses. The mass of an isotope of an element is the same as its nucleon number. This equals the number of protons plus the number of neutrons. The relative atomic mass of the element is the 'weighted average' of the nucleon numbers of its isotopes.

**b** Tellurium and iodine have several isotopes each. The weighted average $A_r$ of tellurium is higher than the average for iodine. Thus, in a table based on relative atomic masses only, tellurium would have been placed higher than iodine.

**9.3** **a** C $1s^2\,2s^2\,2p^2$    Si $1s^2\,2s^2\,2p^6\,3s^2\,3p^2$

**b** Both outer shell configurations are $s^2\,p^2$.

**c** Ge also in Group IV so outer shell is $s^2\,p^2$.

**9.4** The noble gases exist only as individual atoms, not in molecules.

**9.5** Both $P_4$ and $S_8$ are molecular structures with weak bonds between the molecules and these are fairly easily separated at relatively low temperatures. Their molecular masses, however, are much higher than for $Cl_2$ molecules. More energy is needed to move $P_4$ or $S_8$ molecules into the vapour phase than $Cl_2$ molecules. $S_8$ and $P_4$ do not boil until a higher temperature than the boiling point of $Cl_2$.

**9.6** In general, if the attractive forces between the particles are high, more energy is needed to overcome these forces and the melting point is high.

**a** These elements all have a metallic structure. The metallic bonding is stronger moving from sodium to aluminium as there are more outer shell electrons available to be mobile and take part in the bonding.

**b** Silicon has a giant covalent lattice structure like diamond. The melting point is high as the bonding is very strong.

**c** These elements exist as non-polar small molecules (sulphur and chlorine) or as separate atoms (argon). Only weak van der Waals' forces are present, so the melting points are low.

**9.7** **a** Group I to Group III elements are all metals with metallic structure and bonding. The number of shell $n = 3$ electrons which are available to join the conduction band increases from one to three per atom and this gives greater electrical conductivity.

**b** This is due to their metallic structures, with one or more electrons per atom joining a conduction band, which allows electrons to move throughout the whole structure. The p-block elements are molecular in structure with electrons kept in strong covalent bonds; their conductivity is much lower than the conductivity of metals.

**9.8** **a** Electronic configurations are:
Na  $1s^2\,2s^2\,2p^6\,3s^1$
Mg  $1s^2\,2s^2\,2p^6\,3s^2$
Al  $1s^2\,2s^2\,2p^6\,3s^2\,3p^1$
Mg has a higher nuclear charge than Na. This makes it more difficult to remove a 3s electron and thus Mg has a higher first ionisation energy. Al has a lower first ionisaton energy than Mg as the electron being removed is in a 3p orbital, a little further from the nuclear charge (and of higher energy) than the 3s orbital.

**b** Si  $1s^2\,2s^2\,2p^6\,3s^2\,3p^2$
P  $1s^2\,2s^2\,2p^6\,3s^2\,3p^3$
S  $1s^2\,2s^2\,2p^6\,3s^2\,3p^4$
The general increase in ionisation energy is mainly due to the effect of the increasing nuclear charge on the 3p electrons. The first ionisation energy of S is slightly lower than that of P for the same reason as the first ionisation energy of oxygen is lower than that of nitrogen (see text).

**9.9** Francium is the most likely: it has only one electron in an s orbital, distant from the nucleus and well screened by several filled inner shells.

**9.10** **a** Between the fifth and sixth successive ionisation energies.

**b** Group VII (the element is fluorine).

**9.11** Burns with a red flame; white solid produced.
$Ca(s) + \frac{1}{2}O_2(g) \rightarrow CaO(s)$

**9.12** $2S(s) + 3O_2(g) \rightarrow 2SO_3(g)$

**9.13** $Ca(s) + Cl_2(g) \rightarrow CaCl_2(s)$

**9.14** A colourless liquid, $PCl_3$, would be formed.

**9.15** a $Mg(s) + H_2O(g) \rightarrow MgO(s) + H_2(g)$
b $Mg(s) + 2H_2O(l) \rightarrow Mg(OH)_2(aq) + H_2(g)$

**9.16** a Giant ionic lattice
b Simple molecular
c Giant ionic lattice

**9.17** pH 7, neutral

**9.18** a hydrolysis reaction
b $SiCl_4(l) + 2H_2O(l) \rightarrow SiO_2(s) + 4HCl(g)$
or $SiCl_4(l) + 4H_2O(l) \rightarrow Si(OH)_4(aq) + 4HCl(g)$
c White fumes given off, exothermic, white solid produced.

# Chapter 10

**10.1** a (i) the metallic radii increase from element to element down the Group;
(ii) the first ionisation energies decrease from element to element down the Group.
b (i) the radii increase as additional shells of electrons are added going down the Group from magnesium to barium.
(ii) the electron removed is further from the nucleus and shielded by the inner filled shells of electrons. The distance and shielding effects together are able to reduce the effect of the increasing nuclear charge from element to element down the Group. Hence the ionisation energy decreases from element to element down the group.
c As less energy is needed to remove an electron going down the Group from magnesium to barium, the electronegativity will also decrease from element to element down the Group.

**10.2** Magnesium oxide.
0.33 g

**10.3** a $2Sr(s) + O_2(g) \rightarrow 2SrO(s)$
b The metal burns with a red flame and a white solid is formed.
c Each strontium atom loses two electrons and changes oxidation state from 0 to +2. Strontium is oxidised.
Each oxygen atom gains two electrons and changes oxidation state from 0 to −2. Oxygen is reduced.
d Two electrons are lost from each metal atom in the reaction. Down the Group, the first two ionisation energies decrease from magnesium to barium. Consequently, the reactivity of the metals increase increase down the Group as less energy is required to remove the two electrons.

**10.4** a Calcium carbonate dissolves rapidly in dilute hydrochloric acid with the evolution of carbon dioxide.
$CaCO_3(s) + 2HCl(g) \rightarrow CaCl_2(aq) + H_2O(l) + CO_2(g)$
b The calcium hydroxide contains hydroxide ions which will neutralise the acidity in the soil.
c $Mg(OH)_2(s) + 2HCl(g) \rightarrow MgCl_2(aq) + 2H_2O(l)$

# Chapter 11

**11.1** Yes. Lead has a typically metallic appearance, but carbon (either graphite or diamond) does not look metallic.

**11.2** a

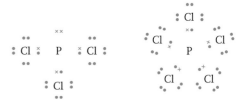

b A phosphorus atom has five electrons in its outermost shell.
■ In $PCl_3$, there is one lone pair and the remaining three electrons form covalent bonds with three chlorine atoms, as shown in the diagram.
■ In $PCl_5$, expansion of the octet occurs. Each of the five electrons in a phosphorus atom forms a covalent bond with each of five chlorine atoms.
■ Expansion of the octet is able to occur because in a phosphorus atom the d orbital is available for holding the extra electrons.

**11.3** Electron-pair repulsion theory predicts that four covalent bonds and no lone pairs will give a regular tetrahedral shape.

**11.4** The bond length increases and the bond strength decreases.

**11.5** Nitric acid. Lead(II) nitrate is soluble. If sulphuric acid is used, insoluble lead(II) sulphate is formed; likewise insoluble lead(II) chloride is formed if hydrochloric acid is used.

**11.6** Yes, this is a redox reaction. Sulphur is oxidised and lead is reduced.

**11.7** No. Tin displaces lead.

# Chapter 12

**12.1** 0, −1, +7, +4

**12.2** See *figure*.

$$\left[Na\right]^{+} \quad \left[\begin{array}{c} {}^{\times\times} \\ {}^{\times}_{\bullet}Cl{}^{\times}_{\times} \\ {}^{\times\times} \end{array}\right]^{-}$$

$$H \overset{\times}{\bullet} Cl \overset{\bullet\bullet}{\underset{\bullet\bullet}{\bullet}}$$

**12.3** The halogens have covalent bonds and they are non-polar molecules. Polar molecules dissolve best in water, which is itself polar. Non-polar molecules dissolve best in non-polar solvents.

**12.4** **a** The orange cyclohexane layer would turn purple:
$Br_2(aq) + 2I^-(aq) \rightarrow 2Br^-(aq) + I_2(aq)$

**b** No change.

**c** Given its position in Group VII, we would expect astatine to be darker in colour than iodine. The orange cyclohexane would turn this dark colour of astatine:
$Br_2(aq) + 2At^-(aq) \rightarrow 2Br^-(aq) + At_2(aq)$

# Chapter 13

**13.1** **a** $[Ar]3d^54s^1$

**b** $[Ar]3d^3$

**c** $[Ar]3d^{10}4s^1$

**d** $[Ar]3d^9$

**e** $[Ar]3d^54s^2$

**f** $[Ar]3d^5$

**13.2** **a** +6          **b** +3

**13.3** **a** See *figure*.

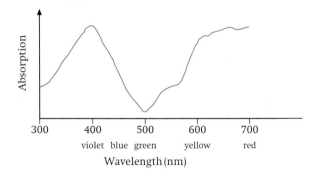

**b** green

**c** $Ni^{2+}$

**13.4** **a** $Ni^{2+}(aq) + 2OH^-(aq) \rightarrow Ni(OH)_2(s)$

**b** $Ti^{3+}(aq) + 3OH^-(aq) \rightarrow Ti(OH)_3(s)$

**13.5** **a** $[FeCl_4]^-$

**b** $[Ti(H_2O)_6]^{3+}$

**13.6** **a** octahedral

**b** octahedral

**c** tetrahedral

**13.7** The colour changes as the $NH_3$ ligands substitute $H_2O$ ligands. (The complexes involved are $[Ni(H_2O)_6]^{2+}$, which is green, and $[Ni(NH_3)_6]^{2+}$ which is dark blue.)

**13.8** **a** a volumetric pipette

**b** a burette

**13.9** 1 $Ni^{2+}$:1 edta

**13.10** $6Fe^{2+} + Cr_2O_7^{2-} + 14H^+ \rightarrow 6Fe^{3+} + 2Cr^{3+} + 7H_2O$

**13.11** **a** 0.28g

**b** 67%

**13.12** **a** yes $E_{cell}^{\ominus}$ = +0.18 V although this value is lower than 0.30 V (see chapter 6) the loss of chlorine from the solution will drive the equilibria to form more chlorine.

**b** no $E_{cell}^{\ominus}$ = +0.03 V for chlorine oxidising chromium(III) ions.

# Chapter 14

**14.1** **a** In a thunderstorm the electrical discharge (lightning) between $N_2$ and $O_2$ is of high energy and breaks the $N \equiv N$ bond.

**b** In a car engine, the high temperature and high pressure are sufficient to overcome the activation energy of the reaction between $N_2$ and $O_2$.

**14.2** Bacteria contain enzymes which catalyse the formation of nitrate ions from nitrogen.

**14.3** $CO_2$ is an acidic oxide, dissolving in water to form carbonic acid, $H_2CO_3$. In the reaction with ammonia, in the absence of water, a base, $NH_3$, reacts with an acidic oxide.

**14.4** Petrol and diesel fuel contain small quantities of sulphur. When these fuels are burned in an internal combustion engine, the sulphur present forms $SO_2$.

**14.5** In the oxidation of $SO_2$ to $SO_3$, the NO is initially used up to give $NO_2$ and then re-formed.

# Chapter 15

**15.1** See *figure*.

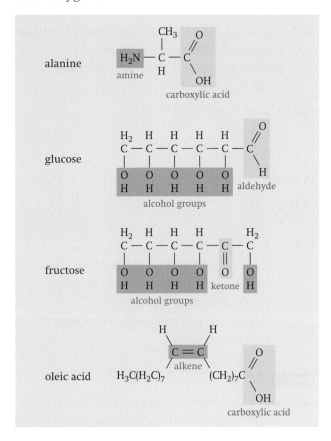

**15.2** a  A  heptane
    B  3-methylhexane
    C  cyclopentane
    D  pentan-3-ol
    E  pentan-2-one
    F  2-methylbutanoic acid
    G  2,2-dimethylpropanal
  b  See *figure*.

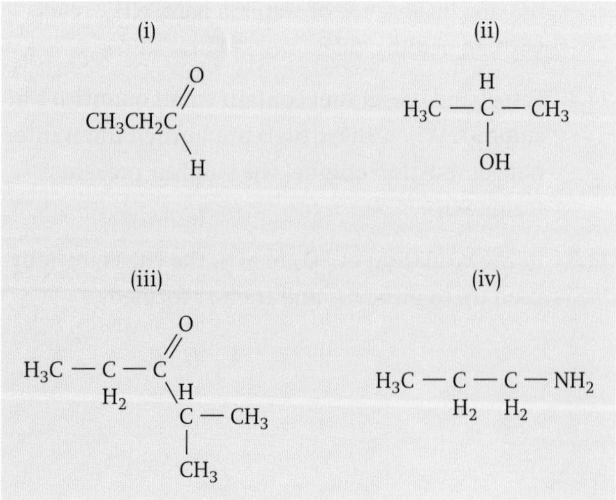

(i)

$$CH_3CH_2C\overset{O}{\underset{H}{\diagdown}}$$

(ii)

$$H_3C - \underset{\underset{OH}{|}}{\overset{\overset{H}{|}}{C}} - CH_3$$

(iii)

$$H_3C - \underset{H_2}{\overset{}{C}} - C\overset{O}{\underset{\underset{CH_3}{|}}{\underset{C-CH_3}{\diagdown}}}H$$

(iv)

$$H_3C - \underset{H_2}{\overset{}{C}} - \underset{H_2}{\overset{}{C}} - NH_2$$

**15.3** See *figure*.

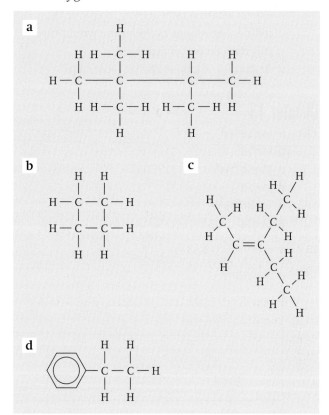

a

b  $(CH_3)_3CCl$

c

d  $C_4H_9Cl$

e

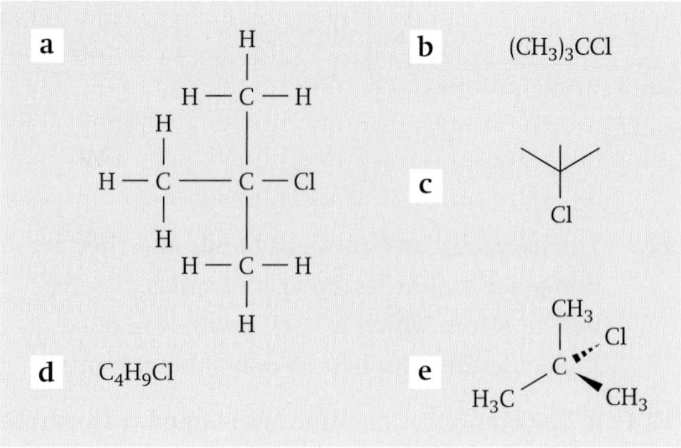

**15.4** See *figure*.

a

b

c

d

**15.5** As 12 g of carbon are present in 1 mol
(= 44 g) $CO_2$,

mass of carbon in $= \dfrac{12}{44} \times 0.4800$ g
0.4800 g of $CO_2$

$= 0.1309$ g

$=$ mass of carbon in **W**

As 2 g of hydrogen are present in 1 mol
(= 18 g) $H_2O$,

mass of hydrogen $= \dfrac{2}{18} \times 0.1636$ g
in 0.1636 g of $H_2O$

$= 0.0182$ g

$=$ mass of hydrogen in **W**

As 14 g of nitrogen are present in 1 mol
(= 17 g) $NH_3$,

mass of nitrogen in $= \dfrac{14}{17} \times 0.0618$ g
0.0618 g of $NH_3$

$= 0.0509$ g

$=$ mass of nitrogen in **W**

Hence

mass of C, H and N $= \begin{array}{l}(0.1309 + 0.0182 \\ + 0.0509)\,\text{g}\end{array}$
in 0.2000 g of **W**

$= 0.2000$ g

As this is the same as the total mass of the sample, **W** contains only C, H and N.

Now we calculate the numbers of moles of C, H and N:

|  | **C** | **H** | **N** |
|---|---|---|---|
| Mass (g) | 0.1309 | 0.0182 | 0.0509 |
| Amount (mol) | 0.1309/12 $= 1.091 \times 10^{-2}$ | 0.0182/1 $= 1.82 \times 10^{-2}$ | 0.0509/14 $= 3.636 \times 10^{-3}$ |

Divide by the smallest amount to give whole numbers:

| Atoms (mol) | 3 | 5 | 1 |
|---|---|---|---|

Hence the empirical formula of **W** is $C_3H_5N$.

**15.6** 1 mol of butan-1-ol will produce 1 mol of 1-bromobutane. The quantity of butan-1-ol will determine the yield as the other reagents are in excess.

1 mol of butan-1-ol, $C_4H_9OH$, has a relative molecular mass of

$4 \times 12 + 9 \times 1 + 1 \times 16 + 1 = 74$ g

1 mol of 1-bromobutane, $C_4H_9Br$, has a relative molecular mass of

$4 \times 12 + 9 \times 1 + 80 = 137$ g

Hence

maximum yield of $= 10 \times \dfrac{137}{74} = 18.5$ g
1-bromobutane

percentage yield $= \dfrac{12}{18.5} \times 100 = 65\%$

**15.7** See *figure*.

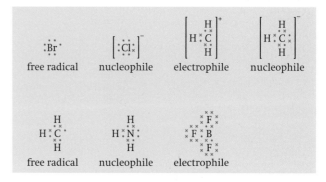

Free radicals have seven outer-shell electrons, electrophiles have six and nucleophiles have eight.

**15.8** See *figure*.

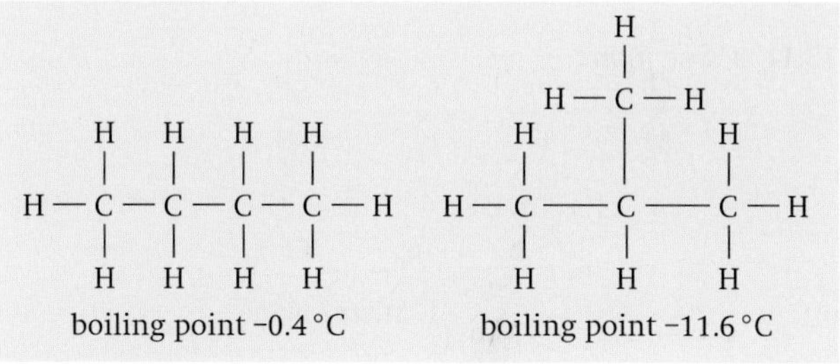

boiling point –0.4 °C        boiling point –11.6 °C

**15.9** See *figure*.

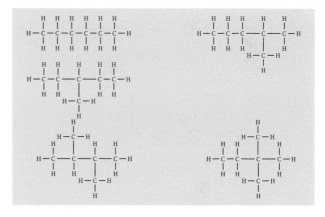

**15.10** See *figure*.

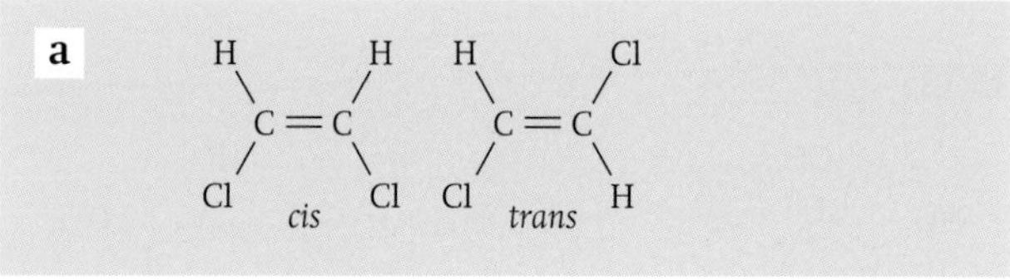

**b**

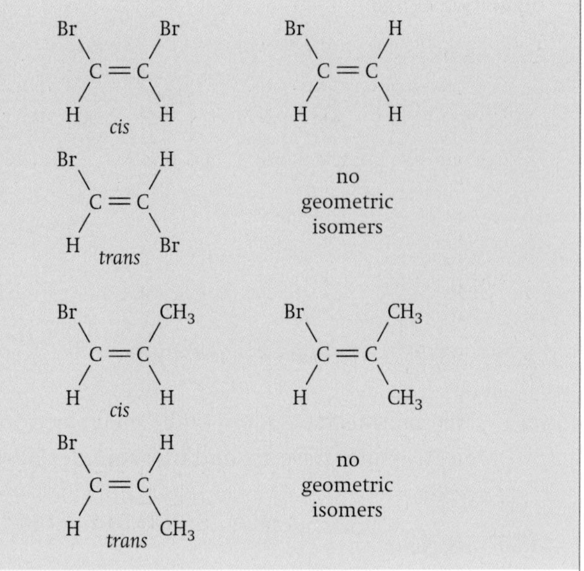

**15.11 a** See *figure*.

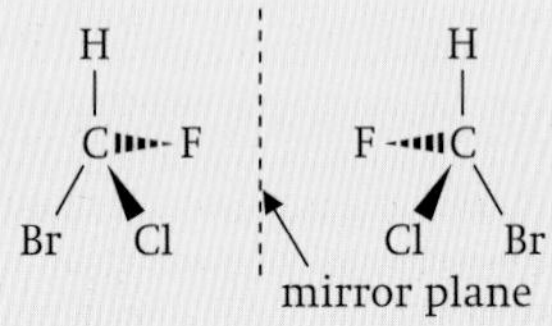

**b** See *figure*.

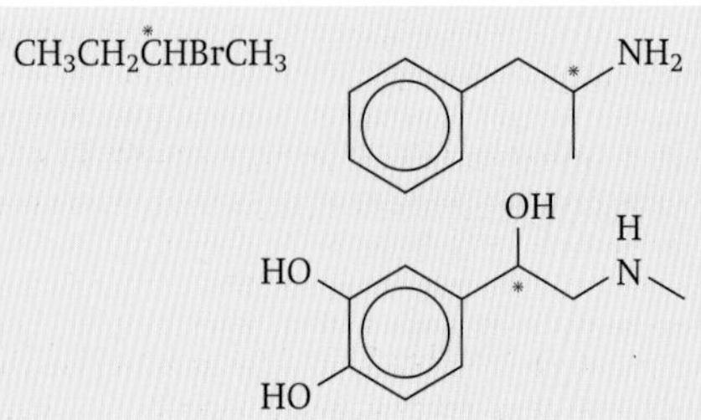

**15.12**

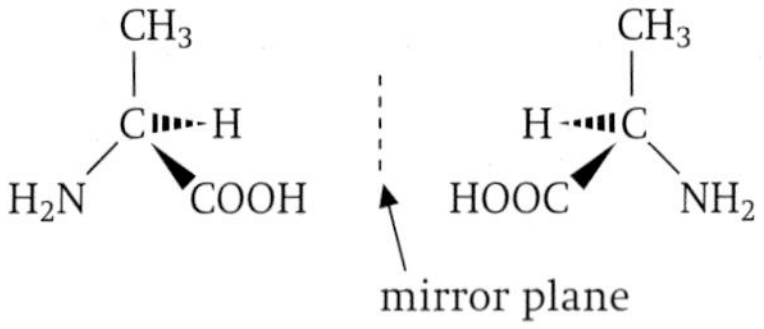

**15.13**

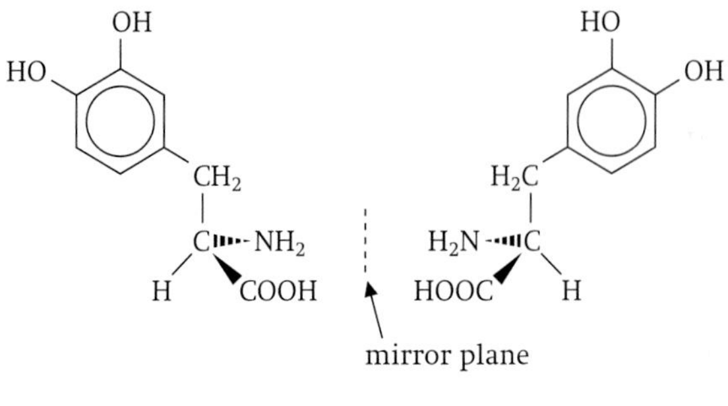

L-dopa          D-dopa

**15.14** See *figure*.

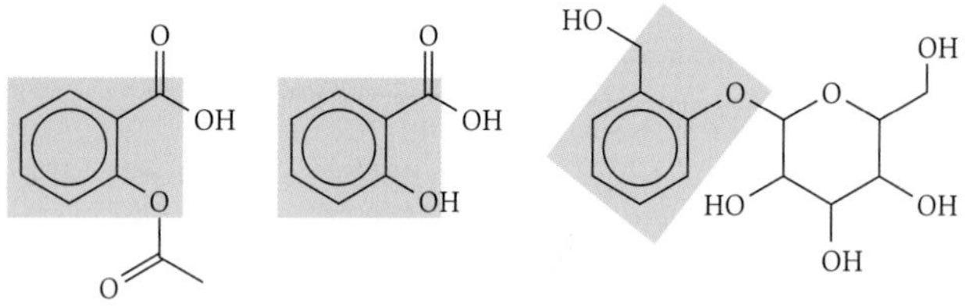

aspirin        2-hydroxybenzoic acid        salicin
               (salicylic acid)

**15.15 A and C.**

**15.16 B.**

**15.17 a**

$$H_2C=CH_2 \xrightarrow{HCl(aq)} CH_3CH_2Cl \xrightarrow[\text{under pressure}]{\text{heat with alcoholic ammonia}} CH_3CH_2NH_2$$

**b**

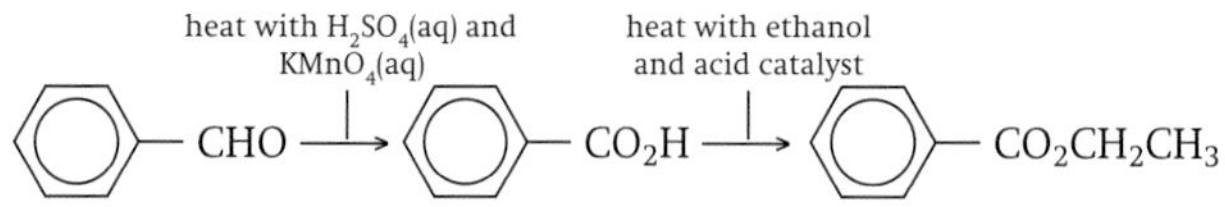

**c**

$$CH_3CH_2CH_2Br \xrightarrow[\text{and ethanol}]{\text{reflux with NaCN(aq)}} CH_3CH_2CH_2CN \xrightarrow{\text{reflux with HCl(aq)}} CH_3CH_2CH_2CO_2H$$

**d**

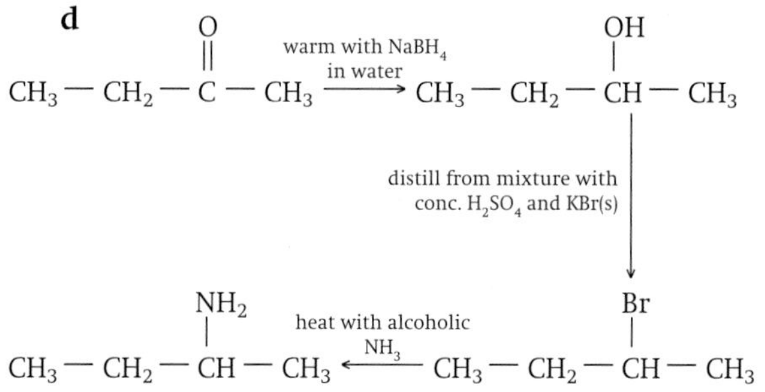

**15.18**

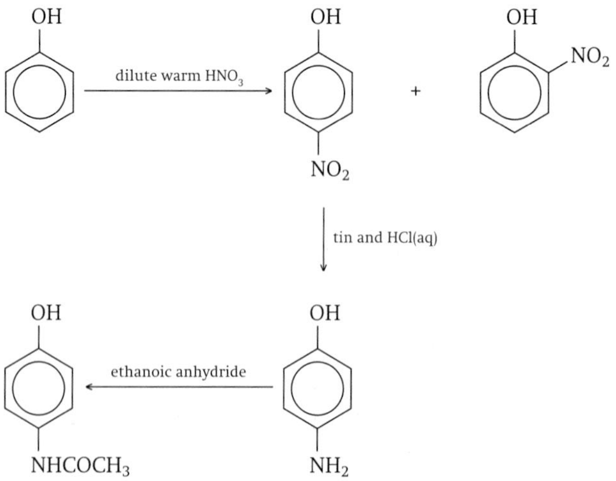

**15.19** $CH_3CH_2OH \xrightarrow[\text{acidified dichromate}]{\text{reflux with excess}} CH_3COOH$

$CH_3COOH + CH_3CH_2OH \xrightarrow[\text{acid catalyst}]{\text{heat}} CH_3COOCH_2CH_3 + H_2O$

For the investigation:

1 Effect of temperature: try equal amounts of ethanol and ethanoic acid **a** with reflux and **b** without reflux.

2 Effect of a catalyst: repeat experiment **1** for each of the following acid catalysts (five drops of the catalyst are sufficient): **a** $H_2SO_4$, **b** $H_3PO_4$ and **c** HCl.

3 Repeat experiments **1** and **2** to check the results.

4 Effect of changing concentration: repeat the experiment that gave the best yield, but this time use excess ethanol. Repeat again with excess ethanoic acid. Repeat this step to check the results.

**15.20** $CH_3CH_2OH + HBr \rightarrow CH_3CH_2Br + H_2O$

$M_r$ for ethanol is 46; for hydrogen bromide it is 81. Hence 2.0 g of hydrogen bromide require:

$\dfrac{46}{81} \times 2.0 = 1.14$ g of ethanol.

**15.21 a** Optical isomerism.

$$\begin{array}{cc}
\text{OH} & \text{OH} \\
| & | \\
C\text{···}H & H\text{···}C \\
H_3C \quad COOH & HOOC \quad CH_3
\end{array}$$

mirror plane

**b** (i) The mechanism is as follows.

$$H_3C \atop H \diagdown \underset{\delta+}{C}=\underset{\delta-}{O} \longrightarrow H-\overset{CH_3}{\underset{CN}{C}}-O\bar{:}$$

:CN⁻

$$H-\overset{CH_3}{\underset{CN}{C}}-O\bar{:} \quad H-CN \longrightarrow H-\overset{CH_3}{\underset{CN}{C}}-OH + :CN⁻$$

(ii) The reaction is catalysed by the presence of a base. Hydrogen cyanide is a very weak acid and the presence of a base increases the concentration of cyanide ions.

(iii) The nucleophilic attack can occur from either side of the ethanal molecule, resulting in equimolar amounts of the two isomers.

# Chapter 16

**16.1** See *figure*.

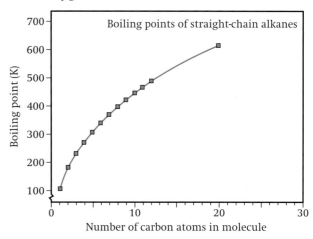

Boiling points of straight-chain alkanes

Both graphs show a gradually diminishing increase in the melting and boiling points of the alkanes with increasing chain length.

**16.2 a** The lack of polarity of alkane molecules means that only weak instantaneous dipole-induced dipole (van der Waals') force are present between molecules.

**b** As the number of electrons increases in the molecule (with increasing numbers of atoms), the strength of these forces also increases. More energy is needed to separate the atoms when melting the solid or boiling the liquid, so the melting and boiling points rise with increasing number of carbon atoms.

**16.3 a** (i) $C_8H_{18}(l) + 8.5O_2(g) \rightarrow 8CO(g) + 9H_2O(l)$
(ii) $C_8H_{18}(l) + 12.5O_2(g) \rightarrow 8CO_2(g) + 9H_2O(l)$
**b** (i) $12.5 - 8.5 = 4$ moles $O_2(g)$
(ii) Volume of oxygen $= 4 \times 24.0 = 96\,dm^3$.
Volume of air $= 96 \times 100/20 = 480\,dm^3$

**16.4 a** $Br_2(l)$ and $Cl_2(g)$ only – the others are in aqueous solution and are already ionised.
**b** $C_4H_{10}(g) + Br_2(l) \rightarrow C_4H_9Br(l) + HBr(g)$
$C_4H_{10}(g) + Cl_2(g) \rightarrow C_4H_9Cl(l) + HCl(g)$

**16.5** See *figure*.

$$\underset{H}{\overset{H}{\diagup}}C \overset{\times\times}{\underset{\times\times}{:}} C\underset{H}{\overset{H}{\diagdown}}$$

$$\underset{H}{\overset{H}{\diagdown}}C = C\overset{H}{\underset{H}{\diagup}} \quad 121° \quad 119°$$

molecule is planar

**16.6 a** D and E can also exist as *cis–trans* isomers.

**b**

CH$_3$CH$_2$ / CH$_3$
C=C
H / H
*cis*-pent-2-ene

CH$_3$CH$_2$ / H
C=C
H / CH$_3$
*trans*-pent-2-ene

**16.7** See *figure*.

**a**

H H
H × C × C × H
× Br ×  ⊕

The positive carbon atom has six electrons in its outer shell. It gains two more by accepting a lone-pair from the bromide ion.

**b**

H   H
C=C
H ↓ H
H δ+
Cl δ−

→

H H
│ │
H—C—C—H
│ ⊕ │
H
Cl:⊖

→

H H
│ │
H—C—C—H
│ │
H Cl

**c** CH$_2$ClCH$_2$Br

**d** Cl$_2$ — Electrophile, polarisable like Br$_2$.

Na$^+$ — No; does not usually form a covalent bond.

F$^-$ — No; negative charge, hence repelled by electron-rich centre.

H$_2$ — No; not sufficiently polarisable.

SO$_3$ — Electrophile, as sulphur will accept more electrons to form a new covalent bond.

ICl — Electrophile, as polar; iodine is positive (electrophilic) end of molecule.

**16.8 a** See *figure*.

H       Cl
$n$  C=C
H       H
chloroethene

→

H Cl
│ │
—C—C—
│ │
H H   $n$
poly(chloroethene)

H
$n$  C=C⟨ring⟩
H   H
phenylethene

→

⟨ring⟩
H │
—C—C—
│ │
H H   $n$
poly(phenylethene)

**b** See *figure*.

**(i)**

H   H
│   │
—C———C—
│   │
H   H—C—H
│
H       $n$
poly(propene)

**(ii)**

H       H
C=C ⟨H⟩
H       C
H H
propene

**16.9**

Possible reactions include:

CH$_3$CH$_2$CH$_2$CH$_2$CH$_3$ ⟶ CH$_3$CH$_2$CH$_3$ + H$_2$C=CH$_2$

⟶ CH$_3$CH$_2$CH$_2$CH=CH$_2$ + H$_2$

⟶ CH$_3$CH$_2$CH=CHCH$_3$ + H$_2$

⟶ CH$_3$CH$_3$ + CH$_3$CH=CH$_2$

⟶ CH$_2$=CHCH=CHCH$_3$ + 2H$_2$

⟶ H$_3$C—C—C=CH$_2$ + H$_2$
         │ H
        CH$_3$

**16.10** C(s) + O$_2$(g) → CO$_2$(g)
CH$_4$(g) + 2O$_2$(g) → CO$_2$(g) + 2H$_2$O(l)
C$_8$H$_{18}$(l) + 12.5O$_2$(g) → 8CO$_2$(g) + 9H$_2$O(l)
CH$_3$OH(g) + 1.5O$_2$(g) → CO$_2$(g) + 2H$_2$O(l)
2H$_2$(g) + O$_2$(g) → 2H$_2$O(l)

**16.11** A kilogram of hydrogen contains 500 moles of H$_2$(g), whereas a kilogram of methane contains 62.5 moles of CH$_4$(g).

**16.12 a** The volume of a liquid is much smaller than the volume of a gas of the same mass.

**b** A spherical shape gives the lowest surface area for the container of any given volume of liquid or gas. This saves material for making the container, and helps to keep the surface area of contents, affected by heating from the Sun, as small as possible.

**16.13** 2NO$_2$(g) + H$_2$O(l) → HNO$_2$(aq) + HNO$_3$(aq)
                    nitrous acid    nitric acid

SO$_2$(g) + H$_2$O(l) → H$_2$SO$_3$(aq)
                    sulphurous acid

SO$_3$(g) + H$_2$O(l) → H$_2$SO$_4$(aq)
                    sulphuric acid

**16.14 a**

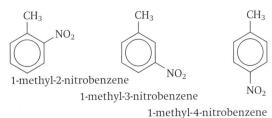

1-methyl-2-nitrobenzene

1-methyl-3-nitrobenzene

1-methyl-4-nitrobenzene

**b**

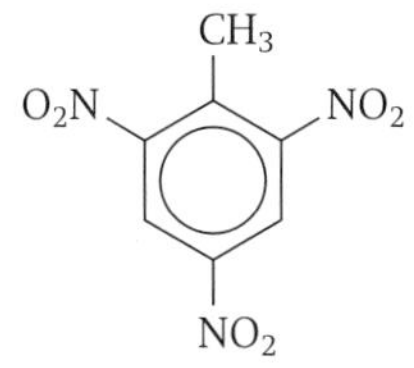

1-methyl-2,4,6-trinitrobenzene (TNT)

**16.15** See *figure.*

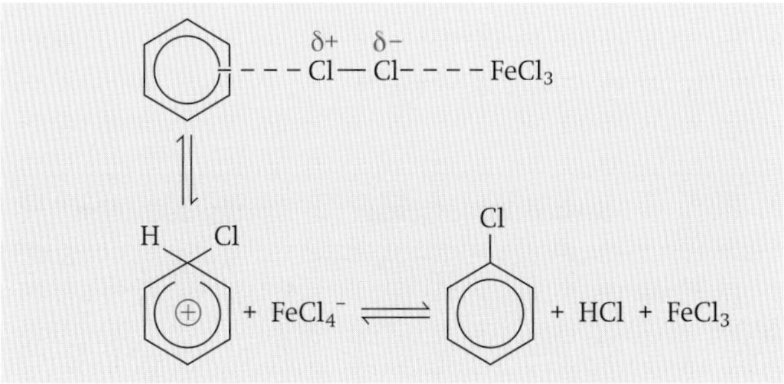

**16.16 a** anhydrous iron(III) chloride or anhydrous aluminium chloride .

**b** 2-chloro-2-methylpropane and benzene.

**c**

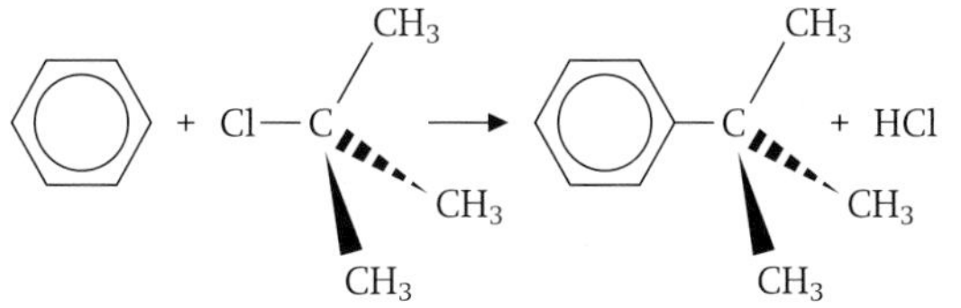

**16.17 a** The attacking species involved in the addition to benzene is a free radical.

**b** The attacking species involved in the addition of chlorine to an alkene is an electrophile.

# Chapter 17

**17.1** $CH_3CH_2CH_2I$: 1-iodopropane;
$CH_3CHBrCH_3$: 2-bromopropane;
$CBrF_2CBrF_2$: 1,2-dibromo-1,1,2,2-tetrafluoroethane.

**17.2** Structural isomerism.

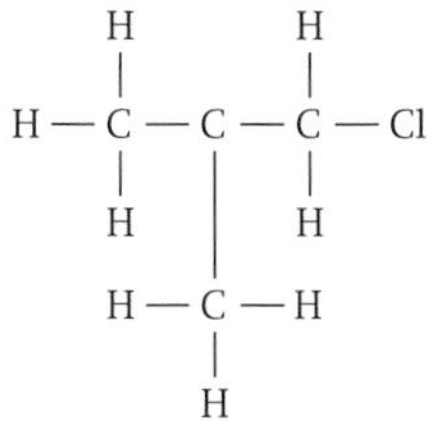

1 chloro-2-methylpropane (primary)

**17.3 a** 1-chloropropane is polar and has dipole–dipole intermolecular forces that are stronger then the instantaneous dipole-induced dipole forces in non-polar butane. More energy is needed to overcome the intermolecular forces in 1-chlorobutane, so its boiling point is higher.

**b** 1-chloropropane attracts water molecules by dipole–dipole forces that are weaker than the hydrogen bonds in water. An input of energy would be required for 1-chloropropane to mix with water and break some of these hydrogen bonds.

**17.4**

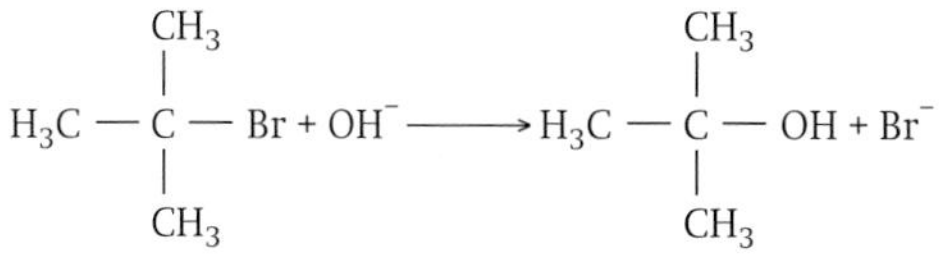

2-methylpropan-2-ol

**17.5** Ammonia behaves as a nucleophile because the nitrogen atom possesses a lone-pair of electrons, which will form a covalent bond to carbon:

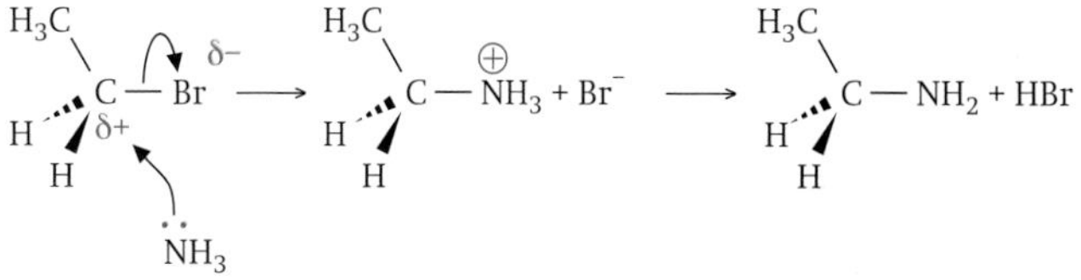

The hydrogen bromide will be neutralised by excess ammonia to form ammonium bromide:

$HBr + NH_3 \rightarrow NH_4Br$

# Chapter 18

**18.1** Energy is absorbed when a bond is broken.
In order from strongest to weakest:
$E(O–H) > E(C–H) > E(C–O) > E(C–C)$

**18.2 a** C–O.

**b** The oxygen atom is very electronegative compared to hydrogen or carbon.

**c** An electrophile has a positively charged atom, which is attracted by an electron-rich centre. A nucleophile has a lone-pair of electrons, which is attracted to a positively charged centre.

**18.3** See *figure.*

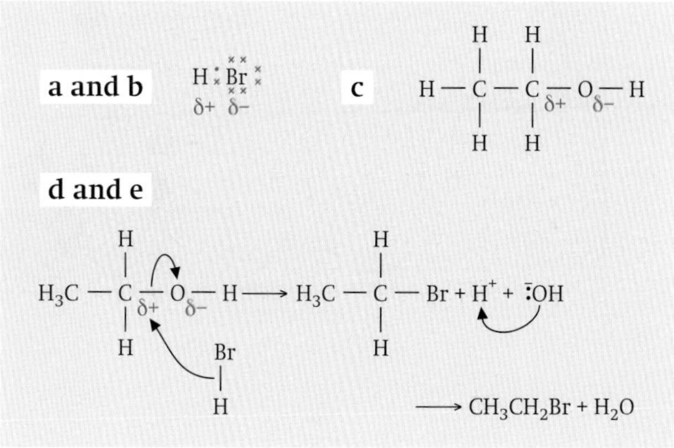

**18.4** The hydrolysis of bromoethane requires aqueous ethanolic alkali and heat. The reverse reaction requires distillation with an excess of sodium bromide and concentrated sulphuric acid (no water is added). In the forward reaction, excess of water moves the reaction in the direction of hydrolysis. In the reverse reaction, absence of water and excess of hydrogen bromide (generated from the concentrated sulphuric acid and sodium bromide) moves the reaction towards the formation of bromoethane.

**18.6 a**

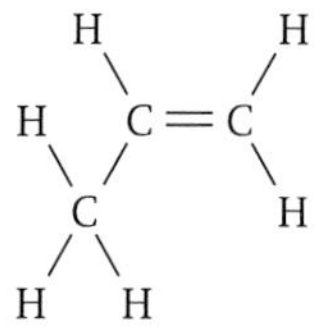

**b** $CH_3CH(OH)CH_3 \rightarrow CH_3CH=CH_2 + H_2O$

**18.7 a**

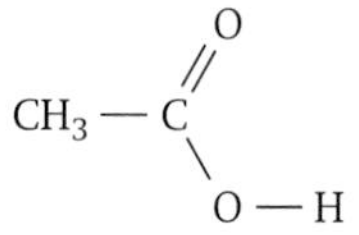

**b** C=O at $1710\,cm^{-1}$, strong and sharp.

**18.5**

| Alcohol | Molecular model | Structural formula | Classification |
|---|---|---|---|
| **a** pentan-1-ol | 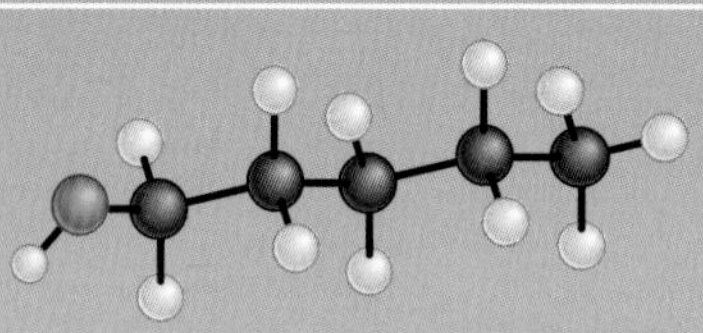 | $CH_3CH_2CH_2CH_2CH_2OH$ | primary |
| **b** pentan-2-ol | | $CH_3CH_2CH_2\overset{\overset{\textstyle OH}{\textstyle \|}}{C}HCH_3$ | secondary |
| **c** 2-methylbutan-2-ol | | $CH_3CH_2\overset{\overset{\textstyle CH_3}{\textstyle \|}}{\underset{\underset{\textstyle OH}{\textstyle \|}}{C}}CH_3$ | tertiary |
| **d** 3-methylbutan-1-ol | 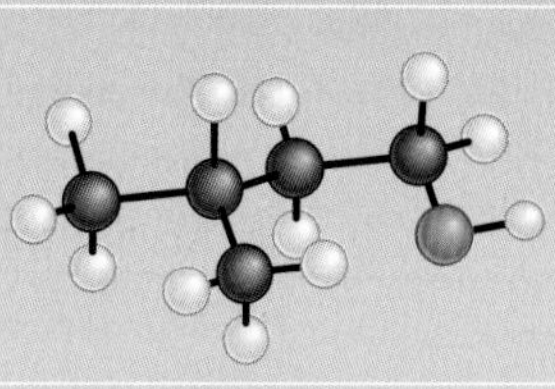 | $CH_3\overset{\overset{\textstyle CH_3}{\textstyle \|}}{C}HCH_2CH_2OH$ | primary |
| **e** 3-methylbutan-2-ol | | $CH_3\overset{\overset{\textstyle CH_3}{\textstyle \|}}{C}H-\overset{\overset{}{\underset{\underset{\textstyle OH}{\textstyle \|}}{}}}{C}HCH_3$ | secondary |
| **f** 2-methylbutan-1-ol | 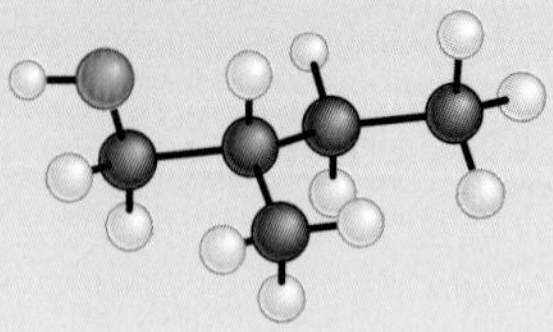 | $CH_3CH_2\overset{\overset{\textstyle CH_3}{\textstyle \|}}{C}HCH_2OH$ | primary |

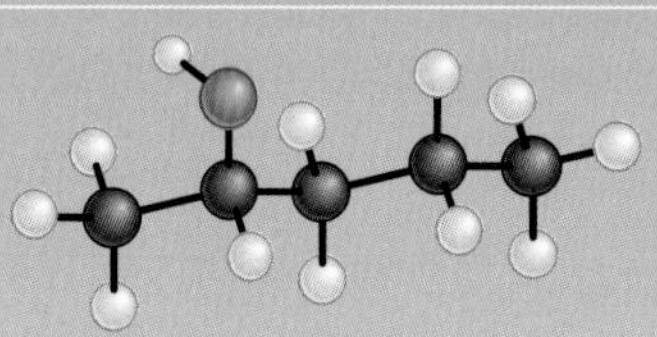

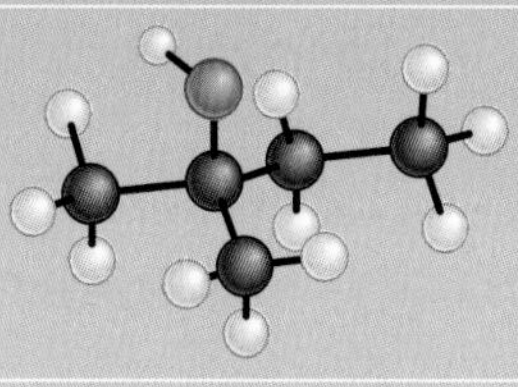

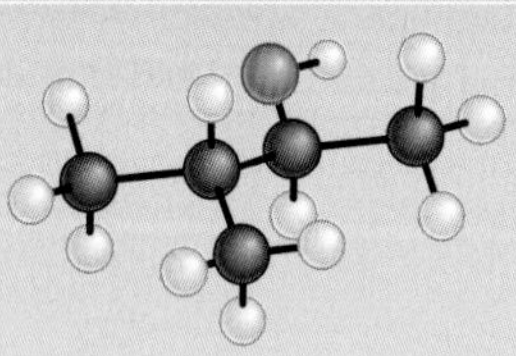

**18.8** In *figure 18.9* **a** is butanone as a strong, sharp absorption is present at 1710 cm$^{-1}$, characteristic of the C=O bond in butanone; **b** shows a strong, broad absorption at 3450 cm$^{-1}$, characteristic of the O–H bond in an alcohol.

**18.9** CHI$_3$ and HCOOH.

**18.10** See *figure*.

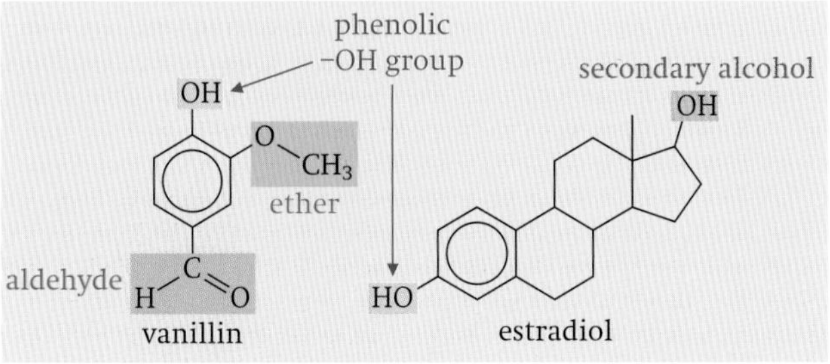

phenolic –OH group

OH

secondary alcohol

OH

O CH$_3$

ether

aldehyde

vanillin

estradiol

HO

**18.11** The bromine molecule is polarised by the delocalised π electrons on phenol. (The enhanced reactivity of the benzene ring, caused by the –OH group, is also required. Aqueous bromine will not react with benzene.)

# Chapter 19

**19.1** See *figure*.

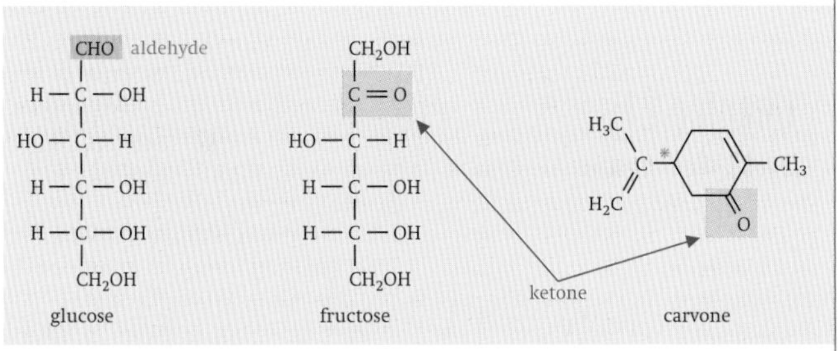

CHO aldehyde

H—C—OH

HO—C—H

H—C—OH

H—C—OH

CH$_2$OH

glucose

CH$_2$OH

C=O

HO—C—H

H—C—OH

H—C—OH

CH$_2$OH

fructose

ketone

H$_3$C

H$_2$C

CH$_3$

O

carvone

**19.2** **a** See *figure*.

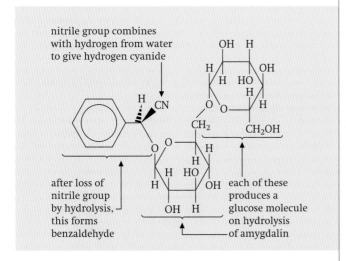

nitrile group combines with hydrogen from water to give hydrogen cyanide

after loss of nitrile group by hydrolysis, this forms benzaldehyde

each of these produces a glucose molecule on hydrolysis of amygdalin

**b** Hydrolysis involves the breaking of a covalent bond by reaction with water.

**19.3** The hydrocarbon part of the molecules is only attracted to other molecules by weak, instantaneous dipole–induced dipole forces. The carbonyl group has a permanent dipole and will hydrogen bond to water molecules. Aldehydes and ketones with less than four carbon atoms are miscible (they mix freely) with water because the intermolecular forces in the mixture are similar in strength to those in the separate liquids. As the length of the carbon chain is increased, the intermolecular forces in the organic compounds decrease and become too weak for the hydrogen bonding between water molecules to be disrupted.

**19.4** **a**

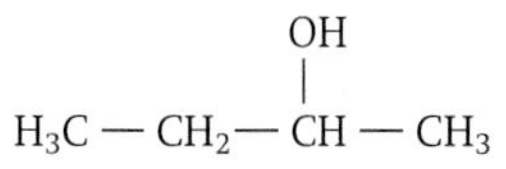

OH

H$_3$C — CH$_2$— CH — CH$_3$

**b**  H$_3$C — CH$_2$— CH$_2$— CH$_2$OH

**19.5**

H  H  H   O

H—C—C—C—C

H  H  H   O—H

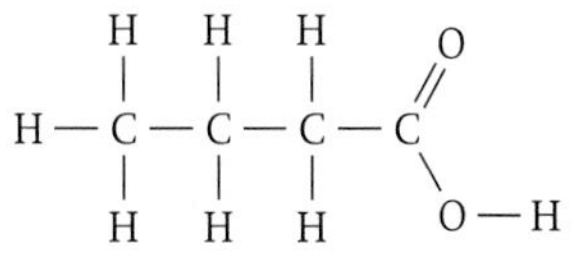

# Chapter 20

**20.1** **a** Ester.

**b** Carboxylic acid.

**c** Ester.

**20.2** **a** COOH

**b** COOH

**c** Octadeca-*cis*-9-*cis*-12-dienoic acid.

**d**

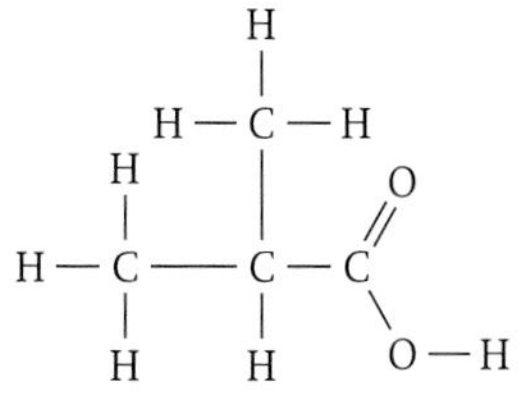

H

H—C—H

H           O

H—C—C—C

H   H   O—H

2-methylpropanoic acid

**e**

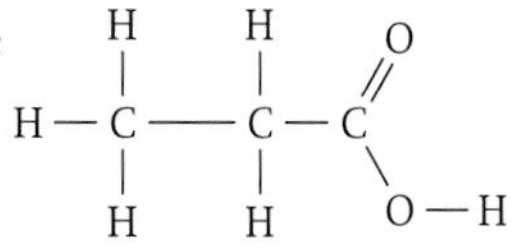

H   H   O

H—C—C—C

H   H   O—H

propanoic acid

**20.3**  **a**  Zn(s) + 2CH₃CH₂COOH(aq)
$$\rightarrow (CH_3CH_2COO)_2Zn(aq) + H_2(g)$$

**b**  Na₂CO₃(aq) + 2HCOOH(aq)
$$\rightarrow 2HCOONa(aq) + CO_2(g) + H_2O(l)$$

**c**  MgO(s) + 2CH₃COOH(aq)
$$\rightarrow (CH_3COO)_2Mg(aq) + H_2O(l)$$

**d**

$$\bigcirc\!\!-COOH(s) + NaOH(aq) \longrightarrow \bigcirc\!\!-COONa(aq) + H_2O(l)$$

**20.4**  **a**

methyl butanoate    propyl ethanoate    butyl methanoate

**b**

1-methylpropyl    2-methylpropyl    1,1-dimethylethyl
methanoate    methanoate    methanoate

1-methylethyl ethanoate    methyl 2-methylpropanoate

Pentanoic acid, CH₃CH₂CH₂CH₂COOH, and structural isomers of this and other acids.

Methoxybutan-2-one, CH₃OCH₂COCH₂CH₃, and structural isomers of this with an ether plus a ketone or an aldehyde group.

Cyclic isomers are also possible. For example:

**20.5**  **a**  (i)

$$CH_3-CH_2-C\overset{O}{\underset{O-CH}{\big<}}\overset{CH_3}{\underset{CH_3}{}}$$

(ii)  Propanoic acid and propan-2-ol.

(iii)

$$CH_3-CH_2-C\overset{O}{\underset{OH}{\big<}} + HO-CH\overset{CH_3}{\underset{CH_3}{}} \longrightarrow CH_3-CH_2-C\overset{O}{\underset{O-CH}{\big<}}\overset{CH_3}{\underset{CH_3}{}} + H_2O$$

**b**  (i)  Butyl methanoate.

(ii)

$$H-C\overset{O}{\underset{OH}{\big<}} + HO-CH_2CH_2CH_2CH_3 \longrightarrow H-C\overset{O}{\underset{O-CH_2CH_2CH_2CH_3}{\big<}} + H_2O$$

**20.6**  **a**

$$\bigcirc\!\!-COOCH_3(l) + NaOH(aq)$$
$$\longrightarrow \bigcirc\!\!-COONa(aq) + CH_3OH(l)$$
sodium benzoate    methanol

**b**  CH₃CH₂COOCH₃(l) + H₂O(l)
$$\rightarrow CH_3CH_2COOH(aq) + CH_3OH(l)$$
propanoic acid    methanol

**20.7**  **a**  Water;  **b**  esterification;  **c**  3.

**d**

$$\begin{array}{l} CH_2OH \\ | \\ CHOH \\ | \\ CH_2OH \end{array} + 3CH_3(CH_2)_{16}COOH \longrightarrow \begin{array}{l} H_2C-O \\ | \\ HC-O \\ | \\ H_2C-O \end{array} + 3H_2O$$

with $C-(CH_2)_{16}CH_3$ groups

**20.8**

$$CH_3CO\overset{OCH_3}{\underset{\big\|}{\bigcirc}}-CH_2CH=CH_2$$

# Chapter 21

**21.1**  See *figure*.

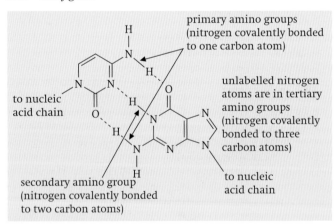

primary amino groups (nitrogen covalently bonded to one carbon atom)

unlabelled nitrogen atoms are in tertiary amino groups (nitrogen covalently bonded to three carbon atoms)

to nucleic acid chain

secondary amino group (nitrogen covalently bonded to two carbon atoms)

to nucleic acid chain

**21.2**

amide functional group

$$N-(CH_2)_6-N\overset{H}{\underset{}{}}-C\overset{O}{\underset{\big\|}{}}-(CH_2)_4-C-$$

repeat unit of a polyamide

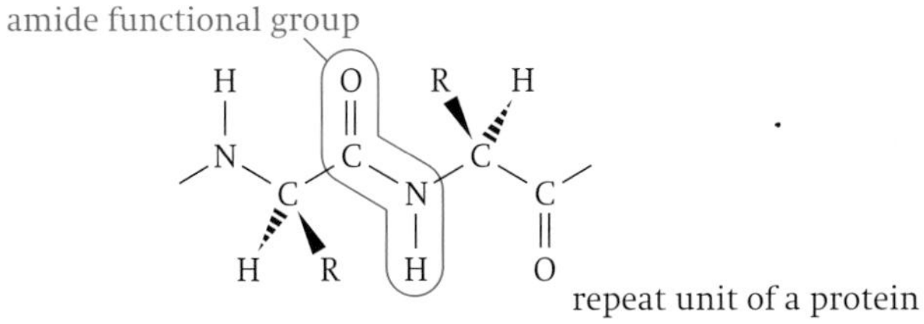

amide functional group

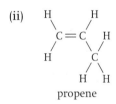

repeat unit of a protein

**21.3** **a** Propylamine, $CH_3CH_2CH_2NH_2$.

**b** 4-aminophenol,

$$H_2N-\langle\ \rangle-OH$$

**21.4** **a** $CH_3CH_2CH_2CH_2NH_2 + HNO_3$
$\rightarrow CH_3CH_2CH_2CH_2NH_3^+NO_3^-$

**b**
$H_2N-\langle\ \rangle-OH + HCl \longrightarrow {}^-Cl^+H_3N-\langle\ \rangle-OH$

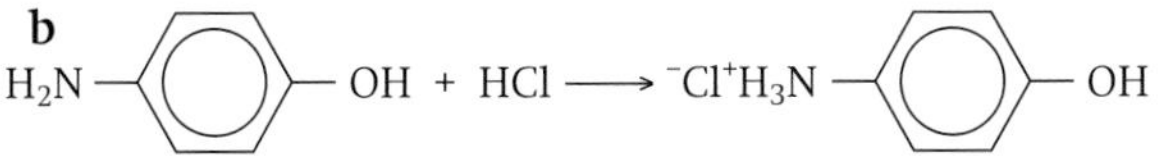

**c**
$H_2N-\langle\ \rangle-OH + NaOH \longrightarrow H_2N-\langle\ \rangle-O^-Na^+ + H_2O$

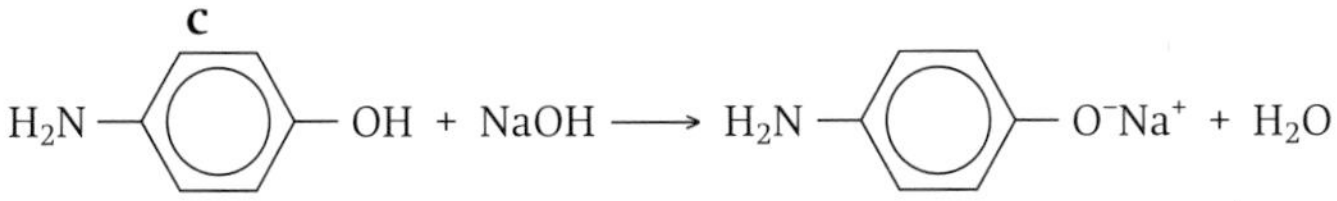

**21.5**

$H-O-\langle\ \rangle-N=N-\langle\ \rangle-O-H$

$HO-\langle\ \rangle-NH_2 + HNO_2 + HCl \longrightarrow HO-\langle\ \rangle-N_2^+Cl^- + 2H_2O$

$HO-\langle\ \rangle-N_2^+Cl^- + \langle\ \rangle-OH \rightarrow HO-\langle\ \rangle-N=N-\langle\ \rangle-OH + HCl$

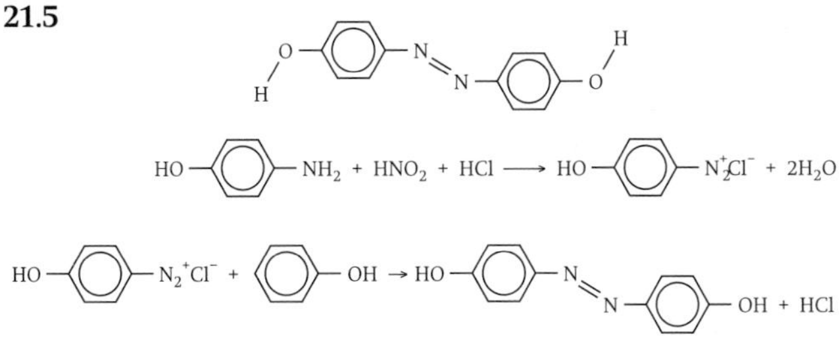

**21.6** **a** (i) $HOOCCH_2NH_3^+Cl^-(aq)$
(ii) $NH_2CH_2COO^-(aq)$

**b** (i) $HOOCCH_2NH_2(aq) + HCl(aq)$
$\rightarrow HOOCCH_2NH_3^+Cl^-(aq)$
(ii) $NH_2CH_2COOH(aq) + NaOH(aq)$
$\rightarrow NH_2CH_2COO^-Na^+(aq) + H_2O(l)$

**21.7** **a**

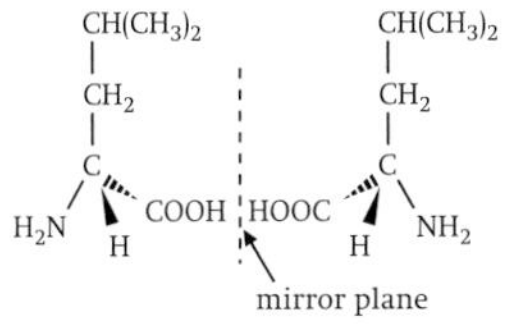

$CH(CH_3)_2$ ... $CH(CH_3)_2$
$|$ ... $|$
$CH_2$ ... $CH_2$
$|$ ... $|$
$H_2N \overset{C}{\underset{H}{\cdots}} COOH$ ┊ $HOOC \overset{C}{\underset{H}{\cdots}} NH_2$
mirror plane

**b**

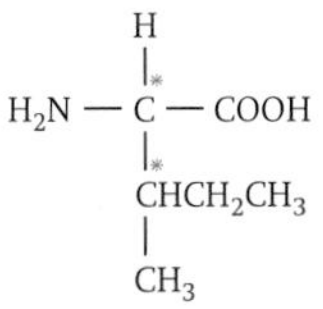

$$H_2N-\overset{\overset{H}{|}}{\underset{\underset{CH_3}{|}}{\underset{CHCH_2CH_3}{|}}{C}}-COOH$$

**21.8** **a**

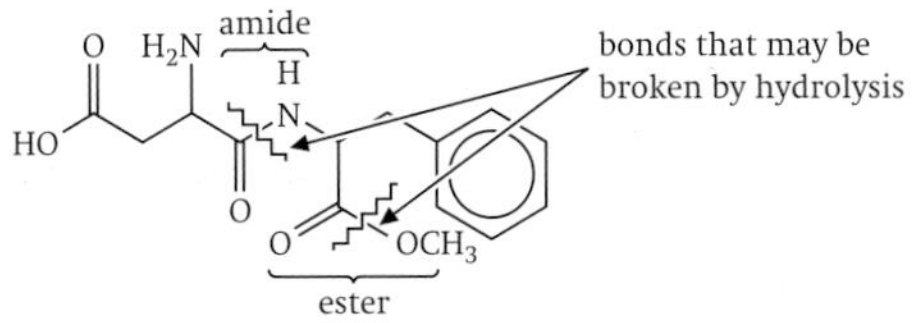

**b**

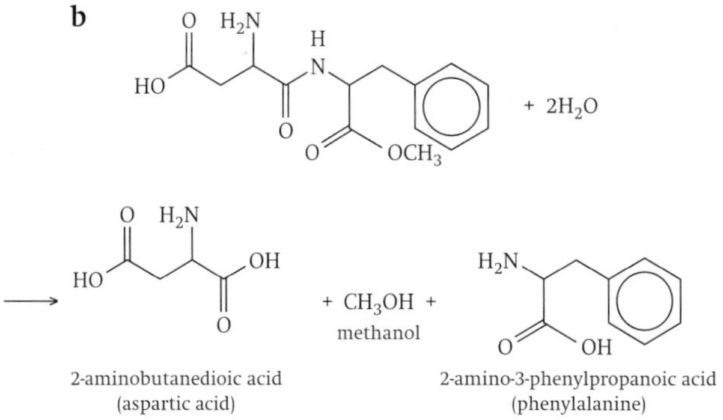

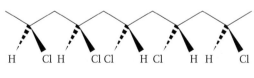

→

2-aminobutanedioic acid
(aspartic acid)

+ $CH_3OH$ +
methanol

2-amino-3-phenylpropanoic acid
(phenylalanine)

# Chapter 22

**22.1** **a**

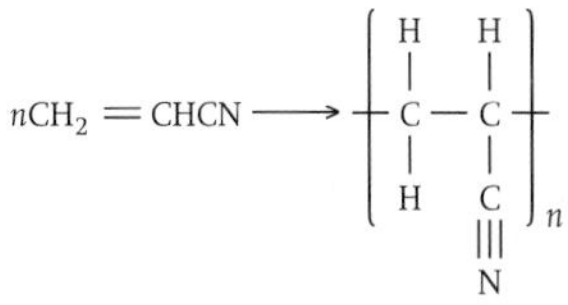

$nCH_2=CHCN \longrightarrow$ 
$\begin{bmatrix} H & H \\ | & | \\ -C-C- \\ | & | \\ H & C \\ & ||| \\ & N \end{bmatrix}_n$

**b** (i)

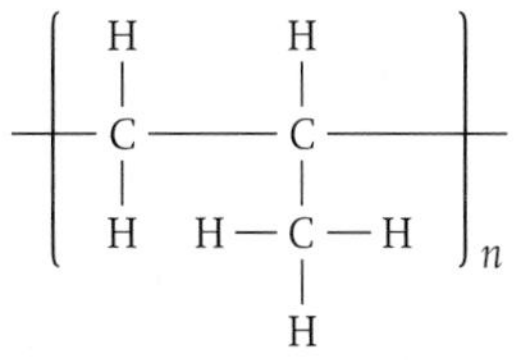

$$\begin{bmatrix} H & H \\ | & | \\ -C-C- \\ | & | \\ H & H-C-H \\ & | \\ & H \end{bmatrix}_n \text{ poly(propene)}$$

(ii)

$$\overset{H}{\underset{H}{}} C=C \overset{H}{\underset{\underset{\underset{H}{|}}{C}}{}}$$
$$\phantom{xxxxxx}\overset{}{\underset{H\ \ H}{}}$$
propene

**22.2** **a**

isotactic pvc

atactic pvc

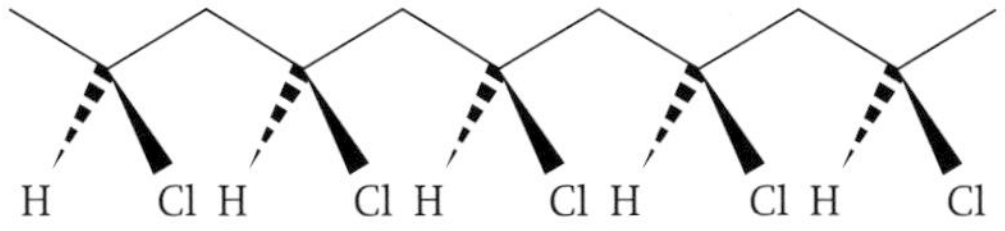

**b** (i) Isotactic pvc will be harder and more rigid, atactic pvc will be softer and more flexible.

(ii) Isotactic pvc will be more heat resistant, atactic pvc will have less heat resistance and melt easily.

**c** The regular structure of isotactic pvc allows the molecular chains to pack more closely (greater crystallinity) than the irregular structure in atactic pvc allows. The dipole-dipole forces of attraction in pvc will thus be greater in isotactic pvc. Hardness, rigidity and heat resistance all increase with increasing intermolecular forces.

**22.3** Ethene, propene and other alkenes together with some longer chain alkanes might be formed on pyrolysis of poly(ethene). The alkenes could be used to make poly(alkene)s or other useful products (such as ethane-1,2-diol from ethene). The alkanes could be used to make petrol or diesel fuel.

**22.4**

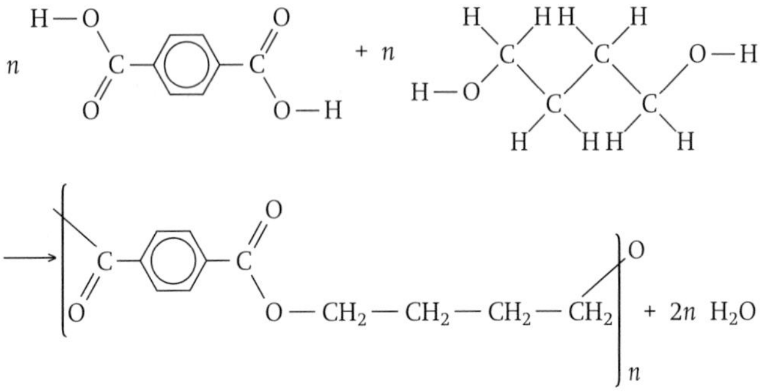

**22.5**

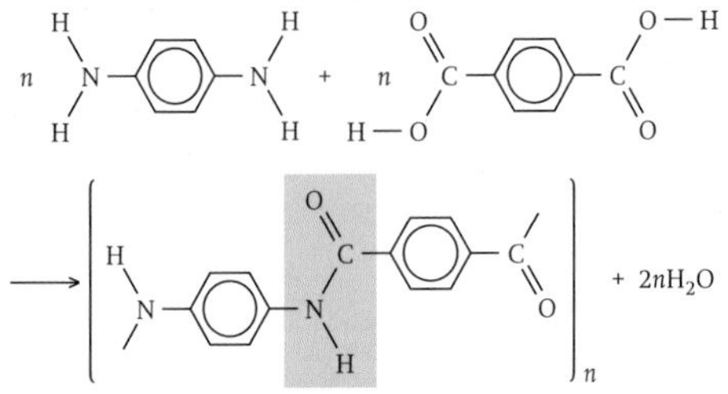

amide link

# Chapter 23

**23.1** –COOH is a carboxylic acid group, –COOCH$_3$ contains an ester group.

**23.2**

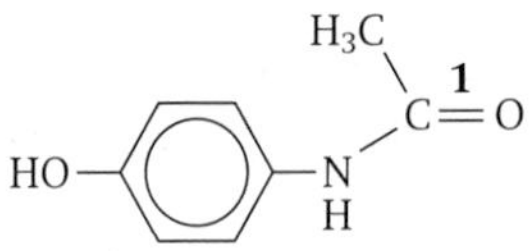

**23.3** $M_r$ (hydrocarbon) = 190

**23.4**

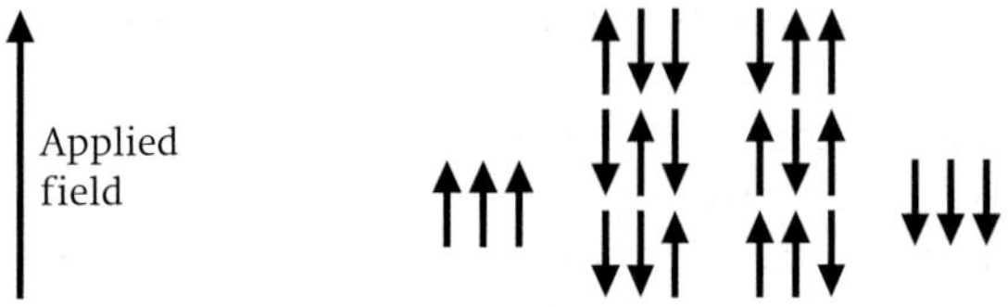

number of
arrangements   1   3   3   1

**23.5 a**

| Chemical shift, δ (ppm) | Relative number of protons | Splitting pattern |
|---|---|---|
| 1.2 | 3 | triplet |
| 1.9 | 3 | singlet |
| 4.0 | 2 | quartet |

**b** From the splitting patterns given, the following can be deduced.
- To produce a triplet, the three protons at chemical shift 1.2 must be adjacent to a –CH$_2$– group.
- To produce a quartet the two protons at chemical shift 4.0 must be adjacent to a –CH$_3$ group.
- To produce a singlet the three protons at chemical shift 1.9 must have no protons on the adjacent carbon atom.

**c** The types of protons are as follows

| Chemical shift, δ (ppm) | Type of proton |
|---|---|
| 1.2 | CH$_3$–R |
| 1.9 | $-\overset{\overset{\displaystyle O}{\|}}{C}-CH_3$ |
| 4.0 | –O–CH$_2$–R |

The presence of the >C=O group is supported by the infrared data as 1750 cm$^{-1}$ is the absorption frequency for this bond.

**d** The structure of the compound is

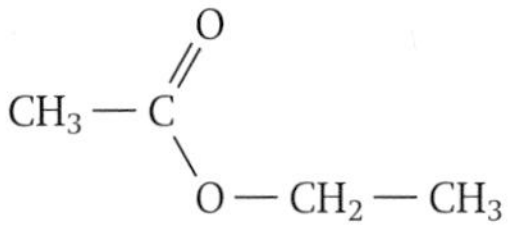

**23.6** Methyl propanoate has the following structure

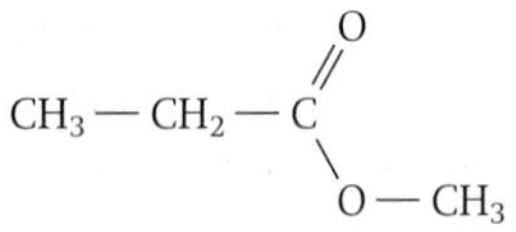

The chemical shifts and splitting patterns are as follows

| Type of proton | Chemical shift, δ (ppm) | Relative number of protons | Splitting pattern |
|---|---|---|---|
| CH$_3$–O | 3.3–4.3 | 3 | singlet |
| CH$_3$–R | 0.7–1.6 | 3 | triplet |
| $-\overset{\overset{\displaystyle O}{\|}}{C}-CH_2-R$ | 2.0–2.9 | 2 | quartet |

# Glossary

**acid** a chemical species which can donate a proton, H⁺. **Strong** acids dissociate fully into ions; **weak** acids only partially dissociate into ions.

**acid dissociation constant**, $K_a$ is the equilibrium constant for a weak acid HA:

$$K_a = \frac{[H^+][A^-]}{[HA]} \text{ mol dm}^{-3}$$

**activation energy** the energy barrier which must be surmounted before reaction can occur.

**addition polymer** a polymer formed by a repeated addition reaction.

**addition reaction** the joining of two molecules to form a single product molecule.

**adsorption** weak bonds forms between, for example, gaseous molecules and atoms at the surface of a solid catalyst.

**aliphatic** an organic compound that does not contain an arene rings.

**alkali** a soluble base.

**allotrope** different crystalline or molecular forms of the same element. Graphite, diamond and $C_{60}$ are allotropes of carbon.

**amide group:**

**amine group:** $-NH_2$.

**amino acids** are naturally occurring building blocks of protein molecules. The structure of an amino acid consists of a carboxylic acid group and an amino group attached to the same carbon atom.

**amphoteric** an amphoteric oxide is a substance that can act both as an acid and as a base. Aluminium oxide is an example.

**anions** negatively charged ions, formed when an atom or group of atoms, gains electrons.

**anode** the positive electrode. In electrolysis, anions are attracted to the anode.

**aromatic** compounds contain one or more arene rings.

**atomic number** the number of protons in the nucleus of each atom of an element.

**atomic radius** half the distance between the nuclei of two covalently bonded atoms.

**Avogadro's constant**, $L$ the number of atoms or molecules in one mole of a substance ($L = 6.01 \times 10^{23}$).

**azo group:**

**base** a base reacts with an acid to form a salt.

**Boltzmann distribution** the distribution of molecular energies.

**bond enthalpy** the amount of energy need to break one mole of a bond in a gaseous molecule.

**Born–Haber cycle** is an enthalpy cycle for the formation of an ionic solid that includes the lattice enthalpy.

**Brønsted–Lowry theory of acids and bases** a Brønsted–Lowry acid is a proton (H⁺) donor; a Bronsted-Lowry base is a proton (H⁺) acceptor.

**buffer solution** is a solution that minimises changes in pH, even when moderate amounts of acid or base are added to it. It consists of a conjugate acid and its base, where one of the pair is weak.

**carbanion** a negatively charged ion that contains carbon; for example $CH_3^-$.

**carbocation** a carbon atom in an organic molecule which has lost an atom or a group of atoms from a carbon atom creating a single positive charge.

**catalyst** a catalyst increases the rate of a reaction but is not itself used up during the reaction.

**cathode** the negative electrode. In electrolysis, cations are attracted to the cathode.

**cations** positively charged ions, formed when an atom or group of atoms, loses electrons.

**chain reaction** a self-sustaining reaction in which the products of one step in the reaction initiate the next step.

**chemical shift** is the δ/ppm value of a signal in an n.m.r. spectrum.

**chiral centre (or chiral carbon)** is a carbon atom in a molecule attached to four different groups.

**chiral molecules** are molecules that cannot be superimposed on each other, but are mirror images of each other.

*cis-trans* **isomerism** arises in alkenes that have two identical groups, one on each of the carbon atoms involved in the double bond. A *cis*-isomer has each set of identical groups on the same side of the double bond. A *trans*-isomer has each set of identical groups on opposite sides of the double bond. *cis-trans* isomerism occurs because a C=C cannot freely rotate.

**closed system** a closed system can only transfer energy to or from its surroundings. Substances cannot be exchanged.

**colorimetry** is an instrumental technique that records the wavelength of visible light passing through a coloured solution.

**complex ion** is an ion containing a central atom or ion to which other atoms, ions or molecules are bonded. In a transition metal complex the central atom or ion is a transition metal. The atoms, ions or molecules are bonded to it with dative covalent bonds and are called ligands.

**condensation polymerisation** is a polymerisation reaction in which the monomers are joined together by condensation reactions.

**condensation reaction** is a reaction in which two molecules join together to form a larger molecule, with elimination of a small molecule such as $H_2O$, HCl, $NH_3$ etc.

**conjugate acid-base pairs.** In an acid-base equilibrium there are two conjugate acid-base pairs:
- the acid in the forwards reaction and the base in the back reaction
- the base in the forwards reaction and the acid in the back reaction.

**coupling reaction** is the reaction between a diazonium salt and an arene to form a dye.

**covalent bonding** involves a pair of electrons between two atoms.

**covalent radius** (atomic radius) half the distance between the nuclei in neighbouring atoms in molecules.

**cracking** the thermal decomposition of an alkane into a smaller alkane and an alkene.

**curly arrows** show the movement of a pairs of electrons in a reaction mechanism.

**dative covalent bond (co-ordinate bond)** a covalent bond where both electrons come from one atom.

**dehydration** a reaction in which a molecule of water is lost; for example alcohols are dehydrated to form alkenes.

**delocalisation** is where electron pairs are shared between three or more atoms as, for example, in benzene.

**desorption** weak bonds break between, for example, gaseous molecules and atoms at the surface of a solid catalyst.

**diazotisation** is the formation of a diazonium salt from a primary amine.

**dipole–dipole force** the force of attraction between polar molecules.

**displacement reaction** a reaction in which one element produces another from an aqueous solution of its ions.

**displayed formula** shows all the covalent bonds and all the atoms present.

**disproportionation** the oxidation and reduction of the same species in one chemical reaction.

**dynamic equilibrium** an equilibrium is dynamic at the molecular level; both forward and reverse processes occur at the same rate; a closed system is required and macroscopic properties remain constant.

**electrochemical cell** an exothermic chemical reaction set up in two half-cells in two separate containers so that the energy released can produce an electric current between them.

**electrochemical series** the list of anions and cations in order of their standard electrode potentials.

**electrode potential** the voltage measured for a half-cell. Another half-cell is essential for this measurement to be made.

**electrolysis** the general term for chemical changes brought about by an electric current. During electrolysis, positive ions (cations) are discharged at the negative cathode and negative ions (anions) are discharged at the positive anode.

**electron** one of the three basic particles in any atom. An electron has negative charge and has a mass about 1/2000th the mass of a hydrogen atom.

**electron affinity (first)** is the enthalpy change when one electron is added to each gaseous atom in one mole, to form one mole of gaseous ions.

**electron-pair repulsion theory** enables predictions of the shapes and bond angles in a molecule to be made from the numbers of bonding pairs and lone pairs of electrons present.

**electronegativity** describes the ability of an atom to attract the bonding electrons in a covalent bond.

**electronic configuration** is the arrangement of electrons in an atom or ion shown in sub-shells – for example; the electronic configuration of Na is $1s^2 2s^2 2p^6 3s^1$.

**electrophile** an atom (or group of atoms) which is attracted to an electron-rich centre or atom, where it accepts a pair of electrons to form a new covalent bond.

**electrophilic addition** addition reaction in which the first step is the attack by an electrophile on the electron-rich part of a molecule; for example the addition to double bonds in alkenes.

**element** elements cannot be broken down further into simpler substances. All the atoms of the same element contain the same number of protons and electrons.

**elimination** when a small molecule is removed from a larger molecule.

**empirical formula** the simplest whole number ratio of the elements present in a compound.

**endothermic** term used to describe a reaction in which heat energy is absorbed from the surroundings (enthalpy change is positive).

**enthalpy,** *H* the term used by chemists for heat energy transferred during reactions.

**enthalpy cycle** a diagram displaying alternative routes between reactants and products which allows the determination of one enthalpy change from other known enthalpy changes using Hess's law.

**enthalpy profile** a diagram for a reaction to show the difference in enthalpy of the reactants compared with that of the products.

**equilibrium** in a dynamic equilibrium reaction, the rate of the forward reaction is equal to the rate of the backward reaction.

**equilibrium constant,** $K_c$, in terms of concentrations for the formation of ammonia from nitrogen and hydrogen, $N_2 + 3H_2 \rightarrow 2NH_3$ is given by

$$K_c = \frac{[NH_3]^2}{[N_2][H_2]^3} \, mol^{-2} \, dm^6$$

**equilibrium constant,** $K_p$, in terms of partial pressures for the formation of ammonia from nitrogen and hydrogen, $N_2 + 3H_2 \rightarrow 2NH_3$ is given by

$$K_p = \frac{p(NH_3)^2}{p(N_2) \times p(H_2)^3} \, kPa^{-2}$$

**esterification** the acid-catalysed formation of an ester from a carboxylic acid and an alcohol.

**exothermic** term used to describe a reaction in which heat energy is transferred to the surroundings (enthalpy change is negative).

**fatty acids** are carboxylic acids obtained from oils or fats. Mono-unsaturated fatty acids contain one carbon-carbon double bond. Poly-unsaturated fatty acids contain more than one carbon-carbon double bond.

**feedstock** a primary source of substance for the production of other chemicals.

**fractional distillation** a method of separating mixtures of similar liquids, which depends on differences in boiling points of the different molecules in the mixture.

**free radical** an atom or group of atoms with an unpaired electron.

**functional group** an atom or group of atoms which gives rise to an homologous series. Compounds in the same homologous series show similar chemical properties.

**general formula** a formula which may be written for each homologous series ($C_nH_{2n+2}$ for alkanes).

**half-cell** half of an electrochemical cell. One half-cell supplies electrons, the other half-cell receives electrons.

**half-equation** describes what is happening in one half-cell. Alternatively, in a redox reaction a half-equation can be used to describe only the reduction reaction or only the oxidation reaction.

**half-life,** $t_{\frac{1}{2}}$ is the time taken for the concentration of a reactant to fall to half its original value.

**halogen carriers** are reagents which increase the rate of reaction of a halogen with an organic compound, for example iron(III) chloride in the reaction of chlorine with benzene to form chlorobenzene.

**Hess's law** the total enthalpy change for a chemical reaction is independent of the route by which the reaction takes place, provided initial and final conditions are the same.

**heterogeneous catalysis** a catalyst that is present in a different phase to the reactants; frequently reactants are in a gaseous phase with a solid catalyst.

**heterolytic fission** when a bond breaks to form a positive ion and a negative ion.

**homogeneous catalysis** the catalyst and reactants are in the same phase, which is most frequently the aqueous phase.

**homologous series** a series of organic molecules with the same functional group.

**homolytic fission** when a bond breaks to form two free radicals.

**hydrocarbons** compounds that contain only carbon and hydrogen atoms.

**hydrogen bond** a weak intermolecular bond formed between molecules containing hydrogen bonded to the most electronegative elements (N, O, F).

**hydrolysis** involves the breaking of a bond by reaction with water.

**ideal gas** an imaginary gas in which the molecules have negligible size, no intermolecular forces and where collisions between molecules are elastic.

**ideal gas equation** $PV = nRT$ where $P$ is the pressure (in Pa or $N \, m^{-2}$), $V$ is the volume (in $m^3$), n is the number of moles of gas, $R$ is the gas constant and $T$ is the temperature (in K).

**inductive effect** is the tendency of a group to push or pull electrons. A group with a positive inductive effect has the tendency to push electrons towards a neighbouring atom. A group with a negative inductive effect has the tendency to pull electrons away from a neighbouring atom.

**infrared spectroscopy** is a technique used to identify the bonds within molecules by passing a beam of infrared radiation through them.

**infrared spectrum** is a chart from an infrared spectrometer showing peaks at different wavenumbers ($cm^{-1}$). The peaks represent the presence of various bonds in the molecules of the sample.

**initial-rates method** of determining the order of a reaction. The initial rate of reaction is measured with several different reactant concentrations in separate experiments.

**initiation** the first step in a free-radical substitution in which the free radicals are generated by heat or ultraviolet light.

**instantaneous dipole–induced dipole forces** another name for **van der Waals' forces**.

**intermolecular forces** the weak forces of attraction between molecules based on instantaneous or permanent dipoles.

**ion** a positively or negatively charge atom or (covalently bonded) group of atoms.

**ionic bonding** the electrostatic attraction between oppositely charged s.

**ionic product of water,** $K_w = [H^+][OH^-] = 1.0 \times 10^{-14} \, mol^2 \, dm^{-6}$ at 298 K.

**ionisation energy** the first ionisation energy is the energy needed to remove one electron from each atom in one mole of gaseous atoms of an element. Successive ionisation energies are the sequence of first, second , third, fourth, etc ionisation energies needed to remove the first, second, third, fourth, etc electrons from each atom in one mole of gaseous atoms of an element.

**isomerisation** the conversion of a straight chain alkane to a branched-chain isomer.

**isomers** isomers have the same molecular formula but the atoms are arranged in different ways.

**isotopes** are atoms of an element with the same number of protons but different numbers of neutrons.

**Kelvin scale** the absolute scale of temperature. To convert from degrees Celsius, you add 273.0 °C = 273 K.

**lattice enthalpy** is the enthalpy change when 1 mole of an ionic compound is formed from its gaseous ions under standard conditions (298 K, 100 kPa).

**Le Chatelier's principle** when any of the conditions affecting the position of a dynamic equilibrium are changed, then the position of that equilibrium will shift to minimise that change.

**ligand** is the atom, ion or molecule which is bonded with dative covalent bonds to the central atom or ion in a complex.

**ligand substitution** is the replacement of one ligand by another in a complex.

**lone-pair** the non-bonding electron-pairs in the outer electron shells of an atom in a molecule. For example, nitrogen in ammonia has one lone-pair of electrons.

**mass number** the total number of protons and neutrons in the nucleus of an atom.

**mechanism** the sequence of stages in a reaction.

**metallic radius** half the distance between the nuclei of neighbouring atoms in metallic crystals.

**molar mass** the mass of one mole of a substance, calculated from its formula.

**mole** the unit of amount of substance (abbreviation: mol). One mole of a substance is the mass that has the same number of particles (atoms, molecules, ions or electrons) as there are atoms in exactly 12 g of carbon-12.

**mole fraction** of a gas in a mixture of gases is the number of moles of the gas divided by the total number of moles in the mixture.

**molecular formula** shows the total number of atoms present in a molecule of the compound.

**molecular ion peak (M)** in a mass spectrum, the peak which represents the unfragmented (whole) ionised molecule. Usually the peak with the highest m/e value is the (M+1) peak, and the next highest m/e value is the M peak.

**molecule** a covalently bonded group of atoms.

**monomer** the small molecule used to build a polymer molecule.

**neutron** one of the three basic particles in any atom. A neutron has no charge and has a mass about the same as a hydrogen atom.

**nitrating mixture** is a mixture of concentrated nitric acid and concentrated sulphuric acid that produces nitration of an arene ring (substitution of a hydrogen atom by the $-NO_2$ group).

**nitrile:** the $-C{\equiv}N$ group.

**nitro compound** is an organic compound containing the $-NO_2$ group.

**n.m.r. spectrum** is a chart from an n.m.r. spectrometer showing signals at different chemical shifts. Each signal indicates a different type of H atom.

**nuclear magnetic resonance (n.m.r.) spectroscopy** is a technique that provides information about the relative numbers and different environments of hydrogen atoms in an organic molecule.

**nucleophile** a chemical that can donate a pair of electrons with the subsequent formation of a covalent bond.

**nucleophilic addition** addition reaction in which the first step is the attack by a nucleophile on the electron-deficient part of a molecule; for example the addition to double bonds in ketones and aldehydes.

**nucleus** the central core of an atom – contains the neutrons and protons.

**optical isomers** are molecules that are non-superimposable mirror images of each other. They contain one or more chiral centres.

**orbital** a representation of the region of space where there is a high probability of finding an electron in an electron subshell. Orbitals in different subshells have different shapes; s-orbitals spherically surround the nucleus in the centre of the sphere, p-orbitals have two spherical lobes either side of the nucleus.

**order of reaction** is the power to which the concentration of a reactant is raised in the rate equation. *Zero-order* indicates the reactant concentration does not affect the rate, rate $\alpha$ $[A]^0$. *First-order* indicates that the reactant concentration is directly proportional to the rate, rate $\alpha$ $[A]^1$. *Second-order* indicates that the square of the reactant concentration is directly proportional to the rate, rate $\alpha$ $[A]^2$.

**oxidation** the loss of electrons from an atom of an element. Oxidation number goes up.

**oxidation state (number)** a number (with a positive or negative sign) assigned to the atoms of each element in an ion or compound. Oxidation states are determined using a set of rules devised by chemists.

**π-bond** a molecular orbital formed from overlap of atomic p orbitals in the formation of a double bond.

**partial pressure** of a gas in a mixture of gases is its mole fraction multiplied by the total pressure of the gas.

**peptide link** is the amide link in polypeptides and proteins.

$$pH = -\log_{10}[H^+]$$

**pH** is the negative logarithm to the base ten of the concentration of the hydrogen ion.

**pharmacophore** is the part of a molecule that gives rise to its pharmacological activity.

**phenols** are aromatic alcohols. They contain a benzene ring with an −OH group attached to it.

**p$K_a$** is the negative logarithm to the base ten of the acid dissociation constant p$K_a$ = $-\log_{10}[K_a]$

**polar molecule** a molecule with an electric dipole.

**polarising power** is the ability of an ion to distort another ion next to it.

**polyamide** polymers in which the monomers are connected by peptide linkages.

**polymer** the long molecular chain built up from monomer units.

**polypeptide** is a length of amino acids joined by condensation polymerisation. A polypeptide is shorter in length than a protein molecule.

**principal quantum shell** electron shells are numbered 1, 2, 3, 4, etc. Each quantum number corresponds to a principal quantum shell.

**propagation** is the second stage of a free-radical mechanism in which the products are formed and the radicals re-generated.

**proton** one of the three basic particles in any atom. A proton has positive charge and has a mass about the same as a hydrogen atom.

**rate constant** is the proportionality constant k in a rate equation (rate = $k[A]^x[B]^y$).

**rate-determining step** is the slowest step in the reaction.

**rate equation** has the form rate = $k[A]^x[B]^y$ which shows how the rate of a chemical reaction depends on the concentration of reactants (A & B) and the rate constant $k$.

**rate of reaction** the amount in moles of a reactant which is used up in a given time.

**reaction pathway** for a reaction, this contains details of intermediate chemical species.

**receptor molecules** are molecules that medicines or other agents bind to in the body.

**redox** reactions which involve reduction and oxidation processes.

**reduction** the gain of electrons by an atom of an element. Oxidation number goes down.

**reforming** the conversion of alkanes to cycloalkanes or arenes.

**relative atomic mass, $A_r$,** of an element is the weighted average mass of an atom of the element relative to the mass of an atom of carbon-12, which has a mass of exactly 12.

**relative formula mass** the weighted average mass of the formula of a compound relative to an atom of carbon-12, which has a mass of exactly 12.

**relative isotopic mass** the mass of an isotope of an atom of an element relative to an atom of carbon-12, which has a mass of exactly 12.

**relative molecular mass** the weighted average mass of a molecule of a compound relative to an atom of carbon-12, which has a mass of exactly 12.

**repeat unit** is the smallest section of a polymer which, when reproduced, gives the polymer.

**salt bridge** a piece of filter paper soaked in potassium nitrate solution used to make electrical contact between the half-cells in an electrochemical cell.

**saponification** the hydrolysis of fatty acids by sodium hydroxide to give the sodium salts of the fatty acids (soaps) and propane-1,2,3-triol.

**saturated hydrocarbon** contains only C−C single bonds.

**shielding effect** the negative charge of filled inner shells of electrons repels electrons in the outer shells reducing the effect of the positive nuclear charge.

**skeletal formula** shows the carbon skeleton only, hydrogen atoms are omitted, other atoms are shown as in a structural formula. For example, the skeletal formula of propylcyclohexane is:

**solubility product** for a salt, this is the product of the concentrations of the ions in a saturated solution of the salt raised to the appropriate powers. Only applies to sparing soluble salts.

**splitting pattern (in n.m.r. spectroscopy)** signals in the spectrum can be split into two (doublets), three (triplets) etc. This splitting gives information on the neighbouring H atoms to the H atom(s) responsible for the peak.

**standard conditions (for electrochemical cells)** a temperature of 298 K, all solutions at a concentration of $1 \, mol \, dm^{-3}$, all gases at a pressure of one atmosphere (100 kPa).

**standard conditions (enthalpy changes)** a temperature of 298 K and a pressure of 100 kPa.

**standard electrode potential** the electrode potential of a half-cell when measured with a standard hydrogen electrode as the other half-cell. All conditions must be standard. If this value is negative the half-cell donates electrons to the standard hydrogen electrode. If this value is positive the half-cell receive electrons from the standard hydrogen electrode.

**standard enthalpy change of atomisation** is the enthalpy change when one mole of gaseous atoms are formed from an element in its standard state.

**standard enthalpy change of combustion** the enthalpy change when one mole of an element or compound reacts completely with oxygen under standard conditions.

**standard enthalpy change of formation** the enthalpy change when one mole of a compound is formed from its elements under standard conditions; both compound and elements are in their standard states.

**standard enthalpy change of hydration** the enthalpy change when one mole of a gaseous ion dissolves in water to give an infinitely dilute solution.

**standard enthalpy change of neutralisation** the enthalpy change when one mole of $H^+$ ions from an acid is completely neutralised by an alkali to give one mole of water.

**standard enthalpy change of reaction** the enthalpy change when amounts of reactants, as shown in the reaction equation, react together under standard conditions to give products in their standard states.

**standard enthalpy change of solution** the enthalpy change when one mole of a solute dissolves in a solvent to give an infinitely dilute solution.

**standard hydrogen electrode** a half-cell in which hydrogen gas at a pressure of one atmosphere is bubbled into a solution of $1 \, mol \, dm^{-3} \, H^+$ ions. Electrical contact is made with a platinum black electrode. This half-cell is given a standard electrode potential of 0.00 V; all other standard electrode potentials are measured relative to it.

**standard reference electrode** a half-cell used as a standard; the electrode potentials of other half-cells are measured relative to it.

**stereoisomers** are molecules containing the same atoms with the same order of bonds but with different spatial arrangements of atoms.

**stoichiometric ratio** the stoichiometric ratio or stoichiometry for a reaction shows the mole ratio of reactants and products in the balanced equation for the reaction.

**strong acid** is an acid fully dissociated into ions in aqueous solution.

**structural formula** shows how the atoms are joined together in a molecule.

**structural isomerism** structural isomers have the same molecular formula but different structural formulae.

**substitution reaction** an atom (or group of atoms) is substituted by a different atom (or group of atoms).

**systematic name** is the name of an organic compound, following internationally agreed rules.

**termination** is the last stage of a free-radical mechanism in which the radicals combine to end the reaction.

**thermal decomposition** a reaction in which a compound is broken down by heat.

**three-dimensional formula** – the structural formula of an organic molecule using wedged lines and dotted lines for bonds (wedged lines = bond pointing forwards, dotted line = bond pointing backwards). A normal line indicates a bond in the plane of the paper. For example the three-dimensional formula of methane is:

**Tollens' reagent** – an aqueous solution of silver nitrate in excess ammonia. It produces a silver mirror with an aldehyde, but not with a ketone.

**transition element** (or transition metal) is an element that forms at least one ion with a partly-filled d orbital.

**unsaturated hydrocarbon** contains one or more C=C double bonds.

**van der Waals' forces** the weak forces of attraction between molecules based on instantaneous or permanent dipoles.

**volatility** a measure of the ease with which a solid or liquid evaporates to a gas. Volatility increases as boiling point decreases.

**weak acid** is an acid partly dissociated into ions in aqueous solution.

**zwitterion** is an 'internal' salt of an amino acid, in which the –COOH group donates a proton to the $-NH_2$ group:
$-OOC-CHR-NH_2^+-$

# Index